BRIBES, BULLETS, AND INTIMIDATION

Drug Trafficking and the Law in Central America

Bribes, Bullets, and Intimidation

Julie Marie Bunck and Michael Ross Fowler

The Pennsylvania State University Press
University Park, Pennsylvania

Cover spot © Shutterstock

Library of Congress Cataloging-in-Publication Data

Bunck, Julie Marie, 1960–
Bribes, bullets, and intimidation : drug trafficking and the law in central america / Julie Marie Bunck and Michael Ross Fowler
p. cm.
Includes bibliographical references and index.
Summary: "Examines drug trafficking through Central America and the efforts of law enforcement to counter it. Details the routes, methods, and networks involved, while comparing the evolution of the drug trade in Belize, Costa Rica, Guatemala, Honduras, and Panama over three decades"—Provided by publisher.
ISBN 978-0-271-04866-6 (cloth : alk. paper)
1. Drug traffic—Latin America—Case studies.
2. Drug control—Latin America—Case studies.
I. Fowler, Michael Ross.
II. Title.

HV5840.L3B86 2012
363.4509728—dc23
2011045324

Printed in the United States of America
Published by The Pennsylvania State University Press,
University Park, PA 16802-1003

The Pennsylvania State University Press is a member of the Association of American University Presses.

It is the policy of The Pennsylvania State University Press to use acid-free paper. Publications on uncoated stock satisfy the minimum requirements of American National Standard for Information Sciences—Permanence of Paper for Printed Library Material, ANSI Z39.48-1992.

This book is printed on Natures Natural, which contains 50% post-consumer waste.

CONTENTS

ILLUSTRATIONS

FIGURES

MAPS

TABLES

ACKNOWLEDGMENTS

This book is the product of many years spent studying the international drug trade in Central America. As we canvassed court records and newspaper accounts and spoke to scores of public officials and others, we amassed considerable debts to many helpful individuals. Those cited by name represent a small fraction of all who gave generously of their time in helping us with our research. We appreciate all the help received, and naturally, no one who assisted us bears any responsibility for the content of this study.

Given how little was known about the bridge-state drug trade and given the secrecy of trafficking activities and certain of the law-enforcement efforts to counter them, few at first believed that this was a viable research project. We would thus like to extend special thanks to Kenneth W. Thompson and the Institute for the Study of World Politics (ISWP) in Washington, D.C., for recognizing the gap in the drug literature that this work might fill, for believing in our ability to bring the project to fruition over the long term, and for providing us with our initial research grant. The Institute of Foreign Policy Analysis at Tufts University then ably administered our ISWP start-up grant. We also specially thank those who read the manuscript, or portions of it, and offered their suggestions on improvements. Along with a number of anonymous reviewers, two retired professors, William O. Walker III of the University of Toronto and Inis L. Claude Jr. of the University of Virginia, offered extremely valuable and greatly appreciated advice.

We also owe much to the generosity of the Council for the International Exchange of Scholars. That organization, through its Fulbright Scholarship Central American Republics Research Program, funded our second major research trip and later enabled us to lay the theoretical foundation for our work and to advance toward a finished product through awards to Japan and Mexico. The Miller Center of Public Affairs at the University of Virginia, the Department of Politics at Australia's Bond University, and the Center for Social Research at Mexico's Universidad de Colima all provided forums for us to present our research and absorb suggestions and constructive criticisms, as did annual conferences of the Latin American Studies Association and the American Political Science Association. We thank our own University of Louisville for a Lewis Fellowship in Latin American Studies and a Project Completion Grant, as well as for its various Panama programs, which helped to finance multiple trips for fieldwork. The university's Department of Political Science, its Brandeis School of Law, and its Muhammad Ali Institute also contributed talented and indefatigable research assistants, including Kevin Fahey, Mikkaka Hardaway, Amelie Quinnec, Chris Rueff, Abi Smith, Holly Wallace, and Ramsey Younis. And no one contributed more time and effort than Carolyn Morgan, whose work with our charts went far beyond the call of duty.

We would also like to thank the wide array of officials from the United States and the Central American republics who assisted one way or another in our research. In particular, the firsthand insights of those contending with the regional drug trade contributed much to our understanding. Without their cooperation, this work would have been much more limited in scope. For example, in Belize on several occasions the Office of the Chief Magistrate permitted us to undertake extensive reviews of court records. Similarly, in Costa Rica the archives of the Judicial Branch supplied opinions from dozens of the most significant drug cases, and the Judicial Branch Office of Statistics directed us to their relevant data on drugs. In Guatemala the Office of the Director of Prisons provided help in the review of public files on drug offenders, and the Office of Statistics of the Judicial Branch undertook a lengthy and informative project to compile statistics on a range of offenses, including various categories of drug cases. In Honduras persons associated with the Commission for the Reform of the Judicial System of Honduras and the Faculty of Law at the National Autonomous University gave freely of their time on repeated occasions, and the Office of the Director of the Penal Establishment allowed us access to personnel, statistics, and records. To supplement this information, Honduran Supreme Court archivists helped us to ferret out relevant information regarding drug-trafficking cases, convictions, and sentencing. In Panama the Solicitor-General's Office and the Center for Juridic Investigation at the Faculty of Law, University of Panama, were singularly helpful in arranging interviews and helping us to find relevant information.

We thank the *Albany Law Review* and the *Suffolk Journal of Transnational Law* for permitting us to draw on early articles that we wrote for them regarding drug trafficking. The numerous detailed maps in the book are the work of our extraordinary cartographer, Erin Greb. We offer special thanks to everyone associated with our publication of this volume through Penn State Press, most particularly our outstanding copyeditor, Susan Silver, and the former Press director, Sandy Thatcher, who cheered us on for many years on this project. Finally, we are most appreciative of all those who encouraged and helped with matters at home, as we traveled to research and write this volume. To all who lent a hand, one way or another, we offer our sincere thanks and our hope that you recognize the imprint of your many contributions in the pages that follow.

Julie Bunck and Michael Fowler
Louisville, Kentucky, 2012

ABBREVIATIONS

BELIZE

AM	*Amandala*
BDF	Belize Defence Force
BT	*Belize Times*
PUP	People's United Party
TR	*The Reporter*
UDP	United Democratic Party

COSTA RICA

LN	*La Nación*
NT	*Nica Times*
OIJ	Office of Judicial Investigations (Organismo Investigativo Judicial)
TT	*Tico Times*

GUATEMALA

CICIG	International Commission Against Impunity in Guatemala (Comisión Internacional Contra la Impunidad en Guatemala)
DOAN	Department of Antinarcotics Operations (Departamento de Operaciones Antinarcóticos)
LH	*La Hora*
LPL	*La Prensa Libre*
PNC	National Civil Police (Policía Nacional Civil)
SAIA	Antinarcotics Analysis and Information Services (Servicio de Análisis e Información Antinarcóticos)
SV	*Siglo Veintiuno*

HONDURAS

LP	*La Prensa*
SETCO	Commander Executive Tourist Services (Servicios Ejecutivos Turistas Commander)

PANAMA

FDP	Panama Defense Force (Fuerza Defensa de Panama)
LP	*La Prensa*
PTJ	Judicial Technical Police (Policía Técnica Judicial)
SMN	National Maritime Service (Servicio Marítimo Nacional)

UNITED STATES

AP	Associated Press
AWACS	Airborne Warning and Control System
BINM	Bureau of International Narcotics Matters (Department of State)
BNDD	Bureau of Narcotics and Dangerous Drugs (Department of Justice)
CIA	Central Intelligence Agency
DEA	Drug Enforcement Administration
FBI	Federal Bureau of Investigation
INCSR	*International Narcotics Control Strategy Report* (Department of State)
IPS	Inter Press Service
LAT	*Los Angeles Times*
MH	*Miami Herald*
NYT	*New York Times*
SLPD	*St. Louis Post-Dispatch*
SPT	*St. Petersburg Times*
UPI	United Press International
WP	*Washington Post*

OTHER

AUC	United Self-Defense Groups of Colombia (Autodefensas Unidas de Colombia)
BCCI	Bank of Credit and Commerce International
EU (MX)	*El Universal* (Mexico)
FARC	Revolutionary Armed Forces of Colombia (Fuerzas Armadas Revolucionarias de Colombia)
PRI	Institutional Revolutionary Party (Partido Revolucionario Institucional) (Mexico)
PRIDE	Parent's Resource Institute for Drug Prevention
THC	Tetrahydrocannabinol

Introduction

Exploring Central American Drug Trafficking

This book explores one distinctly understudied aspect of the international drug trade: the experiences of "bridge countries," that is, states that may neither consume nor produce sizable amounts of illegal drugs but that lie on favored paths carved out between centers of production and key consumer markets. In the 1980s the Central American republics became critically important to the international drug trade and have remained so ever since, with illegal drugs continually transiting en route to North American, European, and various emerging markets. Central America is particularly well suited for one of the first comparative studies of bridge-state trafficking, because its trade in drugs has long been emphatically multipolar.[1] Significant drug transit has occurred not only across the territories but in the skies above each state and through offshore Pacific and Caribbean waters. By studying Central American drug trafficking, we offer a first examination of social, political, and economic phenomena of extraordinary importance to an often overlooked region of the world.

Certainly, by the 1990s massive inflows and outflows of cocaine had come to affect profoundly each small republic. Nevertheless, no sound empirical foundation has yet been compiled, much less have theoretical explanations been offered, to illuminate the manner in which drug traffickers and law enforcement have contended with one another in Central America.[2] One

1. The trail of bridge-state trafficking studies was blazed in Griffith, *Drugs and Security*, but this work deals almost exclusively with Caribbean, not Central American, drug trafficking. For the multipolarity of early twentieth-century cocaine production, culture, and uses, see Gootenberg, *Andean Cocaine*, 190, 248.

2. Addressing the paucity of research, one scholar wrote, "Anyone attempting to do research on drug trafficking in Central America will come up against a dearth of information on this subject. Therefore, research . . . will have to begin at the most basic level." Juhn, "Central America," 389.

leading authority on drugs has written, "The topic of transnational smuggling attracts a good deal of rhetoric but not much that could be called research." Another recent work declares, "Although studies of drug use are numerous and our understanding of local drug markets is growing, our understanding of the multimillion-dollar business of international drug smuggling is considerably less well developed."[3] This book thus aims to fill a gap in the literature by using extensive primary and secondary research to elucidate the dynamics of the Central American drug trade.

The Case Studies Selected

We organized our research around five case studies: Belize, Costa Rica, Guatemala, Honduras, and Panama.[4] Each has served as an important staging point in international drug transit throughout the last decades of the twentieth century and the first of the twenty-first. Although as early as the 1980s transshipment also occurred via El Salvador and Nicaragua, their high levels of instability and violence kept some traffickers at bay and greatly hampered antidrug activities.[5] Throughout that decade, data are scarce, since their authorities were seldom seizing narcotics and even more rarely breaking up significant drug rings.[6] Furthermore, the Nicaraguan and Salvadoran civil wars hampered the U.S. drug investigations usually critically important for seizures and arrests anywhere in the region. The Sandinista government was not prepared to cooperate with the U.S. Drug Enforcement Administration (DEA), and U.S. national security officials reportedly squelched DEA inquiries that involved trafficking related to the Salvadoran military, its bases, and its role in supporting the Nicaraguan contras.[7]

In later chronicling how drug problems had long been ignored, the U.S. State Department reported that El Salvador had seized a single kilogram of cocaine in 1989 and a mere 26 kilos in 1990.[8] Even as late as 1998, of 31.6 metric tons of cocaine seized in Central America, Salvadoran authorities accounted for a mere 41 kilos.[9] Similarly, in Nicaragua neither the right nor the left did much to stem drug passage in the 1980s.[10] Indeed, before 1990 the

3. Reuter, "Political Economy," 128; Decker and Chapman, *Drug Smugglers*, 1.

4. Regions rarely "break easily along neatly perforated lines." Claude, *Swords into Plowshares*, 113. Some might question including Panama, or even Belize, in Central America and wish to exclude them on geographic, historical, or cultural grounds. Vis-à-vis the drug trade, however, it seems to us that both should properly be considered Central American bridge states.

5. The Kerry Commission observed that traffickers want to conduct their business smoothly, which is most readily accomplished in states with stable governments but weak institutions. U.S. Senate, *Law Enforcement: Report*, 10.

6. In 1985 the first DEA agent assigned to undertake undercover work entered El Salvador. He later wrote, "As I leafed through the files, I discovered the drug war in this corner of the globe amounted to piles of reports documenting traffickers' identities and movements, but few seizures and arrests." Castillo and Harmon, *Powderburns*, 112.

7. See generally U.S. House, *Nicaraguan Government*, and Cockburn and St. Clair, *Whiteout*, 283.

8. U.S. Department of State, *International Narcotics Control Strategy Report* (hereafter cited as *INCSR*) (1991), 145. In the early 1990s, one source claims, the Cali cartel bought four 230-kilo cluster bombs from Salvadoran military officials. Strong, *Whitewash*, 267.

9. Metric tons are hereafter referred to simply as tons. "Costa Rica el guardián de Centroamérica," *Siglo Veintiuno* (Guatemala), 14 February 1999, 22.

10. The Kerry Commission concluded that "individuals who provided support for the Contras were involved in drug trafficking, the support network of the Contras was used by drug trafficking organizations, and elements of the Contras themselves knowingly received financial and material assistance from drug traffickers." See U.S. Senate, *Law Enforcement: Report*, 36. Once the Sandinista regime took control, the CIA and DEA, through undercover informant Barry Seal, procured photos implicating Sandinistas in cocaine trafficking. A former internal affairs official in Nicaragua's Interior Ministry, Álvaro José Baldizón Avilés, likewise testified that Nicaraguan officials had trafficked in cocaine. Imprisoned Nicaraguan trafficker Enrique Miranda Jaime stated that from 1981 to 1985 he had been personally involved in Sandinista efforts to raise funds by drug trafficking. And, Medellín insider Roberto Escobar later revealed that Sandinista officials had agreed with the cartel to hide its leading fugitives and to use an

country had never seized a Colombian cocaine plane.[11] Instead, individuals on both sides of the Nicaraguan civil war trafficked narcotics for their own profit or to finance their causes. Thus, although drug transit eventually reached substantial levels in Nicaragua and El Salvador, and each enters our account in relation to trafficking in its neighbors, we chose to examine the five Central American countries in which the most data are available over the longest time frame.[12]

Our research soon revealed that the many transnational criminal organizations active in Central America were putting into effect varied, numerous, and often quite creative drug-smuggling schemes.[13] These aimed to tap the enormous potential profits inherent in the drug trade while avoiding interdiction, that is, the interception and seizure by law-enforcement officials of drugs and traffickers traveling from source to market countries, as well as of the back flow of drug profits.[14] Criminal efforts to establish efficient smuggling routes and methods, followed by official attempts to counter them, have caused the drug trade to evolve, state by state and organization by organization, as traffickers and police have tried to adapt to each other's actions.[15]

In the chapters that follow we explore where, when, and why smugglers have periodically changed their routes and modi operandi to avoid detection. We detail the growing magnitude of the regional trade, and we identify key traffickers in Central America and their organizations. Although the bridge states have shared many experiences, we draw special attention to the aspects of Central American trafficking operations that have varied by drug and by country. In analyzing state efforts to curb the trade, we examine what was typical and what was singular about the historical development of key institutions and how this affected antidrug initiatives.

Although in many respects we have disaggregated the Central American societies, we have also focused on the ways in which this activity is regional as well as national. As we shall show, traffickers, routes, and law-enforcement efforts have often involved more than a single bridge state. For an accurate picture of the Central American drug trade, a panorama must be created, in which developments in the different republics can be set next to one another and compared and contrasted. When approached from that perspective, the challenges of the Central American drug trade have underscored grave deficiencies in countering organized crime in more authoritarian societies and more democratic ones, in civil law and common law judicial systems, in postcolonial and long-independent states, and in countries at very different levels of development.

Empirical and Theoretical Contributions

In examining the complex workings of the Central American drug trade, our book has

---

island for aerial trafficking. See U.S. House, *Nicaraguan Government*, 3; Shannon, *Desperados*, 150–55; CIA, *Allegations of Connections*, 6; and Escobar, *Accountant's Story*, 69, 119.

11. "Central America Fights Its 'Drug Bridge' Image," United Press International, 30 August 1990.

12. In 2007 Nicaraguan authorities seized 20 tons of cocaine, 184 kilos of heroin, and $5.5 million in confiscated assets, a twelve-fold increase over the prior year. "Police Make Record Drug Busts in 2007," *Nica Times* (Costa Rica) (hereafter cited as *NT* [CR]), 11 January 2008, 2. In 1991 Salvadoran authorities seized approximately three tons of Medellín cocaine in a container off a Liberian ship transporting goods from South America for a Mexican company. See "Salvador's Drug Role Growing," *Miami Herald* (hereafter cited as *MH* [US]), 4 December 1991, international ed., 3A, and "Gran decomiso de coca en El Salvador," *La Nación* (Costa Rica) (hereafter cited as *LN* [CR]), 30 October 1991, 30A.

13. Use of the word *transnational* is meant to highlight the fact that nonstate actors engaged in the drug trade are carrying out activities that cross state boundaries, as opposed to the interactions between governments that are the traditional focus of *international* relations. See Farer, *Transnational Crime*, xvi, n1.

14. See Reuter, Crawford, and Cave, *Sealing the Borders*, v, 1n2.

15. See generally Kenney, *From Pablo to Osama*.

empirical and theoretical dimensions.[16] One scholar wrote, "Like plants in nature, theories and explanations grow out of the dirt of observations of reality. . . . Getting your hands dirty with the nitty-gritty details . . . is a good way to test the abstractions of theory, and perhaps to develop alternate theory, or modifications of theories."[17] In that spirit we have aimed to write an empirical book that sets forth and illuminates important data regarding the Central American drug trade, while using inductive observations to provide the first detailed, comparative account of drugs and the law in this region.

Exploring this variety of transnational crime in this region of a globalized world seemed to us to invite an interdisciplinary approach. We are political scientists, but we have also drawn on the disciplines of law, history, geography, economics, and criminal justice. Furthermore, in conducting our fieldwork, we found it necessary to live for a period in each of the five countries, to become closely familiar with the geography, culture, institutions, and procedures of each society; to develop networks of sources; and to begin to ferret out information. We then tried to assemble for scholarly analysis the type of information that, if assembled at all, had heretofore been largely restricted to antidrug and intelligence services.

Our work also has a theoretical dimension in seeking to go beyond laying out facts to pose conceptual questions about the role of bridge states in the international drug trade and to develop a framework to better understand how states have tried to contend with this aspect of transnational crime. From this standpoint this volume continues our past work on the state. In the mid-1990s we collaborated on our first book exploring the role of state sovereignty in international relations. At a time when many scholars were portraying sovereignty as "perforated, defiled, cornered, eroded, extinct, anachronistic, bothersome, even interrogated," we struck off on a different course, arguing that, although the implications of sovereignty for international affairs now vary from past eras, the concept has remained at the center of international discourse.[18] Other scholars then elaborated on that basic theme, arguing that sovereignty has remained viable, though reflective of "organized hypocrisy," or subject to occasional revolutions in meaning.[19]

When the Central American drug trade is viewed through an international relations lens, certain preliminary points stand out. Academics have long agreed that relations between states should no longer be the sole focus of scholarly attention in this field. Furthermore, it is no longer self-evident, as it may once have seemed to be, that states are automatically the chief actors in the international drama with other entities present on the stage but playing bit parts.[20] Drug organizations amount to transnational actors that take on far more than minor roles in these bridge states. Indeed, they contend with, challenge, and sometimes overwhelm bridge-state institutions. This book thus aims to further our understanding of the relationships between states and one important class of nonstate actors.

A study of bridge states is also interesting for students of international relations, because the Central American drug trade accelerated just in the period when the cold war era was succeeded by one marked by expanded trade, diminished militaries, enhanced regional integration, and increased globalization. We wondered how these broader phenomena would affect drug trafficking. While the drug trade via Central America has certainly spotlighted the difficulties of mounting an effective multilateral campaign against agile, wealthy, and opportunistic

16. We are indebted here to Alan Knight's views on empiricism and theory in scholarship regarding Latin America; see his "Modern Mexican State," 177–80.

17. Strange, *Retreat of the State*, xvi.

18. Fowler and Bunck, *Sovereign State*, 2–3.

19. Krasner, *Sovereignty*; Philpott, *Revolutions in Sovereignty*.

20. See Strange, *Retreat of the State*, 68.

nonstate actors, we believed that in such an era of rapid change, it was particularly important to relate drug smuggling through the Central American bridge states to broader international trends.

As the issues of the post–cold war world have become more sharply defined, we became especially interested in another overlooked and underexplored aspect of the clandestine side of globalization: how exactly have governments tried to contend with the illicit dimensions of the global economy?[21] Where in the middle decades of the last century scholars often portrayed states as omnicompetent, if not omnipotent, entities, and international relations was sometimes portrayed in terms that might be likened to leaders moving pieces on a diplomatic-military chessboard, scholarship toward the end of the cold war and throughout the post–cold war era has increasingly focused on the deficiencies and incapacities of states.[22] Indeed, in this age many governments have been unable to discharge even their most basic functions: maintaining law and order, promoting a sound economy, defending territory from foreign depredations, and operating a fair and effective legal system.[23] Increasingly, governments purport to regulate all kinds of activity that they have no real ability to oversee, and in many societies the notion that the state has a legal monopoly on violence seems like a curious abstraction largely irrelevant to daily life. Again, to us these points seemed directly relevant to bridge-state drug trafficking.

Such observations brought us, in turn, to what has been called the most prominent theoretical debate at the close of the twentieth century and outset of the twenty-first: to what extent are states retreating in light of increasingly global markets and increasingly pervasive transnational actors, some of them quite powerful? When confronted with the illicit global economy, states do not abandon the field so much as they retreat, persist, and reassert themselves in different ways.[24] We wondered if this would accurately describe the manner in which Central American bridge states were responding to the transshipment of large quantities of drugs.

In an attempt to explore these more theoretical considerations, while getting our hands dirty with the nitty-gritty details of the subject, we identified a handful of questions regarding bridge-state drug trafficking that have yet to be satisfactorily answered:

- Has the drug trade been confined to particular corners of Central America, or has it blanketed the region? To what extent have early trends, set in the 1980s and before, carried over to the 1990s and the twenty-first century?
- How exactly have wealthy and violent illegal business enterprises chosen to carry out transshipment operations within the Central American bridge states? Which methods have traffickers used, and what routes to market have they blazed?
- Which drug organizations have directed transshipment through Central America and over what time periods? Which Colombian and Mexican cartels have been most active in which countries? What might be concluded of the native drug-trafficking organizations within the bridge states? How have they operated?
- What key characteristics of the Central American states have factored into the drug trade? Have antidrug successes had lasting positive consequences, or have they turned out to be largely ephemeral triumphs?
- How has the drug trade been perceived within the bridge states over time? Have actions matched rhetoric or not? What measures have been adopted to respond to government trafficking? How enthusiastically and how

21. See Walker, "Limits of Coercive Diplomacy," 143; and Friman and Andreas, *Illicit Global Economy*, vii, 2.

22. Cf. Claude, *Global System*, 35.

23. With a few liberties we paraphrase here Strange, *Retreat of the State*, xii.

24. Friman and Andreas, *Illicit Global Economy*, 3.

effectively have policies been implemented? How successful have smuggling organizations been in evading or co-opting authorities?

- What has the extraordinary stress test of the passage to market of many millions of dollars worth of drugs meant for government structures—political, judicial, penal, and law enforcement? What has it meant for people, whether nationals or foreigners, traffickers or law-abiding citizens, politicians, police officers, judges, prison wardens, or other officials?
- Finally, what does the record of bridge-state drug trafficking reveal about international relations in the late twentieth and early twenty-first centuries and, in particular, the efforts of governments to contend with the challenges posed by drug organizations and the role they are playing in the illegal global economy?

Our focus on the Central American bridge states steers our contribution to the now voluminous illegal drug literature away from South American production and North American and European dealing and consumption. However, by focusing on trafficking, our work may shed light on why officials have so often been disappointed by the long-term results of interdiction strategies. Although over the years impressive seizure and arrest totals have accumulated, not enough drugs have been intercepted to raise prices so high as to discourage drug use. Prior studies of drug smuggling and interdiction have largely focused on police efforts at the borders of market states. We look instead to the bridge states and show that here interdiction of large percentages of the drugs in transit has failed to occur. However, the subsequent policy issue of just how many government resources ought to be devoted to trying to curtail supply as opposed to attempting to reduce demand is beyond the purview of this study. We have also chosen not to address the related question of whether states should respond to drug abuse and violence by decriminalizing or legalizing drugs. While our work may provide grist for that mill, the topic has already been well canvassed, with basic arguments readily accessible. Furthermore, until quite recently such potentially dramatic policy changes have had little support within our area of focus—Latin America and particularly Central America.[25]

The Challenges of Studying Bridge-State Drug Trafficking

That scholars have seldom addressed even the quite fundamental issues regarding bridge-state trafficking that we have sought to explore is attributable, in part, to the fact that so much of the trade occurs outside of public view. Transnational criminal organizations have gone to considerable lengths to keep activities secret, attempting to camouflage their routes, personnel, and methods, including the manner in which they have corrupted authorities to ensure the smooth flow of drugs to market. The secrecy that cloaks this subject led many to doubt whether our research project was viable. Certainly, many standard social science tools commonly used to investigate new topics have strictly limited applicability to the drug trade. For instance, apart from a small handful of quite useful studies that have questioned imprisoned traffickers, survey research has revealed little about this brand of transnational criminal activity.[26] Although polling can indicate something about public perceptions of

25. At present, very few Central Americans and no governments favor legalization of all or even most drugs. A 1993 Costa Rica poll, for example, found 93 percent opposed to legalizing drugs. "Ticos opuestos a legalizar venta de drogas," *LN* (CR), 14 October 1992, 1. In 2009, however, the Argentinian and then the Colombian Supreme Court ruled unconstitutional prosecution for possession of drugs for personal use, an approach that may gain traction in Central America. "New Approach to Drugs Seeks Footing in C.R.," *Tico Times* (Costa Rica) (hereafter cited as *TT* [CR]), 16 April 2010, 3.

26. See, for instance, Decker and Chapman, *Drug Smugglers*, and Reuter and Haaga, *Drug Markets*.

drug corruption, the illicit nature of the subject and consequent efforts to cover up activities may well distort mass opinion.

As for statistical analyses, for decades law-enforcement officials have compiled data on drug production and seizures, drug-related arrests, and the confiscation of drug-tainted assets. While drawing on this, we recognize its limitations, various aspects of which have been well documented.[27] Statistics can illuminate certain aspects of bridge-state trafficking, but not others. And, although some figures appear to be reasonably reliable—advanced only after data have been carefully collected, processed, and cross-checked—others are imprecise or even suspect. The validity of drug statistics depends on honest, thorough, and conscientious professionals reporting numbers that are compiled with logical and consistent methodologies across different countries for a number of consecutive years. Unfortunately, these attributes have rarely been evident.[28]

On inspection, certain statistics regarding drugs in Central America turned out to be simply rough estimates. Government data have sometimes been collected and advanced without methodological rigor. The biases of those charged with assembling the facts may have affected some figures, and political agendas may have intervened in the collecting or publicizing of some drug data.[29] Certainly, those reporting figures have often had a stake in inflating or deflating particular numbers, either to gain personal promotions or to enhance the flow of resources from those funding antidrug activities.[30] In any event, many statistics have been publicized without clear explanation, leading to ambiguities and misunderstandings.[31] Moreover, just what many commonly tracked statistics demonstrate can be arguable. For example, that more traffickers are arrested and more drugs interdicted may indicate improving law enforcement, larger amounts of drugs being shipped to market, or some combination.[32] Thus, some drug statistics are flawed, and many are open to varying interpretations.

More broadly, a recurrent problem in investigating Central American drug trafficking concerns finding reliable sources to depend on, whether statistical or otherwise. Across the region officials have failed to keep sufficiently detailed records on drug cases. Material from Central American legal archives has tended to be erratic in quantity and quality, making it difficult to follow a trafficker's career or an organization's life history. In some countries prison and court records have been ambiguous, fragmentary, inaccurate, or missing. Librarians in national libraries have sometimes neglected even to keep legal statutes and codes properly

27. See Robinson and Scherlen, *Lies*; Gootenberg, *Andean Cocaine*, 327; and Reuter, "Mythical Numbers."

28. Consider, for instance, the following exchange recounted in the memoirs of a DEA agent temporarily assigned to a desk job in the Latin American unit. Another agent advised him, "'The other half of the job is makin' up fact sheets and briefing papers—you know statistical bullshit, how we're winnin' the war—so one of these clowns can go on TV or testify before Congress.' 'Where do you get the statistics?' Tom laughed, 'Outta your head, where else?'" Levine, *Big White Lie*, 129. If some DEA statistics have lacked reliability, one must wonder about the data compiled by police forces across Central America that may be less professional still.

29. Here, the situation in Central America has analogues elsewhere in the region. For instance, for the allegation that the U.S. State Department was underestimating Mexican marijuana production for political reasons, see Shannon, *Desperados*, 126.

30. Thoumi, *Political Economy*, 180, 201n4.

31. For example, when annual marijuana seizures are reported without distinguishing between domestic marijuana and Colombian marijuana being transshipped through a country, its utility is reduced for those studying bridge-state trafficking, as it is when annual totals of seized cocaine erratically factor in instances in which traffickers jettisoned their cargo while being pursued or U.S. Coast Guard seizures with national ship riders on board. Statistics can mislead in more subtle ways as well. For instance, much of the marijuana grown in Central America for export is of the *sinsemilla* strain, in which the top is the most valuable portion. However, when governments reported that a certain number of marijuana plants had been eradicated, they did not state whether the tops of the plants had already been harvested, a ploy used by marijuana traffickers in league with corrupt antidrug officials in Mexico. See Poppa, *Drug Lord*, 68.

32. Andreas, *Border Games*, 145.

updated. Archival research can thus be quite challenging.

Despite these many difficulties, this book proceeds from the premise that scholars can go much further in studying the role of bridge countries in the international drug trade than has hitherto been evident. In fact, extraordinary amounts of data on bridge-state trafficking are available in open sources, particularly in the Spanish language, much of it never before synthesized and analyzed.[33] Certain useful government documents, such as the periodic reports of the Costa Rican and Honduran Legislative Commissions on Narcotics Trafficking, are publicly available. Bodies of relevant laws may be reviewed as well, those dealing specifically with drugs as well as those focused on related subjects, such as bail, extradition, and search and seizure. Furthermore, various U.S. government sources, including congressional hearings and reports, once-classified documents published by the National Security Archive, and DEA and Central Intelligence Agency (CIA) materials, can clarify points about regional drug transshipment.

Most important, drug rings operating in the bridge states have slipped up, and the seizures and arrests that have unraveled their operations have exposed many activities. As our extensive Index of Cases attests, much information has been published in case reports and other legal documents from criminal proceedings in market and bridge states alike. Furthermore, antidrug officials have often consented to be interviewed, and a handful have written accounts of the drug trade, as have various traffickers after arrest. And, although few secondary sources deal directly with drug smuggling via the bridge states, much of the drug literature touches indirectly on the subject.

Thus, we took on the task of canvassing a broad array of sources on Central American drug trafficking and then sifting through a wealth of data to determine just how drugs have moved across the region and with what consequences. In conducting dozens of interviews in our five case studies, we spoke with many officials, including ministers of interior and justice, diplomats, legislators, foreign ministers, and even a prime minister. In addition, we contacted a host of officials working at different levels of the criminal-justice systems, including police officers, jurists, prosecutors, defense lawyers, public defenders, human rights observers, and prison wardens. We conversed with social workers, public health officials, and clerics with insights on the drug trade. We interviewed editors of newspapers within the bridge states, along with a range of academic observers, including professors at the region's most highly regarded universities. We met as well with various authorities from the United Nations Latin American Institute for Crime Prevention and the Treatment of Offenders, including the director of the Organized Crime and Drug Traffic program. In each of the five countries we communicated with a slew of individuals on a not-for-attribution basis, including private citizens, foreign diplomats, and law-enforcement officials.

From this research we have tried to weave together many threads—individuals and organizations, places and routes, policies and laws, antidrug failures and successes—into a single fabric that presents the Central American drug trade accurately and holistically, nationally and regionally. Although no research project concerning secret illicit activity can be foolproof, we have attempted to corroborate information by relying on multiple sources, wherever possible, while weeding out material that seemed biased, implausible, or contradictory. In hopes that our work will stimulate others to sift through this information and to qualify, correct,

33. That unclassified information is readily available does not necessarily mean that it "is automatically available to officials who need it, or in the form they need it." Betts, *Enemies of Intelligence*, 5.

and amplify our findings, we have tried to be as thorough as possible in indicating the sources that substantiate our points.

Clarification of Terms

Where preexisting scholarship is scarce, clarifying the terms used takes on particular importance. In this regard, categorizing the Central American countries as bridge states, as opposed to market states, ought to be qualified by the fact that drug consumption has risen sharply in each republic. For many years traffickers have purposefully stimulated domestic markets in the region by compensating bridge-state associates with drugs rather than cash, and these were then often transferred to local dealers in local markets.[34] Furthermore, after traffickers have crashed planes, botched airdrops, or jettisoned cargoes during pursuit at sea, lost drug shipments have often been sold within the bridge countries. In fact, with significant drug use occurring throughout the Americas, the distinction between bridge and consumer states has become blurred. Indeed, because much cocaine headed for Canada passes through U.S. territory or waters, in a sense even the United States has served as a bridge country as well as the leading market state.[35] Nevertheless, the chief role for the Central American countries in the drug trade has been to serve as a route to consumers elsewhere. This distinguishes them from countries that are principally markets.

While the Central American republics are most commonly referred to as bridge states, an alternative metaphor conceives of the Latin American drug trade as a pipeline, with much of the product originating in South America, particularly in Colombia.[36] This image, however, also needs to be qualified and further elaborated. Some Central American countries have produced drugs for export, most notably, opium in Guatemala and marijuana in Belize and Panama. These drugs might be envisioned as entering the pipeline along its course, adding to the main flow from South America. Moreover, most drugs passing through the pipeline have been directed to Mexico, and Mexican traffickers have then transported the drugs across the border into the United States.[37] Hence, the Central American portion of the pipeline has not necessarily emptied into a market country, though it sometimes has. Instead, it has often deposited the drugs into what might be envisioned as the key reservoir state, where supplies have been pooled before being smuggled into the U.S. market.

One might wonder, then, why we chose to confine our case studies to Central America, rather than extend them to Mexico. Unlike the Central American republics, Mexico is not a prototypical transshipment country. Not only does it include a large and growing market of millions of drug consumers but over the past four decades it has housed numerous leading drug syndicates and has thus served as the headquarters for many trafficking ventures. In contrast, although important traffickers and organizations have flourished across Central America, these drug rings have never rivaled, much less overshadowed, Colombian groups, as their Mexican counterparts have grown to do. A quintessential bridge country has one paramount role—to provide passage to market for drugs. Mexico is thus not an archetype of a bridge state but is instead a special case, worthy of separate studies to analyze its various functions in the international drug trade.

34. Although some use the terms *trafficker* and *dealer* synonymously—indeed, some provisions in the laws of bridge states have failed to distinguish clearly between them—we use the former with reference to those moving drugs and the latter with reference to those engaged in retail or wholesale drug sales. An individual could be a trafficker and a dealer, and an organization could be engaged in trafficking and dealing, or these functions could be separated.

35. Andreas, *Border Games*, 17.

36. Chepesiuk, *Hard Target*, 14.

37. *INCSR* (1998), 173.

In clarifying our terms, we come next to the problematic term *cartel*. While an economic cartel is an arrangement among businesses to avoid free competition in a particular market by regulating prices and output, the word has been used differently with respect to the drug trade. Popular use of *cartel* in the drug context dates to 1983, when U.S. authorities had traced the cocaine in dozens of seizures to Medellín kingpin Jorge Luis Ochoa. It appeared that Ochoa and other prominent Medellín traffickers had engaged in some joint decision making and division of tasks. While the phrase *export cooperative* might have been more accurate, the DEA and various federal prosecutors began to use *cartel* to describe the thick web of interconnections that appeared to link Ochoa with other leading Colombian traffickers headquartered in Medellín.[38]

The word *cartel* thus came to signify mostly Colombian and Mexican, even occasionally Bolivian, criminal organizations that over an extended period procured considerable supplies of cocaine, oversaw their transport to market, and reaped significant profits. Certainly, this description makes for an imprecise definition. Determining whether a drug ring of some magnitude has attained cartel status is an inexact science. Nevertheless, the use of *cartel* has become deeply entrenched in discourse about the Latin American drug trade, frequently employed by journalists, politicians, counter-narcotics officials, prosecutors and judges, and many, though not all, scholars.

Given how often *cartel* appears, we adopt its usage as well, though we hasten to add certain clarifications. First, the term does not necessarily imply an ability to thoroughly control the supply of a drug or to form a monopoly or even an oligopoly that so diminishes competition as to permit price fixing.[39] Most drug cartels could not make a strong claim to such activities. In using the word *cartel*, we also do not mean to imply that these are especially monolithic organizations, that is, ones marked by uniformity, solidarity, and pyramidal hierarchies. The Medellín cartel, for instance, has been shown to have been not nearly so centralized and unified as popularly portrayed.[40] Nor has any cartel ever swept a drug-trafficking field of rivals. Given the low barriers to entry, new drug rings have tended to spring up over time. Often, these have drawn on experienced freelancers and the remnants of groups previously taken down by authorities, as well as profit-hungry newcomers, who often have relevant criminal experience outside the drug trade.[41] At times serving as junior partners or paying transit route taxes, smaller organizations have coexisted, and sometimes conflicted, with much larger ones, though only a few have evolved into cartels themselves.

Indeed, perhaps the principal reason that no cartel has monopolized the cocaine trade is that the potential profits for producers, intermediaries, transshippers, and dealers have been so

38. A sealed federal indictment in 1986 declared, "The Medellín cartel . . . consisted of controlling members of major international cocaine and manufacturing and distribution organizations. . . . Through the cartel, major cocaine organizations were able to pool resources, including raw materials, clandestine cocaine conversion laboratories, aircraft, vessels, transportation facilities, distribution networks, and cocaine to facilitate international narcotics trafficking. . . . The cartel members met at 'brokerage houses' in Medellín—private estates where drug lords dickered for pilots and lab service. The cartel maintained inventory control, corrupted officials of foreign governments, and carried out murders to 'protect its business operations and enforce its mandates.'" Gugliotta and Leen, *Kings of Cocaine*, 278.

39. See Zaitch, *Trafficking Cocaine*, 59; Kenney, *From Pablo to Osama*, 26; and Thoumi, *Political Economy*, 142. Although cartels have sometimes been able to influence market prices, supply and demand have remained the main price determinants, because many small organizations provide a significant percentage of the drugs consumed in major markets. Zabludoff, "Colombian Narcotics Organizations," 27.

40. See, for instance, Kenney, *From Pablo to Osama*, 88–89.

41. See Zabludoff, "Colombian Narcotics Organizations," 26, and Thoumi, "Illegal Drug Industry," 119.

lucrative as to encourage entrepreneurs.[42] In an era when U.S. dealers might sell a kilo of cocaine wholesale for $32,000, and their European counterparts for as much as $42,000, yet coca leaves might bring farmers $650 per kilo in Peru, any start-up organization could turn a quick substantial profit.[43] And law-enforcement pressure on leading organizations has increased opportunities for competitors to gain market share. Indeed, an internal dynamic within the drug trade favors smaller organizations, because they are less likely to come to the attention of rivals and law enforcement.[44]

Furthermore, those relatively infrequent occasions when interdiction has succeeded in raising prices have increased the incentive to ship more of the drug.[45] In addition, the closer to the source country interdiction has occurred, the less costly has it been for the traffickers to replace the lost load.[46] Since market-state law enforcement has posed the greatest risk for a drug shipment, much of the value added has come after the cocaine has transited through the bridge countries. This, too, has encouraged entrepreneurs who lack retail distribution abilities but can still sell the drugs wholesale in a market country.[47] Thus, although drug rings have created barriers to entry through violence aimed at maintaining or expanding their market share, even lesser networks prepared to cooperate with cartels, or with sufficient muscle and fortitude to withstand them, have soon accumulated considerable earnings.[48]

Groups of traffickers at work in Central America have sometimes been cells of foreign drug organizations, perhaps with a trusted representative planted in a particular zone to supervise a number of drug ventures.[49] At other times, such groups have been independent, or quasi-independent, entities. For instance, a Belizean network might undertake a service such as refueling cocaine planes for multiple foreign organizations. In parts of Spanish-speaking Central America, such native transshipment networks have been referred to as *cartelitos*, or "mini-cartels." For example, during the 1990s a number of cartelitos developed in Guatemala, each specializing in particular routes and methods and each with its own contacts within the larger Colombian and Mexican organizations.

In this way, Central American groups have contributed to the compartmentalizing of drug operations, enabling organizations to outsource key transportation functions, which has posed even more difficult challenges for law enforcement than more vertically integrated criminal groups doing most trafficking tasks themselves. In addition, a foreign drug organization might be active in a number of Central American countries, supplying, offering logistical support, and coordinating the activities of cartelitos or cells. Indeed, multiple cartels have often been at work simultaneously in the different bridge states, while a host of lesser networks, foreign and domestic, might be

42. For the role of entrepreneurs in the Mexican marijuana industry, see Kamstra, *Weed*, 75, 105.

43. For DEA statistics and U.S. prices, see Reuter, "Political Economy," 130, table 7.3. For European prices in this time frame, see "Tica detenida en París con catorce kilos de cocaína," *LN* (CR), 20 July 1995, 10A. Some scholars have debated whether (or which) groups trafficking drugs have sufficient hierarchy and cohesion to be properly called *organizations* at all, as opposed to a term such as *networks*, which connotes a looser and less vertical structure. Compare Decker and Chapman, *Drug Smugglers*, 15–17; Zaitch, "Post-Fordist Cocaine," 150, 170; and Williams, "Transnational Criminal Networks," 69. We consider all groups of traffickers working together to be *organizations*, although some are much more tightly and extensively organized than others.

44. Reuter and Haaga, *Drug Markets*, 41.

45. Cave and Reuter, *Interdictor's Lot*, v.

46. In 2010, for instance, a kilo of cocaine that cost $1,750 in Colombia might be purchased for roughly $6,000 in Central America, but multiples of those figures in the market countries. See "Carteles mexicanos del narco toman el continente," *LN* (CR), 31 January 2010, 20A.

47. Andreas, *Border Games*, 82.

48. Thoumi, *Political Economy*, 134.

49. See "'Mini carteles' colombianos operan desde Panamá," *LP* (PA), 10 January 2000, 5A.

moving smaller quantities of drugs through that country as well.

Conclusion

In the chapters that follow, we explore the particular deficiencies and abilities of people, governments, and drug organizations interacting in the bridge states. Certainly, the international drug trade is very much concerned with individual and collective incapacities. The rise of the marijuana, heroin, and cocaine industries is undergirded by millions of users unwilling or incapable of freeing themselves from drug use and so reducing the steep demand curve that stimulates trafficking. Within Central America, when confronted by the prospect of quick wealth, many individuals have overlooked the potential long-term costs of involvement in the trade. Not only has there been the risk of arrest or violent death for traffickers, but their friends and family members have frequently been drawn into illegal activities to their ultimate detriment. Participation in the drug trade has also turned facilitators, such as bankers, lawyers, and accountants, into white-collar criminals and has disrupted or ended the careers of many judges, politicians, military and police officers, and other government officials.

Our examination of the Central American drug trade also reveals the extraordinary capabilities of transnational criminal organizations to multiply and thrive in the post–cold war era. Drug rings have been able to adopt for their own purposes practices undertaken by legitimate international businesses. Particular kingpins as well as the leaders of Central American cells and cartelitos have become adept at reorienting when challenged by law-enforcement officials. Equally important, they have found ways to exploit an extraordinary variety of weaknesses or opportunities within different bridge states. Thus, while authorities have compiled records of seizures and arrests that are not unimpressive, the illegal drug industry as a whole continues to prosper—moving immense quantities of drugs to major markets in North America and Europe.

To answer the question of why trafficking through Central America so resists being curbed by national efforts, regional cooperation, or extraregional assistance, we would point, in the first instance, to the power of the bribes, bullets, and intimidation that drug organizations have wielded. Huge flows of drugs have headed to market, and enormous profits have returned to bolster and further motivate their organizations. So long as demand for narcotics remains strong, criminal groups will materialize to try to reap the extraordinary profits, and they will suborn, bully, and kill to protect their interests in the illicit global economy.

Institutional weaknesses help explain why traffickers have penetrated particular countries when they did.[50] Several cardinal factors have characterized government structures in the region. Virtually all lack the resources needed to carry out their functions effectively. Frequently, weak institutions are insufficiently transparent and lack the oversight necessary to ensure that officials are held accountable. Many do not have in place a formal set of operational rules and procedures adequate to provide guidance to those charged with carrying out assigned tasks or to discipline those who neglect their duties. Finally, weak institutions often have no tradition, no institutional culture, of laws, rules, and procedures generally followed and enforced in a consistent and unbiased manner. Naturally, countries with grave institutional weaknesses provide inviting targets for drug traffickers.

50. In developing our points on Central American institutional weaknesses, we found particularly useful Levitsky and Murillo, *Argentine Democracy*.

However, even taken together, the relative weakness of institutions in the different bridge states does not itself suffice to explain why, when, and how much drug trafficking occurs in each country. One might ask, if traffickers simply identify and exploit the countries with the weakest formal institutions, then why did the flow of cocaine actually increase through Panama after the downfall of the Noriega regime brought about governments intent on strengthening previously corrupted institutions? If institutional weakness were the sole variable at work, then one would expect trafficking organizations largely to avoid Costa Rica, the country with the strongest institutions. And yet Costa Rica has long been a critically important bridge state.

We have found that drug organizations can successfully operate in the face of the region's stronger government institutions as well as its weaker ones. Furthermore, institutions are but one factor in determining the extent of bridge-state drug transshipment. We shall see that noninstitutional factors, including geography, also greatly influence trafficking. Moreover, even the stronger and more stable institutions in Central America have often been rigid and inflexible. Institutions that are generally functioning effectively might not have been designed to cope with transnational criminal networks or with the particular stresses imposed by extraordinary drug flows. Their strengths seem not to include the adaptability needed to change to meet drug-trafficking challenges. In the case studies we thus note both the weak institutions and the rigidity of otherwise strong institutions that have helped to determine the extent of the drug trade.

The essence of our argument is that although the Central American bridge states have the power to join with outside powers, and occasionally with one another, to disrupt the operations of any particular criminal group transshipping drugs across their waters, territories, and skies, they have been overwhelmed by the drug trade as a whole. The social, economic, political, and geographic factors that propel this dimension of the illicit global economy—especially the North American and European demand for drugs produced in South America that governments throughout the world have outlawed—are too formidable for these states to counter effectively. When a large array of transnational criminal groups choose to ride these powerful currents toward wealth, Central American states lack the resources needed to stop, or even to dramatically curb, drug transshipment through the region. The balance of forces can thwart the efforts of the strongest countries in the region—newly developed Costa Rica, solidly democratic Belize, and economically dynamic Panama. And it can wreak havoc on the weakest—poverty-stricken Honduras and deeply fractured Guatemala.

The best that these bridge states can do is to try to minimize the bridge-favoring factors that traffickers perceive in sending drugs through their state and to maximize the bridge-disfavoring factors so as to encourage drug rings to shift more of their business to a neighboring state. However, altering certain bridge-favoring factors is impossible. For example, Belize and Guatemala flank Mexico, and Panama borders Colombia, making each of them attractive transshipment sites. Altering other bridge-favoring factors may be possible but also very costly, time-consuming, or uncertain. Consequently, Central American bridge states, even with extraordinary amounts of outside assistance, can devote many resources to countering drug smuggling and yet, despite disrupting many drug rings, can remain incapable of stemming the flow of drugs from South America to North American and European markets.

1

Central America and the International Trade in Drugs

As drug exports from South America initially gathered momentum in the late 1970s, criminal syndicates favored air and maritime routes through the Caribbean, including transshipment via the Bahamas, Cuba, Haiti, and Jamaica. In the early 1980s, however, responding to bloody struggles among cocaine traffickers contesting market shares, U.S. government initiatives in south Florida aimed to curtail air and sea drug imports.[1] At this time, various Caribbean governments, encouraged and pressured by the U.S. government and supported by the U.S. Coast Guard and the DEA, stepped up interdiction. U.S. officials also began to track air traffic headed toward Florida more thoroughly, using military planes equipped with the advanced Airborne Warning and Control System (AWACS).[2] In this way, oversight improved of Florida's air and waters—traditionally the chief target for drug smugglers—as well as of three Caribbean straits: the Mona Passage, Windward Passage, and Yucatán Channel.[3]

With the smooth flow of drugs to market jeopardized, by 1984 significant Colombian traffickers had started to import cocaine across the U.S.-Mexican border. This strategic shift empowered Mexican drug organizations, which brought the Colombians to search for the least risky and most cost-effective routes to transship drugs into Mexico.[4] Here, the skies, territories,

1. See generally Eddy, Sabogal, and Walden, *Cocaine Wars.*

2. According to his brother, however, Pablo Escobar was paying a U.S. Customs agent to provide the schedules of AWACS planes so that his pilots could avoid flying at times or in areas under surveillance. Escobar, *Accountant's Story*, 65–66.

3. See CIA, *Allegations of Connections*, 7, and Shannon, *Desperados*, 322.

4. For DEA official David Westrate's congressional testimony, see Andreas, *Border Games*, 44.

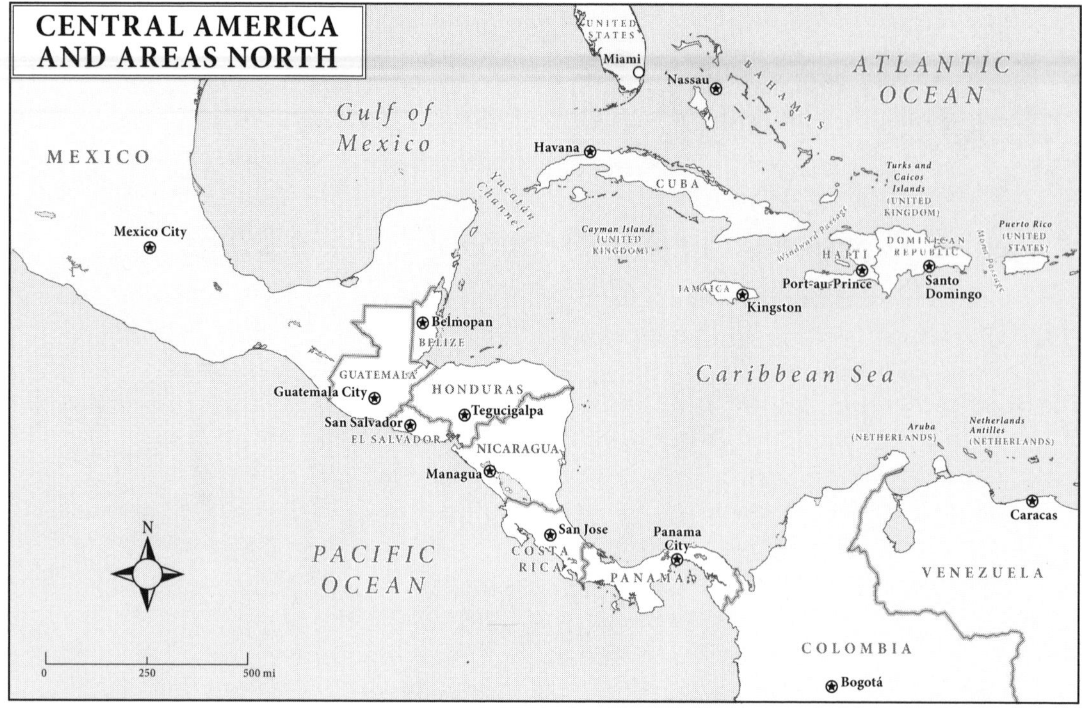

MAP 1.1

and offshore waters of Central American countries proved to have real competitive advantages. Most important, intercepting drugs entering or leaving islands is less difficult than doing so in larger countries with porous land borders and long coastal stretches. Central American transit thus began to eclipse Caribbean routes as the leading pathway for South American drugs, and more cocaine began to enter the southwestern United States than Florida.[5] Cocaine imports to the United States via Mexico rose to one-third of the total in 1989, to more than half in 1992, and to 80 percent by century's end.[6]

By the early 1980s significant cocaine shipments—fifty to three hundred kilograms for that period—were regularly transiting Central America, and by the 1990s Caribbean routes had been relegated to a secondary, though still quite significant, role.[7] Of course, the Central American versus Caribbean choice was not necessarily either/or. A number of routes have involved both regions, as when cocaine has been shipped from Panama to Haiti, flown from Costa Rica to the Bahamas, or sent aboard speedboats from Colombia's resort island of San Andrés to Belize, Honduras, or Costa Rica. Furthermore, in the drug trade, predictability increases the risk of interception, while using a multiplicity of routes spreads bets across the board. Thus, drug routes through the Caribbean have by no means been abandoned,

5. Confidential interviews with U.S. officials familiar with Caribbean basin drug-smuggling patterns, July 1990, Guatemala City, Guatemala, and December 1991, Tegucigalpa, Honduras. See also "U.S. Technology Gleans Data on Drug Corridor," *Washington Post* (hereafter cited as *WP* [US]), 26 June 1992, A26. According to insider Roberto Escobar, the use of AWACS was central to the Medellín cartel's decision to send more drugs through Central America and Mexico. Escobar, *Accountant's Story*, 67.

6. Smith, "Semiorganized International Crime," 195.

7. Efficient routes have long moved drugs through Haiti and the Dominican Republic, while traffickers used Jamaica and the Bahamas intensively at even earlier dates.

although over the last two decades they have not threatened the status of Central America as the leading transshipment zone.

The Stimulus for Central American Drug Trafficking

Geography must stand as the initial factor that has transformed Central America into perhaps the world's preeminent bridge region. These states, squarely situated between South American producers and the immense market of North American consumers, have enjoyed relatively easy access to Mexico—that paramount gateway into the United States. In addition, the lack of sustained, broad-based economic development, coupled with pockets of extreme poverty, has helped to produce ready supplies of collaborators for foreign and domestic trafficking organizations.[8] "For every one arrested," one foreign law-enforcement official declared, "there are a hundred hungry souls eager to take his place."[9] In this way, personal economic travails have aligned with the objectives and operations of international drug-trafficking organizations.

Had those working in Central American drug trafficking confronted modern laws against transnational organized crime, vigilant law enforcement, able prosecution, and stiff penalties, including imprisonment in secure penitentiaries, the potential costs of involvement might have deterred some individuals. In fact, these bridge states have also attracted smuggling organizations because their criminal-justice systems, often antiquated and haphazardly constructed, have usually functioned poorly. Legal institutions have tended to be underfunded and prone to intimidation and corruption, offering wealthy traffickers multiple opportunities to escape conviction or at least lengthy imprisonment. While trying to contend with new and different varieties of crime in rapidly urbanizing societies that have expanded quickly with youthful populations, chiefs of police have often had to stretch their poorly compensated forces to cover their countries as best they could. Transnational criminal networks have thus been able to exploit the grave limitations of domestic law enforcement.

A catalog of cross-regional factors relevant to the drug trade must also include the nationalistic sensitivities, occasionally developing into animosities, that have long divided various Central American peoples. Historical tensions between certain of these countries and the United States have also sometimes resulted in difficult relations. Only infrequently have leading policy makers in neighboring states been simultaneously disposed to prioritize antidrug measures, especially those going beyond rhetoric to require significant outlays of resources.[10] Other domestic and foreign-policy issues, some of which have involved conflicting priorities, have often distracted top officials from countering the drug trade. It is true that, from time to time, collaborative projects involving joint patrols, shared intelligence, and common border monitoring have occurred—sometimes stimulated by outside encouragement or pressure. But, on the whole, intraregional counternarcotics efforts have been slow to develop and have proven to be easily derailed. Few have been especially inspired or creative. While some unofficial transnational networks of mid-level personnel interacting in the implementation of antidrug measures have coalesced, these have tended to be more fragile in Central America than in a more cohesive, developed, wealthy, and technologically advanced region such as

8. According to one authority, "The hundreds of millions of under- or unemployed poor provide a vast seething cauldron in which criminality of all sorts can and does incubate and multiply." Bagley, "Globalisation," 34.

9. Confidential interview, December 1991, Tegucigalpa, Honduras.

10. With reference to the joint antidrug endeavors of Caribbean bridge states, one scholar likewise observed, "Collaboration among states may result in conflict over sovereignty and perception of the nature and severity of threats and, therefore, appropriate responses." Griffith, "Political Economy of Drugs," 107.

western Europe.[11] Given the lack of resources and training, cross-national law-enforcement networks have been prone to lapse into inactivity.

Deep-seated concerns that neighbors or more powerful countries might infringe on sovereignty have also hampered cooperative antidrug initiatives.[12] With seven states sharing a relatively small region, Central America has numerous land and maritime boundaries. Despite increasing interdependence and globalization, borders remain highly relevant to the drug trade and efforts to counter it.[13] Whether on land, sea, or air, borders have tended to be sufficiently fluid to permit traffickers reasonably easy ingress and egress, but they have then bedeviled authorities trying to stop the rapid passage of drug shipments. Furthermore, free trade policies have brought expedited inspections of vehicles, border posts open for longer hours, and ready access to neighboring countries.[14] Criminals have often easily crossed the region's porous borders, either merging into legitimate traffic or simply ignoring customs posts and entering where they liked. Foreign traffickers have suddenly appeared in a country during a transshipment operation and then just as abruptly vanished. The inability of authorities, whether police or military, to cross Central American boundaries in hot pursuit, indeed, to exercise any of a range of law-enforcement functions on another state's soil, has hampered official efforts to contend effectively with transnational organizations able to move speedily and alter plans nimbly.[15]

In addition, across Central America, armed forces have proven to be largely inadequate to provide for national security when confronted with the asymmetrical threats posed by transnational criminal groups. Because for many years patrols of airspace have been inadequate and radar coverage limited, most unauthorized drug flights have proceeded unhindered. For its part, while the U.S. military has long tracked drug planes and forwarded such intelligence to the DEA and national authorities in Central America, the U.S. Air Force has not been constituted as a law-enforcement agency and has been of limited utility in stopping aerial drug smuggling.[16]

Moreover, since the navies and coast guards of these bridge states typically have had only a tenuous grip on offshore activities, local authorities have infrequently intercepted maritime shipments, unless tipped off by the DEA. In any event, as fears of communist subversion have diminished and democracy has taken root, governments across the region have drawn down military forces.[17] In some places the deemphasis of national security has helped to ensure the ready transit of drugs, but in others,

11. For basic information on European Union law-enforcement networks, see Slaughter, *New World Order*, 56.

12. See Joyce, "Transnational Criminal Enterprise," 111. As Joyce observed, "Effective cooperation may require surrender of some of the core prerogatives of statehood in the spheres of criminal justice, law enforcement, and security." U.S. authorities used sovereignty concerns to try to rally support for antidrug measures. "Technology Gleans Data," A25.

13. Cf. Andreas, *Border Games*, 4.

14. See "Police Make Record Drug Busts in 2007," *Nica Times* (Costa Rica) (hereafter cited as *NT* [CR]), 11 January 2008, 2.

15. See, for instance, "Just What the Smuggler Ordered," *WP* (US), 2 August 1998, A1.

16. The 1878 Posse Comitatus Act, 18 U.S.C. §1385, has generally prohibited the U.S. armed forces from engaging in domestic law enforcement. While the U.S. armed forces still lack arrest powers, the legal regime was loosened in the 1980s, with one important step a 1986 directive from President Ronald Reagan that classified drugs as a national security threat. See U.S. House, *Posse Comitatus Act*; "Reagan Order Defines Drug Trade as Security Threat, Widens Military Role," *WP* (US), 8 June 1986, A26; and Andreas, *Border Games*, 43.

17. For the seven Central American republics, the total active military forces, including the paramilitary units of Costa Rica, and eventually Panama and Guatemala, rose from 173,410 in 1985 to 210,200 in 1990, and then dropped to 127,050 in 1995, 101,550 in 2000, and 88,250 in 2005, before rising slightly to 96,850 in 2009. See International Institute for Strategic Studies, *Military Balance* (hereafter cited as *MB*), *1985–1986*, 142–53; *MB, 1989–1990*, 184–99; *MB, 1994–1995*, 200–216; *MB, 1999–2000*, 222–37; *MB, 2004–2005*, 199–212; and *MB, 2009*, 65–88.

officers have searched avidly for opportunities for additional compensation—a boon to drug trafficking in those states in which the military has exercised substantial control. Capitalizing on their extraordinary resources, drug organizations have gained extensive experience in corrupting those who might oppose them, including members of militaries.

At sea the U.S. Coast Guard, the principal maritime antidrug force in international waters off Central America, has not been able to enter the territorial waters of these bridge states to enforce drug laws absent specific agreements authorizing joint operations. Thus, between 1991 and 2003 the U.S. government signed cooperative agreements for maritime counterdrug operations in all five of the countries we studied.[18] These so-called ship-rider agreements typically enabled the coast guard to proceed with patrols or in hot pursuit so long as an official of the state in whose territorial waters the operation was occurring was on board to authorize formally any law-enforcement action. All told, this has proven to be a particularly successful antidrug initiative. Nevertheless, while these treaties were being conceived, negotiated, and approved, maritime drug smuggling soared. In addition, having to follow the procedures laid out has sometimes proven cumbersome.[19] Traffickers have periodically succeeded in evading pursuit, even after a U.S. ship has spotted their vessel and started to give chase, and in Honduras and Panama supplementary implementing arrangements had to be designed to correct flaws in the treaties. Indeed, the ship-rider approach has been ideally suited only for those times when the U.S. Coast Guard was conducting planned operations near a country's territorial waters and could get a local official on board before suspected vessels were sighted.

Within the Central American states, where large drug loads have been seized and leading traffickers arrested, the U.S. government has frequently led the way. Operating through its DEA, the U.S. Department of Justice has had the financial and technological resources needed to develop intelligence on upcoming drug shipments. DEA agents have operated out of U.S. embassies across the region, recruiting informants and cultivating ties with the local authorities in charge of actually arresting traffickers and seizing drugs.[20] However, the DEA, too, has limited resources. The budget for Central America has been modest, and the number of agents assigned to the region has not been large. Their attention has been chiefly directed toward major organizations and trafficking ventures, rather than smaller criminal groups moving lesser quantities.

Although the DEA has been institutionally stable, retaining most policies and personnel despite periodic government transitions and occasional scandals, such has often not been the case with the national police forces with which it has cooperated. In Central America constant turnover in personnel and other institutional difficulties have often led to real discontinuity in antidrug law enforcement. When faced with soaring international trafficking, Central American governments have frequently responded by terminating and then reorganizing counternarcotics institutions when they have

18. See DOS, *Drug Interdiction Agreements*.

19. In a representative instance in 1998 a U.S. patrol plane spotted a suspicious speedboat heading north along the Costa Rican coast. A U.S. Navy guided missile carrier, almost two thousand feet in length, in the area intercepted the go-fast, ultimately firing fifteen warning shots in an unsuccessful effort to stop it. However, the vessel fled into Nicaraguan territorial waters and vanished before the U.S. authorities could get Nicaragua's approval to continue the hot pursuit.

20. Within the Central American republics the U.S. government opened DEA offices as follows: Panama City, Panama, in 1972; San José, Costa Rica, in 1974; Guatemala City, Guatemala, in 1975; Tegucigalpa, Honduras, in 1981; Managua, Nicaragua, in 1989; Belize City, Belize, in 1992; and San Salvador, El Salvador, in 1992. Bartilow and Kihong, "Busting Drugs," 114. Before DEA offices were opened in various of these countries, the office in a neighboring state sometimes covered their counterdrug activities, such as DEA agents stationed in Guatemala operating in Belize.

become discredited. Governments have removed antidrug officials to eliminate suspect individuals, punish lack of success, offer up a scapegoat, or reward political patrons. Whether such turnover has been merited or not, in most of the bridge states the reporting requirements, chains of command, even the names of antidrug units have repeatedly changed. This constant state of flux has contributed to ongoing institutional weaknesses.

Yet another factor promoting Central American drug trafficking has been the conflicting and overlapping law-enforcement jurisdictions. Typically, many national actors have had antidrug responsibilities: customs officials; naval, army, and air force personnel; antinarcotics, anticorruption, and other special units; and multiple police forces, run by the judiciary and by federal or provincial authorities.[21] Many of these units have been secretive, reluctant to share information or otherwise cooperate with one another. Latin American militaries have been especially so and have frequently taken advantage of their distinctive legal status as well.[22] Infighting over turf has then commonly occurred, as different units have grappled with one another for scarce resources, for their vision of strategies and objectives, for public and governmental attention, and on occasion, for assuming the prime position to reap bribes.

Furthermore, the complexities, confusions, sometimes even chaos in enforcement have been overlaid on often patently inadequate laws dealing with drug trafficking. Apart from Belize, which has struggled with a somewhat different set of legal problems, the rest of the region has been firmly rooted in civil law traditions.[23] Their legal systems have not traditionally recognized conspiracy to be a crime, and wiretapping and various undercover operations, including controlled deliveries, have been difficult to undertake lawfully, such that perpetrators can be successfully prosecuted.[24] In addition, traditionally, penalties for trafficking drugs have been much lower than those found in most developed countries. These ingredients, combined, form a recipe for a highly ineffective legal regime versus organized crime.

On top of these factors, after decades of internal violence and civil war plagued Guatemala, El Salvador, and Nicaragua, by the late 1990s an estimated one to two million weapons were circulating through Central America, no longer controlled by regular or rebel armed forces.[25] Not only have traffickers purchased and put to use grenades, high-powered automatic weapons, and other small arms, but these have also contributed to increasingly violent domestic crime. And other criminal activity has often diverted the attention of authorities from drug trafficking. Indeed, some officials have suspected that drug organizations have actively encouraged it for precisely this reason.

Meanwhile, the guerrillas and the paramilitaries engaged in the Colombian civil war have had ready access to cocaine supplies and their own steep demand for weapons. Central Americans have thus participated in numerous arms-for-drugs exchanges, including barter transactions involving combinations of money, weapons, and narcotics.[26] In the late twentieth and early

21. The complex of authorities tasked with antidrug responsibilities has also occasionally proved counterproductive in the United States and other market societies, though the extent of the problems in Central America would be difficult to match.

22. Astorga, "Mexico," 98.

23. For a comparison of the administration of justice in Belize and Guatemala, see Fowler and Bunck, "Legal Imperialism."

24. See Nadelmann, *Cops Across Borders*, 192–94, 225–35. While Nadelmann focuses on the misgivings of European officials regarding undercover operations, the same hesitations have surfaced in Central America.

25. See "Region Takes Aim at Weapons Traffickers," *TT* (CR), 7 December 2001, 5; "The Most Violent Area in the Americas," *TT* (CR), 18 August 2000, 8; and Cragin and Hoffman, *Arms Trafficking*. Between 1979 and 1990 the Nicaraguan government alone distributed 600,000 AK-47 rifles and recovered only 180,000 of them. "Armas sin control en el istmo," *LN* (CR), 1 February 1997, 17A.

26. See Cragin and Hoffman, *Arms Trafficking*, 68.

twenty-first centuries, arms-for-drugs deals have occurred periodically in Costa Rica, Honduras, Nicaragua, and Panama, some of large scale.[27] Capitalizing on this, an undercover U.S. Federal Bureau of Investigation (FBI) agent in a 2002 sting operation arranged to trade an array of Russian-made weapons, including shoulder-fired antiaircraft missiles, nine thousand assault weapons, three hundred thousand grenades, and sixty million rounds of ammunition to the Autodefensas Unidas de Colombia (AUC) in exchange for $25 million in cocaine. In this case twenty-five Costa Rican officers then trapped and arrested the AUC representatives at a hotel meeting arranged, purportedly, to seal the deal.[28] In other cases, however, the authorities have failed to root out arms-for-drugs transactions or have taken action too late to stop them.

A handful of cardinal factors that have affected much of the region have thus greatly stimulated drug trafficking through the Central American bridge states. Arms, poverty, overmatched militaries, weak legal regimes, dismal law enforcement, and ineffective cooperative efforts have joined with geography to create an ideal region for drug transshipment. In addition, in much of Central America the state, historically, "has been used as a means of obtaining and enlarging personal fortunes."[29] This, too, has promoted the extensive narco-corruption through which criminal groups have arranged for drugs to flow through these countries without interruption.

One might at first assume that because our five Central American case studies coexist within a fairly small region and have shared historical experiences and social and economic obstacles, their political, judicial, and law-enforcement systems would closely resemble one another, and the development of the drug trade within their boundaries would follow identical courses. Indeed, the common characteristics of these countries, once derogatorily labeled "banana republics," have gained considerable attention. Observers have pointed to the interference of various Central American militaries in political affairs, the chronic instability of many of the political systems, the pervasive corruption hampering government functions, and the numerous twentieth-century U.S. interventions.

With respect to the drug trade, however, we have been struck as much by the distinctions among our case studies as by their similarities. In terms of geography the Central American bridge states have varying combinations of jungle, mountains, islands, inland waterways, and lengthy coastlines, each of which factors into transshipment schemes in different ways. Indeed, we have coined the phrase "the geotactics of the drug trade" to denote the manner in which drug networks have formulated trafficking strategies by assembling different methods, routes, and logistics, many dependent on geographic factors. To take one of many possible examples, the placid sea dotted with cayes that lies behind the Belizean barrier reef has encouraged speedboat deliveries of cocaine, while narcotics have been routinely shipped via the deep-water ports of Honduras and Panama.

27. Arms worth $1,200 apiece in Nicaragua could bring $2,000 or more in Colombia, and, rather than pay cash, Colombian fighters preferred to trade kilos of cocaine for weapons. In 2001, after a series of weapons confiscations in Panama and Costa Rica, Panamanian authorities noted that Colombian guerrillas were paying for contraband weapons with cocaine. See "Regional Pact Sought to Bust Illegal Drug Trafficking," *TT* (CR), 9 November 2001, 9. In 2004 Panamanian police broke up a barter transaction that apparently was to involve 441 kilos of cocaine for 80.4 kilos of Lodex explosives manufactured in Costa Rica. "Eighty Kilos of Tico Explosives Found in Panama," *TT* (CR), 26 March 2004, 3. The following year Honduran authorities arrested FARC collaborators attempting to arrange arms-for-drugs transactions. "Honduras Arrests Two FARC Agents," *TT* (CR), 1 April 2005, N-3.

28. "Big Bust Nabs Arms Dealers," *TT* (CR), 8 November 2002, 1A.

29. Pérez, "Drugs," 150.

In a private conversation with the director of the United Nations Drug Control Program, a Caribbean police commissioner declared that the drug problems of the twenty-nine countries being discussed "were like fingerprints: no two were identical, and, for that same reason, no two strategies to combat them could be identical either."[30] Likewise, both drug trafficking and counternarcotics activities in the Central American bridge states have varied in notable ways. Political, judicial, and law-enforcement institutions have functioned in somewhat different manners. The degree of transparency; the content of laws, policies, and procedures; the levels of resources and official competence and motivation; the sophistication of institutions; and institutional flexibility and rigidity have differed from state to state. The region, in fact, hosts a spectrum of regime types, each with its own distinctive profile. Although the historical experiences of these countries have paralleled one another in certain significant respects, they have contrasted markedly in others.[31] Each society has provided trafficking organizations and also antidrug policy makers with a particular set of bridge-favoring and disfavoring factors, and while threads of common color reappear, a singular pattern has marked each country.[32]

The Central American experience suggests that, to analyze bridge-state trafficking, one must first grasp the social, economic, and political contexts in which traffickers have been operating, and one must thus explore not simply the commonalities but the many ways in which a region's bridge states have differed. Rather than being confined to operating in a single type of bridge state, drug organizations have shown themselves to be highly adaptable: they have instituted successful trafficking schemes in a range of settings. Thus, as drug syndicates have considered where to concentrate their efforts, the profile of each country has helped to determine the speed with which drug trafficking has taken hold; the manner in which it has evolved; the amounts of different drugs that have been transshipped; and the effectiveness, or lack thereof, of antidrug efforts.

The Principal Drugs Trafficked via Central America

Over the years smugglers have succeeded in slipping through Central America sizable amounts of three primary illicit drugs: marijuana, heroin, and cocaine. Though the particular methods and routes to market have differed, the trail has normally led back to Colombia, which has exported the vast majority of all the psychoactive substances transshipped through the region. However, the passage of each of these drugs has had distinctive features. The period and the ways in which trafficking gathered momentum have by no means been identical, nor have government institutions been equally affected.

30. Calvani, Foreword to *Island*, 1, quoted in Maingot, "Decentralization Imperative."

31. After noting the dramatic differences in Central American politics, one scholar declared that in the 1980s "it would have been difficult to find anywhere in the world three political systems as different as those of El Salvador, Costa Rica, and Nicaragua." Paige, *Coffee and Power*, x, quote on 5.

32. Certain scholars have applied the concepts of competitive advantage and comparative advantage to South American cocaine-producing states. See, for instance, Zaitch, *Trafficking Cocaine*, 35–37, and Thoumi, *Political Economy*, 168–75. The latter author, however, hesitates to use the term, because comparative advantage theories are traditionally couched "in terms of the relative endowment of factors of production . . . [—] natural resources, raw and skilled labor, capital and technology"—as opposed to "institutional factors such as corruption, lack of state legitimacy, and . . . inability to control large regions of the country" (177n5). In addition to these concerns, the term *advantage* may be better employed with respect to states competing against one another for economic primacy, than with the drug trade, which most officials find *dis*advantageous for their countries. Hence, we have coined the terms *bridge-favoring* and *bridge-disfavoring* factors.

Central American Marijuana Trafficking

Marijuana trafficking within Central America has taken two principal forms: direct exports and transshipment of Colombian cannabis. Although much of the marijuana grown in the region is also consumed there—mostly within the producer state, though occasionally in neighboring ones—drug rings have exported some to North America. Transnational criminals have also found it profitable to transport through Central America significant quantities of high-quality Colombian marijuana. While in the mid-twentieth century modest amounts of other drugs transited the region, marijuana was the first to pass through in large shipments. Successful marijuana organizations thus blazed paths, initiated smuggling methods, marshaled networks of associates, and developed other relevant expertise in moving drugs toward market.

The principal psychoactive chemical in *Cannabis sativa L*, or marijuana, is tetrahydrocannabinol (THC), and marijuana potency is measured by the THC percentage found in the dried plants. Traditionally, Mexican varieties of marijuana have tended to be among the cheapest, lowest grade, and most common. Quality has improved over time, as traffickers in Mexico invested in better strains, and a few notable varieties—Acapulco Gold, Zacatecas Purple, Michoacán, and Popo Oro among them—gained early and enthusiastic followings among consumers. However, even after years of effort to develop enhanced Mexican marijuana, its average THC level, as seized along the U.S. border in 2003, measured only 4.8 percent.[33]

In contrast, more potent Colombian marijuana has regularly fetched the highest prices in the North American market.[34] In the 1970s, after eradication curbed Mexican output and the use of paraquat in aerial spraying frightened consumers, American traffickers stimulated the growth of a Colombian marijuana industry by providing seeds, financing, and technical assistance.[35] The cannabis cultivated in the lower Sierra Nevadas on Colombia's Guajira Peninsula then quickly gained an excellent international reputation.[36] Users came to value such varieties as Red Dot, Red Point, and San Miguelito, and the pale yellow strains like Santa Marta Gold and Blue Sky Blonde.[37]

In stark contrast the THC for most Central American marijuana has tended to be rather low, and cannabis from the region has resembled cheap Mexican varieties or the darker and more commonplace strains, such as Mango Viche and La Negra, grown at lower altitudes in southern Colombia. International demand for Central American marijuana has generally been weak. While Costa Rica and Guatemala have occasionally exported the drug, the only Central American strains of marijuana for which significant foreign markets have developed are Belize Breeze and a variant of Red Dot known as Panama Red. During the 1980s cannabis production in Belize crescendoed, as it moved for a period into the first rank of marijuana-exporting countries. And, though in much smaller quantities, producers on Panama's Las Perlas archipelago have long cultivated some marijuana for export.

To move Central American cannabis to the North American market, most traffickers have

33. "Cartels Face an Economic Battle," *WP* (US), 7 October 2009, A01. For information on the development of Mexican marijuana in the 1960s and early 1970s, see Kamstra, *Weed*, 148–50.

34. In the mid-1980s marijuana costing $70 a pound in Colombia might be purchased for $240 a pound wholesale in Miami. Eddy, Sabogal, and Walden, *Cocaine Wars*, 127–28.

35. Thoumi, *Political Economy*, 126.

36. Flanking the Caribbean and Gulf of Venezuela, Guajira is a sparsely populated corner of Colombia, isolated by the Sierra Nevada de Santa Marta, with nearly twenty-thousand-foot peaks and numerous cannabis plantations along its eastern slopes. Riley, *Snow Job*, 128–29.

37. Shannon, *Desperados*, 9, 73. One source observed, "The general rule is, the paler the gold, the stronger the grass. The palest weed is grown at the lowest range of the optimum growing altitude, around 500 meters above sea level, where the sun is hottest (any lower and the humidity saps the vital resins in the plant)." Nicholl, *Fruit Palace*, 9. The naming of different varieties of cannabis has served as a marketing ploy distinguishing the marijuana trade from those in cocaine and heroin. In fact, while many users can distinguish between high- and low-quality cannabis, they are hard-pressed to identify particular strains either by sight or use.

COLOMBIA
0
100
200 mi
N
SAN ANDRÉS Y PROVIDENCIA
Isla de Providencia
Isla de San Andrés
Caribbean Sea
Guajira Peninsula
Aruba (NETHERLANDS)
Netherlands Antilles (NETHERLANDS)
Santa Marta
LA GUAJIRA
Gulf of Venezuela
Barranquilla
Sierra Nevada de Santa Marta
ATLÁNTICO
Cartagena
Maracaibo
Caracas
CESAR
MAGDALENA
Maracaibo Lake
Río Magdalena
PANAMA
Montería
SUCRE
NORTE DE SANTANDER
CÓRDOBA
BOLÍVAR
Cúcuta
VENEZUELA
Turbo
CHOCÓ
ANTIOQUIA
Río Orinoco
ARAUCA
Medellín
SANTANDER
Envigado
BOYACÁ
CASANARE
PACIFIC OCEAN
RISARALDA
CALDAS
CUNDINAMARCA
Guaymaral
Pereira
Bogotá
Río Meta
VICHADA
QUINDÍO
Norte Valle del Cauca
Buenaventura
TOLIMA
VALLE DEL CAUCA
Palmira
Cali
META
Río Guaviare
GUAINÍA
HUILA
CAUCA
Cordillera Central
Cordillera Oriental
Cordillera Occidental
ANDES
Tumaco
GUAVIARE
NARIÑO
PUTUMAYO
CAQUETÁ
VAUPÉS
Quito
Río Caquetá
AMAZONAS
ECUADOR
BRAZIL
Río Amazonas
PERU
Iquitos
Leticia

MAP 1.2

preferred maritime shipments, though smuggling networks once also transported much Belizean marijuana by small plane. As for South American marijuana, while some aerial trafficking has occurred, drug networks have regularly shipped Colombian marijuana to Mexico to be exported overland into the United States, while routing other shipments toward western Europe.[38] Most commonly, however, numerous vessels carrying marijuana through the Caribbean basin have aimed directly for the United States. Rather than employing Colombian vessels, which have the signal drawback of flying the flag of a leading drug-producing state, smuggling rings have often preferred to use boats registered elsewhere, such as Panama or Honduras. Typically older seventy- to ninety-foot fishing trawlers, characterized by extra fuel drums on deck and relatively large crews to assist in unloading, such "mother ships" have sometimes passed through Caribbean and Pacific waters off the Central American coasts.[39]

The U.S. Coast Guard has led international efforts to stem maritime drug passage. Given time and resource constraints and the large number of legitimate commercial ships, making a bust at sea can be challenging without prior intelligence on the vessel, its route, and even the location on board of the drugs.[40] Nevertheless, in their continuous patrols of U.S. territorial waters and of the Gulf of Mexico, Caribbean Sea, and Pacific Ocean, coast guard ships have routinely attempted to do so. Coast guard officials (including navy ships with a coast guard officer on board) are authorized to stop and inspect any boat flying the U.S. flag or located in U.S. territorial waters, that is, within twelve miles of the shore of the United States or one of its possessions. In international waters, however, given the venerable doctrine of freedom of the seas, U.S. authorities cannot board vessels of another state at will. When a coast guard crew suspects drug trafficking, it radios the ship, requesting permission to board to check its documentation or seaworthiness. Signs of drug trafficking might be spotted in the ensuing inspection. If the ship's master refuses boarding privileges or if suspicious matters emerge during the inspection, the coast guard can check information about the vessel with authorities from the flag state. If drug-trafficking suspicions remain, the coast guard may request a Statement of No Objection through the U.S. Department of State, from the country in which the ship is registered, to board, inspect, and enforce appropriate criminal laws on the vessel, using force if necessary.[41]

Central American states have almost invariably cooperated in issuing these statements. Their governments have also been engaged in implementing antidrug policies of various sorts, and collaborating in major seizures can help officials appear vigilant and competent, domestically and internationally. Central American governments have not wanted to seem to be shielding traffickers, which might cause political trouble at home and antagonize the U.S. government, possibly threatening the continued flow of development assistance. Nevertheless, despite international cooperation, considerable U.S. resources, and some immense seizures, drugs continue to be successfully shipped to market. The maritime transit zone is vast—perhaps six million square miles—shipping has been extensive, and patrols cannot cover the region comprehensively.

As for Central American marijuana exports, this dimension of the trade had multiple effects. Colombian traffickers gained dominance in

38. U.S. Department of State, *International Narcotics Control Strategy Report* (hereafter cited as *INCSR*) (1997), 89. See also *INCSR* (1999), 102, noting that the prior year European authorities had seized significant quantities of Colombian marijuana.

39. See the testimony of U.S. Coast Guard officers, found in *United States v. May*, 470 F. Supp. at 388.

40. See Decker and Chapman, *Drug Smugglers*, 73–75, and Riley, *Snow Job*, 227–28.

41. See *United States v. Leuro-Rosas*, 952 F.2d 616.

international cocaine trafficking by adapting methods developed in marijuana smuggling.[42] They thus naturally took note of successful marijuana exports via Central America and drew on already existing domestic drug networks there. In fact, the marijuana trade often established Central American criminal groups and then helped bridge-state traffickers to become more capable and elusive, wealthy and well connected.

Marijuana, however, has not been an ideal drug for transnational criminal enterprises. Because it has to be shipped in bulk, rather than in a concentrated form, and its odor is quite distinctive, authorities have found cannabis fairly easy to interdict. Furthermore, marijuana is not as addictive as harder drugs. Since it is relatively easy to grow, global supplies have usually been plentiful, something that has capped its price and resulted in lower profit margins than heroin or cocaine.[43] Consequently, experienced marijuana traffickers, intent on maximizing profits and with smuggling methods, routes, and networks already in place, have often moved to the transport of hard drugs.[44] Just as marijuana has been a gateway to more dangerous drugs for users, so it has often led to more lucrative drug smuggling for traffickers.

Central American Heroin Trafficking

The Central American heroin trade has diverged from that of marijuana in numerous respects. Traditionally, Europe has been the leading western market for diacetylmorphine, or heroin, originally supplied largely by producers in South and Southeast Asia. Even in North America, Asian producers controlled the heroin supply for many years, with the drug often imported via couriers or inside shipping containers.[45] In the late 1950s Colombians did engage in some heroin trafficking, cultivating ties with the U.S. mafia in pre-Castro Havana.[46] However, not until the late 1960s and early 1970s did more substantial heroin transshipment occur through Latin America.[47] Traffickers came to capitalize particularly on Panama's role as a busy commercial crossroads and international air hub and on members of its political elite, who could use their influence and social stature to help ensure uninterrupted transit.

Another noteworthy development occurred in Mexico. Here, early in the twentieth century Chinese immigrants had introduced opium poppies (*Papaver somniferum L.*), hardy and adaptable plants well suited to tropical and semitropical regions.[48] With the development of processing and refining skills, Mexican heroin made inroads in the U.S. market. In the 1950s and 1960s Mexican heroin accounted for an estimated 10–15 percent of U.S. consumption, a market share that climbed rapidly in the 1970s, as Turkish authorities curtailed production there.[49] Although opium cultivation increased substantially over the next two decades, Mexican civil and military authorities vigorously eradicated it in the mid-1970s and again from 1985 to 1990.[50] Nevertheless, the

42. Wilson and Zambrano, "Commodity Chains," 304.

43. By the early twenty-first century U.S. growers were harvesting fully ten thousand tons of cannabis, with another five thousand tons produced in Canada and Mexico. *INCSR* (2003), 2:7.

44. Medellín trafficker José Cabrera testified that although he had originally shipped marijuana, increased risks caused him to shift to aerial cocaine trafficking. "Continúa hoy el testimonio de José Cabrera en juicio a Noriega," *La Prensa* (Panama) (hereafter cited as LP [PA]), 21 October 1991, 1A.

45. "Drug Smugglers Join Shipping's Box Revolution," *Journal of Commerce*, 12 April 1988, 1A.

46. Eddy, Sabogal, and Walden, *Cocaine Wars*, 44. For the early role of Cuba in international drug trafficking, see also Meyer and Parssinen, *Webs of Smoke*, 261–62.

47. For the development of heroin transshipment, see Clark and Horrock, *Contrabandista*, esp. 177–212.

48. Childress, *Heroin Trade*, 8.

49. Andreas, *Border Games*, 40. Harry Anslinger, director of the U.S. Federal Bureau of Narcotics, testified that as early as 1941 Mexico was producing five tons of opium a year. *Extradition of Ignacia Jasso Gonzales (La Nacha) from Mexico* (case cited in ibid.).

50. See Riley, *Snow Job*, 128; Toro, *Mexico's "War,"* 20, 23–25, 42–44; and Smith, "Semiorganized International Crime," 194–95.

ease of smuggling heroin across the Mexico-U.S. border counterbalanced the relatively high costs of Mexican production.[51] In addition, Mexican heroin proved difficult to stamp out, because a handful of powerful, readily identifiable groups has never controlled it.[52] Instead, the heroin industry has been highly fragmented, opportunistic, and marked by shifting ad hoc arrangements among farmers, processors, and traffickers.[53] The lack of vertically integrated, multipurpose organizations has precluded the "decapitation" of heroin-trafficking groups by killing or capturing kingpins, a strategy commonly employed against cocaine cartels.

In the drug trade widespread trafficking in one country often comes to profoundly affect its neighbor. As one U.S. Customs agent observed, "Agents and police can't change [the drug business]. . . . It's like trying to stab a piece of mercury with an ice pick. It just goes someplace else."[54] When counternarcotics authorities pressured Mexican opium producers, some figured turning south would be the best way to maintain profits and outlast antidrug campaigns. Thus, from the mid-1980s to the mid-1990s and again in the early twenty-first century, significant opium crops were cultivated in the mountains of northwestern Guatemala along the Mexican border.

Then, in the 1990s the prospect of creating a lucrative South American heroin industry attracted attention from many criminal organizations, including remnants of the Medellín cartel looking to increase profits and regain past prominence.[55] While two years would elapse before a newly planted coca bush would become productive, and while high-quality coca came only from the Andes, opium poppies were annual plants, could be grown in many places, and had a short 120-day growth cycle. Although most Colombian producers aimed for two crops a year, some found three annual harvests to be possible. And, because immediate replanting after spraying had occurred was economically viable, antidrug authorities could be quickly put on the defensive again, and production could continue.

Just as important, heroin has been the easiest of the major drugs transiting Central America to hide and transport. Since in a typical year heroin might retail at $1,700 per gram, cocaine at $170, and marijuana at $12, to reach identical sales levels a heroin trafficker would have to transport to market only a hundredth of the product of a marijuana trafficker and a tenth of that of a cocaine trafficker.[56] Small shipments of heroin, tasteless and odorless, could be slipped past police, customs inspectors, and even trained drug-sniffing canine units more easily than either marijuana or cocaine.[57] Furthermore, Colombian syndicates had the wherewithal to hire Southeast Asian narcotics chemists with expertise in the formulas and refining techniques needed to produce high-quality heroin.[58] They could also capitalize on some preexisting trafficking strategies and channels for wholesale and retail distribution and marketing. And, while a drug like cocaine

51. Reuter, Crawford, and Cave, *Sealing the Borders*, 18.

52. U.S. officials noted, "A mix of opium farmers, heroin processors, and small-scale trafficking groups operating independently or in mutually supportive business relationships controls Mexican heroin production." *INCSR* (2007), 169.

53. Note the parallel to legitimate agriculture, where "U.S. grains tend to be handled by major agribusiness firms while fresh vegetables are moved by many specialized, small-scale distributors." Zabludoff, "Colombian Narcotics Organizations," 22.

54. Shannon, *Desperados*, 72.

55. See "Hermanos ligados a cartel de Medellín," *La Nación* (Costa Rica) (hereafter cited as *LN* [CR]), 5 August 1998, 10A.

56. For calculations relying on 1997 prices, see Zabludoff, "Colombian Narcotics Organizations," 22.

57. See "Aumenta el tráfico de heroína," *LP* (PA), 15 August 2002, 5A.

58. "Colombian Cartels in Asia Connection," *South China Morning Post* (Hong Kong), 18 April 1993, 3. In noting that a "good chemist is like a good chef," one counternarcotics agent observed, "Samples we are getting supposedly from Colombia show a similarity in composition to Southeast and Southwest Asian heroin." Ibid.

Fig. 1.1 Cultivation of opium in Colombia and Mexico, 1991–2009

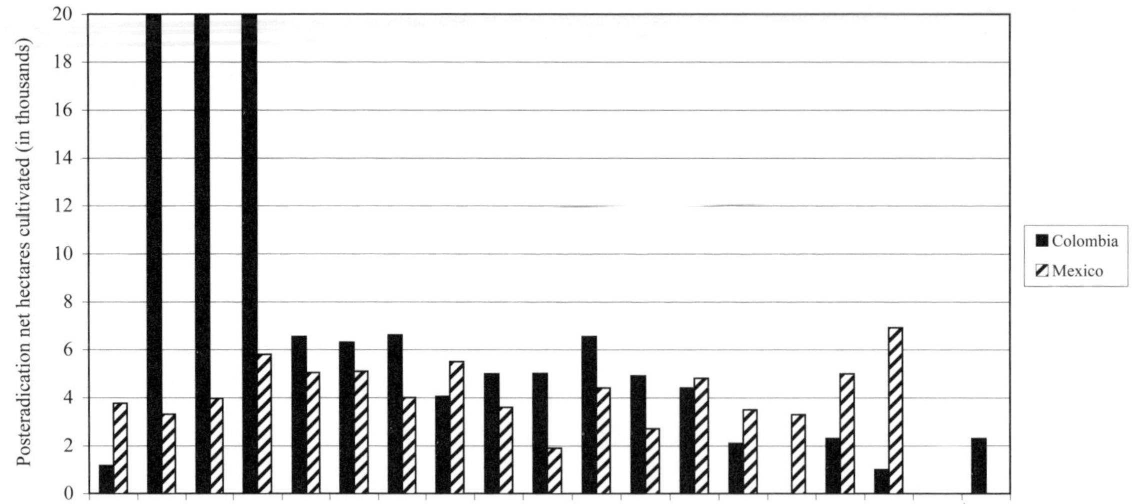

Sources: *INCSR* (2009), 33; *INCSR* (2000), 54; *INCSR* (2010), 196.

Note: Figure 1.1 tracks the *net* of hectares cultivated, that is, total hectares cultivated less hectares eradicated. Although satellite imagery helped to determine the number of hectares cultivated, analysts concentrated their efforts "on those areas that are most *likely* to have cultivation," and not "the entire country for any hint of illicit cultivation." *INCSR* (2009), 30. Note further that the statistics do not reflect the fact that some hectares could be replanted after eradication had occurred.

is a stimulant that addicts often take for five years or less before becoming overwhelmed, heroin is a depressant that an addict can use over a longer time frame. This has helped to ensure stable demand.

The bulk of heroin production occurs far from the North American market, but it has commanded such high prices that transporting a relatively small amount to consumers has brought tremendous profits. With prices reaching $200,000 a kilo in U.S. cities in the early 1990s, the trafficking through Central America of high-purity Colombian heroin climbed thereafter.[59] Poppies were first cultivated in Colombia in 1986.[60] Two years later, Colombian counternarcotics police destroyed the first heroin laboratory, as well as the largest poppy fields that had ever been found in the country. In 1991 U.S. Customs authorities first seized Colombian heroin, and during the 1990s Colombian producers came to dedicate more than eight thousand acres to opium poppies.[61] As Colombian production climbed, the Central American states became immersed in the transshipment of South American heroin. By 2001 it was being sold for $60,000 to $125,000 per kilo, depending on purity, and heroin supplies regularly moved through Central America, by land, by sea, and especially by air, usually toward the key U.S. market.[62]

59. *INCSR* (1992), 6.

60. Colombian National Police report "Amapola: Producción," quoted in Thoumi, "Illegal Drugs in Colombia," 74.

61. "Colombia's Drug Lords Sending Heroin to U.S.," *New York Times* (United States) (hereafter cited as *NYT* [US]), 14 January 1992, A10. See also "Poppy Plants in Colombia Raises Spectre of S. A. Heroin," *The Reporter* (Belize) (hereafter cited as *TR* [BZ]), 18 July 1988, 16. If producers succeeded in harvesting a hectare of opium poppies the maximum of three times annually, they could produce ten kilos of opium gum or one kilo of pure heroin. *INCSR* (1999), 103.

62. DEA, *Illegal Drug Price.*

Fig. 1.2 Projected heroin production in Colombia and Mexico, 1995–2009

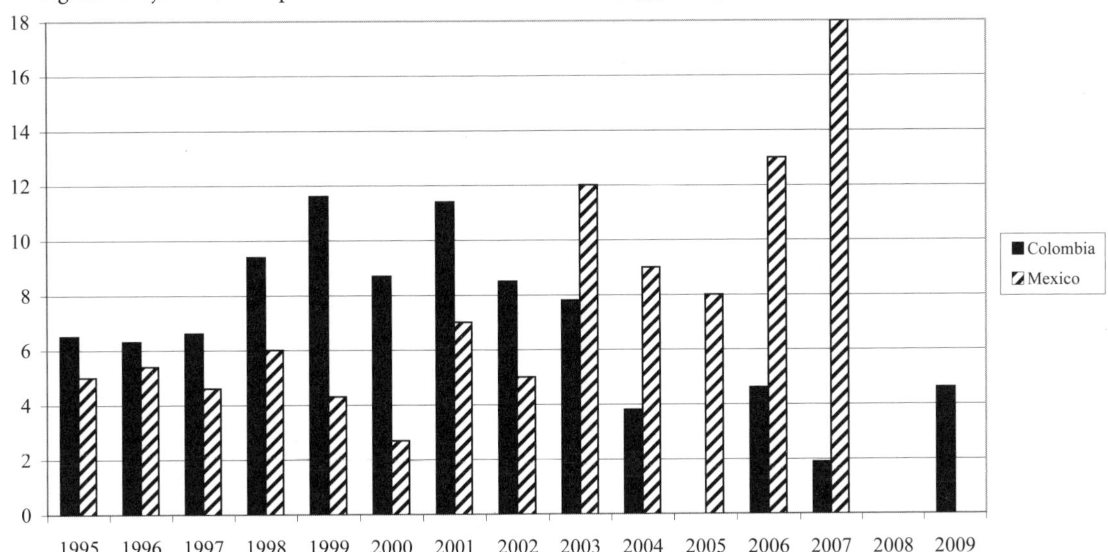

Sources: *INCSR* (1996), 85, 149; *INCSR* (1997), 14, 22, *INCSR* (1998), 13, 20; *INCSR* (1999), 15, 19–20, *INCSR* (2000), 47, *INCSR* (2001), http://www.state.gov/g/inl/rls/nrcrpt/2000/888pf.htm, *INCSR* (2002), 2:5, 2:14; *INCSR* (2003), 2:5; *INCSR* (2004), 99; *INCSR* (2005), 129; *INCSR* (2006), 25; *INCSR* (2007), 32, 120; *INCSR* (2008), 124; *INCSR* (2009), 208, 419; *INCSR* (2010), 196.

Note: Before 1995 the U.S. government did not include in its reports estimated heroin production figures, as opposed to related data such as hectares under cultivation and production of opium gum. Because supporting statistics had been provided by the governments of Mexico and Colombia only up through November of particular years, the State Department was unable to immediately calculate for its annual reports the potential heroin yield in either Mexico or Colombia for 2003 or for Mexico in 2004. However, the statistics were later reported for Colombia in *INCSR* (2007), 120, and for Mexico in *INCSR* (2009), 181.

From the mid-1990s into the early twenty-first century, about 60 percent of the heroin seized in the United States originated in Colombia, and in 2000 the Colombian market share climbed further, given drought and eradication in Mexico.[63] Although the underlying statistics are not precise, figs. 1.1 and 1.2 illustrate that by 1992 Colombia had decisively overtaken Mexico as the largest poppy and heroin producer in the Americas, a position it generally maintained for a decade.[64] Most recently, an intensive eradication campaign, financed by the U.S. government, reduced net acreage in cultivation and reversed the trend of increased

63. In 1996 the estimate was 62 percent, while in 2001, 59 percent of heroin submitted to DEA's Heroin Signature Program was Colombian. *INCSR* (2002), 4:25, and *INCSR* (1997), 89. However, for statistical uncertainties associated with the HSP, see Childress, *Heroin Trade*, 14n10.

64. For numerous reasons, projected heroin yields are considerably less precise than figures for hectares cultivated. First, production depends on harvest size, and yet, as the U.S. government noted, "Small changes in soil fertility, weather, farming techniques, and disease can produce widely varying results from year to year and place to place." Second, because the figures assume no losses between the opium harvest and its processing into opium gum, they estimate potential: they assume that the entire crop is duly processed into drugs. Third, the efficiency with which opium gum is processed into heroin may not be a constant variable, as is typically assumed. The DOS noted, "Differences in the origin and quality of the raw material used, the technical processing method employed, the size and sophistication of laboratories, the skill and experience of local workers and chemists, and decisions made in response to enforcement pressures all affect production." Fourth, a 2001 research project found that yield and efficiency had improved in Colombia, further suggesting that potential heroin production had been underestimated for quite some time. Fifth, the DOS

Fig. 1.3 Heroin seizures in key Central American bridge states, 1991–1999

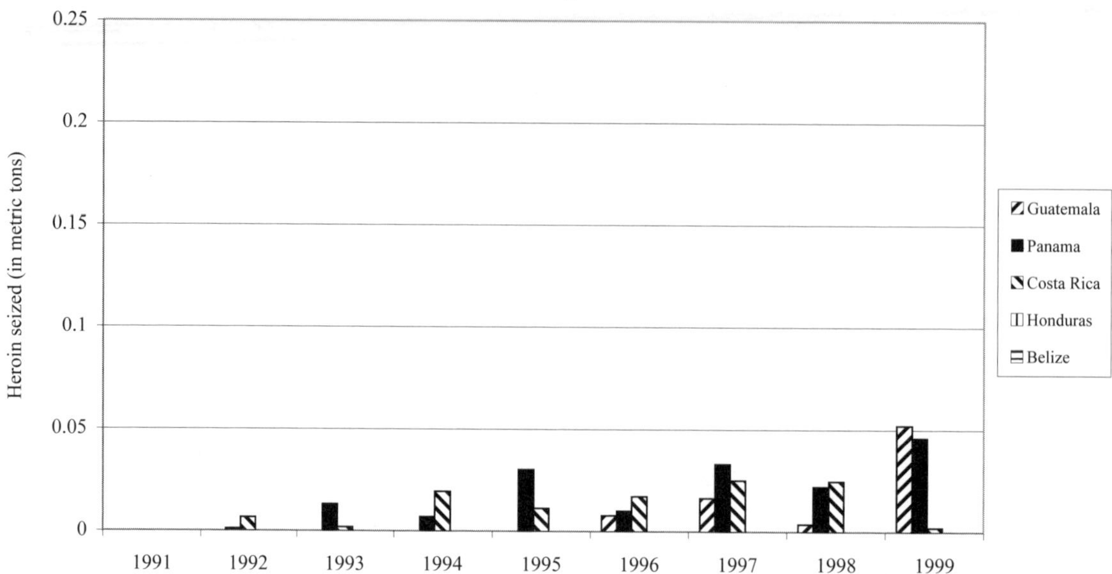

Sources: DEA, *Resources, Costa Rica* (2000), 1; DEA, *Resources, Costa Rica* (2003), 2; DEA, *Resources, Guatemala* (2001), 2; DEA, *Resources, Guatemala* (2003), 3; DEA, *Resources, Panama* (2000), 3; DEA, *Resources, Panama* (2001), 2, with the gaps in these data filled in by the country reports in *INCSR* (1991) to *INCSR* (2010).

Colombian heroin trafficking. In particular, the U.S. Congress passed Plan Colombia, signed into law in 2000. This comprehensive $1.3 billion assistance package aimed to encourage the Colombian peace process while supporting counternarcotics measures, instituting judicial and democratic reforms, and protecting human rights.[65] It was followed in 2001 by the Andean Counterdrug Initiative, which further expanded an array of narcotics policies, including intensive poppy-eradication campaigns.

Although Colombian heroin transshipment initially occurred primarily via Panama and Guatemala, it was not so confined for long, and by the early twenty-first century, officials across Central America had uncovered significant heroin-trafficking operations.[66] While the drug can be transported in many ways, the most typical method has been by courier flown out of the major Colombian airports in Bogotá, Cali, and Medellín, and occasionally Barranquilla. After a layover somewhere in Central America, a different courier, whose documents would not alert customs officials to recent passage from Colombia, would carry the heroin to market. The drugs might be taped to the body; concealed in shoes, clothes, or suitcases; or swallowed in pellets of eight to ten grams, encased in wax or latex. In the early twenty-first century, drug networks started to transship larger individual loads: twenty to thirty kilos, with cocaine and heroin sometimes combined in a single shipment. As figs. 1.3 and 1.4 illustrate, Central American heroin confiscations steadily rose

initially based its figures on pure heroin yield; however, the yield of mere "export-quality" heroin would be markedly higher, and it appears that when figures were recalculated to correct for prior underestimating, the U.S. standard also shifted from pure to export-quality heroin. A further complication is that black tar heroin has also sometimes been exported and yet would require even less pure heroin than would export-quality. Quotes from *INCSR* (2009), 31–32; see also *INCSR* (2002, 2:14) and DEA, *Special Report.*

65. See Crandall, *Driven by Drugs*, 123–34.

66. See *INCSR* (1997), 89; *INCSR* (2001), available at http://www.state.gov/g/inl/rls/nrcrpt/2000/888pf.htm; and *INCSR* (2002), 4:25.

Fig. 1.4 Heroin seizures in key Central American bridge states, 2000–2010

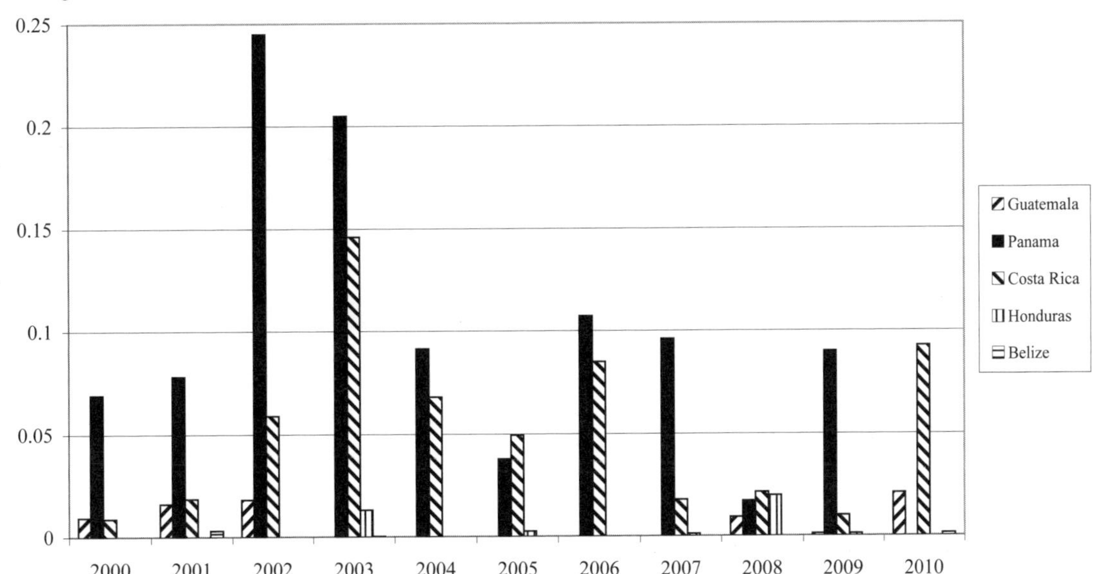

Sources: DEA, *Resources, Costa Rica* (2000), 1; DEA, *Resources, Costa Rica* (2003), 2; DEA, *Resources, Guatemala* (2001), 2; DEA, *Resources, Guatemala* (2003), 3; DEA, *Resources, Panama* (2000), 3; DEA, *Resources, Panama* (2001), 2, with the gaps in this data filled in by the country reports in *INCSR* (1991) to *INCSR* (2011), 137, 206, 272.

through the 1990s and into the twenty-first century, until opium-poppy eradication dramatically reduced the heroin flow from Colombia.

Central American Cocaine Trafficking

Although marijuana and heroin exports have helped to initiate extensive drug shipments via Central America, the transshipment of cocaine hydrochloride truly elevated the stature of these small republics within the international drug trade. As early as the late 1970s Colombian traffickers came to grasp the vast, highly profitable potential of dealing in cocaine. Unlike marijuana, cocaine could be compactly packaged for transport. And, to turn a substantial profit, much less had to be stowed in a light plane, making for safer transshipment.[67] Authorities periodically noted that the annual supply for all U.S. consumers could be carried by perhaps six to nine tractor trailers, depending on demand in the year in question.[68] Cocaine also lacked marijuana's distinctive smell; indeed, only specially trained police dogs could sniff out cocaine.[69] Even more advantageous, in preparation for sale, pure cocaine could be mixed with other ingredients to increase its volume, thus adding profits.[70] Most important, the narcotic was highly addictive and resistant to medical treatment, and its alluring image brought

67. Kirkpatrick, *Turning the Tide*, 39.

68. See "Marijuana of the Eighties," *Los Angeles Times* (United States) (hereafter cited as LAT [US]), 4 December 1985, 2, and the testimony of U.S. attorney Alan Bersin, U.S. House, *Border Security*, 17, quoted in Andreas, *Border Games*, 75.

69. After the 1988 seizure in Miami of almost 5.5 tons of marijuana in a shipping container, Michael Shaheen of U.S. Customs noted it could be smelled blocks away. "Drug Smugglers Join," 1A.

70. Note, however, that virtually pure cocaine brought the highest price and most enhanced the seller's business reputation.

cocaine to be referred to as "the champagne of drugs."[71] One U.S. source declared, "In a competitive, achievement-addicted, 'Type-A society,' cocaine's ability to make us feel empowered, euphoric, energetic, and ebullient fits our culture like a glove."[72]

Criminal enterprises discovered that South American cocaine production could be readily expanded. Furthermore, they came to see that if cocaine could be supplied in sufficient quantities and at moderate prices, other drug users might well shift to it. Indeed, production rose, prices fell, and demand grew.[73] The Rand Corporation estimated that 38–68 tons of cocaine had been smuggled into the United States in 1981, but four years later cocaine imports had increased to 111–153 tons. In 1985 the U.S. cocaine market peaked at 5.7 million users. These developments spurred competition among dealers, and cocaine purity climbed spectacularly. In 1983 the average purity of cocaine on U.S. streets stood at about 35 percent; by 1986 that figure had risen to 65 percent. In that year the U.S. State Department estimated that Latin American coca growers were producing fully 377 tons of cocaine. A decade later, a national narcotics intelligence committee figured potential cocaine production at 760 tons.[74]

And so, notwithstanding the lengthy history of marijuana transshipment or the extraordinary profits associated with the heroin trade, cocaine smuggling offered drug rings considerable competitive advantages. Most important, South American criminal organizations had easy access to supplies of coca, which were readily expanded as demand grew. For Central Americans the passage of immense quantities of cocaine immersed their countries in the drug trade. Although marijuana could readily be grown in the hills and mountains of Central America, producers failed to follow suit with coca plants (*Erythroxylon coca*), perennial natives of the eastern slopes of the Bolivian and Peruvian Andes. Rather, the steps to grow and process coca tended to occur in South America, and its link to Central America was almost exclusively in cocaine transshipment.

The lower reaches of the Andes were thought to provide the ideal location for farmers intent on large-scale coca-leaf cultivation with the requisite high alkaloid levels.[75] While Panamanian authorities periodically found and eradicated minor plantations right along the Colombian border, significant modern production never really took hold outside of South America. Instead, the soil, climate, and long growing seasons favored Bolivian, Peruvian, and eventually Colombian coca farming. So, too, did the legions of poor subsistence farmers available to tend the crops, and the long-standing, and entirely legal, tradition within much of the Andean region of cultivating coca to chew to provide vitamins and energy and to ward off the cold and fatigue of high altitudes.

In the 1970s first Chilean and then Bolivian traffickers, most notably Roberto Suárez Gómez, helped to initiate the rapid growth of

71. "Conspiracy to Corrupt," *Financial Times*, 14 February 1987, 1.

72. Waldorf, Reinarman, and Murphy, *Cocaine Changes*, 281–82, quoted in Wilson and Zambrano, "Commodity Chains," 299.

73. See *INCSR* (1998), 9; Shannon, *Desperados*, 374, 388; "Drug Smugglers Join," 1A; and "Stemming the Drug Flow," *TT* (CR), 3 December 1999, 17.

74. The most authoritative U.S. estimate, a 2006 interagency assessment, concluded that 517–732 tons of cocaine were departing South America for the United States annually, with more directed to Europe. *INCSR* (2007), 15–16.

75. Coca shrub leaves contain fourteen alkaloids, that is, psychoactive compounds naturally found in various plants. Although coca will grow in tropical lowlands and has been cultivated in such places as Africa, India, Taiwan, Okinawa, and Indonesia (Gootenberg, *Andean Cocaine*, 73, 125–31), there "'life is too easy.' . . . In the intense and humid heat it produces dense foliage, but the leaves have little potency. Lower-altitude plantations are also prey to a butterfly, the ulo, whose larvae feed on the leaf, and to various destructive lichens." Nicholl, *Fruit Palace*, 296. "In the mist-filled valleys on the eastern slope of the Andes . . . water vapor from the Amazon rain forest rises upward, providing the proper warmth and wetness for the shrubs that bear the coca leaf." Gugliotta and Leen, *Kings of Cocaine*, 120.

the cocaine trade.[76] Then, through the latter 1970s and into the early 1980s Colombian organizations rose to dominance.[77] Just as geographic variables are key to understanding the evolution of bridge-state drug trafficking, so they influenced Colombian ascendancy in cocaine production. Not only did Colombia's Amazon jungle abut the coca-producer states of Peru and Bolivia, but Colombia featured long Caribbean and Pacific coastlines with multiple deep-water ports.[78] Traffickers from Colombia also jumped in to fill the vacuum created when General Augusto Pinochet expelled nineteen leading Chilean traffickers to the United States.[79] Moreover, Colombian drug rings tapped into abundant national entrepreneurial and commercial know-how as well as long experience in importing such contraband as whiskey, textiles, appliances, and cigarettes, while exporting sugar, coffee, and emeralds, and eventually marijuana.[80]

Initially, the Colombian syndicates served as intermediaries, buying drugs from the existing Andean producers and then working out their delivery to market. Eventually, however, Colombian drug cartels encouraged Colombian farmers to plant coca to diminish the costs and risks inherent in importing coca base from Bolivia and Peru. According to the CIA, by the mid-1990s Bolivia and Peru produced about 85 percent of the world's coca, with 15 percent originating in Colombia and elsewhere.[81] Thereafter, the Colombian share of coca production climbed steadily, and by 2001 Colombia had become the world's leading center of coca cultivation.[82]

After being harvested, coca then has to be processed into cocaine hydrochloride. To isolate the key alkaloid that drug users value, cocaine production proceeds through two lengthy stages: from leaf to paste and from paste to crystal. Here, Colombian organizations had taken the lead by the late 1960s, thereafter refining 80–90 percent of the cocaine exported to foreign markets.[83] Coca grown outside of Colombia has thus been flown or transported overland from Peru, Bolivia, and sometimes Brazil into refining laboratories in Colombia, where drug rings for many years then dominated transportation to market as well. Colombian traffickers usually exported it from Colombian soil, but to avoid detection they sometimes first shipped it to a neighboring South American state such as Venezuela or Brazil. Then, much of the cocaine would be transported via the land, sea, or air space of the bridge states to market. While the retail sale of cocaine has often been left to others, Colombian cartels have created their own distribution networks, taking payment in market countries from wholesale buyers, or through narcotics brokers, who for a fee have held shipments and contacted or searched out such buyers. Indeed, in the late 1980s authorities estimated that the U.S. distribution infrastructure of Colombian

76. For Suárez Gómez, see Gamarra, "Criminal Organizations," 175–83, and Henkel, "Bolivian Cocaine Industry." While Bolivian and Peruvian organizations undertook some international transshipment, as Colombian syndicates assumed a dominant position, the Suárez organization came to supply Pablo Escobar.

77. A DEA agent who worked undercover in South America during the late 1970s noted that Colombian traffickers would then buy base in Bolivia to convert to cocaine in Colombia because Bolivians grew the most potent coca. Levine, *Deep Cover*, 34. He estimated that Bolivia's "Santa Cruz Mafia" supplied 80 percent of the world's coca at that time. Levine, *Big White Lie*, 10.

78. Wilson and Zambrano, "Commodity Chains," 304.

79. Gootenberg, *Andean Cocaine*, 303–4.

80. Zaitch, *Trafficking Cocaine*, 29, 37.

81. CIA, *Allegations of Connections*, 7. The U.S. Southern Command likewise figured that in 1995 Peruvians had cultivated 115,300 hectares of coca (54 percent of world production), Colombians 50,900 (24 percent), and Bolivians 48,680 (22 percent). "EU mantiene centro antidrogas desde 1992," *LP* (PA), 26 September 1996, 2A. For earlier figures, see *INCSR* (1992), 27.

82. See *INCSR* (2002), 2:3, and "Colombia produce dos tercios de hoja de coca en el mundo," *LA* (PA), 23 January 2001, 4A.

83. In 1998 the U.S. government reported that Colombian organizations were refining 80 percent of the world's cocaine, a figure that rose to 90 percent by 2004. *INCSR* (1999), 3; *INCSR* (2005), 13.

drug organizations consisted of about 200 individual groups, including 120 in Florida alone.[84]

The Central American share of the cocaine-transshipment business has varied over time and is, in any event, impossible to gauge with great precision, particularly on a state-by-state basis.[85] This does not mean, however, that no statistics exist. When their superiors, the media, or politicians demand facts, officials have made educated guesses as to amounts transiting one country or another. They have triangulated from seizures actually made, information gleaned from court cases and informants, and judgments as to production and consumption to try to determine about how many tons have passed through each bridge state annually. Although cocaine transit via Central America has plainly increased markedly, the rise in exports has not proceeded in linear fashion. Drug organizations have been nimble and proactive, frequently changing the location of transshipment schemes within a bridge state and between different bridge states. The amounts sent via any particular route in any particular period have thus depended on a constellation of factors favoring or disfavoring shipping through one country or another.

Among the credible estimates, the judge who heard the most major drug cases in Honduras in the late 1980s concluded that cocaine traffickers were then shipping about 35 tons annually through his country.[86] In 1990 Guatemalan sources believed that drug syndicates exported approximately 50 tons from that country.[87] In 1991 the Costa Rican director of narcotics, the U.S. ambassador, and other sources estimated that 40–60 tons of cocaine transited Costa Rica each year.[88] That same year, a leading Panamanian official figured that, even soon after General Manuel Noriega's ouster, 24 tons of cocaine passed through Panama.[89] In 1993 U.S. and Colombian law-enforcement sources estimated that about a quarter of the U.S. narcotics trade involved Central America and that drug organizations were transshipping a combined 165–275 tons of narcotics through all the Central American bridge states annually.[90] That figure continued to rise over the years. In 2001 the DEA estimated that 300–400 tons of cocaine passed through the Central American corridor to Mexico and the United States, and the figure of 400 has repeatedly been cited thereafter.[91] As the new century approached, an estimated 60–65 percent of U.S. cocaine imports entered the country via this critically important bridge region.[92]

Given the sheer size of the cocaine trade and the considerable law-enforcement resources

84. For an estimate by a former member of the Federal Commission on Organized Crime, see "Colombian Chieftains Rule Drugs in U.S.," *Chicago Tribune*, 3 April 1988, 6, and for a statement by the FBI assistant director of intelligence, see U.S. Senate, *Structure*, 46.

85. CIA analysts frankly conceded, "There are no authoritative estimates of the quantities of cocaine moved through Central America in the 1980s." CIA, *Allegations of Connections*, 7.

86. For Judge Miguel Izaguirre's estimate, see "En dos años Honduras puede ser como Panamá en asuntos de drogas," *La Prensa* (Honduras) (hereafter cited as LP [HO]), 2 July 1988, 5.

87. See "Una tonelada semanal de cocaína pasa por el país," El Gráfico (Guatemala), 30 May 1990, 7. For the U.S. estimate of one ton weekly, see "Guatemala Seen Slipping into a Haven for Drugs," LAT (US), 30 August 1989, 1. See also "Guatemala: A Major Cocaine Player," *TR* (BZ), 12 April 1992, 4.

88. See "Investigan base 'narco' en el Pacific Sur," *LN* (CR), 2 June 1991, 10A, and "Embajador critica lucha antidroga," *LN* (CR), 13 September 1991, 6A.

89. "Ruta de centroamérica preferida para los carteles de la droga," *La Hora* (Guatemala) (hereafter cited as LH [GU]), 8 June 1991, 11.

90. "'Narcos' suramericanos abren nuevas rutas en centroamérica," *LP* (HO), 2 April 1993, 46.

91. DEA, *Resources, Guatemala* (2001), 5–6. For references to the four-hundred-ton figure, see, for instance, *INCSR* (2003), 5:21.

92. By late in the 1990s the CIA estimated that traffickers shipped only about 10 percent of the U.S. cocaine supply directly from South America. Another 30 percent was transshipped via Caribbean islands, and the remaining 60 percent traversed the Central America–Mexico corridor (land territory and adjacent sea lanes). CIA, *Allegations of Connections*, 7. For nearly identical U.S. Army Southern Command figures, see "Drug Cops Agree to Cooperate," *TT* (CR), 3 March 2000, 1A.

Fig. 1.5 Cocaine seizures in key Central American bridge states, 1990–1999

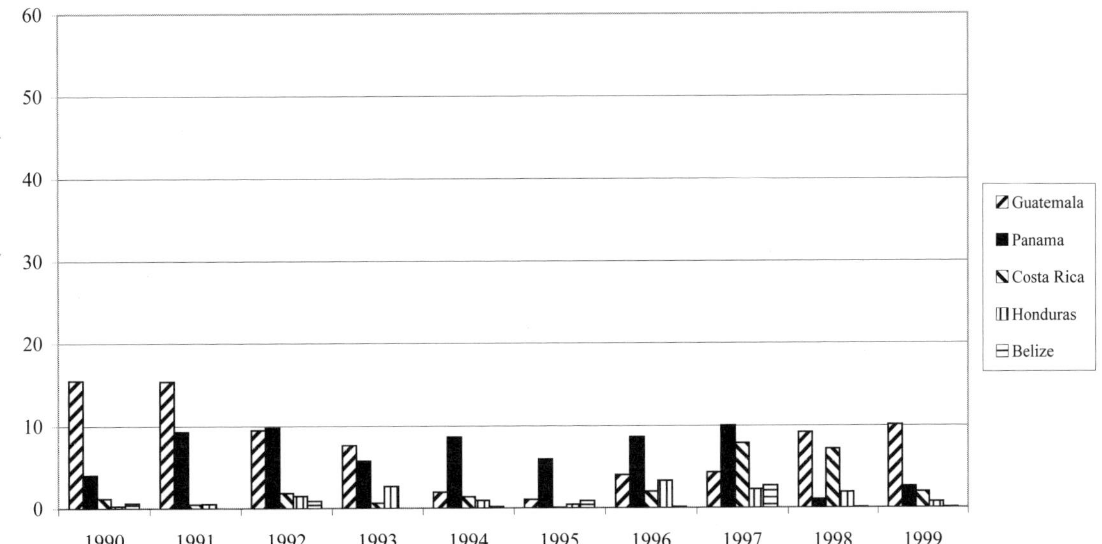

Sources: *INCSR* (2000), 154, 170; *INCSR* (1999), 190; *INCSR* (1997), 160; *INCSR* (1996), 139; *INCSR* (1994), 172; *INCSR* (1991), 136, 138, 150, 187; *INCSR* (1990), 184, 174; *INCSR* (1989), 100; *INCSR* (1988), 184, 127, 121; DEA, *Resources, Belize* (2000), 1; DEA, *Resources, Costa Rica* (2000), 2; DEA, *Resources, Guatemala* (2001), 2; DEA, *Resources, Honduras* (2000), 1; DEA, *Resources, Panama* (2000), 3.

ranged against it, some trafficking ventures were bound to fail. In the 1980s most cocaine seizures occurred in the United States: two tons in 1981, twenty-seven tons in 1986, and one hundred tons in 1989.[93] By the 1990s, however, as fig. 1.5 illustrates, Central American authorities, regularly acting on DEA information, were confiscating sizable quantities of cocaine each year. But, as fig. 1.6 demonstrates, seizure figures had risen substantially by 2006 and thereafter. As our case studies detail, they were also arresting some substantial drug traffickers as well as large numbers of local drug dealers and users.[94] Figs. 1.5 and 1.6 also demonstrate that, taken as a group, the Central American bridge states were not surrendering to transnational organized crime; rather, the states were persisting in law-enforcement efforts and then vigorously reasserting themselves, with considerably larger seizures occurring over time.

Nevertheless, the cocaine interdicted in Central America en route to market has amounted to a small fraction of all that has passed through these countries. The most optimistic estimates have authorities interdicting 10–15 percent of the narcotics heading to the United States through this bridge region.[95] The estimate of 5 percent is, perhaps, more realistic, and various law-enforcement authorities have declared that the actual figure might be a mere 2 percent.[96] Thus, Central American seizures have lagged well behind estimated

93. Andreas, *Border Games*, 43.

94. According to the Inter-American Drug Abuse Control Commission of the Organization of American States, in 1995 the Central American states, including Belize, arrested 5,582 persons for drug offenses. CICAD, *Total de detenidos*, 2.

95. See U.S. Senate, *Law Enforcement: Report*, 1–2. For similar estimates, see "Agents Take Record Haul of Cocaine," *St. Petersburg Times* (United States) (hereafter cited as *SPT* [US]), 20 November 1987, 1A, and "Aims of 'Drug War' Questioned," *TT* (CR), 21 May 1999, 1A.

96. At an antidrug conference in San José, Costa Rica, in March 1998 both Guatemalan and Costa Rican counter-narcotics authorities declared that they would be satisfied to intercept 2 percent. "Heroin: A Growing Threat," *TT* (CR), 27 March 1998, 1.

Fig. 1.6 Cocaine seizures in key Central American bridge states, 2000–2010

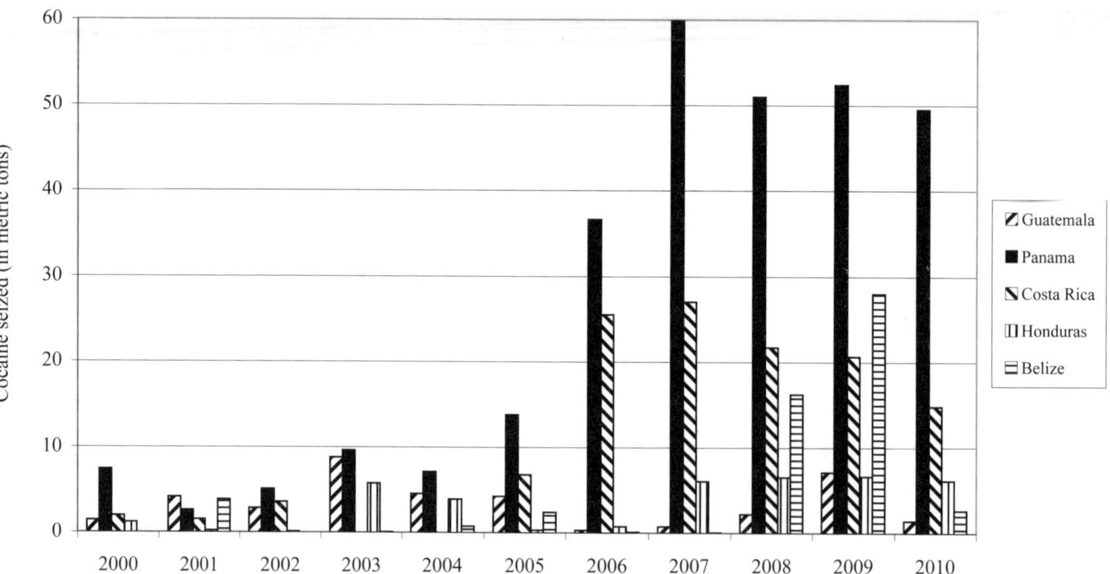

Sources: *INCSR* (2011), 137, 206, 272, 293, 439; *INCSR* (2010), 219, 308, 498; *INCSR* (2009), 150, 210, 289, 467; *INCSR* (2008), 154, 162, 168, 185; *INCSR* (2007), 19, 147, 154, 160; *INCSR* (2006), 129, 136, 142; *INCSR* (2005), 160, 170; *INCSR* (2004), 132, 155; *INCSR* (2003), 5:4, 5:29; *INCSR* (2002), 5:3, 5:27, 5:25; *INCSR* (2001), 5:23; DEA, *Resources, Belize* (2003), 3; DEA, *Resources, Costa Rica* (2003), 2; DEA, *Resources, Honduras* (2001), 1.

interception rates in market countries of 10–25 percent.[97] Consequently, while many seizures have occurred, the contribution made by bridge-state interdiction has been too modest to deter criminal groups from transshipping drugs through these countries.

Methods of Trafficking Drugs Through Central America

"Ant Traffic"

In the 1970s drug enterprises routinely employed individual couriers, so-called mules or burros, who carried small amounts of drugs to market in their luggage or on their persons.[98] In addition to the few duped into transporting drugs, mules ranged from poor individuals to students to wealthy elites, all enticed by promises of "easy money." Over time, courier techniques became more elaborate, with some couriers even carrying drugs in their stomachs or body cavities.[99] Trafficking organizations naturally came to favor those least likely to arouse the suspicion of customs authorities, such as diplomats or members of ship or plane crews. Members of groups such as the elderly or pregnant women have had the added bonus of being able to avoid x-ray screenings at many security checkpoints.[100] A popular variant on air couriers has had underlings driving cars or pickups outfitted with hidden compartments. The steady march of

97. See Farrell, "Global Rate of Interception," and Zaitch, *Trafficking Cocaine*, 93.

98. See, for instance, *United States v. Grayson*, 597 F.2d 1225; *United States v. Navarro-Varelas*, 541 F.2d 1331; and *United States v. Gomez*, 457 F.2d 593.

99. See "Embarazadas . . . de marihuana," *LP* (HO), 18 October 1989, 29, and Centro, "Narcotráfico en Honduras," 8.

100. "Cargaba heroína en su estómago," *LP* (HO), 2 September 2009, 66.

small quantities of drugs via Central America came to be termed "ant traffic," and the carriers, while insignificant singly, have together carried considerable amounts of drugs, especially cocaine and heroin.[101]

Air Transport

Although drug networks, particularly minor ones, have continued to rely on these time-tested courier methods, the principal organizations, intent on moving larger quantities, soon turned to the widespread use of propeller planes.[102] By 1977 Colombian traffickers had started to transship a significant percentage of cocaine exports by air, and by the mid-1980s authorities estimated that 80–90 percent of the U.S. cocaine supply arrived aboard aircraft.[103] Smugglers outfitted fleets of small planes with extra fuel tanks, long-range navigation systems, and sophisticated communications technology, and aerial shipments of four hundred to eight hundred kilos of drugs soon became commonplace.[104]

Although a light plane with additional fuel bladders can fly from Colombia to the United States directly, such a route is much more vulnerable to being tracked on radar and intercepted.[105] The smaller the aircraft, the more difficult it is for authorities to follow its course, but the more heavily loaded, the slower it will fly and the shorter the distance it can travel before refueling. Thus, to evade radar and maximize payload, traffickers might load a Cessna 310 with perhaps five hundred kilos of cargo and fly it at low altitudes for up to eight hours at 240–360 miles per hour, then refuel.[106] By incorporating a bridge-state pit stop, drug rings have been able to transport larger quantities more successfully than by using direct flights. But this method requires advance arrangements for logistical support en route. Planes that carry drugs north might return empty, or, to repatriate profits, they might carry weapons, merchandise, or cash.

Interim stops in the different Central American countries thus became a vital ingredient in the successful transit of drugs. While some flights headed from Central America to the United States, more commonly their destination was northern Mexico. By the mid-1980s U.S. Customs agents knew of five hundred Mexican airstrips and 132 stash houses within a hundred miles of the U.S. border.[107] The Medellín cartel alone regularly employed eight different named routes, while sometimes experimenting with new flight plans and also combining portions of existing, well-tested ones. In looking back over the decade of Medellín preeminence, one cartel insider declared, "At the beginning there were maybe two or three flights a week, but by the end airplanes were almost continually taking off and returning with cash."[108]

When interdiction during refueling has threatened, aerial smugglers have moved to touch-and-go landings or to airdrops, in which a plane would descend to a couple hundred feet and parachute duffel bags of cocaine to boats or waiting ground crews. They have also frequently combined tactics, as when vacuum-sealed and waterproof packages have been tossed into the sea to be picked up by speedboats and eventually moved along by truck, boat, or plane. Over time, to increase efficiency and payoffs, drug

101. See "Detienen a cinco mexicanos por introducir cocaína," *LP* (PA), 7 January 1997, 5A.

102. CIA, *Allegations of Connections*, 7.

103. See Dinges, *Our Man in Panama*, 126; "U.S. Plans to Call Out National Guard," *Christian Science Monitor* (US), 29 March 1989, 7.

104. For the alteration of planes to accommodate drug shipments, see *United States v. Lee*, 743 F.2d at 1244, and *United States v. Nichols*, 741 F.2d 767.

105. Decker and Chapman, *Drug Smugglers*, 69, and Reuter, Crawford, and Cave, *Sealing the Borders*, 46.

106. See "U.S. Radar System Detects Illegal Flights Here," *TT* (CR), 9 August 2002, 8, and "Capturado avión con cocaína en Quepos," LN (CR), 3 July 1987, 10A.

107. Shannon, *Desperados*, 322.

108. Escobar, *Accountant's Story*, 64.

organizations have sometimes employed large jets able to fly from Colombia to North America and even Europe.[109] During flights from Panama to Mexico in 2006, drug planes were reported to have refueled while airborne for the first time.[110]

Maritime Transport

During the late 1980s rivals in Cali began to supplant the Medellín traffickers who had pioneered cocaine smuggling by air, and their specialty came to be maritime drug transport. In 1985 the U.S. Coast Guard had first started to seize shipments amounting to thousands of kilos of cocaine, and by the end of the decade aerial cocaine transit had decreased to an estimated 40 percent of the total.[111] Colombian cocaine has often been exported by sea from the country's five principal ports: Santa Marta, Barranquilla, Cartagena, and Turbo, on the Caribbean, and Buenaventura on the Pacific. Maritime-trafficking schemes have employed an array of vessels—yachts, speedboats, fishing and coastal-supply boats, ocean-going freighters, and eventually even semisubmersibles and submarines—with some ventures combining motorboat transit with that by fishing vessel or container ship.[112] Of these, the most important method over the decades has been to send drugs on commercial ships, with smugglers taking advantage of the millions of containers that enter the United States annually with at best abbreviated customs inspections of the goods inside.[113]

Here, drug organizations have governments in a bind. Key measures enhancing modern maritime commerce—expedited customs inspections, deregulated shipping industries, and privatized port facilities—have also encouraged smuggling by sea.[114] Although the Container Security Initiative program of 2002 has brought U.S. officials into certain foreign ports to work with customs officials to inspect suspicious cargoes, drug shipments have managed to evade the screening process or pass through it undiscovered.

Traffickers have appreciated not only the low interception rates but the sheer bulk of drugs that could be forwarded by ship and soon were moving quite large quantities. Thus, in one six-month period in 1987, U.S. authorities seized sixty-six maritime cargo containers packed with multiple tons of cocaine, including a 3.1-ton seizure in Palm Beach, 2.5 tons in Chicago, and 2 tons in Miami and in San Juan, Puerto Rico. That same year, agents in Port Everglades, Florida, discovered nearly 4 tons of cocaine, transshipped through Honduras, and in 1988 a similar load was interdicted in Tarpon Springs, Florida. In 1989 Mexican authorities made the largest cocaine confiscation ever recorded, seizing a 4.8 ton shipment. Thereafter, as anti-drug officials repeatedly eclipsed this record, vessels registered in Central American states were frequently involved. Among the largest busts, in 1995 the U.S. Coast Guard intercepted the Panamanian vessel *Nataly I*, carrying 12

109. For the Michael Horn statement, see U.S. Senate, *Drug Cartels*, 37. One U.S. prosecutor proceeding against air-cargo companies engaged in bulk cocaine imports observed, "What began as single-engine Cessnas island-hopping 100-kilo loads into Florida rapidly evolved into four- to eight-ton loads in Boeing 727s." "Drug Cartels' Big Planes Are Big Problem," *WP* (US), 6 February 1995, C11.

110. See "Narcotráfico en la frontera Tico-Panameña," *LP* (PA), 18 April 2006, 6A.

111. Reuter, Crawford, and Cave, *Sealing the Borders*, 31; "U.S. Plans," 7.

112. See *INCSR* (2002), 4:25; *INCSR* (2011), 49; Kenney, *From Pablo to Osama*, 68–69; and Escobar, *Accountant's Story*, 68–69. The range of vessels used is illustrated by *United States v. Garate-Vergara*, 942 F.2d 1543; *United States v. Castro*, 874 F.2d 230; and *United States v. Alvarez*, 810 F.2d 879. For submersibles, see "Cocaine-Toting Sub Busted in Pacific Ocean," *TT* (CR), 19 September 2008, 8; "Drug Traffic Beneath the Waves," *WP* (US), 6 February 2008, A4; and "Cops in Colombia Find Drug Sub," *TR* (BZ), 17 September 2000, 23.

113. Until technology improved after the September 11, 2001, terrorist attacks, a five-agent U.S. Customs unit might spend three hours inspecting a single container of a size that would fit behind a tractor trailer. Bartilow and Kihong, "Free Traders," 124. See also "Drug Smugglers Join," 1A, and "Drug Cartels Have Best Technology Money Can Buy," Associated Press, 4 June 1997, 12A.

114. See Andreas, "Smuggling Wars," 89.

tons.[115] Enormous cocaine seizures at sea continued in the twenty-first century. In 2001 and 2004 authorities stopped two Belize-flagged ships, taking nearly 12 tons from one and more than 11 from the other. And, in the Pacific Ocean U.S. authorities seized nearly 20 tons from a Panamanian vessel in 2007.[116]

But, to focus on the enormous drug busts alone risks overlooking the constant stream of smaller loads, whose significance, in sum, may well have outweighed even the most immense single shipment. In the summer of 1998, the U.S. Customs Service, operating in Florida's noncontainerized shipping zone on the Miami River that serves small Caribbean freighters, made a 500-kilo cocaine seizure on a Honduran-registered vessel, another of more than 700 kilos from a Belizean ship, and yet another of almost 2.3 tons from a Panamanian freighter.[117] Organizations trafficking drugs by ship have usually secreted them within shipping containers holding such products as wood, crates of hammocks, barrels of butane, and bags of coffee and sesame seeds.[118] Perishable items such as flowers, meat, seafood, fruits, and vegetables have often been favored because they can be subject to expedited customs inspection.[119] Alternatively, criminal groups have hidden drugs in secret compartments under the decks or inside tanks.[120] In one case Costa Rican authorities uncovered a scheme using divers to insert sealed cocaine packets into the outer hulls of ships headed to the United States.[121]

Whether hidden within a container or inside the ship itself, cocaine has often been brought onto vessels in Central American ports. Alternatively, drugs have sometimes been loaded in South America and have then passed through Central American territorial waters, sometimes transferred from one vessel to another. In addition, drugs have often been carried on ships registered as part of the merchant marines of different Central American states. The region's ports and free trade zones have thus factored into many transshipment schemes, with the colossal duty-free port at Colón, Panama, the most significant of all.

By the end of the twentieth century, speedboats, often termed cigarette boats or simply go-fasts, were in vogue, carrying cocaine up the Caribbean and Pacific coasts to destinations in Mexico, Guatemala, or Belize. Unlike freighters, fishing vessels, or yachts, which ordinarily fly the flag of a state, go-fasts are not typically registered in that way: a speedboat found in some distant place is very likely engaged in criminal activity. Hence, as stateless vessels, they are subject to U.S. jurisdiction when intercepted far from home. Their low, open hulls and powerful engines make them exceptionally fast and difficult to detect. The speediest boats could outrun most vessels they might meet. While antidrug authorities have confiscated numerous go-fasts, operating them for routine police patrols has often been judged too expensive.[122] Thus, criminal enterprises moving

115. For the 1987 through 1995 data, see "Mayor decomiso de cocaína en EEUU," *LN* (CR), 20 November 1987, 8A; "U.S. Plans," 7; "Massive Drug Load Seized in Pinellas," *SPT* (US), 5 May 1988, 1A; "Abren nuevas rutas para la cocaína a través de México," *El Gráfico* (Guatemala), 16 March 1989, 24; and "Castrillón Henao dirigía vasta red de narcotraficantes," *LP* (PA), 25 April 1996, 45A.

116. "Drugs Found on Boat Flying Belize Flag," *TR* (BZ), 3 October 2004, 1, and "Droga no pasó por el canal," *LP* (PA), 23 March 2007, 8A.

117. "Drug-Busting X-ray Units Land at Port of Miami," *Journal of Commerce*, 21 August 1998, 1A.

118. See, for instance, "En Guatemala extraditan a narco reclamado por E.U.," *LP* (PA), 15 December 1990, 6A; "Hallan cocaína en barco hondureño," *LP* (HO), 20 November 1987, 1; "Coca decomisada vale c. 55 millones," *LN* (CR), 15 July 1989, 10A; "Cops Find Cocaine in Butane Gas Tanks," *TR* (BZ), 26 July 1987, 10; and "Policía decomisó cocaína en barco norteamericano," *LN* (CR), 24 July 1985, 10A.

119. See, for instance, "Autoridades decomisaron unos 12 mil kilos de cocaína," *LN* (CR), 5 October 1986, 10A; "Perú: Intentaban mandar droga a Italia en el interior de pescados," *LH* (GU), 12 July 1991, 20; and Kenney, *From Pablo to Osama*, 70.

120. See Decker and Chapman, *Drug Smugglers*, 70, 75–78.

121. "En firme causa contra buzos por narcotráfico," *LN* (CR), 29 October 1992, 12A.

122. See "Cien lanchas capturadas se desperdician por líos legales," *LN* (CR), 13 August 2007, 14A.

cocaine by cigarette boats have had a decided edge, not usually available to those pursuing them. Helicopters or planes have been able to keep tabs on suspicious speedboats, yet these have also been expensive to operate and not always available.

As speedboats have headed north from South America, they have sometimes stayed within the coastal states' territorial seas, but, particularly in the Pacific, they have at times veered dozens or even hundreds of miles offshore, well into the exclusive economic zones of Central American countries or even into international waters beyond. However, for the traffickers, all of these offshore routes have raised considerable logistical difficulties. Most important, speedboats are gas-guzzlers and need to be periodically resupplied with fuel. Central American associates have often assisted, stockpiling gasoline on fishing boats so that refueling can occur far out at sea.

Whether the drug loads have traveled by container ship, freighter, fishing vessel, speedboat, or even yacht, the cumulative total of small, medium, and large drug transit by sea has certainly been vast. By 1996 the CIA estimated that traffickers were smuggling three times more cocaine by sea than by air. And by 2004 the DEA calculated that drug syndicates were shipping a hundred tons of cocaine through Central American waters annually.[123]

Ground Transport

Alongside air and sea trafficking, the ground transport of drugs north through Central America has amounted to a third principal transshipment method. Occasionally, cocaine heading to Europe might be brought for a short distance by car or truck to a convenient port or airport, but cocaine being transported overland through multiple countries has normally been headed to the United States.[124]

Overland drug trafficking has sometimes been used to shift drugs between neighboring bridge states, for instance, from Panama to Costa Rica or from Honduras to Guatemala, prior to export. Ground transport has also been a vitally important method of getting drugs from the bridge states of Belize and Guatemala into Mexico, that key gateway to the U.S. market. And, of course, drugs have often crossed the U.S. border by land. Most significant for the bridge states, drugs have sometimes been trucked, or transported by car, the length of Central America. This approach soared in importance in the 1990s. Before that time the civil wars in Nicaragua, El Salvador, and Guatemala had obstructed long-range ground transit, but the free trade arrangements of the post–cold war era eased it.[125]

With time, overland drug shipments have grown markedly in size, as leading drug organizations have come to favor tractor trailers rather than pickups or passenger cars. Large quantities of drugs can be hidden behind false walls or within the merchandise inside eighteen-wheelers. As commerce has increased, the legitimate flow of goods has helped drug trucks heading north to escape detection. Only in the late 1990s were certain authorities able to respond with mobile X-ray units to help inspectors find false compartments in vehicles and containers, and there were not enough of these to do more than curb cocaine trucking to some modest extent.

Continuing Interdiction Difficulties

Across the different smuggling methods, the threat of interdiction has caused drug rings to turn to ever more inventive schemes to try to

123. "DEA se reúne con empresarios de Zona Libre," *LP* (PA), 13 January 1994, 3A; CIA, *Allegations of Connections*, 7; and "Region Defines Maritime Drug-Prevention Plan," TT (CR), 25 June 2004, 13.

124. As former DEA agent Michael Garland testified, cocaine headed to Europe would not ordinarily be sent overland into northern Central America. *United States v. Martinez*, 476 F.3d at 969.

125. Aguilera Peralta, "Fighting the Dragon," 221.

outwit authorities.[126] In the later 1980s one group crafted plastic imitation yams and stuffed them full of drugs, another inserted 560 kilos of cocaine in a shipment of antique machine guns, and still another packed dead armadillos with narcotics.[127] In both the United States and Europe, authorities have found sacks of tropical fish that also contained clear bags of pure, liquefied cocaine.[128] In the early 1990s, as authorities more commonly called on canine units to sniff out drugs and even drug earnings, traffickers attempted to mask the telltale odors with such items as dog food, spoiled seafood, beeswax, grease, glue, wine, and car and truck batteries.[129] In 1992 Honduran police determined that a corpse being sent to the United States for burial had been filled with cocaine, and in 1995 Panamanian Customs authorities, acting on a DEA tip, discovered liquid heroin inside thirty-three-gallon containers of perfume.[130] In 1997 the U.S. Southern Command director of counterdrug operations observed that traffickers had been making furniture and even a bathtub out of material containing cocaine, intending to extract the drugs upon their arrival in the United States.[131]

The most salient point is that, rather than deterring many traffickers, interdiction created a dynamic that encouraged additional production of cocaine, more ingenious smuggling methods, and the use of numerous drug routes through different bridge states. As this occurred, shipment size steadily increased. Indeed, within a span of about a dozen years, cocaine-trafficking organizations had shifted from typical loads of less than five kilos to those of hundreds of kilos with the occasional shipment of multiton quantities.[132] While authorities within Central America have made numerous significant drug seizures, the sheer quantities of drugs being exported have overwhelmed the capacity of law enforcement. After reviewing the profusion of ways in which drugs can be effectively moved—couriers, planes, vehicles, and vessels, one observer declared, "These varied forms of travel have created a byzantine maze of air, land, and water routes, making it virtually impossible for a significant portion of their shipments to be intercepted."[133]

Central American Drug Traffickers

As the cocaine trade developed into an illicit commercial enterprise that earned billions of dollars a year, it came to involve a host of criminal enterprises. Some groups have focused on only a single type of drug, but many have capitalized on available opportunities to become polydrug organizations. As early as 1985 DEA charted several hundred drug-trafficking rings in Mexico and Colombia alone that could together move tons of cocaine and marijuana per month.[134]

126. Precisely when traffickers first used these schemes is often difficult to determine, because the police discovering a new smuggling method often lags behind its first use by months or years. Gootenberg, *Andean Cocaine*, 335.

127. See Abrams, "Drug Wars," 79; "Gigantesco decomiso de cocaína en España," *LN* (CR), 25 April 1988, 22A; and "Armadillos rellenos de marijuana," *LP* (HO), 20 June 1989, 20.

128. "One of the bags in a big shipment leaked and killed all the fish, or we wouldn't have discovered it," DEA Special Agent Jack Hook said. "Who knows how much moved that way before we caught it?" "The Mexico Connection," *LAT* (US), 13 April 1989, 1. See also Zaitch, *Trafficking Cocaine*, 139n7.

129. See "Incautan otro cargamento con ocho millones de dólares," *LP* (PA), 7 March 1992, 1A; "Costa Rica ligada al blanqueo de narcodólares," *LN* (CR), 2 August 1994, 10A; "'Somos inocentes,' dicen tripulantes de avioneta," LP (HO), 16 May 1992, 5; "Cerca de L. 100 millones en coca habría enviado a EUA, ex militar," *LP* (HO), 12 September 1992, 19; "Banda trasegó 550 kilos de cocaína," *LN* (CR), 19 July 1994, 10A; United States v. Bristol, 964 F.2d 1088; and "Descubren otra forma de transportar drogas," *LP* (PA), 18 January 2004, 9A.

130. See "Decomisan cadáver cargado de coca," *LP* (HO), 16 November 1992, 50, and "Cae cargamento de heroína líquida," *LN* (CR), 3 February 1995, 10A.

131. "Best Technology."

132. Zabludoff, "Colombian Narcotics Organizations," 23.

133. "Stemming the Drug Flow," 17.

134. Shannon, *Desperados*, 420–21.

Certainly, the fortunes of individual enterprises within the Latin American drug business have constantly waxed and waned. Yet considerable demand coupled with high profit margins have ensured that new criminal groups could make the quick earnings needed to branch off from established drug organizations or to spring up in place of those the authorities had disrupted.[135] Thus, as particular groups have fallen on hard times, entrepreneurial successors have quickly replaced them, forming a virtually seamless web of traffickers intent on moving drugs to market as effectively as possible.

Although a range of foreign and domestic criminal organizations—some large, others small—have moved drugs through Central America, Colombian and Mexican enterprises have played the most critically important roles. Active for many years, these organizations have moved the largest shipments and fostered a good deal of the drug-related corruption and violence. Kingpins have sometimes used a bridge state, most often Panama or Costa Rica, to meet with others to arrange the details of drug deals.[136] They and their closest associates have made key decisions regarding which bridge states to use and how frequently, which routes to employ and for how long, and which smuggling methods to rely on and when to alter them.[137]

Colombian and Mexican traffickers have sometimes created local cells within the bridge states to assist in their operations, that is, permanent or semipermanent representatives stationed in that country working on transshipment. Alternatively, to transport drugs as efficiently and cost-effectively as possible, they have sometimes outsourced jobs to existing Central American networks that might do business with multiple foreign drug rings. Because the fingerprints of leading Colombian and Mexican traffickers are evident in numerous drug-transshipment schemes in the bridge states, we turn next to an overview of the principal cartels active in Central America.

Drug Enterprises Within Central America

Even the largest and most profitable foreign drug organizations at work in Central America have had relatively few permanent employees, as compared to legitimate businesses. The degree to which a drug organization was vertically integrated varied from one group to another and from one period to another, but none was like a multinational corporation with a dense, hierarchically organized, Weberian bureaucracy at its headquarters.[138] Rather, drug organizations tended to be lean, decentralized, and highly compartmentalized criminal groups. Kingpins, advised by family members and other inner-circle associates, might determine business strategy and make key decisions regarding routes and methods, which tasks ought to be handled in-house and which ought to be delegated to subcontractors, and when to employ violence, intimidation, and bribery. Associates would procure drug supplies and oversee bridge-country transit, market distribution, security, and money laundering.

To ensure business efficiency, drug smuggling has often functioned as a "fronted-goods business." That is, as one trafficker put it, "A small amount of money is paid up front, but everyone does not get paid in full till the money flows back down from the ultimate user. That means everyone has a stake in the success of the mission."[139] Beyond this, at home, in the bridge countries, and in markets, drug rings have used

135. Because a kilo of cocaine, costing about two thousand dollars per kilo in Colombia, might be sold wholesale in the United States for fifteen thousand dollars per kilo, even small smugglers enjoyed extremely high profit margins. Thoumi, *Political Economy*, 150n27.

136. See "Policía confirma reunión de narcotraficantes aquí," *LN* (CR), 25 December 1985, 10A, and Levine, *Big White Lie*, 227, 249.

137. See Duzán, *Death Beat*, 110.

138. See Lee, "Colombia's Cocaine Syndicates," 7–8, and Zabludoff, "Colombian Narcotics Organizations," 27–37.

139. Lee, "Transnational Organized Crime," 2.

the "stick" of violence against those who let them down and the "carrot" of extraordinary compensation for jobs well done. Family members of even low-level, expendable employees have stood as collateral, readily killed by the organization if the employee were to try to cheat it or reveal its secrets to competitors or the authorities.[140] Drug groups have also used bribes, bullets, and threats to suborn, dispense with, or intimidate judges, police officers, politicians, prosecutors, customs officials, prison wardens, and a host of others who might stand in their way. Consequently, one DEA agent declared of the Medellín traffickers at the height of their power, "There isn't a cop that will arrest them; there isn't a judge that will try them; there isn't a jail that will hold them."[141]

The Era of Medellín Cartel Preeminence

Through much of the 1980s the world's leading cocaine smugglers were from Medellín, accounting for as much as 80 percent of the cocaine entering the United States.[142] While organizations headquartered in Bogotá, in Pereira, along the north coast of Colombia, and especially in Cali also held shares of the cocaine trade, Medellín was preeminent, and the loose links among its traffickers solidified to some extent over time.[143] Specifically, the principals cooperated in moving drugs and shielding their operations from law enforcement. By pooling the resources of different producers and refiners, they were able to provide a regular cocaine supply. They also minimized risk by coinsuring or cofinancing transportation, partnering to send shipments to market that contained cocaine from multiple groups.[144] By using an array of pathways and avoiding putting too much of any one trafficker's cocaine in any single load, even allowing for losing one or more shipments, a considerable overall annual profit might still be registered.

As between Medellín traffickers and their Cali counterparts, these criminal enterprises sometimes acted cooperatively, and sometimes competitively. Both of the leading Colombian cartels shared interests: for instance, shaping antidrug laws, resisting extradition to the United States, intimidating investigative journalists, and stopping left-wing guerrillas from kidnapping their people for ransom.[145] Not only did top Colombian drug organizations sometimes recognize and act on such shared interests, they often peacefully resolved their differences, particularly in the early 1980s and before. For a period Medellín and Cali traffickers even jointly financed and operated a Panamanian bank deeply involved in money laundering. And, on occasion, the different Colombian cartels agreed, at least tacitly, to divide particular markets geographically, rather than to shed blood competing with one another.[146] For a period Cali traffickers dominated New York, Medellín traffickers took the lead in south Florida, and a number of Colombian syndicates

140. For more on this mindset, see Mazur, *Infiltrator*, 45.The more important the cartel managerial position, the more likely is the individual to be related to a kingpin by blood or marriage or will "at least have [family] roots in the region a capo comes from." Chepesiuk, *Hard Target*, 146.

141. U.S. Senate, *Law Enforcement: Report*, 30.

142. Shannon, *Desperados*, 106, 346, and Kenney, *From Pablo to Osama*, 88.

143. According to testimony by Carlos Lehder Rivas, after joining the Muerte a Secuestradores organization to counter the threat of left-wing hostage taking, he and nine other Medellín traffickers grew to cooperate closely: Pablo Escobar Gaviria, Jorge Luis Ochoa Vásquez, Gustavo Gaviria, José Gonzalo Rodríguez Gacha, Rafael Cardona Salazar, Pablo Correa Arroyave, Alonso Cárdenas, and Rodrigo Murillo. "Lehder confirma relación de Noriega con el cartel," *LP* (PA), 20 November 1991, 1A.

144. See *INCSR* (1987), 91; Lee, "Transnational Organized Crime," 18; Thoumi, *Political Economy*, 142, 145; Gugliotta and Leen, *Kings of Cocaine*, 95.

145. See Lee, "Colombia's Cocaine Syndicates," 5, and Clawson and Lee, *Andean Cocaine Industry*, 91–122. For the joint efforts by Medellín and Cali traffickers to eliminate such kidnapping, see Mermelstein, *Man*, 123; Gugliotta and Leen, *Kings of Cocaine*, 92; and Shannon, *Desperados*, 104–5.

146. See the Horn Statement in U.S. Senate, *Drug Cartels*, 37, and Castillo, *Jinetes de la cocaína*, 115.

competed in California, which eventually became, principally, Cali territory.[147]

Nevertheless, the Medellín and Cali cartels were competitors as well: alternative business entities within a single illegal capitalist industry. They typically utilized separate transshipment with distinctive security, financial, and intelligence arrangements. To gain market share, they sometimes tipped law-enforcement officials to their counterparts' operations. And, at length, the principal Medellín traffickers lost their grip on the cocaine trade on account of pressure from rivals as well as authorities. Treachery within organizations occurred as well. In 1987 Colombian officials arrested Carlos Lehder Rivas, who had masterminded many transshipment schemes, especially aerial ones, and his own colleagues were thought to have turned him in.[148]

According to the DEA, Cali traffickers often had better intelligence information on their Medellín counterparts than did the police.[149] Early in 1988 Cali kingpin Hélmer Herrera Buitrago instigated a damaging turf war and eventually assisted authorities in tracking down Medellín's leaders.[150] Thereafter, Gonzalo Rodríguez Gacha was killed in 1989, and the Ochoa brothers—Jorge Luis, Fabio, and Juan David—surrendered in 1990. Then, as the Medellín cartel disintegrated during the intense hunt for Pablo Escobar, Cali kingpins were actively engaged in the so-called People Persecuted by Pablo Escobar (or Los Pepes) death squad that murdered scores of Escobar's associates, "stripping away the layers of protection around him."[151] Finally, in December 1993 police snipers killed Escobar, definitively ending the Medellín cartel's reign.

For our purposes, Medellín kingpins were critically important in the decision to shift trafficking operations from the Caribbean to Central America, and Medellín operatives went to work in each of the bridge states that form our case studies. Antidrug officials across the region pointed to the cartel as having opened an array of cocaine-transshipment routes through their countries, with aerial trafficking of particular importance. Thus, the era of Medellín preeminence was closely tied to the rise of Central American bridge-state trafficking.

The Era of Cali Cartel Preeminence

As the principal Medellín smugglers fell, the Cali cartel—best thought of as a "loose association of five major drug syndicates"—grasped the opportunity to grow in scope and stature.[152] Cali traffickers eventually initiated even more intensive Central American operations than their Medellín counterparts had. They gained a reputation for conducting their drug-smuggling ventures in a low-profile, businesslike, and less flamboyant style.[153] The head of the DEA office in Colombia noted that Cali traffickers "always tried to avoid attention. . . . They killed people left and right—law enforcement, informants and their own people who did not play by the rules—but they always managed to cover it up or make it look as if someone else did it. In Medellín, if Escobar killed someone, he left his calling card as a warning. While Escobar seemed to be concentrating on openly intimidating the

147. Chepesiuk, *Drug Lords*, 63–64.

148. For more on Lehder, see generally Kirkpatrick, *Turning the Tide*, and Lee, "Colombia's Cocaine Syndicates," 9–10.

149. DEA officials made this point in a December 1992 interview. Thoumi, "Illegal Drug Industry," 134, 138n30.

150. "Sicario asesina a jefe del cartel de Cali," *LP* (PA), 7 November 1998, 13.

151. Bowden, *Killing Pablo*, 269. For allegations that Los Pepes was using U.S. government intelligence information funneled through the Colombian Army, see pages 196–98, 217, 270. For skepticism regarding the extent to which the U.S. government was knowingly involved, see "The Fugitive," *NYT* (US), 17 June 2001, 18.

152. Decker and Chapman, *Drug Smugglers*, 34.

153. Cali kingpin Gilberto Rodríguez Orejuela once declared, "We don't kill judges or ministers; we buy them." Lee, "Transnational Organized Crime," 8. See also Zaitch, *Trafficking Cocaine*, 54.

government through terrorism, the Cali crowd was penetrating and buying the government while concealing its terrorist-type activity."[154]

Under the leadership of the Rodríguez Orejuela brothers, Gilberto and Miguel, and José Santacruz Londoño Cali traffickers thus succeeded in becoming the next dominant force in cocaine exporting. Of course, even at the apex of its power, the Cali cartel could not form an entirely unified, multilayered enterprise that set prices or otherwise controlled the cocaine trade. Instead, numerous other groups played significant roles in cocaine trafficking. Nevertheless, by the mid-1990s U.S. law-enforcement officials declared that Cali accounted for 70 percent of the cocaine imported to the United States and 90 percent of that trafficked to Europe.[155] In 2000 DEA international-operations chief William Ledwith testified to Congress that the Cali cartel had become "the most powerful organized crime group in history."[156]

The very prominence of Cali traffickers, however, caused U.S., Colombian, and Central American authorities to join forces against them, helped along by jealous rivals. In February 1988 the DEA received three anonymous letters, later traced to the Medellín cartel and reportedly to Pablo Escobar's brother, Roberto, that revealed that the Cali cartel was smuggling cocaine into the United States from the Amazon hidden in hollowed-out lumber. In March 1988 a ship carrying lumber from Leticia, Colombia, in the Amazon docked in New Orleans. U.S. agents intercepted two tractor trailers transporting the cargo and found large quantities of cocaine. Soon thereafter, another ship carrying lumber from the Amazon arrived in Saint Petersburg, Florida. The shipment was transported to a nearby warehouse, where DEA agents watched a forklift separate 701 cedar boards into a separate pile. When agents moved in, 3.3 tons of cocaine were found hidden in those boards. The forklift operator, who also owned the New Orleans and Saint Petersburg warehouses where the cocaine had been found, as well as the ships that traveled from Colombia to the United States, was Mike Tsalickis, a Florida native who had been appointed by the U.S. Embassy in 1967 to serve as U.S. consul in Leticia. Once featured in a *National Geographic* book, Tsalickis had earned a living in the Amazon running a zoo, hotel, and sawmill, while exporting wildlife. When Cali kingpin Gilberto Rodríguez Orejuela was arrested in Spain in 1984, he was carrying an address book containing Tsalickis's home and work phone numbers. A U.S. federal court eventually convicted Tsalickis of drug trafficking, sentencing him to twenty-seven years.[157]

Although Tsalickis had declined to cooperate with authorities, law-enforcement operations continued to seize Cali cocaine and arrest Cali traffickers, including in 1992 Harold Ackerman, the cartel's point person in Miami. Information and evidence accumulated, and in major police operations during the summer and fall of 1995, seven top Cali traffickers were arrested and one killed.[158] Behind the scenes, Cali Cartel security chief Jorge Salcedo and Guillermo Alejandro Pallomari González, the chief accountant for the Rodríguez Orejuela brothers, fearing for their lives, surrendered to U.S. authorities, providing DEA with key informants prepared to divulge further details of Cali trafficking.[159] These

154. Strong, *Whitewash*, 225.

155. Kenney, *From Pablo to Osama*, 88.

156. "Target: Cali Cartel," *Tampa Tribune*, 17 June 2001, 1.

157. *Taylor v. United States*, 1991 U.S. Dist. LEXIS 18099; *Confesiones secretas*, 49–60; "The Cali Connection," *SPT* (US), 31 July 1995, 1A; "The Downfall of Jungle Mike," *SPT* (US), 12 September 1993, 1F; "Pieces in Local Drug Puzzle Point to Cartel," *SPT* (US), 8 May 1988, 1A; "Man Accused in Smuggling Once Called One-Man Peace Corps," *SPT* (US), 5 May 1988, 4A; "Tsalickis Gets Twenty-Seven Years for Smuggling Cocaine," *SPT* (US), 17 February 1989, 1B; Schreider and Schreider, *Exploring the Amazon*, 134–35, 141–43, 152–53.

158. Although Santacruz Londoño escaped from prison in January 1996, Colombian police killed him in less than two months.

159. Rempel, *At the Devil's Table*, pp. 305, 315. After secret DEA negotiations, Pallomari flew to the U.S. and voluntarily surrendered for fear of being killed by Cali Kingpins for his knowledge of their operations. "Top Cali Aide

law-enforcement moves fractured the efficient logistical systems that had characterized Cali transshipment operations, diminishing the cartel's competitive edge.

The highly compartmentalized structure of Cali operations, which had long hampered counternarcotics efforts against the cartel, also slowed the transition to the next generation of kingpins, led by Herrera Buitrago and Joaquín Mario Valencia Trujillo.[160] In any event, their reign was much briefer, as Panamanian authorities arrested key operator José Castrillón Henao in 1996 and extradited him to the United States two years later. At length, Castrillón became an extraordinarily valuable government witness.

As the case studies that follow demonstrate in detail, Central America was at the center of many Cali cartel transshipment operations. As Cali traffickers and the law contended with another, the Central American bridge states were central to important developments. Deeply involved in Cali trafficking, they were the site of key arrests and seizures that disrupted the organization and built legal cases against its kingpins.

The Post-Cali Cartel Era

The Rodríguez Orejuela brothers, especially Gilberto, and José Santacruz Londoño had provided direction to and cohesion for the Cali cartel. Within the Colombian cocaine industry, their downfall led to increasing fragmentation and intense competition over market share. In general, the larger and more hierarchical and vertically integrated drug organizations have been, the more readily have top leaders been identified for arrest and prosecution, while an array of smaller networks subcontracting many operations has been even more challenging for law enforcement.[161] Simply put, pursuing multiple criminal groups can spread resources thin. When asked to comment on the dismantling of the Cali cartel, one Colombian intelligence source analogized: "Hit [mercury] . . . with a hammer and it splatters into tiny drops which are much more difficult to spot, but it doesn't stop being mercury."[162] By 1999 U.S. intelligence estimated that Colombia alone contained more than three hundred active drug-smuggling networks.[163]

At first, traffickers from the Northern Valley cartel came to the fore. Initially an offshoot of Cali, this extremely violent organization at its height held sway over much of Colombia's Pacific coast, smuggling enormous quantities of cocaine while diversifying into heroin.[164] And yet even as the configuration of forces in the cocaine trade shifted, bridge-state transit remained vitally important. Not only did Northern Valley traffickers often utilize Central American transshipment routes, but various of their kingpins spent considerable periods in Panama, where certain notable arrests occurred.

As had been true at one point of Medellín traffickers, as it rose to prominence, the Northern Valley cartel sometimes cooperated with Cali. In 1994 Cali kingpins are thought to have persuaded Northern Valley counterparts to contribute along with them to Colombian presidential candidate Ernesto Samper's election campaign.[165] A U.S. Senate 1996 staff report observed that the Northern Valley worked with Cali counterparts to serve common business interests. For instance, for a time the Northern Valley group leased certain airstrips it controlled

Surrenders to U.S. Officials," *WP* (US), 22 September 1995, A1. See also *Confesiones secretas*, 61–68, 188–90, and Kenney, *From Pablo to Osama*, 37–38.

160. See *United States v. Klimavicius-Viloria*, 144 F.3d 1249.

161. Farer, *Transnational Crime*, xiv.

162. "Latin America's Fragmenting Narcotics Industry," *Guardian* (United Kingdom), 28 November 1997, 13.

163. For Defense Intelligence Agency information, see Chepesiuk, *Hard Target*, 276.

164. For the statement by rear admiral Joseph Nimmich, see "Drug Suspect's Arrest Hailed," *LAT* (US), 13 September 2007, A4.

165. Castillo, *Jinetes de la cocaína*, quoted in Thoumi, "Illegal Drug Industry," 119. For Cali contributions to Samper, see Crandall, *Driven by Drugs*, 83–88.

to Cali.[166] Similarly, Castrillón later reported that Cali's Valencia Trujillo had offered the services of Castrillón's maritime cocaine-smuggling network to Northern Valley traffickers.[167] Nevertheless, when agreements disintegrated, when threatening actions occurred, or when tempting opportunities to gain market share arose, the cartels violently clashed.

As for Northern Valley leadership, in 1992 Colombian authorities arrested initial kingpin Iván Urdinola Grajales. While serving a plea-bargained seventeen-year prison term, he died in a Colombian prison a decade later. In 1995 police gained custody of another kingpin, Henry Loaiza Ceballos, who, harried by Cali rivals and law enforcement alike, turned himself in. The Henao Montoya brothers then rose to the fore. After José Orlando Henao Montoya surrendered to authorities in 1997 and then was murdered in prison the following year, Arcángel de Jesús Henao Montoya stepped up, until his 2003 arrest in Panama. At length, the Northern Valley organization split into three blocs, whose internal strife brought on considerable bloodshed.[168] Eventually, Eugenio and Diego León Montoya Sanchez took charge, until their arrests in 2007, and in 2010 Venezuela expelled Carlos Alberto Rentería Mantilla, the last of the Northern Valley kingpins not already imprisoned or killed.[169] At its apex the Northern Valley cartel may have controlled as much as 70 percent of the cocaine exported from Colombia annually, but other significant Colombian groups continued to traffic narcotics during Northern Valley's period of dominance.[170] In the early twenty-first century certain Cali traffickers rebounded for a period, and even remnants of the Medellín syndicate, now under Fabio Ochoa's leadership, carried out major operations in Belize, Guatemala, Honduras, and Panama.[171]

In the meantime, the irregular forces in the Colombian civil war took to cocaine trafficking to finance their operations. By the mid-1990s the Revolutionary Armed Forces of Colombia, or Fuerzas Armadas Revolucionarias de Colombia (FARC), regularly demanded fees for protecting coca crops, while imposing "taxes" on drug enterprises active in southwest Colombia.[172] Notwithstanding fundamental ideological differences between the revolutionaries and many leading traffickers, the realities of power distribution in rural Colombia, coupled with the prospect of lucrative profits, overwhelmed conflicting politics.[173] A 2001 U.S. government report on foreign terrorist organizations estimated—conservatively, according to later officials—that the FARC was receiving $300 million annually from the drug trade. By this time the FARC was controlling local markets in coca base and had started to supply drug rings with cocaine. Before long its operatives were moving narcotics across Central America, often through its Frente 58 unit. Eventually, FARC arms-for-drugs deals came to light in Honduras,

166. U.S. Senate, *Corruption and Drugs*, 7, cited in Jordan, *Drug Politics*, 168.

167. See the affidavit filed by FBI special agent Roderick D. Huff in *United States v. Valencia-Trujillo*, No. 8:02-CR-329-T-17-EAJ (hereafter cited as "Huff affidavit"), 44.

168. More than 1,300 people were killed in the first ten months of 2004 alone. Chepesiuk, *Drug Lords*, 264.

169. "Reputed Cocaine Boss Arrested in Colombia," *WP* (US), 11 September 2007, A13. For Northern Valley cartel infighting, see Garzón, *Mafia and Co.*, 36–41.

170. "Colombian Drug Lords Toppled," *Christian Science Monitor* (US), 13 September 2007, 6.

171. See "EEUU congela bienes a capo ligado a empresas en Guatemala," *Siglo Veintiuno* (Guatemala) (hereafter cited as SV [GU]), 29 March 2007, 8. At Fabio Ochoa's 2003 trial U.S. federal prosecutors argued that between 1997 and 1999 Ochoa's operation had exported 30 tons of cocaine a month. "Ochoa culpable," *LP* (PA), 29 May 2003, 2A.

172. See *INCSR* (2001), 2:4, 4:18, and "Intelligence Network Threatens to Drop Country," *TT* (CR), 26 October 2007, 7.

173. Francisco Thoumi observed, "The illegal [drug-trafficking] . . . industry and the guerrillas have been strange bedfellows. At times the government has been their common enemy, but they have fundamentally opposite goals. The industry represents a crude, unrestrained form of capitalism, while guerrilla organizations have their origins in the fight against the unfair, crude capitalism that has prevailed in Colombia. The conflict between the long-term goals of these two social groups is irreconcilable." Thoumi, *Political Economy*, 159. See also Lee, "Colombia's Cocaine Syndicates," 17.

Costa Rica, and Panama, while Nicaragua granted asylum to FARC leader Nubia Calderón de Trujillo, termed a drug kingpin by the U.S. government.[174]

For its part, as the right-wing Colombian paramilitary organization United Self-Defense Groups of Colombia, or Autodefensas Unidas de Colombia (AUC), grew to control sizable tracts in northern Colombia, it too became deeply involved in cocaine trafficking.[175] AUC cocaine transshipment first occurred under the leadership of Carlos Castaño, eventually murdered in an internal power struggle.[176] In 2003 when the AUC was negotiating with the Colombian government to dismantle nine fronts in exchange for provisional amnesty, the fact that U.S. prosecutors had already indicted three AUC leaders on drug charges complicated negotiations. Although by 2008 the AUC had largely demobilized, many of its former commanders then capitalized on their expertise and connections to continue to traffic cocaine, still sending much of it through Central America.

Just as the connections of the Medellín, Cali, and Northern Valley cartels affected bridge-state trafficking, so too did the repercussions of the Colombian civil war and the increasing involvement of the FARC and the AUC. However, mention of these more prominent drug organizations should not divert attention from the broader trend in twenty-first-century Colombian trafficking. The fewer and somewhat more vertically integrated criminal syndicates of the 1980s and 1990s have given way to numerous drug rings that relate to one another horizontally, with Colombian brokers generating cocaine loads, and numerous so-called offices independently outsourcing activities to specialists in transportation, laundering, and other functions, including another set of brokers in the United States who take charge of arranging distribution.[177]

The Preeminence of Mexican Cartels

Mexican traffickers, with their unparalleled abilities to move drugs across the border into Texas, New Mexico, Arizona, and California, had been greatly benefited by the shift away from Caribbean cocaine trafficking. Marijuana, grown in Mexico from the nineteenth century on, had traditionally dominated the Mexican drug trade, with the U.S. market its most lucrative outlet.[178] In their efforts to reap the even larger profits of cocaine smuggling, Mexican criminal groups could call on strong existing organizational infrastructures, years of experience in marijuana and human trafficking, and a two-thousand-mile border flanking the largest cocaine market.

Colombian traffickers soon recognized the business advantages to subcontracting to Mexicans the job of getting the cocaine into the United States, the phase at which so many arrests and seizures occurred. Thus, starting with a 1984 agreement brokered by Honduran trafficker Juan Ramón Matta Ballesteros, Mexican drug rings began to charge Colombians one thousand to two thousand dollars per kilo for cross-border transportation. This worked so well that by 1987, according to Robert Bonner, former DEA administrator and U.S. Customs commissioner, 80–90 percent of U.S. cocaine had been smuggled via Mexico. This

174. "U.S. Government Identifies FARC 'Kingpin' Operative Here," *NT* (CR), 10 October 2008, N2.

175. *INCSR* (2004), 18, and *INCSR* (2008), 120.

176. A useful source on Castaño's career, written by Pulitzer Prize–winning Colombian journalist Gerardo Reyes, is Nuestro hombre en la DEA. Castaño was killed in 2006, allegedly on orders of his brother Vicente. See also "Castaño, asesinado por su hermano," *LP* (PA), 25 August 2006, 30A, and "Policía y ejército buscan a Castaño," *LP* (PA), 14 October 2006, 6A.

177. See Decker and Chapman, *Drug Smugglers*, 35–36, and Garzón, *Mafia and Co.*, 107.

178. Indeed, as late as 2006 the White House Office of National Drug Control Policy estimated that of the $13.8 billion that Mexican syndicates had amassed in total annual revenues, more than 60 percent, or $8.6 billion, continued to come from marijuana. "Economic Battle."

arrangement, however, caused the Mexican groups to grow in wealth and strength, while multiplying their connections in South and Central America and the United States.[179]

Perhaps most important, by the early 1990s Colombian cartels were often providing their Mexican associates with a commission of a percentage of the drugs being moved, in lieu of cash payments.[180] The DEA traced this policy change to a 1989 dispute between Colombian traffickers and Mexican transporters, who had brought tons of cocaine into Sylmar, California, for temporary storage.[181] When Colombian distributors attempted to repossess the cocaine, the Mexicans refused to release it while awaiting full payment for their services. But, before the stalemate could be resolved, the DEA raided the Sylmar warehouse and in the largest U.S. cocaine seizure confiscated 21.5 tons. Thereafter, Colombian and Mexican traffickers agreed that the Mexicans would take a percentage of each future drug shipment as compensation. This, however, entrenched Mexican traffickers in U.S. cocaine distribution, bringing them yet more influence within the cocaine industry.[182] In 1992, for instance, Cali traffickers sent about 100 tons of cocaine far out into the Pacific Ocean on mother ships to rendezvous with Mexican vessels. Mexican smugglers then brought the drugs to shore and oversaw their transit across the U.S. border. After returning some of the cocaine to Cali representatives for distribution, the Mexicans took possession of about half the entire shipment to distribute through their own networks.[183]

The next cardinal factor contributing to the rise of Mexican cocaine-smuggling networks was the passage of the North American Free Trade Agreement (NAFTA) in 1994, markedly expanding traffic along the border.[184] In the mid-1990s, poised for aggressive expansion and bridling at their long subordinate status vis-à-vis Colombian groups, Mexican traffickers increased their presence in the bridge states, while threatening to buy directly from Andean producers unless the Colombians came to more favorable terms for cross-border transit.[185] Although Colombians continued to dominate cocaine refining, Mexican muscle flexing brought on renegotiation.[186] Colombians directing cocaine shipments through Mexico began to pay considerably more to their Mexican associates. Furthermore, certain Mexican enterprises did begin to work directly with suppliers, buying cocaine in South America and moving the drugs to the U.S. market themselves.[187] And, in response, some Colombian drug rings looked to move more cocaine to the United States by circumventing costly Mexican assistance.[188]

Each of these developments had significant consequences for Central America. Deftly capitalizing on their advantages, Mexican organizations soon rose to become the new leaders of

179. Zabludoff, "Colombian Narcotics Organizations," 29; *INCSR* (1998), 4; Bonner, "New Cocaine Cowboys," 36–37.

180. See Bonner, "New Cocaine Cowboys," 37, and *INCSR* (1998), 4.

181. DEA, *History Book, 1985–1990.*

182. CIA, *Allegations of Connections*, 7.

183. Huff affidavit, 43–44.

184. For NAFTA's effect on trafficking and interdiction, see Andreas, *Border Games*, 74–82; The trade liberalization marked by Mexico's 1986 accession to the General Agreement on Tariffs and Trade also stimulated cross-border trade.

185. "Mexican Drug Traffickers Eclipse Colombian Cartels," *WP* (US), 30 March 1997, 1A.

186. In 1996, despite instability within its cocaine industry, the Colombian minister of justice estimated that Colombia continued to export 80 percent of the world's cocaine. "Colombia, primer exportador de cocaína," *LP* (PA), 2 April 1996, 3A.

187. "Fragmenting Narcotics Industry," 13.

188. FBI agent Huff stated of the Cali cartel kingpin: "Valencia was relentless in his exploration of other smuggling routes and methods . . . particularly . . . in a direct route from Colombia to the United States, as this would eliminate the high cost and periodic treachery associated with dealing with Mexican smugglers and traffickers. Valencia was weary of his Mexican associates' lack of discipline and reliability in delivering cocaine pursuant to their agreement with him." Huff affidavit, 49.

MAP 1.3

the Latin American cocaine trade.[189] Because Mexico borders two Central American countries and its traffickers had ties throughout the region, the shifting configuration of power further enhanced the importance of this key bridge region. And, just as the drug trade within Colombia was distributed geographically, with certain traffickers predominant in Medellín, others in Cali or Bogotá, so the same was true of Mexico. Criminal groups staked out their turf and then fought tenaciously to retain or expand it. Thus, while Mexican drug-related violence as well as Mexican drug-trafficking schemes has long been evident in Central America, each now climbed markedly.

Particular Mexican Cartels Active in Central America

One Mexican drug organization of some note in the early years of the Central American drug trafficking boom was the cartel headquartered in the far northern state of Sonora. Originally led by Rafael Caro Quintero, Sonoran traffickers focused especially on the export of Mexican marijuana, rather than smuggling cocaine via Central America. However, they allied with counterparts in Guadalajara for a period, and Caro's close links with Guadalajara kingpin Miguel Ángel Félix Gallardo extended to both men participating in the 1985 kidnapping of DEA agent Enrique Camarena.[190] The agent's torture and murder then factored into the development of the Central American drug trade. Honduran kingpin Matta Ballesteros was deeply involved, and gaining custody of Matta became a key DEA objective. Moreover, while the target of a worldwide hunt, Caro fled to Costa Rica, where he was arrested and extradited to Mexico in the spring of 1985. As for the Sonora cartel, although Rafael's brother Miguel

189. "Mexican Drug Traffickers Eclipse," 1A.

190. Among U.S. federal cases the murder spawned were *United States v. Alvarez-Machain*, 504 U.S. 655; *United States v. Verdugo-Urquidez*, 494 U.S. 259; and *United States v. Caro-Quintero*, 745 F. Supp. 599.

took over, leading it until his arrest in 2001, repeated clashes with the Gulf cartel steadily diminished its importance.

The Guadalajara cartel, founded in the 1970s by Alberto Sicilia Falcón, also gained very early prominence. Guadalajara kingpins long supervised marijuana and opium cultivation in Mexico's "Golden Triangle"—the mountains of Sinaloa, Durango, and Chihuahua, where most of the country's drugs are produced—and it frequently trafficked drugs into the U.S. Southwest. As Guadalajara traffickers entered the cocaine trade, they reached out from their traditional territory in northwest Mexico to become active in Baja California, in the Pacific ports of Acapulco and Lázaro Cárdenas, and as far east along the U.S. border as Nuevo Laredo. Cocaine kingpin Félix Gallardo and heroin kingpin Ernesto Fonseca Carrillo built up the cartel. Once Félix was apprehended in 1989, however, the organization split apart. One center of power shifted to Culiacán where Joaquín "El Chapo" Guzmán Loera developed the Sinaloa cartel. This organization controlled routes within Mexico that ran from Chiapas all the way to the U.S. boundary, and Sinaloan traffickers launched transshipment schemes across Central America with a major presence in Costa Rica.[191]

The Juárez cartel also grew out of Guadalajara's fragmentation, and it came to be led by the nephews of Fonseca Carillo—Amado, Cipriano, and Vicente. The most able of the three, Amado Carillo Fuentes, initially seized control, gaining the nickname "Lord of the Skies" for moving large cocaine shipments by air.[192] For a period in the 1990s Juárez dominated Mexican cocaine smuggling, enjoying the allegiance of other Mexican cartels and cultivating relationships with Cali and other Colombian traffickers. However, with Carillo's death in mid-1997 during a botched plastic-surgery operation, bloody struggles among Mexican drug enterprises eventually ensued, as an initial truce ruptured and contenders vied for primacy. With Vicente Carillo Fuentes in charge, the Juárez cartel clashed violently with the Gulf and Tijuana cartels, which had temporarily allied. Not only did Tijuana traffickers fight with Juárez counterparts, but both struggled with Sinaloa for dominance in the Chihuahua–Ciudad Juárez–El Paso, Texas corridor.[193] In the course of this bloody violence, the Juárez cartel shifted more of its operations south, with its southeast cell, headquartered in the Yucatán, taking a central role in drug transit via Belize. However, starting in the latter 1990s, law-enforcement successes, pressure by rival Mexican cartels, and eventually Mexican military operations left Juárez a shadow of what it once had been.

The final consequence of the splintering of the Guadalajara cartel was that Félix Gallardo's nephews, the Arellano Félix brothers, came to lead the Tijuana cartel, sometimes simply termed the Arellano Félix organization. For Tijuana traffickers the Tijuana–San Diego corridor has been critically important to importing drugs into the United States. And for receiving cocaine, the Tijuana cartel has had interests in trafficking all along Mexico's Pacific coast, including Baja California. In mainland Mexico, Tijuana's tentacles have extended into Sinaloa and Sonora, and its ambitions have overlapped with those of the Sinaloa cartel, with which it has feuded. Twenty-first-century U.S. and Mexican law-enforcement efforts have diminished Tijuana; one brother (Francisco Rafael) was arrested in 1993, another (Ramón) was killed in 2002, a third (Javier) was arrested in 2006, and a fourth (Eduardo) was apprehended in 2008. Then, after Teodoro García Simental gained

191. Grayson, *Mexico's Struggle*, esp. 68–85, and Garzón, *Mafia and Co.*, 98. See generally Grayson, *Mexico.*

192. See Jordan, *Drug Politics*, 151, and "Tons of Cocaine Reaching Mexico in Old Jets," *NYT* (US), 10 January 1995, A1, A8.

193. For the 1993 Guadalajara airport shoot-out between Tijuana and Sinaloa traffickers that killed Catholic cardinal Juan Jesús Posadas Ocampo, who was meeting the Vatican's ambassador arriving from Mexico City, see Rotella, *Twilight on the Line*, 150–60.

control, the Mexican Federal Police promptly captured him. Over the years, however, Tijuana has been quite active in Central America. Its traffickers have run numerous drug transshipments through Costa Rica and Guatemala, for instance, and in recent years have clashed violently with Gulf cartel counterparts in Guatemala.

From the Central American perspective, the Gulf cartel, one of Mexico's most long-standing, has eclipsed Sonora and Tijuana in importance, while rivaling Juárez and Sinaloa.[194] Contraband smuggling along the coast of the Gulf of Mexico, dating at least to the 1940s, when it was identified with the border city of Matamoros, first developed smuggling networks, routes, and methods. The Gulf cartel has long specialized in moving drugs, first marijuana, then cocaine as well, especially through the Nuevo Laredo–Laredo, Texas corridor. One of the first Mexican kingpins, Juan Nepomuceno García, initially led the organization, but eventually his nephew Juan García Abrego took over operations, expanding its size, functions, and reach and extending its connections in Mexican politics and in the Colombian cartels. Once closely allied with the Cali cartel, Gulf traffickers have long relied on routes through Central American bridge states, including Belize and the Caribbean side of Costa Rica, and they have diversified from cocaine trafficking into the transshipment of precursor ingredients for methamphetamine.

The Gulf cartel has also been especially important for spawning another significant Mexican drug ring: Los Zetas. In 1996 García Abrego was captured and expelled to the United States, and thereafter the Gulf cartel's long-standing strategy of corrupting key military, political, and law-enforcement figures faltered. Threatened by rivals and federal authorities and facing internal dissension, the new kingpin Osiel Cárdenas Guillén formed his own special forces, recruited from an elite Mexican Army unit that had received U.S. training. This Los Zetas group acted at first as the Gulf cartel's enforcers, intimidating potential informants, deserters, and debtors, while clashing with other cartels and Mexican law enforcement alike. In the twenty-first century the upper echelons of the Gulf cartel came under pressure with the arrest of José Albino Quintero Meraz in 2002 and Cárdenas Guillén in 2003. Although for some years Cárdenas continued to run many Gulf operations from his cell, he was extradited to the United States in 2007, and shortly thereafter Los Zetas branched off on its own.[195]

Headquartered first in central and eastern Mexico—Tamaulipas, Nuevo León, Coahuila, and Zacatecas—Los Zetas had fought its way into the front ranks of Mexican drug organizations by 2009, employing extreme cruelty to intimidate rivals and the public. At first, it lacked the connections to thrive on its own, so for a short period Los Zetas allied with the Salvadoran Mara Salvatrucha gang, more expert in certain aspects of moving and distributing drugs. With time, however, Los Zetas gained such a reputation for violence and such a capacity to traffic drugs effectively that it has threatened other Mexican cartels. It has also become deeply involved in drug transportation via northern Central America with extraordinary influence in Guatemala, where it has recruited former Guatemalan soldiers, the elite *kaibiles*, established training camps, and fought local authorities, Mexican rivals, and Guatemalan associates alike.

For its part, La Familia, headquartered in Michoacán, has shunned the term *cartel*, preferring to project an image of being God-fearing, community-spirited, Michoacán locals, employing the poor and the dispossessed and awakening them to fundamentalist evangelical

194. For the evolution of the Gulf cartel, see Garzón, *Mafia and Co.*, 82–89. For its ties to top Mexican judicial and federal police officials, see Jordan, *Drug Politics*, 85–86.

195. "Top Mexican Cartel Chief Sentenced to Prison," *Wall Street Journal* (United States) (hereafter cited as *WSJ* [US]), 27–28 February 2010, A12.

Protestantism.[196] In truth, while sometimes blaming others for crimes its people have perpetrated, La Familia has engaged in terrorism, launching the 2008 grenade attack on Independence Day in Morelia that killed 8 and injured 110, and it has viciously attacked rival traffickers, torturing and murdering them, sometimes with dismemberment or decapitation. Before his killing in a two-day shoot-out in late 2010, Nazario Moreno González led La Familia, alongside José de Jesús Méndez Vargas. Under their tutelage the organization came to dominate the import of drugs, including large quantities of cocaine, through the major Pacific port of Lázaro Cárdenas. One specialty has been in trafficking methamphetamines: importing pseudoephedrine and exporting and distributing meth. In 2009 La Familia reportedly helped the Sinaloa and Gulf cartels against Los Zetas, dispatching lieutenants and hit men in coordinated attacks in Veracruz and elsewhere. As part of this arrangement, La Familia has apparently advised Sinaloa on producing meth, while Sinaloan traffickers have permitted La Familia to transport cocaine along its routes, including via Guatemala, without paying them a transit fee.[197]

While these principal Mexican drug organizations have been vitally important to bridge-state trafficking, an array of other Mexican criminal groups has been at work in Central America as well. In 2001, while identifying the Juárez, Gulf, and Tijuana cartels as predominant, the DEA reported that of the fifteen to twenty leading drug organizations, nine were Mexican. In 2003 DEA statistics suggested that Mexican cartels were responsible for 77 percent of the cocaine entering the United States, a figure that jumped to 92 percent by the following year. In 2004, at a time when illegal drug sales were grossing $65 billion, regional DEA director Larry Holyfield declared, "The largest groups of narcotics traffickers are in Mexico. They are the most dangerous, the strongest, and they have incredible trafficking networks."[198]

As was the case with the Cali and Medellín cartels, law-enforcement authorities have been able to kill or arrest numerous kingpins. And some high-level Mexican traffickers have been arrested in Central America, further disrupting operations. However, again, new leaders have sometimes taken charge and fragments of once-dominant syndicates have grown to prominence themselves. Instability has encouraged both entrepreneurs and extreme violence, as contenders have tried to grasp control and gain market share. In 2001 antidrug officials noted that some major arrests had stimulated the rise of sixty new trafficking groups, some paying fees to larger organizations to gain access to the U.S. drug market.[199] In 2007 the U.S. Government Accountability Office reported that Mexican traffickers, including The Federation, were at work across the United States, amassing $23 billion in drug profits.[200] During a forty-four-month law-enforcement operation against La Familia that concluded in 2009, U.S. authorities seized 12 tons of drugs and $32.8 million and arrested more than 1,200 associates, while discovering that the Mexican organization had cells in nearly every U.S. state. In 2010 U.S. officials ended another two-year operation, in which they seized $154 million, 2.5 tons of cocaine, 69 tons of marijuana, and more than 630 kilos of heroin, while arresting 2,200.[201]

196. Note that some originally used the term La Familia to denote the close ties in the early 1980s between the Guadalajara and Sonora cartels. See Toro, *Mexico's "War,"* 79–80, 80n78.

197. Grayson, *Familia Drug Cartel*, esp. iii, 3, 42–43, 58–60.

198. "Según la DEA: La mitad de los principales cárteles de drogas del mundo son mexicanos," *LP* (HO), 23 April 2001, 39A; "El poderío de los cuatro cuarteles," *LP* (PA), 26 May 2007, 5A; "DEA privilegiará lucha contra narcos mexicanos," *LP* (PA), 26 May 2004, 2A.

199. "Surgen sesenta grupos de narcotraficantes," *SV* (GU), 15 July 2001, 13.

200. The Federation refers to cooperation among Pacific-coast Mexican organizations, including the Sinaloa cartel, after a 2002 meeting in Cuernavaca. Garzón, *Mafia and Co.*, 100.

201. "Mexican Drug Cartels Move North," *WP* (US), 20 September 2007, A14; "U.S. Strikes Blow Against Mexican Cartel," *WSJ* (US), 23 October 2009, A3; "U.S. Arrests Hundreds in Mexican Cartel Sweep," *WSJ* (US), 11 June 2010, 1.

The rise to dominance of Mexican traffickers has been especially significant for the Central American bridge states, which were ideally situated for the scores of transshipment schemes aimed at transferring drugs from South America to Mexico. There, Mexican cartels could take charge of transport into the United States, relying on their own methods and secure routes within Mexico proper and along the U.S. border.[202] All of the Central American bridge states, and especially neighboring Belize and Guatemala, have had the experience, connections, and location needed to play vitally important roles for Mexican drug rings.

Anatomy of a Central American Bridge State

Since transferring tons of drugs from farmer to consumer requires extensive activities en route, smuggling organizations have carried out numerous functions within the bridge states. Drug enterprises have hired truck drivers, mechanics, loaders, bodyguards, and longshoremen. They have employed pilots familiar with flying small aircraft around Central America, preferably with a daredevil or outlaw mentality, often paying a per-kilo price to transship drugs.[203] They have also contracted with local captains to traverse coastal waters, avoiding law enforcement and hidden hazards alike. At sea, Central American fishing vessels have refueled speedboats. On land, associates have supplied aviation fuel to drug planes. Indeed, the essential bridge-country function has been to serve as a pit stop, where aircraft, ships, and vehicles could be refueled, repaired, or serviced. During ongoing transshipment, safe houses have been provided for traffickers so that drivers, pilots, captains, and crews could be rested or rotated. After drugs have been imported, bridge states have functioned as forward staging bases, in which supplies could be warehoused while awaiting shipment to market.[204]

Some Central Americans have been hired to perform discrete tasks, such as leasing a private airstrip. Others have become more integral and multipurpose members of an organization, taking on different jobs in a series of aerial, maritime, or overland drug ventures. Leading bridge-state traffickers have even invested in transshipment schemes or masterminded aspects of them.[205] Mid-level associates have hidden drugs in legitimate merchandise or repackaged them to make their transit more secure, such as vacuum-sealing them for water drops. When transshipment operations have gone awry, drug rings have called on Central American cells or cartelitos to salvage what they could from botched deliveries or compromised shipments. Sometimes an organization's fugitives have been hidden from the DEA or other foreign police forces. Central American colleagues have assisted pilots and route supervisors looking to evade capture or to flee from jails and prisons. They have plotted out escape plans and furnished plane tickets, false passports, and new identities.

202. In 1997 retired DEA agent Donald Ferrarone testified to Congress that "every indicator now and over the last 20 years reveals the government of Mexico consistently works together with the major drug-trafficking families, seeing to it that the drugs . . . are offloaded securely, protected, shipped cross-country under convoy, stored and safely transported to our border." Jordan, *Drug Politics*, 142. For a corroborating statement by a Medellín trafficker to an undercover U.S. agent, see Mazur, *Infiltrator*, 65. In 1998 a 230-page confidential assessment by Swiss officials investigating money laundering reportedly alleged that President Carlos Salinas de Gortari's brother Raúl had taken "control of practically all drug shipments transiting Mexico" during the Salinas administration. Jordan, *Drug Politics*, 259n42. Raúl Salinas was later convicted of ordering the assassination of his brother-in-law, president of the PRI; however, in 2009 the investigation of his alleged drug trafficking was closed. See Astorga, "Mexico," 94, and Garzón, *Mafia and Co.*, 84n118.

203. See generally Gross, *Drug Smuggling*, and Escobar, *Accountant's Story*, 64.

204. See "Drugs: Central American Region a Cocaine Warehouse," Interpress Service, 21 April 1999.

205. Lee, "Perversely Harmful Effects," 191.

Valuable Goods and Services

Before his murder, U.S. trafficker Barry Seal, a convicted cocaine smuggler turned government witness, appeared before the President's Commission on Organized Crime and claimed that the Medellín cartel was "as professional as any Fortune 500 company."[206] Certainly, the leading Colombian drug organizations once ranked among the wealthiest multinational businesses, with resources that could outstrip those that any state in the region could devote to combating them. With transit costs a small fraction of potential profits, traffickers have had money to finance tasks such as sending operatives to spread disinformation, while keeping tabs on the authorities, the competition, and informants.[207] To determine changes in police tactics and strategies, drug organizations have developed informants within law enforcement and recruited local people—janitors, clerks, cab drivers, prostitutes, gang members, low-level employees—to assist in surveillance or provide useful tips.[208] Major drug organizations have had the ability to bug phones and intercept and record conversations.[209]

While social scientists may be disinclined to focus attention on technological factors,[210] the ability of transnational criminal groups to acquire and utilize high-technology items has vitally affected the manner in which traffickers and law enforcement have contended with one another in the bridge states. One reason that drug organizations have posed such a challenge to those aiming to curb their activities is their ability to spend lavishly on goods as well as expertise. They have purchased automatic weapons and such accessories as night-vision goggles and laser-equipped guns, most far superior to those of Central American authorities.[211] Drug rings have invested in electronics: global-positioning systems, cell phone encrypting devices, voice-disguising scramblers, and spy equipment, sometimes employing former intelligence officers to operate them.[212] Planes with sea-sweeping radar have been sent out in front of large maritime cocaine loads to try to ensure that the way was clear for following speedboats.[213] These planes, some costing six-figure sums, have been outfitted with multiple 200- or 300-horsepower engines, enabling maximum speeds of up to fifty knots that provide the ability to outrun local pursuers.[214]

To maximize effective trafficking while minimizing losses of product and personnel in transit, drug rings have cultivated links to officials in the bridge states, including judges, politicians, military personnel, and law-enforcement agents. The most prominent traffickers, whether domestic or foreign, have routinely developed networks of friends and acquaintances from whom favors might be expected. They have aimed to extend their influence by giving generously to needy

206. "Marijuana of the Eighties," 1.

207. In 1994 the DEA discovered on a $1 million IBM computer, confiscated from José Santacruz Londoño, extensive telephone records, including those of the U.S. Embassy and its DEA office, and all of Colombia's motor-vehicle records. This enabled Cali traffickers to gain clues as to the identity of informants. Chepesiuk, *Drug Lords*, 239–40.

208. U.S. Senate, *Law Enforcement: Report*, 139.

209. "Cartels Have Best Technology," 12A.

210. Strange, *Retreat of the State*, 7.

211. Drug czar General Paul Gorman told the U.S. Senate that Medellín traffickers, in certain respects, were better equipped than the U.S. Air Force. U.S. Senate, Law Enforcement: Report, 33. Barry Seal demonstrated Medellín communications equipment to the President's Commission on Organized Crime, stating, "I don't believe there's any paramilitary group better equipped than my former associates." "Marijuana of the Eighties," 2. See also "Equipo satelital controlaba trasiego de droga por mar," *LN* (CR), 9 August 2007, 18A; "Cartels Have Best Technology," 12A; and "Stemming the Drug Flow," 17.

212. See Huff affidavit, 111; U.S. Senate, *Laundering in Panama*, 34–35; and "Gozan de impunidad sin costo," *LP* (PA), 23 January 1999, 6A. In arresting a Salvadoran trafficker in 1998, Guatemalan authorities found an encryption device and equipment to monitor police conversations. "Desmantelan red telefónica que servía a narcotraficantes," *LP* (HO), 13 July 1998, 71A.

213. "Target: Cali Cartel," 1.

214. See "Patrols Push Drugs into Deeper Waters," *TT* (CR), 20 February 2004, 12, and "Ticos Tour U.S. Anti-drug Ship," *TT* (CR), 16 August 2002, 1A.

individuals, political campaigns, and particular communities. Drug rings have thus taken full advantage of the patron-client relationships long ingrained in Latin American life, expanding business contacts, utilizing extended families, and nurturing relationships with the influential.

Associates within the bridge states have assisted in identifying targets for bribery, and local "bagmen" have delivered payoffs. A great range of corrupted officials have then worked to thwart the seizure of drugs and the arrest and imprisonment of traffickers. However, drug organizations at work in the Central American republics have been so intent on increasing their profits and market share that their political interests have been strictly limited. Central American traffickers have not aimed to overthrow regimes, create parallel government functions, or overtly install themselves in political power, objectives that have occasionally influenced the substance of local and national politics elsewhere in Latin America.[215] Rather than seeking to destroy the political system, as a terrorist might, drug rings operating in Central America have opted to work within the established social order, manipulating it to their benefit.[216]

Drug organizations have also frequently wielded violence and intimidation in the bridge states. Of course, this is an industry naturally prone to bloodshed: possible prosecution discourages written records; criminal transactions often go sour; discreetly informing on a partner or competitor may well benefit a trafficker; and, at least in certain places, drug loads are regularly stolen.[217] All such activities have spilled into Central America, causing drug-related violence to soar. Moreover, to coerce the support of reluctant officials and to interrogate, cow, or eliminate rivals, untrustworthy or uncooperative employees, and others who might potentially threaten their activities, drug rings active in Central America have utilized thugs and gunmen.[218] While foreign drug enterprises have sometimes dispatched their own professional hit men to the bridge states, they have also employed local associates to strong-arm people or even to carry out contract killings.[219] In these activities present or former members of the police and military have often had access to weapons and useful local knowledge, including contacts among gangs and arms and drug dealers. They have often been eager to supplement painfully inadequate salaries, and some have had extensive experience in intimidating officials, frightening the populace, and carrying out extrajudicial killings.

In the face of this rash of organized crime, authorities in the bridge states have not been idle. As transnational drug enterprises have amassed wealth and experience, they have been forced to contend with new and improved police strategies and techniques, usually spearheaded by the DEA. However, as evident in much transnational crime, including human trafficking, increased law enforcement tends to lead to enhanced criminal skill, organization, and sophistication.[220] In the case of the drug organizations active in the bridge states, the most important response has been increasing

215. La Familia has developed certain parallel state functions in Mexico. See Grayson, Familia Drug Cartel, viii, 61–62. In Honduras drug money was involved in the 1978 coup and 1984 attempted coup. However, the extent of penetration by Honduran traffickers and of their ambitions may be distinguished from Bolivia's cocaine coup of 1980, sometimes characterized as a cartel buying an entire government. See Scott and Marshall, *Cocaine Politics*, 54, and Shannon, *Desperados*, 475.

216. Garzón, *Mafia and Co.*, 29, and Bagley, "Dateline Drug Wars," 158.

217. Here, we paraphrase Thoumi in *Political Economy*, 141.

218. For information on sicarios, see Duzán, *Death Beat*, 202–15; Salazar, *No nacimos pa' semilla*; and Krauthausen and Sarmiento, *Cocaína y Co.*, 85–90.

219. In 2009 Costa Rica's chief prosecutor, Francisco Dall'Anese, observed, "The truth is we have cases of hit men every day." "Dall'Anese: It's Easy to Traffic Drugs Here," *TT* (CR), 30 January 2009, 2. For the downfall in a Honduran DEA operation of alleged Medellín assassin Guillermo León Velásquez, suspected of seven Florida killings and others in Colombia, see "Capturan en Tegucigalpa pistolero del 'Cartel,'" *Tiempo* (Honduras), 18 May 1990, 3.

220. Andreas, *Border Games*, 23.

specialization.[221] Deal makers have assembled the pieces of transactions, while brokers have brought buyers and distributors together.[222] Upper-level managers have acquired aircraft, supervised the shipment of particularly profitable loads, or overseen continual shipping through certain zones.[223] Mid-level facilitators have taken on tasks ranging from obtaining beepers and cell phones for associates to renting vehicles, apartments, and stash sites, to otherwise coordinating conspirators.[224]

Screening Off Activities

While traffickers have had to attend to all such business exigencies, the illegal nature of these transnational ventures has required layers of complexity well beyond those found in legitimate commercial undertakings. To hinder law enforcement, functions have routinely been compartmentalized so that conspirators know little about activities other than their own tasks.[225] Then, to keep their assets from being seized as the fruits of crime, trafficking organizations have constantly worked to hide the true source of their wealth. Implementing elaborate money-laundering schemes has been one cost of doing business. And, while Panama has served as the epicenter of financial operations for drug organizations, the cleansing of assets that could be traced to drug transactions has come to concern authorities across Central America. Indeed, couriers have regularly flown from the United States into all the Central American states, transporting extraordinary quantities of cash.

While criminal enterprises have often used profits to buy cars, planes, furniture, jewelry, and real estate, they have also frequently deposited drug profits in bank accounts, which, to hinder investigators, have usually been numbered or placed in the name of mistresses, relatives, or fictional or shell companies. The funds have then typically been transferred electronically through multiple accounts in multiple banks, often in different countries.[226] At length, many of these funds have landed in some legitimate investment that would bring a return to the kingpins not obviously related to drug transactions. Trafficking organizations needing to camouflage large sums of drug profits have been particularly attracted to commercial undertakings with high cash flows: hotels, restaurants, flea markets, art dealerships, construction companies, car-and-boat dealerships, casinos, internet-betting operations, and currency-exchange and investment houses. Drug earnings have thus been unobtrusively merged into legitimate businesses operating in the region.[227]

In laundering money, multiplying their earnings, and further entrenching themselves in society as apparently legitimate business executives, major traffickers have had to interact with the global economic system. While often in dire need of expert counsel, rather then maintaining the in-house professionals routinely

221. For the statement of Ana Martes, former director of prosecutors, Colombian Attorney General's Office, see "Por la fuga de dos extranjeras suspenden a director del COF," *SV* (GU), 25 June 1996, 12.

222. As the Eleventh Circuit explained, "A 'broker' in the drug trade is a middle-man who for a fee will take on a consignment basis large shipments of drugs smuggled into this country to find a buyer for them." *United States v. Corona*, 885 F.2d 766. See also Decker and Chapman, *Drug Smugglers*, 39–45, 55–56, and Levine, *Big White Lie*, 150. For the operations of one Cali cocaine broker, see Huff affidavit, 45–47.

223. See, for instance, *United States v. Torres-Teyer*, 322 F. Supp. 2d at 365. A New York federal court declared, "[Jorge] Torres-Teyer quite literally organized the Belizean trans-shipment operation. . . . He did not act as a mere manager or supervisor, but as a high-level operative who recruited, supervised, and directed dozens of individuals and organized their activity."

224. *United States v. Mejia*, 448 F.3d at 447.

225. See U.S. Senate, *Drug Cartels*, 42. For compartmentalization in a Colombian cartel's New York distribution network, see Natarajan, "Understanding the Structure," 273–98.

226. Bank employees, particularly those evaluated on the daily number of clients serviced, have sometimes failed to record electronic-transfer data conscientiously.

227. Loría Quirós, *Caro Quintero*, 244, 247–50.

employed by legitimate corporations, they have preferred to subcontract for white-collar matters.[228] And, given their wealth, traffickers have had few difficulties in finding eager assistance. Bankers and accountants within Central America have looked after business interests, while financiers and real estate agents have assisted with investment strategies. Lawyers, too, have played a vital part in ongoing operations. While primarily serving as defense counsel for imprisoned conspirators, attorneys have also frequently facilitated the business affairs of drug organizations. They have helped traffickers to buy legitimate enterprises, create shell companies, defeat asset-seizure laws, and handle underlings and inquiring officials alike.[229]

In detailing how leading foreign drug rings have recruited local attorneys, one former defense lawyer reported, "I was asked by someone who was to appear before the [Legislative] Drug Commission [of Costa Rica] to represent him. Ask for any amount of money, he said, and it will be on your desk. Just ask; just name a price. And if you don't want it delivered to your desk, it can go to a bank account in the United States or Switzerland or Panama. He said to me, 'I'm not asking you to do anything wrong, just appear with me, and it can all be yours: money, five-star hotels, travel, entertainment.'"[230] Recognizing that traffickers have sometimes trapped attorneys by paying excessively for legal work but then later demanding help in illegal ventures, this attorney chose to turn down the offer. But, other lawyers have failed to reject extralucrative enticement, and some have later found that they lacked the willpower to resist demands for unlawful behavior, particularly when those were paired with threats or blackmail. Certain lawyers have turned to assisting criminal syndicates with activities well removed from the practice of law. Attempts to curry favor with wealthy clients have entwined lawyers in other criminal activity, occasionally through "fee" arrangements. Some attorneys have been convicted of directly trafficking drugs, and for a period the so-called lawyers' cartel took a prominent role in the drug trade in central Honduras.[231] The occasional report has even surfaced of a lawyer acting as a hit man for a drug ring.[232]

Much more frequently, lawyers have been used as bagmen and messengers delivering threats. From their headquarters in Cali, the Rodríguez Orejuela brothers used noted U.S. and Colombian defense lawyers to "encourage" captured associates not to reveal operations to authorities and certainly not to implicate the kingpins.[233] A carrot-and-stick approach helped to maintain a rigid code of silence. The cartel would cover the expenses of arrested employees, including supporting their families and paying their attorneys, as long as they refused to divulge information on its activities. Yet it would threaten to murder them and family members should cooperation with the authorities occur.[234] The cartel called on its attorneys to deliver cash payments to imprisoned associates and their families and to visit arrested employees

228. Lee, "Transnational Organized Crime," 17.

229. For one case of a Costa Rican arrested after transferring property to a shell company, see "Detienan a abogados," *LN* (CR), 23 September 1998, 10A.

230. Confidential interview with official, May 1990, San José, Costa Rica.

231. See, for instance, "En fuga abogado de Mario Valverde," *LN* (CR), 13 March 1997, 5A.

232. For instance, Guatemalan attorney Javier Barba Hernández, eventually killed in a shoot-out with Mexican police, was a reputed executioner for the Guadalajara cartel. Shannon, *Desperados*, 280, 448. A prominent Mexican defense lawyer showed a British journalist the U.S.-manufactured grenades that narcotics suspects had given him in lieu of pay. "Conspiracy to Corrupt," 1.

233. In particular, Cali employees were supposed to sign sworn affidavits, soon after arrest, "disavowing knowledge of, or involvement with, [Miguel] Rodríguez-Orejuela." *United States v. Abbell*, 271 F.3d at 1291. For cases involving confidential informants against Cali traffickers intimidated into stopping their cooperation, see Chepesiuk, *Drug Lords*, 156–57; *United States v. Orjuela* [sic], 809 F. Supp. at 196; and "Cartel's Lawyers, Legal Profession Also on Trial in Miami," *SPT* (US), 1 August 1995, 1A.

234. *United States v. Abbell*, 271 F.3d at 1291. See also Huff affidavit, 111.

in jail, reminding them of the code of silence and its strict enforcement.[235]

U.S. Policy Responses vis-à-vis the Bridge States

The U.S. government has employed vigorous diplomatic-political tactics to try to coerce bridge-state governments judged to be insufficiently vigilant or enthusiastic toward more effective antidrug efforts.[236] In particular, in the 1980s the United States began to link U.S. aid, loans, and trade preferences to counternarcotics assistance by foreign governments.[237] Under §490 of the Foreign Assistance Act, the U.S. Congress has required presidents to certify annually that states are fully cooperating with U.S. counternarcotics efforts aimed at curbing drug production, trafficking, and consumption.[238] While humanitarian and drug-control assistance would not be affected, a decertified state would ordinarily be ineligible for most U.S. military and development aid. Congress has also mandated that the U.S. government vote no on loan applications by decertified countries appealing to multilateral development banks.

This apparently strict regimen, however, has been tempered somewhat in practice. U.S. representatives have lacked the authority to veto proposed development-bank projects, and U.S. diplomats have not, traditionally, lobbied other governments to block loans on account of U.S. decertification.[239] Furthermore, Congress has supplied the Executive Branch with a national-interest waiver, and this has often been used for states not satisfactorily cooperating in counternarcotics ventures, but in which decertification might adversely affect other U.S. national security concerns. Most frequently, U.S. diplomats have employed the process of deciding whether or not to certify as a means of sending stern messages to foreign officials that more tangible action is expected. In fact, most Central American countries, most of the time, have shown some antidrug efforts and successes each year, although occasionally, as in Belize in 1997, or Guatemala and Honduras in 2003, the U.S. government has publicly protested lackluster performance. Only after seizures rose were the countries again certified as fully cooperating partners in the effort to stop international drug trafficking.

The antidrug laws that have passed, the antidrug policies that have been implemented, and the antidrug resources that have been marshaled against drug networks have by no means been insignificant. In the bridge states considerable seizures have occurred. Many midrange and low-level associates and a few kingpins have been captured. Authorities have disrupted one organization after another, and even the largest and most powerful drug syndicates have failed to become permanent fixtures on the Central American scene. However, the relentless demand for illegal drugs and the consequent enormous profits to be made in their supply have continued to entice individuals into the drug trade. While the U.S. government has offered compensation for useful information via authorized payments by DEA agents or initiatives such as the State Department's Narcotics Rewards Program, those cooperating

235. *United States v. Abbell*, 271 F.3d at 1294. The Harvard-educated Michael Abbell, former prosecutor for the Department of Justice, was eventually convicted of money laundering for major Cali traffickers. See Chepesiuk, *Drug Lords*, 163.

236. The U.S. government was not alone in publicly condemning lackluster performance. In 2001 the Grupo de Acción Financiera Internacional (GAFI) blacklisted Panama for failing to cooperate against laundering, and in 2007 the Organization for Economic Cooperation and Development greylisted Panama for withholding financial information. "Gobierno panameño se reúne hoy con funcionarios antinarcóticos de EU," *LP* (PA), 4 January 2001, 2A; "Panamá y EU firman acuerdo," *LP* (PA), 1 December 2010, 1A.

237. See Lee, *White Labyrinth*, xiv.

238. For discussions of the certification process, see Crandall, Driven by Drugs, 38–40, and "The Process Has Become an Annual Charade," *WP* (US), 21 March 1999, B3.

239. See Thoumi, "Illegal Drug Industry."

with traffickers, rather than authorities, might earn even more considerable sums, with less risk.[240] When drug rings have detected an informant, they have often acted brutally, torturing and murdering the individual and sometimes exacting further vengeance on relatives.

Thus, even though the U.S. government proclaimed a War on Drugs and has devoted hundreds of millions of dollars to it, the overall drug supply has remained ample. Indeed, despite hundreds of tons that have been routed to Europe, and despite increasingly impressive annual seizures in the United States and in producer and transit countries, market prices have rarely spiked upward.[241] In 1997 U.S. counternarcotics authorities conceded that there had been "little discernible effect on price or availability," even after the seizure of a hundred tons of cocaine that year.[242] For all of the money devoted to antidrug activities, for all of the crops eradicated, shipments seized, traffickers taken down, and networks dismantled, drug organizations have succeeded in sending plentiful quantities of drugs through Central America every year from the mid-1980s to the present. For consumers the price of these drugs has remained relatively stable and in some cases has actually decreased, even as drug purity has risen.

The North American and European Markets

A final noteworthy dimension of bridge-state trafficking involves the consumers to whom the drugs have been directed. The size of drug markets has largely determined the quantities of drugs that have passed through Central America, and the manner in which drugs have finally entered those markets has been the ultimate stage of the transshipment schemes that so often featured the bridge states. Of course, the United States has always been the leading market for Latin American illegal drugs. By the 1980s millions of Americans had tried marijuana and cocaine, and more than half a million had used heroin. In the following decades, however, drug use climbed significantly in neighboring countries as well. While a cocaine market developed more slowly in Canada, by the mid-1990s an estimated 250,000 Canadians used cocaine annually and 35,000–40,000 were on heroin, with Health Canada reporting in 2003 that approximately 1 million Canadians consumed illegal drugs.[243] That same year, 3.5 million Mexicans were thought to be on drugs, a figure that increased by another million before the decade had elapsed. Indeed, between 2003 and 2009 the estimated number of Mexican drug addicts nearly doubled to 307,000.[244] Thus, by the twenty-first century, marijuana, heroin, and cocaine traffickers were targeting all of the North American countries.

Despite extended efforts over three decades, the Central American bridge-state governments, even with the aid of the United States and other interested developed countries, have been unable to overwhelm the capabilities of the many

240. For the alleged terms of one DEA deal with a British confidential informant in the ship-repair business, see *Daly v. Hubner*, 2001 Ch.D. 1, although note that the court merely assumed that Terence Daly was accurately testifying to his DEA arrangement.

241. Although in a single week in 1989 U.S. authorities seized fully 30 tons of cocaine, higher street prices of cocaine did not follow. Thoumi, *Political Economy*, 195. U.S. cocaine prices did temporarily spike after the major Tranquilandia seizure. They also rose 19 percent between February and September 2005, and wholesale prices climbed again in 2007–8. See Strong, *Whitewash*, 142; *INCSR* (2006), 104–5; and Gootenberg, *Andean Cocaine*, 315.

242. *INCSR* (1997), 9.

243. See *INCSR* (1997), 125, and *INCSR* (2003), 5:10. Note, however, that in supplying Canadian drug users, heroin typically arrived in Canada from Asia and cocaine via the Caribbean, not Central America, and much marijuana was produced domestically. For Medellín's difficulties in opening a Canadian cocaine market, see Escobar, *Accountant's Story*, 74.

244. "Mexico Eases Ban on Drug Possession," *WSJ* (US), 22–23 August 2009, 1. In 2004 Mexico's National Council Against Addictions reported that 1.3 million Mexicans were addicted to some illegal drug, and in 2005 that 1.68 percent of the population between twelve and sixty-five had admitted using illegal drugs in the past year, which would amount to 911,000 users. For statistics on earlier Mexican drug use, see Toro, *Mexico's "War,"* 47–49.

organizations smuggling drugs through the region. Clear evidence of this has been the abundant supply of high-quality narcotics in the markets at the end of the drug pipelines. Between 1981 and 1996 the prices of cocaine and heroin in the United States fell by about two-thirds, while purity rose by 44 percent and 83 percent, respectively.[245] A clearer testament to the overall success of traffickers in getting their product from its point of origin to market is difficult to imagine. Furthermore, drug production has been sufficiently large that even the seizure by authorities of enormous shipments has failed to diminish perceptibly the availability of drugs. At most, successful interdiction might cause very occasional temporary price increases, but drug users, undergirded by those who are addicts, make for a demand curve that remains largely unresponsive to modestly higher prices, particularly those of short duration.[246]

The U. S. Market

While U.S. demand for illegal drugs is not as high as it once was, large numbers continue to use drugs, and the most recent statistics indicate that use is once again rising.[247] The U.S. market is well supplied because consumers have the money to buy drugs, which can enter the United States from many directions and through many methods. Indeed, with boundaries stretching almost ninety thousand miles in circumference and the world's largest economy, the United States has been an exceedingly inviting target for traffickers. As early as the mid-1980s the U.S. Customs Service estimated that 682,000 commercial flights and 4 million shipping containers entered the country annually. By 1998, 86 million cars and 4 million trucks crossed the Mexico-U.S. border each year, as did 278 million people. Drug smugglers have long been able to either evade inspection or simply merge into the private and commercial traffic and get drugs past the DEA, customs, the border patrol, local police, and other authorities.[248]

Initially, the most popular method to smuggle drugs into the United States was on board light planes. In the mid-1980s officials estimated that some eighteen thousand unauthorized flights penetrated U.S. borders annually. Through most of the 1980s, drugs primarily arrived in the United States through Florida, as much as 70–80 percent of the cocaine, according to official estimates. As Central American transshipment increased, more flights were directed to remote airstrips across the U.S. border neighboring Mexico or flanking the Gulf of Mexico. Furthermore, as authorities caught on to simple aerial-import schemes, drug syndicates adapted with more sophisticated tactics, such as having drug planes evade radar by flying just above the water's surface or dodging into the regular path of helicopter flights coming ashore from offshore oil operations. A technique known as "mating" involves two small planes flying so close to one another that they show up on radar screens as a single blip. One pilot in a clean plane would then land legally at a major airport, while the other would abruptly split off and drop a drug load elsewhere.[249]

As for maritime trafficking, many shipments of marijuana and cocaine have arrived via the Florida coasts, though with time, U.S. destinations, particularly for marijuana imports, have ranged all along the Gulf of Mexico and up the Atlantic coast to the Carolinas and even to New

245. Lee, "Transnational Organized Crime," 3.

246. See Reuter, Crawford, and Cave, *Sealing the Borders*, v.

247. The U.S. Department of Health and Human Services' *National Survey on Drug Use and Health* reported that 8 percent of Americans twelve and over had used illegal drugs in 2009, as opposed to 8.7 percent in 2010. *INCSR* (2011), 13.

248. Eddy, Sabogal, and Walden, *Cocaine Wars*, 100, and Andreas, *Border Games*, 4n3. See also "The New Frontier in the War on Drugs," *U.S. News and World Report* 109, 3 December 1990, 22. For U.S. transportation methods of Medellín traffickers, see *United States v. Mendoza*, 78 F.3d 460.

249. Shannon, *Desperados*, 477n15. For DEA and Customs Service estimates, see Eddy, Sabogal, and Walden, *Cocaine Wars*, 100. See also "Mexico Connection," 1.

Fig. 1.7 Estimated marijuana users in the United States, 1979–2009

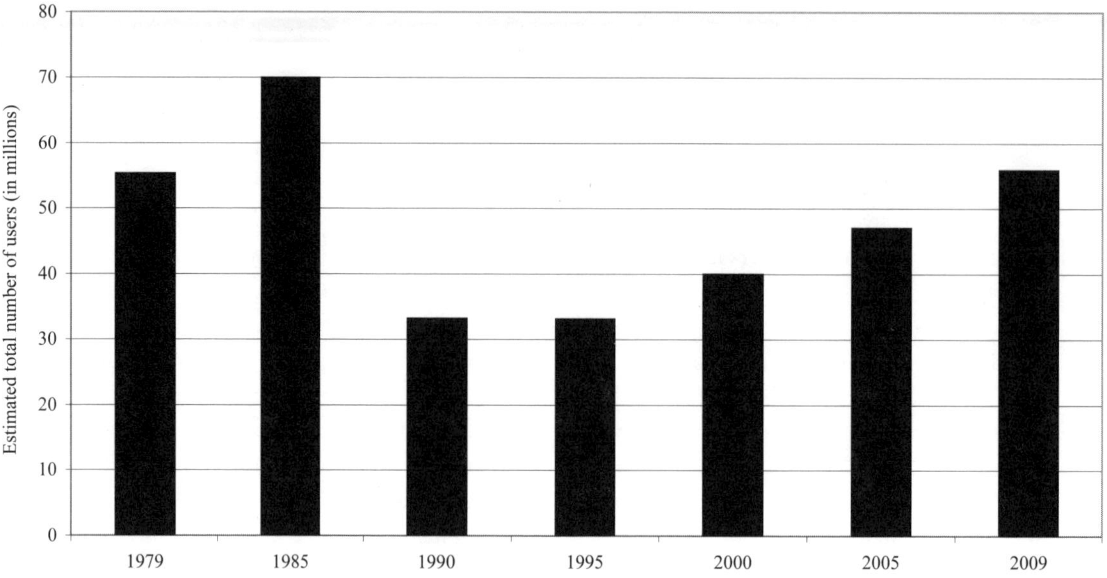

Sources: DHHS, *Household Survey, 1979, 1985, 1990, 1995, 2000, 2005*.

Note: Given the large number of marijuana consumers, we have used a scale of 80 million, as opposed to 20 million for heroin and cocaine users. Data from the National Survey on Drug Use and Health from 1979, 1985, 1990, 1995, 2000, and 2005 were obtained from the Inter-university Consortium for Political and Social Research (ICPSR) and compiled using SPSS to find the estimated number of drug users in the United States in the listed years. These findings, however, are estimates and do not represent the actual number of drug users in the population. Usage of marijuana, cocaine, and heroin was defined in terms of having used the drug within the past year. This method was preferred over "ever using," as it shows the demand for the particular drug, thereby eliminating respondents who experimented once with the drug. The population estimate is based on the percentage of respondents to the survey (number of "yes" respondents/sample size). This percentage, multiplied by the total population according to the U.S. Census, determines the estimated number of users. The margins of error in each of the six studies were relatively small, primarily on account of the large sample size relative to the population.

England. A mother ship might steer for a prearranged rendezvous point twenty to two hundred miles offshore. There, associates could approach in small vessels, and after an all-clear signal, the drugs would be off-loaded. The coastal boats would then scatter, either heading to remote locations along the shore or simply merging into the regular water traffic entering nearby ports. During the summer months, entry along U.S. coasts was particularly easily accomplished because offshore waters were full of pleasure boats, and drug deliveries could blend into offshore boating and sport fishing.[250]

When hidden cocaine has arrived secreted in a container vessel bound for a major U.S. port, associates might be poised to unpack it upon arrival or wait until it reaches its final destination. As a U.S. Customs official noted, "There are virtually thousands of individuals employed by ocean carriers, . . . as longshoremen, freight forwarders, brokers and in companies working in the importation or transportation industries,

250. See Gross, *Drug Smuggling*, 45. A smuggler who had conducted extensive maritime operations declared, "They haven't invented the radar yet that can tell the difference between a boat that is carrying dope and one that isn't; they're all blips on a screen." Eddy, Sabogal, and Walden, *Cocaine Wars*, 100.

Fig. 1.8 Estimated heroin users in the United States, 1979–2009

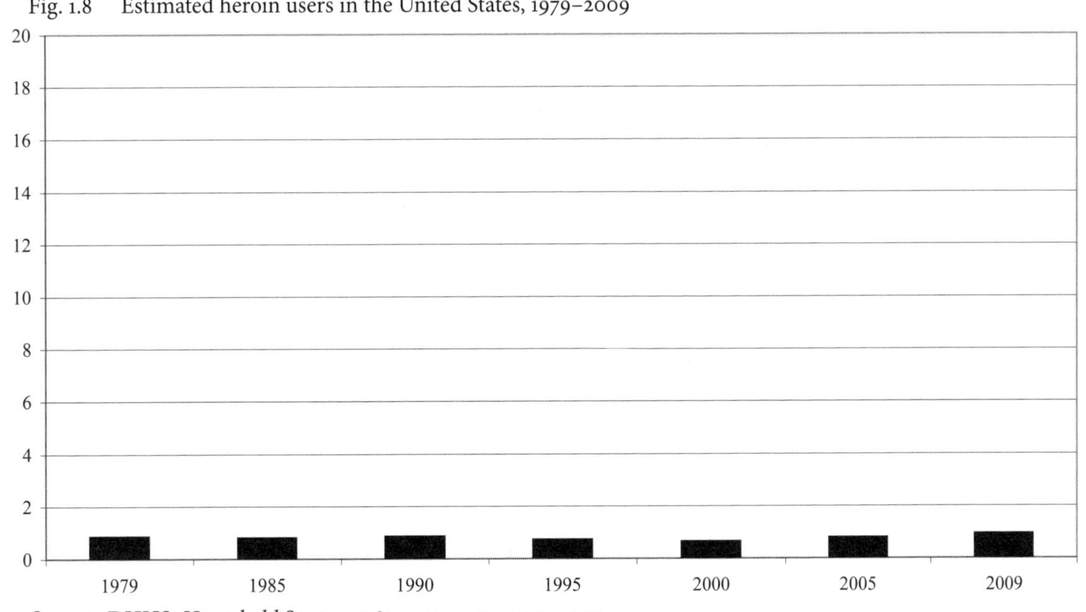

Sources: DHHS, *Household Survey, 1985, 1990, 1995, 2000, 2005.*

who know how, where, and when Customs examines cargo."[251] Thus, drug rings could create or tap into networks closely familiar with the shipping industry to off-load drugs and to provide counterintelligence on customs operations.

For the United States, marijuana has been the least important of the three principal psychoactive drugs trafficked via Central America, although the U.S. cannabis market has been large and stable and far more people have consumed marijuana than any other illicit drug. As fig. 1.7 shows, between 1979 and 2009 the number of U.S. marijuana users varied from just over thirty million to about seventy million.[252] In addition, considerable profits have been made supplying the North American market with transshipped Colombian marijuana or high-quality Central American cannabis. However, many countries have produced marijuana; indeed, very large quantities have been grown in North America itself. In the early twenty-first century, to revive and add value to the marijuana trade, Colombian drug rings began to export a potent mixture of marijuana, glue, and additives known as *pegón*. This rose to become a noteworthy problem in Panama and has concerned officials in Costa Rica, Honduras, and Guatemala as well. Some pegón has even been exported to the United States. Nevertheless, over the last three decades only a modest portion of the international marijuana trade has originated in Central America or been transshipped through it.

The morphine in heroin, exceptionally addictive, has resulted in a market with a steep demand curve. Through much of the 1980s and 1990s, U.S. antidrug officials estimated that half a million people were using heroin annually in the United States, but the data shown in fig. 1.8 suggest rather higher numbers: that between

251. See the Hoglund Statement in U.S. Senate, *Drug Cartels*, 57.

252. While use surveys are perhaps the best data available, their utility may be questioned. Apart from the accuracy of answers, as Francisco E. Thoumi has pointed out, "Typical questions asked in those surveys are: Have you ever consumed a particular drug? Have you consumed it within the last year? Within the last month? These questions do not provide good data about frequency, patterns, and amounts consumed each time." "Illegal Drug Industry," 137n8.

Fig. 1.9 Estimated cocaine users in the United States, 1979–2009

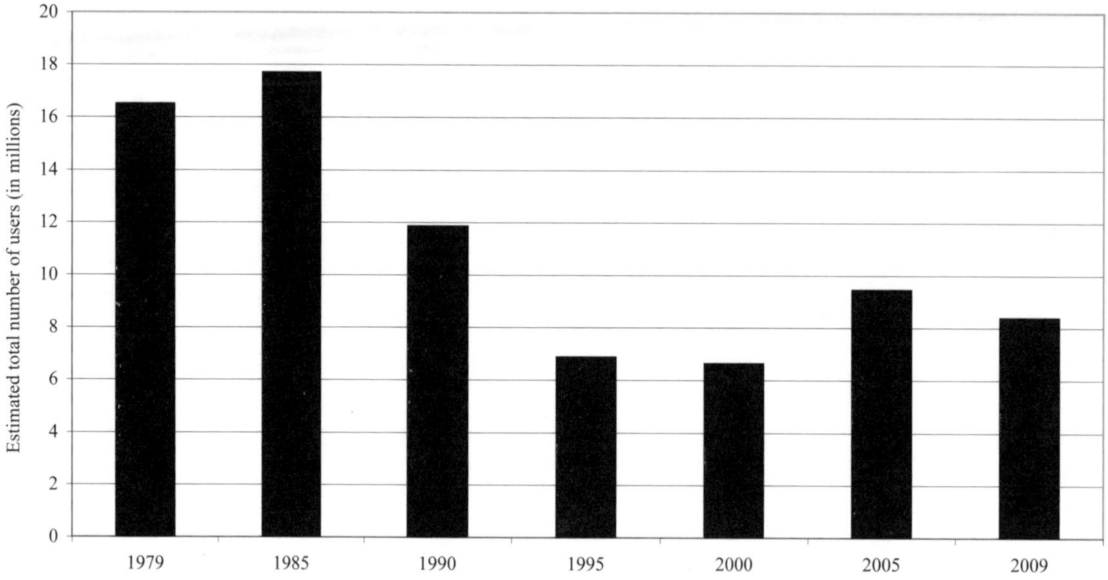

Sources: DHHS, *Household Survey, 1985, 1990, 1995, 2000, 2005.*

1979 and 2009 a total of 650,000 to about 930,000 users consumed heroin each year.[253] At length, U.S. counternarcotics officials came to agree that earlier figures had been flawed, concluding that by 1998 the numbers of heroin users had actually reached at least 980,000 and perhaps 1.2 million, if casual users were included.[254]

Fig. 1.8 also illustrates that U.S. heroin consumption has remained at significant levels from the 1970s through the first decade of the twenty-first century. Just as the high price of cocaine made that drug a status symbol in the 1980s, so heroin eventually became more of an elite drug than it once was. By the later 1990s the purity of Colombian heroin had climbed from 60 to 95 percent, enhancing its allure, with one Costa Rican counternarcotics official observing, "Its quality is now better than that of the traditional Asian producers, and it's gaining popularity in the United States, where addicts no longer need to inject it, but can inhale it (cocaine style)." Indeed, once heroin could be sniffed, like cocaine, or smoked, like marijuana, users no longer had to worry about contracting HIV/AIDS through contaminated needles.[255]

While heroin from Asia, often trafficked by Chinese and Nigerians, long dominated the U.S. market, developments in Latin America radically altered the dynamics of the U.S. heroin trade.[256] Between 1995 and 1999 Colombian and Mexican heroin largely displaced Asian heroin across much of the country. Mexican heroin took over markets in the western United States, while heroin consumed east of the Mississippi River was usually Colombian. Some Mexican heroin originated in the poppy fields of Guatemala, and a substantial percentage of Colombian

253. *INCSR* (1997), 12.

254. *INCSR* (2000), 45.

255. "Heroin: A Growing Threat," 1; "Heroin Seizures Have Nearly Doubled," TT (CR), 31 October 2003, 3; *INCSR* (1997), 12.

256. Although quite significant in the United States, Latin American producers held only a small portion of the global heroin trade. Given enormous crops in South and Southeast Asia, the cultivation of opium poppies by Colombian and Mexican producers combined amounted in 1997 to less than 4 percent of the world's total estimated opium-poppy production. *INCSR* (1998), 1–2. As detailed in the Guatemalan case study, Guatemalan production was a fraction of Mexican and Colombian.

heroin had reached the United States after transshipment via Central American bridge states.[257]

However, for all of the significance of Central America in the trafficking of other drugs, the chief role of the bridge states in the international drug trade has been to ensure that a plentiful supply of cocaine reaches U.S. and European markets. Over the last several decades the United States has been home to the most significant cocaine consumers (fig. 1.9).[258] Inhaling powdered cocaine has appealed to middle- and upper-class users, while those on society's lower economic rungs have opted for the cheaper smokable variety known as crack, which has proven to be one of the most highly addictive drugs. As the twenty-first century approached, combining drugs gained popularity. For example, heroin was increasingly used "to cushion the 'crash' that follows the euphoria of using crack."

The European Market

As the U.S. cocaine market started to get saturated in the mid-1980s, the wholesale price dropped by 70–80 percent.[259] With bloody competitive struggles breaking out among dealers and their suppliers, such leading traffickers as Jorge Luis Ochoa, Gilberto Rodríguez Orejuela, and Juan Ramón Matta Ballesteros spent considerable time investigating European business opportunities and then capitalizing on their new connections to supply cocaine to European markets in Spain and other countries.[260] U.S. Customs agent Robert Mazur, working undercover with top Medellín traffickers, reported that by 1987 Colombians had chosen to move decisively into the European market. In fact, the cocaine flow into Europe climbed rapidly at just this time. Between 1986 and 1987, seizures across Europe doubled; nevertheless, between September 1987 and February 1988 wholesale per-kilo profits dropped by two thousand dollars, indicating a rapidly rising cocaine supply.[261]

The criminal syndicates supplying growing European markets already had well-oiled transshipment operations active in Central American bridge states such as Costa Rica, Guatemala, and Panama. Drug organizations thus started to rely on Central American associates to launch large shipments toward Europe as well. Starting in the late 1980s, authorities in the primary European narcotics gateways—Spain, Italy, and the Netherlands—and then in such secondary entry points as France and Germany, even Poland, Romania, and Russia, uncovered multiple trafficking conspiracies via Central America.[262] As the Colombian drug organizations reached toward distant markets that lacked the dense distribution networks laboriously built up in the United States, their traffickers infiltrated expatriate communities, such as Amsterdam's Colombian population.[263] Many also opted to integrate into their operations European criminal

257. *INCSR* (2000), 46; *INCSR* (1997), 3; *INCSR* (1999), 15; and Chappell, "Colombian Heroin Threat."

258. For an estimate that the United States absorbed roughly two-thirds of the world's cocaine, see *United States v. Klimavicius-Viloria*, 144 F.3d at 1249.

259. Zabludoff, "Colombian Narcotics Organizations," 24.

260. Chepesiuk, *Drug Lords*, 64. For early activities of Colombian drug entrepreneurs in Europe, see Zaitch, *Trafficking Cocaine*, 78–79. Roberto Escobar alleged that, during Colombia's violent struggles in 1987, Gilberto Rodríguez Orejuela asked a Basque terrorist he had met in a Spanish prison to train Cali associates to manufacture the large bomb used to destroy Escobar's Bogotá residence. Escobar then hired the same individual to train Medellín's bomb makers and later trafficked cocaine into Spain using the Basque's network. Escobar, *Accountant's Story*, 164–67.

261. Mazur, *Infiltrator*, 77, and "Narcotráfico apunta ahora hacia Europa," *LN* (CR), 12 November 1987, 28A.

262. See Zaitch, Trafficking Cocaine, 4. For Sicilian-Colombian links, see Jordan, *Drug Politics*, 77–78. For a comprehensive overview of trafficking methods into the Netherlands, see Zaitch, *Trafficking Cocaine*, 138–42. While European criminal syndicates tended to engage in numerous illegal activities, including stealing cars and running prostitution rings, Mexican and Colombian networks tended to focus on drug trafficking alone. Williams, "Transnational Criminal Networks," 70–71.

263. See generally Zaitch, *Trafficking Cocaine*.

networks, from the Sicilian mafia to Russian organized crime.[264]

From this foothold, the cardinal events of the early 1990s—both the Soviet Union's disintegration and the European Union's consolidation and growth—contributed to climbing European cocaine trafficking.[265] Borders across the continent became more easily and frequently traversed, making them at least appear to be more porous, thus encouraging the drug trade.[266] The extensive arms trafficking involving former Soviet-bloc states engendered weapons-for-drugs deals.[267] And, as fledgling democracies replaced police states in the former Soviet Union and Eastern Europe, enterprising Colombian traffickers hurried in, sometimes using them as a back door to enter more lucrative western European markets.[268] Thus, through the 1990s cocaine imports soared in Europe, and by 2001 users in the European Union states consumed an estimated 100–130 tons.[269] The steadily rising purity of seized cocaine in Europe attested to successful imports, and U.S. officials went so far as to argue that by 1998 Europe was "running a close second" to the United States as an international cocaine market.[270] In 2007 the United Nations calculated that the United Kingdom had more than 980,000 cocaine consumers, and Spain more than 820,000.[271] Thus, by the early twenty-first century very substantial numbers of European consumers had come to contribute to booming Central American cocaine transshipment.

Conclusion

In the 1970s marijuana and cocaine trafficking through Central America began to climb. By the early to mid-1980s cocaine had become the most important drug passing through these bridge states. In the 1990s cocaine trafficking truly took flight, becoming an immense export-import enterprise within Central America, albeit an illegal one. And, that same decade, Colombian heroin production brought on more drug smuggling. The five countries that are the subjects of our case studies—Belize, Costa Rica, Guatemala, Honduras, and Panama—thus developed into critically important bridge states, with drug rings finding ways to capitalize on bridge-favoring factors in each Central American republic.

For their part, the governments of Central American states have responded in different ways and with varying efficiency and effectiveness to the millions of dollars in drugs transiting the region. In each country notable efforts to curb the trade have occurred, with numerous arrests and some large individual and annual seizures. However, drug rings have adapted with agility and flexibility to antidrug strategies, and for every route temporarily blocked by antidrug officials, traffickers have opened new pathways.[272] New organizations have quickly sprung up to replace those taken down by authorities.[273] This might be thought a natural condition of the drug trade, in which processes

264. See Bartilow and Kihong, "Free Traders," 120; Bagley, "Globalisation," 36, 40–41; and Krauthausen and Sarmiento, *Cocaína y Co.*, 172–73.

265. Chepesiuk, *Drug Lords*, 113. Note that in the first three months of 2004 European authorities seized 4,200 kilos of cocaine as opposed to 2,300 kilos in the first three months of 1993.

266. See Estievenart, "European Community," 58–59, and Joyce, "Transnational Criminal Enterprise," 100.

267. Although drugs and arms have typically been exchanged in complex multiparty transactions, they occasionally have been dealt bilaterally, as when the Camorra syndicate in Naples traded weapons to Basque Fatherland and Liberty (ETA) terrorists for cocaine. See Federal Research Division, "Nexus Among Terrorists," 9, 21.

268. DEA, *History Book, 1990–1995*.

269. See Zaitch, *Trafficking Cocaine*, 81n15. "For at least half a decade, the South American cocaine syndicates have been shipping hundreds of tons to Europe." *INCSR* (1997), 9.

270. Zaitch, *Trafficking Cocaine*, 84; *INCSR* (1999), 11.

271. United Nations Office on Drugs and Crime, *World Drug Report 2007*, quoted in Garzón, *Mafia and Co.*, 119.

272. Kenney, *From Pablo to Osama*, viii.

273. In 1997 Michael Horn, DEA chief of International Operations, testified to Congress, "The drug trafficking arena is in a constant state of change: restructuring organizations, adapting to law enforcement efforts, responding to demand, and incorporating new trafficking groups that bring specialties or advantageous distribution networks to the trade." See the Horn Statement in U.S. Senate, *Drug Cartels*, 44.

of fragmentation and amalgamation occur constantly and, often, simultaneously. As one scholar put it, "What is being defined and redefined, in reality, is the configuration of the criminal organizations that control the market."[274]

Furthermore, instead of causing traffickers to recalculate the cost-benefit equation and abandon shipping drugs altogether, the interdiction of large shipments has often simply brought them to explore different routes and methods. Rather than disheartening members of a drug ring, loads that go astray have often stimulated redoubled efforts to make up for the lost profits.[275] Confronting a large array of drug-trafficking groups, many wealthy, sophisticated, and determined, these bridge-state governments have often been discouraged and frustrated. Transshipment has highlighted many of their deficiencies, inadequacies, and incapacities, and ultimately such large quantities of drugs have transited without interception that market prices have remained too low to discourage consumption. Thus, the drug flow has not markedly tapered off. Continually prodded by the U.S. government to do more and further stimulated by the evident problems large-scale trafficking is posing for their societies, bridge-state governments have often fallen into a pattern of retreating, persisting, redoubling efforts, and then falling back again.

Trafficking groups have found that unpredictability paired with logistical efficiency has often been rewarded by a successful transhipment operation, leaving frustrated counter-narcotics officials in its wake. In 1991 Guatemalan police officer Evin Linares observed, "Every time we think we have made a dent, we turn around and they are one step ahead of us again." In 1998, in noting that traffickers are "able to switch night and day," a U.S. official in Belize remarked, "If they see something's not working in this area, they have a second plan, a backup. That's why it seems as though we are always playing catch-up."[276] By 2003 State Department officials noted ruefully, "Battling the international drug trade is a complex, dynamic process. Contrary to expectations, it does not get easier with time. Every time we score a major success—and over the past decade we have scored many—the drug trade learns from it." They concluded, "As successful counter-narcotics operations eliminate the less agile drug syndicates, those that survive get smarter and more sophisticated, adopting ingenious new strategies for concealment and survival. We have seen this already with the emergence of hundreds of small, less targetable syndicates that filled the void left by the destruction of Colombia's Medellín and Cali cartels."[277]

The most common responses by the Central American bridge states to extensive drug trafficking have been to try to create more disincentives and to launch institutional reforms. Politicians have fashioned drug laws to provide for more severe trafficking and money-laundering penalties.[278] Although transshipment, rather

274. Garzón, *Mafia and Co.*, 57.

275. As major heroin trafficker Kon Yu-Leung testified before the U.S. Senate, "I think it is important for you to know that although we lost half of our heroin shipments to law enforcement or stealing, that did not discourage us from continuing in the business. It only pushed us to smuggle more drugs to make up for our losses." "The confessions of a heroin smuggler," *South China Morning Post* (Hong Kong), 9 August 1992, 3.

276. "Guatemala Is Latest Battlefield in War on Drugs," Associated Press, 12 May 1991; "Just What the Smuggler," A1.

277. *INCSR* (2003), 2:11.

278. See Belize's Misuse of Drugs Act (1990; *Laws of Belize*); Costa Rica's Law no. 7233, Law on Drugs, Psychotropic Substances, Drugs of Non-authorized Use and Related Activities (1991; *Ley sobre estupefacientes*); Guatemala's Law Against Drug Activities (1992; *Ley contra la narcoactividad*); Honduras's Law on the Undue Use and Illicit Traffic of Drugs and Psychotropic Substances (1990; *Código penal de Honduras*); and Panama's Law no. 13 (1990; *Código penal de la República*). Particular provisions of these laws were sometimes later amended or additional laws were passed to form a more elaborate legal regime. See, for instance, Guatemala's Law Against Narcoactivity (2005; *Ley contra la narcoactividad*) and Law Against the Laundering of Money or Other Activities and Their Regulations (2005; *Ley contra el lavado*).

than production, has been at the heart of the regional drug problem, authorities have embarked on energetic eradication policies, often successful ones, targeting marijuana cultivation as well as the production of opium in the Guatemalan highlands and coca in the southern border region of Panama.

Less auspicious have been most of the efforts aimed at strengthening weak judicial and penal systems and buttressing the police, customs, coast guard, and air force. While drug syndicates have strategized as to which officials to bribe, which institutions to target, and which weaknesses to exploit, governments have encountered long-ingrained and often quite intractable problems. Many officials have been reluctant to alter traditional ways of doing things. Resources have almost always been scarce. Enthusiasm for reform has tended to wax and wane. Corruption has been evident. While changes in the capabilities of government institutions have, in fact, occurred, these have tended to take place slowly and unevenly. The Central American activities of trafficking organizations have thus represented extraordinary stress tests for the region's governments. Just as a structurally unsound dike might spring leak after leak, bridge states have often succumbed to immense pressure, and drugs have poured through.

As bridge states have tried to withstand traffickers and reassert their authority, they have often looked hopefully toward international cooperation. In the 1990s Central American leaders held various summit meetings that aimed to enhance regional security against drug trafficking and other threats. With great fanfare, joint strategies were plotted, declarations against the drug trade were pronounced, and broad agreements to blend national and regional security were rolled out.[279] While these occasions provided photo opportunities and perhaps some modest domestic political advantage, the tangible consequences of these initiatives have been more difficult to trace. The familiar problems of multilateralist approaches seem to have afflicted these efforts: free-riders, differing strengths of feeling, and a tendency toward the "least common denominator," that is, toward adopting only those measures that all members of the group wholeheartedly support.

More important than the multilateral efforts, governments have negotiated bilateral extradition and mutual legal assistance treaties, especially with the United States, to try to better administer justice: to render suspects more often and more efficiently and to enhance the transfer of the evidence needed to convict traffickers. Ship-rider agreements have aimed to bring U.S. naval power to bear on maritime trafficking off Central American coasts, while still respecting the sovereignty of the bridge states by acknowledging that foreign law-enforcement efforts can take place in their executive jurisdiction only by prior agreement and under at least nominal local supervision. Often using foreign aid, officials within the bridge states have improved drug-detection methods at ports, airports, and border crossings. Extensive training programs, usually funded from abroad, have attempted to professionalize or add expertise to prosecutors, judges, prison officials, special police units, and others on the front lines of antidrug efforts. While some real progress on all of these fronts has certainly occurred, international cooperation has not been sufficiently rapid, thorough, or far-reaching to stem the drug trade. Bridge states have resisted and persisted, but they have not gained the upper hand.

A notable aspect of the problem has been that microdecisions have too often trumped macropolicies. That is, when confronted by extensive drug trafficking through their states, public officials in the police force, customs, politics, and the judiciary, and private actors ranging from farmers, loaders, and couriers to lawyers, bankers, and accountants have had to

279. Aguilera Peralta, "Fighting the Dragon," 222–24, includes a useful review of these developments.

make personal choices regarding the drug trade. Should technicians, manual laborers, and other blue-collar workers shun employment offers by drug organizations? Should professional services be confined to legal activities, such as providing an alleged trafficker with the best defense possible? Or, should illegal activities be undertaken as well? What are the potential benefits and risks involved in participation? Do the possible costs of joining in the drug trade—stress, arrest, imprisonment, danger to loved ones, even death—outweigh the prospect of substantial additional income? Should an individual be concerned about the drug trade's impact on a local community and on national society?

Human nature suggests that an immediate return of benefits will often overwhelm concerns of potential future costs. In addition, the evident successes of transnational criminals and the evident weaknesses of the bridge-state institutions and procedures have, no doubt, entered these individual calculations. Transnational criminal groups, ranging from the large and powerful to the nimble and savvy, have grasped even fleeting opportunities to transship marijuana, heroin, and cocaine. Indeed, while the overall record of Central American businesses has often been disappointing, the enviable efficiency of Central American drug transshipment has stood out. One reason may be that, in contrast to the typical workings of multinational corporations with their foreign managers and their drive to profit distant shareholders, drug-trade earnings have cascaded downward through a relatively small number of local associates, providing an immediate and tangible monetary incentive to work effectively. In addition, the "outlaw mentality" may drive drug-trade participants to demonstrate that they are sufficiently strong and clever to beat the system and outwit law enforcement. And, there is that very real fear of death or imprisonment, should people act in sloppy or foolish ways as their organizations try to forward drug shipments to market.

Because the vast majority of the illegal drugs passing through Central America have originated elsewhere, it is perhaps natural that traffickers abroad have often directed the operations of smuggling networks. However, as we shall see in the case studies that follow, the brains and muscle involved in transshipment have never been wholly Colombian or Mexican. Over time, Central Americans themselves have done considerably more than simply take and implement instructions from foreign overseers. This fact is well illustrated by the careers of Central Americans prominent in drug-trafficking circles. These have included not merely such notorious figures as General Manuel Noriega of Panama or Juan Ramón Matta Ballesteros of Honduras, but also a host of lesser, though still very significant, players in the other primary bridge states. Furthermore, although sufficient quantities of narcotics transit each of the Central American republics that a smuggling operation might be under way virtually anywhere in the region at any time, trafficking in each country is marked by certain time-tested sea and air routes and overland trails. These we also identify in the subsequent case studies, starting with the distinctive part played by Belize.

2

Belize

British novelist Aldous Huxley wrote what became perhaps the single most oft-quoted statement about Belize, formerly British Honduras: "If the world had any ends, British Honduras would certainly be one of them. It is not on the way from anywhere to anywhere else. It has no strategic value. It is all but uninhabited." Huxley's subsequent observation has been much less widely publicized: "and when Prohibition is abolished, the last of its profitable enterprises—the re-export of alcohol by rum-runners, who use Belize as their base of operations—will have gone the way of its commerce in logwood, mahogany and chicle."[1] Who could have foreseen that the illegal drug trade would become exponentially more profitable than its rum-running predecessor? In fact, at an early date the Central American drug trade encompassed Belize, with notable repercussions for Belizeans, for others in the region, and for North American drug users.

Our first case study involves a country unique among the Central American states. Its roots are British, not Spanish, and relative to its neighbors, Belize is a newly independent society, wedged among countries that gained sovereignty much earlier. In British Honduras, calls for independence grew after World War II. The Belizean nationalist movement that blossomed in the 1950s then bore fruit in the following decade, as Great Britain granted self-government in 1964. The state took the name Belize in 1973, attaining full independence in 1981.[2] Thus, as Central American drug transshipment soared,

1. Huxley, *Beyond the Mexique Bay*, 35. For the activities of one such Belizean rum runner, see the international arbitration case *The I'm Alone*. Note that, alongside Belize, Colombia was one of the few Western Hemisphere states that exported considerable contraband, as opposed to the more common import smuggling, and that this contributed to the rise of early Colombian drug trafficking. Thoumi, *Political Economy*, 73.

2. Great Britain's declaration that Belize was its colony did not occur until 1840, informally, and 1862,

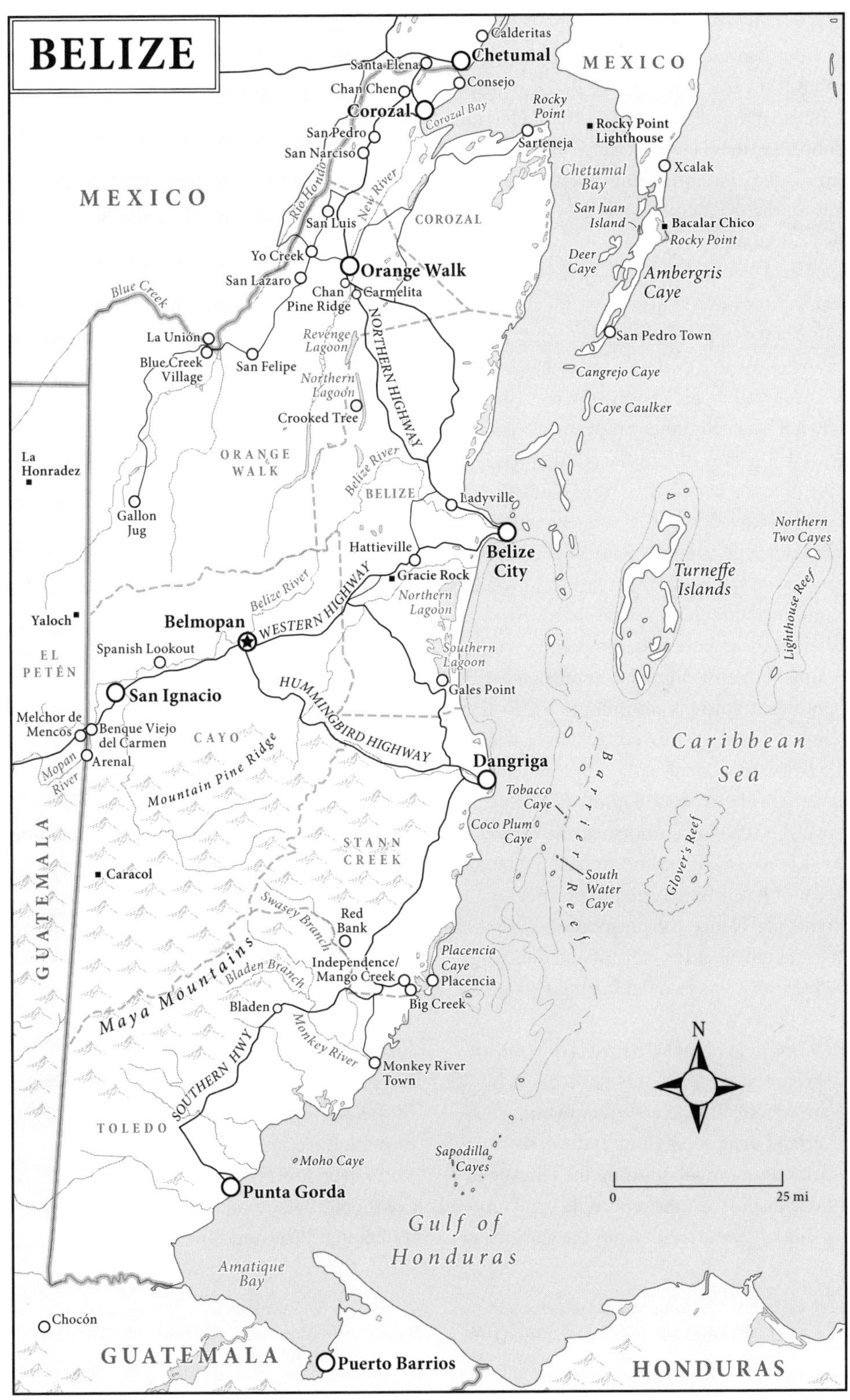
BELIZE
Calderitas
Chetumal
MEXICO
Santa Elena
Consejo
Chan Chen
Corozal
Corozal Bay
Rocky Point
Rocky Point Lighthouse
San Pedro
San Narciso
Sarteneja
Chetumal Bay
Xcalak
Rio Hondo
New River
MEXICO
San Luis
COROZAL
San Juan Island
Bacalar Chico
Rocky Point
Yo Creek
Deer Caye
Orange Walk
Ambergris Caye
San Lazaro
Chan Pine Ridge
Carmelita
Blue Creek
Revenge Lagoon
NORTHERN HIGHWAY
La Unión
San Pedro Town
Blue Creek Village
San Felipe
Cangrejo Caye
Northern Lagoon
Caye Caulker
Crooked Tree
La Honradez
ORANGE WALK
Belize River
BELIZE
Ladyville
Gallon Jug
Northern Two Cayes
Hattieville
Belize City
Gracie Rock
Turneffe Islands
Northern Lagoon
Yaloch
Belize River
WESTERN HIGHWAY
Belmopan
Lighthouse Reef
EL PETÉN
Spanish Lookout
Southern Lagoon
San Ignacio
Gales Point
HUMMINGBIRD HIGHWAY
Melchor de Mencos
Benque Viejo del Carmen
CAYO
Caribbean Sea
Arenal
Mopan River
Mountain Pine Ridge
Dangriga
Barrier Reef
Tobacco Caye
Coco Plum Caye
STANN CREEK
GUATEMALA
Caracol
South Water Caye
Glover's Reef
Swasey Branch
Red Bank
Placencia Caye
Independence/ Mango Creek
Placencia
Bladen Branch
Maya Mountains
Big Creek
Bladen
Monkey River
N
SOUTHERN HWY
Monkey River Town
TOLEDO
Moho Caye
Sapodilla Cayes
Punta Gorda
0
25 mi
Gulf of Honduras
Amatique Bay
Chocón
GUATEMALA
Puerto Barrios
HONDURAS

MAP 2.1

the last two decades of the twentieth century marked for Belize the period just after its transition to full sovereign statehood. Equally important, Belize differed from its Central American neighbors in that its laws, judicial and political systems, and Commonwealth of Nations (British Commonwealth) membership duly reflected its British colonial past.

Certain aspects of Belizean society might appear to have been inauspicious for the advent of significant drug trafficking. The country has never experienced a civil war. Instead, decolonization occurred in a relatively orderly fashion, and no leftist revolutionary movement has ever coalesced. The lack of internal conflict has sharply differentiated Belize from Guatemala, as well as El Salvador and Nicaragua, which have suffered not only from deep internal divisions but from extensive postconflict turmoil, including the continued circulation of weapons. Also unusual for the region, Belizean political culture, including both anticolonial elements and social and political traditions common to the British Caribbean, has long stressed civilian leadership. While Belize has a small army, its role in society has invariably been strictly limited.[3] Firmly controlled by civilian authorities, the Belize Defense Force (BDF) has never become bloated in size, nor has it intervened in political or economic life. Hence, the prospect of corrupting a powerful officer corps has not enticed drug traffickers, as it has in neighboring Guatemala and Honduras.

In terms of geography Belize is the only of these bridge countries that is not crossed by the Pan-American Highway, that major artery for overland drug smuggling. Indeed, its road network is quite small, limiting the efficacy of ground transport. Traffickers could much more easily ship or fly narcotics from the Caribbean coasts of Honduras and Guatemala than send them overland across Belize. Thus, certain bridge-favoring factors common to much of Central America have been notably absent in Belize

Furthermore, particular aspects of Belizean society might be postulated as discouraging transshipment—bridge-disfavoring factors. Ordinarily, the Belizean government has enjoyed warm and friendly relations with Great Britain and the United States, both eager to assist in stemming regional trafficking. Two parties have contended vigorously for political power, and the media has never been cowed by government authorities or drug traffickers. Moreover, Belize has had a largely respected and independent judiciary, with cases heard in open court, sometimes before juries. This greater transparency might be expected to curtail opportunities for corruption to infect the legal system. Belize also has the smallest economy in the region, with the fewest connections to other Central American states.

And yet, by the 1990s Belize had become a key Central American bridge state. Powerful Latin American drug syndicates were frequently calling on homegrown Belizean smuggling expertise, and foreigners were deeply involved in initiating and supervising as well as participating in drug trafficking. While networks of Americans often bought and transported marijuana in the heyday of that trade in Belize, Colombian and eventually Mexican cartels used their extensive resources to stimulate a cocaine-transshipment boom starting in the late 1980s. Thereafter, leading drug-smuggling rings have regularly sent large cocaine loads through the country.

To date, however, very little scholarship has examined the development of Belizean drug trafficking. Why and how have foreign and

formally, more than two centuries after settlement by the British loggers called the Baymen. Waddell, *British Honduras*, 30. As Belizean scholar Assad Shoman has pointed out, however, "for many years before that [declaration] the British government treated the territory, in most respects, as if it were a colony." *Thirteen Chapters*, 43.

3. The Belizean military grew from 610 soldiers and other personnel in 1985 to 700 in 1990, and 950 in 1995, before leveling off at 1,050 in the twenty-first century. See International Institute for Strategic Studies, *Military Balance* (hereafter cited as *MB*), *1985–1986*, 142 ; *MB, 1989–1990*, 184; *MB, 1994–1995*, 200; and *MB, 1999–2000*, 222.

domestic networks turned Belize into a prominent Central American bridge state? How exactly has the Belizean drug trade evolved? To what extent has it become truly extensive? How has it differed from the trade in other Central American countries? Which routes and methods have drug traffickers operating in Belize preferred, and why? Which principal organizations have operated within the country? Which Belizeans and foreigners have figured most prominently in the trade, and how have they interacted? This chapter addresses these often overlooked questions.

Bridge-Favoring Factors Relevant to Belize

Geography

The geography of Belize is strikingly well suited for drug-trafficking ventures by sea and air. Traffickers opting for maritime delivery have capitalized on the Belizean coastline, stretching for two hundred miles along the Caribbean Sea. The barrier reef, the longest in the Western Hemisphere, might be envisioned as the spine of Belizean territorial waters. It encompasses hundreds of small, deserted islands, many covered by dense mangrove swamps. The country's tropical climate and frequent rainfall have proven to be ideal for cannabis production, and years of substantial marijuana exports have developed domestic expertise in smuggling by ship and plane.

Belizean antidrug officials have had a difficult time tracking small planes in Belizean airspace. Drug rings have used aerial transportation extensively within Belize, utilizing the country's many airstrips servicing remote farms or communities. Not only are local radar resources quite limited, but the inland Maya Mountains, densely covered with jungle and over 3,600 feet in height, run north to southwest, east of the Guatemalan border. Belize has the lowest population density in all Central America, and its sparsely populated interior, covered in large tracts by tropical forest, has itself amounted to a bridge-favoring factor. With respect to air transit, the wild terrain and meager transportation infrastructure have greatly challenged law enforcement, while advantaging those transshipping drugs, or growing and moving them to market. Likely named for the Mayan word *baliz*, meaning muddy waters, Belize also features numerous swamps, lakes, slow-moving rivers, and fresh- and salt-water lagoons.[4] These, too, have factored into drug-trafficking schemes involving drops from aircraft.

As a general proposition, law-enforcement officials and imprisoned traffickers alike have acknowledged that traffickers tend to favor bridge states that are closer to markets over those farther away.[5] Colombian and U.S. drug syndicates have found Belize to be situated sufficiently far north in Central America that planes could import drug loads into the United States without further refueling stops in Mexico.[6] This feature of Belizean geography has attracted traffickers looking to eliminate interception in Mexico or another round of payoffs to Mexican traffickers.

In fact, the other cardinal characteristic of Belizean geography is its position flanking Mexico, a drug market to be reckoned with and the prime gateway for drugs entering the United States. The easily forded Blue Creek, which becomes the Río Hondo, delineates Belize's northwestern boundary with Mexico. Furthermore, the boundary line between Belize and Mexico, which continues south to divide Belize and Guatemala, runs through dense jungle. Consequently, even by regional standards, Belizean borders have traditionally been

4. Everitt, "Growth and Development," 77.

5. Interviews with two traffickers imprisoned in Florida and two Jamaican counternarcotics authorities, quoted in Bartilow and Kihong, "Free Traders," 130.

6. See *United States v. Evans*, 865 F.2d 261.

quite porous. Any government contending with Belizean geography would be hard-pressed to strictly control what crossed its borders, and that task has proven to be impossible given Belizean technology, resources, and political culture. Mexican cartels have thus found neighboring Belize to be a convenient stepping stone for drug shipments that would then cross Mexico by land or air.

Economy

While enjoying the significant advantages of a mostly literate populace and a political culture wedded to democracy and largely respectful of human rights, Belize has always been quite poor, marked by extensive unemployment and underemployment. This lack of economic vitality has helped to create large pools of potential collaborators for drug traffickers. In 2003 more than a third of Belizean inhabitants lived below the poverty line, and the annual per capita income stood at just over $2,600. By 2009, 43 percent of the population was classified as poor, earning less than $1,800 per year. In light of the limited economic opportunities and few legitimate avenues for personal advancement, some Belizeans have looked to earn pay from drug rings for a wide range of services. Furthermore, the potential for an individual to gain considerable money for cooperating with drug syndicates has greatly outweighed the likelihood of arrest and serious punishment. This fact of life has been plainly evident to poor citizens, government officials, and wealthy elites alike, and it certainly has not escaped the notice of cartels plotting out Caribbean basin routes.[7]

The nature of Belize's largely rural and undeveloped economy has attracted drug-smuggling organizations as well.[8] From independence forward, postcolonial governments have struggled to bring their citizens a higher standard of living, while making the political and legal systems function adequately despite severe budgetary constraints brought on, in part, by foreign debt that reached $144 million in 1991 and exceeded $1 billion by 2006. In the 1990s well over a third of the country's gross domestic product was required to service Belize's burgeoning debt.[9] In this respect, Belize has typified many newly independent yet poverty-stricken postcolonial societies that have borrowed extensively to try to meet high social expectations.

Because Belize has by far the smallest population in Central America, an inadequate tax base has led to chronically insufficient revenues. Indeed, up until the early twenty-first century, when a Mennonite farmer digging a shallow well struck a modest oil deposit, the country has lacked very substantial income-producing natural resources.[10] Sugar, rice, citrus, and banana operations have not delivered extensive wealth or employment, nor have shrimp, lobster, and other fisheries. Tourism, especially on the cayes and ecotourism inland, has been promising, though with limited impact for much of the population. At the macroeconomic level, ongoing balance-of-payments difficulties have contributed to persistent economic instability, and the always sizable ranks of the unemployed have swollen further when export prices fall, as has happened periodically. Continuing economic woes have thus underlaid many tangled problems of governance.

While these difficulties have constrained antidrug efforts, other national concerns and policies have actually subverted them. One scholar has noted, "The elaborate apparatus of

7. DEA, *Resources, Belize* (2003), 2; Reddy, *Statistical Abstract*, 92; "Looking for a Bail-Out, Belize Turns to Venezuela," *The Reporter* (Belize) (hereafter cited as *TR* [BZ]), 7 May 2006, 1; and "Over Fifty Thousand More Poor," *Amandala* (Belize) (hereafter cited as *AM* [BZ]), 29 January 2010, 1.

8. Note that these same characteristics attract drug producers. See Vellinga, "Political Economy," 5.

9. Griffith, "Political Economy of Drugs," 110.

10. See "Rumble in the Jungle Over Oil," *TR* (BZ), 16 April 2006, 35, and "Spanish Lookout Oil Reserves Estimated at 11 Million Barrels," *TR* (BZ), 2 December 2007, 1. For key changes in the Belizean economy between 1970 and 2002, see Thomson, *Belize*, 180–84.

offshore banks, shady lawyers, and anonymous corporations in Panama and the Caribbean obviously benefits the criminal underworld, but it was largely created by upperworld business leaders anxious to avoid regulations, reduce taxes, and maintain government secrecy."[11] In a similar vein, Belizean government decisions, primarily focused on other public-policy issues, have nonetheless created circumstances advantageous to drug networks.[12] For instance, not only has the government pegged the currency to the U.S. dollar, but Belizean officials have repeatedly attempted to enhance their country's revenue streams with plans and policies that have indirectly encouraged the drug trade. For instance, to attract offshore investors, Belizean legislators have fashioned rather lax banking and corporate laws. By the mid-1990s officials had registered thousands of offshore companies under the International Business Companies Act.[13]

Officials have also earned money for the government, and perhaps some for themselves as well, by selling Belizean citizenship to foreigners, including individuals who turned out to be criminals, and by supplying flags of convenience to vessels, including some engaged in trafficking.[14] This has resulted in embarrassing incidents when authorities have discovered immense drug shipments on board.[15] In 2001 authorities patrolling the coast of Mexico seized 8.8 tons of cocaine off the Belize-registered vessel *Forever My Friend*. That same year, in a case illustrating the globalized nature of major illegal undertakings in the twenty-first century and the manner in which organized crime linked to the former Soviet Union has penetrated the Western Hemisphere, 13 tons were seized a thousand kilometers south of Acapulco off a Belize-flagged Russian fishing trawler, the *Zvezda Maru*, run by a crew of Ukrainians and Russians. Then, in 2004 officials found 5 tons of cocaine on the *Lugo*, located near the African coast, and 4.5 and 11.6 tons on Belize-registered vessels near Mexico.

Other particular characteristics of the Belizean economy have affected the drug trade as well. For instance, Belize City—far and away the country's largest urban area—has always tended toward commercial, rather than industrial, pastimes. Historians have described it as serving as an entrepôt port as early as 1815, and again during extensive trade with the Confederacy during the U.S. Civil War.[16] Traditionally, a small merchant class has dominated the city, whose larger businesses have depended on imports and a handful of exports, such as lumber, citrus, and sugar, subject to considerable price fluctuations.[17] While the lack of manufacturing has largely precluded the passage of precursor chemicals, the export-import trade has screened certain trafficking endeavors and provided opportunities for others.

By the 1990s drugs had been found in various of the city's warehouses, businesses, and hotels. In market countries, stashing drugs awaiting sales has been a particularly risky stage of the drug trade.[18] If traffickers within a bridge state relatively near sizable markets could offer reasonably secure storage, this has amounted to a notable bridge-favoring factor. While speed of

11. Lee, "Transnational Organized Crime," 25.

12. For a similar observation concerning Mexico, see Andreas, *Border Games*, 12.

13. "Subregion Grows as a Transit Route," *Latin American Weekly Report*, 22 August 1996, 380.

14. For information on the Belize Economic Citizenship Program—suspended, though incompletely, in 2002—see "No More Buying of Belizean Citizenship," *TR* (BZ), 10 February 2002, 3, and U.S. Department of State, *International Narcotics Control Strategy Report* (hereafter cited as *INCSR*) (2003), vol. 3.

15. See "Drugs Found on Boat Flying Belize Flag," *TR* (BZ), 3 October 2004, 1; "Ten Thousand Lbs. of Cocaine Found on Belize Registered Ship," *TR* (BZ), 18 July 2004, insert C; "Belize Registered Cocaine Ship Found Off African Coast," *TR* (BZ), 29 February 2004, 6; and "U.S. Coast Guard Seizes Drug Boat of Belizean Registry," *TR* (BZ), 20 May 2001, 10. For the *Zvezda Maru* case, see Bagley, "Globalisation," 36. See also "Belize-Flagged Vessel Busted with $2.5 Million in Cocaine," 14 May 2000, http://www.belizemall.com/amandala/archives/may_14_2000.html#A.

16. Everitt, "Growth and Development," 87, 93.

17. Grant, *Making of Modern Belize*, 68.

18. Zaitch, *Trafficking Cocaine*, 85.

transit through a bridge state is one variable of interest to trafficking organizations as they determine how much of a drug to send through a country, an additional factor involves another dimension of logistics: whether secure warehousing is available in a bridge state close to targeted consumers.

Finally, with the development of the cocaine trade, money laundering has cropped up more regularly in Belize, involving much larger sums. For instance, in 2007 the suspicions of DEA and Belizean law-enforcement officials were aroused by Moises Cal, former Belmopan politician and ambassador to Guatemala, who was making frequent trips to Guatemala and Panama and had gained expensive assets that seemed out of line with his government salary. On one of his fifty trips into Panama over a two-year period, Panamanian authorities stopped Cal, who was traveling on a diplomatic passport, and found him carrying $500,000 in cash.[19] Cal reportedly attempted, unsuccessfully, to bribe the officials with $110,000. In a different laundering incident late the following year, the new Belizean Financial Investigations Unit searched the Belize City residence of a family operating a MoneyGram International business and found $1.5 million in cash.[20] By 2009 the U.S. State Department was listing Belize as a major money-laundering state, defined as one "whose financial institutions engage in currency transactions involving significant amounts of proceeds from international narcotics trafficking."[21]

Law Enforcement

Drug-trafficking rings have often exploited underfunded and underdeveloped law-enforcement and criminal-justice institutions. In this respect, until 2005 Belize completely lacked a coast guard, much less a navy, relying instead on the Fisheries Department and a tiny BDF maritime division to patrol its territorial waters.[22] While Belize has a relatively high number of police per capita, the force has lacked weapons, training, and technology adequate to counter wealthy transnational criminal networks.[23] And, on land as well as at sea, authorities have been spread quite thin. By the 1990s they had proven incapable of containing the simultaneous challenges of considerable growing urban violence, much of it tied to youth gangs, and rising rural violence, often stimulated by the influx of poor immigrants. Violent crimes directly linked to the drug trade thus came to permeate the country, as substantial cocaine loads passed through, as local drug markets vastly increased in scope, and as domestic and foreign trafficking organizations vied with one another.

Belize is sufficiently small that authorities, often drawing on outside government support, could fly over, identify, and then eradicate fields of marijuana reasonably successfully, but in many other matters the grip of authorities has been quite tenuous, particularly away from the country's handful of cities and towns. Postcolonial Belize has been not so much a purposefully decentralized state as one that has yet to be fully integrated. To this day, the country's infrastructure is poorly developed. Its roads are still narrow, few, and slow. Much of the country remains inaccessible: tropical forest covers much of the interior; swamps and lagoons, the bulk of the coast; thick mangroves, most of the islands. In 1992 Belizean authorities estimated that the country had 140 airstrips

19. See "Moises Cal 'Busted' in Panama!," *AM* (BZ), 20 February 2007, 1; "Dinero de Cal tenía rastros de explosivo," *La Prensa* (Panama) (hereafter cited as *LP* [PA]), 6 March 2007, 8A; and "Cincuenta entradas de ex diplomático Beliceño," *LP* (PA), 12 March 2007, 8A.

20. See "Money Laundering Case Delayed in Supreme Court," *TR* (BZ), 23 April 2010, 1, and "Million Dollar Money Laundering Case Gets Under Way, October 9," *TR* (BZ), 10 February 2009, 1.

21. "U.S. Narcotics Report Lists Belize Among 'Major Money Laundering' Countries," *AM* (BZ), 3 May 2009, 1.

22. "GOB Picks Berland to Command Coast Guard," *TR* (BZ), 26 December 2004, A.

23. By 2009 Belize had a police officer for every 252 inhabitants, second only to Panama in Central America and far more than in Guatemala (1/641) or Honduras (1/791). PNUD, *Informe, Ámerica Central*, 232, quoted in "Centroamericanos, cada vez más desprotegidos," *LP*

serving isolated settlements, and the government's radar coverage has never extended beyond thirty miles from the Belize City airport.[24]

As distance from Belize City increases, the reach and efficacy of law enforcement has tended to tail off dramatically. And, for purposes of stemming the drug trade, distance cannot be measured in miles as a bird might fly, but in the time it might take officials to reach a particular location. The coordination of the few police assigned to remote parts of Belize has posed continuing difficulties. Effective oversight and accountability have been infrequent, and officers have sometimes felt more loyalty to local acquaintances, with whom they might share ethnicity, kinship ties, or cultural characteristics, than to officials in far-off Belize City or in the capital of Belmopan.[25] The lack of national integration has adversely affected antidrug work, as traffickers have been able to choose from multiple routes in places unlikely to attract much official attention.

It is true that a trip wire of British military forces has long been stationed in Belize, conducting jungle training and other exercises from bases in the country, and for a time soldiers from British bases periodically interrupted drug-trafficking schemes. In the 1980s and early 1990s British forces sometimes assisted Belizean law enforcement with backup and logistics, while supplying radar, helicopters, and explosives to disable unauthorized airstrips.[26] In other cases, British forces stumbled upon drug-trafficking activity.[27] However, in 1994 the British Forces Belize garrison was largely withdrawn, and by the mid-1990s only small numbers of British military and intelligence personnel remained, which diminished one modest deterrent to transshipment.[28]

Even more important, the largely undistinguished record of Belizean antidrug operations can be attributed to inadequate resources, competing government priorities, and official corruption that has particularly afflicted the police force, which has been underpaid, few in number, and sometimes outgunned. By 2003 the Belize Antidrug Unit contained only thirty-five officers. While reasonably well armed, the unit has been largely absorbed with crime in Belize City, and it has sometimes been diverted from narcotics duties to contend with other violent crimes.[29] Furthermore, an array of fundamental law-enforcement problems, plainly evident at independence, still afflicted Belizean society decades later. In 2009 Harold Crooks, a former leading Jamaican police official, filed a lengthy report, commissioned by the government, that sharply criticized many aspects of the Belizean force. The Crooks report identified "an unrecognized crisis of indiscipline" among the rank-and-file police. It termed case file preparation methods "obsolete," noting the absence of "formal mechanisms to periodically reopen serious cases." And it called attention to the deficiencies of sporadic on-the-job training and the absence of effective coordination among

---

(PA), 26 December 2009, 6A. Not until 2002 did the Serious Crimes Unit gain automatic rifles and semiautomatic handguns. "Increased Police Fuel Budget Pays Off," *TR* (BZ), 9 June 2002, 5.

25. Due west from Belize City on an inland plain away from the hurricane-ravaged coast, Belmopan is the centrally planned capital city. However, moving government functions did not bring about a major population transfer, as relatively few Belizeans have chosen to live in this dull, functional, and often vacant place. As one of the world's smallest capitals, consisting chiefly of government buildings and a supporting population of about four thousand, Belmopan has remained of negligible importance to drug trafficking.

26. "British Forces May Have Back-Up Role in Belize War Against Drugs," *TR* (BZ), 22 May 1988, 1, and "UK Troops Help Belize Drugs Drive," *Belize Times* (Belize) (hereafter cited as *BT* [BZ]), 18 August 1985, 1.

27. For example, in 1989 British forces played a vital role in the seizure of 1,453 kilos of processed marijuana in Orange Walk. See "O. W. Authorities Make Major Marijuana Bust," *TR* (BZ), 2 April 1989, 6B.

28. See *INCSR* (1995), 119, and "Dark Forces," *Scotsman*, 24 July 1999, 11.

29. *INCSR* (2004), 131.

agencies and ministries. In singling out the lack of the infrastructure needed to investigate complex organized crime successfully, the Crooks report observed that, rather than developing intelligence on the drug trade, the uniformed antidrug unit simply patrolled in an effort to interdict shipments. What information on organized crime existed, Crooks concluded, was of poor quality, could be accessed only by senior officers, and focused excessively on low-level operatives.[30]

Although Belizean legal institutions have certain notable strengths, they, too, have been ill-suited for combating sophisticated transnational criminals. In a region marked by many poorly functioning civil law legal systems that have largely failed to prosecute crime openly and expeditiously, the different common law tradition has been deeply rooted in Belize. As elsewhere in the Commonwealth of Nations, the Belizean legal system has featured prosecutors who function extensively in open court rather than penal and investigating judges who operate largely behind closed doors. Furthermore, from independence forward, the country has been able to draw on connections to other Commonwealth states.[31] These have helped to shape Belizean law and have buttressed traditions of respect for judges and judicial independence. Of great use for a postcolonial developing society that has lacked lawyers, the British Loan Service has supplied Belize with experienced judges and prosecutors from elsewhere in the Commonwealth, who have rotated into the country for defined terms.

However, from the perspective of traffickers, bridge-favoring factors related to the Belizean judicial system have outweighed these disfavoring matters. Forensic capabilities have been negligible, no law specifically addresses narco-corruption, and evidence gleaned from the use of wiretaps has not been available to prosecutors. Bail has traditionally been granted at quite low sums, a policy instituted when Belize was a small, isolated tropical backwater, in which family and community ties were paramount and significant crime was infrequent. Bail practices were not formulated with powerful trafficking organizations in mind. To them, depositing a large sum to spring an associate would be a routine business cost. Hence, judges and legislators have been challenged to adjust traditional thinking about bail to suit the new reality of transnational organized crime. Furthermore, prison terms for drug trafficking have been lenient, something remarked on even by Colombian authorities, themselves not noted for stiff drug sentencing.[32]

Throughout the 1980s the penalties that could be assessed for international trafficking were, in the words of one foreign diplomat, "nothing more than a flea bite" for substantial drug networks.[33] Even in the 1990s international drug trafficking carried relatively modest penalties of between five and ten years in prison and a fine of up to fifty thousand dollars.[34] Furthermore, the 1990 Drugs Act contained so many loopholes that, as one leading judge prophetically stated, "lawyers are going to have a field day with it."[35] Within this context drug

30. See "Crooks Report Says Belize Police Need to Modernize," *TR* (BZ), 1 February 2009, 3. The Crooks Report proved to be controversial not so much for its content, but because the government failed to make the report public and disclose its cost. Then, just over a year after filing the report, Crooks fled Jamaica for Canada after an alleged sexual assault. See "The Harold Crooks Report Still Mostly Secret," *AM* (BZ), 30 January 2009, 1, and "Ex-Cop, Harold Crooks Flees Jamaica Amid Allegation of Sex Crime," *TR* (BZ), 26 March 2010, 1.

31. Until 2010 the ultimate court of appeal in the Belizean legal system was the British Privy Council, but thereafter, it became the Caribbean Court of Justice in Trinidad and Tobago. See "Belize to Move Away from Privy Council," *TR* (BZ), 22 January 2010, 1, and "Goodbye Privy Council, Aloha Caribbean Court," *TR* (BZ), 14 May 2010, 1.

32. "Stung by U.S. Censure, Belize Seeks International Help in War Against Drugs," *TR* (BZ), 3 August 1997, 9.

33. Confidential interview, 16 February 1990, Belize City, Belize.

34. "Colombians Sentenced to Five Years Imprisonment," *TR* (BZ), 6 December 1992, 1.

35. "Wake Up Belizeans! We Have a Very Serious Cocaine Problem," *TR* (BZ), 7 July 1996, 11. For the bill that eventually became the Misuse of Drugs Act, see

networks, aided by certain politicians as well as by many of the country's finest and most expensive lawyers, have been able to thrive. Belizean institutions and procedures were carried over from the country's colonial past and have then been only partially amended or reformed to deal better with organized crime. For example, until 2010 a prisoner was compelled to serve only a quarter of his or her sentence before becoming eligible for parole.[36] In addition, even after Belizean laws came to provide for the forfeit to the state of assets connected to criminal activity, in practice, the police have received only a quarter of the sales price of each item of seized property. The lion's share has gone instead to the many law-enforcement needs other than antidrug initiatives.[37]

Further along in the administration of justice, poor training and inadequate technical and human resources have gravely damaged criminal prosecution. More than twenty-five years after Belizean independence, the U.S. State Department observed that "the Office of Public Prosecutions remains under-trained, under-staffed, and under-funded."[38] Typically, less than half of all criminal trials have resulted in convictions.[39] And, while conviction rates remain above those in neighboring legal systems, acquittals in high-profile drug cases have periodically rankled Belizean law enforcement as well as DEA officials and U.S. diplomats. Not only has witness intimidation stood out as a chronic problem, but drug networks have had the means to bribe or threaten jurors, whose pictures and personal information the local media has sometimes published.[40] Prosecutors have feared that some jurors might be drug users themselves, and in any event the state has been unable to afford to sequester jurors, much less to offer them, or witnesses, credible protection from criminals.

For these reasons the government has routinely opted to send drug cases, even those involving international trafficking, to bench trials in the magistrates courts, rather than to Supreme Court jury trials. This, however, has funneled efforts to corrupt and intimidate toward the least educated, least prestigious, least compensated, and most vulnerable level of the judiciary. Moreover, such innovations as the creation of drug courts or the rotation of judges have not been tried; indeed, the office of chief magistrate tends to be occupied by the same person for lengthy periods. Even more important, given the strictly limited number of prosecutors, time and again lay magistrates have had to decide drug cases with the government represented only by so-called police prosecutors. In 1990 then chief magistrate John "Troadio" González noted that well-prepared defense lawyers have tended to "sail over" baffled and sometimes "terrified" police officers trying to act as prosecutors.[41] All of these matters suggest that while Belizean criminal justice might appear to be a bridge-disfavoring factor at first glance, the manner in which the system actually works encourages organized crime.

Furthermore, rather than firmly adhering to a rule-of-law ideal, the Belizean legal system has continually overlooked the transgressions of elites. Citizens of influence have infrequently

---

"Under New Get-Tough Legislation Drug Traffickers May Soon Face Fines of Up to Half Million Dollars," *TR* (BZ), 22 July 1990, 1; "New Anti-drug Law Will Give Courts Right to Seize Property," *TR* (BZ), 29 July 1990, 8; "Government Introduces New Anti-drug Law," *BT* (BZ), 4 November 1990, 1; and "House Passes Tough Anti-drug Law," *TR* (BZ), 4 April 1990, 20. This 1990 act was later amended, in part, by the Belize Criminal Justice Act of 1994, no. 22.

36. "Cabinet Amends Prison Rules," *TR* (BZ), 26 March 2010. The amendment mandated that at least half the prison term be served.

37. *INCSR* (2006), 136.

38. *INCSR* (2007), 147.

39. See "Espat Scolds Cops," *TR* (BZ), 21 January 2001, 4, and "Murders Increase, Few Arrests and Even Fewer Convictions," *TR* (BZ), 20 August 2000, 10.

40. "CJ Defines Rule of the Press in Court Cases," *TR* (BZ), 28 September 1997, 9.

41. Interview, 7 March 1990, Belize City, Belize.

been arrested and even more rarely prosecuted, convicted, and sentenced to prison terms. On various occasions officials have ignored rumors or allegations that prominent people have committed crimes. For their part, elites have sometimes compensated, strong-armed, or otherwise persuaded underlings to shoulder the blame for them. Although Belize has one of the most vibrant and deeply entrenched democracies in the region, such antidemocratic norms have undermined efforts to combat crime and have invited elite participation in lucrative transnational criminal activities. Not only have these problems aided cartels looking to transship drugs smoothly through the country, but they have helped to fertilize the soil within which domestic drug organizations could sink their roots and grow into formidable entities in their own right.

The difficulties that kinship ties and compartmentalized operations have posed for counternarcotics institutions with weak intelligence capabilities have been compounded by the fact that all law enforcement in postcolonial Belize has been severely underfunded. At one point, with the government encouraging more police patrols by foot and bicycle in Belize City, officials acknowledged that police there had been restricted by a monthly gasoline quota of forty gallons per vehicle per month. Because a police car patrolling all day might use fifteen to twenty gallons, many vehicles were grounded early in the month.[42] The situation was no better at sea. In 1997 a senior official reported of drug enforcement in the south: "We have no boats. We have raised this with the ministry, but so far all we can do is concentrate on what happens inland. And if we get things, the maintenance is expensive and we have no money. . . . Yes, there are people making fortunes mysteriously. . . . Yes, there is more violence as drug trafficking increases. But we are doing what we can, and that is not much."[43]

Population Flows

During that typically difficult transition period that follows independence for formerly dependent states, Belize has also had to contend with serious regional problems that spilled over into its territory. In this regard, cross-border population flows, one significant aspect of the regional civil wars and of globalization more broadly, have also contributed to drug trafficking. Illegal immigration into Belize triggered jumps in population from 120,000 in 1970 to 205,000 in 1993 to 266,000 in 2003.[44] From independence on, the country, long viewed as a lightly populated oasis of peaceful stability in Central America, has had to contend with refugees escaping from conflict in El Salvador, Guatemala, and Nicaragua and with economic immigrants from those countries and Mexico and Honduras as well. Democratic Belizean society, predominantly English speaking and marked by sociopolitical values akin to the British Caribbean Islands, has had to absorb, at least temporarily, scores of poverty-stricken, Spanish-speaking, undocumented immigrants, many fleeing from far more violent and authoritarian cultures.

These intraregional population migrations have hampered assimilation and contributed to unemployment and the rise of gangs, to petty and serious crime, and to overburdened health, education, and penal systems.[45] With jobs scarce, some of these immigrants have become deeply immersed in the drug trade—growing and trafficking cannabis and providing protection

42. "Police Fuel Rationed," *TR* (BZ), 10 February 2002, 8.

43. "Belize by Sea," *Washington Post* (United States) (hereafter cited as *WP* [US]), 10 June 1997, A27.

44. Thomson, *Belize*, 184, and DEA, *Resources, Belize* (2000), 1.

45. In 1990 solicitor-general Gian Ghandi attributed soaring crime levels to the "influx of very violent persons from other Central American countries." Interview, 5 March 1990, Belize City, Belize.

and enforcement as hired muscle for marijuana and cocaine networks.[46] Indeed, numerous foreigners involved in the Belizean drug trade have been killed after deals went sour. In commenting on the double murder of refugees who had been trying to buy marijuana seeds, a Belizean journalist wrote, "The story . . . is depressingly familiar. Bodies are discovered, drugs are involved, nobody is ever arrested, tried, or convicted. Most of the time they involve aliens from Guatemala, Mexico, and Salvador."[47]

The transnational movement of people affected Belize in another way as well. Tens of thousands of Belizean economic immigrants have moved north to the United States, and communities of expatriate Belizean Americans have risen to forty thousand in Los Angeles alone. Communities of fairly recent immigrants, perhaps especially those in urban areas, tend to be both poverty-stricken and reluctant to cooperate with police, factors that contribute to their playing key roles in the import and dealing of drugs.[48]

Some Belizeans, transplanted to urban areas such as Los Angeles, Miami, New Orleans, New York City, and Washington, D.C., have become involved in gangs and drug distribution.[49] This has resulted in an increasing stream of criminals being deported to their native country, who have then used their experiences abroad within Belizean gangs.[50] The process of emigration and repatriation has also led to a widening network of Belizean contacts within the world's largest drug market. In recent years gang activity has resulted in Belize repeatedly setting and then eclipsing national murder records, and by 2010 the per capita murder rate had reached nearly forty per one hundred thousand citizens, with U.S. officials noting that most were gang related and many narcotics related.[51] The population flows often identified as a salient feature of globalization have thus amounted to yet another bridge-favoring characteristic.

International Cooperation

Flawed international cooperation that might have done more to check drug transit has been a final significant factor encouraging Belizean drug trafficking. Here, the country has stood out among its neighbors as being at once a part of and distinctly separate from the remainder of Central America. In light of Guatemala's longstanding claim to its territory and the presence of a garrison of British troops even after independence, some in the region have seen the very existence of Belize as depending on foreign intervention.[52] Indeed, its British cultural heritage and Commonwealth membership have led many Central Americans to consider Belize really to be a Caribbean state. The country has not shared with its neighbors their history of Spanish colonialism and its key consequences: the Spanish language, Catholic religious tradition, civil law legal system, and centralized corporatist political model. Consequently, at first, other Central American governments routinely excluded Belize from their gatherings.

Reflective of this state of affairs, Belizean independence did not immediately translate

46. See, for example, "Two Killed in Gangland Slaying," *TR* (BZ), 18 October 1987, 1; "Arrested for Drugs," *TR* (BZ), 1 February 1987, 13; "Serious Crime Squad Uncovers Seven Marijuana Fields," *TR* (BZ), 21 February 1988, 12; and "Shoot-out in Ramonal!," *TR* (BZ), 18 December 1988, 9.

47. "Two Petville Corpses," *AM* (BZ), 12 January 1997, 8. See also "Guatemalans Abducted and Questioned About Drugs," *AM* (BZ), 12 January 1997, 8.

48. See Reuter, "Political Economy," 135.

49. See "Cops Crack Down on Belize Gang in Harlem," *TR* (BZ), 9 November 1997, 11; "Visiting Belizeans with Cocaine," *BT* (BZ), 17 November 1985, 1; and "DEA Triggers Arrest of Five Belizeans in Miami and New Orleans," *TR* (BZ), 24 January 1985, 1. For a representative case concerning a Belizean distributing cocaine in the United States, see *United States v. Flowers*, 2008 U.S. Dist. LEXIS 97390.

50. See, for instance, "Repatriation Contributes to Crime," *BT* (BZ), 20 March 1994, 15, and "11 Belizeans Deported," *BT* (BZ), 18 February 1996, 24.

51. *INCSR* (2011), 136.

52. For a summary of the territorial sovereignty dispute with Guatemala, see Thomson, *Belize*, 165–78.

into extensive multilateral activity. Not until 1991, for instance, did Guatemala recognize Belize to be an independent state, a pivotal step in the country's bid for membership in the Organization of American States, which occurred that same year.[53] And, within a region in which effective counternarcotics cooperation has occurred infrequently, Belize at first forged few links with neighboring police forces.[54] Relations with Guatemala have customarily been strained and sometimes downright hostile, and thus joint antidrug initiatives have occurred rarely with this neighboring state, vitally important to regional trafficking.[55] With a small handful of exceptions, collaborative efforts to curb trafficking were at first largely confined to bilateral undertakings and agreements with Mexico, Great Britain, and the United States.[56]

Here, the bilateral antidrug moves between Belize and the United States have been by far the most significant. In the 1980s, though at first from headquarters in the U.S. Embassy in neighboring Guatemala, DEA agents operated in Belize, working in conjunction with the Belizean police force and its Serious Crimes Squad. From that time on, the vast majority of significant antidrug seizures and arrests have come through U.S. intelligence, most often tips on incoming shipments passed from the DEA to Belize police. In 1991 the United States and Belize established a Joint Information Coordination Center, later hailed as a prototype.[57] A Memorandum of Understanding, followed by a 1992 agreement, authorized the U.S. Coast Guard and Navy to patrol Belizean waters when a Belizean "ship rider" was aboard or when hot pursuit of suspects led into territorial waters.[58] This culminated in additional U.S. financial support for the BDF Maritime Wing.[59]

Notwithstanding these bilateral ties, only in the late 1990s, fully a decade and a half after drug transit started to climb, did Belize begin to participate in significant multilateral antidrug undertakings. After years of resistance, Belize opted in 1996 to sign the 1988 United Nations Drug Convention.[60] Three years later, Belize hosted an international drug-enforcement conference. Thereafter, increasingly, Belizean officials have attended and even taken leadership positions in related multilateral forums.[61]

53. Despite recognition, Guatemala continued to claim roughly half of the country's territory, and Guatemalan politicians repeatedly aroused nationalist support by raising the Belize question.

54. See *INCSR* (1993), 136, and "Central Americans Meet to Chart Anti-drug Tactics," *TR* (BZ), 7 March 1993, 7.

55. One exception was Operation Triangle 95, in which Mexico, Belize, and Guatemala collaborated on an antidrug initiative. Aguilera Peralta, "Fighting the Dragon," 228.

56. In 1993 Belize hosted a day-long drug-trafficking summit for Central American leaders. "Central Americans Vow War on Drugs at Belize Summit," *Los Angeles Times* (United States) (hereafter cited as *LAT* [US]), 20 February 1993, A11. Belize also participated in the regional counternarcotics effort known as Operación Unidos II. When tensions with Guatemala subsided, some joint counternarcotics efforts planning and activities occurred. *INCSR* (1997), 121–22. See also "Belize and Guatemala Embrace Joint Patrols," TR-BZ, 6 January 2002, 7. For bilateral work with Mexico, see "Belize/Mexico Anti-drugs Accord Signed," *BT* (BZ), 18 February 1990, 3; "Belize and Mexico Attack Drugs," *BT* (BZ), 11 August 1991, 1; and "Belize Enters Historic Partnership with Mexico," *TR* (BZ), 11 August 1991, 1. For work with Great Britain, see "Britain Pledges Funds to Fight Drug Traffic," *TR* (BZ), 10 December 1989, 9; "U.K. Assists Belize with Drug Problem," *TR* (BZ), 11 October 1992, 6; and "Brit. Officers Conduct Drug Enforcement Course," *AM* (BZ), 12 February 1993, 9. For work with the United States, see "U.S. Planes for Belize's Drug War," *AM* (BZ), 13 March 1992, 10; "Three Hundred Thousand Dollars U.S. for Belize War on Drugs," *TR* (BZ), 5 September 1993, 1; "Americans Donate to Police and BDF's Anti-narcotics Efforts," *AM* (BZ), 21 January 1996, 20; "U.S. Vehicles to Fight Narcotics," *TR* (BZ), 18 February 1996, 10; and "Barrow to Extradite More Belizeans to the U.S.," *BT* (BZ), 12 January 1997, 3.

57. See *INCSR* (1992), 142, and *INCSR* (1996), 121.

58. "Agreement Between the Government of Belize and the Government of the United States of America Concerning Maritime Counter-Drug Operations," *Treaties and Other International Acts* 11914 (1992).

59. See *INCSR* (1994), 137; *INCSR* (1995), 119; and "U.S. Deal on Hot Pursuit an Old Story, Says Foreign Affairs," *TR* (BZ), 4 August 1996, 21.

60. United Nations Convention Against Illicit Traffic in Narcotic Drugs and Psychotropic Substances, UN Doc., E/CONF., 82/15 (1988).

61. Belizean officials, for instance, attended the Caribbean Regional Drug Control Conference, sent officers abroad

Yet, though cooperation had certainly intensified by the turn of the century, drug routes and networks had already become firmly established. The year 2000 brought new extradition and mutual legal assistance treaties with the United States as well as expanded overflight privileges.[62] By 2002 Belize had become a full-fledged member-state on the Permanent Central American Committee on Anti-drug Activities, and the following year the government initiated a series of anticorruption seminars, funded by Canada, and held a national, OAS-sponsored, anticorruption conference.[63] In 2005 Belize joined the Cooperating Nations Information Exchange System, sponsored by the U.S. Army Southern Command, which has assisted in tracking and intercepting suspicious aircraft. Some significant bilateral cooperation has also started to occur in drug cases involving Mexico, Colombia, or Guatemala, leading to a handful of successes.[64]

The crowning point here is that cooperative police efforts that Belize has shared with its neighbors and North American and European states have been too few and started too late to meet the law-enforcement goal of choking off cocaine transshipment. Indeed, counternarcotics relations with the United States have suffered rocky periods, during which drug trafficking and corruption became even more entrenched. In assessing the record of international cooperation, one might point out that postcolonial societies often have sensitivities with respect to relations with larger powers that more established states may feel less acutely. In this respect, Belize has certainly faced starkly different circumstances than has a country like Costa Rica, long independent and newly developed, with legislative and judicial systems that for many years have functioned relatively smoothly, at least by regional standards.

In contrast, in their first several decades of independence, Belizeans have had a weak and inadequately funded law-enforcement system with poorly trained personnel; a court system in which prosecutorial assistance has been spread far too thin and that has relied on inexperienced lay magistrates, some of whom have been corruptible; and a shoddy penal system, crowded with inmates, that long featured antiquated facilities and has been run by outnumbered and underpaid officials. In short, confronted with an enormous number of competing priorities that have often stymied effective antidrug efforts, Belizean officials have had to try to contend with the extraordinary stress test that wealthy criminal syndicates have posed for the country's institutions, with very few budgetary resources at a very challenging period in national history. Under these circumstances, urging by U.S. diplomats and law-enforcement officials to take on additional tasks, to cooperate more extensively, and to function more effectively was likely to raise tensions on occasion. In any event, while certain useful counternarcotics links and institutions have been established between the United States and Belize, a robust Belizean drug trade has developed despite the resources offered and joint efforts launched.

The Evolution of Drug Trafficking in Belize

From at least the 1960s, when the country first produced high-quality marijuana for export, moving drugs out of Belize has been the most prominent aspect of the country's underground economy. And, although the vast majority of the marijuana exported from Belize has been homegrown, the occasional export of Guatemalan or even Panamanian marijuana has also

for financial training, and hosted U.S. officials in counternarcotics and investigation training seminars. Police commissioner Ornell Brooks was elected and then reelected as president of the International Association of Chiefs of Police.

62. *INCSR* (2002), 5:5.Note, however, that the government of Belize did not implement the mutual legal assistance treaties until 2005.*INCSR* (2009), 151.

63. See "Belize to Strengthen its Anti-drug System," *TR* (BZ), 25 August 2002, 15, and "Serious About Government Corruption," *TR* (BZ), 1 September 2003, 1.

64. See *INCSR* (2000), 152; *INCSR* (1999), 139; and *INCSR* (1998), 140.

occurred.[65] Dealing in contraband has a lengthy history in Belize among elites as well as other classes. To some Belizeans, perhaps drawing on cultural traits that stretch back to colonial times, marijuana smuggling has not been a wholly disreputable occupation but has been viewed instead as a profitable undertaking that also evades, circumvents, or ridicules state authority.[66]

By the late 1980s, however, the Belizean drug trade was definitely evolving toward significant cocaine transshipment, supplemented in the 1990s by the very occasional passage of heroin. With the increasing transit of harder drugs and such evident consequences for society as soaring crime rates and crack-cocaine abuse, many Belizean citizens have lost their prior tolerance for trafficking. Nevertheless, by then domestic marijuana production had already laid the groundwork for Belize to become a prominent bridge state in the cocaine trade. In this respect, the Belizean experience has differed from that of all the other Central American states.

The Marijuana Trade

Successful drug-eradication efforts in one country, it has been observed, frequently lead to additional drug-production problems in another.[67] In this regard Mexico's extensive marijuana- and opium-suppression campaign, known as Operation Condor, cut that country's share of the U.S. marijuana market from more than 75 percent in 1976 to less than 10 percent in 1980.[68] This, in turn, created opportunities for others. In Belize not only had cannabis long been grown, but by the 1980s it was being produced virtually throughout the country.[69] In 1985 Belize police chief Maxwell Stephens noted, "We are twice the size of Jamaica, sparsely populated, and well watered. . . . This is ideal for marijuana cultivation."[70] As early as the 1970s high-quality varieties of Belizean marijuana, under such labels as Belize Breeze, had gained an international reputation for potency, with THC levels reaching 11 percent.[71] Not only did Belizeans have a valuable product to export, but Belize was much closer to the U.S. marijuana market than was Colombia. This proximity has been particularly advantageous for smugglers, because marijuana is the bulkiest drug to transport, a fact that increases the likelihood of its interdiction and raises costs and risks.[72]

Just after the country completed its transition to independence, these various factors led to a stage of extremely large-scale marijuana production in Belize, as fig. 2.1 illustrates. Indeed, the U.S. Department of State's Bureau of International

65. In 1968 a freighter from British Honduras arrived in the United States, carrying twelve tons of high-quality Panama Red marijuana. Kamstra, *Weed*, 239.

66. A similar factor has been identified with respect to the rise of Colombian drug trafficking. One scholar noted, "Years and years of contraband generated [a] certain social legitimacy and broke traditional social stigmas related to this activity." Zaitch, *Trafficking Cocaine*, 38.

67. See Nadelmann, "Case for Legalization," 9, and Bagley, "Colombia," 73–74.

68. See Andreas, *Border Games*, 41, and Smith, "Semi-organized International Crime," 195.

69. DEA, *Resources, Belize* (2003), 3. The southern Toledo district was not known for marijuana cultivation, at least until 1988. See "Toledo Advances as Marijuana Center," *TR* (BZ), 28 August 1988, 12. In fact, finer strains of marijuana grow best at about five hundred meters above sea level and up, and with much of Toledo at less-than-optimal height, only small plots took hold. See "525 Weed Trees Destroyed by Police," *BT* (BZ), 25 February 1996, 21.

70. "Belize: Concerned by Growing Drug Traffic," Inter Press Service, 11 March 1985.

71. See "Belize Breeze Is Potent Marijuana," *TR* (BZ), 17 March 1985, 5. By "Belizean marijuana" we mean marijuana grown in, not native to, Belize. Police Chief Maxwell Stephens noted, "This is a professional operation. [Traffickers] are growing the finest 'sinsemilla' varieties here. The seeds are not local; they were imported by the growers." "Belize: Concerned." The few seeds on a sinsemilla (in Spanish "without seed") plant fall off readily as it dries. This hybrid variety of marijuana grows best south of the Tropic of Cancer and was developed on the U.S. West Coast by pinching back female plants to prevent flowering, which causes resin to be concentrated in the leaves and leads to high potency. See Kamstra, *Weed*, 158, and Shannon, *Desperados*, 3.

72. Thoumi, *Political Economy*, 169, and Kirkpatrick, *Turning the Tide*, 39.

Fig. 2.1 Marijuana production in Belize, 1982–1990

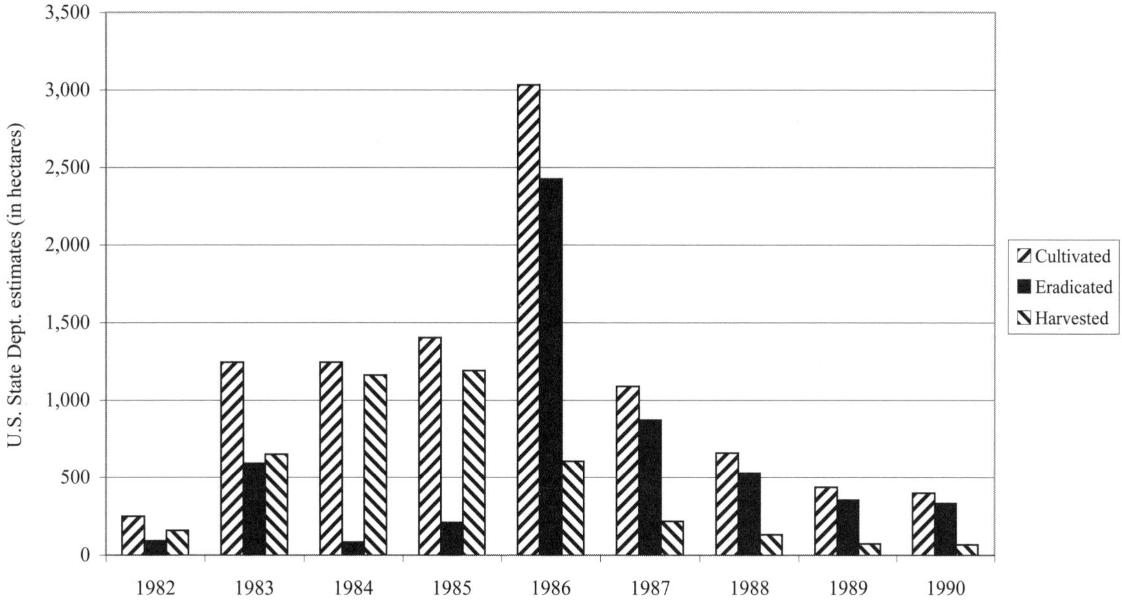

Sources: *INCSR* (1993), 145; *INCSR* (1992), 133, 135; *INCSR* (1989), 116; *INCSR* (1985), 42–43.

Note: After 1991, with international attention focused more single-mindedly on cocaine and heroin, the U.S. government noted in annual drug reports that the amount of cannabis being cultivated in Belize was unknown.

Narcotics Matters (BINM) estimated that in 1984 the yield of the Belizean marijuana crop had reached 1,053 tons. As fig. 2.2 demonstrates, only a relatively small amount was consumed domestically, and of the remainder, 85 percent was exported to the United States and 14 percent sent to other countries, including Mexico.

The Belizean marijuana industry long capitalized on the country's lack of integration. Producers recruited illegal aliens to tend fields, typically located in quite remote areas, such as the jungles along the Guatemalan boundary or bordering the New River south of Orange Walk.[73] Indeed, the New River zone has witnessed continuing violence, including numerous clashes between rival growers.[74] The unevenly populated northern Orange Walk district and the Red Bank region south of Dangriga also became noted for considerable cannabis production. In contrast to the enormous, extensively fertilized and irrigated marijuana plantations that authorities discovered in rural Mexico at this time, Belizean marijuana farmers traditionally planted plots of about a hectare, or roughly two and a half acres, hidden in the jungle or within fields of legitimate crops.[75] As a U.S. government report noted, Belizean marijuana "is normally grown using the slash-and-burn technique of clearing fields. A grower employed by a trafficker will hike into a remote jungle area, hack out a plot,

73. See DEA, *Resources, Belize* (2003), 3; "Shootout at Revenge Bags Ganja Grower," *TR* (BZ), 4 April 1999, 4; and "Marijuana Fields Coming into Full Production," *TR* (BZ), 6 June 1993, 15.

74. See, for instance, "Mini Massacre at Indian Church Believed to be a Revenge Killing," *TR* (BZ), 24 September 2010, 1, and "Three San Carlos Villagers Ambushed," *AM* (BZ), 24 September 2010, 1.

75. While marijuana plantations of fifty acres or more were found in the Mexican states of Nayarit and Chihuahua, the prototypical example was El Búfalo ranch near Chihuahua, where thousands of tons of marijuana were grown and stored. See Toro, *Mexico's "War,"* 30–31, 39, and Shannon, *Desperados*, 117–20.

Fig. 2.2 Marijuana yield and exports from Belize, 1982–1990

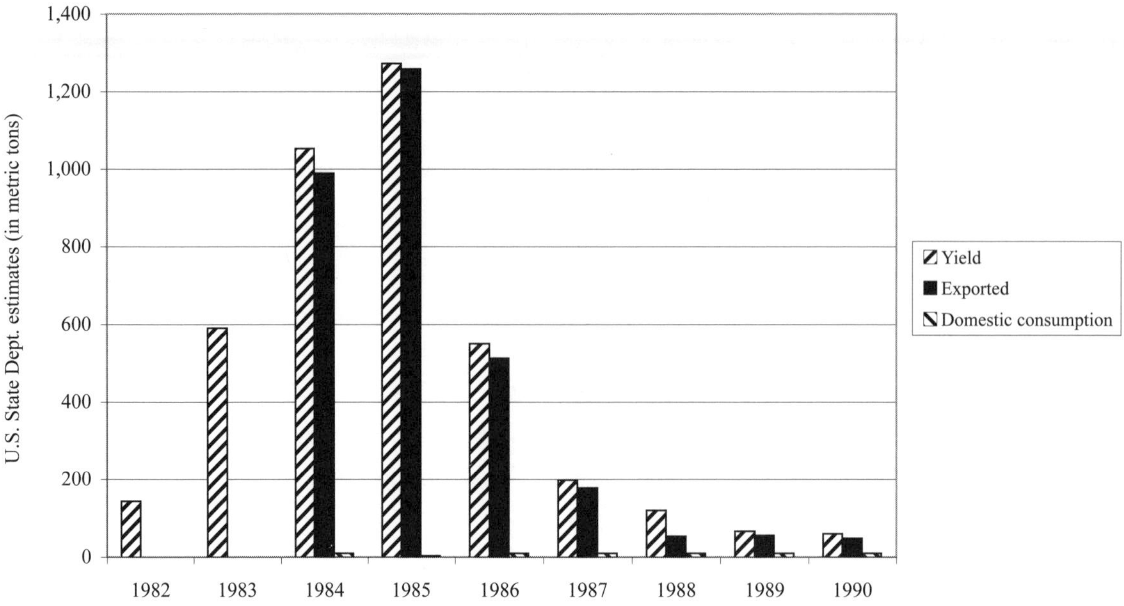

Sources: *INCSR* (1990), 167; *INCSR* (1991), 136.

Note: The estimates of Belizean and U.S. authorities differed a bit, disagreeing, for instance, on whether the best estimated yield in 1986 was 550 or 605 tons, and in 1987, 198 or 220 tons. See "Belize Bucks Regional Trend in Drug Production," *TR* (BZ), 27 March 1988, 12, and "'Drug Problem Is Alarming,' Says PRIDE Director," *BT* (BZ), 17 December 1989, 3, 27. The differences were not marked, however, and a high-level U.S. official with responsibilities in Central America declared, "The statistics in the [Belizean] newspapers on crop eradications and crop seizures appear to us to be fairly accurate. Belize is too small a country for the statistics to be misleading and no one to suspect [it]. The statistics match up pretty well with computer programs tracking drugs coming from Latin America." Confidential interview, 1990.

burn the debris, and plant marijuana. After the crop matures, he harvests and delivers it to the trafficker."[76]

As in the Colombian marijuana industry, small, hard-to-locate plots minimized risk.[77] When authorities might need to hike for much of a day to reach a cannabis field previously identified from the air, those cultivating the site were often forewarned and fled. Although arrests linked to marijuana production occasionally occurred, these tended to snare unwary individuals hired to guard or plant small plots. In part because the poverty-stricken farmers involved have often been viewed sympathetically, neither the Belizean legislature in passing drug laws nor the courts in sentencing offenders have seriously penalized marijuana production. Cannabis has frequently been grown on public land, and when fields turned up on private holdings, owners have routinely disclaimed all knowledge. In fact, absentee owners might be collecting substantial fees to permit marijuana production; however, with their strictly limited investigative resources, authorities have found this difficult to prove. And, lacking a strong rule-of-law tradition, officials have usually been disinclined to pursue elites when marijuana has been found on their land. Thus, apart from the

76. *INCSR* (1988), 115. A Mexican marijuana smuggler likewise noted that growers planted fields hours from home to make denials of ownership more plausible if caught by authorities in the area. Kamstra, *Weed*, 158.

77. See Thoumi, *Political Economy*, 137.

peons caught tending marijuana fields, those involved in cannabis production have rarely faced prosecution, much less conviction and serious penalty.[78]

On the national scene, although no strong movement has ever coalesced to legalize growing and trafficking marijuana, whether stamping out enhanced production would become a top government priority immediately after independence was unclear. At the time other pressing tasks and problems occupied politicians. Some appreciated the foreign exchange and employment that the marijuana industry delivered, and a number were beholden to the trade, either corrupted by it or cognizant of its influence within the communities they represented. Moreover, the chief marijuana organizations have traditionally been headquartered in northern and southern Belize. Law enforcement there has been even more erratic than in central Belize, with the influence of elites, kinship networks, and patron-client relationships exceptionally strong. And, some doubted whether an unintegrated new state lacking financial resources and robust institutions could counter marijuana traffickers very effectively.

The economics of the marijuana trade proved to be nettlesome as well. By the early 1980s, even as sugar profits slumped, Belizean intermediaries paid producers fifteen to thirty dollars a pound for marijuana and then charged foreign syndicates fifty to a hundred dollars per pound when it was packaged and prepared for export. Cannabis could be harvested in both the fall and spring, and it eventually helped support numerous small farmers.[79] In addition, those who could furnish airstrips, weapons, laborers, aviation fuel, mechanical skills, and alike skimmed considerable sums from the trade.[80] In 1985 one Belizean citizen commented, "Almost everyone you meet in this country is at least tangentially involved in the marijuana trade. Most never see the stuff. But they may rent a plane or an airstrip to someone. Or a truck. They may lease out some land or ignore someone's use of it."[81] In fact, with Belize ranked as the fourth largest exporter of marijuana to the United States, its annual crop was estimated in the mid-1980s to be worth $350 million, a figure more than triple the country's $111 million in legal exports.[82]

Nevertheless, within two years of independence, the government had moved decisively to stem the trade. The prime incentive involved the country's bid to cultivate positive U.S. relations. To gain enhanced foreign assistance, Belizean officials felt that marijuana production had to be curtailed. Determining the best strategy to do this, however, proved problematic. As one outside consultant put it, "Destruction of the marijuana by personnel on the ground [was] thought to be prohibitively slow, expensive, and dangerous."[83] By contrast, spraying weed killer from the air was markedly more effective, but also considerably more controversial.[84] In the first year of spraying, starting in 1982, officers

78. See DEA, *Resources, Belize* (2000), 2, and *INCSR* (1997), 123. For a marijuana field arrest, see "Fined Two Hundred Thousand Dollars for Marijuana," *TR* (BZ), 1 November 1987, 10. For a Guatemalan farmer killed by an antidrug patrol inside the Caracol Archaeological Reserve near the Guatemalan border, see "Another Guat Dead," *AM* (BZ), 30 January 2000, 1.

79. *INCSR* (1985), 38. In 1984 Police Chief Stephens stated, "We can add one and one to make two. . . . We know what the farmers have done." "Belize: Concerned."

80. A U.S. federal court identified Belizean Johnney Crawford not only as a prominent marijuana supplier, but as manager of a marijuana-loading operation. *United States v. Adams*, 1 F.3d at 1569. For an Orange Walk couple arrested for possessing thirty-three gallons of aviation fuel along with crack cocaine, an unlicensed shotgun, and eighty-one kilos of marijuana, see "Two Arrested in Police Raid," *BT* (BZ), 10 December 1989, 24.

81. "Belize: No More the World's Dead End," *WP* (US), 27 January 1985, C2.

82. MacDonald, *Dancing on a Volcano*, 89, 99. In 1985 the DEA similarly concluded that Belize had exported $150 million of marijuana versus $90 million in legitimate exports. "Marijuana Now Belize's Main Cash Crop," United Press International (United States) (hereafter cited as UPI [US]), 7 December 1985.

83. Webster, "Honey Production Problems," 1–2. At least in Mexico, ground eradication was thought to be more conducive to corruption as well, because police came face-to-face with producers. Shannon, *Desperados*, 62.

84. See "Aerial Spraying of Marijuana Fields," *BT* (BZ), 27 January 1985, 1; "Twelve Million Pounds of Belizean Marijuana Destroyed Since 1983," *TR* (BZ), 5 April 1987, 8; and "Ganga Growers Split," *TR* (BZ), 13 August 1989, 14.

of the BDF Air Wing flew two loaned U.S. crop dusters and destroyed about 85 percent of the crop. Furthermore, U.S. authorities seized certain sizable marijuana shipments that Belizean traffickers had managed to export. For instance, in 1983 U.S. Customs officials hid a transponder on a Cessna 404 airplane; tracked from Belize to New Mexico, it contained 1.1 tons of marijuana.[85]

It has been theorized that increased antidrug law enforcement often has the effect of "cartelizing" a drug industry.[86] That is, enhanced eradication and interdiction adversely affect the smaller and less-capable traffickers first, thwarting or eliminating them and strengthening their larger, better-organized, more influential, and often violent competitors, who gain market share. This dynamic occurred in Belize. While more vulnerable rings—small Belizean or U.S. operators exporting marijuana—fell during law-enforcement campaigns, the most entrenched Belizean drug organizations carried on. These were primarily headquartered in Orange Walk in the north and Big Creek in the south, and they capitalized on their connections not only to continue to export marijuana but to diversify to cocaine transshipment.

Thus, major Belizean drug rings persevered, despite the government's antimarijuana campaign. In 1983 the country's cannabis production rose to an estimated seven hundred tons, and though authorities eradicated almost six million marijuana plants, growers then doubled the acreage planted, while aggressively irrigating and fertilizing to improve yields.[87] Many in Belize objected vigorously to the aerial-eradication campaign—largely funded by the United States but including some support from Mexican helicopters and crews—arguing that the spraying occurred haphazardly or hampered legitimate activities.[88] While marijuana producers and exporters may have engineered certain complaints, others appeared to be genuine and troublesome. Belizeans in widely scattered settlements declared that crop dusters were releasing weed killer where no marijuana plantations existed, harming fruits and vegetables, fish and animals.[89] During the early years of heavy aerial spraying, the Belize Honey Producers Federation commissioned a study by an American entomologist that linked the widespread application of weed killer dropped by planes on or near marijuana fields to beehive damage and slumping honey production.[90]

At the end of 1983 the government halted aerial spraying, with authorities then relying solely on search-and-destroy missions on the ground. Yet manual operations destroyed a much smaller percentage of the crop. The estimated thirty-five tons exported in 1983 approached and then exceeded a thousand tons the next two years. Judith Bertini, DEA chief of operational intelligence, noted that the 85 percent exported to the United States would supply 8 percent of the U.S. market.[91] Indeed,

85. *United States v. Erickson*, 732 F.2d 788, and *Erickson v. Commissioner of Internal Revenue*, 937 F.2d 1548.

86. Toro, *Mexico's "War,"* 17.

87. See DEA, *Resources, Belize* (2000), 13, and "Drug Crops Are Up in Export Nations, State Department Says," *New York Times* (United States) (hereafter cited as *NYT* [US]), 15 February 1985, A1.

88. Thomas, "International Campaign," 50.

89. For complaints of damage to corn, beans, plantains, papayas, avocados, pears, and coronets, see "Collapse of Honey Production and Sickness Likely Caused by Careless Marijuana Spraying," *BT* (BZ), 10 July 1988, 1. See also "Round-up Aerial Spraying," *BT* (BZ), 16 April 1989, 9.

90. Webster, "Collapse of Honey Production," 1. The study, by Dr. Thomas Webster of the University of California at Davis, eliminated other possible causes for damage to the honey industry, from bee diseases to antimalaria campaigns, because only marijuana spraying could account for the findings in such widely scattered areas. Webster concluded, "Comments and complaints from beekeepers across the country follow a pattern that would be highly unlikely if most were not telling the truth." The report recommended that application methods be changed and government inspections improved. "Honey Production Problems," 1. See also "Honey Industry Faces Extinction," *BT* (BZ), 29 January 1989, 1.

91. *INCSR* (1985), 35. See also "Twelve Million Pounds," 8; "Belize: No More," C2; "Marijuana Raise-Up in Campaign Must Now Pay-Up," *BT* (BZ), 10 March 1985, 12; "Belize: Fourth Ranking Producer of Marijuana," *TR* (BZ), 3 April 1985, 14; and "Belize's Main Cash Crop."

a U.S. federal district court concluded that in about the last half of 1984, a single marijuana-trafficking organization, led by Randall Garrett, succeeded in importing into the United States more than three tons of Belizean marijuana.[92]

Certainly, government policies regarding the marijuana trade interested numerous Belizeans and, hence, could have resounding political impact. The People's United Party (PUP) administration of George Price had initiated aerial spraying, but by the 1984 election year it was embattled on corruption charges, and leading PUP politicians concluded that further air eradication was politically untenable. In fact, many Belizeans at this time were prepared to tolerate fairly extensive marijuana use and trafficking. One estimate suggested, conservatively, that about ten thousand Belizeans smoked it; another postulated that between ten and thirteen tons of Belizean marijuana were consumed domestically each year. Furthermore, a widespread perception existed that prior spraying had occurred on a politically selective basis, with marijuana going untouched so long as it was situated on land owned by PUP supporters.[93]

Behind-the-scenes struggles within the Price government illustrate just how interrelated were personal, national, and international interests with respect to drug issues. Certain cabinet members, including Elijio "Joe" Briceno, an influential Orange Walk politician then serving as minister of energy and communication, opposed aerial eradication. With time, hidden motives behind Briceno's political stance came to light. In 1984 a DEA special agent learned that Briceno, responsible for supervising airports, traffic, and communications, was also involved in the drug trade. Indeed, Briceno met the agent and offered to store and supply high-quality marijuana, to provide a clandestine airstrip for marijuana exports, and to ensure that police not interfere. He even arranged for visiting pilots, in reality undercover DEA agents, to tour possible runways that might accommodate DC-3 planes. Briceno eventually promised to deliver two thousand kilos of marijuana a month in exchange for a 10 percent commission on sales. In April 1985 Briceno flew to Miami to collect more than thirty-two thousand dollars in seed money. After meeting with undercover agents at the Columbia Hotel and discussing security arrangements and the price and availability of marijuana in Belize, Briceno was arrested. Eventually convicted of conspiring to import marijuana and cocaine, among other charges, he was sentenced to seven years in prison and a fine of fifty thousand dollars.[94] While this incident ended Briceno's political career, his son eventually launched a political career and in recent years has risen to lead the People's United Party.

By the mid-1980s a DEA official called drug trafficking "more significant in Belize than in any other country in Latin America," in light of its modest population and economy.[95] While an overstatement given developments in Colombia and elsewhere, numerous Belizeans were quite attracted to the potential remuneration associated with the drug trade.[96] With corruption rife, trafficking occurred blatantly. Planes touched

92. *United States v. Evans*, 865 F.2d at 261, and *United States v. Evans*, 951 F.2d at 729.

93. Griffith, *Drugs and Security*, 33; *INCSR* (1991), 167; and "Belize: No More," C2. Widely recognized as the father of Belize for his central role in the independence movement, George Price became a social democrat whose political accomplishments included organizing the PUP and designing an effective system of church-state primary education. Shoman, *Party Politics in Belize*, 69.

94. See *United States v. Briceno*, 814 F.2d 655, and "U.S. Accuses Ex-minister from Belize in Plot to Import Marijuana," *NYT* (US), 9 April 1985, A15. See also "'I Have Brought Shame on My Family, My Friends and My Country,' Says Contrite Briceno," *TR* (BZ), 22 September 1985, 1; "Briceno Gets Seven Years for Conspiracy to Smuggle Drugs," *TR* (BZ), 15 September 1985, 1; "Former Belize Minister Gets Seven Years on Drug Charges," UPI (US), 10 September 1985; and "DEA 'Sting' Exposes Big Potato!," *TR* (BZ), 14 April 1985, 1.

95. "Intrigue at Land's End," *WP* (US), 27 January 1985, C1.

96. Cf. Thoumi, "Illegal Drugs in Colombia," 70.

down on the principal highways or even at the international airport without eliciting an official response. An informant pilot testified in a U.S. federal court case that in 1983 he had landed at the Belize airport to find trucks loaded with marijuana guarded by an American trafficker and several local residents armed with automatic weapons. In describing how the marijuana trade permeated life in Belize, an airport baggage handler placed the constant drug smuggling in sharp perspective: "Big plane land here, pick up dope. Big plane land in highway, pick up dope. Everybody getting rich but the little people."[97]

In fact, although light planes exported most Belizean marijuana during the heyday of production, traffickers also shipped considerable quantities by sea. At its widest, Belizean territory is about sixty-five miles across, so marijuana need not be transported far to reach the coast. This, coupled with such attractive features of offshore waters as the barrier reef and its cayes, encouraged maritime marijuana trafficking.[98] In one case that eventually brought about the conviction and resignation of corrupt U.S. federal district judge Robert F. Collins, American Gary Young pled guilty to charges that in 1985 he had conspired to send a maritime delivery of more than 1.1 tons of Belizean marijuana to the United States.[99] Then, in the late 1980s U.S. prosecutors exposed a network that had been sending thousands of kilos of Belizean marijuana from Misteriosa Bank off Rocky Point Lighthouse, near Sarteneja, toward Marco Island, Florida.[100] In 1990 combined British-U.S.-Belizean maritime operations interdicted fully 7.89 tons of marijuana.[101] Whether sent by air or sea, the constant marijuana exports developed capable Belizean drug rings that came to operate quite skillfully, frequently outfoxing authorities by changing routes.

On the national scene, despite having halted the antidrug aerial-eradication program, the PUP lost the 1984 election. The incoming, more conservative United Democratic Party (UDP) administration and prime minister Manuel Esquivel soon confronted renewed U.S. pressure concerning marijuana exports.[102] In 1985 Esquivel declared, "The cultivation and trafficking of marijuana has been converted into a serious problem that threatens the country's security."[103] The UDP government then agreed in principle to resume aerial spraying, though it temporarily refrained from doing so, awaiting the results of U.S. legal proceedings that had challenged the government-sanctioned spraying of paraquat as harmful to the health of marijuana smokers.[104] At length, Belize opted to use Roundup, and after a period of limited measures, the government ordered full spraying to resume in 1986.[105] Not only did the renewed campaign destroy

97. Quoted in "Belize: No More," C2; see also *United States v. Lee*, 743 F.2d 1240.

98. For a similar observation about maritime marijuana trafficking in Mexico, see Kamstra, *Weed*, 204.

99. See *United States v. Collins*, 972 F.2d 1385, and *In Re Robert F. Collins*, 645 So.2d 1131. For allegations that trafficker Earl Henry Benjamin corrupted a Florida state judge after arrest for smuggling 386 kilos of Belizean marijuana, see "Ex-judge Took Bribe, Convicted Felon Says," *St. Petersburg Times* (United States) (hereafter cited as *SPT* [US]), 29 July 1989, 1B.

100. See *United States v. Gonzalez*, 940 F.2d at 1417–18. In 1988 the U.S. Coast Guard boarded one of this enterprise's ships, the *Sea Viking*, and discovered 7,045 kilos of marijuana. At trial the *Ross and Bess* was shown to have already successfully imported at least 13.6 tons.

101. *INCSR* (1992), 141.

102. Organizer of the more right-wing UDP, Esquivel had been a forty-four-year-old junior college physics professor when elected prime minister. Among Belize's growing Spanish-speaking communities, Esquivel capitalized on his Hispanic ethnicity. His party advocated replacing the PUP's old-boy network with younger politicians, while promoting a capitalist, free-enterprise system to attract foreign investment.

103. "Belice, serio problema de narcotráfico," *LP* (HO), 29 April 1985, 26.

104. "Belize: Concerned." See also "Belize Warily Considers Marijuana Herbicide," *NYT* (US), 27 October 1985, A9.For contending views on paraquat, see "Herbicide Once Again Under Fire," *Tico Times* (Costa Rica), 2 March 2001, 1, 9. In his memoirs U.S. attorney general Griffin Bell wrote, "We have gone so far as to ban the use of foreign aid funds for Paraquat—on the flimsiest of evidence that it would have damaging side effects—while allowing Florida to spray 61,000 pounds of it on its food crops in 1980." *Taking Care*, 161.

105. For the resumption of spraying, see Griffith, *Drugs and Security*, 33; Webster, "Honey Production Problems," 1; "Aerial Spraying of Marijuana Fields," 1; "P. M. Supports

more than 2.2 million kilos that year and 2.7 million the next, but the government also embarked on a much-publicized effort to use explosives to destroy some of the most suspicious unlicensed airstrips.

These measures, coupled with drought, took a considerable toll on the Belizean cannabis industry, and marijuana production declined steeply from 1986 to 1990. Fig. 2.1 illustrates that, while much more marijuana was cultivated in 1986 than at the beginning of the decade, much more was eradicated as well. Thus, after 1985 exports steadily fell, with eradication reducing the amount available to be shipped abroad from 512 tons in 1986 to 48 tons in 1990. George Price and the PUP then took office again and opted to retain the UDP's fundamental eradication policies, resulting in a further decrease to 36 tons in 1991. By 1992 the U.S. government declared that by cutting marijuana production 90 percent over five years, Belize had suppressed cultivation to the maximum extent possible.[106]

Despite these considerable setbacks, Belizean drug networks did not discontinue all efforts to export marijuana. Eradicating fields of cannabis failed to disrupt the long-lived, well-connected, and historically successful domestic networks that had been financing, producing, and transporting the drugs. The attraction of the trade persisted, as did the routes, infrastructure, international connections, and consumer demand that had supported their operations. In 1987 Prime Minister Esquivel observed that so high was foreign demand, traffickers were actually bartering cocaine for Belizean cannabis.[107] In addition, significant Belizean producers relocated operations into Guatemala's El Petén region and substantial quantities of marijuana began to cross the Guatemalan border.[108] Nevertheless, while curtailing drug production in one country did lead to enhanced output in its neighbor, the overall result was a decrease in marijuana production in this corner of Central America.

The next noteworthy development occurred in 1994 when, in a cost-cutting measure, the U.S. government removed its spray planes from Belize. This left the BDF Air Wing to attempt to identify marijuana fields and send in ground units to eradicate the crops. Although the United States was prepared to return the planes the following year, the Belizean government chose, on environmental grounds, not to initiate a new spraying campaign, seeking instead to continue aerial reconnaissance and manual eradication. Thus, destruction of cannabis fields by hand became, once again, the centerpiece of the Belizean campaign to curb the marijuana trade.[109] After eradicating a mere 12,700 plants in 1994, Belizean authorities took out nearly 300,000 in 1997, and over 200,000 and 270,000 in the following two years.

In response, marijuana farmers tried to confound the authorities with various tactics. Some turned to fast-growing varieties of indica marijuana, which could mature in four months or fewer. Many worked to hide their crop better by interplanting corn stalks with the cannabis plants or by employing the "underbrush method," in which they cleared low-lying vegetation for cannabis cultivation but retained larger trees to screen fields from detection. Growers also took advantage of the Belizean climate, especially its

Spraying of Marijuana Fields," *BT* (BZ), 28 April 1985, 12; "Twelve Million Pounds," 8; "Belize Breeze Potent Cannabis Linked to Cocaine," *TR* (BZ), 12 April 1987, 5; and "Drug War in the North?," *TR* (BZ), 8 May 1986, 10.

106. "A Practical Alternative," *TR* (BZ), 17 January 1988, 2; "Toledo Marijuana Field Torched," *TR* (BZ), 14 August 1988, 9; and *INCSR* (1992), 142–43.

107. "Belize Breeze Potent Cannabis," 5. In fact, an undercover DEA agent broke up just such a barter deal. See *United States v. Kaufman*, 858 F.2d 994.

108. "Ganga Growers Split," *TR* (BZ), 13 August 1989, 4. The U.S. BINM reported in 1993, "Although seizures of domestic marijuana are down, intelligence indicates the continuing transit of significant quantities of marijuana." *INCSR* (1993), 140.

109. See DEA, *Resources, Belize* (2003), 3; DEA, *Resources, Belize* (2000), 2; *INCSR* (1993), 139; "War on Marijuana 95 Percent Effective," *TR* (BZ), 9 April 1989, 11; and Griffith, *Drugs and Security*, 33–34

regular and plentiful rainfall, planting cannabis seedlings and then leaving them until harvest.

Thus, some cannabis cultivation, transit, and export persisted.[110] Moreover, even as the industry declined, particular large shipments were still prepared for export, with few repercussions for local traffickers. In 1986 police operating on the outskirts of Belize City discovered that a large shipping container, marked "Empty," actually contained more than 3.5 tons of compressed marijuana. Businessman Jaime Perdomo was arrested, convicted, and sentenced to a $37,500 fine.[111] In 1990, after authorities at Belize City Port searched another shipping container bound for Miami, marked "Empty" and yet holding more than 1.6 tons of marijuana, two Mennonite businessmen were arrested, but later acquitted, and no one else was held responsible.[112] Similarly, in 1998 authorities discovered 3 tons of compressed marijuana in another supposedly empty shipping container that had brought imported goods to a Mennonite community and was then trucked around the Orange Walk district before being returned to the Port Authority shipping compound.

This record suggests a number of points. To the surprise of many onlookers, significantly curtailing the Belizean marijuana industry was not a hopeless undertaking. Belizean yields and exports did taper off substantially from the enormous crops of the early to mid-1980s, a testament to national eradication efforts. U.S. and Belizean officials hailed the curbing of the Belizean marijuana trade as an example of highly effective national antidrug actions, stimulated and supported by U.S. aid. However, just as Belize increased its market share with the Mexican antimarijuana campaign of the late 1970s, so Guatemalan producers gained ground as the Belizean yield fell. Even more important, to a much greater degree than occurred in any other Central American state, the extensive export of homegrown cannabis had developed organizations, infrastructure, and know-how in Belize that could be applied to the transit of South American narcotics. Whether antidrug successes against marijuana could be duplicated very much remained to be seen.

The International Trade in Narcotics

Even as the government of Belize trumpeted what had indeed been an impressive campaign to thwart the domestic marijuana industry, a far more serious problem grew rapidly in scope: the transit of cocaine shipments headed from South America toward Mexico and the United States. It soon became apparent that as official pressure on the domestic marijuana industry had crescendoed, various prominent Belizean drug networks had shifted into cocaine transshipment. In retrospect, while successes in eradication and interdiction played the most important part in stemming Belizean marijuana

110. For additional details, see *INCSR* (1993), 140; *INCSR* (1994), 135; *INCSR* (1995), 120; *INCSR* (1998), 119; DEA, *Resources, Belize* (2003), 2; and *INCSR* (1998), 138. For representative export cases, such as a Canadian extradition case involving 591 kilos of marijuana smuggled from Ambergris Caye to Destin, Florida, see *United States v. Lacey*, 23 W.C.B. 427. In 1994 police near Cangrejo Caye interrupted the transfer of more than 100 kilos of Belizean marijuana, dropped into the sea to be retrieved by a Florida-registered boat. "Police Bust Marijuana Ring," *TR* (BZ), 20 February 1994, 1. See also *United States v. Knowles*, 66 F.3d at 1154.

111. "Record Drug Bust Exposes Container Racket," *TR* (BZ), 26 January 1986, 1; "Drug Trial Continues," *BT* (BZ), 16 March 1986, 1; and "Perdomo Fined Seventy-Five Thousand Dollars [Bz] for Container Load with Marijuana," *TR* (BZ), 6 April 1986, 1. If Perdomo could not pay the fine, the court ordered three years in prison. See "Privy Council Rejects Perdomo Appeal," *AM* (BZ), 12 June 1992, 3, and "Perdomo Loses Drugs Appeal," *TR* (BZ), 28 July 1991, 5.

112. For this and the 1998 Mennonite case, see "US-bound 'Empty' Container Found with 3,689 Lbs. of Weed!," *TR* (BZ), 3 June 1990, 1; "Accused of Trading in Marijuana, Mennonites Deplore Cruel Twist of Fate," *TR* (BZ), 17 June 1990, 7; "Weed Goes Up in Smoke," *BT* (BZ), 24 June 1990, 1; "Five Walk Free in Marijuana Container Case," *TR* (BZ), 25 November 1990, 1; "Businessmen Implicated in Marijuana Operations," *TR* (BZ), 14 June 1998, 1; and "One Man Left to Face Charges of Weed Trafficking," *TR* (BZ), 28 March 1999, 10.

exports, another key factor was the aim of Belizean organizations to increase their earnings by trafficking even more profitable drugs.

The most arresting fact concerning the evolution of the Belizean drug trade is how significant prior marijuana trafficking was in preparing for later cocaine transit. Although a U.S. federal court once noted, "Marijuana and cocaine are different drugs in terms of sources, channels of distribution, methods of shipment and processing, and customers," this general principle does not accurately encapsulate the Belizean experience.[113] Here, drug organizations adapted for use in cocaine smuggling the very routes, methods, and logistics first developed in moving marijuana. Colombian, American, and Mexican cocaine traffickers found well-oiled export machinery in Belize, as well as a plentiful supply of experienced potential collaborators. The existing drug-smuggling infrastructure thus abetted the sweeping transformation of the Belizean drug trade.

As for the characteristics of the Belizean networks involved, a U.S. intelligence report stated, "Most Belizean trafficking organizations are small, tightly knit groups, and their members often are related. A trafficker often divides a large cocaine shipment among several smaller groups to transport it, thus minimizing his risk. Some organizations act solely as support teams to refuel aircraft and go-fast boats, or to transport cocaine overland."[114] Colombian cocaine cartels that had learned of successful marijuana export from Belize paid top dollar to use the same airstrips and networks of collaborators. For instance, a 1992 U.S. federal court case identified Frederick Pou as both a source of marijuana in Belize and an intermediary arranging refueling stops in Belize for aircraft traveling between Colombia and the United States.[115]

For Belizean traffickers the transition from marijuana to cocaine smuggling often occurred incrementally, rather than as an abrupt switch. In diversifying their operations, various Belizean organizations at first dabbled in moving cocaine. In the 1970s and 1980s some helped to transship very modest amounts of the narcotic, while still mostly concentrating on marijuana exports.[116] A few helped to transport much larger cocaine loads. Indeed, U.S. court records reveal that from at least the late 1970s notable cocaine shipments periodically transited the country. For instance, Claude Griffin, a marijuana and cocaine trafficker who eventually turned state's evidence, described for U.S. authorities three cocaine flights in 1982 that proceeded from Colombia into Belize for refueling and then on to Raceland, Louisiana, carrying a total of 600 kilos of cocaine.[117] In general, however, over a period of many months, for one group after another, cocaine transshipment increased as marijuana smuggling diminished.

For that era, the transport of hundreds of kilos amounted to striking cocaine-trafficking ventures. In using Belize as an intermediate stop for flights in small planes, such smugglers did not normally off-load the drugs to be stored or forwarded via another method; instead, they simply refueled and continued north into Mexico or directly into the United States. One ring,

113. *United States v. Pallais*, 921 F.2d at 687.

114. The report continued, "Smaller trafficking organizations and support groups usually are paid in cocaine instead of cash." DEA, *Resources, Belize* (2000), 4.

115. *United States v. DeShaw*, 974 F.2d 667. For allegations that in the 1980s a former Cuban politician moved from marijuana to cocaine trafficking via Belize and the Bahamas, see "Trafficker of Drugs Did Business with GMCT [Guinness Mahon Cayman Trust] and John Furze," *Irish Times*, 9 July 2002, 5.

116. In 1978 a U.S. informant named a Belizean cattle farmer as a cocaine supplier; however, the plane sent to collect a small cocaine shipment returned with almost 273 kilos of marijuana. *United States v. Neal*, 692 F.2d 1296. For additional drug allegations concerning the JaBo Cattle Company, see *United States v. Neal*, 1992 U.S. App. LEXIS 15385. In 1981 and 1982 a major Houston trafficking ring led by Dempsey Buford Merida organized the smuggling of marijuana and some cocaine paste from Belize. See *United States v. Merida*, 765 F.2d at 1211, and *United States v. Dunn*, 775 F.2d 604.

117. *United States v. Nichols*, 741 F.2d 767.

broken up by authorities in Miami in 1984, was transshipping cocaine from Colombia right through Belize International Airport. There, with protection from airport and police officials, refueling occurred, prior to an onward flight into Florida.[118] Indeed, by the early 1990s various U.S. federal court cases showed cocaine being transported by air from Colombia through Belize and into the United States.[119] One prominent network, headed by Richard Lynn, smuggled numerous loads of more than six hundred kilos of cocaine into the southern United States via Belize. In 1988, after police in Marion, Alabama, interrupted a cocaine transfer, authorities captured two of the ring's pilots, who eventually opted to become government informants. At trial, the pilots testified that in 1987 and 1988 they had often flown to Colombia and returned to the United States after refueling in Belize.[120]

In fact, since the first substantial Belizean cocaine seizure did not occur until 1990, more can be learned about the country's early cocaine trafficking by examining U.S. court records. Indeed, to this day, most cocaine-transshipment schemes involving Belize have come to light through seizures abroad, and detailed information about prior successful transshipment ventures have frequently emerged from the testimony of police, informants, and others at foreign trials. This, in turn, reflects the fact that Belizean authorities soon discovered that curbing cocaine transit was a far more difficult challenge than curtailing marijuana production. A cannabis field offered an immoveable target that could be identified, sometimes with foreign technological assistance, approached by air or ground, and expeditiously dealt with. In contrast, opportunities to intercept cocaine were fleeting and required better intelligence and more nimble responses. The Colombian and Mexican cocaine networks have also been considerably more dangerous—more wealthy and sophisticated, more adept at wielding bribes and intimidation, and more violent and paranoid—than were the U.S. marijuana-trafficking rings that they supplanted.[121]

In conjunction with this growing trade, the 1980s also witnessed mounting cocaine consumption within Belize and the advent of crack-cocaine markets. The DEA reported,

> Cocaine first surfaced in Belize in 1985, when an airplane laden with cocaine from Colombia crash-landed in the Orange Walk District in northern Belize. Several local drug traffickers stole the cocaine and sold it locally. Seeing the potential profits . . . some marijuana traffickers changed their operations to the more profitable business of working with Colombian groups to import cocaine . . . for further transshipment to the United States. The cocaine flow into Belize increased along with local abuse of crack cocaine. . . . Several known Belize traffickers own or control airfields and support drug flights by providing fuel and security for which they are paid in cocaine by international traffickers.

The development of domestic cocaine markets, in turn, furthered the growth of urban gangs and drug-related violence, although it also

119. For a Colombia-Belize-Louisiana cocaine route, see *United States v. Grant*, 734 F. Supp. at 769. For a Colombia-Belize-Alabama route, see *United States v. Eyster*, 948 F.2d 1196. For other examples, see *United States v. Goff*, 847 F.2d 149; *United States v. Simpson*, 901 F.2d 1223; and *United States v. Weaver*, 905 F.2d at 1468.

120. Convicted on five counts, Lynn received life imprisonment without parole. In 1990 he escaped from custody, but was later recaptured. During the investigation another conspirator corroborated much of the information revealed by the pilots, who had received immunity from prosecution despite earning between seven hundred thousand and one million dollars. Two additional flights linked to Lynn were unsuccessful. In 1986 police found 711 kilos of cocaine stuffed in burlap sacks near a Waynesboro, Mississippi, airstrip, and in 1987 a cocaine plane crash-landed, exploding at a small Alabama airport. *United States v Eyster*, 948 F.2d at 1199–1200, 1200n2.

121. For paranoia and the cocaine trade, see Porter, *Blow*, 166..

enhanced the commitment to curb trafficking by some Belizean authorities.[122]

As the Medellín cartel rose to dominate the cocaine trade, their leaders looked to Belize as a particularly promising bridge state. The former key transportation strategist for the Medellín cartel, Carlos Lehder Rivas, originally tipped to certain of the country's bridge-favoring characteristics by an imprisoned American doctor familiar with the country, targeted Belize as ideal to manipulate through bribes and violence.[123] A close past associate later testified that Lehder had planned to "take over" Belize and turn it into a criminal paradise.[124] Toward that end, the Colombian kingpin hoped to appeal to Belizeans on ideological grounds, while intimidating authorities and thoroughly corrupting institutions, all to enable the regular transit of large cocaine shipments.[125] This was a formula he had already employed in another recently independent, postcolonial, formerly British state—the Bahamas.[126]

Although Lehder was arrested in 1987 in Colombia and extradited to the United States, Medellín traffickers had already initiated plans to ship cocaine through Belize, with Police Commissioner Bernard Bevans noting in early 1988 "a great upsurge in drug trafficking."[127] At a mid-1989 press conference U.S. Ambassador Robert Rich declared, "A major narcotic network built on the groundwork of the languishing marijuana trade and having strong connections with an international drug ring is responsible for the increase in cocaine trafficking and distribution in Belize."[128] The cocaine trade through Belize then climbed rapidly in the following decade. In 1993 U.S. antidrug officials reported of the country, "Intelligence and seizure statistics indicate continuous or even increasing cocaine transshipment. Main routes are by air or sea from Colombia, often with stopovers in Honduras and/or Guatemala, as well as overland to Guatemala. Most major shipments move on to Mexico en route to the U.S."[129]

While the initial surge of Belizean cocaine transshipment occurred through the use of small planes, cocaine soon came to be frequently trafficked at sea. In 1992 a U.S. federal court sentenced American lawyer James Timonere to forty-five years in prison and a $1 million fine

122. DEA, *Resources, Belize* (2000), 3; "American Drug Habit," UPI (US), 24 March 1985.

123. In 1974 the doctor, serving time for Medicaid fraud at the Danbury Federal Correctional Institute, had attracted Lehder's attention by touting Belize's lack of an extradition treaty with the United States. Porter, *Blow*, 112, and Gugliotta and Leen, *Kings of Cocaine*, 31. In fact, however, even before signing its own extradition treaty with the United States, Belize could extradite individuals under a 1972 United States–United Kingdom treaty.

124. See *United States v. Lehder*, 955 F.2d 1510. Lehder's plan for Belize was spelled out at his 1987 U.S. federal trial on charges of importing 3.3 tons of cocaine, largely via the Bahamas. George Jung, a cellmate in Danbury in 1974 and later the groomsman at his wedding, testified about Lehder's designs on Belize. See "Conquista de Belice en planes de Lehder," *LP* (HO), 18 November 1987, 25, and "Jacksonville Drug Trial," *TR* (BZ), 7 February 1988, 4. See also Porter, *Blow*.

125. Lehder organized Colombia's National Latin Movement, writing in a 1985 letter drafted to send to Soviet diplomats in Bogotá: "What I know today, after many years of political and revolutionary experiences, after having become familiar with the brother governments of Cuba and Nicaragua, of the Bahamas and Belize, of Puerto Rico and Haiti, as well as the countries of Latin America, as well as Central America [is that] . . . their economic and social problems are caused by the imperialist gringo industrialists." Shannon, *Desperados*, 114–15, 264–65. See also Strong, *Whitewash*, 88.

126. See generally Kirkpatrick, *Turning the Tide*, and Porter, *Blow*, 177–95.

127. "Now in Place: A Belize SWAT Team to Stop Drug Trafficking and Fight Crime!," *TR* (BZ), 24 January 1988, 1. Ironically, the other Medellín kingpins lost faith in Lehder because of erratic behavior stemming from drug abuse. At a U.S. court hearing Lehder's public defender stated, "Your Honor, we understand that he was turned in to the police by an underworld figure, Pablo Escobar." Gugliotta and Leen, *Kings of Cocaine*, 320. This was corroborated by General Miguel Maza, director of Colombia's Departamento Administrativo de Seguridad. No reprisals followed Lehder's extradition, and George Jung later claimed to have asked Escobar, through intermediaries, if he should testify, and Escobar assented. See Mollison, *Memory of Pablo Escobar*, 125–26; and Porter, *Blow*, 292–93. Also see Escobar, *Accountant's Story*, 303.

128. "Medellín Drug Connection in Belize?," *TR* (BZ), 16 July 1989, 1.

129. *INCSR* (1993), 140–41.

for shipping 2 tons of Colombian cocaine via Belize into a marina near Dunedin, Florida. The following year, a DEA sting involving more than 900 kilos of Colombian cocaine transported by yacht from Belize led to thirteen arrests and the downfall of a ring that over a decade had imported an estimated 35 to 50 tons of cocaine from around the Caribbean basin into the United States. In 2000 DEA agents in Florida seized 479 kilos of cocaine and uncovered another network, led by a U.S. grandmother, that had also been shipping cocaine from Colombia through Belize into the United States.[130]

A significant portion of this trade has involved drug ventures that piggybacked on regular intra-Caribbean shipping. Thus, in one typical case U.S. Customs inspectors found nearly 70 kilos of cocaine on the Belize-registered freighter *Layenda*, after its arrival in Miami from Haiti. At the close of the twentieth century the DEA concluded,

> Most of the cocaine transported overland to or through Belize is hidden in containers or concealed in bulk commercial shipments, such as lumber or concrete. Cargo smuggled into Guatemala, Honduras, and El Salvador via maritime vessels also is shipped overland to Belize or Mexico for onward transshipment. . . . Drug traffickers also transport cocaine through Belize to Mexico via containerized cargo. Belize has two seaports capable of berthing container shipments. A common practice for drug traffickers is to conceal cocaine in fresh fruit and seafood, both regular exports. Vessels transporting food are rarely checked thoroughly by customs due to the perishability of the foodstuffs, and inability of customs to pay for the cargo, should no drugs be found and the goods ruined.[131]

The next development of signal importance in maritime cocaine trafficking through Belizean waters involved the much more frequent use of speedboats. In the 1990s go-fasts carrying large cocaine loads came up the Central American coast, perhaps via the Islas de la Bahía (Bay Islands) of Honduras, or they headed directly to Belize from the island of San Andrés off Colombia. Alternatively, Belizean speedboats might take to sea to load cocaine brought on a mother ship or dropped by planes. Whatever the route, go-fasts often transited the territorial seas of Belize at night, using the cayes to camouflage their activities further. The DEA reported, "Go-fast boats are refueled and unloaded by support teams, which usually use a different location for each operation. Drug traffickers in Belize are known to rotate their operations from the Northern Districts to the Southern Districts in order to avoid detection."[132]

In relation to available maritime counternarcotics resources, Belizean territorial waters are vast. And the scores of cayes on both sides of the barrier reef, coupled with the many coastal swamps and lagoons, have made for a plethora of potential hiding places. Belizean authorities have lacked the boats and fuel to patrol their waters at all thoroughly, with the ocean side of the barrier reef especially neglected, and large U.S. Coast Guard vessels have been more effective in deep offshore waters than in coastal shallows. Hence, as confounding a task as

130. "Tarpon Lawyer Gets Forty-Five Years," *SPT* (US), 18 January 1992, 1; "U.S. Indicts Nineteen in Drug Inquiry," *Fort Lauderdale Sun-Sentinel*, 29 September 1994, 1B; and "DEA: Grandma Led Cocaine Ring," *Fort Lauderdale Sun-Sentinel*, 2 March 2000.

131. *United States v. Estupinan-Yesquan*, 2005 U.S. App. LEXIS 23171; *United States v. Montana-Batalla*, 2005 U.S. App. LEXIS 23178; and DEA, *Resources, Belize* (2000), 3.

132. *INCSR* (2002), 5:4, and DEA, *Resources, Belize* (2000), 3. For a report on traffickers using low-slung thirty- to forty-foot wooden boats to evade radar, see "Cocaine Cartel Now Trying Stealth Boats," *TR* (BZ), 1 March 1992, 7

keeping tabs on air traffic in Belize has been, authorities have found it even more problematic to determine what exactly is happening offshore. In particular, small planes have often operated with the disadvantage of entering Belizean airspace flown by foreign pilots with limited knowledge of the country's landing strips. Furthermore, hiding a plane that arrived early to a rendezvous could be problematic. In contrast, Belizeans intimately familiar with offshore hazards and hiding places and the patterns of local law enforcement have taken charge of trafficking through coastal waters and, on the whole, have managed it quite successfully.

Low interception rates then encouraged more maritime narcotics-transshipment schemes. Over time, while aerial smuggling has still been employed, traffickers have more frequently employed water drops, in which sealed cocaine packages have been tossed into the sea or into lagoons or other bodies of water to be collected by associates. Plainly, the most opportune moment for authorities to capture a loaded plane and its occupants is when they are on the ground. In a properly executed water drop, however, the pilot need not land at all or can touch down for refueling with an empty plane, having already left the drugs some distance away.[133] Thus, hybrid aerial-maritime routes using water drops have reduced the arrest of pilots, a highly skilled, expensive asset of drug organizations.

Traffickers operating in Belize have also allied to move drugs more efficiently and outmaneuver authorities. In the mid- to late 1990s Colombian and Mexican cocaine-smuggling networks began to collaborate more closely, and Belize proved to be a convenient intermediate staging point.[134] Where the Colombians' responsibility was to oversee the cocaine shipments out of South America, the Mexicans would take charge of transport into the United States. Belizeans became intermediaries, receiving and then reexporting the drugs. Thus, during this period Belizean associates increasingly warehoused narcotics. The stored cocaine could be exported when buyers were ready, or divided into smaller loads, thus reducing the risk that an entire shipment would be seized.

By 1994, when the UDP and Manuel Esquivel once more ousted Price and the PUP, even more cocaine-trafficking organizations were at work in the country.[135] These groups varied substantially in size from Mexican and Colombian cartels, to long-standing Belizean operations, to drug ventures by growing Belize City gangs, to opportunistic enterprises by individuals. As fortunes waned for the Medellín kingpins, Cali traffickers stepped in, markedly intensifying operations that actually dated to the early 1980s.[136] Then, when arrests by U.S. and Colombian authorities broke up the Cali cartel, the void was filled by traffickers linked to exceptionally violent competitors: Colombia's Northern Valley and Mexico's Juárez cartel.[137] By 2000 leading Belizean trafficking groups had assisted various of the principal Mexican and Colombian cocaine syndicates, helping them to transport shipments of many hundreds and sometimes thousands of kilos.

With cocaine supplies readily available and distributors eager for more drugs, Belizean entrepreneurs have entered the cocaine trade as well. Although these smaller operations have

133. See "Police Drug Trap Catches Family of Ten," *TR* (BZ), 5 September 1993, 3.

134. DEA, *Resources, Belize* (2000), 3, and *INCSR* (2003), 5:5.

135. For one example affirming Nevada convictions of Iván Benítez and Jairo Humberto Moreno for a multimillion-dollar cocaine import-and-distribution scheme via Belize, see *United States v. Benitez*, 1993 U.S. App. LEXIS 22056.

136. See "Police Seize $16.5 Million Worth of Cali Cocaine," *TR* (BZ), 15 January 1995, 1, and *INCSR* (1996), 120. For a 1982 case relating to Cali traffickers, see *United States v. Nichols*, 741 F.2d at 769.

137. "Belize Caught in the Middle of Drug War," *LAT* (US), 25 July 1997, A5. See also "C. A. Drug Link Straining with Recent Arrests in Colombia," *TR* (BZ), 9 July 1995, 14. Although sometimes referred to as the "Southeast cartel," this organization was actually a Juárez-cartel arm.

not initially been able to finance the purchase and transport of very sizable cocaine loads, kilograms of cocaine have been readily procured, and the successful trafficking of modest quantities has been an effective route toward building capital and contacts. The risk posed by local authorities has been tolerable as well. While U.S., Mexican, British, or Canadian customs and police might uncover small trafficking schemes, Belizean officials have not been especially vigilant.[138] Hence, so long as the principals in a Belizean drug ring found others to assume the risks of crossing borders and otherwise operating abroad, they might stay in business for quite some time.

A courier operation set up by Belizean brothers in the mid-1990s exemplifies this variety of trafficking. Authorities alleged that Dwayne, Mark, and Gary Seawall at first used the postal service to move cocaine into Columbus, Ohio. To increase the scope and profits of their undertaking, they turned to offering free vacations and a thousand dollars in cash to dozens of young American couriers, who had to return to the United States wearing shoes with a pound or two of cocaine hidden inside.[139] Eventually, the U.S. government requested the brothers' extradition on multiple charges of trafficking and money laundering, and Dwayne Seawall eventually pled guilty and was sentenced to seventeen years in prison.[140] Of course, any single courier engaged in such a smuggling operation would be moving a tiny fraction of the cocaine found in one major shipment. Nevertheless, the activities of such entrepreneurial organizations, regularly sending couriers north, added to the stream of cocaine flowing from Belize.

With time, cocaine smuggling led, in turn, to some heroin transshipment. In 1996 Belizean authorities, assisted by the DEA, made the first seizure.[141] By 2000 the DEA determined that, on occasion, Colombian networks were shipping heroin along with cocaine loads, and the next year a number of heroin-trafficking arrests involving Belize occurred.[142] In 2005, in the country's first such case, two Belizean couriers, carrying heroin from Panama, died when the glass test tubes wrapped in latex that they had swallowed ruptured in their stomachs.[143] However, Belize was not a renowned international air hub, as Panama was. Belize had only a fraction of the tourist trade of Costa Rica. And, the country was far less suited than Guatemala for opium production, none of which occurred. Thus, for Belize the heroin trade has remained of quite modest proportions.

Instead, in the twenty-first century, a new drug-trafficking threat developed from the

138. In 2003 elderly Canadian Ed Shaw, once hailed for selfless humanitarian work in Belize, testified that two years earlier he had transported cocaine across the Mexican border into the United States for Belizean traffickers, an escapade he attributed to curiosity about how the drug trade functioned. See "Canadian Crusader Convicted," *New Orleans Times-Picayune*, 19 June 2003, 1, and "Humanitarian Admits He Ferried Drugs to U.S.," *Toronto Star*, 5 September 2003, A8.

139. See *United States v. Henderson*, 209 F.3d 614. See also "Thirty-Five Charged with Smuggling Drugs," *Columbus Dispatch*, 11 October 1997, 1B; "Plot to Smuggle Cocaine in Shoes Trips Up Drug Ringleaders," *TR* (BZ), 4 November 2007, 4; and "Seawall Bros. Await Extradition Hearings," *TR* (BZ), 25 February 2007, 1.

140. See "One of 'Belize's Most Wanted,' Gary Seawall, Thirty-Three, Captured in Esperanza," *AM* (BZ), 2 December 2010, 1; "Chief Magistrate Rules Against Mark Seawall," *AM* (BZ), 29 April 2009, 1; and "GOB says Dwayne Seawall Should Be Returned to Belize for Extradition Hearings," *AM* (BZ), 23 February 2007, 1.

141. See *INCSR* (1997), 122; "First Ever Heroin Bust Worries Belize Police," *BT* (BZ), 31 March 1996, 1; "Couple Pleads Not Guilty to Possession of Heroin," *BT* (BZ), 31 March 1996, 1, 3; "Nigerian Granted Bail of Ten Thousand Dollars," *BT* (BZ), 7 April 1996, 1; and "Pasqual Mekowalu Fined Twenty-Five Thousand Dollars in First Heroin Case," *BT* (BZ), 22 December 1996, 1A. Note that the case involved a Belizean resident who was a Nigerian expatriate.

142. DEA, *Resources, Belize* (2000), 1. See also Nigerian Woman Held for Heroin," *TR* (BZ), 20 August 2000, 10; "Cops Bag Heroin Smugglers," *TR* (BZ), 15 April 2001, 8; "African Man Caught Smuggling Heroin," *TR* (BZ), 15 July 2001, 5; and "Heroin in Belize! Lots of It," *TR* (BZ), 19 August 2001, 10. For the role of Nigerians in international heroin smuggling, see Chepesiuk, *Hard Target*, 167–75.

143. See "Two Belizeans Smuggling Drugs in Body Died from Overdose," *AM* (BZ), 16 March 2005, 1, and "Drug Mules Lose Life," *TR* (BZ), 20 March 2005, 4

passage of large quantities of pseudoephedrine, a decongestant used in manufacturing methamphetamine. Mexico's Gulf cartel became deeply involved in Central American transshipment of pseudoephedrine, and it had already cultivated excellent contacts in Belize. In October 2009 authorities located a million dollars' worth of pseudoephedrine in a Belize City house. The following month, the Belize Customs Department declared that the Gulf cartel had threatened inspectors who might uncover pseudoephedrine transshipment. After a Gulf contact in Belize informed Gregory Gibson, comptroller of customs, that his department had been targeted, Gibson declared, "We don't sleep well at night. Too few people are in the fight and too many people are afraid."[144]

As they investigated the pseudoephedrine trade, Belizean Customs officials noted that various trucks, either while in the customs compound or shortly after leaving it, and carrying trailers later suspected of containing pills, had been hijacked and vanished or were recovered empty. It further developed that a shipping container brought to Belize on the Chinese ship *Palencia* had been irregularly cleared through customs, and investigators came to believe that it had included 10 million tablets of pseudoephedrine. Shortly thereafter, a container off another Chinese ship, *Paranga*, was found to contain 4.8 million pseudoephedrine pills. The shipment had been consigned to a company called Me Agape, with a Corozal Free Zone office and directors that included prominent Corozal politician Florencio Marin Jr. along with two of his relatives. Me Agape, however, denied all knowledge of the shipping container, and the investigation stalled. By the end of 2009 Belize reported that 423 kilos of pseudoephedrine had been seized.[145]

While heroin and pseudoephedrine smuggling via Belize has occurred, cocaine trafficking has dwarfed the transit of all other narcotic drugs. In examining the peaks and valleys of cocaine seizures from 1990 to 2010, as illustrated by fig. 2.3, one sees the Belizean state not entirely collapsing in the face of intensive cocaine trafficking but instead displaying a marked pattern in which it periodically reasserted itself in counternarcotics work. In general, however, one should bear in mind that interdicting cocaine being transshipped through the country was not so much a hit-or-miss proposition as one that was mostly misses. Peak years often reflected a single large cocaine seizure, almost invariably the result of DEA information.[146] The typical difficulties faced by an emergent society contending with scarce law-enforcement resources grievously hampered counternarcotics operations. In 1998 a diplomat in Belize observed, "They have no radar, they have no helicopters, their air force has three planes, their navy has 50 people and an annual maintenance budget of [about US$25,000] to keep the fleet afloat and patrol more than 200 islands. . . . Their chances of catching anything are pretty slim."[147]

The record thus raises grave doubts about the efficacy of an interdiction strategy in Belize. Typically, while Belizean officials have occasionally intercepted drugs, the incapacities of the criminal-justice system have been brought into sharp relief, as authorities have struggled to identify and break up the networks behind the transactions. In light of the significant

144. See "Forty Boxes of Suspected Pseudo-ephedrine Seized," *AM* (BZ), 10 August 2009, 1; "Gulf Cartel Targets Belize Customs!," *AM* (BZ), 9 September 2008, 1; "Three Customs Officers Arraigned on Forgery of Official Document Charges," *AM* (BZ), 26 September 2008, 1; and "The Ephedrine Container Epidemic and the Free Zone," *AM* (BZ), 26 September 2008, 1.

145. *INCSR* (2010), 150.

146. The fact that the Glover's Reef seizures do not appear in the 2003 statistics indicates that these figures fail to include U.S. Coast Guard drug confiscations in Belizean territorial waters. Of the 734.5 kilos confiscated in 2004, Belize police seized more than 700 from a single plane. *INCSR* (2005), 161. Of the 2,386 kilos seized in 2005, all but ten came in one DEA-assisted seizure. *INCSR* (2006), 129.

147. "Just What the Smuggler Ordered," *WP* (US), 2 August 1998, A1.

Fig. 2.3 Cocaine seizures in Belize, 1990–2010

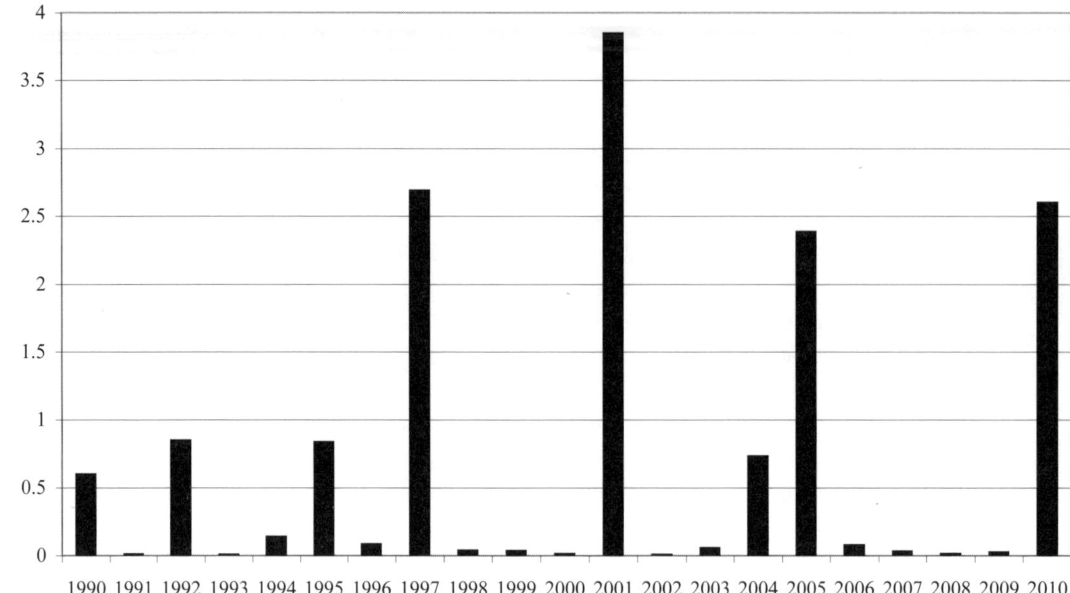

Sources: *INCSR* (2011), 137; *INCSR* (2009), 150; *INCSR* (2008), 154; *INCSR* (2007), 147; *INCSR* (2006), 129; *INCSR* (2005), 160; *INCSR* (2004), 132; *INCSR* (2003), 5:4; *INCSR* (2002), 5:3; *INCSR* (2000), 154; *INCSR* (1991), 136; DEA, *Resources, Belize* (2003), 3; DEA, *Resources, Belize* (2000), 1.

vulnerabilities of Belizean law enforcement, the magnitude of annual cocaine seizures was often correlated to the state of Belize-U.S. relations.

Belize–United States Relations

Over the years most Belizean administrations have valued a strong relationship with the United States government. Not only has the United States served as the country's principal trading partner, but U.S. tourists have contributed in increasingly important ways to the Belizean economy. Thanks in large part to its strong democratic traditions, Belize has also frequently led the region in U.S. foreign assistance per capita.[148] In turn, U.S. policy makers have normally viewed Belize as a particularly friendly neighboring state. Indeed, although numerous requests occurred, the U.S. government had never lost an application to have a suspected criminal extradited from Belize to the United States, until a technical mishap derailed an extradition bid in 2005.[149] Very few states could match that record of international cooperation with the United States in transnational criminal matters.

Nevertheless, just as drug transshipment via Belize climbed in the mid-1990s, Belizean interception rates and other counternarcotics work fell precipitately, straining Belize-U.S. relations. In 1995 the U.S. government bluntly declared that the government of Belize "does not give high priority to anti-drug efforts." In an unusually frank interview the following year, U.S. deputy chief of mission Gerard Gallucci told

148. "Drug Crops Are Up," A1. In 1985 U.S. economic and military aid stood at $24–34 million.

149. See "Kidnapped! Two Belize Men Flown to NY for Trial," *TR* (BZ), 4 May 2003, 1. For the first extradition application that the United States lost, see "U.S. Extradition Fails!," *TR* (BZ), 25 September 2005, 7; "More Fireworks, More Adjournments in Papa Brown's Extradition Case," *TR* (BZ), 14 August 2005, 1; and "Andrew 'Pawpa' Brown Wanted by the U.S.," *TR* (BZ), 24 July 2005, 1.

the media, "Belize is essentially uncontrolled territory. It is possible for drug traffickers to work with almost complete impunity. . . . The allure of Belize as a staging area for cocaine transfers has become great." In 1997 the Clinton administration notified Congress of the Belizean government's lackluster performance in countering the drug trade, stating, "Narcotics are transiting the country with little resistance." Assistant secretary of state Richard Gelbard cited inadequate seizures, high-level corruption, mismanaged investigations, and the failure to prosecute high-profile defendants. The State Department noted that Belizean traffickers were collaborating with Mexican organizations to transship Colombian cocaine to the United States and that the ability of Belizean officials "to combat them was severely undermined by deeply-entrenched corruption, which reaches into senior levels of government."[150]

Such critical comments emerged during the annual process through which the U.S. Congress has compelled the State Department to certify those countries cooperating in antidrug endeavors. Since denying Belize certification might threaten multilateral development bank funding supportive of democracy and development, the administration opted to invoke the national-interests exception. And U.S. criticism did prompt significant Belizean action aimed at raising interception rates. Later in 1997 Belizean officials organized and financed Operation Ides of March, through which seizures of 1,323 and 1,083 kilos helped to set an annual confiscation record.[151]

U.S. pressure, followed at first by Belizean denials and resistance and then by additional antidrug efforts, thus played into the larger process observed in various Central American bridge countries in which a state, confronting the wealth and power of transnational drug networks, retreats, persists, and at length reasserts itself in relation to the illicit global economy.[152] In Belize, the 1998 elections then brought to power a new PUP administration, which publicly ranked "combating narcotics trafficking and associated crime as a top priority," increasing the prospects for more sustained national antidrug efforts.[153] By March 1999 the U.S. government was again certifying Belize as cooperative.[154] More bilateral counternarcotics initiatives ensued, with the new extradition treaty coming into force in 2001, a mutual legal assistance agreement in 2003, and a Caribbean antidrug accord the following year.[155]

Certain tangible results followed renewed U.S.-Belizean cooperation. In 2001 Belizean authorities granted permission to the U.S. Navy to board the Belizean-flagged vessel the *Zvesda Mardu*, off the Mexican coast, leading to the seizure of twelve tons of cocaine, at the time the largest maritime cocaine bust ever recorded.[156] Yet the underlying problems that made Belize such an attractive bridge state remained unaddressed. In 2004 U.S. counternarcotics officials complained, "After five years in power, the People's United Party continues to advocate combating drug trafficking and associated crime as a top priority, but avoids providing the appropriate units with resources." They

150. *INCSR* (1997), xxxv; *INCSR* (1995), 119; "Belize Outraged at U.S. Criticism," *TR* (BZ), 9 March 1997, 1; "Corruption Seen in High Places," *BT* (BZ), 9 March 1997, 1; "U.S. Warns: The Gloves Are Off on Drugs, Stolen Cars, Smuggled Aliens," *TR* (BZ), 30 June 1996, 1; and "Belize Caught," A5. Although under the U.S. Foreign Assistance Act of 1961, codified as amended at 22 U.S.C. § 2151 (1994), the administration was obligated to report to Congress on Belizean antidrug actions, Belize lodged a formal diplomatic protest with the U.S. State Department concerning Galluci's remarks. "Diplomatic Row," *Latin American Weekly Report*, 25 July 1996, 336.

151. "Stung by U.S. Censure," 9.

152. See Friman and Andreas, *Illicit Global Economy*, 3.

153. *INCSR* (2000), 152.

154. See "U.S. Says It Is Satisfied with Belize's Efforts Against Drugs," *TR* (BZ), 7 March 1999, 9; and "Belize Taken Off Clinton's Black-list," *TR* (BZ), 21 November 1999, 1.

155. For the Agreement Concerning Co-Operation in Suppressing Illicit Maritime and Air Trafficking in Narcotic Drugs and Psychotropic Substances, see "Belize Ratifies Anti-drug Accord," *TR* (BZ), 17 October 2004, 6.

156. See *United States v. Savchenko*, 201 F.R.D. 503, and "Coast Guard in Record Drug Bust," *CBSNEWS.com*, 14 May 2001, www.cbsnews.com/2003-201_162-0-3974.html.

noted that an array of U.S. intelligence sources active in the narcotics field continued "to gather increasing evidence and information pointing to the fact that the [government of Belize] suffers from serious corruption problems at all levels."[157]

Thus, although U.S. pressure influenced the priorities of the Belizean government and stimulated increased cooperation, it did not dramatically alter Belize's place within the multipolar system of Central American drug trafficking. While occasional busts and arrests have occurred, foreign and domestic law enforcement efforts within Belize have yet to stem the flow of hard drugs for a sustained period. Although the U.S. government has provided particular useful resources—computers, a coast guard vessel, refurbished speedboats—such assets did not lead to steadily increasing interception rates, nor did they alter the fundamental institutional weaknesses that prevented more effective counternarcotics campaigns from being launched.

Drug-Trafficking Routes and Organizations in Belize

As Central American drug transit climbed, foreign and domestic criminal syndicates used an array of routes to try to slip drugs past Belizean authorities. Although the drug trade eventually touched virtually all parts of the country, the five most prominent centers of activity were Belize City, the Guatemalan border and western Belize, Orange Walk in northern Belize, Big Creek in southern Belize, and Ambergris and the other Belize cayes. Examining them illuminates how and when the marijuana and cocaine trades enveloped much of the country and spotlights certain of the principal actors.

Belize City

Long maligned by its critics for its inadequate sewage and extensive petty crime, while hailed by its supporters for its rakish tropical charm, Belize City has traditionally stood as the country's largest urban area and chief port. The city's flaws have been well chronicled: "the destruction of periodic tropical storms, overcrowding, narrow streets, open sanitary sewers, poor health conditions, inadequate water supply, continual subjection to insects, rats, pests, invasions of land crabs, extreme heat, and high humidity."[158] Nevertheless, by the 1990s Belize City, located just north of the midpoint of the Belizean coastline, contained nearly fifty thousand residents, or roughly a fifth of the population. After observing that Belize City inhabitants "are not in an easy position to obtain any kind of wealth," one scholar noted that "much of the population . . . gains its income mainly from informal opportunities."[159] Unsurprisingly, as Central American drug-trafficking increased the city swiftly became a vital drug-transshipment hub.

In words strikingly applicable to Belize and Belize City, one authority has written of narco-criminality in Caribbean states, "Drug barons, dons, . . . 'bigmen,' and international entrepreneurs all have connections with government, commercial houses, and political party bosses. Overlapping, vertically-integrated chains of patron-client relationships, ripple throughout society connecting top to bottom, eventually to the unemployed, disaffected youth who hustle, scrap, scuffle, retail, and kill each other."[160] By the early 1990s serious gang activity, fueled by international cocaine trafficking and a booming domestic crack-cocaine market, very much plagued Belize City, particularly its poverty-stricken south side. While Rastafarians and others had long dealt marijuana, the more lucrative local crack distribution stimulated deadly competitive contests.[161] Furthermore, for at least the past two decades, gangs have provided muscle for international trafficking ventures, while increasingly participating in moving drug shipments, at first largely within

157. *INCSR* (2004), 134.
158. Odaffer, "Three Capitals," 14.
159. Everitt, "Growth and Development," 110, and 110n175.
160. Brana-Shute, "Narco-criminality," 109.
161. See, for instance, "Thirty-Eight of Forty-Five Belize City Murders on Southside!," *AM* (BZ), 1 September 2009, 1.

the city's vicinity and then much farther afield over time.[162] Foreign connections of Belizean gangs have also involved members in distribution abroad, and, with time, certain gang leaders have risen to international prominence in the drug trade.[163]

For many years significant drug loads have transited right through Belize City, either via air, over land, or through speedboats, small freighters, or coastal fishing and supply vessels. One striking trend has been the ever-larger individual shipments involved. A U.S. federal court case in 1964 detailed marijuana smuggling inside foot lockers.[164] By the mid-1980s typical trafficking in central Belize involved luggage or boxes containing at most 100 or 200 kilos of marijuana, directed through the port or airport.[165] Eventually, cocaine transshippers adopted the very paths through the Belize City area once established by marijuana smugglers.

As these routes proved successful, drug syndicates utilized them for bigger shipments. In a key drug case in 1988 the Serious Crimes Squad found about 5.5 kilos of cocaine at a motel just outside of Belize City.[166] Two years later, authorities intercepted nearly 190 kilos of cocaine just north of the city; discovered flight plans, cash, and another 55 kilos in a city hotel; and broke up a Miami-based operation involving Colombians, Hondurans, and Belizeans.[167] In 1991, 273 kilos of cocaine slipped past the authorities when a plane transiting the country landed for refueling at the municipal, not the international, airport.[168] Over the next two years cocaine smugglers sent into Belize from Honduras on commercial airliners a series of 100-kilo shipments inside filters for hot-water heaters.[169] In 1995 the Belize police confiscated 650 kilos of Cali cartel cocaine, hidden in the ceiling of a city apartment.[170] Considerable rhetoric followed, with promises of tougher enforcement and joint Belize-U.S. law-enforcement missions. In 1996, however, the smell of drugs so thoroughly overcame a U.S. counternarcotics canine unit, sent to Belize City's central port buildings, that the dogs suffered from sensory overload and had to be pulled out of the warehouses![171]

Two leading twenty-first-century cocaine-trafficking cases, one centered on a foreign trafficker, another on a Belizean, illustrate both the growing magnitude of drug-transshipment operations through Belize City and notable characteristics of this dimension of the Belizean drug trade.

Jorge Torres Teyer

In 2001 Belizean authorities stumbled onto Jorge Torres Teyer, alleged to be, since 1995, the Mexican trafficker in charge of transshipment through Belize for the Southeast cell of the Juárez cartel.[172] On the run from Mexican

162. See "Belize Caught," 5A. "At [their] highest levels, gangs are used to move and distribute drugs. But at the intermediate and lower levels gangs provide infrastructure—manpower for errands, lookouts, enforcement." "Gang Proliferation in Belize City Symptom of a Much Bigger Problem!," *TR* (BZ), 7 February 1993, 4.

163. See, for instance, "Steve 'Insect' Reneau Nabbed in Miami on Drug Charges," *TR* (BZ), 31 July 2005, 11, and "Belizean Executed in Washington, D.C.," *TR* (BZ), 8 April 2001, 1.

164. *United States v. Stadter*, 336 F.2d at 326.

165. See, for instance, "Police Holding Two Strangers for Suitcase of Marijuana," *TR* (BZ), 10 November 1985, 1; "Dominican Republic Pair Fined One Hundred Thousand Dollars for Drugs," *TR* (BZ), 1 December 1985, 6; and "Charged for Trying to Export Marijuana," *TR* (BZ), 27 March 1988, 15.

166. "Big Cocaine Haul," *BT* (BZ), 31 July 1988, 16, and "Cocaine Bust Yields Twelve Lbs.," *TR* (BZ), 31 July 1988, 1.

167. See "Belize Strikes at Colombian Connection," *BT* (BZ), 14 October 1990, 1, and "Six Hundred Lbs. of Refined Cocaine is a Prize too Hot to Handle," *TR* (BZ), 14 October 1990, 1.

168. See "Drug Planes at Municipal!," *TR* (BZ), 7 October 1990, 1, and "Police Bribery Case," *TR* (BZ), 3 February 1991, 1.

169. See "One Hundred Kilos Cocaine Discovery," *AM* (BZ), 21 September 1992, 7; "Authorities Target TAN/SAHSA for Contraband Coke," *TR* (BZ), 23 August 1992, 1; "Cops Destroy Cocaine Worth $5 Million," *TR* (BZ), 14 March 1993, A; and "Eighty-Nine Kilos of Cocaine Found at International Airport," *AM* (BZ), 14 August 1992, 1.

170. "Major Drug Bust," *BT* (BZ), 15 January 1995, 1.

171. *INCSR* (1997), 122. See also "Belize by Sea," A28.

172. See *United States v. Torres-Teyer*, 322 F. Supp. 2d 359; *United States v. Torres-Teyer*, 2006 U.S. Dist. LEXIS 88150; and *United States v. Magana*, 147 Fed. Appx. 200. See also "Mexico's Most Wanted in Hattieville Prison," *TR*

police Torres had gained Belizean citizenship for fifteen thousand dollars just eight days before his arrest. He was initially brought into custody after police stopped him for driving the wrong direction on a one-way street in Belize City, and the trafficker attempted to bribe the officers with cocaine. After further inquiries, authorities conducted a predawn raid that netted 1,532 kilos of cocaine at an apartment complex just north of Belize City, which led, in turn, to the arrest of Torres, three other Mexicans, and a Belizean.[173]

The network's modus operandi involved speedboats dispatched from Colombia as well as larger Colombian vessels that off-loaded Medellín cocaine shipments, usually of about 1,500 kilos, to smaller Belizean boats. After entering Belizean territory, the drugs were next directed toward the small Mexican town of Calderitas, just north of Chetumal on the Yucatán coast, for shipment on to the United States. The drug ring included Belizeans Liston McCord, a former senior patrol officer of the Fisheries Department with extensive knowledge of Belizean territorial waters, and George Enrique Herbert, who owned a boat-building business and, over time, had developed extensive Mexican and Colombian connections. Herbert was also deeply involved with one of the country's most violent gangs, the George Street Crew of Belize City.[174]

Most "chilling" in the view of the U.S. federal judge who oversaw his trial were Torres's handwritten instructions to the boat captains he employed: "If purported customers did not give the correct password, they should 'shoot them all and kill them.' Similarly, if those claiming to be customers did not deliver the appropriate amounts of money, in correctly colored suitcases handed over in the previously agreed sequence, Torres instructed his subordinates to 'kill them all.'" This was, indeed, an extensive and extremely violent criminal network.

According to Mexican investigative journalists, Torres also masterminded a stolen-car ring in Chetumal, working with Belizean partner Harold Sheran to supply to Belizean elites luxury cars, outfitted with false vehicle identification numbers. Sheran may also have been linked to the drug trade, as authorities searching his ranch found aviation fuel, a thirty-one-foot Mexican skiff, and sophisticated radio-communication equipment. In 2001 gunmen in a convoy of vehicles with tinted windows suddenly arrived at the Belizean farm where Sheran was staying, abducting him and his brother-in-law as well as a farm assistant and his wife. All disappeared without a trace, with the kidnappers overlooking only a Salvadoran cook, hiding on the premises. That same day, unknown assailants in Chetumal strangled Sheran's wife to death. This rash of violence is typical of the settling of accounts that has regularly occurred within and between drug-trafficking organizations in Central America.[175]

Prominent Medellín trafficker Mauricio Ruda Álvarez reportedly supplied much of the cocaine to the Torres network, and, at length, this collaboration turned violent as well. In 2002 Ruda, suspicions aroused by a stolen cocaine shipment, reportedly ordered George Herbert to be seized. Four gunmen, armed with assault rifles, kidnapped Herbert at his Belize City office. A boatyard employee witnessed the assault and followed in a high-speed chase that eventually two police cruisers joined. After a shoot-out that injured one officer, the kidnappers tried to force Herbert onto a boat on the Belize River, but he dove into the water and

(BZ), 21 October 2001, 1; "Belize: Three Mexicans Who Faced Drug Charges Are Deported to USA," BBC Monitoring Latin America, 27 August 2002; "Friends of Herbert and McCord Threaten Cops and Ministers!," *AM* (BZ), 30 April 2003, 1; and "Sparks Fly in Moreno Drug Trafficking Case," *BT* (BZ), 5 March 2002.

173. See "Cops Seize 1,500 Kilos of Cocaine in Pre-dawn Raid," *TR* (BZ), 14 October 2001, 3.

174. See "Kidnapped!," 1; "George Herbert Seeks Court Order," *TR* (BZ), 19 October 2003, 1; and "Federal Jury Convicts Herbert," *TR* (BZ), 19 December 2004, 1.

175. "After a Six-Month Investigation, Police Discover a Scapegoat," *TR* (BZ), 12 May 2002, 11.

eluded capture. Some weeks later, Ruda himself was murdered, his corpse found stuffed in a car trunk in Medellín. Within two months of Torres's arrest, the headless corpse of David Reyes, reportedly an informant in the case, bobbed up in the Belize River. This, then, resulted in the suspension of two other police officers, since Reyes had been enrolled in a clearly ineffective police-protection program.[176]

Although Belizean authorities held Jorge Torres Teyer for trial for many months, it became increasingly clear that the legal system was unlikely to successfully prosecute, convict, and securely imprison such a prominent Mexican trafficker. According to the country's leading newspaper, at a court appearance in April 2002, Torres smirked when chief magistrate Herbert Lord postponed the trial on grounds that a court interpreter had turned out to be "unavailable" on account of sickness. By the following month, not only had the trial been adjourned twice for lack of translation services in a largely bilingual country, but charges had been dropped against McCord, in whose van much of the seized cocaine had been discovered. Then, in July Lord suddenly announced that in light of the illness of Bernard Pitts, former chair of the Belize Bar Association and a prominent lawyer handling the case, the trial would again be adjourned, not resuming until September. The *Reporter* recounted that the courtroom then rocked "with mirth" as the "not-so-sick Pitts walked into the courtroom to be informed by the Chief Magistrate that the trial was being adjourned because of his sickness."[177]

In August, after Belize officials were tipped that Torres planned to use explosives to break out of Hattieville Prison, they gave up on the prosecution, instead deporting the trafficker forthwith to the United States. At his U.S. trial Torres eventually pled guilty to conspiracy to import cocaine, as did various accomplices, and he was sentenced to serve thirty-eight years in prison.[178] A U.S. federal court concluded, "The evidence easily supports a finding that Torres Teyer's activities involved the importation of 15,000 kg, maybe more."[179] George Herbert and Mexican colleague Víctor Manuel Adán Carrasco received terms of thirty-four and a half years and twenty years, respectively, while Liston McCord was sentenced to ten years.

Robert Hertular

Another notable Belize City trafficker was Robert Hertular, who, with his brother, joined Herbert in the George Street Crew.[180] Not only does his career further illustrate the involvement of Belize City gangs in weighty cocaine shipments, but it demonstrates their international ties, influence within Belize, and ongoing efforts to corrupt and intimidate domestic and foreign officials.

Although over the years Hertular had numerous encounters with the Belizean police force, including arrests for forgery and shooting at a patrol car, he was never confined to prison for any lengthy term.[181] Authorities finally developed

176. "Cartel War Declared!," *TR* (BZ), 1 September 2002, 1, and "Kidnapped Man Escapes Abductors," *TR* (BZ), 8 September 2002, 14.

177. "Cocaine Trial Delayed," *TR* (BZ), 28 April 2002, 10; "McCord Walks," *TR* (BZ), 26 May 2002, 1; "Teller-Moreno Trial in a Holding Pattern," *TR* (BZ), 14 July 2002, 4; "Drug Kingpin Deported to the U.S.," *TR* (BZ), 1 September 2002, 4; and "Chetumal's Teflon Don A Killer at Heart!," *TR* (BZ), 8 September 2002, 4.

178. See *United States v. Torres-Teyer*, 2006 U.S. Dist. LEXIS 88150; "Guilty in New York!," *TR* (BZ), 15 June 2003, 1; and "George Herbert Breaks the Silence," *TR* (BZ), 4 January 2009, 1.

179. *United States v. Torres-Teyer*, 322 F. Supp. 2d at 371. A coconspirator that a U.S. federal court termed a "highly credible" cooperating witness testified that Torres had given orders relating to "more than a dozen cocaine shipments, generally in amounts of at least 1500 kilograms" (364).

180. See *United States v. Hertular*, 562 F.3d 433. See also "$70 M Cocaine Bust," *TR* (BZ), 13 May 2001, 1; "U.S. Wants Hertular to Stand Trial," *TR* (BZ), 1 February 2004, 4; and "Robert Hertular Convicted of Threats," *TR* (BZ), 5 March 2006, 35.

181. See "Hertulars Come Under Fire," *TR* (BZ), 20 October 1991, 12; "Accused Kidnapper Claims Sour Drug Deal to Blame," *TR* (BZ), 14 July 1996, 26; "Clever Forger Gets Caught and Sentenced," *TR* (BZ), 29 November 1998, 10; "Death Threats Send Belize Cops into Overdrive," *TR* (BZ), 4 May 2003, 1; and "Hertular Brothers Charged with Attempted Murder," *TR* (BZ), 21 September 2003, 3. In a

a solid case when DEA information led to a 2001 cocaine raid on a warehouse, uncovering more than 580 kilos of cocaine and producing the arrest of Hertular and four others. Information gained during interrogation led to a follow-up raid in Ladyville, just north of Belize City, where police found 570 kilos in an empty lot next to the Hertular family home. Both loads were thought to be en route to Mexico. Further U.S. investigations revealed that Hertular had dealt with both Mexican and Colombian traffickers. Indeed, the kingpin eventually admitted that he had arranged these and four other shipments, totaling more than 5 tons of cocaine, through his "personal friend" Carlos Castaño, leader of the Autodefensas Unidas de Colombia (AUC).[182]

Released on $125,000 bail, Hertular then surprised Vincent Williams, who directed the DEA office at the U.S. Embassy in Belize, by calling the agent's unlisted personal cell phone number to suggest a meeting. The two met, and Hertular admitted to transshipping large quantities of cocaine via Belize by sea and air, with the assistance of various high Belizean officials. He also presented to Williams a VHF radio and satellite phone that he claimed had been used to coordinate a recent cocaine shipment. The DEA, however, chose to decline Hertular's offer of additional information in exchange for leniency.

In 2003, as the Hertular case proceeded through the Belizean court system, Williams was conducting surveillance at a DEA confidential informant's house when Hertular arrived. The informant later reported that Hertular told him that a DEA car was outside and demanded to know whether he was cooperating with the U.S. government. When the informant denied it, Hertular ordered him to get rid of the surveillance. The gang leader offered hand grenades and then said he could do the job himself. When the informant rejected these "drastic options," Hertular left. Shortly thereafter, he and Williams confronted one another in a nearby parking lot, with Hertular declaring that he was tired of the DEA and the U.S. Embassy and was willing to kill an agent or other official, presumably to intimidate the authorities and short-circuit the case against him.

By the end of 2003, however, the DEA and federal prosecutors in New York were building a major cocaine-trafficking case against Hertular. As evidence was being assembled, the trafficker called DEA agent Raymond Kelly, recently assigned to Belize, again using an unlisted cell phone number. Perhaps to illustrate his extensive knowledge of counternarcotics personnel operating in Belize, Hertular suggested that he and Kelly meet near another DEA agent's residence. When Williams and Kelly met the Belizean trafficker, Hertular stated that he knew all about the impending U.S. legal action. After Kelly denied that an indictment was forthcoming, Hertular told him that his organization had tapped DEA's telephones, both landline and cellular. To prove it, he played a tape recording of a conversation between Kelly and a confidential informant regarding the alleged involvement of a senior Belizean official in the drug trade. Hertular also told the agent that he had sources within the U.S. Embassy providing him information, including the identities of DEA informants.

After raising again his offer of cooperation with the United States in exchange for dropping the federal indictment, Hertular revealed that for sixteen years he had participated in a Belizean organization that trafficked drugs and laundered money and, he alleged, was led by past and present officials at the very pinnacle of the government. Hertular told the agents that if they did not back off their investigation, he would have to protect his interests, and he

case for possessing 2.2 kilos of cocaine in 1990, on appeal, Hertular and codefendant James Swan were fined $17,500 each, or in default six years of imprisonment. *Broaster v. Swan and Hertular*, Sup. Ct. of Belize, Inferior Ct. App. No. 14.

182. See "Drug Target Is Extradited from Belize," *New York Daily News*, 27 July 2004, 32.

claimed that his network would not hesitate to support him by hiring Colombian or Mexican hit men to kill them.[183] Once again, however, the DEA agents turned Hertular down, opting instead to proceed with the case against him.

In 2004 a New York grand jury indicted Robert Hertular on charges of narcotics trafficking, obstruction of justice, and forcibly impeding and attempting to intimidate a federal officer. Within three weeks Belizean officers had arrested Hertular. In most Central American countries the rendition of a national citizen accused of international drug trafficking would be extremely difficult to accomplish. At the least, it would be highly controversial. And yet, in another example of Belizean-U.S. cooperation during a period of normal relations, Hertular was swiftly extradited and in 2006 found guilty at a jury trial.[184] A federal appellate judge who had reviewed the case later observed, "The trial evidence convincingly demonstrated that in the period between 2001 and January 2004, Belizean national Robert Hertular conspired with others to import more than six tons of cocaine into the United States."

Western Belize

Drug rings operating in Belize City have relied on all of the city's legitimate activity to mask smuggling, while taking advantage of the poverty, gangs, and local drug markets as well. Traffickers operating outside of the city have frequently exploited the country's lack of national integration, directing transshipment toward out-of-the-way places: vacant coastlines and jungle clearings, swampland and solitary farms and ranches, infrequently traveled roads and distant inland lagoons and other waterways. Not only is much of western Belize quite remote, but this is a fluid border region: Belize shares with Guatemala a 165-mile boundary, and with Mexico, a 155-mile boundary.[185]

Among the handful of notable urban areas in western Belize, San Ignacio is a small city located in the Mountain Pine Ridge foothills of the Maya Mountains, approximately twenty miles west of Belmopan and near the midpoint of the country's boundary with Guatemala. Once a quiet center for cattle farming and various trades in the Cayo district, San Ignacio long played a modest part in marijuana trafficking, with some cannabis being grown locally, especially in the hills and jungle south of the city.[186] With time, the cocaine trade reached San Ignacio: by the 1990s crack houses had sprung up.[187] Then in 2010 alleged major Guatemalan trafficker Otoniel Turcios Marroquín, found to be quietly living with his family in San Ignacio, was arrested and expelled to the United States.[188]

In fact, networks exporting and importing drugs had long capitalized on the porous border region. As Belizean eradication efforts increased in the 1980s, considerable marijuana came to be

183. After this conversation was reported to the embassy, the U.S. government then instituted more stringent security measures to protect DEA personnel and diplomats in Belize, traditionally considered a low-risk post.

184. While, on appeal, Hertular persuaded the appellate court that the evidence had been insufficient to show that he had the present ability to inflict injury to the DEA agents, thus obviating the charge related to forcibly impeding or intimidating a federal officer, his convictions for obstructing justice and importing and distributing drugs were upheld. *United States v. Hertular*, 562 F.3d at 433, 435.

185. CIA, *World Factbook, 1991*, 31.

186. See, for instance, "Anti Drug Forces Destroy Arenal Marijuana," *TR* (BZ), 8 November 1987, 10; "Police Destroy 4,307 Ganja Trees," *TR* (BZ), 11 June 1989, 8D; "Cayo Drug Raid," *BT* (BZ), 23 July 1989, 20; "Police News," *BT* (BZ), 12 November 1989, 8B; and "Using 'All Means Available,' Marin Vows to Punish Drug Traffickers," *TR* (BZ), 29 October 1989, 1.

187. See "Cayoans Express Concern over Drug-Peddling Menace," *TR* (BZ), 3 February 1991, 5; "Notorious Crack Houses," *AM* (BZ), 20 March 1992, 23 (lengthy letter to the editor by a San Ignacio resident); and "Police Seize Abandoned Coke," *TR* (BZ), 17 December 1995, 3.

188. "Police: Wanted Drug Dealer Was Arrested in Belize and Expelled," *AM* (BZ), 1 November 2010, 1, and "Accused Guatemalan Drug Lord Expelled from Belize," *AM* (BZ), 2 November 2010, 1.

imported from Guatemala's vast El Petén region, flanking the Cayo district.[189] Along the border, logging tracks and other dirt roads cut through the dense tropical forest, approaching and even crossing the boundary. In this area marijuana has been smuggled into Belize in vans stolen in Guatemala or, during the rainy season, in four-wheel-drive vehicles.[190] In March 1991, for instance, Belizean police confiscated 924 and 1,160 kilos of marijuana from a van and a hiding place off a Cayo district road, then in the succeeding two months authorities stopped three vehicles in the San Ignacio vicinity, seizing 1,711 kilos of marijuana in one and a total of 1,063 kilos in the other two, all imported from El Petén.[191]

While Belizean traffickers for a time are likely to have imported tons of Guatemalan marijuana into Belize undetected, some cannabis and much cocaine came to flow in the opposite direction as well: from Belize into Guatemala. In fact, as Central American transshipment surged, both Guatemala and Mexico emerged as key stepping stones toward the U.S. drug market. Thus, small communities on Belizean borders, such as Blue Creek Village, across the Río Hondo from La Unión, Mexico, and Arenal and Benque Viejo del Carmen, facing Guatemala, became deeply entangled in the drug trade.[192] In 1991 the leading Belizean newspaper reported, "La Unión, a deceptively sleepy village perched on a curve of the Río Hondo, has become a major contraband port. At nighttime the river becomes a bustling waterway for all types of contraband, ranging from whiskey and television sets to diesel and gasoline motor fuel. On the outflow Belize exports cocaine and marijuana."[193] Eventually, though to little avail, the Mexican government tried to pressure Belize to stem the flow of Colombian cocaine from Orange Walk into Mexico via La Unión.

In truth, traffickers in western Belize could capitalize on the spotty international cooperation noted earlier. If joint police work between Belize and Mexico left much to be desired, the outlook for cooperation with Guatemalan officials was nothing short of dismal. As Guatemalan politicians disputed with Belizean counterparts over territorial claims, counternarcotics authorities rarely shared information, and the countries' respective border patrols much more frequently clashed with one another than joined forces against drug rings active in this zone. Hence, on those rare occasions when authorities have come upon smugglers, they have often simply fled across the boundary to

189. For the statement by U.S. ambassador Robert Rich, see "Medellín Drug Connection," 1. See also "Marijuana from El Petén Means Problems for Belize," *TR* (BZ), 3 March 1991, C; and "Ganga Growers Split," 14. For a representative case of a police roadblock intercepting 190 kilos of Guatemalan marijuana, see "Three Belizeans Freed, Guat Convicted of Western Highway Weed," *AM* (BZ), 25 October 1991, 4.

190. DEA, *Resources, Belize* (2000), 4. For marijuana eradication in the vicinity of the remote Caracol archaeological site, a significant cannabis production zone since the early 1990s, see "Guats Livid over Border Shooting," *TR* (BZ), 30 January 2000, 1, and "Another Guat Demand," *AM* (BZ), 30 January 2000, 1.

191. See "Drug Busts," *BT* (BZ), 17 March 1991, 1; "Border Patrol Finds 3,300 Pound Stash of Marijuana," *TR* (BZ), 17 March 1991, 1; "Police Capture Van with a Ton of Weed," *TR* (BZ), 17 March 1991, 5; "Cops Seize Van with 3,560 Lbs. of Marijuana," *TR* (BZ), 7 April 1991, 4; "Western Highway Drug Bust," *BT* (BZ), 7 April 1991, 1; "More Arrests in Major Drug Bust," *BT* (BZ), 14 April 1991, 1; "Drug Plane Crashes," *BT* (BZ), 26 May 1991, 1; "Narcotraffickers Burn Damaged Aircraft!," *TR* (BZ), 26 May 1991, 16; and "Serious Crimes Squad Foils Another Van-Load of Weed," *TR* (BZ), 16 June 1991, 6. The following January authorities seized 739 kilos traveling east from Guatemala. "BDF Soldier on Trial for Drug Trafficking," *AM* (BZ), 10 January 1992, insert. Note that the five seizures alone belie the assertion of the U.S. BINM that a mere 800 kilos of cannabis were seized in Belize in 1991. *INCSR* (1999), 141. Indeed, this thriving intraregional drug trade seems to have largely escaped the notice of U.S. officials compiling statistics on Belizean marijuana trafficking.

192. For a 1,500-kilo marijuana discovery just off the Arenal–Benque Viejo road and one of more than 580 kilos on the Western Highway, with the arrest of the driver, a Benque Viejo resident, see "Border Patrol Finds 3,300 Pound Stash," 1, and "Another Successful Drug Bust," *BT* (BZ), 16 June 1991, 1.

193. "Narcotraffickers Burn," 1.

avoid capture.[194] Equally problematic, Belizean traffickers have sometimes tried to insulate themselves from possible murder charges by employing foreign hit men, whom the Belize police have found much more difficult to identify, trace, arrest, and prosecute.[195] In 1998 senior superintendent Malicio Uk of the Police Intelligence Unit, Special Branch, reported that Belizean drug organizations had been employing Guatemala's Mano Negra gang as enforcers: gunmen had been contacted in Guatemala and provided with information and a plan; they had then carried out the hit, collected compensation, and returned home. A key lesson here is that transnational organized crime thrives where politics inhibit cross-border police work.

Furthermore, Belize and Guatemala were interdependent in the sense that drug-trade developments in one often deeply affected the other. In the 1990s Guatemala established itself as the preeminent Central American cocaine-transshipment target, with efficient domestic trafficking organizations employing well-established routes into Mexico and the United States. Hence, once cocaine reached Guatemala, the vast bulk proceeded north to the U.S. market. Thus, unsurprisingly, the same pattern identified elsewhere in the country—cocaine trafficking succeeding that of marijuana—marked the evolution of the drug trade in this Cayo district.[196] At the same time, however, cocaine loads that doubled back into Belize have not only supplied local drug markets but varied drug-smuggling patterns and in that way helped traffickers to evade official detection.[197] Thus, while cocaine has primarily flowed in a northerly direction, a countercurrent has passed through the region around San Ignacio.

Northern Belize

Although central and western Belize have played notable roles in developing the marijuana and cocaine trades, the northern region has long eclipsed them. Historically, northern Belize was closely tied to Mexico's Yucatán Peninsula. In the mid-nineteenth century the British supported the revolt by Yucatán natives against the colonial government, and during the long fighting in the Caste War (1847–1901), British Honduras provided refuge for people fleeing the Yucateco Army trying to reimpose the governor's authority. Indeed, these very Mexican refugees helped to settle Ambergris Caye as well as much of the Corozal and Orange Walk districts, and family and commercial links to the Yucatán have been maintained ever since.[198]

It has often been hypothesized that free trade policies encourage drug smuggling, although extensive supporting evidence is less frequently offered. The situation in northern Belize, however, is certainly one case in point. This region depends on the Yucatán for much of its imports and exports. Chetumal, the capital of Mexico's Quintana Roo state and a city of 120,000, has long been a Mexican "free port," and the Belizean government eventually designated Corozal, the closest town to the northern border and the third largest in Belize at eight

194. In one such 1991 incident, authorities surprised six Guatemalan smugglers, who dropped sixty-six kilos of marijuana and swam across the border to evade pursuit. "Traffickers Drop Booty and Swim," *TR* (BZ), 27 January 1991, 15. For a similar case involving a smaller amount of marijuana, with Guatemalan smugglers caught crossing the Mopan River, see "Women Held for Drug Possession," *TR* (BZ), 8 November 1992, 3.

195. See "Guatemalan Was the Hired Gun," *TR* (BZ), 6 July 1997, 1, and "Mano Negra Gang Now Active in Belize," *TR* (BZ), 21 June 1998, 6. For Mexican hit men active in Belize, see "Zetina Shot Dead Execution Style," *TR* (BZ), 14 May 2006, 1, and "Mennonite executed in Corozal Free Zone," *AM* (BZ), 22 August 2008, 1.

196. See *INCSR* (1992), 141, and DEA, *Resources, Belize* (2000), 2.

197. For a representative case in which police found twenty-four kilos of cocaine in a pickup that entered Belize from Melchor de Mencos and sped through a road block, see "Cayo Cops Impound Truck with Cocaine Bricks," *TR* (BZ), 26 February 2010, 1.

198. See "Bad News from Isla Bonita," *AM* (BZ), 23 March 2010, 1

thousand inhabitants, a commercial free zone as well. These development policies increased border traffic, easing the challenge of masking illicit goods within the flow of legitimate commerce. The key drug connections in northern Belize have joined Belizean traffickers with counterparts in Chetumal, a leading drug-transshipment center. Indeed, as early as the 1980s a steady traffic of couriers, planes, and vehicles had started to export drugs from northern Belize into Quintana Roo. With Mexican traffickers having thoroughly penetrated the U.S. market, a sizable slice of Belizean marijuana exports and a significant portion of transshipped cocaine traveled north into the Yucatán overland or by sea.

Drug-trafficking organizations capitalize on a sense of futility among officials, which as in this customs post, leads directly to lack of effort as well as to corruption. Encouraging vigilance among poorly compensated and undertrained officials is a common problem afflicting border customs officials across the region. On the Belize-Mexico border, customs authorities at Santa Elena have been lax, earning long-standing suspicions of corruption. However, dedicating scarce resources to improving drug interdiction at the border has seemed futile, when anyone wishing to avoid the officials could select from scores of remote crossings that had no controls whatsoever.[199] Once again, severe budgetary constraints have hampered counternarcotics policies, while the impossibility of trying to seal off borders has demoralized officials.

Reflective of considerable overland drug export, villages neighboring Corozal, including San Pedro, San Narciso, and Chan Chen, gained reputations as trafficking centers.[200] In a typical 1986 case, customs officials at Santa Elena intercepted an American and two Belizeans attempting to export to Mexico 137 kilos of marijuana.[201] The following year Corozal police discovered a storehouse holding 569 kilos of marijuana.[202] As cocaine trafficking took hold, law enforcement discovered increasingly large quantities being moved through far northern Belize. Thus, where authorities found 212 kilos of cocaine being stored in villages near Corozal in 1992, nine years later they located fully 1,161 kilos near Carmelita.[203] It may be that when confronting a porous border with no choke point through which drug shipments must be funneled, antidrug operations aimed at uncovering storage sites near the border may produce more seizures than trying to redouble efforts at lackluster, corrupted, or frequently bypassed customs posts.

Also at the northern extreme of Belize, the towns of Sarteneja and Consejo became notable drug conduits. Perched on the tip of a remote and swampy peninsula just across Chetumal Bay from Mexico, Sarteneja is easily reached by water or air, although authorities might take three hours or more to traverse the forty-mile road from Orange Walk. This tiny settlement exemplifies the remote Belizean settlements, far off the tourist track and historically dependent on subsistence fishing, which have been especially vulnerable to the drug trade. Early on, Sarteneja came to serve as a drug-trafficking hub, with authorities regularly discovering drugs, paraphernalia, aviation fuel, and suspect boats and planes.[204] Despite the settlement's very small population, notable busts elsewhere in the country have frequently included the

199. *INCSR* (2002), 5:4.

200. For trafficking in San Pedro, just southwest of Corozal, see "Village Shootout Baffles Police," *TR* (BZ), 31 March 1991, 1. A 1988 bust near Chan Chen, northwest of Corozal, turned up 182 kilos of marijuana leaves, 6.4 kilos of seed, and five hundred mature marijuana plants. "Chan Chen Raid Snares Three," *TR* (BZ), 16 October 1988, 4.

201. See "Cops Nab Three for Marijuana," *TR* (BZ), 16 November 1986, 6, and "Two Freed, One Fined for Marijuana," *TR* (BZ), 8 March 1987, 12. For a similar case, see "Cops Hold Texan for Marijuana," *TR* (BZ), 11 October 1987, 14.

202. "Police Seize 1,252 Pounds of Marijuana in Town House Raid," *TR* (BZ), 8 March 1987, 4.

203. See "Legal Arguments Slow Cocaine Case," *TR* (BZ), 23 August 1992, 1, and "Herbert and McCord," 1.

204. See, for instance, "Police Discover Aviation Fuel," *BT* (BZ), 3 March 1996, 27; "Drug Traffickers Were Tipped Off," *BT* (BZ), 5 May 1996, 1; and "Caye Hunt Finds $3 M[illion] of Cocaine," *TR* (BZ), 16 February 1997, 1.

arrest of its residents.[205] In the late 1980s the suspicious activities of one Colombian alien living in Sarteneja included a hidden compartment in his vehicle, reported airdrops onto his property of a white powder the man claimed was screwworm medicine for what turned out to be a nonexistent cattle herd, and the unauthorized bulldozing of a concrete barrier the government had erected to prevent planes from landing on the nearby airstrip. Although these incidents led to the Colombian's deportation, trafficking through Sarteneja continued to climb, with occasional large busts interspersed with regular suspected visits by drug planes, including one in October 2010.[206]

Consejo is also well suited for trafficking ventures: on the coast at the end of a road angling northeast from Corozal. Speedboats can cover the fifteen miles to Chetumal in twenty-five minutes. In a representative 1996 case a light Colombian-registered aircraft attempted to land on the Corozal-Consejo road. Although the BDF, tipped by the DEA, was poised to intercept, a collaborator hidden nearby fired two shots to warn off the pilot. When authorities discovered the plane, crash-landed in Sarteneja, they located more than 368 kilos of Cali cartel cocaine, although the pilot and the remainder of the load had disappeared.[207] Two police officers, members of the Corozal Quick Response Unit, were strongly suspected of involvement in this and other suspicious incidents, including one in which authorities in charge of a highway drug checkpoint seized one of the officers' cars, after a wild chase in which the occupants fled into the bush. Although the vehicle contained five kilos of cocaine and thirty-four thousand dollars, chief magistrate Herbert Lord acquitted the officers for insufficient evidence in a "dramatic and unexpected outcome," according to the country's leading newspaper. A follow-up police inquiry also failed to assemble a convincing case against the men.[208]

While Corozal, Sarteneja, and Consejo were part of the drug trafficking machinery in northern Belize, drug organizations in the inland city of Orange Walk have traditionally been the engine driving the trade. About forty miles northwest of Belize City and twenty-five miles from the border, it long functioned as the seat of a sizable marijuana production and export trade. Although the country's second-largest city, Orange Walk contained a mere twelve thousand inhabitants, according to the 1993 census. Nevertheless, it emerged as such a vibrant center of cocaine consumption and transshipment that the U.S. government termed Orange Walk "the leading area of drug activity in Belize." U.S. dollars were said to circulate more freely than Belizean dollars, and the *Belize Times* lamented the city's many prominent citizens imprisoned in the United States or Mexico on narcotics charges.[209]

In the 1980s small airplanes frequently landed around Orange Walk to be packed with marijuana, much of it grown nearby, and

205. See, for example, "Cops Expose Belize Hub of Drug Operation," *TR* (BZ), 11 May 1997, 1, and "Colombians Go to Jail, Mexicans Are Deported," *TR* (BZ), 27 July 1997, 9.

206. "Expulsion Order to Jaime Muñoz Gonzalez," *Belize Government Gazette*, 27 January 1990, 81–82. After officials reviewed these suspicious activities, they filed an expulsion order, stating, "[it is] for the welfare of the country that you be so expelled." See also "Colombian Drug Suspect Deported," *BT* (BZ), 28 January 1990, 1, and "Suspected Drug Plane Lands in Sarteneja Village?," *AM* (BZ), 15 October 2010, 1.

207. See "$30 M[illion] in Cocaine Abandoned as Drug-Running Planes Forced Down," *TR* (BZ), 5 May 1996, 1, and "Drug Traffickers Were Tipped Off," *BT* (BZ), 5 May 1996, 1.

208. See "Cops Escape Drug Charges," *TR* (BZ), 13 February 2000, 10; "Corozal Cops Shed Trafficking Charges," *TR* (BZ), 18 April 1999, 6; and "Rogue Cops on the Lam," *TR* (BZ), 6 July 1997, 1, 3.

209. See *INCSR* (1997), 124, and "Orange Walk," *BT* (BZ), 31 August 1986, 14.See also "DEA Says Drug Plane Loaded with Cocaine Passed Through," *TR* (BZ), 17 December 1989, 1; "In the Republic of Orange Walk the Drug Barons' Men Are Taking Over," *TR* (BZ), 4 November 1990, 1; "O[range] Walk Cocaine Capital of Belize!," *TR* (BZ), 16 February 1992, 6; and "Key Arrest Follows Inquiry into Orange Walk Drug Ring," *TR* (BZ), 26 May 1996, 1.

flown on to the U.S. market. Indeed, marijuana smugglers carried on their operations so brazenly as to delay traffic on district roads, including even the Northern Highway, while drug planes landed, loaded, refueled, and took off.[210] Although the government erected large poles along the shoulders of favored stretches of roads, smugglers routinely avoided or destroyed them.[211] In a representative 1988 case, one evening patrolling police spotted a twin-engine Cessna plane that had touched down on a secondary road north of Orange Walk.[212] As they approached, the plane took off, but the police seized abandoned vehicles nearby, including a pickup truck containing nearly three hundred kilos of compressed marijuana. Two members of the locally prominent Campos family were soon arrested, with media reports indicating that Fortunato Campos had left his passport in a car found at the scene. Several months earlier, authorities had accused Urbano Campos of bribing police and the BDF to ignore another drug plane landing in these environs, to which the DEA had tipped the Belizean government. Although suspicions persisted that the Campos family had been involved, the authorities failed to compile evidence sufficient to prove that any family member had participated in these cases.[213]

Certainly, drug networks extensively employed numerous clandestine airstrips in the Orange Walk vicinity, relying on foreigners as well as local residents, usually heavily armed, to guard them.[214] Typically located within large or quite isolated farms and ranches, the runways were often surrounded by jungle or dense crops such as corn or sugar cane. In 1988 a Belizean newspaper observed, "The tall cane fields make a perfect cloak for clandestine operations since the aircraft can only be seen during landing and takeoff operations. At all other times the refueling can take place in broad daylight with reasonable secrecy."[215] With business thriving by the mid- to late 1980s, the busiest of these runways could service a half-dozen planes over several days.[216]

Incidents such as one in 1989, in which British Forces Belize seized a truck near Orange Walk containing 1,453 kilos of marijuana, demonstrate how large were some of the cannabis loads handled by these traffickers.[217] Furthermore, DEA information, elicited through undercover work, confidential informants, government witnesses, and wiretaps, exposed rampant drug trafficking and corruption.[218] Such

210. See "Belize: No More," C2; "Police Intercept Drug Delivery but Pilot and Runners Escape," *TR* (BZ), 24 July 1988, 5; "Highway Shootout Near Buena Vista," *TR* (BZ), 20 January 1991, 1; "O. W. Kidnap Victim Returns After Week's Disappearance," *TR* (BZ), 29 July 1991, 1; and "Minister's House Cased for Drugs," *BT* (BZ), 26 May 1996, 1.

211. "Crack, L.A.-Style Gangs Trouble Torpid Belize," *WP* (US), 19 September 1989, A23.

212. See "Police Intercept Drug Delivery," 5, and "Police Arrest Trio for Weed Plant Caper," *TR* (BZ), 31 July 1988, 5.See also "Attempting to Bribe BDF, Police," *BT* (BZ), 24 April 1988, 16; "Bribery in BDF," *BT* (BZ), 17 April 1988, 1; "BDF Gang of Five Held for Court Martial," *TR* (BZ), 8 May 1988, 1; "San Narciso Family Safe After Kidnap Experience," *TR* (BZ), 7 February 1993, 1; and "Pays Ten Thousand Dollars Ransom for His Son," *AM* (BZ), 5 February 1993, 1.

213. Rivals often threatened Belizean traffickers more than the criminal-justice system did. Five years later, Fortunato Campos was kidnapped, along with five family members, in a dispute allegedly involving another drug deal, this one gone sour. In 1999 Armando "Warran" Gomez, termed the area's "richest and most powerful drug lord," was shot in the head and eventually died. "O[range] Walk Drug Boss Dies Following Week-Long Coma," *TR* (BZ), 25 April 1999, 1.

214. For an example of an Orange Walk district shootout between police and five Hispanic gunmen using Uzi submachine guns and .357 caliber revolvers, see "Shoot-out with Narcos Frustrate Police Mission," *TR* (BZ), 17 February 1991, 4.

215. "Guinea Grass Execution Traced to Drug Plane," *TR* (BZ), 26 June 1988, 1.

216. For the informants' testimony of how the drug deal was delayed because four other planes were scheduled to fly to the designated airstrip, see *United States v. Lee*, 743 F.2d at 1243. Villagers at Chan Pine Ridge, south of Orange Walk, noted four drug plane landings in a week in 1989. "Drug Plane Stuck at Chan P. Ridge but Three Others Flew Clear!," *TR* (BZ), 19 November 1989, 1.

217. See "Major Marijuana Bust," 6B. For an Orange Walk residence doubling as a marijuana warehouse, see "Home Bust Yields 250 Lbs. Marijuana," *TR* (BZ), 17 May 1987, 9.

218. See, for instance, *United States v. Clem*, 2000 U.S. App. LEXIS 6395.

sources produce revealing snapshots of significant Orange Walk smuggling operations. For instance, in the early 1980s one farm, known as Rancho Grande, served as headquarters for a marijuana-export business, operative for many years.[219] From 1982 to 1984 the network, which came to include a government informant, imported at least five substantial marijuana shipments into the United States.[220]

Working out of the limelight but at the center of operations that were moving drugs through northern Belize were men like Perry and Paddy Franks, Canadian nationals residing in northern Belize during the 1980s.[221] In 1986 authorities broke up their ring when an individual contacted the DEA with information about a marijuana-smuggling conspiracy headed by James Gregory Smith. U.S. officials persuaded the contact to become an informant and then had an undercover agent pose as a conspirator claiming to be able to provide clandestine airstrips and support services. The informant traveled to Chetumal to meet the Franks brothers, who were to supply the marijuana and help arrange the landing site in Belize. Eventually, DEA agents loaded more than 360 kilos of marijuana into their own twin-engine plane and flew it to a Texas airstrip. At an Austin warehouse American conspirators weighed the drugs and were paying off the undercover agent when authorities moved in to arrest them. Shortly thereafter, Mexican Federal Police arrested the Frank brothers in Chetumal for a venture to import marijuana into Louisiana. Mexican authorities then expelled the pair to the United States. A Texas federal court convicted both of conspiring to import marijuana, and Perry Franks was also found guilty of marijuana trafficking into Louisiana.

Over time, more lucrative and violent cocaine trafficking completely overshadowed the earlier marijuana trade in northern Belize. In the mid- to late 1980s Medellín traffickers moved aggressively into Orange Walk, paying top dollar to use its drug rings to assist in forwarding large cocaine shipments.[222] Although most of the narcotics escaped interdiction, trafficking ventures were sometimes exposed. Occasionally, DEA informants or undercover operations led to major busts. At other times, local police happened upon crashed aircraft or drugs being stored or transported to an airstrip, or they managed to stop transshipment during vulnerable phases of the operation, such as refueling. In still other cases, foreign authorities seized drugs at their destination and determined that an Orange Walk route had been utilized.[223] Thus, in 1989 federal agents in Westchester, New York, seized 2,033 kilos of Medellín cocaine off a plane that had refueled near Orange Walk. The following year authorities confiscated nearly 360 kilos of cocaine after a plane accident at a clandestine airstrip off the Northern Highway.[224] In 1991 a suspected

219. "Owner Tells Court O.W. Rancho Grande Farm Was Used in Marijuana Smuggling Operations," *TR* (BZ), 1 April 1990, 1.

220. *United States v. Lindell*, 881 F.2d 1313. At least one shipment was a controlled delivery in which authorities allowed the drugs to proceed under surveillance to learn more about the entire trafficking-and-distribution network. In later court proceedings the informant named as the gang's Belizean suppliers Isaac Dyck and Rancho Grande owner Badner Hassan, leading a Texas grand jury to indict Hassan on six drug counts.

221. See *United States v. Kaufman*, 858 F.2d at 998–99. "Chetumal Authorities Grab Franks Brothers," *TR* (BZ), 27 July 1986, 1; and "DEA Agent Russ Reiner Strikes Again," *BT* (BZ), 27 July 1986, 1.

222. For U.S. ambassador Robert Rich's press conference, see "Medellín Drug Connection?," 1.

223. See, for instance, "Arrests Imminent," *BT* (BZ), 24 July 1989, 2, and "Orange Walk Drug Bust," *TR* (BZ), 2 June 1985, 1. For a vehicle seized with ninety-one kilos of marijuana, off-loaded from the wreck of a small plane, see "Drug Runners in Orange Walk Put Crashed Plane to the Torch," *TR* (BZ), 12 April 1987, 1. See also "Belize Weed?," *BT* (BZ), 9 April 1989, 1; "Marijuana Plane from Belize with Six Hundred Pounds of Dope Crashes in Houston," *TR* (BZ), 22 December 1985, 1; and "Narcotraffickers Burn," 1.

224. "DEA Says Drug Plane," 1; "Major Cocaine Seizure, Arrests Announced," UPI (US), 11 December 1989; "BDF-Police Seize Coke," *BT* (BZ), 27 May 1990, 1; "Narcotraffickers Burn," 1; "BDF-Police Seize Coke: 790 Lbs. Valued at $27.5 Million," *BT* (BZ), 27 May 1990, 1.

Colombian drug plane crashed on another such strip in San Felipe, about fifteen miles from Orange Walk, just after the BDF had partially destroyed a runway.

Through the 1990s cases related to the northern Belize cocaine trade multiplied. In 1991 the DEA used an undercover sting operation to penetrate a Medellín operation that was shipping cocaine into Belize and on for U.S. East Coast distribution. The organization was allegedly led by Pedro Libardo Ortegón Ortegón, identified at trial as "directly below the highest level of the cartel," and was being assisted by Belizean traffickers led by Armando Grajales of Orange Walk.[225] That same year, after a cross-border cocaine deal went sour, a Chetumal kingpin orchestrated a kidnapping of Belizeans.[226] In 1992 the DEA and an elite Belizean counternarcotics team captured 212 kilos of cocaine in two villages near Corozal, and in 1995 Corozal police seized a sport-utility vehicle and arrested its two occupants, headed toward the border with 114 kilos of cocaine.[227] In 1996 authorities found a rough runway, aviation fuel, and a weapons cache at Revenge Lagoon, on the edge of the Orange Walk district in the wilderness north of Crooked Tree.[228]

Cocaine transshipment put an even greater premium than had marijuana export on corrupting police and politicians to preclude interdiction. When drug networks operated in remote areas of an unintegrated state like Belize, they might be confident of avoiding official detection without assuming the risk and expense of corrupting authorities. However, in light of the violence freely wielded by Colombian and Mexican cartels, as the size and value of cocaine shipments increased, so, too, did the risk of undertaking trafficking without systematically corrupting counternarcotics officials ahead of time. Hence, evidence of extensive drug corruption in northern Belize increasingly surfaced. For instance, in 1991 a notepad belonging to the pilot of a drug plane captured in this area was found to contain the name, address, and phone number of a Serious Crimes Squad officer with detailed knowledge of antidrug operations and intelligence.[229]

In another notorious case in 1996 a police car, parked several miles from Orange Walk, was set on fire and burned, destroying documents that reportedly implicated relatives of government minister Elito Urbina in a large drug-transshipment scheme.[230] Although the destroyed evidence effectively thwarted prosecution, the U.S. government then canceled the visas of Urbina's son and son-in-law and raised the case during the 1997 controversy over certification. As for police inspector Lamberto White, responsible for the destroyed vehicle, authorities investigated and suspended him.[231] Then, five years after having been compelled to take early retirement, White was arrested in Nicaragua for possessing several kilos of cocaine and numerous Ecstasy pills.[232]

225. See *United States v. Diaz*, 1993 U.S. App. LEXIS 2704, and "Five Miamians Charged in New York Cocaine Bust," *MH* (US), 12 December 1989, B2.

226. See "Drug Plane Crashes," *BT* (BZ), 26 May 1991, 1, and "Chetumal 'Boss' Frees Belize Drug Hostages," *TR* (BZ), 25 August 1991, 1.

227. See "$6 Million Corozal Drug Bust," *AM* (BZ), 12 June 1992, 1; "Police Nab Big Fish," *TR* (BZ), 14 June 1992, 14; "Bail Order for Colombians Revoked," *AM* (BZ), 14 August 1992, 8; "Policía arresta a dos por 250 libras de cocaína," *TR* (BZ), 15 January 1995, 11; and "Cali Cartel," *BT* (BZ), 15 January 1995, 20. In 1994 authorities seized two Mexican visitors carrying eleven kilos of cocaine in the spare tire of their Datsun. "Border Bust Retrieves Eleven Kilos of Cocaine," *TR* (BZ), 24 April 1994, 7.

228. "Revenge Lagoon—New Drop for Drugs," *TR* (BZ), 7 January 1996, 1.

229. "Police Investigation Targets Two!," *TR* (BZ), 3 February 1991, 1.

230. See "Drug Investigation Sabotaged," *BT* (BZ), 17 March 1996, 1; "Minister's House Cased," 1; "As Close to Cabinet as a Son-in-Law," *AM* (BZ), 26 May 1996, 1; "Police Inspector Suspended During Mystery-Fire Probe," *TR* (BZ), 6 October 1996, 1; and "Drug File Destroyed, Minister's Son-in-Law Set Free," *BT* (BZ), 8 December 1996, 1.

231. See "Senior Cop Gets the Axe," 20 April 1997, 4, and "Ecstasy Excess!," *TR* (BZ), 24 March 2002, 1.

232. Nicaraguan police simultaneously arrested Juan Cantun of San Narciso Village, reportedly involved in marijuana exports from northern Belize in the 1980s. In

Over time, trafficking networks operating in northern Belize altered their methods either to perfect techniques or to stay ahead of authorities. By the early 1990s various operators had shifted from ground transport to speedboats and focused aerial delivery on water drops over bays, lakes, and lagoons.Unpredictability in methods as well as routes minimized interception. Thus, after authorities seized 2,700 kilos of cocaine in 1997, for a time Colombian and Mexican organizations reverted to clandestine landings on Orange Walk roads and airstrips. In 1998, as reports of suspected drug flights increased, two senior BDF officers were arrested for allegedly assisting drug planes landing around the Orange Walk district, and one trafficking network was found to have employed heavy construction equipment to widen two miles of road into San Luis village to accommodate aircraft touching down for refueling.[233]

One example of this trafficking occurred in 2003, when a drug plane landed near Blue Creek Village, an area largely inhabited by Mennonite farmers.[234] Several times, the propeller-driven Russian cargo plane appeared but flew away without setting down. Finally, after dark, collaborators on the ground signaled the plane to approach, and five pickup trucks turned on their headlights to illuminate a landing strip. Within forty minutes handlers had removed an estimated 1.8 tons of cocaine that were thought, then, to have crossed the nearby Río Hondo into Mexico, the river there being shallow enough to be readily forded. As this operation occurred, Blue Creek residents repeatedly called the Orange Walk police and politicians, including the mayor. However, no officials appeared until the next morning, twelve hours after the cocaine had disappeared. This case underscores how unintegrated was the Belizean state and how unresponsive its northern authorities tended to be. Despite the logistical problems encountered by the traffickers and the repeated efforts of local people to tip officials, a large cocaine shipment transited without seizure or arrests.

The following year the Anti drug Unit patrolling near San Lazaro village, ten miles west of Orange Walk, received reports of another low-flying airplane. As the plane approached a rough air strip in a cane field, the pilot spotted the authorities and tried to abort the landing. The heavily loaded aircraft did not respond quickly enough, however, and the pilot crash-landed. The six traffickers involved, armed with automatic weapons, then engaged in a fifteen-minute shoot-out with the police. Ultimately, while just over seven hundred kilos of cocaine were seized, all the traffickers escaped, apparently with the help of a circling helicopter, thought to have been sent from Mexico to assist in exporting the drugs.[235]

Over time, drug syndicates grew even more daring. In 2004 a drug plane undertook a water drop in the busy early afternoon hours, right in the heart of Corozal Bay, in fact, within the town limits.[236] Three waiting boats gathered up dozens of packages and sped across the water to Mexico. The police were caught unprepared, and speedy and effective international cooperation with Mexican counterparts failed to materialize. Although authorities intercepted the boats on their return to Belize, the cargo—evidence needed for successful prosecution—had disappeared. Such incidents demoralized law enforcement,

---

1987 Corozal police raided an underground bunker in San Narciso, seizing 425 kilos of marijuana and 330 gallons of aviation fuel and arresting Cantun, who pled guilty to marijuana and illegal-fuel charges and was sentenced to pay twenty-five thousand dollars, or serve four years. "Corozal Cops Seize Underground Weed Bunker," *TR* (BZ), 25 January 1987, 12.

233. See "Drug Barons Back to Plan A," *TR* (BZ), 26 April 1998, 1, and "O.W. Drug Barons Convert Public Road as Landing Strip for Drug Planes," *TR* (BZ), 3 May 1998, 1. Charges were dropped after a key prosecution witness failed to appear in court. "Drug Charge Dropped Against BDF Major," *TR* (BZ), 7 November 1999, 8.

234. "Mexicans 'Invade' Belize in Airborne Drug Stunt," *TR* (BZ), 7 September 2003, 1.

235. "Cops Seize Plane and U.S. $15 M[illion] of Coke," *TR* (BZ), 8 August 2004, 14.

236. "Cocaine Traffickers Getting Bolder," *TR* (BZ), 30 May 2004, 2.

while criminal networks gained confidence that counternarcotics operations were unlikely to interfere with their schemes, however blatant.

In 2008 one Orange Walk transshipment ring was so bold as to land a drug plane at about two in the morning right on the Northern Highway.[237] Heavily armed masked men dressed in black stopped traffic while a shipment estimated at more than a ton of cocaine was unloaded and a refueling truck carrying 1,200 gallons of aviation fuel serviced the aircraft. Army and police, alerted by an oncoming driver's cell phone call, rushed to the scene, but, apparently unwittingly, passed the truck heading north packed full of drugs. During the ensuing shoot-out with traffickers carrying AK-47 assault rifles, police shot the driver of the refueler truck, which crashed, and eventually nine other individuals were arrested, although the pilots escaped.

In countries with well-developed criminal-justice systems, prosecutors have used the threat of conviction and lengthy imprisonment to persuade conspirators to provide information in exchange for more lenient treatment. Given the lesser resources and abilities of Belizean authorities, climbing "up the chain" in this manner occurred much less frequently. In this Northern Highway case, too, the government proved to be largely impotent. The Belizean authorities never located the drugs and could only speculate on their probable route out of the country, while those Belizeans who had masterminded the venture were never publicly identified, much less successfully prosecuted.

Juárez Cartel Activities

Mexican cartels, cooperating with Belizean networks, have been behind many of the air and maritime ventures in northern Belize, far overshadowing the Colombian organizations that had moved in during the initial stage of Belizean cocaine transshipment. The most important of the Mexican syndicates came to be the Southeast cell of the Juárez cartel. While Juárez long had a presence in Belize and the Yucatán, its activities here mushroomed in the late 1990s. This illustrates how broader developments within the drug trade often had critically important consequences for Central American bridge states. After the 1997 death of Juárez kingpin Amado Carrillo Fuentes, bloody struggles ensued within and among the principal cartels active in northern Mexico. Feeling intense pressure from the Arellano Félix brothers leading the Tijuana cartel, Vicente Carrillo, Amado's brother, shifted many Juárez operations into the Yucatán.[238]

Headquartered in Quintana Roo, the Southeast cell of the Juárez cartel was directed by José Albino Quintero Meraz ("Don Beto") and former Mexican federal police officer Alcides Ramón Magana ("El Metro"). Before Magana's 2001 arrest by the Mexican Army, this smuggling ring became one of Mexico's most violent narcotics networks, dominating the Chetumal and Cancún drug trade. The U.S. government went so far as to direct its consul in Cancún to leave Mexico after his life was threatened.[239] Indeed, by 2000 Cancún had become a regional drug center. Servicing the beach resorts out on the peninsula, the city had grown to 750,000 inhabitants, including surrounding slums, and the booming tourist industry provided exceptional opportunities both to launder money and to camouflage cocaine transshipment. The Southeast cell was deeply involved in both, and routes through neighboring Belize gained prominence.

In early 1999 a Mexican federal police report declared that Chetumal traffickers were transporting cocaine for Colombians into northern

237. "Plane Makes 2 a.m. Landing on Northern Highway," *AM* (BZ), 14 March 2008, 1; "The Big Haul," *TR* (BZ), 16 March 2008, 5; and "Cops Hold Copo," *TR* (BZ), 20 April 2008, 29.

238. See Jordan, *Drug Politics*, 248n47.

239. Astorga, "Mexico," 97.

Belize by air and sea. The narcotics were then being imported into Mexico, either via the Río Hondo or by shipment into nearby ports and oil refineries. The Mexican investigation also revealed that a pair of Belizean police officers in Corozal was assisting passage of the drugs. Most important, the network had support at the top echelons of Mexican politics. It had corrupted Mario Ernesto Villanueva Madrid, governor of Mexico's Quintana Roo state from 1993 to 1999 and a member of the then nationally dominant Partido Revolucionario Institucional party.[240]

Villanueva Madrid, who had extensive contacts in Panama linked to the Cali cartel, was on the payroll of the Southeast cell as well.[241] His trusted subordinates had taken charge of importing and transporting drugs through Quintana Roo toward northern Mexico and the United States. Juárez traffickers had been provided with official credentials and with access to planes, hangars, and airstrips, as well as with heavy equipment to construct clandestine runways. In exchange, prosecutors later declared, Villanueva was receiving a per kilo kickback. In one incident a small plane carrying cocaine being transshipped from Barranquilla, Colombia, to the United States developed engine trouble. Traffickers reportedly capitalized on the governor's influence and had the drugs off-loaded and moved up the coastal highway from Chetumal to Cancún. According to witnesses, state police and a judicial police chief accompanied the drug shipment as it traveled overland within Quintana Roo.

This organization eventually succeeded in moving immense quantities of cocaine through Quintana Roo. Authorities came to believe that between 1994 and 2002 it exported hundreds of tons to the United States, and some of this cocaine was transshipped through Belize.[242] In fact, a critical break in the U.S. federal case against the Southeast cell leaders came when U.S. government informants at a northern Belize airstrip loaded 550 kilos of cocaine onto an airplane owned by the Quintana Roo governor's office to be flown into Mexico.

After spending many of his last months in office denying links to the drug trade, Governor Villanueva abruptly disappeared from Mérida.[243] For many months he eluded Mexican officials who had prepared a forty-count indictment, alleging drug charges and abuse of high office. However, an investigative reporter located Villanueva, interviewing him for the weekly Mexican news magazine *Milenio*. Interpol eventually reported that the former governor had fled south, immediately crossing the border into Belize and following the Río Hondo toward Blue Creek Village. The fugitive then seems to have relied on friendly Belizean political and business elites, and he reportedly lived for a time at two farms and a tourist resort in Orange Walk, Yo Creek, and Gallon Jug. To disguise his identity, Villanueva grew a beard and long hair, and he moved regularly, crossing from Belize into the Maya Biosphere Reserve of northern Guatemala, near the archaeological sites of Yaloch and La Honradez, just west of the Belizean border.

240. For information on the Villanueva case, see "Mexican Governor Denies Drug Trafficking Allegations," *TR* (BZ), 17 January 1999, 1, and "Villanueva colocó a narcos en gobierno," *El Universal* (Mexico) (hereafter cited as *EU* [MX]), 29 May 2001, 1.

241. See "De Veraguas a Quintana Roo," *LP* (PA), 17 January 1999, 6A, and "No necesito dinero del narcotráfico," *LP* (PA), 16 January 1999, 4A.

242. For the words of a DEA spokesman, see "U.S. Indicts Three in Drug-Ring Probe," *Washington Times*, 28 June 2002, A6.

243. For Villanueva's time as a fugitive, see "Más de dos años evadió a la justicia," *EU* (MX), 25 May 2001, 1; "Belize Played Pivotal Role in Protecting 'El Chueco'—Mexican Journalist Claims," *TR* (BZ), 2 September 2001, 10; "Ex-governor Fesses Up," *TR* (BZ), 17 June 2001, 1; "U.S. Wants a Piece of Mario Villanueva," *TR* (BZ), 24 June 2001, 9; "Mexican Press Involve Belize Politicos in the Adventures of Rogue Governor," *TR* (BZ), 24 June 2001, 9; "Protegían empresarios a 'El Chueco' en Belice," *EU* (MX), 29 May 2001, 1; "Fue Centroamérica su refugio," *EU* (MX), 28 May 2001, 1; "Se refugió Villanueva en Belice, informa Interpol," *EU* (MX), 28 May 2001, 1; and "A Mexican Official's Account of His Back-Door Escape," *NYT* (US), 15 February 2000, A4.

After Villanueva had successfully avoided capture for two years, the election of Vicente Fox of the National Action Party changed the Mexican political landscape. Fox immediately vowed to root out corruption and enhance counternarcotics cooperation. With the Institutional Revolutionary Party out of office, whatever lingering protection the former governor might have been enjoying vanished.[244] Soon thereafter, authorities in Cancún captured Villanueva and prepared to try him in the Mexican courts.[245] In the meantime, U.S. authorities announced their own federal case against him. Mary Jo White, U.S. attorney for the southern district of New York, and Donnie Marshall, DEA director, accused Villanueva of participating in a conspiracy between 1994 and 1998 to import into the United States and distribute more than two hundred tons of cocaine. Félix Jiménez, chief of the DEA New York field division, publicly reported that Villanueva Madrid had been receiving five hundred thousand dollars for every five hundred kilos of cocaine successfully transshipped through his state.

At his 2007 trial in Mexico, despite extensive witness testimony that the governor had protected drug smugglers while in office, a lower court cleared Mario Villanueva Madrid of trafficking and organized-crime charges, convicting him only of money laundering.[246] The court then ordered his release, because he had already served more than six years in prison. However, prosecutors immediately appealed, and a higher Mexican federal court over-turned that decision, eventually convicting the ex-governor of fomenting drug trafficking and sentencing him to thirty-six years. Then, in 2010 Mexico extradited Villanueva to the United States to face further drug charges.

The Villanueva Madrid case shows how northern Belize became enmeshed in cocaine transshipment for a leading Mexican cartel, extraordinarily well connected within Belize as well as the Yucatán. It also reveals something of the economics of the cocaine trade. The return of profits has been so lucrative that extraordinary sums have been available to corrupt high officials. Bribery has frequently occurred, incrementally, on a case-by-case basis, when a particular problem arose, such as the arrest in a bridge state of a valuable pilot or a prominent trafficker. But, the larger organizations have also corrupted systematically, when traffickers formulated shipping plans through a certain zone that were sufficiently ambitious that problems were bound to occur. Here, prudence dictated that prominent officials be corrupted in advance to create a network of collaborators ready to spring into action.

Southern Belize

One might anticipate that southern Belize, which had long lagged behind the central and northern regions in development, accessibility, and population and which lacked the extensive historical links to Mexico found in the north, might also have trailed in the drug trade. In fact, however, the distinctive profile of the south afforded foreign and domestic trafficking rings

244. Former DEA administrator Robert Bonner, who also served as commissioner of U.S. Customs and Border Protection, noted that Mexican cartels had a "cozy relationship" with the PRI government, given "entrenched corruption," "lack of accountability," and "weak law enforcement agencies, which could not take effective action against major cartel leaders even when the political will to do so existed." "New Cocaine Cowboys," 38–39.

245. For Villanueva's arrest, see "Villanueva, formalmente preso y sujeto a proceso," *EU* (MX), 2 June 2001, 1; "Mexico Arrests," 1; and "Former Mexican Governor Indicted for Drug Trafficking in New York," Agence France Presse, 26 May 2001. For the capture of Alcides Ramón Magana, see "Big Smuggler of Cocaine Is Arrested, Mexico Says," *NYT* (US), 14 June 2001, 15A.

246. For Villanueva's trial and extradition, see "Mexican Court Sentences Ex-governor to Thirty-Six Years in Prison for Fomenting Drug Trafficking," Associated Press Worldstream, 5 June 2008; "Sentencian a Mario Villanueva a treinta y seis años de prisión," *EU* (MX), 4 June 2008, 1; "Emergen las huellas del narcotráfico," Inter Press Service, 27 May 2009; and "Former Governor of Quintana Roo Extradited to the U.S.," *AM* (BZ), 10 May 2010, 1.

significant opportunities. This highlights the point that different sets of bridge-favoring factors were sometimes present *within* a single Central American state. Furthermore, where drug trafficking in northern Belize took advantage of the neighboring Petén and Yucatán, southern Belize flanked the corner of the Caribbean busy with trafficking into southeastern Guatemala and northern Honduras.

Belize and Honduras have no common boundary, but the Honduran border lies only about forty miles from southern Belize, and the Gulf of Honduras and, especially, Amatique Bay provide ready access by sea. As elsewhere in the Caribbean basin, cocaine was by no means the first variety of contraband to traverse this region. Belizeans traditionally smuggled some seafood into the Islas de la Bahía and southern Honduras, and despite their inability to match the quality of much Belizean cannabis, Honduran traffickers occasionally exported marijuana for consumption within Belize.[247] Cocaine could thus move down routes established by earlier smuggling. By the early 1990s authorities were finding cocaine stashes in the Toledo district, and the DEA eventually reported that traffickers were using speedboats to transport cocaine into Belize from Caribbean ports in Honduras and Guatemala.[248] Fronting Amatique Bay, the small Belizean port of Punta Gorda not only had its own air strip but was connected by regular ferry service to Puerto Barrios, Guatemala, a magnet for significant drug trafficking. Furthermore, Toledo was the country's poorest district; consequently, the incentives for participating in transshipment schemes were especially acute. However, given negligible antidrug resources, police uncovered only a small handful of incidents.

Here, too, local elites have been surpassingly influential, and some have turned to drug trafficking. For their part authorities have at times seemed more concerned with protecting local reputations than enforcing the law. For example, in 2008 police stopped and searched a car emerging from a farm on Hummingbird Highway. Although 13.9 kilos of cocaine worth $325,000 were confiscated from the driver, reportedly a former police officer with ties to Mexican drug dealers, the police failed to divulge the name of the farm's owner. Thereafter, the Belizean media urged the government toward more transparency, arguing that the practice of omitting mention of prominent people who might be involved in significant drug cases ought to be discontinued.[249] However, discernible changes failed to occur.

Indeed, the incapacities of law enforcement have been pronounced in southern Belize. Spread thin, underfunded, and sometimes intimidated, local officials have rarely interrupted the aerial or maritime operations of drug organizations. In addition, problems of insufficient national integration have been especially serious. The south has fewer roads, many inaccessible in the rainy season, and settlements are even smaller and more scattered. The largest town in southern Belize is Dangriga. Perched on the coast and by 1993 containing about seven thousand persons, it has long been a center of the Garífuna, or Black Carib, ethnic group.[250] We have already seen multiple ways in which geographic considerations have factored into the Belizean drug trade. In Dangriga, on account of the swampy coastline, no road has ever been built directly to Belize City, located about thirty miles north.

247. Centro, "El narcotráfico en Honduras," 4, 7.

248. See "Toledo Trafficker Fined One Hundred Thousand Dollars," *TR* (BZ), 2 July 1992, 4, and DEA, *Resources, Belize* (2003), 5.

249. "Two Charged for Griga Coke Bust Worth BZ$650,000," *AM* (BZ), 25 April 2008, 1.

250. In 1991 Garífuna comprised 7.6 percent of the Belizean population. CIA, *World Factbook, 1991*, 31. Many in this ethnic group moved north into Belize from the more southern Central American states (Shoman, *Thirteen Chapters*, 10), especially the Caribbean coasts of Nicaragua and Honduras and the Honduran Islas de la Bahía. See generally England, *Afro Central Americans*.

Rather, a northern spur leads to the isolated village of Gales Point, which flanks one of a series of inland lagoons. Gales Point is then linked to the small settlement at Gracie Rock. To avoid these rough roads, most overland traffic endures the long detour on Hummingbird Highway to Belmopan before turning east to the coast, a trip of several hours. By the mid-1980s these infrequently traversed roads and unpopulated lagoons had attracted drug smugglers.

In 1986 hundreds of water-tight packages containing a kilo each of cocaine were found floating in the Northern Lagoon, north of Gales Point. The following year a plane carrying 560 kilos of marijuana crash-landed on Dangriga's Pelican Beach Hotel airstrip, and authorities elsewhere caught a Gales Point man heading toward Chetumal with marijuana. In 1988 a Belizean citizen who frequently drove from Gracie Rock to Gales Point wrote to the *Belize Times*: "On many of my trips to the area I have personally seen planes landing in broad daylight on the road. I understand from other people who also travel the area that the planes land at night, too. It is generally believed that the cargo is drugs." Indeed, by 1990 antidrug officials had identified Gales Point as a frequent target for aerial-trafficking schemes, especially cocaine water drops.[251]

While Dangriga could not avoid serious problems of addiction and drug-related violence, to call it "the new cocaine capital of Belize," as one newspaper did in 1997, is hyperbole.[252] In fact, the largest drug ring operating south of Belize City long had its center of operations farther south in the coastal Stann Creek district. By the 1980s one of the country's prime marijuana-production areas had been established on the Swasey Branch of the Monkey River near Red Bank.[253] More important, the two small neighboring towns of Big Creek and Independence/Mango Creek and the nearby offshore beach and fishing village of Placencia soon became immersed in various trafficking ventures, although antidrug successes were sporadic at best.[254] Big Creek has formed the hub of the country's citrus and banana trade and has ranked as its second-busiest deepwater port.

As for Placencia, it sits at the tip of a twenty-three-mile-long peninsula, dividing the sea behind the barrier reef from a lagoon ideal for water drops.[255] In this period this small beach community began to host significant influxes of tourists, whose activities might distract onlookers from trafficking activities, and some of whom consumed drugs as well. In 1997 a single police constable had responsibility for all law enforcement around Placencia, flanked by that lengthy lagoon and surrounded by many miles of remote coves, swamps, and cayes, ideal for drug transshipment. He had no boat, no vehicle, no close backup, and a slew of duties that had nothing to do with narcotics. "I am responsible for all this beach," officer Manuel McFarzen observed plaintively, "but I am only one person."[256]

While the scarcity of law enforcement was one problem, police corruption was another. One

251. "Police Sting Nets Five Lbs. of Cocaine," *BT* (BZ), 16 September 1990, 1; "Gales Point Lagoon: Bridgehead for Cocaine Shipments?," *TR* (BZ), 8 July 1990, 1; "The Drug Planes," *BT* (BZ), 15 May 1988, 6; "Fined Four Thousand Dollars [Bz] for Marijuana," *TR* (BZ), 22 February 1987, 14; "Mystery Plane Crashes in Dangriga," *TR* (BZ), 22 November 1987, 1; "Weed Plane Crash Lands," *BT* (BZ), 22 November 1987, 1; and "Floating Cocaine Packets Down South," *TR* (BZ), 9 March 1986, 1.

252. "Trial in Dangriga," *TR* (BZ), 16 November 1997, 1. For a representative case of Dangriga cocaine trafficking, see "Two Charged."

253. "Marijuana Fields," 15.

254. For a 1987 seizure at the Big Creek airfield of 295 kilos of compressed marijuana, see "Anti Drug Force Seizes Two Small Planes," *TR* (BZ), 26 July 1987, 1.

255. In 1995 Belizean investigative journalists concluded, "Colombian cocaine packaged in water-tight containers is regularly dropped off into Placencia Lagoon near Independence, where Belizean 'mules' collect it. The drugs are then smuggled into Mexico from where they continue on their illegal way to the United States." "Bodies and More Cash Found as Southern Drug Ring Falls Apart," *TR* (BZ), 8 October 1995, 1. See also "Cocaine Washing Up on the Beach of Placencia," *TR* (BZ), 28 August 1994, 3, and "Belize by Sea," A27.

256. "Belize by Sea," A27.

day in November 2010 at two in the morning, traffickers used fourteen logs to block off a section of Southern Highway, near the Bladen Branch of the Monkey River.[257] A twin-engine turboprop Beechcraft plane touched down on the highway but clipped its left wing on trees during the landing. Hearing the aircraft's approach, residents of Bladen Village alerted Independence police, who responded, causing the traffickers to flee. In a high-speed chase police pursued a suspicious white van for twenty-one miles. Inside, they discovered a firearm, Antidrug Unit uniforms, a Belize City Customs officer, and four police officers from Belize City and Belmopan, including the governor-general's chauffeur and a former Belize Antidrug Unit member. During an all-day search in the plane's vicinity, officials later found makeshift landing lights, a semiautomatic assault rifle, a satellite phone and global-positioning system, a truck with hundreds of gallons of aviation fuel, and 2,604 kilos of Colombian cocaine, amounting to the largest seizure in Belizean history.

For drug networks operating in southern Belize, the tiny population has meant not only that the law-enforcement presence has been small and spread thin but also that elites have been positioned to influence the administration of justice. In this context, trafficking operations have long been carried out, brazenly and successfully, supervised by wealthy locals with extensive international connections. One scholar of the developing world has noted that "the organization of society, even in remote areas, may dictate the character and capabilities of politics at the center."[258] This statement encapsulates nicely the interplay of drug trafficking and the law in southern Belize. Political elites in Belmopan and Belize City could fashion policies and make antidrug pledges of various kinds to the United States and other governments, but, in truth, the state has had limited capacity to implement those policies and carry through with those pledges, particularly in outlying areas. That life in southern Belize has long encompassed significant drug trafficking is illustrated by the career of Angel John Zabaneh.

Angel John Zabaneh

In 1981 the extensive drug trafficking in southern Belize gained publicity when Texas Narcotics Division agents broke up a marijuana-smuggling ring, apprehending three suspects. One identified his supplier as Angel John Zabaneh, a well-known citrus and banana farmer from a prominent Belizean family of Lebanese descent.[259] The following year, Belizean authorities arrested Zabaneh after finding a warehouse containing processed marijuana in Independence. However, two foreigners accepted responsibility for the seized drugs, and Zabaneh was acquitted, though not cleared of suspicion.[260] A DEA agent who worked in Belize in the mid-1980s later termed Zabaneh "the biggest doper in the country," noting his involvement in a marijuana trafficking and distribution conspiracy.[261]

257. For information on this bust, see "BZ$131 Million Worth of Cocaína!," *AM* (BZ), 17 November 2010, 1; "Drug Plane Lands $140 Million Cargo," *TR* (BZ), 18 November 2010, 1; "Police Destroys Narco Cargo," *TR* (BZ), 26 November 2010, 1; and "Five Read Additional Charges for Southern Hwy Drug Plane," *AM* (BZ), 10 December 2010, 1.

258. Migdal, *Strong Societies*, xvii.

259. For the Zabaneh case, see *United States v. Zabaneh*, 837 F.2d at 1254, and Castillo and Harmon, *Powderburns*, 128–29. See also "DEA Gets John Zabaneh in Guatemala," *TR* (BZ), 17 November 1985, 1; "Dallas Court Convicts Zabaneh Seven Out of Eight," *TR* (BZ), 20 July 1986, 1; "Texan Court Convicts John Zabaneh," *BT* (BZ), 20 July 1986, 1; "Jury Has Drug Case with Unlawful Arrest," *Houston Chronicle*, 15 July 1986, 10; "From a Texas County Jail John Zabaneh Pleads for Help," *TR* (BZ), 9 March 1986, 9; and "'Kidnapped' Belize Drug Suspect Jailed in Houston," *BT* (BZ), 8 December 1985, 8.

260. For another plan to have two underlings paid off to accept the blame for cocaine shipments "and accept a prison sentence of three or four years, while . . . [the principals] would receive favorable treatment based on their bribery of the presiding magistrate," see *United States v. Torres-Teyer*, 322 F. Supp. 2d at 375n8.

261. Castillo and Harmon, *Powderburns*, 128–29.

Zabaneh's downfall came after Belizean counterintelligence officials, in a notable example of cooperative antidrug work with U.S. law enforcement, wiretapped his telephone line, learned that he planned to fly into Guatemala on business, and passed that information to the DEA. In Guatemala City police officials and a DEA agent met the plane, and Guatemalan airport authorities held Zabaneh overnight as an undesirable. By design, his ticket out of the country took a Guatemala-Houston-Belize route, and he was seated next to a DEA agent, who duly arrested him as the plane approached the Houston airport.[262] Although indictments in Louisiana and Mississippi were eventually dismissed, a Texas jury in 1986 found Zabaneh guilty of conspiring to import marijuana and of possessing and distributing 527 kilos of it.

In a related case that same year a federal grand jury, acting on U.S. Customs Service information, indicted Charles Bell and Ronnie Page for smuggling 1,090 kilos of marijuana into Arkansas.[263] The indictment stated that the Zabaneh ring had supplied the marijuana. Citing court documents, the *Dallas Times Herald* then reported that informants had told DEA agents, "Zabaneh and his family were responsible for one-third to one-half of all the drugs smuggled into the United States from Belize—a total of about 100,000 pounds of marijuana and 3,000 kilograms of cocaine since 1978."[264] The leading Belizean newspaper reported, "According to DEA reports, John Zabaneh is the leader of the marijuana brokers in the south of Belize and perhaps the biggest in the country, supervising a vast network of cultivators and runners," and U.S. federal officials labeled Zabaneh a "godfather" of the drug trade.[265]

In noting that Belizean elites have usually acted with impunity, few could recall an instance when a leading figure had been seriously penalized for criminal behavior. And, the Zabaneh family very much stood out in Belize, with particular members having risen in business, politics, and society over the years. While much of the family took no part in illegal trafficking activities, the extent of the involvement of others soon became a matter of public controversy. In 1994 police learned of cocaine trafficking on Coco Plum Caye, an island south of Dangriga, and owned by the Zabanehs.[266] Officers put the caye under surveillance and soon observed suspicious activities. An attempt to interrupt a major drug transaction backfired, however, when police moved in too quickly. Authorities had spotted Michael Zabaneh in his speedboat in the vicinity, and although they did not capture him, he eventually chose to turn himself in. Meanwhile, police did arrest Richard Sjogreen, who described himself as a former Zabaneh family employee. After finding 3 kilos of cocaine in Sjogreen's boat, they discovered 225 kilos buried in the sand nearby.

In spite of this evidence the legal case soon fell apart. Even after Sjogreen jumped bail, fled the country, and then was rearrested on his return to Belize months later, no conviction was attained. The case was heard in Dangriga and presided over by Supreme Court judge

262. U.S. officials used a similar strategy in gaining custody of another Belizean drug suspect, arrested in the Guatemalan border town of Melchor de Mencos in 1989. See "The Loskot Kidnapping," *BT* (BZ), 19 November 1989, A1, and *United States v. Laskott*, 900 F. Supp. 411.

263. "Two Indicted Are Accused in 'Pot' Case," *Arkansas Democrat-Gazette*, 18 March 1986, 1.

264. "Legal Twist Holds Suspect Captive," *Dallas Time Herald*, 14 July 1986, 1, 8A.

265. See "DEA Gets John Zabaneh," 6A, and "Belize Man Convicted on Federal Drug Charges," *Dallas Morning News*, 16 July 1986, 27A.

266. For the Coco Plum case, see "Police Seize 250 Lbs. of Cocaine," *BT* (BZ), 27 March 1994, 1; "Serious Crime Squad Hooks Big Fish!," *TR* (BZ), 27 March 1994, 1; "New Twist to Dangriga Drug Mystery," *TR* (BZ), 8 October 1995, 1; "Jury Acquits Cocaine Boatman," *TR* (BZ), 3 December 1995, 1; "Impeach DPP Sooknandan!," *TR* (BZ), 18 December 1994, 1; and "Belize: Main Staging Post for Cocaine," *BT* (BZ), 5 March 1995, 1. Note that Sjogreen was a Nicaraguan national who become a naturalized Belizean citizen without a security clearance check after Michael Zabaneh had vouched for his character.

George Meerabux, who was impeached on corruption charges many years later and became the first judge in the history of Belize to be involuntarily removed from office. Evidence in the impeachment inquiry undertaken by the Belize Advisory Council reportedly suggested that in the Sjogreen case Judge Meerabux had thoroughly frustrated the work of Crown counsel Dionne Gallimore. In the judicial disciplinary proceedings, police constable Lincoln Jones, Meerabux's driver, testified that during the Sjogreen trial he had found a stack of one hundred dollar bills four inches thick in a bag in the judge's room, of which Meerabux gave him two hundred dollars. He also testified that en route back to Belize City, Judge Meerabux declared, "Jonesy, if I get five more years contract, I will be a millionaire."[267]

But, even this was not all the fallout from the Coco Plum Caye case. In a decision that infuriated U.S. Embassy personnel and brought about calls within Belize for his impeachment, acting director of public prosecutions Latchman Sooknandan opted to drop the case against Michael Zabaneh. Although Sooknandan cited lack of evidence and police bungling, a police inspector closely familiar with the case had observed, "We are convinced that there is enough evidence to take this matter to court," and acting attorney general Wilfred Elrington stated conclusively, "The case ought to have been left to be determined by a court of law." At length, attorney general Dean Barrow chose to accept Sooknandan's decision, although, to some, this determination was tainted because Barrow's brother, Denys, was representing the accused. Although the theory that bribery or intimidation may have been involved was never proven, suspicions lingered.[268]

The Coco Plum Caye case illustrates how Belizean authorities failed to prosecute successfully substantial trafficking that allegedly involved local elites. Law enforcement botched the controlled delivery. A jury would not convict even the suspect caught with the drugs. Pressure may have been applied within the criminal-justice system, and a prominent Belizean caught up in the case never had to face charges in court. This type of high-profile case then had rippling consequences as individual Belizeans considered whether to participate in or resist the drug trade. The Coco Plum Caye case stood for the proposition that large sums could be pocketed, while serious repercussions were sidestepped, if one assisted the key networks transshipping cocaine through Belize.

The Cayes

The Coco Plum Caye case fits into another significant category as well: the many cocaine-trafficking ventures that have involved the Belize cayes. In fact, the more than one thousand islands, islets, and sand spits found in Belizean territorial waters have frequently factored into the geotactics of bridge-state drug trafficking. While most cayes are positioned inside the barrier reef that parallels the 255-mile Belizean coastline, others are located outside it, within the Turneffe Islands', Lighthouse, and Glover's

267. "Judge Fights Impeachment Verdict in Supreme Court," *TR* (BZ), 20 January 2002, 1; "The Impeachment of a Judge," *TR* (BZ), 20 January 2002, 5; "Meerabux Won a Battle, But Lost the War!," *TR* (BZ), 3 March 2002, 1; and "Dwindling Hopes for Ex-judge Meerabux," *TR* (BZ), 7 July 2002, 11.

268. In 1989 U.S. authorities arrested one Mohammed Assad on drug charges. The case stalled when Assad jumped bail, moved to Belize, and married a Belizean. When the DEA ultimately located Assad, though thwarted in gaining the fugitive's return to the United States, agents persuaded him to become an informant. Assad was then responsible for several important drug busts, including that on Coco Plum Caye. In 1996 an assailant fatally shot him, and the DEA offered a considerable reward for information about the murder. However, although officials searched for a Guatemalan for questioning, they never succeeded in bringing anyone to trial, and Assad's killing was never conclusively linked to the Coco Plum bust. See "U.S. Steps Up War on Drug Mobsters," *TR* (BZ), 29 September 1996, 1; "Drug Informant Shot in O.W.," *AM* (BZ), 9 September 1996, 1; "Cops Search for Trial Farm Hitmen," *TR* (BZ), 8 September 1996, 1; and "Guatemalan Hunted for Murder of Assad," *TR* (BZ), 13 October 1996, 1.

reef systems. Belize has no coastal radar system to track vessels transiting its waters.[269] The barrier reef and surrounding cayes are a distinctive feature of Belizean geography, and drug rings have taken full advantage in plotting maritime trafficking schemes.

For several reasons many of the largest cocaine loads to pass through Belize have been transshipped through or via particular cayes. First, the shallow waters and many islands have made "for an intricate maze where pilots drop their loads to waiting 'go fast' speedboats that can outrun and outmaneuver most larger navy vessels."[270] Dense mangroves cover most cayes, and many are entirely uninhabited or only very sparsely populated by subsistence fishermen, often at sea. Perhaps most important, law enforcement has lacked the resources needed to patrol effectively the length and breadth of Belizean territorial waters, much less watch for suspicious activities in and around all the cayes. Although sizable cocaine loads have often entered these waters at night, traffickers operating in broad daylight have also succeeded in outmaneuvering or outrunning approaching vessels or temporarily hiding their boats and shipments in the mangroves.

Woefully outnumbered authorities have faced the challenge of interdicting drugs in transit on a large array of vessels. Not only have the cayes been the seat of the Belizean shrimping and fisheries industries, but they have gained an international reputation for diving, snorkeling, and sport fishing. The tourist trade and commercial fishing have camouflaged trafficking ventures, while water drops have further challenged law enforcement. By the early twenty-first century enough water drops had gone awry or speedboats being pursued by authorities had jettisoned their cargoes that, as one Belizean newspaper observed, "Fishermen and others regularly comb . . . [the] stretch of coastline north of Belize City on the lookout for bales of cocaine floating in the water or lodged in the mangrove."[271]

Glover's Reef, thirty-six miles off the Belizean coast, has amounted to one nearly ideal site to carry out air-water transshipment. An atoll, with several small and usually deserted islands to windward, Glover's is located on the distant, open-sea side of the barrier reef, yet features a reasonably quiet saltwater lagoon. A Belizean newspaper noted, "Water in the lagoon is flushed out over the reef wall at every high tide, but between high tides anything dropped in the lagoon is likely to remain there until recovered."[272] In 2003 a U.S. Coast Guard ship was trailing a speedy vessel, likely from Colombia, that deposited an estimated 750 kilos of cocaine in the Glover's Reef lagoon and then vanished. The coast guard could not catch the traffickers, clearly quite familiar with Belizean waters, but the crew did retrieve twenty-six cocaine packages, and Belizean authorities, another two packets.[273]

Twenty-four miles farther offshore lies Lighthouse Reef. One of the several islands along this atoll, Northern Two Cayes features a resort with a small landing strip. In 2010 a drug plane missed this runway and sunk in the deep seas south of the island. Several days later, authorities discovered the corpse of an unidentified Hispanic man, floating near the caye. The coroner determined that he had been tortured, inflicting multiple injuries, and after death his body had been cut to pieces and thrown into the

269. *INCSR* (2011), 138.

270. "What the Smuggler Ordered," A1.

271. "Two Dead in Stake Bank Massacre," *TR* (BZ), 6 July 2003, 5. See also "Finder Not Keeper of Twenty-Five Kilos of Cocaine," *TR* (BZ), 18 January 2009, 1. Late in 1992, after traffickers botched one such water drop, British soldiers collected almost twenty kilos of cocaine floating near southern Moho Caye, about ten miles east of Punta Gorda. See "Brit Soldiers Find One Million Dollars in Cocaine," *AM* (BZ), 31 December 1992, 1, and "Cocaine Fortune Found Off Moho Caye, Toledo," *TR* (BZ), 3 January 1993, 1.

272. See "Coast Guard Cocaine Find Shows Mexican Cartel Still 'At It' in Belize," *TR* (BZ), 6 June 2003, 12.

273. "Coast Guard Cocaine Find," 12.

sea.[274] In all likelihood, much more trafficking was taking place on these distant cayes and reefs than has gained police notice. As was true of remote jungle locations, Belizean possessions far offshore have tended to be beyond the reach of effective law enforcement.

Indeed, only a handful of the Belize cayes have been permanently inhabited, and fewer still have police forces. While investors have built resorts on a small number of the cayes, only Ambergris and the smaller neighboring island of Caye Caulker have been developed for significant tourism.[275] With time, both of these were transformed from minor drug-dealing centers to the locations of major transshipment and drug storage. In 1992 authorities seized nearly 545 kilos of cocaine from a group headquartered in Corozal, finding the drugs on San Juan Island, actually an inaccessible peninsula on the leeward side of northern Ambergris.[276] The ensuing case highlights the chronic problems of the Belizean legal system vis-à-vis drug prosecutions. Between the arrest of Faustino Moh and Antonio Pérez and their initial sentencing to four years in prison and twenty-thousand-dollar fines, fully five years elapsed, and four prosecutors, three defense attorneys, and three magistrates passed the case from one to another. Then, within a week of their convictions, Moh and Pérez had appealed and been released on bail. Modest penalties, inept police work, liberal bail policies, inefficient prosecution, and justice that is at least greatly delayed have been hallmarks of Belizean criminal law exploited by drug organizations.

In geographic terms, Ambergris Caye, situated to the far north of the barrier reef, has been particularly well suited for drug trafficking. Flanking Mexico's territorial waters, Ambergris could serve as a springboard to such Yucatán entry points as Xcalak and Bacalar Chico, and Chetumal is close at hand. At Rocky Point, on the island's northern end, the reef curves into the caye: an excellent target for pilots executing water drops.[277] Ambergris has remote areas, uninhabited and rarely patrolled, as do such small nearby islands as Deer Caye. However, this largest of the Belize islands also contains the country's busiest seaside tourist locale—San Pedro Town. The town has provided cover for the import of supplies, the arrival and departure of speedboats, and other drug activities, including storage and money laundering. Most important, large cocaine shipments have been directed toward Ambergris as well.[278]

In 2005 the Antidrug Unit was tipped to a Colombian vessel nearing San Pedro. When the boat spotted the BDF plane, it reversed course, fleeing toward international waters. However, a Mexican rapid response team then located the vessel and, after a shoot-out, seized more than 1,350 kilos of cocaine, while arresting four Belizeans and a Honduran.[279] By early in the twenty-first century, the DEA reported that drug organizations were storing cocaine on Ambergris. With the narcotics has come more violence, as when three Belizeans, one clearly a gang member, were killed in northern Ambergris and buried in shallow graves in a 2009 drug-trafficking dispute.[280]

274. "Intrigue at Sea," *TR* (BZ), 16 April 2010, 1.

275. See "Drug Bust at Caye Caulker," *BT* (BZ), 11 March 1990, 1. For the arrest of a crack cocaine dealer on Caye Caulker, see "Young Belizean Women—Trapped by the Drug Cult?," *TR* (BZ), 4 August 1991, 5. See also "Caye Caulker Cocaine Poisoning Belize City Streets," *TR* (BZ), 22 August 1993, 3.

276. For this case, see "Corozalenos Held in Cocaine Bust," *TR* (BZ), 19 July 1992, 1; "Longest Running Case Ends in Belize," *TR* (BZ), 31 August 1997, 1; and "Moh and Pérez Out on Bail, Two Hundred Thousand Dollars Each," *TR* (BZ), 7 September 1997, 1.

277. "Rocky Point Massacre!," *TR* (BZ), 8 February 2009, 1.

278. See DEA, *Resources, Belize* (2000), 3, and DEA, *Resources, Belize* (2003), 3.

279. "Cops Seize 16 Million Dollars of Cocaine in San Pedro Waters," *TR* (BZ), 7 August 2005, 5.

280. "Rocky Point Massacre!," 1, and "George Street's Pinky Tillett Linked to San Pedro Murders," *TR* (BZ), 22 February 2009, 14.

Yet, although Ambergris has been one focal point for drug transshipment, the authorities, whether Belizean, British, or U.S., have repeatedly interdicted cocaine all along the cayes.[281] Thus, in 1995 when the U.S. Coast Guard chased two speedboats into Belizean territorial waters, traffickers abandoned 1.1 tons of Cali cocaine as they tried to escape. The following year Belizean officials interrupted an effort to transship a large cocaine load on the far southern Sapodilla Cayes. In 1997 Belizean authorities found 1,768 kilos of cocaine on a Colombian-registered skiff on South Water Caye. In 2001 the British Royal Navy alerted the BDF maritime wing to a go-fast boat. After a chase four traffickers escaped; the fifth, from Sinaloa, Mexico, was captured, and more than 1,000 kilos of cocaine were seized. Then, in 2005 a BDF-DEA joint operation located 2,376 kilos of cocaine buried under a humble wooden house on stilts on Tobacco Caye, east of Dangriga, near one of the principal channels through the barrier reef.

In another revealing case of cocaine transit through the cayes, in 1997 Belizean authorities, working with the DEA, broke up an operation that had been moving cocaine from Colombia through Belize and into Mexico, apparently supervised by José Nelson Urrego Cárdenas of the Northern Valley cartel.[282] The police confiscated a Colombian-owned boat and 1,183 kilos of cocaine hidden in a mangrove swamp in the Turneffe Islands, on the reef's windward side. Belizean conspirator Albert Gordon claimed to be a simple fisherman, yet his house contained twenty-five thousand dollars; expensive communications equipment, including high-frequency radios; and a global positioning system for pinpointing air traffic. Authorities also discovered, attempting to hide in Gordon's house, two Mexicans, two residents of Sarteneja, and four Colombians who had entered the country illegally, including one whose brother had been imprisoned for five years in a notable 1991 cocaine-trafficking case.[283]

Once again, however, the government failed to prosecute the suspects successfully. Police inspector Daniel Itza had found a key at the Gordon residence that fit the boat that had carried the cocaine. However, the officials discharged Itza for improper conduct in another case, and he suddenly disappeared from his next job, as a Belize City taxi driver, thus failing to receive a summons and bench warrant to testify. Chief Magistrate Lord thereupon threw the entire case out of court, absolving Gordon and ordering the Colombians deported, after paying six-hundred-dollar fines for illegal entry. The Belizean media questioned Lord's decision to give the police twenty-four hours to locate Itza, then terminate the case, less than six months after the arrests had occurred. The country's leading newspaper observed, "For people and organizations concerned about the immense influence of the drug barons in Belize, this entire scenario by the police, the

281. See "U.S. Links Belize to Cali Cartel," *BT* (BZ), 24 March 1996, 1; "Accused Colombians Are Singing," *BT* (BZ), 23 June 1996, 19; "Cops Seize Colombian Drug Delivery Boat with $38.8 Million Cocaine Cargo!," *TR* (BZ), 30 March 1997, 1; "Stung by U.S. Censure," 9; "Drug-Runner Held," *TR* (BZ), 16 September 2001, 3; "5,238.183 Lbs. of Cocaine Found Near Tobacco Caye," *AM* (BZ), 14 September 2005, 1; "$112 M[illion] of Coke Seized," *TR* (BZ), 9 September 2001, 1; and "Cops Capture Cocaine Treasure!," *TR* (BZ), 18 September 2005, 11.

282. For this case, see "Belize Caught," 5A; "Cocaine Bust Yields 1,183 Kilos," *BT* (BZ), 18 May 1997, 1; and "Cops Expose Belize Hub," 1. Police sources claimed that Urrego Cárdenas had served as the Northern Valley's chief contact on San Andrés before going underground after drug-trafficking charges in Bogotá and Barranquilla and a Cali assault charge. For Gordon's prior criminal record, see "Cocaine Charges Against Gordon, Roca Withdrawn," *AM* (BZ), 25 September 1992, 7.

283. The brothers were Carlos Cabeza, arrested in 1992, and Velásquez Cabeza Archbold, arrested in 1997. The cocaine in this case also originated in San Andrés and was headed to Caye Caulker and on to Sarteneja. See "No Bail for Colombians," *AM* (BZ), 21 September 1992, 17; "Colombians Await Magistrate's Verdict," *TR* (BZ), 15 November 1992, 4; and "Colombian Beats Drug Trafficking Charge," *TR* (BZ), 1 November 1992, 1.

prosecution, and the judiciary leaves a bad taste in the mouth."[284]

Conclusion

Scholars may never be able to determine, with real precision, which bridge state has held what slice of the Central American drug trade over what period. Nevertheless, the record clearly demonstrates that Belize has exported considerable quantities of drugs over the past three decades. It is very likely to continue to do so in the future. Further development and future reforms could certainly raise average seizure levels, as could improved counternarcotics policies. For instance, law enforcement could better focus maritime resources on the geographic choke points represented by the limited number of channels through the barrier reef. Police officials could develop more extensive working relationships with counterparts in Mexico and Guatemala such that mid-level personnel facing common problems could cooperate more frequently. The government could urge other Commonwealth states to press forward with the plan "to develop a regional cadre of experienced drug prosecutors, who would be readily available to assist any of these countries in prosecuting traffickers."[285] Nevertheless, the positive results of implementing any revised interdiction strategy in the Belizean circumstances are likely to be limited because cocaine transshipment is already firmly established and an array of bridge-favoring factors will continue to attract traffickers.

The Belizean state has by no means been completely helpless in countering the drug trade. A state's capacity has been defined as its ability "to implement official goals, especially over the actual or potential opposition of powerful social groups."[286] Here, despite elite participation in the marijuana trade, cannabis eradication proved astonishingly successful. Moreover, with U.S. assistance, over the years Belizean authorities have made truly significant arrests and broken up quite a few organizations involved in the passage of large cocaine loads through the country. Yet by their own admission national officials have intercepted only a very modest percentage of all the drugs in transit. Citizens have continually reported suspicious low-flying planes, many of which have then touched down on secluded roads and airstrips to be fueled and often to deposit drugs or collect them. Authorities have also regularly happened upon crashed, abandoned, burned, or sunk aircraft and speedboats.[287] All this suggests that much more trafficking is occurring than police are interrupting.

In 1997 a Belizean journalist declared, "Drug trafficking and drug use are so pervasive in Belize today that not a single district, not a single village is completely free of this scourge."[288] By the late 1990s the drug trade had indeed engulfed the country, dominating its informal economy and deeply affecting its urban and rural areas. Neither its border zones with Mexico and Guatemala, nor its offshore territorial waters and inland waterways, nor even its air space have been spared. The trade has come to involve Colombian traffickers, especially those from the

284. For the trial, see "Former Police Inspector Daniel Itza Could Sabotage Drug Case," *TR* (BZ), 21 September 1997, 5, and "$10 M[illion] Drug Case Thrown Out of Court," *TR* (BZ), 28 September 1997, 1.

285. Griffin, "Democracy and Political Economy," 131.

286. Skocpol, "Bringing the State," 9, quoted in Friman, *Narcodiplomacy*, 2.

287. See *INCSR* (2004), 131, and DEA, *Resources, Belize* (2003), 5. In 2004 authorities seized fifteen speedboats and six aircraft. *INCSR* (2005), 160. One plane confiscated in 2003 was a Russian Antonov cargo plane, suspected of having imported two thousand kilos of cocaine, whose landing gear became stuck in the mud at a runway near Blue Creek. See also "Five Arrested Following Drug-Plane Crash," *BT* (BZ), 31 January 1993, C; "On the Trail of Drug Plane Cops Overturn Ranger," *TR* (BZ), 18 April 2004, 9; and "Helicopter Abandoned in Toledo," *TR* (BZ), 6 June 2004, 30.

288. "In the Face of Pervasive Drug Culture, Police and BDF Work On," *TR* (BZ), 12 October 1997, 3.

Medellín, Cali, and Northern Valley cartels, as well as Mexicans from the Juárez, Sinaloa, Tijuana, and Gulf cartels.

The structure of the criminal entities involved in this largely successful trade has been revealing. While vastly larger, foreign organizations have shared certain characteristics with their Belizean partners. For instance, just as the principal Colombian and Mexican drug syndicates have been turf based, with headquarters and spheres of influence in different regions of their countries, so Belizean networks have followed suit, with key rings located in Orange Walk, Belize City, and Big Creek. In these countries transnational criminals have taken advantage of the lack of integration. The regional dominance of different drug rings has also been partly the result of the personalistic, patron-client, kinship-oriented modes of behavior long associated with Latin American societies and the consequence of criminal enterprises competing vigorously and violently for market shares within an extraordinarily lucrative illegal industry. Regional divisions within the drug industry seem to have worked well for trafficking organizations looking to co-opt, intimidate, or outfox authorities in different areas.

More broadly, Colombian and Mexican cartels, looking to establish routes through Central America, have found in Belize notable bridge-favoring factors. Certain of these characteristics have been shared with the region's other bridge states. For instance, poverty has stimulated the drug trade, as have inadequate government resources and a weak criminal-justice system. As elsewhere in the region, narco-corruption has tainted particular police officers, prosecutors, and judges, as well as politicians. Making sustained headway against international drug trafficking has been particularly difficult, however, because transnational criminal networks have also capitalized on characteristics peculiar to Belize.

In particular, the country has had almost uniformly difficult relations with its immediate neighbor. Continuing friction over Guatemalan territorial claims, and such derivative tensions as clashing border patrols, have seriously undercut prospects for joint operations, and drugs have readily crossed the Belizean-Guatemalan border. While relations between Belize and Mexico have been generally positive, over the past several decades coordinated law-enforcement, either to seize shipments or to investigate and arrest traffickers, has occurred infrequently. Most important, drug trafficking and corruption in Belize have sometimes disrupted even the usually strong working relationship between Belizean and U.S. officials. Unlike the situation in Panama, Costa Rica, or even Guatemala, drug exports via Belize have been almost invariably destined for U.S. consumers. When Belizean seizures have dipped to abysmal levels and blatant cases of narco-corruption have gone unaddressed, relations have suffered.

As for geography, Belize's proximity to Guatemala and Mexico stands out as one singular factor. Its location in far northern Central America, relatively close to the U.S. market, further differentiates Belize from Panama and Costa Rica. The country's geography has featured boundaries running through remote areas covered by jungle or divided in the north and the south by easily forded rivers and readily traversed bays. This has greatly encouraged drug trafficking, as have Belize's unintegrated and sparsely populated outlying regions, with their many unsupervised air strips.

As the most enterprising drug organizations began to transship increasing amounts of cocaine by sea, countries came under particular pressure if they had geographic characteristics especially conducive to transshipment, such as offshore archipelagos, deepwater ports, or lagoons appropriate for airdrops. No other Central American country apart from Belize has a barrier reef stretching more than two hundred miles, with a protected sea behind it replete with dozens of small, mostly uninhabited islands, many covered by dense mangroves. As trafficking organizations have assembled combinations of methods, routes, and logistics, often dependent on geographic variables, with the aim of creating an effective overall drug-trafficking strategy that moves the most drugs at the least risk, Belize has appeared to be a most promising bridge state. Geography has ensured, and in all likelihood will continue to ensure, that trafficking organizations look to fashion connections through the country.

Thus, when smuggling rings have weighed the advantages and disadvantages inherent in moving drugs via Belize, the country's distinctive profile has often attracted them. Opportunities have outweighed potential problems. While scholars to date have tended to overlook the impact of the drug trade on Belize, citizens looking back on their first several decades of independence have seen their new country saturated with illegal drugs, a common complaint reflected in the country's principal newspapers.[289] As trafficking organizations began to pay off conspirators in drugs, rather than dollars, cocaine transshipment created flourishing domestic markets, particularly in crack, that further taxed already tremendously overburdened health-care and prison systems. Drug trafficking has also contributed significantly to the growth of urban gangs and to soaring rates of kidnappings, murders, and other serious crimes. Not only has drugs-driven crime adversely affected Belizean tourism, tarnishing one of the few bright spots in the economy, but the extraordinary levels of violence reached by the 1990s would have seemed almost unimaginable to many living in the more peaceful and tranquil Belize of the 1970s.[290] Ultimately, many Belizeans have come to see drug transit as one of the greatest challenges that their country faces.

289. One of the foremost accounts of Belizean history, published in 2004, fails to focus on how narcotics have affected Belizean society, simply noting, "The pernicious effects of drug trafficking and consumption have begun to make themselves felt." Thomson, *Belize*, 185.

290. Griffith, "Political Economy of Drugs," 118.

3

Costa Rica

For some years Costa Rica represented the paradigmatic Central American state: the first, for instance, to grow coffee and bananas with commercial success. Over time, however, the country has proceeded down political and economic paths unusual for the region. Modern Costa Rica differs markedly from its Central American neighbors, and drug-trafficking organizations and law-enforcement agencies have both had to operate in a distinctive environment. Comparing the evolution of the drug trade in Costa Rica with that in Belize underscores the flexibility of the many transnational criminals trafficking drugs in the late twentieth and early twenty-first centuries. They could successfully smuggle drugs through bridge states with dramatically different characteristics. And, for the first time in 2010, U.S. officials placed Costa Rica in the category of major drug-transit countries.[1]

After a short though bitter civil war in 1948, Costa Ricans chose to abolish their military in their new constitution. In the post–civil war era José Figueres Ferrer and his National Liberation Party (PLN) contended with the Social Christian Unity Party (PUSC) of his chief opponent, Rafael Ángel Calderón Guardia. The more liberal PLN policies tended to feature a somewhat larger government role, and the PUSC came to favor more market-oriented economics. However, both agreed that the regime should feature civil liberties, offer considerable social programs, and stake out an officially neutral international posture, tempered by long-standing close ties, political and economic, to the United States. Most important, political elites committed themselves to free elections and respect for human rights, and they came to share political power within a highly competitive democracy.

1. U.S. Department of State, *International Narcotics Control Strategy Report* (hereafter cited as *INCSR*) (2011), 204.

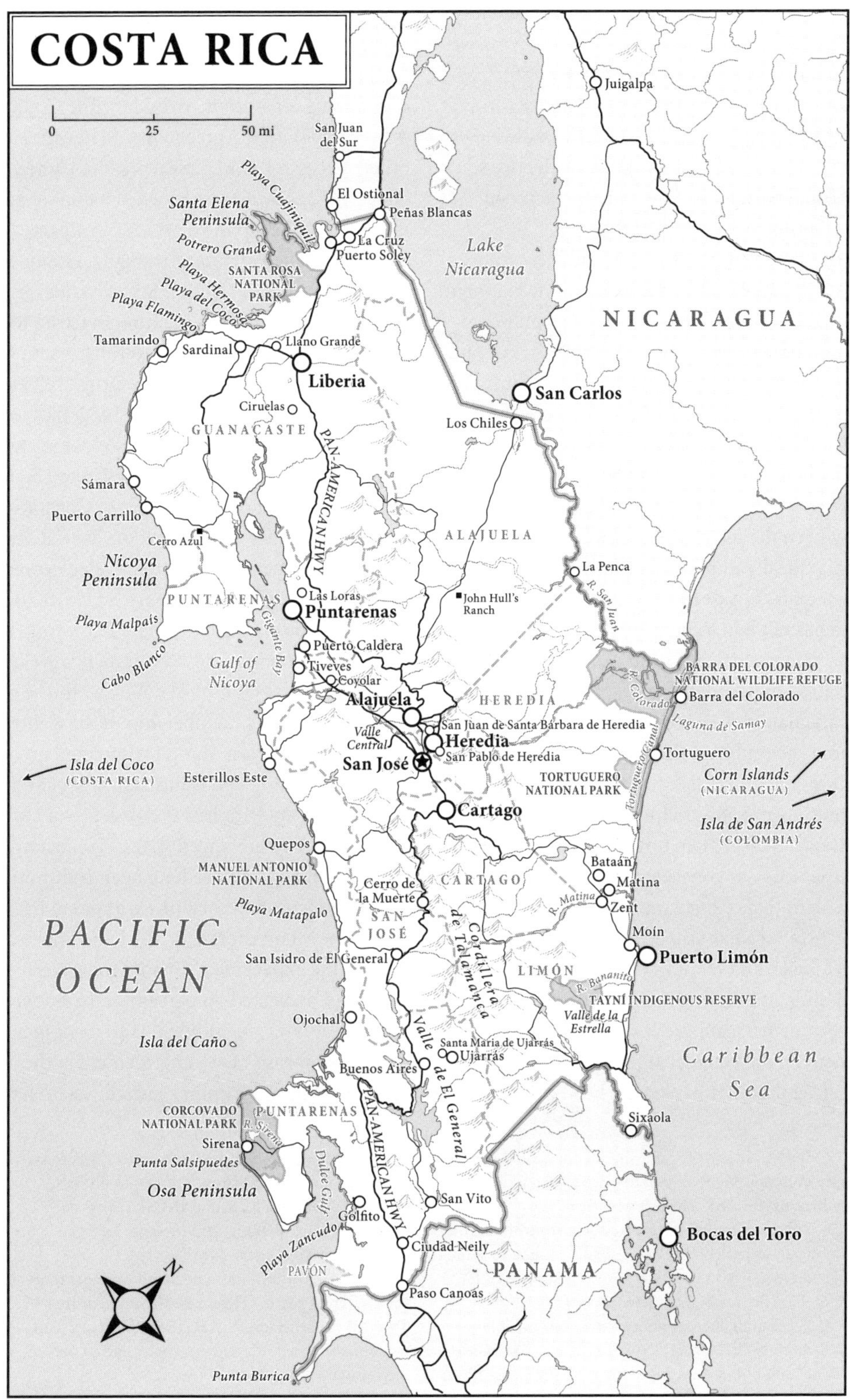
COSTA RICA
0
25
50 mi
Juigalpa
San Juan del Sur
Playa Cuajiniquil
El Ostional
Peñas Blancas
Santa Elena Peninsula
Potrero Grande
La Cruz
Puerto Soley
Lake Nicaragua
SANTA ROSA NATIONAL PARK
Playa Hermosa
Playa del Coco
Playa Flamingo
NICARAGUA
Tamarindo
Sardinal
Llano Grande
Liberia
San Carlos
Ciruelas
GUANACASTE
PAN-AMERICAN HWY
Los Chiles
Sámara
Puerto Carrillo
Cerro Azul
ALAJUELA
Nicoya Peninsula
La Penca
R. San Juan
PUNTARENAS
Las Loras
John Hull's Ranch
Puntarenas
Playa Malpaís
Gigante Bay
Puerto Caldera
Cabo Blanco
Gulf of Nicoya
Tiveves
BARRA DEL COLORADO NATIONAL WILDLIFE REFUGE
Coyolar
R. Colorado
Barra del Colorado
Alajuela
HEREDIA
Laguna de Samay
San Juan de Santa Bárbara de Heredia
Valle Central
Heredia
San José
San Pablo de Heredia
Tortuguero Canal
Tortuguero
Isla del Coco (COSTA RICA)
Esterillos Este
TORTUGUERO NATIONAL PARK
Corn Islands (NICARAGUA)
Cartago
Isla de San Andrés (COLOMBIA)
Quepos
Bataán
MANUEL ANTONIO NATIONAL PARK
Matina
Cerro de la Muerte
CARTAGO
R. Matina
Zent
Playa Matapalo
SAN JOSÉ
Cordillera de Talamanca
Moín
PACIFIC OCEAN
San Isidro de El General
Puerto Limón
LIMÓN
R. Bananito
TAYNÍ INDIGENOUS RESERVE
Valle de la Estrella
Ojochal
Isla del Caño
Valle de El General
Santa María de Ujarrás
Ujarrás
Caribbean Sea
Buenos Aires
CORCOVADO NATIONAL PARK
PUNTARENAS
R. Sirena
Sixaola
Sirena
Punta Salsipuedes
Dulce Gulf
Osa Peninsula
San Vito
Golfito
Bocas del Toro
Playa Zancudo
Ciudad Neily
PAVÓN
PANAMA
N
Paso Canoas
Punta Burica

MAP 3.1

With a culture attuned to face-saving and constitutionalism, Costa Ricans have prided themselves on civilized resolutions of political conflict, and policy makers and peaceful transitions have invariably followed electoral defeats.[2] Thus, although the PLN has prevailed in the most elections, opposing parties have never been excluded from power.

In the second half of the twentieth century, Costa Ricans carefully tailored an international reputation for having a safe, stable, and peace-loving country. During the cold war the country managed to avoid the internal ethnic conflict and violent convulsions that characterized much of Central America. Because the relatively small indigenous population had been decimated during Spanish colonialism, the country has long been the most homogenous in the region.[3] Also critically important, unlike post–civil war Guatemala, El Salvador, and Nicaragua, Costa Rica has not had to manage the socioeconomic consequences of once thoroughly militarized societies. In particular, apart from certain Nicaraguan immigrants, Costa Rica has been spared the problematic presence of demobilized soldiers and guerrillas and the circulation of numerous weapons following years of fighting. This may help explain how the Costa Rican murder rate has consistently remained a fifth or a sixth that of once war-torn neighbors.[4]

Costa Rica has also differed from Belize, Guatemala, and Honduras in that it has never had difficult antidrug relations with the U.S. government. Costa Rica's strong commitment to democratic values, coupled with an elite antidrug unit that has largely been competent and effective, professional and trustworthy, has led the United States to be forthcoming with training and equipment. For example, capitalizing on a productive Maritime Counter-drug Cooperation Agreement and decades of other successful joint endeavors, the United States in 2005 and 2006 invested a total of $2.3 million to build up the Costa Rican Coast Guard.[5] Unlike Panama, Nicaragua, Honduras, and Guatemala, the United States has never launched a military intervention in Costa Rica. One result has been that no lingering resentments have created ongoing tensions. Drug-trafficking networks have thus had to contend with the bridge-disfavoring factor of an unusually close relationship between Costa Rica and the United States.

The socioeconomic situation in Costa Rica has set it apart from its neighbors as well. As early as the nineteenth century, coffee exports, primarily to England, transformed Costa Rica with railroad construction and other infrastructure improvements, and it eventually developed into the region's wealthiest country.[6] In the early 1960s Costa Rica's membership in the Central American Common Market stimulated growth in manufacturing and industrialization, and by the 1970s Costa Rica had become one of Latin America's more advanced states.[7] Electricity and running water have long been commonplace, and a modern health-care system has led to low infant mortality and Latin America's highest life expectancy.[8] By 1981 the government had dedicated 70 percent of the budget to social programs, including health insurance and medical care.[9] Law-enforcement authorities and others in the criminal-justice system have

2. Indeed, a Costa Rican who offended another's dignity or honor might be sent to prison for ten to fifty days. Biesanz, Biesanz, and Biesanz, *Ticos*, 7–9.

3. The 2000 census categorized sixty-four thousand Costa Ricans as indigenous. See "Japanese Embassy Funds Indigenous Schools," *Tico Times* (Costa Rica) (hereafter cited as *TT* [CR]), 31 March 2006, 1.

4. See "Istmo: País repunta en muertes violentas," *Siglo Veintiuno* (Guatemala) (hereafter cited as *SV* [GU]), 6 March 2009, 2. Between 2006 and 2008 the Costa Rican murder rate rose from eight to eleven per hundred thousand, in contrast to El Salvador's from fifty-five to sixty-six per hundred thousand, Honduras's from forty-six to sixty-eight, and Guatemala's from fifty-one to fifty-six.

5. *INCSR* (2006), 8, and *INCSR* (2005), 12.

6. Biesanz, Biesanz, and Biesanz, *Ticos*, 1.

7. Seligson, "Costa Rica," 455–56.

8. Costa Ricans' life expectancy averages more than seventy-eight years. "Ticos' Life Expectancy Tops in L.A.," *TT* (CR), 29 June 2001, 1A. By the 1980s more than 80 percent of households had electricity and 95 percent, running water. Honey, *Hostile Acts*, 2.

9. Glassman, *Costa Rica*, 17.

tended to be better educated, trained, and equipped than their counterparts elsewhere in Central America. And the population, which reached about 3.8 million in 2000, has largely been spared the depths and the breadth of the region's poverty.[10]

Yet serious problems of governance have remained. While Costa Rica has frequently been touted as "the Switzerland of Central America," novelist Graham Greene caustically observed that this was something of "a libel on Switzerland," and eventually Costa Ricans themselves began to question the slogan's accuracy.[11] Even as the country cultivated its positive reputation, serious difficulties abounded. Although the Costa Rican Constitution extolled the family, domestic violence has been an enduring problem, as has child sexual abuse.[12] Despite the region's highest literacy rate, access to education has lagged.[13] Between 1950 and 1985 the population tripled. And the consequences of neighboring problems spilled into the country as refugees and economic migrants flooded Costa Rica, contributing to rising unemployment.[14] Although the serious gang problems that afflicted Belize, Guatemala, Honduras, and in quite recent years, Panama, have been avoided, Costa Rican crime rates have nonetheless climbed steadily.[15]

Although drug traffickers have sometimes designed their ventures somewhat differently in Costa Rica, for a quarter century cartels have succeeded in avoiding, contending with, or attempting to subvert the country's strengths, while exploiting its weaknesses. Despite considerable seizures, the country has proved to be a remarkably effective transshipment center, especially for cocaine.[16] The Costa Rican experience strongly suggests that political and economic development alone cannot resolve the drug-trafficking problems of bridge states. However, a more advanced bridge state may be able to interdict larger quantities of drugs and to contend somewhat more effectively with the violence and corruption that typically accompany extensive drug trafficking.

To date, however, very little has been written about the nature and details of drug and counter-drug operations in Costa Rica. What aspects of Costa Rican society have attracted drug organizations, which networks have been most important, and why? How might the Costa Rican drug trade best be characterized, and how has it evolved? Which drugs have been produced in the country, and which transshipped through it? What routes have smuggling organizations favored? How deeply have the different regions of the country been embroiled in the drug trade, and in what ways have Costa Rica's strengths and vulnerabilities affected it?

Bridge-Favoring Factors Relevant to Costa Rica

In much of Central America, drug organizations have exploited underdevelopment and, in

10. For the 2000 census figures, see "Census: Population Increase Due to Immigrant Flood," *TT* (CR), 2 February 2001, 1A. As of 2003, Costa Rican per capita income was $4,060, compared with $3,260 for Panama, $2,750 for Belize, $2,040 for El Salvador, $1,640 for Guatemala, $1,570 for Nicaragua, and $900 for Honduras. Allen and Leppman, *Student Atlas*, 141–43.

11. See "Is C.R. Still 'Little Switzerland'?," *TT* (CR), 27 August 1999, 1A. For the Greene quote, see Cockburn, *Out of Control*, 21.

12. See "Family Violence No Stranger in Tico Homes," *TT* (CR), 5 September 2008, 6, and "Child Sex Trade Fueled by Fear," *TT* (CR), 14 June 2002, 1A.

13. By 1980 the Costa Rican literacy rate stood at 93 percent, but a quarter century later the United Nations ranked Costa Rica 112th of 173 countries in access to education. See Honey, *Hostile Acts*, 2; "C.R. Leads Region in Education, but Still Lags," *TT* (CR), 20 April 2001, 8; and "U.N. Rankings Show Room for Improvement," *TT* (CR), 9 September 2005, 11.

14. For the population tripling, see Biesanz, Biesanz, and Biesanz, *Ticos*, 5. See also "C.R. Leads as Refugee Host," *TT* (CR), 2 March 2001, 1A.

15. Crimes investigated increased from 26,514 in 2002 to 61,884 in 2008; see, for instance, "Courts Overwhelmed by Rising Crime Rates," *TT* (CR), 14 August 2009, 4.

16. In 1985 U.S. diplomat George Jones reported that Colombian traffickers were aggressively moving in, looking to establish new routes north. See "Afirman que por Costa Rica se trafican toneladas de cocaína," *La Nación*

countries such as Belize and Guatemala, the lack of national integration. In Costa Rica drug syndicates have capitalized on quite different sets of factors. What is particularly striking about Costa Rican drug trafficking is that various of the country's strengths—its considerable economic activity, highly competitive democratic system, equitable laws and judicial system, even its positive international reputation—have led to real opportunities for drug smuggling. Costa Rica's experience thus underscores the adaptability of these transnational nonstate entities that have so successfully challenged Central American governments in the late cold war and early post–cold war periods by trafficking enormous quantities of illegal drugs across their territories.

Geography

The geographic advantages that Costa Rica has offered drug organizations may not be so immediately evident as those in other Central American bridge states. Costa Rica differs from Belize and Guatemala in having no common border with Mexico, that vitally important U.S. gateway. Nor does it flank Colombia, that formidable engine of drug exports, as Panama does. Not only does the country lack the barrier reef and scores of cayes that have made Belize such an inviting target for maritime trafficking, but it actually has relatively few islands. The country has no equivalent to such Central American archipelagos as the Islas de la Bahía off Honduras and Panama's San Blás and Las Perlas chains. While Costa Rica certainly has remote areas, by the early to mid-1980s, the country was more integrated than most Central American states.

Nonetheless, the long-standing popularity of Costa Rica among drug-smuggling organizations may be attributed in no small measure to geographic characteristics. Traffickers have found that, with respect to the aerial transshipment of South American cocaine and heroin, Costa Rica is quite conveniently situated. Roughly a quarter of the length of Central America northwest of Colombia, Costa Rica could serve as an intermediary stop for airplanes heading from South America to Mexico or the United States. Overland trafficking ventures have taken advantage of Costa Rica's fluid border zones. The boundaries with Panama and Nicaragua run through lightly populated areas, mostly characterized by jungles and thick forests, with mountains in the south and inland waterways in the north. Three rugged mountain chains and an extensive elevated plateau dominate much of the interior, and, away from the Valle Central, numerous Costa Rican towns and villages, farms and ranches, have remained quite isolated.[17] As in Belize, traffickers have found advantageous the combination of poorly policed hinterlands and a thriving tourist trade that might explain sudden activity at odd times and places. Drugs have frequently been transshipped via Costa Rica's wetlands and national parks, where gunrunning, clandestine meetings, and even drug-related murders have also occurred. Indeed, given its extensive jungle, highland rain forests, northern flatlands, and irregular topography, those trafficking drugs could easily rendezvous in Costa Rica without being detected.[18]

As for maritime-transshipment schemes, Costa Rica is not far from Colombia, with which it has had long-standing connections.

(Costa Rica) (hereafter cited as *LN* [CR]), 23 May 1985, 1, and "Costa Rica Faces Drug Threat, U.S. Warns," *TT* (CR), 24 May 1985, 1.

17. The Talamanca chain, site of Costa Rica's highest mountain, has been repeatedly associated with drug activities. See, for instance, "Tres bandas de narcos operan en Talamanca," *LN* (CR), 11 November 1992, 10A.

18. For instance, in 2009 a helicopter crash occurred in thick forests flanking Cerro de la Muerte near the Pan-American Highway between San José and San Isidro de El General. Authorities discovered in the wreckage 347 kilos of cocaine and two dead traffickers, including a pilot who had worked for fifteen years in the Public Security Ministry. "Cocaine Found at Site of Fatal Helicopter Crash," *TT* (CR), 8 May 2009, 5.

Ships have regularly traversed the Caribbean between Puerto Limón, the center of Costa Rica's sea trade, and such Colombian ports as Cartagena. Even more important, speedboats have frequently traveled from Limón to Colombia's Caribbean island of San Andrés. Furthermore, unlike Belize and El Salvador, Costa Rica has lengthy Caribbean and Pacific shorelines. Indeed, it trails only Panama for the longest coasts among Central American states. Costa Rica owns the uninhabited Isla del Coco far offshore, 340 miles west, which positions it along a prime Pacific drug-trafficking corridor. And, with respect to coastal waters, the Pacific side includes two large bays, the Dulce Gulf and Gulf of Nicoya, offering traffickers shelter in rough weather or to off-load drugs. Given Costa Rica's twin coasts, traffickers have sometimes employed intercoastal transshipment schemes, in which drugs enter on the Pacific side and depart from the Caribbean.[19] Thus, drug organizations have seized on a distinctive set of geographic characteristics in fashioning smuggling ventures.

Political System

In various respects Costa Rican political development has led the region. Its regime has come to feature strong civic institutions, a real commitment to the rule of law, and popular faith in key principles of democratic governance. Moreover, the country's media, especially its investigative journalists, have excelled at bringing attention to drug smuggling and corruption. Politicians have been prepared to devote considerable resources to countering the drug trade through the exposure of narcotics corruption and the interdiction and prosecution of traffickers.

Nevertheless, drug organizations have repeatedly taken advantage of particular aspects of the Costa Rican political system. As elsewhere in Latin America, politics in Costa Rica have traditionally depended on patronage, on the influential capitalizing on the ability to get things done, and on favor granting for friends, sometimes referred to as *amigoismo*.[20] Not only have cartels successfully recruited present or former mid-level officials, but they have found that a genuine democracy sporting a highly competitive political system could be manipulated through sizable contributions to candidates. Hotly contested elections and elaborate and costly political campaigns have enabled "narcodollars," at least for a period, to infiltrate campaign finances.[21] One former president, Daniel Oduber Quirós, was embarrassed and eventually suspended by his own party in a scandal involving American trafficker James Lionel Casey, who had donated to PLN election coffers.[22]

Blatant corruption, however, has contravened ingrained values in Costa Rican political culture, and rooting it out has garnered broad public support. The political system has shown itself to be sufficiently competitive, the law-enforcement system sufficiently effective, the media sufficiently vigorous, and the judicial system sufficiently independent to be able to publicize and react to corrupt behavior that might never surface or be punished in many other Central American states. By the beginning of the twenty-first century, three Costa Rican presidents were in prison or exile after cases involving bribery in

19. See the comments by Costa Rica's chief prosecutor Francisco Dall'Anese, who concluded, "It's a country that's difficult to get caught trafficking drugs in." "Fear of More Drugs in C.R.," *TT* (CR), 17 April 2009, 1.

20. See Biesanz, Biesanz, and Biesanz, *Ticos*, 76.

21. Contributions aimed to garner behind-the-scenes assistance with future problems, at least so long as links did not become public knowledge. For interviews of officials from Colombia, Jamaica, and Trinidad and Tobago concerning the likelihood of trafficking when outsiders regularly influence elites, see Bartilow and Kihong, "Busting Drugs," 105.

22. "Casey dió 1 millón de colones a Oduber en campaña," *LN* (CR), 27 January 1989, 4A; "Oduber reconoció donaciones a Casey," *LN* (CR), 27 January 1989, 5A; "Oduber admite que usó dinero de Casey," *LN* (CR), 28 January 1989, 4A; and "PLN sanciona a Oduber," *LN* (CR), 25 April 1990, 4A.

the health, construction, and telecommunications sectors. These cases stimulated real political dissatisfaction, with increasing voter absenteeism and disillusionment.[23] Eventually, the scandal-ridden PUSC declined precipitously in popularity, and the country's political landscape fragmented. Polls showed deep concerns with government that would have astounded Costa Ricans a generation before. Pessimism, cynicism, despair, and shame sprouted within a Costa Rican society that had traditionally exhibited real citizen pride in its governance.

Yet part of the inner strength of the Costa Rican system has involved a resilient capacity to adapt and to reform. The "deep democratization" that has starkly contrasted with the more shallowly rooted democratic values in much of Central America has been evident in the speed with which politicians have responded.[24] This may be seen not only in the convening of legislative drug commissions charged with uncovering narco-corruption, but in the extent of their investigations, their publicizing of suspicious activities, and their operational recommendations, such as barring suspect foreigners from future entry and tainted officials from further government service. It was eventually reflected as well not simply in the passage of laws against money laundering and illicit enrichment, but in the actual prosecution of official corruption.[25]

The Costa Rican government has proven itself able to move more nimbly than have neighboring political regimes in fashioning laws to respond to problems and to better align them with core popular values. While laws against organized crime have lagged, Costa Rican legal reforms have influenced the extent and consequences of drug corruption as well as money laundering. Although in certain respects Costa Rica might have provided a model for other Central American states to emulate, intraregional tensions and jealousies have curtailed the impact of the Costa Rican example, which has in any event been uneven in its response to drug trafficking.

Economy

In the northern Central American states, extensive poverty, coupled with a lack of economic opportunities, has greatly enhanced the pools of potential collaborators for drug syndicates. Here, too, Costa Rica has been something of a singular case. By the 1980s Costa Rica was developing into one of the most advanced economies in the Caribbean basin, consistently ranking among its leaders in foreign trade.[26] Indeed, in this period Costa Ricans could claim to have become part of the newly developed world.[27]

In particular, Costa Rica has long enjoyed a thriving tourist trade, with more than a half

23. For more on political dissatisfaction, see ombudswoman Sandra Piszk's four-hundred-page report, arguing that Costa Rica needed to "redemocratize" to counter corruption, power concentration, and lack of transparency and access to courts and government services. "Report: C.R. Democracy Imperiled," *TT* (CR), 16 June 2000, 1A. According to a 1995 poll, 65 percent believed problems would be exacerbated that year, with 71 percent predicting that the new government would make matters worse. "Pesimismo domina a ticos," *LN* (CR), 13 June 1995, 10A. By 2001 almost 80 percent of respondents in a National University poll agreed that Costa Rican democracy had deteriorated, citing "loss of values, fraud, and government corruption." "Ticos Doubt Democracy," *TT* (CR), 10 August 2001, 1A.

24. Deep democratization involves "not just elections but vigorous contention over real issues among people and groups capable of defending themselves politically and of reaching political settlements sustained by their own lasting interests. Such contention and the social 'ownership' of institutions it fosters, helped create democracy in societies where it is now strong." Johnston, *Syndromes of Corruption*, 3.

25. By 2006 the severity of the new Costa Rican law against official illicit enrichment led U.S. officials to conclude that "Costa Rica's commitment to combat public corruption appears to have been strengthened by the scandals." *INCSR* (2007), 5.

26. J. Bell, *Crisis in Costa Rica*, 71.

27. In 2005 the U.N. ranked Costa Rica, with a per capita income of $9,600 (fifty-seventh highest globally), as the forty-seventh most developed state. "U.N. Rankings Show Room," 11.

million arriving annually by the 1990s to enjoy its ecotourism, tropical beaches, and national parks. North American, South American, and European tourists, as well as expatriate retirees, have delivered significant hard currency, much more than has Honduran or Nicaraguan tourism. Furthermore, the nutrient-rich waters off Costa Rica's coasts led the commercial-fishing industry to grow by 1,175 percent between 1980 and 2000, bringing more than $100 million in export earnings by 2006.[28] Agriculture, another critically important sector, modernized relatively quickly, and the remainder of the economy became more diversified than those of various other Central American states. For instance, Costa Ricans have engaged in the assembly of high-technology items: integrated circuits and other electronics, as well as microchips that are exported for Intel. By the early twenty-first century, eighteen free trade zones promoted the export of Costa Rican seafood, produce, and textiles, as well as the reexport of medicines.[29]

Ironically, however, the very economic and political development and positive international reputation that have attracted so many foreigners to Costa Rica have also contributed to its extensive involvement in the drug trade. Given the country's reputation, traffickers not only have come to value false Costa Rican passports, but have frequently scheduled meetings in the country.[30] A relatively high per capita income has encouraged the establishment of local drug markets.[31] Most significant, cartels have perceived a comparative advantage in using the country to export cocaine. Traffickers have believed that customs inspectors in the market states view with less suspicion an individual coming from Costa Rica or a load of flowers or seafood or other Costa Rican export than one arriving directly from Colombia or from any other Central American country.[32] Since expedited customs inspections often miss hidden drugs, criminal syndicates have seen the positive Costa Rican reputation as a substantial bridge-favoring factor.

Opportunistic drug organizations have capitalized on other strengths of a newly developed society and a reasonably vibrant economy as well. A more sophisticated, rapidly developing economy could be used to invest and launder drug profits. It could also serve as cover for conspirators looking to buy aviation fuel, arrange safe houses, deal with mechanical or other logistical problems, or export precursor chemicals to South America.[33] The country's infrastructure has come to include numerous airstrips and a better road network than found in poorer neighbors, both important for speedy transit. A reasonably modern communications system has also been a factor. On account of the strict compartmentalization of trafficking operations, the ability to communicate efficiently has

28. "Country's Fisheries Dangle by Thin Line," *TT* (CR), 7 September 2007, 8. Of the 15.5 million kilograms of seafood, just over 60 percent was exported to the United States.

29. *INCSR* (2006), 5; "Exports Drop 22 Percent," *TT* (CR), 9 March 2001, 6; and "Spoils System Is Hurting C.R.," *TT* (CR), 2 March 2001, 2.

30. See "Creen que red trafica pasaportes," *LN* (CR), 13 March 2005, 16A, and "Colombians Nabbed in Germany," *TT* (CR), 2 March 1990, 22. For a Medellín trafficker using a Costa Rican passport while attempting to smuggle 123 kilos of cocaine into Spain, see "Mujer presa en España resultó ser colombiana," *LN* (CR), 21 November 1990, 10A, and "Tica era cabecilla de traficantes en España," *LN* (CR), 20 November 1990, 4A. In 1990 Interpol reported thirteen traffickers used false Costa Rican passports to import cocaine into Italy, Spain, Belgium, Switzerland, Germany, and the Netherlands. "Bandas de 'narcos' usan falsos pasaportes ticos," *LN* (CR), 4 January 1990, 10A.

31. Two imprisoned traffickers interviewed in 2002 noted that "the level of wealth among countries through which they smuggled was a critical aspect of the incentive structure of drug trafficking." Bartilow and Kihong, "Free Traders," 130.

32. For a trafficker directing a subordinate, in fact an undercover agent, to use Costa Rican ships to move cocaine because they would not be checked so carefully, see "Jenne Urges Port Crackdown," *Fort Lauderdale Sun-Sentinel*, 17 April 1998, 1A. For earlier evidence of this, see "Bust Yields Record Cocaine Haul," *TT* (CR), 10 July 1987, 4, and Luis Fishman's statement in "Coca en furgón iba hacia Miami," *LN* (CR), 23 November 1993, 10A.

33. In 1985 authorities discovered fifty-nine tons of ether, a chemical used in cocaine processing, in Caldera en route to Colombia. "Afirman," 1.

assisted conspirators acting within Costa Rica or coordinating activities with associates abroad.

In addition, drug networks aiming to camouflage operations have often utilized the country's largest metropolitan area, San José and surrounding environs. About two-thirds of the population live in the densely populated Valle Central—the approximately twenty-by-fifty-mile upland area centered on the capital of San José and the neighboring cities of Alajuela, Cartago, and Heredia.[34] This large metropolitan area has enabled the temporary storage of narcotics, as traffickers have consolidated loads for export.[35] During the 1990s, those engaged in international commerce generally and in the cocaine trade in particular put a premium on "flexibility, the development of a capacity of immediate response to changes in demand, transportation, distribution, and law enforcement activity."[36] Drug rings operating in Costa Rica were particularly well situated in these respects.

Yet another feature of the Costa Rican economy relevant to drug trafficking involves commercial air traffic. A number of airlines have regularly flown not only from Costa Rica to major U.S. gateways but from San Andrés, Bogotá, Medellín, and other drug-exporting hubs to the Juan Santamaría International Airport in Alajuela. The relatively advanced economy has ensured that considerable air cargo, within which narcotics might be secreted, has constantly left the country.[37] Trafficking networks directing multiple shipments through Juan Santamaría have sometimes tried to ensure smooth transit by recruiting airport employees working in customs or handling baggage or air freight and looking to supplement their regular incomes.[38]

Individual couriers on commercial flights have also frequently carried drugs into and out of the country, on their persons, in their stomachs, or in their luggage.[39] This "ant traffic"

34. Biesanz, Biesanz, and Biesanz, *Ticos*, 3. In the 1980s the San José population exceeded seven hundred thousand and, with other sizable surrounding cities, created a significant metropolitan area on the central plain.

35. See DEA, *Resources, Costa Rica* (2000), 5. For a representative case, in which in 1988 authorities found sixty-four kilos of cocaine stored in a San José house prior to planned export through the airport, see "Incautados sesenta y cuatro kilos de cocaína," *LN* (CR), 7 July 1988, 10A.

36. Vellinga, "Political Economy," 14.

37. In 1983 airport authorities seized 490 kilos of cocaine and arrested three who had flown the drugs from Colombia. "El mayor cargamento," *LN* (CR), 4 July 1987, 8A. In 1994 Miami antidrug agents found 200 kilos of cocaine on an Iberia flight arriving from Costa Rica. In 1996 Dallas authorities seized 27 kilos of cocaine off an American Airlines flight from San José, and shortly thereafter Costa Rican officials discovered a like shipment heading to Dallas. The following year agents seized 86.5 kilos of cocaine on an American Airlines flight heading from San José to Miami. See "Incautan doscientos kilos de cocaína en Miami," *LN* (CR), 16 October 1994, 10A; "Procesados funcionarios del aeropuerto," *LN* (CR), 31 October 1994, 10A; "Cocaína en avión," *LN* (CR), 23 March 1996, 11A; "Caen doscientos kilos de coca," *LN* (CR), 9 July 1996, 10A; "Hallan cocaína en avión de American," *LN* (CR), 22 April 1997, 10A; and "Amplían procesamiento contra Leonel Villalobos," *LN* (CR), 24 April 1997, 6A.

38. In 1995 DEA agents used a confidential informant to penetrate a Colombian network transshipping cocaine from Costa Rica to Florida by air. See *United States v. Gonzalez*, 183 F.3d 1315. When former Costa Rican official Ricardo Alem turned informant, he reported that various airport employees had been on his network's payroll to assist in cocaine transshipment, including fifteen loads of at least fifty kilos directed to the United States. "Red traficó una tonelada de coca," *LN* (CR), 7 March 1997, 4A. Periodically, authorities implicated airline and airport personnel in other trafficking ventures. In a representative 1987 case, officials seized seventy-six kilos of cocaine from one airline employee's luggage. "Caen 950 millones en cocaína," *LN* (CR), 24 March 1987, 1.

39. For representative cases of cocaine mules caught entering Costa Rica from San Andrés, see "Localizan cocaína en aeropuerto," *LN* (CR), 9 November 1985, 10A; "Detenida costarricense con cinco kilos de cocaína," *LN* (CR), 4 November 1989, 10A; "En fuga presunto jefe de banda," *LN* (CR), 24 November 1989, 10A; and "Mujer con droga," *LN* (CR), 24 December 2002, 10A. For couriers carrying drugs in their stomachs, see, for instance, "Italian Drug-Runner Busted with Coke in Her Stomach," *TT* (CR), 29 February 2008, 8, and "Smuggling Drugs Not for the Weak of Stomach," *TT* (CR), 28 March 2008, 13. In 1989 antidrug authorities seized 137 kilos from a drug ring sending cocaine to Miami in suitcases containing 25 kilos apiece. See "Carga de cocaína entró por Sixaola," *LN* (CR), 14 November 1989, 12A; "Remiten a Alajuela causa por 137 kilos de coca," *LN* (CR), 22 November 1989, 10A; "Intensifican pesquisas sobre presos por coca," *LN* (CR), 23 November 1989, 10A; and "La meta era cuatro cargamentos semanales," *LN* (CR), 26 November 1989, 10A.

has enticed smuggling organizations for its low risk. Each courier carries only a small amount of drugs, and the "mules" themselves are viewed as expendable and easily replaced. Moreover, organizations can compartmentalize courier operations so that authorities have trouble prosecuting and convicting anyone other than the person caught with the drugs.[40] Despite the fact that Costa Rican officials, added by X-ray machines and drug-sniffing canine units, have regularly arrested couriers, this method has retained its popularity over time.[41]

In fact, ample numbers of Costa Ricans have been unemployed or underemployed or simply eager for drug-trade earnings. It is true that Costa Rica has not had to contend with the breadth of poverty found elsewhere in the region: about 18 percent of the population has been judged to be below the poverty line, as opposed to 80 percent of Hondurans.[42] Nevertheless, for all the progress made, the country's economic picture has never been entirely rosy, and the sometimes precarious position of the Costa Rican economy has long contrasted with the stability of its political regime. One significant problem has been that, traditionally, too much of the economy has focused on a narrow range of primary commodities subject to serious price fluctuations: principally coffee, bananas, sugar, and beef, supplemented by such specialties as nuts, flowers, and ornamental fruits and plants. Moreover, significant deforestation has occurred, and a steady consolidation of agricultural enterprises has contributed to a rural population in which many do not own the land that they work.[43]

Indeed, just as Colombian cocaine-trafficking organizations began to favor Central American routes over Caribbean ones, Costa Rica was concluding a period of grave economic troubles. During the global recession from 1979 to 1982, high government spending and large foreign debt, coupled with rising costs of oil and other imports and declining agricultural export prices, brought on a wrenching economic downturn. This was marked by high unemployment, the collapse of the Costa Rican currency, and inflation that rose to 64 percent.[44] As world markets recovered, however, the country's economy regained its footing, and its balance of trade improved. In part, this rebound reflected the foreign aid that poured into Costa Rica from the World Bank, the International Monetary Fund, the Inter-American Development Bank, and the United States.[45] Deeply concerned by the Nicaraguan civil war, the U.S. government looked to shore up Costa Rica against Marxist influence, while assisting contras battling Sandinistas from Costa Rican soil.

Nonetheless, the serious dislocation that has periodically struck the Costa Rican economy, whether taking the form of low wages and inflation or the distress of particular sectors, has regularly replenished the pool of unskilled labor ready to assist in drug transshipment,

40. Since couriers often know little about their organization, they cannot usually reduce their sentences by serving as useful witnesses. Instead, their lawyers often advise plea bargaining, because proceeding to trial might risk a penalty of ten years of prison time. "Narcos les pintan castillos en el aire," *LN* (CR), 15 January 2006, 21A.

41. Between 2000 and 2005, 471 couriers from 37 countries were caught, most at the airport. "Ambición destruyó la vida de 472 'burros' del narcotráfico," *LN* (CR), 15 January 2006, 20A.

42. After calculating the cost of a food basket of forty-two basic products, plus supplements for minimal housing, clothing, education, and health care, the National Statistics and Census Institute judged 17.7 percent below the poverty line in 2008, one percentage point higher than in 2007. In assessing households, the institute considered a family poor if it earned less than $122 per person per month and extremely poor if less than $56 per month. "Ninety-Five Thousand More Poor People in 2008," *TT* (CR), 31 October 2008, 6. See also "National Report Gives Good News and Bad," *TT* (CR), 23 November 2007, 3.

43. See Honey, *Hostile Acts*, 159, and Biesanz, Biesanz, and Biesanz, *Ticos*, 40.

44. See "Pope and Reagan Visited, Colón Collapsed," *TT* (CR), 19 May 2006, S23.

45. For a period in the 1980s Costa Rica was the second highest per capita recipient of U.S. economic aid, trailing only Israel. Biesanz, Biesanz, and Biesanz, *Ticos*, 5, 62. For information on the first downturn, see pages 4 and 56. For a table summarizing foreign assistance from 1980–90, see page 62.

serving as lookouts, off-loaders, informants, and hired muscle.[46] Similarly, as offshore pollution and depleted fisheries led to dwindling catches, an "alarming increase" was noted "in fishermen turning to coastal drug running." In fact, Costa Rica has long had a worrisome economic gap: in 2005, for instance, the richest 20 percent controlled 51.5 percent of the wealth and the poorest 20 percent divided a mere 4.2 percent.[47] Both the lure of "easy money" and the fear engendered by criminal organizations could motivate as readily in Costa Rica as in its neighbors.

The Criminal-Justice System

Costa Rica has also differed in important respects from other Central American countries in the manner in which justice has been administered. In general, its civil law legal institutions have functioned much more effectively than those in its neighbors. Morale has been better, sensible reforms have periodically been implemented, and those working in the system have had more resources than those in poorer countries. An office of public defenders has helped to ensure counsel for indigent defendants. Judges have been better paid and more respected, and their independence and rectitude have been questioned less frequently. While problems have cropped up in the rank-and-file police, the DEA has cooperated quite closely with the judiciary's elite counternarcotics unit from the Office of Judicial Investigations (OIJ), long considered one of the best in Latin America.

For all of its strengths, however, the Costa Rican criminal-justice system as a whole has failed to deal as effectively as might be hoped with the drug trade. In countering organized crime, a chain of institutions is limited by its weakest links. The strengths of the antidrug police have thus provided traffickers with additional incentives to corrupt penal, customs, political, and other officials.[48] Even more important, the principal institutions administering justice have not been well tailored to combat transnational crime, with law enforcement laboring to counter traffickers using antiquated criminal laws and procedures. In 2009 chief prosecutor Francisco Dall'Anese termed his country "very vulnerable" to the drug trade, pointing to inadequate "laws that don't correspond with the reality of organized crime." In noting the presence of new laws and policies in this field in Guatemala, Nicaragua, and Panama, Dall'Anese lamented, "What's going to happen to Costa Rica? It'll be like a building that gets fumigated on every floor except one: all the rats go to the non-fumigated floor. . . . This country hasn't taken the [appropriate] legal, economic, or immigration measures. . . . It doesn't have a clear policy regarding organized crime, and networks have already entered."[49]

Numerous particular procedural and institutional flaws have hampered efforts to resist organized crime. For example, while police have tapped phones in numerous drug-trafficking cases, prosecutors have often not been able to use the evidence to gain convictions.[50] Indeed, in 1990 the Supreme Court ruled unconstitutional the use of wiretaps and resulting evidence, a decision that undermined scores of drug cases dating back to a 1973 court decision that had allowed them.[51] The Legislative Assembly was then compelled to amend the constitution and

46. "Country's Fisheries Dangle," 8.

47. This statistic is derived from the UN Development Programme's Human Development Index. "U.N. Rankings Show Room," 11.

48. For this point with respect to increased Mexican drug enforcement, see Andreas, *Border Games*, 13, 23, 61.

49. "Dall'Anese: It's Easy to Traffic Drugs Here," *TT* (CR), 30 January 2009, 2.

50. For a useful summary of Costa Rican wiretapping laws, see Duartes Delgado, *Jurisprudencia sobre narcotráfico*, 107–31.See also "Corte reguló allanamientos e intervenciones telefónicas," *LN* (CR), 1 September 1988, 16A.

51. "Court Bans Use of Phone Bugs," *TT* (CR), 19 October 1990, 10. For cases involving whether to free a prisoner given use of wiretap evidence, see "Primera resolución tras anularse prueba telefónica," *LN* (CR), 31 October 1990, 10A, and "Ordenan liberar a dos presuntos narcotraficantes," *La Prensa* (Panama) (hereafter cited as *LP* [PA]), 2 November 1990, 2A. For the effect of the Supreme Court decision on a U.S. trafficking case, see *United States v. DeRewal*, 1991 U.S. Dist. LEXIS 9281.

pass implementing legislation regulating wiretap use, a time-consuming process that wreaked havoc with more drug-trafficking investigations and prosecutions.

A traditional strict prohibition against police engaging in any variety of criminal activity has long hampered undercover operations. Although the legislature created a legal framework to combat money laundering, it at first proved to be simplistic and easily evaded.[52] The practice of bounty hunting, or returning fugitives to a state for compensation, has been illegal in Costa Rica, and the constitution has not only completely prohibited the extradition of Costa Rican citizens but offered a range of strong legal protections to defendants.[53] In fact, the judicial system has been so overwhelmingly focused on zealously guarding civil liberties that it has seriously disadvantaged law enforcement and greatly benefited drug networks able to hire leading defense lawyers.[54]

Drug rings have taken full advantage of those aspects of the criminal-justice system that have not yet modernized. The police have traditionally been underpaid and, apart from the elite antinarcotics unit, poorly trained and vulnerable to bribery.[55] A proposal to create a witness-protection program did not emerge until 2008 and was not well endowed.[56] In fact, for a time budget cuts kept the police from making international phone calls, curtailing potential cooperation with neighboring countries, the United States, and Europe. Costa Rican officials have not formulated an effective system that enables the state not merely to seize the assets of criminals but to hold them in conditions that minimize their diminution in value and then sell them after trial at fair market value with the proceeds reverting to the government. Instead, negligence and mismanagement combined with lengthy delays in the court system have caused many seized assets to be wasted. As for prisons, although by 2006 new space had alleviated chronic overcrowding, the penal system has long been a national embarrassment, plagued by a lack of resources and professionalism.[57] Unsurprisingly, notable traffickers have escaped.

The Evolution of Drug Trafficking in Costa Rica

While Costa Rica's balance sheet of bridge-favoring and bridge-disfavoring attributes has been singular in many respects, plainly the country's geography, political system, economy, and criminal-justice system have attracted the attention of large and small drug rings alike. As trafficking evolved, the successful passage of large drug shipments encouraged organizations to try an array of methods and routes.

52. For additional details about the 1998 drug law, see the document DEA prepared for the Costa Rican Legislative Assembly—"Evaluación de la amenaza."

53. See "State Can't Pay for Fugitive's Return," *TT* (CR), 8 April 2005, 1. One frustrated prosecutor declared, "The whole Costa Rican system is set up to avoid convicting and incarcerating people," and a police press release read, "Foreign criminals consider Costa Rica a paradise to commit crimes in, given the lack of severity of the law's application." See "Criminals Guffaw at Tico Justice," *TT* (CR), 22 February 2008, 1, and "They Said What? . . . Voice from '08," *TT* (CR), 24 December 2008, 48. From 1997 to 2007 conviction rates fell from one in five cases to one in forty. "Crime Weighs Heavily on Costa Rican Minds," *TT* (CR), 24 December 2008, 43.

54. For interviews with Canadian and U.S. drug agents concerning systems strong on civil liberties disadvantaging police, see Bartilow and Kihong, "Free Traders," 131. See also Wisotsky, *Breaking the Impasse*, 117–39.

55. See "Narco insiste en infiltrar los cuerpos policiales," *LN* (CR), 27 June 2008, 5A, and "Once policías detenidos por aliarse con narcotraficantes," *LN* (CR), 27 June 2008, 4A.

56. The witness-protection program had a 2009 budget of $112,000. "OIJ Faces External and Internal Turmoil," *TT* (CR), 20 November 2009, 5. See also "Drug Seizures Grease Justice System's Wheels," *TT* (CR), 2 May 2008, 5, and "Crime Bill Advances in Legislative Assembly," *TT* (CR), 3 October 2008, 7.

57. See "Prisons Below Capacity for First Time," *TT* (CR), 19 May 2006, 4; DOS, *2009 Human Rights Report*; and "U.S. Report Cites C.R. Human Rights Issues," *TT* (CR), 6 March 2009, 5.

The Costa Rican Marijuana Trade

Cannabis has been the only illegal drug grown in Costa Rica. Harvested biannually, often mixed with legitimate crops, and typically cultivated in small, rather dispersed fields, Costa Rican marijuana traditionally came from the inland hills of Limón Province, flanking the country's Caribbean coast.[58] As the drug rose in popularity, and small farmers faced increasing economic difficulties, cannabis came to be planted across Costa Rica, including in the Guanacaste and Puntarenas Provinces on the Pacific side.[59] Particularly notable areas of cannabis cultivation have been the southern part of the Talamanca mountain range and two valleys—lower, warmer, and much less populated than the Valle Central—the Valle de la Estrella to the southwest of Puerto Limón and the Valle de El General, near the town of Buenos Aires. To cultivate, protect, and harvest the marijuana, traffickers have frequently employed poverty-stricken indigenous growers, who have intimate knowledge of the terrain and few other economic opportunities.[60] In the most rugged portions of Talamanca, authorities on foot might take eight days to reach the least accessible areas, providing plenty of time for advance warning.

Drug networks have consistently directed much of the Costa Rican marijuana crop toward a substantial internal market; however, the harvest has periodically exceeded domestic consumption levels.[61] In 1985 Ron Thomas, U.S. assistant secretary of state for International Narcotics Matters, listed Costa Rica and Belize as the key Central American marijuana-trafficking countries, noting a significant jump in Costa Rican cannabis exported to the United States.[62] In 1988, after conceding that Costa Rican marijuana production had long been underestimated, the U.S. State Department referenced the belief of local antidrug officials that as much as 75 percent of the crop might be exported. Although this may well have been an overestimate, when Costa Rican drug producers have exported marijuana, it has normally exited by sea, with the U.S. the prime market and Panama a secondary one.[63]

Despite earnest official efforts to curb the marijuana harvest, the crop has been sufficiently lucrative that growers have consistently responded to eradication by increasing acreage. As fig. 3.1 illustrates, marijuana cultivation leaped six-fold between 1985 and 1990. In 1990 alone more than

58. Former cabinet minister and UN ambassador Dr. Carlos José Gutiérrez Gutiérrez, then working for the UN Latin American Institute for Crime Prevention and the Treatment of Offenders, recalled, "As far back as I can remember, . . . you could not find two issues of the weekly Limón newspaper without a confiscation of marijuana. Marijuana has since raised its status. In those days, marijuana addiction was found in the lowest part of the lowest class. Then it became fashionable for university people. Always a lot." Interview, 25 May 1990, San José, Costa Rica. Note that this contradicts the assertion that Costa Rican cannabis cultivation dates only to the 1970s. See Weir, "Costa Rica," 459.

59. For U.S. government assessments of where marijuana was being grown, see *INCSR* (1988), 119, and DEA, *Resources, Costa Rica* (2000), 4. For Costa Rican sources, see "Police Uproot 125,000 Marijuana Plants," *TT* (CR), 26 August 2005, 6; "Indian Boys Running Marijuana," *TT* (CR), 14 July 2000, 4; "U.S. Teams Help Uproot Marijuana," *TT* (CR), 28 April 2000, 10; and "Confiscan marihuana," *LN* (CR), 12 September 1997, 10A.

60. See "Narcotraficantes introducen una marihuana más adictiva," *LN* (CR), 5 January 2009, 14A, and "Narcos se aprovechan de los indígenas," *LN* (CR), 5 January 2009, 14A.

61. *INCSR* (1993), 148, and *INCSR* (1992), 147. Estimates of how many Costa Ricans smoke marijuana have varied substantially. In 1985 the U.S. State Department reported that since 1982 between 200,000 and 250,000 Costa Ricans had used marijuana annually; however, its narcotics reports issued between 1990 and 2003 cited a mere 30,000 marijuana users. In 2010 the Costa Rican Ministry of Public Security estimated 400,000 users. See *INCSR* (1985), 83; *INCSR* (1990), 174; *INCSR* (2011), 206; and "Narcotraficantes introducen," 14A.

62. "Costa Rica y Belice exportan marihuana a EE.UU.," *LN* (CR), 28 June 1985, 24A.

63. *INCSR* (1988), 118. For a Costa Rican, once the chauffeur of foreign traffickers, who allegedly moved to direct his own marijuana-export operation to the United States, see "Narcotráfico desde prisión," *LN* (CR), 27 February 1997, 10A. For marijuana exports to Panama, see "Dos detenidos con sesenta y ocho kilos de marihuana comprimida," *LN* (CR), 25 January 2009, 12A

Fig. 3.1 Marijuana cultivation, eradication, and yield in Costa Rica, 1985–1991

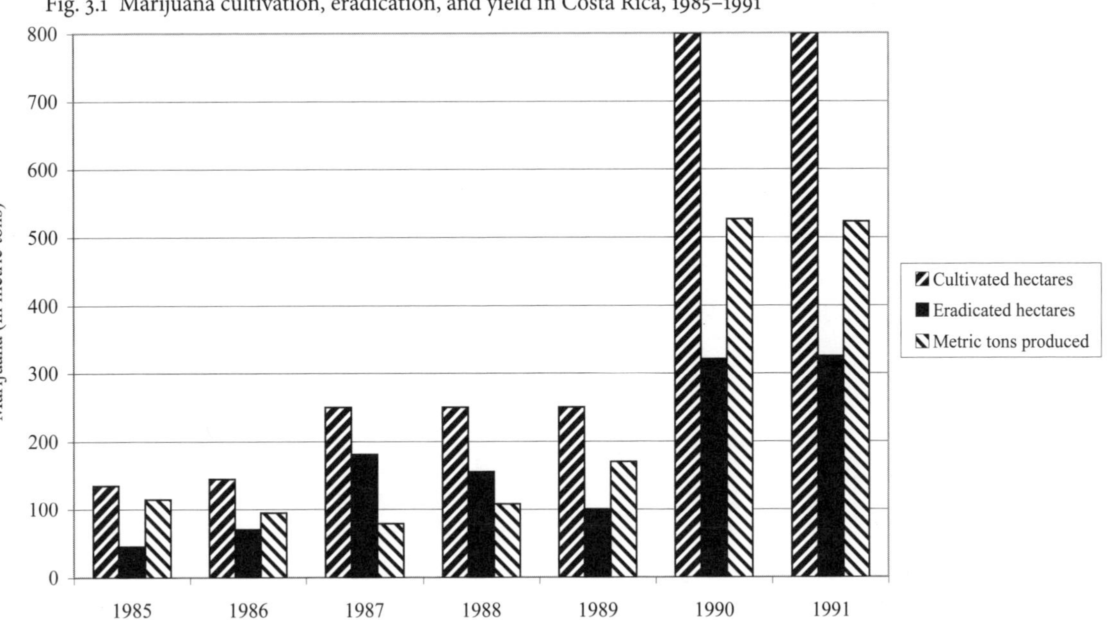

Sources: *INCSR* (1988), 121; *INCSR* (1992), 150; "Diez mil a veinte mil kilos de coca cruzan el país," *LN* (CR), 21 May 1990, 5A.

Note: After 1992 the State Department no longer published estimates of eradicated hectares and metric tons, although for the following two years it continued to estimate that eight hundred hectares were being cultivated. *INCSR* (1993), 148; *INCSR* (1994), 143.

three million plants were destroyed, and yet, in the following years, farmers more than tripled the acreage being cultivated.[64] New plantings came along the northern border with Nicaragua and in Talamanca, where eradication has been quite difficult without helicopters to transport personnel.[65] The resulting potential yield, which fig. 3.1 shows at more than five hundred tons, plainly exceeded the marijuana likely to be consumed domestically.[66]

The new millennium found Costa Rican farmers planting even more marijuana, and counternarcotics authorities straining to keep pace using aerial eradication. Fig. 3.2 illustrates not only that significant numbers of cannabis plants have been destroyed but that the eradication totals rose and fell sharply. This occurred as marijuana producers presented the state with different challenges and as the policies and priorities of antidrug officials shifted. Of particular note, in a 1999 regional antidrug program called Central Skies Operation Chokehold, Costa Rican officials, using U.S. technology, eliminated more than 2.1 million cannabis plants, with 4.2 million taken out in 2000. The following year another million marijuana plants were eradicated, a number that doubled once again in 2002.[67] Nevertheless, Costa Rica has thus far failed to restrict marijuana production either as rapidly or as dramatically as did Belize in the 1980s.

64. *INCSR* (1991), 138.

65. *INCSR* (1992), 148. In 1998 the Special Support Police (or "Mountain Police") of the Public Security Ministry destroyed more than 510,000 marijuana plants, some twelve feet high, using helicopters stationed at Soto Cano Air Force Base in Honduras. *INCSR* (1999), 147.

66. *INCSR* (1992), 150.

67. For the eradication figures, see DEA, *Resources, Costa Rica* (2000), 4; *INCSR* (2000), 159–60; *INCSR* (2001), 6; and DEA, *Resources, Costa Rica* (2003), 2.

Fig. 3.2 Eradication of marijuana plants in Costa Rica, 1992–2010

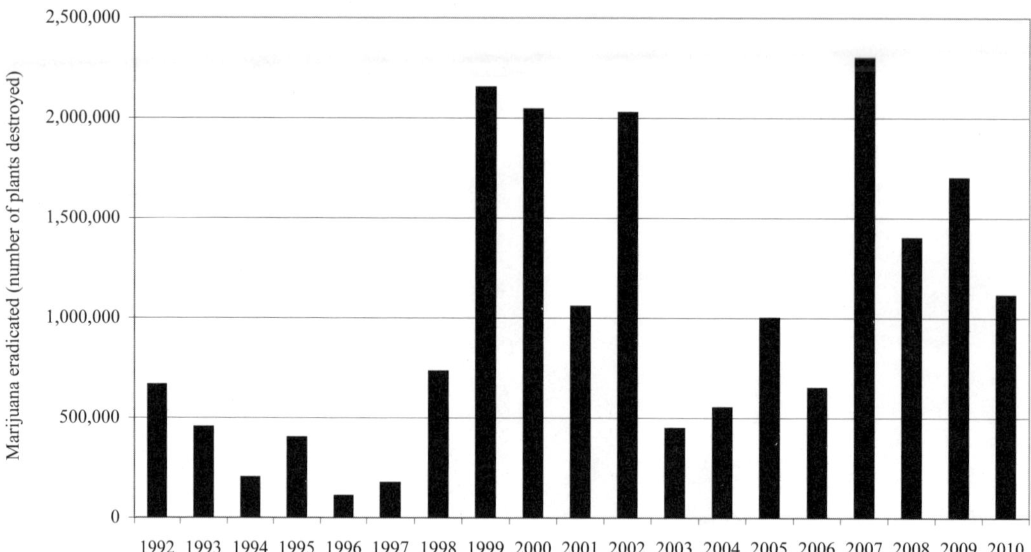

Sources: INCSR (2011), 206; *INCSR* (2010), 214; *INCSR* (2009), 210; *INCSR* (2008), 162; *INCSR* (2007), 154; *INCSR* (2006), 137; DEA, *Resources, Costa Rica* (2003), 2; DEA, *Resources, Costa Rica* (2000), 3.

Note: Before 1992 the U.S. government opted to estimate the hectares of marijuana that had been eradicated in Costa Rica, rather than the number of eradicated cannabis plants (see fig. 3.1).

Even after significant eradication campaigns, extremely large marijuana seizures have occasionally occurred. In 2004, for instance, law-enforcement agents in the far southern city of San Vito inspected a truck carrying manure and found 2,475 kilos of marijuana.[68]

Of even more concern internationally, smuggling networks have periodically transshipped foreign-grown marijuana, most frequently Colombian in origin, which traversed Costa Rican waters or traveled in Costa Rican vessels to its ultimate destination. In 1985 and 1987 Mexican and U.S. officials seized Costa Rican ships carrying 15 and 20 tons of cannabis.[69] Costa Rican police have also engineered very large marijuana busts. In 1993 authorities captured a 3.5-ton shipment in the country's territorial waters, heading from Esmereldas, Ecuador, to Canada in a Mexican-financed operation.[70] Antidrug officials came upon a ship anchored off Isla del Caño, a biological preserve off the Osa Peninsula, located along a well-known maritime drug route. After learning that the *Phoenix* had long been suspected of trafficking, authorities took the ship to Golfito to be searched, and drug-sniffing dogs eventually located the marijuana.

Other notable seizures followed. In the mid-1990s U.S. authorities broke up what a federal appellate court called a "large and intricate marijuana importation and distribution network," in which tons of cannabis had been transferred

68. "Two Tons of Marijuana Seized in Southern Zone," *TT* (CR), 14 May 2004, 3. In 2007 officials reported seizing a total of 2,881 kilos of processed marijuana. *INCSR* (2007), 5.

69. In 1985 the Mexican Navy seized *El Triunfador*, as did U.S. authorities the *Ana Bell* in 1987. See "Decomisan quince toneladas de 'hierba' en barco 'Tico,'" *La Prensa* (Honduras) (hereafter cited as *LP* [HO]), 29 April 1985, 16; "Investigan a dueños de barco detenido en EE.UU.," *LN* (CR), 11 June 1987, 10A; and "Cae barco tico con marihuana," *LN* (CR), 10 June 1987, 1.

70. "3,5 toneladas de marihuana en barco," *LN* (CR), 20 February 1993, 12A, and "Leve condena a tripulación del *Phoenix*," *LN* (CR), 25 February 1994, 10A.

from Colombian suppliers to American transshippers off Costa Rica's Isla de Monterosa. In 1999, 1,440 kilos of marijuana were seized on a small island in the Gulf of Nicoya. And in 2008 coast guard officials captured a vessel that was transporting 4.4 tons of Colombian marijuana, worth approximately $106 million, through Costa Rican waters to the United States.[71]

The significance of Costa Rica for international marijuana trafficking should be neither overlooked nor overstated. Given the modest potency of Costa Rican cannabis and the ready availability of higher-quality marijuana, foreign demand has remained strictly limited.[72] Indeed, just as the purity levels of cocaine and heroin sold in the foremost market countries rose over time, so did the THC levels of marijuana.[73] Thus, over the decades the international competitive disadvantage faced by producers of low-quality Costa Rican marijuana has obstructed the export trade, although it should be noted that the THC levels of Costa Rican cannabis seem to be rising.[74]

Nevertheless, as in Belize, the marijuana trade has fueled the growth of domestic drug networks and has kept some occupied in between narcotics-transshipment jobs. Here, Colombian marijuana has sometimes been imported to or via Costa Rica, occasionally combined in a shipment with cocaine, both to satisfy local demand and for reexport.[75] Moreover, by 2009 traffickers had imported a more potent strain of South American cannabis for growers to produce in Costa Rica. Smaller than the marijuana traditionally grown, these plants have proven to be more easily camouflaged among other crops and more difficult to spot from the air. They are also able to mature in three months, without much fertilizer or care in cultivation.

While Costa Rica has never accounted for an appreciable slice of the North American or European marijuana trades, authorities have proven to be unable to halt its domestic production or its export. Furthermore, over the years, a significant portion of the attention and budgets of Costa Rican antidrug officials has been devoted to countering domestic marijuana production. And, although greatly overshadowed by other Costa Rican drug problems, the marijuana trade has played a role in the evolution of national drug trafficking.

The Costa Rican Cocaine Trade

For all of the troubles posed by marijuana, by the mid-1980s the sheer magnitude and immense value of transshipped cocaine brought that narcotic to eclipse all other Costa Rican drug problems. While traffickers who hailed from Costa Rica have retained a firm grasp on cannabis farming and export, foreigners have usually taken charge of cocaine transshipment, calling on Costa Rican associates to help with discrete tasks. "Colombians, Mexicans, Cuban-Americans, other U.S. citizens, and Venezuelans," according to U.S. antidrug officials, have led effective, sophisticated, and often violent smuggling rings.[76] As the Central American bridge states rose to prominence in cocaine trafficking, Colombians quickly established the largest presence in Costa Rica, moving the most kilos. Indeed, Daniel Moritz, a DEA agent who penetrated a key transshipment network while

71. *United States v. McCarthy*, 97 F.3d 1562; DEA, *Resources, Costa Rica* (2003), 4; "Lancha escondía cuatro toneladas de marihuana comprimida," *LN* (CR), 23 December 2007, 14A; "'Joint Effort' Pays Off," *TT* (CR), 4 January 2008, 2.

72. DEA reports and Costa Rican antidrug police statements, quoted in "Country Becomes Drug Destination," *TT* (CR), 2 April 2004, 1A.

73. THC levels in the United States rose from an average of 1.5 percent in 1970 to reach 7.6 percent in the 1990s, with sinsemilla varieties frequently in the 8–19 percent range and the most potent marijuana registering almost 30 percent. DEA, *History Book, 1990–1995*.

74. *INCSR* (2011), 205.

75. See, for instance, "Golpean a narcos que se abastecían en el Caribe," *LN* (CR), 13 May 2005, 16A.

76. *INCSR* (1988), 118, and DEA, *Resources, Costa Rica* (2003), 2.

Fig. 3.3 Costa Rican seizures of cocaine, 1982–1995

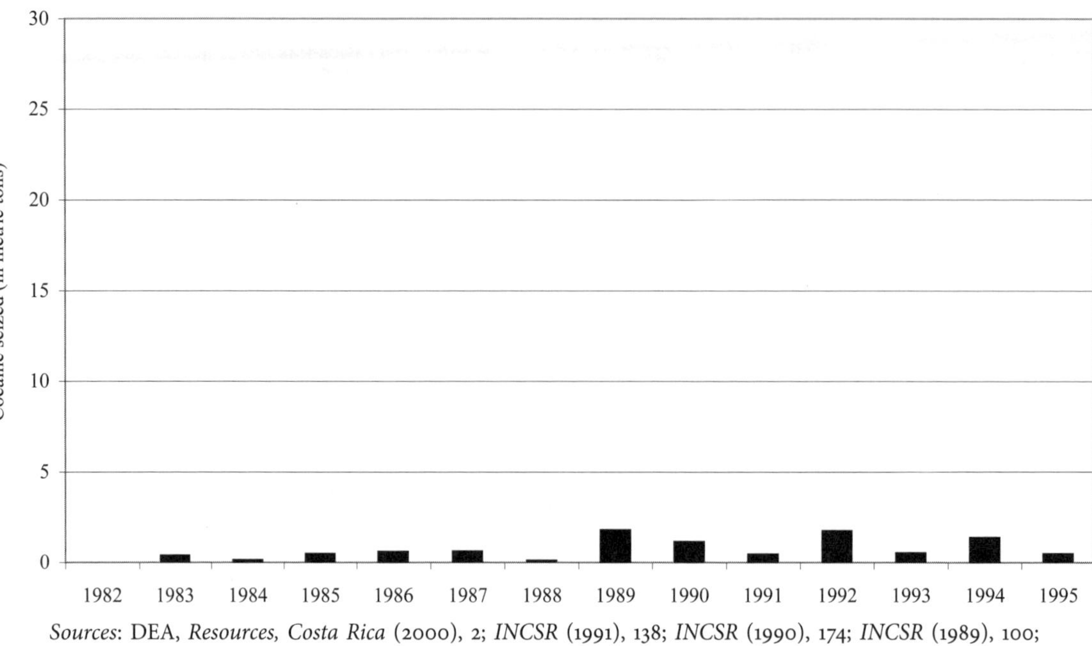

Sources: DEA, *Resources, Costa Rica* (2000), 2; *INCSR* (1991), 138; *INCSR* (1990), 174; *INCSR* (1989), 100; *INCSR* (1988), 121.

Note: On occasion, the U.S. government updated prior estimates or numbers, and in those cases we have used the later, corrected statistic. For 2003 and 2004 the U.S. government failed to include annual cocaine seizure totals for Costa Rica in the yearly *International Narcotics Control Strategy Reports*; hence, for those two years we have used the figures supplied by Costa Rica to the United Nations. See United Nations Office on Drugs and Crime, *World Drug Report 2006*.

working undercover, reported that by 1984 the "tentacles" of the Medellín cartel had already extended into Costa Rica.[77]

In cataloging the rising Costa Rican seizures of cocaine from 1982 to 2010, figs. 3.3 and 3.4 illustrate both the spectacular growth in cocaine transshipment and the way in which the state responded, reasserting itself with increasing vigor, with improved counternarcotics work leading to some extraordinary twenty-first-century annual seizure totals. In 1982 Costa Rican authorities confiscated a single kilo of cocaine. Then, from the approximately 140 kilos intercepted in 1984 and 120 kilos in 1988, officials came to seize nearly 3 tons in 1989 and 1990 combined.[78] But even this seems to have been a small fraction of the cocaine passing through. In 1989 U.S. officials variously estimated that Costa Rica exported annually 6–12 tons, or even 10–20 tons, of cocaine, while the figures offered by Costa Rican antidrug officials were even higher—18–24 tons a year.[79] Thus, while total seizures rose, the annual interception rate—that is, the fraction interdicted of all the cocaine passing through the state—seems likely to have been much less impressive.

77. "Cartel de Medellín con nexos en Costa Rica," *LN* (CR), 20 May 1989, 10A.

78. See *INCSR* (1985), 82; *INCSR* (1989), 100; and *INCSR* (1991), 141. For calculations using Costa Rican government statistics, see "Arias Makes Drug Control Top Priority," *TT* (CR), 10 March 1989, 10.

79. Compare *INCSR* (1989), 97, with "Diez mil a veinte mil kilos de coca cruzan el país," *LN* (CR), 21 May 1990, 5A, and "Dos toneladas de cocaína pasan mensualmente por Costa Rica," *La República* (Costa Rica), 17 April 1990, 1.

Fig. 3.4 Costa Rican seizures of cocaine, 1996–2010

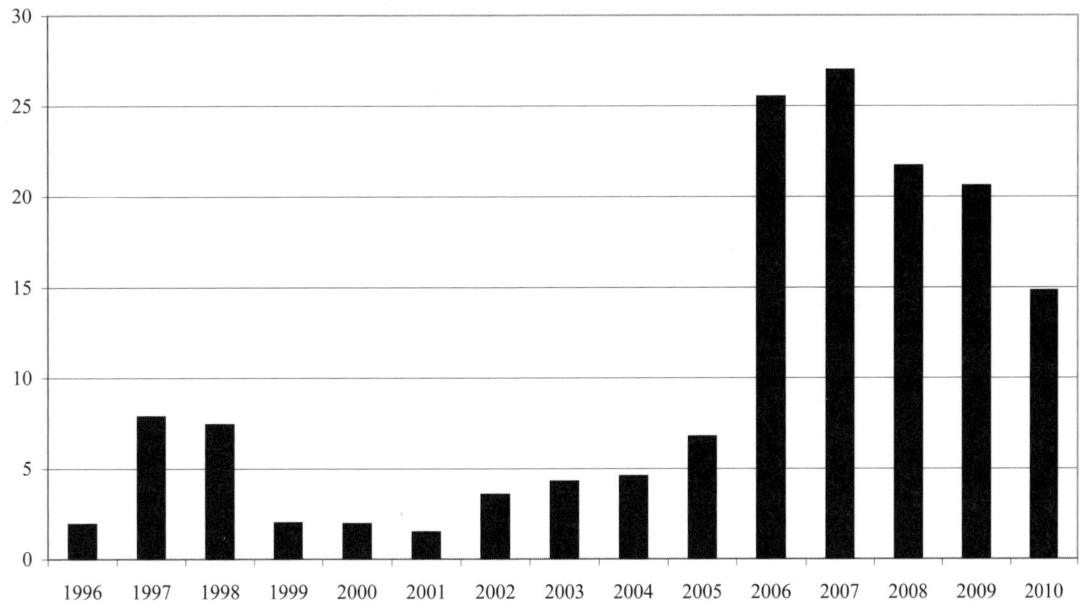

Sources: *INCSR* (2011), 206; *INCSR* (2010), 219; *INCSR* (2009), 210; *INCSR* (2008), 162; *INCSR* (2007), 154; *INCSR* (2006), 136; *INCSR* (2005), 170; DEA, *Resources, Costa Rica* (2003), 2.

Over time, estimated cocaine exports continued to rise. In 1990 the country's top antidrug police officer, Gonzalo Bado Zúñiga, noted that a kilo of cocaine, worth perhaps fourteen thousand dollars in Miami, could be acquired for four thousand to five thousand dollars in Costa Rica. The arithmetic of the drug trade thus encouraged entrepreneurs. Even more important, however, drug enterprises with the ability to move large quantities determined that Costa Rica offered significant advantages compared to other potential bridge states. Just as Belize was affected by developments in the Mexican and Guatemalan drug trades, so the trade in Costa Rica was influenced by events in Panama and Colombia. Interior minister Luis Fishman observed, "The end of Panamanian benevolence toward the drug trade under [General Manuel] Noriega meant the traffickers had to find new bridges for their shipments, and more of them came to us." Successful transshipment brought ever larger individual loads as well as greater cumulative quantities. By 1991 Costa Rican authorities estimated that 48 tons of cocaine annually were flowing across their borders.[80]

The drug rings at work in Costa Rica were opportunistic, constantly probing for flaws in law enforcement or criminal justice that might be turned to their advantage. For instance, while coca processing traditionally occurred in Colombia, it would have been convenient for a cartel to have associates in Costa Rica with the capacity to refine coca paste into cocaine. In 1984 the DEA had traced barrels of precursor chemicals, secretly outfitted with transponders, to the Colombian Amazon site known as Tranquilandia, bringing on a Colombian police raid that closed an enormous Medellín cartel refining

80. The statements by Bado Zúñiga and Fishman appear in "Cocaine a New Threat to the Peaceful Life in Tiny Costa Rica," *Miami Herald* (hereafter cited as *MH* [US]), 16 December 1990, 27A. For the 1991 estimate, see "Cuatro mil kilos de coca cruzan el país al mes," *LN* (CR), 12 February 1991, 10A. See also "Embestida infernal," *LN* (CR), 10 September 1995, 4A

complex there and caused the price of cocaine to rise in Miami for the first time in years.[81] In response, Colombian traffickers moved to use mobile laboratories for a time, and then that same year, the Panamanian military discovered and raided a cocaine-processing laboratory in the Darién jungles of Panama, close to the Colombian border.[82]

Offshore refining in a bridge state like Costa Rica could have potentially served as another innovative way for traffickers to stay ahead of authorities. Certainly, the import and use of precursor chemicals would have been subjected to much less scrutiny in Costa Rica. Likewise, police and the DEA might not have been watching for a cocaine laboratory in Central America. And, establishing a Costa Rican refining lab would have diversified the cartel's operations, enabling traffickers to bypass Colombia, useful during periods of intense counternarcotics efforts there. Finally, it would have permitted regular cocaine exports from a country with a very positive reputation much closer to the United States.

In fact, Colombian traffickers attempted to create just such a Costa Rican operation.[83] In 1986 police raided a clandestine cocaine-refining laboratory being set up in the Cordillera de Talamanca near the small village of Santa Maria de Ujarrás. The officers discovered eighty-seven kilos of raw coca paste, as well as barrels of the precursor chemicals ether and sulfuric acid, needed to cook the paste. This turned out to be no experiment by a fledgling entrepreneur; rather, the mastermind was later found to be Justo Pastor Perafan Homen, then kingpin of the Bogotá cartel.[84] In 1997 he was captured in Venezuela and extradited to the United States, where he was eventually convicted of importing more than 20 tons of cocaine and laundering tens of millions of dollars.[85]

Perafan Homen's plan, overseen in Costa Rica by Colombian Abelardo Camelo Cárdenas, was to import raw coca paste from South America, then export high-purity cocaine to the U.S. market at a projected rate of about two hundred kilos per week. The coca paste seized at the lab was thought to have traveled from Colombia into Panama and then crossed the border into Costa Rica in compartments hidden in the roof of a truck. A Panamanian conspirator told police that customs authorities had been corrupted to ensure that the drugs not be intercepted at the border, with code phrases used to signal that this was one of the organization's trucks.[86]

As the lab was being completed, however, Camelo Cárdenas made the mistake of entering the United States, eliciting DEA attention. Upon his return to Costa Rica, police agents followed him to a meeting with Carlos Ernesto Cuervo Herrera, identified by the DEA as another drug suspect. Costa Rican police investigated, closed in on the lab, and arrested seven Colombians and a Panamanian, each eventually sentenced to fourteen years in prison, as well as nine

81. See DEA, *History Book, 1980–1985*, 11. See also Gugliotta and Leen, *Kings of Cocaine*, chapter 12.

82. Strong, *Whitewash*, 122.

83. Medellín cartel insider Roberto Escobar reported that in 1984 his brother Pablo had also negotiated with the Sandinista government to establish a cocaine-processing laboratory on a Nicaraguan island. Escobar, *Accountant's Story*, 69. See also Dinges, *Our Man in Panama*, 184–85.

84. For information on who masterminded the scheme, see "Ubican en Colombia a jefe de laboratorio," *LN* (CR), 8 October 1986, 1; "Proceso detenidos en laboratorio de cocaína," *LN* (CR), 7 October 1986, 10A; and "Reconocen apellido de implicado en laboratorio," *LN* (CR), 10 October 1986, 10A. See also "Traficantes tenían más nexos en el país," *LN* (CR), 9 March 1988, 10A.

85. See "Extraditarán a narco colombiano a EE.UU.," *LN* (CR), 23 May 1992, 11A; "Cae narco más buscado de Colombia," *LN* (CR), 19 April 1997, 16A; and "De panadero a millonario," *LN* (CR), 19 April 1997, 16A.

86. "Cayó laboratorio de cocaína," *LN* (CR), 21 September 1986, 2; "Mafiosos colombianos involucrados en el laboratorio de coca," *LN* (CR), 22 September 1986, 1; "Ubican en Colombia," 10A; "Jefe de laboratorio no tiene antecedentes," *LN* (CR), 9 October 1986, 11A; and "Colombians Get Stiff Sentences," *TT* (CR), 18 March 1988, 18. During the police operation one suspect allegedly offered a police agent fifty thousand dollars to buy his freedom. "Comenzó juicio por cocaína," *LN* (CR), 2 March 1988, 10A.

Costa Rican associates. This well-publicized triumph seems to have short-circuited other plans to develop coca-refining capacity in the country, a point that underscores how drug organizations adapted to counternarcotics successes as well as failures.[87]

While Costa Rica has avoided hosting such laboratories, in other respects the country has become ever more deeply immersed in the international cocaine trade. For instance, by the 1990s very large quantities of cocaine came to pass offshore. Speedboats, fishing trawlers, and other vessels carrying cocaine shipments transited Costa Rican territorial waters or its exclusive economic zone, often en route to destinations in northern Central America or Mexico. In one 2005 case authorities discovered more than 2.5 tons of cocaine buried on a remote beach in Limón Province after a Colombian speedboat developed engine trouble and then ran aground.[88] In 2006, a year in which Costa Rica interdicted fully 25.5 tons of cocaine, U.S. authorities captured 3 tons of it off a semisubmersible near Isla del Coco, and then officials made the largest cocaine bust in the country's history, taking 7.8 tons off a Costa Rican fishing vessel.[89] In 2008 six of the annual total of 21.7 tons of cocaine were seized from another semisubmersible offshore.

Costa Rica's facilities to temporarily store drugs amounted to yet another bridge-favoring factor, developing into a significant feature of the Costa Rican cocaine trade. Trafficking networks imported numerous smaller shipments, including hundred-kilo quantities that could be hidden in sport-utility and passenger vehicles, and later consolidated them into larger loads for export. By the late 1990s Costa Rica seems to have trailed only Guatemala among the bridge states in which traffickers maintained cocaine supplies. And, over time, the amounts stockpiled reached impressive proportions.[90] In 2007, for instance, Costa Rican authorities arrested seven Mexican traffickers linked to warehouses holding 2.2 tons of cocaine.[91]

As fig. 3.4 illustrates, while Costa Rican cocaine seizures have mounted rapidly, the increases have not been linear. After capturing less than five tons in 2003, Costa Rica interdicted more than 60 tons of cocaine in the first twenty months of the new administration of Oscar Arias, with annual totals reaching 25.5 tons by 2006. As in other Central American states, interdiction successes have often been significantly affected by the degree of cooperation occurring with the DEA and the U.S. military's Southern Command. Thus, U.S. ambassador Mark Langdale explained the low 2003 seizure totals by stating that Costa Rica had become "unplugged" from U.S. regional security efforts.[92] Some argued that this was reflected in the government's decision to allow entry to twelve thousand Colombian refugees, two thousand of whom public security minister Fernando Berrocal later claimed to be linked to drug trafficking.[93]

Although the United States has always been the largest foreign market, cocaine traffickers working through Costa Rica have long directed

87. Thereafter, while rumors occasionally surfaced regarding Costa Rican cocaine laboratories, none were ever confirmed, nor did other arrests occur for attempting to establish refining labs.

88. "2.5 Tons of Cocaine Discovered," *TT* (CR), 29 April 2005, 4.

89. For information on the seizures off semisubmersibles, see "Cocaine-Toting Sub Busted in Pacific Ocean," *TT* (CR), 19 September 2008, 8. For the largest seizure, see *INCSR* (2007), 6.

90. DEA, *Resources, Costa Rica* (2003), 2; *INCSR* (1997), 127, 129; "Narcos almacenan droga aquí," *LN* (CR), 25 March 1997, 3A.

91. "Cartel de Sinaloa planeaba liberar a reo," *LN* (CR), 13 June 2008, 16A. The following year the Sinaloa cartel designed a scheme to free the group's leader, though police thwarted it.

92. "Free Trade, Drug Busts Make U.S. Envoy Proud," *TT* (CR), 11 January 2008, 11.

93. "Flap over FARC Fires Up Arias," *TT* (CR), 4 April 2008, 1. Berrocal ignited political controversy by declaring that "something other than altruism" had been involved in the refugee decision. See also "Still Fussing over FARC," *TT* (CR), 23 May 2008, 2.

cocaine to European destinations as well, with mounting quantities sent over time. For many years Costa Ricans, often posing as tourists, have continually moved small quantities of cocaine into Western Europe. In 1987 German police determined that networks operating in Costa Rica had supplied a substantial amount of the cocaine circulating in their country.[94] From the 1990s forward Costa Rican police as well as various European law-enforcement bodies have arrested scores of couriers acting on behalf of smuggling rings exporting narcotics via Costa Rica to Britain, Spain, Italy, Germany, France, Greece, and the Netherlands, among other destinations.[95] In 2009 Costa Rican authorities arrested fifty-six couriers, forty-five of them foreigners, and most of the drugs were headed to Europe.[96]

Cocaine traffickers eventually shipped much larger narcotics loads to Europe via the Costa Rican gateway. In early 1990 Portuguese authorities discovered that a Costa Rican cargo, sent from Puerto Limón, contained 80 kilos of cocaine. After police captured the Colombian ringleader, further investigations revealed that the vessel had made various prior suspicious trips to the United States and then to Europe, and officials came to believe that 180 kilos had been dropped in Genoa, Italy, before the ship had arrived in Lisbon. In a related case later that year Spanish police seized an additional 123 kilos and arrested a Costa Rican woman who allegedly helped to direct a network linked to the Medellín cartel.[97] In 1997 Costa Rican counter-narcotics officials, in cooperation with the DEA, exposed a major ring that had smuggled 400 kilos of cocaine to Spain.[98]

Over time, Costa Rica was found to be playing a key role in trafficking operations in numerous countries in western and eastern Europe. In 1993 Costa Rican counternarcotics officials broke up another Colombian group that had just sent at least 194 kilos of cocaine to the Netherlands.[99] Shortly thereafter, authorities discovered Russian criminals to be distributing cocaine that had traveled from San Andrés to Puerto Limón and then on to Europe.[100] In 1994 the OIJ broke up a ring shipping cocaine into the Czech Republic, via Germany, in containers of bananas.[101] Then OIJ found another, associated with Colombia's Pereira cartel, that had moved at least 720 kilos of cocaine into other European destinations.[102] Cocaine transshipped via Costa Rica fanned out in

94. "Mafiosos alemanes llevan varios años de actuar aquí," *LN* (CR), 6 July 1987, 8A. For the Costa Rica–to-Germany connection, see also "Revés a narcomafia alemana," *LN* (CR), 27 March 1995, 10A.

95. Between 2000 and 2005 Costa Rican authorities arrested the following European national citizens acting as mules: seventeen Dutch, sixteen Spaniards, fourteen Germans, twelve Rumanians, ten British, and a total of eleven from the Czech Republic, Austria, France, Hungary, and Switzerland. "Ambición destruyó la vida," 14A. Various of the 110 Costa Rican couriers and 78 Colombians arrested in that period were headed to European destinations. See "Drug Smugglers' Use of 'Mules' Is Climbing," *TT* (CR), 19 September 2008, 13.

96. "Creció detención de traficantes de droga en el Juan Santamaría," *LN* (CR), 4 January 2010, 12A.

97. "Cae con drogas barco que salió de Limón," *LN* (CR), 5 January 1990, 9A; "Barco dejó cargas de cocaína en Limón," *LN* (CR), 6 January 1990, 10A; and "Tica era cabecilla," 9A.

98. After a trial featuring heavily armed police surrounding the courthouse, a Costa Rican penal court convicted Colombian ringleader Manuel Salvador Zapata Valencia, sentencing him to eighteen years in prison, while four Colombian associates received fifteen-year terms and two Spaniards, who had eventually cooperated with police, got ten-year terms. "Imponen fuerte condena a narcos," *LN* (CR), 25 January 1997, 10A.

99. "Narco a debate," *LN* (CR), 15 July 1993, 12A. This followed a 1992 cocaine seizure of thirty kilos from the *Tuscan Star*, a Cypriot ship headed to Europe. The following October twenty-three kilos were discovered on the same ship with the same captain, this time heading to Belgium. Two Costa Rican crew members fled, and one was later arrested on drug charges. See "Decomisan barco con veintitrés kilos de cocaína," *LN* (CR), 16 October 1991, 12A; "Detenido sospechoso de trasegar cocaína," *LN* (CR), 26 October 1991, 10A; and "Liberan barco," *LN* (CR), 23 November 1991, 12A.

100. "Desarticulada banda internacional del narco," *LN* (CR), 11 September 1993, 12A.

101. "Costa Rica Police Destroy Drug Trafficking Ring," Xinhua News Agency, 25 December 1998.

102. See "Atrapada banda de narcotraficantes," *LN* (CR), 20 March 1994, 10A. See also "Police Investigate Links Between Dismantled Drug Group and Colombian Cartel," BBC Summary of World Broadcasts, 22 March 1994.

distribution channels across Europe. Carlos Manuel Alvarado Alvarado, sentenced by a Costa Rican court in 1997 to eight years in prison for international drug trafficking, belonged to a network thought to have shipped more than 700 kilos of cocaine from Colombia into Panama, overland into Costa Rica, and on to destinations in Italy, France, Germany, Spain, and the Netherlands.[103]

The cardinal point here is that Costa Rica's distinctive set of bridge-favoring factors has served the purposes of cocaine traffickers intent on opening European markets as well as moving drugs to North America. Alongside the ability of networks to gain access to large cocaine supplies, the country's clean image and vibrant tourist industry as well as its developed economy and inflow of investors have helped Costa Rica to become a vital cog in the machinery exporting cocaine to Europe. Thus, Costa Rica's versatility, serving as a bridge to both U.S. and European cocaine markets has sharply distinguished Costa Rican cocaine trafficking from that in Belize, always focused on supplying the U.S. market.

Costa Rican Heroin Connections

Significant Costa Rican ties to international heroin traffickers further differentiate its narcotics transshipment from that in Belize. As early as the 1980s major figures linked to the heroin trade lived or operated in Costa Rica.[104] Restaurateur Roberto Antulio Fionna Fionna resided in Costa Rica from 1981 until his 1988 extradition to France on heroin-trafficking charges, for which he was soon convicted.[105] In 1988, when U.S. authorities arrested the Chinese-born Kon Yu-Leung—just before the U.S. attorney for Brooklyn characterized him as "one of the two or three biggest heroin dealers in the world"—he was found to be carrying a false Costa Rican passport.[106] Investigators concluded that he had visited Costa Rica in 1981 and 1986, using an alias, and had bribed high officials there and in Panama. Then, in 1990, after authorities discovered 290 grams of heroin and arrested two Chinese men, investigations revealed that Chinese organizations in Panama had been opening a route from Hong Kong to the United States via Panama and Costa Rica, establishing a bridge to U.S. heroin consumers while also aiming to develop local markets.[107]

Eventually, however, the vast majority of heroin transiting Costa Rica came to originate in Colombia. South American heroin couriers usually arrived by air from Panama or Colombia, carrying one- or two-kilo shipments, headed for U.S. and European destinations.[108] In the 1990s law-enforcement authorities in Costa Rica and abroad found heroin transshipped through the country in suitcases and carry-on luggage, strapped to the bodies of couriers, inside capsules in their stomachs, or stored in the soles of their shoes. Traffickers have

103. "Ocho años de cárcel a narcotraficante," *LN* (CR), 26 April 1997, 10A.

104. See "Inculpados de 'narco' estuvieron en el país," *LN* (CR), 27 May 1989, 8A.

105. "Fionna condenado a quince años en Francia," *LN* (CR), 29 November 1989, 10A.

106. "Top U.S. Target in Heroin Trade Seized at Hotel," *New York Times*, 15 March 1988, 5. Kon Yu-Leung, also known as "Johnny Kon," was indicted for smuggling more than 450 kilos of heroin, an enormous amount compared to the French connection case (roughly 32 kilos) and the Pizza connection (roughly 90 kilos). "Asian Tagged as No. 1 Heroin Target Is Arrested in N.Y.," *St. Petersburg Times*, 15 March 1988, 4A. Yu Leung became a government witness and was sentenced to twenty-seven years. *United States v. Yu-Leung*, 51 F.3d 1116. For articles concerning his false passport, see "Zar de la heroína usó pasaporte tico," *LN* (CR), 22 April 1988, 8A; "Officials to Probe Alleged 'Mafia Network,'" *TT* (CR), 22 April 1988, 16; and "Official Suspended in Probe," *TT* (CR), 6 May 1988, 5. For more information on Yu-Leung's heroin operation, see *United States v. Yu-Leung*, 910 F.2d 33, and *United States v. Routollo*, 1988 U.S. Dist. LEXIS 15565.

107. See "Dos chinos procesados por tráfico de heroína," *LN* (CR), 28 October 1990, 10A, and "Caen c. 155 millones en heroína," *LN* (CR), 28 September 1990, 10A. For more on Chinese criminal gangs in Panama and Costa Rica, see "Mafia china opera en C.A.," *Al Día* (Guatemala), 13 May 1997, 11.

108. See DEA, *Resources, Costa Rica* (2000), 5; *INCSR* (1994), 142; and "Confiscan seis kilos de heroína," *LN* (CR), 5 March 1997, 10A.

Fig. 3.5 Costa Rican seizures of heroin, 1992–2009

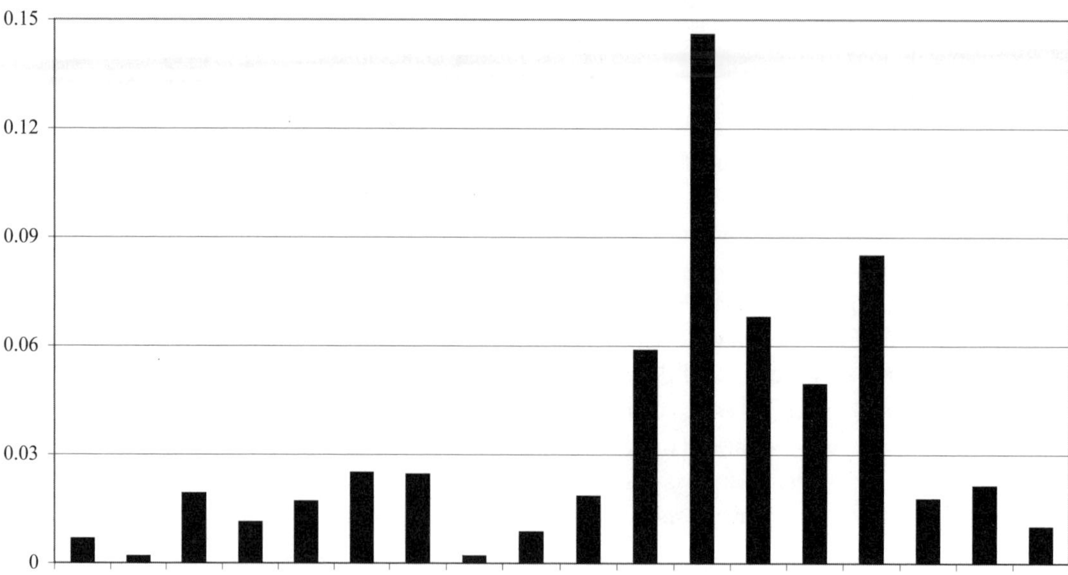

Sources: *INCSR* (2011), 206; *INCSR* (2010), 219; *INCSR* (2009), 210; *INCSR* (2008), 162; *INCSR* (2007), 154; *INCSR* (2006), 136; *INCSR* (2005), 170; DEA, *Resources, Costa Rica* (2003), 2; DEA, *Resources, Costa Rica* (2000), 2.

attempted to screen from detection heroin secreted in luggage by incorporating fiberglass sides in the suitcases, wrapping the drugs in paper printed with cartoons that might distort X-ray images, and masking the scent with another substance, such as glue.[109]

Given the dynamics of this trade, Costa Rican airports have been very much at the center of international heroin smuggling. In 1994, for instance, antidrug agents broke up one notable network transshipping heroin through the international airport and captured couriers employed by other heroin-trafficking gangs as well.[110] In the late 1990s several incidents suggested that traffickers were using the small domestic airport of Tobías Bolaños, serving the San José metropolitan area and lacking much official vigilance, for heroin and also cocaine trafficking as well as the import of money derived from drug sales.[111] In 2002, despite years of extensive interdiction efforts, Costa Rican antidrug officials expressed their concerns that Juan Santamaría Airport was again "becoming a major hub for international drug couriers."[112]

In fact, during the 1990s and into the new century, as Colombian cartels stimulated large-scale opium production, heroin trafficking through Costa Rica grew rapidly. This is reflected in the growing seizures noted in fig. 3.5. In 1990 Costa Rican antinarcotics officials made an

109. See *United States v. Sharon*, 187 F.3d 17.

110. For the network transshipping through the airport, see "Cayó poderosa red de narco," *LN* (CR), 23 March 1994, 18A; "Trasiego de heroína por Costa Rica," *LN* (CR), 9 August 1994, 10A; "Dos colombianos traían droga," *LN* (CR), 5 October 1994, 16A; and "Treinta y tres años por traficar coca," *LN* (CR), 6 October 1994, 10A. For the captured couriers, see "Condena por narco," *LN* (CR), 13 May 1993, 10A; "Heroína decomisada en el Santamaría," *LN* (CR), 7 August 1994, 10A; "Decomisan 6,5 kilos de heroína en el Santamaría," *LN* (CR), 4 October 1994, 10A; "Decomisan heroína," *LN* (CR), 31 January 1995, 10A; and "Capturan a matrimonio con 12 kilos de heroína," *LN* (CR), 31 May 1996, 16A.

111. "Narco halla otra puerta fácil," *LN* (CR), 23 August 1998, 6A.

112. *INCSR* (2002), 7.

initial seizure of South American heroin, half a kilo in size. Much more regular transshipment of heroin was in the offing. Authorities confiscated 6.7 kilos in 1992, a number that grew to more than 25 kilos in 1997 and 1998.[113] Meanwhile, investigations of heroin dealing in the United States repeatedly revealed transportation via Costa Rica.[114] In a notable 1996 case authorities in Orlando, Florida, arrested and eventually convicted Costa Ricans Franklin García Muñoz and Rolando Ugalde Arguedas, formerly Costa Rica's director of immigration, in connection with three kilos of heroin seized en route from Costa Rica to New Jersey, possibly to be shipped on to Germany. Further police inquiries suggested that this drug network, which also included conspirators from Colombia, Honduras, and the Dominican Republic, had also trafficked in cocaine.[115]

Similarly, in 1998 the DEA broke up a Medellín ring, charging its members with smuggling heroin into Miami via Costa Rica.[116] Occasionally, authorities have confiscated much larger heroin loads, sometimes alongside cocaine. In 2003, for instance, authorities at a checkpoint near Paso Canoas discovered in the hidden compartment of a pickup truck fully 40 kilos of heroin, as well as 101 of cocaine.[117] Even individual couriers started to carry larger amounts, as in the Guatemalan arrested at the airport in 2006, arriving from Venezuela with 3.9 kilos of heroin in a suitcase.[118]

By early in the twenty-first century, heroin smuggling via Costa Rica had grown quite prominent, with 58.8 kilos seized in 2002 and more than 100 kilos in the first ten months of 2003. In 2001 a joint police operation broke up a heroin-smuggling ring with arrests in the United States and Costa Rica, and in 2004 Costa Rican authorities made six arrests in Puerto Limón for exporting heroin to Canada and the United States. The record of the Costa Rican heroin trade suggests that traffickers have been attracted by the country's busy airport, its sparkling international reputation, and its extensive international linkages. These bridge-favoring factors helped to establish Costa Rica as a principal transshipment site in the South American heroin trade.[119]

Drug-Trafficking Routes and Organizations in Costa Rica

Although heroin has normally passed through the international airport, and marijuana has most often been shipped through Costa Rican waters, more complex patterns have characterized cocaine passage through the country. Not only have the principal routes and networks involved in cocaine transshipment changed over time, but long-standing Colombian dominance has yielded to Mexican preeminence. In the 1980s and 1990s the leaders of cocaine-trafficking networks in Costa Rica were typically Colombians linked to the Medellín or Cali cartels, but by 2004 oversight of air, maritime, and overland cocaine shipments often came

113. *INCSR* (1991), 137; *INCSR* (1993), 146; and *INCSR* (1998), 128.

114. See, for instance, *United States v. Arango*, 1999 U.S. Dist. LEXIS 21135, and *United States v. Sharon*, 187 F.3d 17. For another Costa Rican network dealing in cocaine and heroin in the United States, see "Drug 'Cell' Busted with Arrests Here and in Costa Rica," *Boston Herald*, 3 November 2001, 6.

115. See "Four Plead Guilty to Smuggling Heroin at Orlando Airport," *Orlando Sentinel*, 8 August 1996, D5; "Investigan tráfico de heroína," *LN* (CR), 27 April 1996, 10A; "Golpe a supuesta red de narco," *LN* (CR), 10 July 1996, 10A; and "Caen más cabecillas de red narco," *LN* (CR), 11 July 1996, 10A.

116. "Hermanos ligados a cartel de Medellín," *LN* (CR), 5 August 1998, 10A.

117. DEA, *Resources, Costa Rica* (2003), 5.

118. "Policía decomisa 3.9 kilos de heroína," *LP* (PA), 11 October 2006, 37A.

119. DEA, *Resources, Costa Rica* (2000), 2; "Detenidos presuntos miembros de red narco," *LN* (CR), 6 November 2001, 10A; and "Police Arrest Six with Links to Drug-Smuggling Ring," *Orlando Sentinel*, 28 April 2004, A7. See also the heroin case detailed in "Cinco años de cárcel," *LN* (CR), 4 November 2001, 12A.

from the principal Mexican cartels, which had taken over an estimated 80 percent of the cocaine trade by 2010.[120] According to OIJ statistics, between 2005 and 2010 sixty-one Mexicans were arrested on drug-trafficking charges in Costa Rica and 16.3 tons of cocaine were seized from Mexican cartels.[121] Mauricio Boraschi, director of Costa Rica's Drug Institute, has hypothesized that by 2008 law-enforcement successes against Colombian drug rings had caused Mexican cartels to lose confidence in their partners and move more of their own organizations into Costa Rica. That same year public security minister Gerardo Lazcares divulged Costa Rican intelligence information suggesting that the Mexican cartels had met and carved up the country to minimize friction. The Tijuana cartel was to be supreme on the Pacific coast, Sinaloa traffickers were to dominate land transit, and the Gulf cartel was to control the Caribbean.[122]

As for the methods used, as Central American trafficking gained momentum in the 1980s, light aircraft moved the bulk of the cocaine transiting the country.[123] San José had the sole airport with a significant law-enforcement presence, and even here the corruption of customs agents and airport security was a continuing problem. More important, even the most cautious estimates counted at least 250 small and unpoliced airstrips servicing out-of-the-way communities. In 1985 public security minister Benjamin Piza noted, "every farm has an airstrip, and we don't have the resources to control every flight."[124] Five years later, interior minister Luis Fishman frankly declared, "Our skies and seas are open to drug traffickers because we have no resources to stop them."[125] In fact, until 1992 the country's single radar system, located in San José, initially had a range of eighteen to twenty miles and thereafter of forty miles or less.[126]

Eventually, moving drugs through Costa Rica by truck and ship grew to supplant passage via the early air routes. The civil war in Nicaragua had stimulated aerial cocaine smuggling, with the frequent flights of materiel into northern Costa Rica providing camouflage. Thus, the peace settlement in Nicaragua, capped by the 1990 elections, removed one factor that had encouraged cocaine transit by light plane. Furthermore, the Medellín cartel had specialized in aerial smuggling, and by the early 1990s its influence had diminished relative to its rivals, bringing other trafficking methods to the fore. In addition, with time, drug rings intent on flying cocaine toward the United States had developed contacts in more northerly Central American states, especially Guatemala, that offered even more attractive competitive advantages for air smuggling.[127]

Equally important, trafficking networks came to appreciate just how easily they could truck or ship even larger cocaine loads than light aircraft could carry. As the 1990s commenced, by regional standards Costa Rica had a reasonably well-maintained road system, lax border controls, and little vigilance by highway patrols or checkpoints. These circumstances favored overland transport, particularly because cocaine could be

120. "Costa Rica: El centro neurálgico para negociar las drogas," *LN* (CR), 31 January 2010, 22A.

121. "Costa Rica, punto para narcos," *LP* (HO), 14 December 2009, 114.

122. For Boraschi's and Lazcares's quotes in this paragraph, see "Mexican Cartels Penetrating C.R. Drug Trade," *TT* (CR), 9 May 2008, 3.

123. See DEA, *Resources, Costa Rica* (2000), 5.

124. "Contras Deal Drugs for Cause," *Chicago Tribune* (hereafter cited as *CT* [US]), 21 December 1985, 1C.

125. "Cocaine a New Threat, " 27A.

126. *INCSR* (1992), 145. Luis Fishman noted that the Arias administration had not immediately accepted a U.S. offer of new radar, to forestall further deterioration of relations with the Sandinistas. By the time Costa Rican officials opted to agree, another government had already taken the offer. Eventually, however, the U.S.-funded Caribbean Basin Radar Network included a new facility at Cerro Azul. See "U.S. Radar System Detects Illegal Flights Here," *TT* (CR), 9 August 2002, 8; "Innocents Fight Off Drug Traffic," *San Diego Union-Tribune*, 12 March 1989, A43; "Inauguran radar para control antidrogas," *LN* (CR), 4 July 1992, 8A; and *INCSR* (1993), 146.

127. DEA, *Resources, Costa Rica* (2003), 5.

readily and inexpensively imported to Panama. With respect to maritime transport, the fact that Costa Rica has busy ports and fishing fleets did not escape the attention of traffickers, nor did the country's lengthy Caribbean and Pacific coasts.[128] Indeed, the Pacific shoreline is marked by so many peninsulas, points, bays, and inlets, as to total more than 750 miles of coastline, much of it secluded.[129] With minimal risk of interdiction, traffickers could organize water drops by circling planes or maritime transfers involving foreign and local vessels. By the late 1990s cartels began to send cocaine by speedboat off Costa Rican coasts, calling on local associates to assist with offshore refueling, a method that minimized exposure to law enforcement.

As drug organizations varied their modus operandi, they came to operate virtually throughout Costa Rica, including its airspace and waters. Hernán Vargas, a Costa Rican counternarcotics officer, observed, "The traffickers have an infinity of routes. They are gamblers. They spread their bets all over the board. For every route we cut off, they get through on ten others."[130] Costa Rica's competent counternarcotics authorities, closely cooperating with the United States, have interdicted considerable quantities. Yet so many drug networks trying their luck on so many different pathways have greatly challenged law enforcement. Both foreign and domestic law-enforcement officials have conceded that far more drug shipments have passed through undetected than have been intercepted. Even the most optimistic estimate was that only 10 percent of the drugs flowing through were being seized.[131]

A close examination of the Costa Rican drug trade over several decades helps to explain the modest success of interdiction in a state that was, in many respects, the best positioned in the entire bridge region to intercept drug shipments. Ongoing and particularly extensive trafficking first occurred in the northern zone of Costa Rica centered on Guanacaste, then in and around Puerto Limón on the Caribbean, in the capital city of San José and elsewhere in the Valle Central, and via the Pan-American Highway. By the twenty-first century many of the largest shipments were passing off the Pacific coast. We turn next to explore these notable drug-trafficking routes.

Northern Costa Rica

Unlike the center of the country, Costa Rica's northern border zone has long been poor, with subpar infrastructure; furthermore, it flanks what have been the extremely poverty-stricken southernmost departments of Nicaragua.[132] And, even within Central America's most developed country, pockets of poverty have provided traffickers with the same opportunities found in countries with much lower per capita gross national incomes. Ironically, however, for a country that had abolished its armed forces, even more important than this economic factor was a military one. In the 1980s the dry, flat, spare grasslands of Guanacaste Province and northern Alajuela and Heredia Provinces played a key role in the Nicaraguan civil war. This border zone was critically important to the effort to funnel significant supplies to the contra forces trying to establish a southern front. Not only did both sides in the fighting need to finance combat operations, but both had individuals eager to profit from the drug trade.[133] Some

128. Bartilow and Kihong, "Free Traders," 129.

129. U.S. officials stated, "The difficulty of maritime interdiction in Costa Rican waters is exacerbated by a total maritime jurisdiction that is more than eleven times the size of Costa Rica's land mass." *INCSR* (2004), 8. The almost unbroken Caribbean coast measures approximately 130 miles, while the Pacific coast accounts for more than 600 miles.

130. "The Mexico Connection: Cocaine Cuts New Routes North," *Los Angeles Times* (United States) (hereafter cited as *LAT* [US]), 13 April 1989, 1.

131. See "Fear of More Drugs," 1, and "Besieged, Country Steps Up Crime Fight," *TT* (CR), 24 December 2009, Y4.

132. See "Poverty in Border Areas Focus of Forum," *TT* (CR), 16 February 2001, 6.

133. In 1987 the director of the Central America Task Force for the CIA testified to Congress: "With respect to [drug trafficking by] the Resistance Forces . . . it is not a couple of people. It is a lot of people." U.S. Senate, *Law Enforcement: Report*, 38. Top DEA official David Westrate

contra associates in Costa Rica were involved in the drug trade as well.[134]

A Costa Rican government investigative report concluded that in 1984 and 1985 contra supply networks had transshipped 5 tons of cocaine through the country.[135] In particular, Colombian cartels learned that particular runways serving remote northern farms and cattle ranches could be rented to traffic cocaine, just as the contras found that certain owners or managers of these strips had been eager to lease them for arms shipments.[136] Various of the experienced pilots employed to fly weapons, clothing, and other supplies south out of Miami and into Costa Rica were also trafficking drugs north to the United States.[137] George Morales, a champion speedboat racer who also ran a large aerial cocaine-trafficking operation, testified before the U.S. Congress that after his second arrest on drug-smuggling charges, southern front military commander Adolfo "Popo" Chamorro and two other contra officials asked for his assistance and promised help with his indictment.[138] Morales then began to work for the contras, who used his pilots in supply missions.

In the mid-1980s Nicaraguan Juan Norwin Meneses Cantarero was reputed to be "one of the largest drug traffickers in Costa Rica." According to the CIA, he was known as "the Nicaraguan Mafia, dealing in drugs, weapons, smuggling and the laundering of counterfeit money." A 1986 CIA document charged that, during the Anastasio Somoza regime in the mid-1970s, while his brother served as chief of police in Managua, Meneses became "the kingpin of narcotics traffickers in Nicaragua." With the rise of the Sandinistas, Meneses moved first to San Francisco, then to Miami, and then in 1985 to Costa Rica. At least six convicted traffickers claimed that he had supplied them with drugs. Indeed, even his own nephew, arrested for cocaine possession in the United States, described his uncle as a major trafficker, with a monthly income of $1.65 million, who gained additional income distributing 20 to 30 kilos per month. After authorities arrested Meneses in Managua in 1991 for trying to ship 764 kilos of Cali cocaine to the United States, he was convicted and sentenced to more than twelve years in prison. One of the trafficker's closest associates, Enrique Miranda Jaime, also arrested in that case, told CIA investigators that Meneses had told him that during the Nicaraguan civil war, Colombian cocaine had been flown into Costa Rica and transferred to planes that had delivered weapons to the contras. The cocaine loads would then be shipped to a site near Fort Worth, Texas, before being transported overland to California.[139]

Cocaine was frequently transshipped through various Costa Rican runways used to supply the contras. U.S. pilot Tosh Plumlee provided maps and detailed accounts of repeated flights carrying weapons and drugs through the Santa Elena airstrip in Guanacaste near two contra camps. A contra leader alleged that he had visited the

---

likewise testified, "It is true that people on both sides of the equation (in the Nicaraguan war) were drug traffickers, and a couple of them were pretty significant." U.S. Senate, *Law Enforcement: Report*, 38.

134. The Kerry Commission report pointed to "substantial evidence of drug smuggling through the war zones on the part of individual Contras, Contra suppliers, Contra pilots, mercenaries who worked with the Contras, and Contra supporters throughout the region." U.S. Senate, *Law Enforcement: Report*, 2. See also Cockburn, *Out of Control*; Scott and Marshall, *Cocaine Politics*; P. Scott, "Honduras"; and Castillo and Harmon, *Powderburns*.

135. Marshall, *Drug Wars*, 84n181.

136. See generally Scott and Marshall, *Cocaine Politics*, and Honey, *Hostile Acts*, 406.

137. A DEA agent later observed, "Nobody knew the terrain like drug pilots, and their dive-and-dump flying skills perfectly matched the job description for covert operations." Castillo and Harmon, *Powderburns*, 139.

138. Ibid., 141.

139. For the information on Menses Cantarero, see CIA, *Allegations of Connections*, 3–6; "Cocaína hunde su garra en el país," *LN* (CR), 23 November 1986, 8A; and "Nica residente aquí es supuesto jefe de banda," *LN* (CR), 1 December 1986, 1. A confidential DEA report also identified Norwin Meneses as a Managua cocaine supplier. See "Country Buzzing as Dope Revelations Continue," *TT* (CR), 5 December 1986, 8.

Guanacaste farm of Cuban American Adolfo Jiménez, reportedly linked to arms and drug trafficking, and found a smoothly running operation that included payoffs to top Rural Guard and Civil Guard officials to ensure their cooperation. A leading Costa Rican authority revealed his government's belief that Armando López Estrada, a Cuban American military trainer on Jiménez's farm who traveled frequently to Colombia, was tied to cocaine trafficking. This information led to his deportation in 1986.[140]

U.S. and Costa Rican investigations have shed additional light on the thriving drug trade in northern Costa Rica during the Nicaraguan civil war. Marcos Aguado, who directed contra commander Eden Pastora's air force, testified to the U.S. Congress that drug organizations "took advantage of the anti-communist sentiment which existed in Central America . . . and they undoubtedly used it for drug trafficking."[141] DEA personnel in Costa Rica noted, "some ranchers in Costa Rica who have landing strips on their property permit small aircraft to land and refuel thinking that they belong to the Contras, when in fact they are used to smuggle cocaine into the United States."[142] Eventually, the purported involvement of a CIA operative living in Costa Rica brought public attention to the role of the Guanacaste region in drug trafficking.

John Hull

In the 1970s John Hull, a farmer from Vincennes, Indiana, began to visit Costa Rica and, with time, to invest his and other Americans' money in purchasing northern ranches. Although Hull in fact managed, rather than owned, various of these large tracts, the properties were often referred to as "John Hull's ranch," and they included at least six airstrips. A staunch anticommunist, Hull became well situated to help move items across the nearby Nicaraguan border, and by the early 1980s, as Hull and the CIA station chief in San José later declared, the rancher was actively collaborating with the CIA, assisting in the contra-supply effort. In 1983 Hull requested Costa Rican citizenship, received it the following year, and thus came, de facto, to hold dual nationality.[143] As U.S. officials spearheaded the effort to build up a Nicaraguan southern front, the CIA reportedly provided Hull with bodyguards, and the rancher hosted mercenaries from the United States, Britain, and France, while inviting contra forces to use his property for training and the delivery of weapons and medical supplies.[144]

As Hull's activities in Costa Rica became publicized, controversy was further inflamed by repeated accusations that he was also involved in cocaine transshipment. Various individuals alleged that weapons and munitions would be flown south and narcotics shipped north, all through Hull's ranch, to supply the contras and finance their operations. All told, in hearings before the U.S. Senate five witnesses testified to Hull's involvement in the drug trade. In the late 1980s American journalists Martha Honey and Tony Avirgnan interviewed Panamanian trafficker Floyd Carlton Cáceres in La Reforma Prison and reported that Carlton had declared that he knew of flights from Miami to Hull's ranch that returned with cocaine. In 1990 cartel insider Carlos Lehder affirmed that Medellín traffickers had used Hull's property to transport drugs to the United States. Former DEA agent Celerino

140. Honey, *Hostile Acts*, 277–78, 406, and "Officials: Law Will Help Keep the Bad Guys Out," *TT* (CR), 15 August 1986, 8.

141. U.S. Senate, *Law Enforcement: Report*, 37.

142. "Hull in the Headlines—Four Years of Controversy," *TT* (CR), 20 January 1989, 9.

143. Costa Rica's citizenship laws require foreigners who become naturalized Costa Ricans to renounce their original citizenship. While a government office records such statements, it does not automatically forward them to other countries. See "Does Costa Rica Recognize Dual Citizenship?," *TT* (CR), 21 September 2007, 26. Costa Rican authorities claimed that Hull had renounced his U.S. citizenship at the time but failed to divulge this to U.S. officials. Comisión Especial, *Segundo Informe*, 66.

144. U.S. Senate, *Law Enforcement: Report*, 54; Comisión Especial, *Segundo Informe*, 66–69.

Castillo reported that in 1986 he had received a cable from his DEA colleague in Costa Rica, Robert Nieves, relaying suspicions that cocaine was being trafficked on contra-supply runs from Hull's ranch to hangars 4 and 5 at El Salvador's Ilopango Air Base.[145]

A number of pilots deeply involved in the Central American drug trade have stated that the rancher had permitted cocaine-trafficking networks to use airstrips on the property he controlled. Werner Lotz, a Costa Rican pilot for Mexican kingpins Miguel Ángel Félix Gallardo and Rafael Caro Quintero, told the U.S. Senate that Colombian and Panamanian pilots had reported to him that their organizations had paid Hull to use his runways for refueling.[146] Before his death in a car crash in Colombia shortly after his release from a U.S. prison, George Morales repeatedly alleged that pilots on arms-for-drugs runs had used Hull's ranch.[147] Former U.S. Navy pilot Gary Betzner, who had worked for Morales, went further, stating not only that he had twice delivered weapons to Hull's ranch in 1984 but that he had exchanged them for cocaine in the rancher's presence.[148] Betzner testified that in July 1984 John Hull met with him at an airstrip on Hull's ranch, and the two watched a weapons shipment be unloaded, and then seventeen duffel bags and five or six square boxes of cocaine be packed into the plane for the return flight to Lakeland, Florida. Two weeks later, according to Betzner, the two repeated the operation at another nearly airstrip: he and Hull were present again as weapons were exchanged for five hundred kilos of cocaine. Thereafter, in the 1990 trial of Medellín trafficker José Rafael Abello Silva, pilot Fabián Ernesto ("Tito") Carrasco claimed that he also had made drug runs in 1984 that landed at Hull's ranch.[149]

For his part, John Hull consistently and steadfastly denied any participation in drugs-for-arms deals, claiming that communists and criminals were conspiring against him.[150] Indeed, he eventually instituted defamation proceedings in Costa Rica to try to clear his name. At the trial the court took testimony from witness Carlos Rojas Chinchilla, a point of contact between journalists Honey and Avirgnan and a Nicaraguan source named David, who had information about operations on Hull's ranch. Since David could not himself appear at trial, having been kidnapped and killed years earlier, Rojas Chinchilla was asked whether David had spoken to him of Hull's ranch being used to

145. U.S. Senate, *Law Enforcement: Report*, 54; Avirgnan and Honey, *John Hull*, 185–86; "Lehder liga Hull con narcotráfico," *LN* (CR), 26 November 1991, 10A; and "Hull Mentioned in Trial," *TT* (CR), 29 November 1991, 22. Lehder also claimed that the cartel had contributed $20 million to the contra cause, though contra spokesperson Adolfo Calero vehemently denied it. "Drug King Fingers Rancher," *TT* (CR), 18 May 1990, 9. For Celerino Castillo's statement, see Cockburn and St. Clair, *Whiteout*, 296.

146. U.S. Senate, *Law Enforcement: Report*, 54. Subcommittee witnesses testified under oath. They did not get reduced sentences for testifying, but were liable to be prosecuted for perjury for false testimony (6).

147. "Piloto revela vuelos con armas y drogas," *LN* (CR), 14 January 1989, 5A. One account has Hull arranging an arms-for-drugs deal with Morales on a June 1983 trip to Miami. Honey, *Hostile Acts*, 363–64.

148. For Betzner's statements, see U.S. Senate, *Law Enforcement: Report*, 55; "OIJ ratifica nexos de Hull con rebeldes," *LN* (CR), 15 January 1989, 5A; "Traficante usó pista tica para dejar armas," *LN* (CR), 8 April 1988, 4A; "Traficantes admiten que ayudaron a la 'contra,'" *LN* (CR), 10 April 1988, 6A; and "Hull Denies Charges of Drug Trade," *TT* (CR), 10 April 1987, 4. For Betzner's testimony, conviction, and sentence to twenty-seven years, see "'Correo' mortal de ida y vuelta: Armas y aromas," *LN* (CR), 8 April 1988, 19, and "Traficante usó pista tica para dejar armas," *LN* (CR), 8 April 1988, 4A.

149. "Cocaine Runs at Hull's Ranch Cited," *TT* (CR), 19 October 1990, 8, and Honey, *Hostile Acts*, 366. Abello Silva was eventually convicted of importing cocaine and marijuana and sentenced to thirty years and a $5 million fine. See *United States v. Abello-Silva*, 948 F.2d 1168, and *United States v. Abello-Silva*, 107 F.3d 22.

150. See, for instance, "Hull Denies Charges," 1. For a summary of allegations regarding Hull, see "Indiana Farmer Helped Contras," *St. Louis Post-Dispatch* (United States) (hereafter cited as *SLPD* [US]), 9 December 1987, 13A. In terming the case against Hull "strong," Senator John Kerry observed, "While some of the information does come from convicted criminals, many of these people have been used by federal prosecutors for other cases or have passed a lie detector test regarding Hull's involvement." "U.S. Senate Report to Clear Rebels, Name Hull," *TT* (CR), 7 April 1989, 24.

traffic drugs. He testified, "Yes, he told me that Hull was involved in the traffic of arms and drugs and that planes landed with drugs and arms at his ranch. David told me that Hull had relations with the CIA and with the Nicaraguan Democratic Force and they had relations with narcotics traffickers."[151] Hull thereupon lost the defamation action. He has not, however, ever been convicted on drug charges.

On the heels of an official inquiry by the Costa Rican Legislative Assembly's Narcotics Subcommittee, the Costa Rican judicial police launched their own investigation of the drug charges. They learned that in 1983 Hull had indeed contacted George Morales, who had put Hull in touch with two pilots: Marcos Aguado and the Costa Rican Gerardo Durán Ayanegui. In 1986 authorities arrested Durán on DEA information in connection with cocaine flights that used Guanacaste airstrips protected by Rural Guard members.[152] After once jumping bail, he was eventually arrested and convicted.[153] Costa Rican officials believed that Hull and Durán had been involved in a scheme to deliver arms to the contras in exchange for their assistance in transshipping a cocaine load.[154] The OIJ report stated that aircraft would land at Hull's farm, refuel, and swap weapons for narcotics, concluding, "This situation occurred during the daytime and was known by Hull."[155] Thereafter, Costa Rican prosecutors formally accused Hull of collaborating in the export of two five-hundred-kilo cocaine shipments to the United States.[156] Nevertheless, a Costa Rican court could not find admissible evidence to support such drug allegations, although it failed to dismiss the charges that by violating Costa Rican neutrality he had committed hostile acts.[157]

In January 1989 OIJ agents arrested John Hull. While incarcerated, Hull claimed to have a serious heart condition, and Costa Rican authorities allowed him to leave jail on bail. On July 19, 1989, Hull jumped bail, reportedly fleeing Costa Rica at first for Haiti, evidently with the help of a rogue DEA agent. This occurred immediately before the Legislative Assembly issued its second report on narcotics trafficking and corruption in the country, which repeatedly alluded to Hull and his activities.[158] Eventually, John Hull turned up in Juigalpa in central Nicaragua, where he was friendly with the bishop and various former contras, renting a house and pursuing opportunities in farming, livestock, and forestry.[159]

Floyd Carlton Cáceres

Whether John Hull's farm was used in cocaine transshipment and whether the farmer himself

151. Avirgnan and Honey, *John Hull*, 62.

152. See "En Guanacaste: Piloto y guardias detenidos por el tráfico de cocaína," *LN* (CR), 12 January 1986, 10A, and "Capturan a otros implicados con drogas en Guanacaste," *LN* (CR), 12 February 1986, 10A. Police believed that, despite these arrests, the network succeeded in exporting most of this cocaine, with 450 kilos flown out of the Llano Grande airstrip toward the Bahamas in January 1986. See "Policía busca a piloto ligado con narcotráfico," *LN* (CR), 11 March 1987, 10A, and "Procesan a pilotos por tráfico de droga," *LN* (CR), 12 May 1988, 10A.

153. See "Detienen a piloto vinculado a drogas," *LN* (CR), 28 March 1987, 10A; "Testimonios débiles contra pilotos," *LN* (CR), 26 November 1992, 10A; "Fiscal pide diez años de cárcel para pilotos," *LN* (CR), 4 December 1992, 10A; and "Penas leves a pilotos por narcotráfico," *LN* (CR), 15 December 1992, 12A. For the controversy over the lack of prison time, see "Cómplices del narco con mínima sentencia," *LN* (CR), 19 January 1995, 16A.

154. "Procesados John Hull y Gerardo Durán Ayanegui," *LN* (CR), 2 March 1989, 10A. For more information on Hull and Durán, see "Hull to be Tried," *TT* (CR), 3 March 1989, 9; "Pilot Jailed in Probe of Drug Flight," *TT* (CR), 3 April 1987, 1; and Comisión Especial, *Segundo Informe*, 75.

155. "Report Links Hull to Bizarre Plots, Meetings," *TT* (CR), 24 February 1989, 9.

156. "Judge Asks More Detail in Hull Case," *TT* (CR), 9 June 1989, 16.

157. "Falta de mérito y procesamiento a Hull," *LN* (CR), 2 August 1989, 10A.

158. "OIJ detuvó a John Hull," *LN* (CR), 13 January 1989, 5A; "Hull Shucks Jail," *Village Voice*, 22 October 1991, 36; "U.S. Probing Drug Agent's Activities in Costa Rica," *San Francisco Chronicle*, 14 August 1991, 8A; "John Hull está en Nicaragua," *LN* (CR), 5 December 1990, 10A; "Prensa reitera que Hull está en Nicaragua," *LN* (CR), 10 December 1990, 10A; Comisión Especial, *Segundo Informe*, esp. 66–73.

159. About six months after fleeing Costa Rica, Hull was charged with murder by Costa Rican authorities investigating the May 1984 bombing of a press conference held by contra commander Eden Pastora at the remote

knew of it were issues regarding drug trafficking in northern Costa Rica that have never been finally resolved in a court of law. Such was not the case with another drug ring operating in this area, that of Panamanian Floyd Carlton Cáceres. This close associate of Manuel Noriega led one of the most notorious of the networks that shipped cocaine through Central America in the early to mid-1980s. Court documents recorded how Carlton's group had used airstrips in Guanacaste and on the Nicoya Peninsula to transship thousands of kilos of Medellín cartel cocaine.

Floyd Carlton's entry into the drug trade illustrates the continuing importance of patronage within Central American societies. While shining shoes at the Panama airport, the teenaged Carlton reportedly made the acquaintance of Noriega, then a young military officer. Some years later, when Carlton was working in the judicial system in David, Panama, he allegedly did Noriega a favor by "losing" records in a civil case brought against the officer. With increasing frequency over the next decade Carlton did errands for Noriega and eventually, in Noriega's own words, carried out his "dirty work." He also learned to fly. As Noriega rose to become chief of the National Guard's G-2 intelligence branch, he called on Carlton to handle various matters regarding arms smuggling into El Salvador and Nicaragua, this time on the side of leftists.[160] In particular, at Noriega's behest Carlton and pilot Cesár Rodríguez funneled Cuban weapons and other supplies through Guanacaste airstrips to the Sandinistas.[161] Then, in 1979 and 1980 the pair flew into El Salvador at least seventeen times, furnishing Salvadoran rebels with arms in exchange for payoffs.[162]

Key Colombian traffickers came to know of Floyd Carlton and his close links to Manuel Noriega. In 1977, when Carlton took a group of Colombians to the United States to learn to fly, all of the men were arrested on suspicion of drug trafficking. When the evidence proved too thin to prosecute, U.S. authorities sent Carlton back to Panama, where he was briefly imprisoned and questioned by DEA agents. In fact, thanks to Noriega's intervention, Carlton spent his days in the Department of Narcotics playing cards, returning to jail at night. Carlton remained within his patron's inner circle, and in 1979 he was photographed piloting the plane transporting the exiled shah of Iran around the country, a

village of La Penca, who had fallen from favor with U.S. officials. In 1991, after asking Nicaragua to deliver Hull and finding he had already moved to Orlando, Costa Rica formally requested his extradition. However, the Department of Justice rejected the application on technical grounds. See "Hull Shucks Jail," 36, and "U.S. High Court Rejects Penca Appeal," *TT* (CR), 17 January 1992, 5. While theories have abounded regarding La Penca, the most recent evidence suggests that a Sandinista intelligence operation caused the killings.

160. See generally "Floyd Carlton vincula a Torrijos y a Noriega con tráfico de armas," *LP* (PA), 2 October 1991, 1A.

161. Rodríguez was later assassinated in Colombia after infuriating Noriega and Pablo Escobar. Bilonick testified that the seizure of one of Medellín's borrowed planes containing a secret cocaine-storage compartment caused Escobar's rage at Rodríguez. See "S. Ferro comparece en juicio de co-acusados de Noriega," *LP* (PA), 6 March 1991, 22A, and "Declara Bilonick: Noriega recibía medio millón por cada cargamento de cocaína," *LP* (PA), 19 November 1991, 1A. For Cuban weapons, see Dinges, *Our Man in Panama*, 105. Although Fidel Castro hesitated to send arms directly to the Sandinistas for fear of provoking U.S. intervention, he reportedly approved Torrijos's suggestion, relayed by Noriega, that arms be channeled through Panama (104–5).

162. "Carlton implica a Noriega en contrabando de armas," *LP* (PA), 26 September 1991, 1A. On the final trip into El Salvador, Carlton piloted his plane there safely, but Rodríguez crashed his. Before Salvadoran military helicopters discovered the accident, Carlton located the downed plane and departed for Panama with the injured Rodríguez. Salvadoran officials who found that a plane registered to the Panamanian government had been supplying the guerrillas strongly protested to Noriega, who prevailed upon Carlton and Rodríguez to declare that they had stolen the aircraft. In fact, Bilonick owned it and rented the plane for rebel supply runs. See "Del Cid delata," 1A, and "Ricardo Bilonick se confiesa," 1A. For the points in the rest of this paragraph, see "Del Cid delata a Noriega," *LP* (PA), 20 September 1991, 1A; "La Fiscalía presenta testimonio de Erick Guerra y Floyd Carlton," *LP* (PA), 26 September 1991, 2A; Dinges, *Our Man in Panama*, 105; and Scott and Marshall, *Cocaine Politics*, 69. Bilonick relayed the "dirty work" quote. "Ricardo Bilonick se confiesa cómplice de Manuel A. Noriega," *LP* (PA), 15 November 1991, 1A.

Panamanian government undertaking whose oversight had been assigned to Noriega.[163]

Then, in 1982 Colombian trafficker Francisco Chávez Gil reportedly accompanied Carlton from Panama City to Medellín to introduce him to kingpins Pablo Escobar Gaviria and Gustavo de Jesús Gaviria Rivero.[164] They proposed that Medellín traffickers begin to fly cocaine shipments through Panama, delivering bribes to Noriega to gain his cooperation.[165] Carlton brought the proposal to his patron, and in early 1983, after some haggling over terms, Noriega is thought to have agreed to the arrangement.[166] In August General Noriega became commander in chief of the National Guard, ideally situating him to assist in the drug trade. In this way Floyd Carlton served as an original intermediary between Noriega and Medellín kingpins.[167]

The drug-smuggling operation built up by Carlton relied on small, well-equipped planes that took off from Montería in northern Colombia packed with three hundred to five hundred kilos of cocaine.[168] From late 1982 into 1984 Carlton's pilots undertook periodic cocaine flights, in which Colombian planes would touch down in Panama with the G-2 providing security. In return for safe passage, Carlton delivered bribes to the general that may eventually have amounted to millions of dollars.[169]

In the middle of 1984, however, at a time when Noriega was looking to consolidate political power and did not wish to add to rumors circulating regarding his involvement in the drug trade, Colombian traffickers agreed, for a time, to curb the flow of cocaine through Panama. At this point Carlton moved his transshipment operation north, first to Nicaragua, where he was promptly arrested and deported, and then to northern Costa Rica, where he developed an extensive cocaine-smuggling operation.[170] Rather than simply carrying out Noriega's errands, Carlton was working directly with Medellín kingpins, reportedly charging three thousand dollars per kilo to transport cocaine from Colombia to south Florida.[171]

Under Carlton's overall management, the ring employed various pilots, allegedly with Cecilio Sáenz Barria in charge of Costa Rican operations and with Spaniard Miguel Alemany Soto overseeing the ring's affairs in Miami.[172]

163. "La Fiscalía presenta testimonio," 2A; Dinges, *Our Man in Panama*, 246.

164. For background on Chávez, see Dinges, *Our Man in Panama*, 132. For the Florida grand jury indictment mentioning Chávez, see *United States v. Noriega*, 1990 U.S. Dist. LEXIS 1.

165. Scott and Marshall, *Cocaine Politics*, 69. Escobar's personal pilot David Rodrigo Ortíz Hermida, formerly of the Colombian Air Force and later convicted of drug trafficking, provided additional flight training to Carlton. "Co-acusado se declara culpable y será testigo en caso Noriega," *LP* (PA), 7 August 1991, 1A.

166. At Noriega's trial Carlton conceded on cross-examination that he had not told Noriega when or where his planes would land as he imported drugs from Colombia into Panama in November and December 1982. "Rubino ataca credibilidad de Carlton," *LP* (PA), 1 October 1991, 1A.

167. See "Many Costa Rican Links to Noriega Charges," *TT* (CR), 12 January 1990, 13. At Noriega's trial Max Mermelstein testified that in September 1983 he met Floyd Carlton in a Paitilla Airport hangar to discuss buying a Panamanian island for Medellín cocaine transshipments. Carlton told him, "No problem. Pick the island you want." "Vinculan a Balbina Herrera con Noriega y el Cartel de Medellín," *LP* (PA), 18 September 1991, 1A. See also "El testimonio de Luis Del Cid," *LP* (PA), 24 September 1991, 2A.

168. Former Noriega adviser José Blandón alleged that by 1985 Carlton was also smuggling drugs for Cali traffickers. "Traficantes compran protección policial," *LN* (CR), 24 November 1986, 10A. See also Scott and Marshall, *Cocaine Politics*, 110.

169. Carlton conceded as much in testimony. "Many Costa Rican Links," 13. At the Noriega trial Ortiz Hermida corroborated Carlton's account. See "At Noriega Trial in Miami: Second Pilot Details Drug Flights," *MH* (US), 4 October 1991, 3A.

170. See Scott and Marshall, *Cocaine Politics*, 69, and Comisión Especial, *Segundo Informe*, 76.

171. See Dinges, *Our Man in Panama*, 210.

172. Other pilots reportedly part of this network included Mexican Alejandro Benítez Fuentes, and Panamanians Aníbal Antonio Aizprua, Ricardo Bilonick, Eduardo Pardo, Enrique Pretelt, and César Rodríguez Contreras. See Comisión Especial, *Segundo Informe*, 76–78, and "Contra-interrogatorio de Pardo," *LP* (PA), 16 October 1991, 2A. Ortiz Hermida testified to participating in two cocaine flights with Carlton. See "At Noriega Trial," 3A, and "Co-acusado se declara culpable," 1A. For Aizprua's grand jury testimony mentioning the Spaniard, see *United States v. Golb*, 69 F.3d 1417.

Carlton's fleet of light planes landed for refueling either at La Flor Ranch near Guanacaste's principal town of Liberia, a ranch previously owned by Costa Rican president Daniel Oduber Quirós, or at Tamarindo, Sardinal, or other coastal airstrips along the Nicoya Peninsula.[173] Here, planes were serviced, and the pilots retired to nearby beach houses to rest and rotate.

A corrupt leader of the Costa Rican Rural Guard, regional commander Edwin Lorenzo Viales Rodríguez, helped to protect the Costa Rican portion of this multimillion-dollar operation.[174] At the time, Viales and rancher Carlos Eduardo Zapporolli Zecca were participating in the transfer of military supplies to the contras.[175] On the side, Viales and Zapporolli assisted Carlton's drug network in transshipping cocaine via Costa Rica, perhaps as much as fifteen tons annually.[176] Later investigations revealed that, after departing Costa Rican airspace, the organization's pilots flew the drug loads to runways near Villahermosa or Monterrey, Mexico, for transshipment to airstrips near Brownsville, Texas, and finally on into the Florida Everglades.[177]

For each flight the Carlton network sent through Guanacaste, it paid Viales ten thousand dollars in cash to cover fuel and protection, while Zapporolli earned a five-thousand-dollar bribe each time the conspirators touched down at the La Flor ranch that he administered.[178] Both men then received bonuses of twenty thousand dollars and seven thousand dollars if the drug run succeeded. Viales procured aviation fuel by telling sellers that he needed it for contra-supply runs. Given the weapons and material constantly being forwarded to the contras, this proved to be a convincing cover story, and one viewed favorably by the many Sandinista opponents living in northern Costa Rica.[179]

With time, DEA undercover agent Daniel Moritz succeeded in infiltrating the Carlton ring. In early 1985 a financier in trouble with U.S. authorities agreed to introduce Moritz to Alfredo Caballero, a Cuban American Bay of Pigs veteran who had lived in Nicaragua during the Somoza regime and over the preceding two years had reportedly supplied arms and planes to contra commander Eden Pastora.[180] Caballero had become president of DIACSA, a Cessna airplane distributorship and parts supply company that had become deeply involved in contra resupply.[181] An informant alleged that Caballero supplied Carlton with planes and was "the man in charge of operations" for Carlton's

173. The Costa Rican Legislative Drug Commission noted the use of strips at Ciruelas, Coyolar, Las Loras, and Llano Grande. Comisión Especial, *Segundo Informe*, 75. Traffickers had reportedly arranged to use La Flor ranch. "Traficantes compran protección," 10A.

174. "Many Costa Rican Links," 13.

175. Zapporolli, who also supervised a Guanacaste furniture factory, had originally helped to provide arms to Eden Pastora when Pastora was fighting for the Sandinistas against Somoza. See ibid., 13, and "Cocaína hunde su garra," 1A.

176. So estimated Costa Rican police sources. Carlton's federal court indictment listed sixteen cocaine shipments, totaling 6.4 tons. "Drug Control Chief Denies Charges," *TT* (CR), 30 January 1987, 8.

177. See ibid. and "Paper Details 'C.R. Connection,'" *TT* (CR), 28 November 1986, 1. Ultimately, distributors stored the cocaine in a Coral Gables's safe house before dealing it from motor homes. "Traficantes compran protección," 9A.

178. According to convicted Mexican trafficker Cecilio Sáenz, identified as having supervised Costa Rica for the Medellín cartel, Viales and Zapporolli also agreed to protect and refuel cocaine planes for Alberto Audemar's Panamanian network. However, after Mexican authorities interdicted the first flight, Audemar could not pay his Costa Rican associates. Hence, in early 1985 Carlton agreed to pay up front one-half of Viales and Zapporolli's fees. "Many Costa Rican Links," 13, and "Cartel de Medellín," 10A.

179. "Many Costa Rican Links," 13; "Cuatro mil kilos," 10A; and "Witness: Guard Sought Airstrip for Drugs," *TT* (CR), 19 May 1989, 15. The bribe figures come from testimony at the Viales-Zapporolli trial.

180. For the information on Caballero, see Dinges, *Our Man in Panama*, 243; "Many Costa Rican Links," 13; and "En Panamá se tejía red criminal," *LN* (CR), 9 January 1990, 5A. In September 1985, after Florida authorities had intercepted the 409-kilo Carlton-network cocaine flight, federal prosecutors indicted Caballero for conspiring to import the seized narcotics and to launder $2.6 million of proceeds. After choosing to cooperate, Caballero was sentenced to five years of probation. Scott and Marshall, *Cocaine Politics*, 11, 70, 110.

181. See U.S. Senate, *Law Enforcement: Report*, 125.

drug-smuggling business. In March 1985, after DEA agent Moritz presented himself as skilled in money laundering, Caballero introduced him to Floyd Carlton.[182]

Within a brief period the agent had penetrated the inner workings of Carlton's smuggling network. At first, he offered to turn illicit drug profits into large cashier's checks and international wire transfers without tipping the U.S. government by filing the requisite forms.[183] After pretending to help Carlton with such financial matters, the agent managed to document six cocaine-smuggling flights totaling many thousands of kilos. Among the information the DEA investigator gleaned, at times by riding in the plane and taking pictures, was the fact that the Carlton network had bought off key members of the Rural Guard in northwestern Costa Rica.

In the meantime, in the mid-1980s U.S. officials had organized and overseen the secret construction of a long airstrip in Potrero Grande in northern Costa Rica, designed to permit the entry of larger contra supply planes. Costa Rican minister of security Benjamin Piza, who had endorsed the plan for his government, turned to Colonel José Ramón Montero Quesada, at that time Civil Guard director in Liberia, to provide security at the airstrip. According to CIA station chief Joe Fernandez, nine flights between April and September 1986 deposited many thousands of pounds of military supplies to transfer to the contras.[184]

In May 1985 Edwin Viales allegedly met with Colonel Montero to propose that Montero stay away from this airstrip two nights a week to free it for drug trafficking. On nights when no military supplies were being shipped, Carlton's drug-trafficking flights would touch down for refueling.[185] Although Montero, earning only seven hundred dollars a month, and with certain prior suspect dealings, would have gained seven thousand dollars per flight, he decided to contact the DEA and the Costa Rican Public Security Ministry.[186] That same month, Carlton ran into trouble with his Colombian suppliers when Teófilo Watson, one of his most experienced pilots who had also flown for Manuel Noriega, mysteriously disappeared, along with a load of 537 kilos of cocaine.[187] After departing from Tamarindo, Watson had landed in Pereira, Colombia, and the cocaine had been loaded. However, after taking off and heading north, Watson disappeared.[188] When informed, Colombian traffickers reacted vigorously to the loss of such a large shipment.[189] The infuriated suppliers, reportedly Colombians Luís José Ospina

182. "Se tejía red criminal," 5A.

183. Dinges, *Our Man in Panama*, 244.

184. Comisión Especial, *Segundo Informe*, 60–61; "Testigo compromete a ex Guardia Rural," *LN* (CR), 16 May 1989, 10A; and "Witness: Guard Sought Airstrip," 15. According to the Costa Rican Drug Commission, in June 1984 Reagan administration officials promised direct aid to Costa Rica for contra support. In July 1985 U.S. ambassador Lewis Tambs, CIA station chief Joe Fernandez, and Costa Rican minister of security Benjamin Piza planned a contra-supply airstrip that a U.S. private group was supposed to finance. Later that summer, Costa Rican president Luis Monge Alvarez authorized its construction in exchange for a pledge of U.S. support should Nicaragua attack Costa Rica.

185. This evidence comes from Montero's testimony at Viales's trial. "Witness: Guard Sought Airstrip," 15.

186. Montero's business relationships were sufficiently suspicious that the Costa Rican Drug Commission recommended that he never again be appointed to public office, noting his purchase of a car from a former U.S. Embassy official using a check for eighteen thousand dollars in payment. Comisión Especial, *Segundo Informe*, 76, 86. However, U.S. congressional investigators found that in the first half of 1986 alone Montero had been paid almost two hundred thousand dollars from Iran-contra bank accounts for contra support services, making him, according to Contra officials, "one of the CIA's highest paid Costa Rican collaborators." Honey, *Hostile Acts*, 253, 406. Hence, Montero may have gained his extra money from other sources.

187. Comisión Especial, *Segundo Informe*, 73.

188. One explanation has Watson being radioed to land at John Hull's ranch, where he was either killed in a plane accident or murdered. See "Se tejía red criminal," 5A.

189. After being placed in the Federal Witness Protection Program, Medellín trafficker Max Mermelstein noted of another missing cocaine shipment, "Without press confirmation of the find by lawmen, there would be more than passing suspicion that the load had been appropriated by either the pilots, the ground crew, or others. . . . If these suspicions became too strong, the Colombian shooters

and Leopoldo Rodríguez, were thought to be connected with the Pereira cartel.[190]

For his part Carlton suspected Zapporolli. He speculated that the rancher had radioed Watson to land at a different airstrip and that the pilot had then been murdered and the drugs stolen. Carlton believed that one of the pilots who regularly supplied the contras had then flown the cocaine to a ranch used in the resupply effort, perhaps a runway on Hull's ranch. At that point, Carlton believed that the cocaine had been exported to finance additional contra arms purchases.[191] The Colombian suppliers, however, favored a simpler explanation. They accused Carlton of double-crossing them by stealing the shipment for his own profit. Carlton went to Medellín and appealed personally to Pablo Escobar to save his life. Although a hit man had already been dispatched, Escobar is said to have had him recalled, and Carlton disappeared, fleeing to Miami.[192]

With Watson dead and Carlton vanished, the suppliers were left to their own devices to investigate the loss.[193] Their thugs, reportedly led by Panamanian Alberto Audemar, kidnapped, tortured, and interrogated one of Carlton's relatives and his wife and used a backhoe to tear up a newly landscaped yard on Carlton's farm near David, Panama.[194] Ultimately, Panamanian authorities arrested Audemar and his associates and sent him to the United States to face narcotics charges, where he was eventually killed in a botched prison escape. Nevertheless, the run of bad fortune for Carlton's network continued. While Carlton was hiding in Miami, an informant's tip led U.S. Customs to capture one of his planes, carrying 409 kilos of cocaine, and eventually its pilot, Antonio Aizprua.[195] In October 1985 Carlton returned to Panama, only to be arrested and imprisoned by the National Department of Investigations, controlled by Noriega through his subordinate, Nivaldo Madriñan. Over the next months the department kept Carlton in custody, and hence away from the DEA and from Colombian hit men alike, while attempting to erase evidence that might link Noriega to the Carlton network.[196]

In January 1986 a Panamanian judge ordered Carlton's release, stating that the authorities had found no cocaine to support the trafficking charges. However, fearing that his smuggling organization was in deep trouble and that either Colombian traffickers or the Noriega regime would soon have him killed, Carlton contacted the DEA agent in charge in Panama City.[197] The trafficker outlined the information he could give the DEA against Manuel Noriega—"money laundering, drugs, weapons, corruption, assassinations"—and proposed a deal: testimony against Noriega in exchange for immunity from U.S. prosecution. According to Carlton, the DEA representative became flustered at the possibility of "taking down" Noriega, and once the DEA rejected his proposal, Carlton again went into hiding.

At the end of July 1986, Carlton returned to Costa Rica to attend a meeting with Alfredo

---

would be given their orders to kill." Mermelstein, *Man*, 50. See also the debriefing of Cali kingpin Miguel Rodríguez Orejuela in *Confesiones secretas*, 39.

190. See Dinges, *Our Man in Panama*, 211;"Traficantes compran protección," 9A; "Incomunicados supuestos narcotraficantes," *LN* (CR), 1 March 1987, 10A; and "Witness: Guard Sought Airstrip," 15. For Escobar's alleged role in the conspiracy, see "Se tejía red criminal," 5A.

191. "Se tejía red criminal," 5A.

192. Scott and Marshall, *Cocaine Politics*, 70, and Dinges, *Our Man in Panama*, 211.

193. Accounts differ on the location of Watson's death. See Murillo, *Noriega Mess*, 404–6; Honey, *Hostile Acts*, 362; "Se tejía red criminal," 5A; "Traficantes compran protección," 9A; and "Many Costa Rican Links," 13.

194. See "Se tejía red criminal," 5A; "Carlton termina testimonio," *LP* (PA), 1 October 1991, 2A; "Traficantes compran protección," 9A; "Many Costa Rican Links," 13.

195. For Aizprua's grand jury testimony and other information regarding his employment piloting drug flights for Carlton, Colombian Cuco Rodríguez, and Dr. Fidel Kosonoy, see *United States v. Golb*, 69 F.3d at 1430–31.

196. Dinges, *Our Man in Panama*, 245–46.

197. For information on this meeting, see "Se tejía red criminal," 5A; "Many Costa Rican Links," 13; and Dinges, *Our Man in Panama*, 246. See also Scott and Marshall, *Cocaine Politics*, 170 (which erroneously dates the meeting January 1987).

Caballero, this one at the luxury Cariari Hotel outside of San José.[198] However, instead of discussing the purchase of more planes, Carlton found himself trapped in a sting operation organized by the DEA and OIJ. Upon his arrest, Carlton complained of Caballero: "Apparently he had problems with the American judicial system, and he exchanged me for his freedom." Early the following year Costa Rica extradited Carlton to the United States, and by early 1988 his testimony had helped to indict Manuel Noriega.[199] Eventually, Carlton served as a prosecution witness against Noriega and entered the Federal Witness Protection Program himself.[200] In the meantime, in May 1989 a Costa Rican court convicted Edwin Viales and Carlos Zapporolli of helping to ship through Costa Rica 2,334 kilos of cocaine. Each was sentenced to serve ten years.[201]

The Significance of Trafficking in Northern Costa Rica

The Guanacaste region thus played a notable role as the Costa Rican drug trade developed. As early as the mid-1980s the airstrips used in efforts to supply and support the Nicaraguan contras proved useful for cocaine traffickers, as did collaborators prepared to import arms and to assist in cocaine transshipment. The conflict in Nicaragua provided excellent cover. This was particularly so because many in Costa Rica and within its government supported the contras and the clandestine efforts to assist them. Indeed, leading Costa Rican law enforcement figures later reported that they had been "instructed to keep their narcotics investigations away from the Nicaraguan border during the Sandinista Revolution. Even when they had received hard information about drugs in the aircraft delivering the weapons, the officials, in an effort to avoid controversy regarding the war, ignored the tips and let the flights go."[202] In 1989 the Costa Rican Legislative Narcotics Commission concluded that the opening of the contra's southern front had initiated large-scale drug trafficking in the country.[203] That same year, former president Oduber, a longtime property owner in the area, stated that even as the fighting wound down, the Nicaraguan frontier remained critically important to the drug trade.[204]

Nevertheless, trafficking organizations would likely have discovered the advantages of flying drugs into northern Costa Rica even without the stimulus of the Nicaraguan civil war. This region has always been thinly populated, inadequately patrolled, and poor, with significant cross-border flows.[205] Thus, by the 1990s traffickers sent increasingly large cocaine shipments overland to the northern border, and speedboat passage along the Pacific often included refueling along Costa Rica's northern coast.[206]

Indeed, as the drug trade through Costa Rica evolved, shipments by sea came to eclipse

198. See Dinges, *Our Man in Panama*, 250, 380. Certain accounts have Carlton meeting with Alfonso Caballero's son, Luis, a DIACSA vice president, who was visiting Costa Rica at about this time. See "Traficantes compran protección," 9A, and "Extradición de panameño lista para su ejecución," *LN* (CR), 11 January 1987, 10A.

199. "Many Costa Rican Links," 13. See also "Noriega protegía embarques de cocaína del 'Cartel de Medellín,' revela Carlton," *LP* (PA), 11 February 1988, 1A.

200. See "Noriega y 'la conexión sórdida,'" *LP* (PA), 27 September 1991, 2A.

201. See "Dos condenados por narcotráfico," *LN* (CR), 19 May 1989, 10A, and "Traffickers Sentenced to Ten Years," *TT* (CR), 26 May 1989, 9. Prosecutors lacked evidence sufficient to convict Fernando Loaciga, another Rural Guard member named in Carlton's indictment, who was absolved but fired. "Destituyen a Guardia Rural sospechoso de narcotráfico," *LN* (CR), 25 November 1986, 10A.

202. U.S. Senate, *Law Enforcement: Report*, 40.

203. Comisión Especial, *Segundo Informe*, 78. See also "A Contra Legacy," *Boston Globe*, 4 August 1989, 10.

204. "Ex-president Again Vows to Name Traffickers," *TT* (CR), 17 March 1989, 15.

205. Costa Rican pilot Werner Lotz, after his drug conviction, testified that "Costa Rica has got only civil guards, underpaid and easily bought. . . . To be very clear . . . our guard down there is barefoot, and you're talking about maybe 50 men to cover 400 kilometers." U.S. Senate, *Law Enforcement: Report*, 40.

206. At first Colombian fishing vessels sometimes looked after refueling and supplying speedboats off Costa Rican shores. See, for instance, *United States v. Sinesterra Colorado*, 170 Fed. Appx. 689. Employing Costa Rican boats, however, proved less risky and more cost-effective.

aerial schemes, with maritime trafficking along the Caribbean coast capitalizing on what the U.S. government once termed the weakest interdiction capabilities in the region.[207] While authorities continued to uncover occasional export operations through Guanacaste, by the 1990s Caribbean maritime drug-trafficking routes had soared in importance.[208] In assessing the evolution of the drug trade in Costa Rica, one might flag, then, the important role that the northern zone played in initiating aerial drug smuggling and the transshipping of large quantities of Colombian cocaine.

The San Andrés and Puerto Limón Links

Puerto Limón and its Caribbean links, especially Isla de San Andrés, dominated the early maritime cocaine trade in Costa Rica. For historical and geographic reasons, Colombia's resort island of San Andrés has been an ideal gateway for drugs being exported from South America. Quite densely populated, San Andrés is located approximately 480 miles northwest of Colombia's Caribbean coast but only 200 and 140 miles off Costa Rican and Nicaraguan shores.[209] In fact, until 1928 Nicaragua claimed title to San Andrés, although many considered the island a part of Panama.[210] And for much of the nineteenth century, Panama stood as the rebellious northernmost province of Colombia, although it did enjoy various brief periods of quasi independence.

In the mid-1950s, to promote trade and tourism on the island, the Colombian government converted San Andrés into a duty-free port. Colombia's highly protectionist economic policies then created incentives for the island's inhabitants to smuggle an array of goods to the mainland.[211] For many years most islanders were so-called *raizales*: people of African descent speaking English and Creole and sharing cultural characteristics with the Afro-Caribbean communities strung along the Central American coastline. Over time, however, on account of steady immigration from the Colombian mainland, their percentage has decreased to just over a quarter of the island's population. In light of ethnicity, history, and geography, both the raizales and the Hispanic groups on San Andrés have cultivated connections with various Central Americans, especially Costa Ricans and Nicaraguans from the Corn Islands, less than one hundred miles away. Colombian drug networks have thoroughly penetrated San Andrés, and Costa Rica's extensive links to the island have amounted to another bridge-favoring factor for that country.

As for typical transshipment schemes, traffickers have frequently flown drugs to San Andrés from mainland Colombian airstrips situated near refining laboratories. Alternatively, they have shipped narcotics to the island via Colombia's principal Caribbean ports: Turbo, Santa Marta, Cartagena, and Barranquilla.[212] In good weather the most powerful speedboats could then make a round trip to Costa Rican territorial waters from San Andrés in less than a day, and small planes could even more easily hop across the Caribbean.[213] Cocaine came to flow along this route so efficiently that

207. Cf. *INCSR* (1998), 128.

208. For an example of cocaine hidden under the floor boards of an abandoned boat on Playa Guanacaste near the Nicaraguan border, see "Caen trescientos kilos de cocaína en lancha," *LN* (CR), 13 August 2007, 14A. For the mailing of cocaine to Memphis and Toronto inside books and wooden statues, see "Caen tres por tráfico de cocaína hacia EE.UU. y Canada," *LN* (CR), 23 December 2004, 4.

209. About eighty-five thousand people live in an area measuring just over ten square miles.

210. In 1928 Nicaragua ceded its claim to San Andrés to Colombia, though in 1980 it contested that treaty's validity, because the Nicaraguan government had been under U.S. military occupation at the time. See "San Andrés Stuck in Custody Battle, "*Nicaraguan Times* (Costa Rica) (hereafter cited as *NT* [CR]), 21 September 2007, 3.

211. Thoumi, *Political Economy*, 100. Indeed, such a thriving illegal trade developed that, to this day, those engaged in contraband in Colombia are commonly called "San Andresitos."

212. See "Cocaína acosa Puerto Limón," *LN* (CR), 7 August 1986, 1. See also "Cargamento de cocaína," *LN* (CR), 15 May 1994, 22A.

213. See "Narcotráfico converge en Limón," *LN* (CR), 25 September 1989, 8A.

by 1993 Costa Rican police estimated that the island could be exporting 80 percent of the cocaine arriving in their country.[214]

Far and away the favorite Costa Rican destination for drug rings at work in Caribbean waters was Puerto Limón, the country's chief port, located about seventy-five miles east of San José. A full 80 percent of Costa Rica's foreign trade, including all of its oil supplies, as well as a considerable fishing fleet, contributed to substantial maritime traffic.[215] As a rough port city, Limón did not enjoy the rapid development of the Valle Central, and it has long been Costa Rica's poorest and most violence-prone city.[216] Indeed, a soaring population that far outpaced local-government resources underlay many problems of governance. From 1984 to 2000 the population rose from 50,000 to 340,000 inhabitants, an increase of almost 6.5 percent annually.[217] In the 1980s a camp for exiled Nicaraguans developed on its outskirts, and Limón soon became "the unofficial capital for black and Miskito Indian contras and refugees."[218] No other Costa Rican city had such a substantial proportion of minorities, including the indigenous, as did Limón, and black Costa Ricans approached a third of the population. Limonses, as residents of Limón were known, proved to be quite vulnerable to national economic downturns, and the experience of Limón reminds us that development did not extend equally across the country, nor to all ethnic groups.[219]

Especially lax and venal coast guard and port authorities plagued law enforcement in Limón and Moín, just to the north. Moreover, corrupt and inadequate city police forces long neglected law enforcement, boosting petty and organized crime alike. In 1993 authorities fired several local OIJ police and suspended twelve Limón officers for corruption.[220] However, such periodic crackdowns had limited positive consequences, given serious underlying problems: poor morale, inadequate pay, and deficient training. Furthermore, cultural differences between Limonses and Hispanic Costa Rican officials in San José complicated law enforcement. All of these factors caused violence, much of it drug-related, to grow rapidly.[221]

Furthermore, Puerto Limón has long had a particularly close relationship with Colombia—highlighted by trade with San Andrés and ferry service to Cartagena—and it has had road connections and other long-standing links with Panama as well. Hence, Colombians, Panamanians, and Nicaraguans engaged in trafficking ventures with Costa Rican associates have found Limón to be readily accessible: they could blend into crowds or expatriate communities without attracting undue notice. It is thus not surprising that drug networks discovered, early on, the advantages to smuggling via Limón. Officials on the take, who had once turned a blind eye to "crates of arms and supplies for the contras, much of it concealed

214. "El narco en el bote, la policía a nado," *LN* (CR), 13 June 1993, 6A.

215. "Port Authority Under Pressure," *TT* (CR), 6 March 2009, 1.

216. In 1991, though already quite run-down, Limón was devastated by an earthquake. See "Limonses Skeptical of Plan," *TT* (CR), 19 November 2004, 1A.

217. "Census: Population Increase," 1A.

218. Honey, *Hostile Acts*, 205. The president of the Caribbean Federation of Tourism Chambers in Limón noted, "Immigrants come to Limón because they know [the police] won't bother them here." "Census: Population Increase," 1A.

219. Over 1995 and 1996 the city's unemployment rate increased by 60 percent, and by 2004 residents of Limón Province earned 37 percent less than the average national income. "Limón: Epicentro de pobreza," *LN* (CR), 23 March 1997, 4A, and "Limonses Skeptical," 1A.

220. "Narco en el bote," 6A.

221. Stimulated by extensive marijuana and crack-cocaine dealing, Limón's homicide rate had reached 17.5 per 100,000 inhabitants by 1995, and the rate rose to 36 per 100,000 in 2007 and 48 per 100,000 in 2008. See "Limón: Epicentro," 4A, and "Tico Towns' Murder Rates Spike," *TT* (CR), 30 January 2009, 1. See also "Un estigma llamado Limón," *LN* (CR), 15 May 1993, 8A; "¢60 millones de coca en Limón," *LN* (CR), 15 May 1993, 10A; "Marijuana que escandaliza," *LN* (CR), 5 August 1986, 1, 8A; and "Limón se asfixia en la droga," *LN* (CR), 4 August 1986, 1.

as agricultural equipment," found it even more lucrative to collaborate in the cocaine trade.[222]

During the 1980s, Colombia to Costa Rica via Puerto Limón turned into one of Central America's most noted drug thoroughfares. Cartels moved in, led by Cali traffickers.[223] By the late 1980s Limón was acting as a cocaine clearinghouse with drug loads warehoused, awaiting shipment. Traffickers could secrete narcotics in containers, some to be forwarded directly to the United States and others moved indirectly via other Central American bridge states or Mexico. Still others combined Central American and Caribbean transit, traveling via islands immersed in the drug trade, such as Haiti, Jamaica, and the Dominican Republic. Occasionally, narcotics that have arrived in Costa Rica via Limón have then taken an overland trip to the capital to depart by air from San José or to be trucked overland across the Nicaraguan border.[224]

The San Andrés–Limón route first came to public attention during the 1980s. In one notable case investigators discovered that a drug ring was sending Costa Rican fruits and vegetables to San Andrés, with the vessels returning with hidden cocaine cargoes. Police followed up on leads by tapping the telephones of various suspects, although without judicial authorization, and at length, in 1988 authorities managed to intercept ten kilos of cocaine on board the *Chaparral*.[225] Captain Stanley Garrón Figuls, a former public security employee in the maritime section, turned out to be second cousin to the public security minister.[226] Among the arrested were also an associate from Spain, another from Costa Rica, and ringleader Alberto Duarte Bernal, a Colombian fugitive suffering from an advanced case of AIDS, who within eight months had managed to escape from a Limón jail.[227] Eventually, various of the sentences handed to his associates, including Garrón Figuls, were overturned for illegal use of wiretaps.[228] The *Chaparral* case illustrates, however, not only how Colombian networks employed well-connected Costa Rican associates to move drugs from San Andrés to Limón, but the ways in which traffickers took advantage of the Costa Rican criminal-justice system: its staunch support for civil liberties and its porous prisons.

The San Andrés connection was confirmed the following year when Miami DEA agents intercepted 1,346 kilos of cocaine hidden among fruit in a ship hailing from Puerto Limón.[229] Investigations by U.S. and Costa

222. Honey, *Hostile Acts*, 205. In 2004 U.S. officials identified yet another institutional problem, noting that "clear legal authority for onboard inspection of containers and ships has yet to be established." *INCSR* (2004), 8.

223. For an OIJ estimate that Cali traffickers were shipping through Limón 400 kilos a month, of which 5 percent was being consumed locally, see "Cartel de Cali controla a Limón," *LN* (CR), 4 June 1993, 10A. See also "Narco en el bote," 6A, and "Banda trasegó 550 kilos de cocaína," *LN* (CR), 19 July 1994, 10A.

224. See "Descubierta empacadora de cocaína en Moravia," *LN* (CR), 18 July 1994, 10A, and "Desarticulada banda internacional," 12A.

225. See "Hallan diez kilos de cocaína en lancha," *LN* (CR), 6 November 1988, 10A; "Excarcelan a marinos vinculados con drogas," *LN* (CR), 28 May 1991, 10A; and "Anulan sentencia por narcotráfico," *LN* (CR), 7 January 1995, 16A. In 1988 the Costa Rican Supreme Court issued search-and-seizure regulations, stating that the OIJ must solicit permission to wiretap from judicial authorities with written justification in each case. "Corte reguló allanamientos e intervenciones telefonicas," *LN* (CR), 1 September 1988, 10A.

226. "Drugs Dominate Local News," *TT* (CR), 11 November 1988, 14. See also "Confirmado juicio por carga de coca en lancha," *LN* (CR), 7 January 1990, 10A, and "Cocaína vale c. 40 millones," *LN* (CR), 8 November 1988, 10A. For the case's resolution, see "OIJ vincula a imputados con mafia internacional," *LN* (CR), 16 December 1993, 10A, and "Condenan a cuatro por narcotráfico," *LN* (CR), 16 December 1993, 10A.

227. "Confirmado juicio por carga de coca en lancha," *LN* (CR), 7 January 1990, 10A; "Sin rastros de traficante colombiano," *LN* (CR), 23 October 1989, 10A. See also "Cocaína vale," 10A.

228. "Anulan sentencia por narcotráfico," *LN* (CR), 7 January 1995, 16A.

229. For information on this case, see "Decomisan camión por caso de embarque de coca," *LN* (CR), 23 April 1989, 12A; "Decomisan mapas de ruta para introducir cocaína," *LN* (CR), 1 May 1989, 10A; "Court Bans Bail on All Drug Cases," *TT* (CR), 5 May 1989, 9; "Excarcelan a

Rican antidrug officials turned up maps in one trafficker's apartment showing cocaine being flown from Medellín to San Andrés, then taken by speedboat to the mouth of the Río Matina, fifteen miles north of Limón, and finally on to the little town of Zent before being stored in Limón. Investigators believed that a worker at a Costa Rican company, Exportadora de Alimentos Atlanticos, assisted in hiding the cocaine in the shipment of plantains and chayotes. At great length, owners Carlos Maria Durán Durán and his brother Luis Javier were convicted of international drug trafficking and sentenced to twelve and ten years in prison.

During the 1980s authorities uncovered at least eight other cocaine-trafficking schemes through Limón.[230] One network using the Limón-Miami route was thought to have shipped 1,000 kilos in frozen vegetables before police intercepted a 500-kilo load in 1987.[231] Then, in 1989 authorities seized 67.5 kilos from a group as it sent 300 kilos to the United States. An alert customs official at the San José airport found it suspicious that an export company would ship an ordinary product like hammocks in quite carefully constructed crates. Close inspection showed cocaine hidden in the double walls. Investigations revealed that traffickers had sent the drugs from the Colombian mainland to San Andrés and on to Limón, using water drops from small planes to waiting speedboats.[232]

As the San Andrés–Limón route became publicized, local authorities came under pressure to scrutinize the port's shipping, both boats hailing from San Andrés and vessels leaving the port.[233] In 1992 police caught a team of divers that had been carrying drugs underwater to a ship called the *Edith L*, unfastening suction grates and inserting the drugs into the hull. Sixty kilos of cocaine were seized, and the seven conspirators arrested included the alleged Colombian ringleader, Oscar Cano Elorza, and three members of Limón's port authority.[234]

As a result of such counternarcotics triumphs, certain networks started to vary their tactics. Some avoided San Andrés by directing drug vessels to sail from Colombian or Panamanian ports up the coast to Limón.[235] Others continued to export cocaine from Limón but stopped importing directly into the port.[236] Instead,

imputado con tráfico do drogas," *LN* (CR), 7 May 1990, 10A; "OIJ identifica a foráneos ligados con red de cocaína," *LN* (CR), 12 May 1989, 10A; and "Two Sentenced in Drug Case," *TT* (CR), 10 January 1992, 26.

230. For a 1983 five-hundred-kilo seizure of cocaine hidden in plantains shipped from Limón to Miami, see "Two Drug Busts, New Charges Shake Country," *TT* (CR), 21 April 1989, 10. For five other examples of cocaine transshipped from San Andrés to Limón in 1988 and 1989, see "Narcotráfico converge en Limón," 8A.

231. See "Cocaína sería enviada en furgones a Miami," *LN* (CR), 4 July 1987, 1, and "Two Drug Busts," 10.

232. For information on this case, see "Veinte kilos de cocaína," *LN* (CR), 14 July 1989, 10A; "Coca decomisada vale c. 55 millones," *LN* (CR), 15 July 1989, 10A; "Empresa exportadora de pescado y hamacas," *LN* (CR), 15 July 1989, 10A; "Planeaban enviar trescientos kilos de coca," *LN* (CR), 18 July 1989, 10A; and "Narcóticos detuvo a delegado de la GAR," *LN* (CR), 21 July 1989, 10A. The ring had already sent at least two shipments of sixty to seventy kilos. "Narcos enviaron dos cargamentos," *LN* (CR), 19 July 1989, 10A.

233. Yet another seizure, this one of twelve kilos of cocaine, occurred in 1989 off a San Andrés boat. "Otro decomiso de coca en Limón," *LN* (CR), 17 September 1989, 10A. The following July authorities seized another forty-seven kilos off the *Curridibat* ship in Limón. "Pesquisas sobre tres tráficos de cocaína," *LN* (CR), 8 July 1990, 11A.

234. See "Sospechan que dos barcos fueron cargados con coca," *LN* (CR), 13 August 1992, 10A, and "En firme causa contra buzos por narcotráfico," *LN* (CR), 29 October 1992, 12A.

235. In 1993 Costa Rican authorities discovered 248 kilos of cocaine bound for the U.S., hidden in a container of bicycles loaded at Las Minas Bay, Panama, just east of Colón. "Coca en furgón iba," 10A. In 1996 officials seized 138 kilos from a group smuggling the drugs by speedboat from Colombia, up the Caribbean coast to the Río Bananito just south of Limón. "138 kilos de cocaína decomisadas en Limón," *LN* (CR), 7 December 1996, 10A. For a similar route, see "29 kilos de cocaína," *LN* (CR), 22 October 1991, 10A.

236. In 1985, when a Colombian plane crashed at the old banana settlement at Bataan, near Limón, the pilots fled before authorities could respond, though leaving behind seventy-five kilos of coca paste. Although this led to suspicions of a clandestine refining lab, none was found. See "Decomisan cocaína por un valor de c. 5.000 millones," *LN* (CR), 7 June 1985, 1, and "Sospechan que cocaína incautada iba a ser procesada in el país," *LN* (CR), 8 June 1985, 1..

small Colombian planes would deliver loads somewhere in the vicinity. In 1989, for instance, undercover DEA and OIJ agents infiltrated a Barranquilla drug ring operating in just this manner for at least ten months.[237] They then convinced the traffickers that, to ensure uninterrupted transit, Limón officials ought to be bribed. Upon the drug plane's arrival, police seized the pilots, 569 kilos of cocaine, and a $1.5 million payoff. In 1992, however, inhabitants of the Tayní indigenous reserve located in an inland valley just fifteen miles southwest of Limón complained that the drug trade was so extensive that traffickers routinely failed to respect their rights.[238]

To interdict drugs officials can lie in wait along favored routes or at a particular site after being tipped or otherwise gaining inside information. Altering routes can stymie authorities, who end up expecting a shipment in the wrong place. This point is illustrated by the creativity and flexibility that transnational criminal enterprises showed in designing geotactics to ensure the continued success of trafficking around Limón. For instance, rather than being shipped or flown from San Andrés, cocaine came to be trucked into Puerto Limón from the south. The drugs were delivered by air or sea into northern Panama near Bocas del Toro and then transported to Limón via the Sixaola border post and the coastal highway.[239] One group brought 393 kilos of cocaine hidden in trucks through Sixaola, planning to reverse the normal course: that is, to ship the drugs out to San Andrés and transfer them to a speedboat for the next leg to Guatemala.[240] Other trafficking schemes took advantage of Costa Rica's dual coasts and narrow width. Traffickers shipped Colombian cocaine up the Pacific coast into northern Panama, imported it through the Paso Canoas customs post into Costa Rica, and then sent the drugs across to the Caribbean for shipment out of Limón.[241]

Still other cocaine-trafficking schemes opted for more circuitous sea routes, such as from San Andrés south into Panama and then north to Costa Rica.[242] Small boats carrying cocaine from Nicaragua have also traveled south to Limón, with the drugs then packed into containers to be shipped to the United States.[243] The Cali cartel arranged for boats from San Andrés to travel to the Corn Islands or Bluefields, which, along with Puerto Cabezas farther to the north, ranked as Nicaragua's key Caribbean ports.[244] Coastal vessels would then bring the drugs to Limón before they were sent to market.[245]

The Moín port is the terminus for the Tortuguero Canal, which, along with about a hundred miles of flanking canals, rivers, and estuaries, extends practically to the Nicaraguan border. As the chief transportation route into Costa Rica's wild, swampy, often rainy, and largely

237. See "Captura 'record' de coca," *LN* (CR), 2 November 1989, 1, 10A, and "Five Hundred Kilos of Cocaine Nabbed in Quepos Bust," *TT* (CR), 23 March 1990, 30. The pilots eventually received twelve-year sentences. "Doce años de cárcel a colombianos," *LN* (CR), 15 June 1990, 10A.

238. "Narcos son nuevos conquistadores," *LN* (CR), 18 October 1992, 6A.

239. "Introducen droga a Costa Rica por Panamá," *LP* (PA), 18 March 1996, 7A. A network allegedly headed by Plinio Trujillo, nephew of former dictator Rafael Trujillo, used Panama and Limón to send cocaine to the Dominican Republic. For additional information, see chapter 6 of this volume.

240. "Abren causa criminal contra dos panameños en Costa Rica," *LP* (PA), 2 February 1997, 2A.

241. See, for instance, "Fuerte golpe a narcotráfico," *LN* (CR), 26 November 1996, 8A, and "Procesados por tráfico de cocaína," *LN* (CR), 10 December 1996, 10A.

242. For an example of cocaine traveling from San Andrés south to Panama and then into Costa Rica overland, see "Tráfico de cocaína," *LN* (CR), 2 July 1985, 10A.

243. "Cartel de Cali," 10A.

244. See *INCSR* (1995), 126; "Un estigma llamado Limón," 8A, and "Nicaragua, C.R. Agree on Drug Control," *TT* (CR), 22 September 1989, 5. For the San Andrés-to-Bluefields-to-Limón route, see "Decomisan trece kilos de cocaína," *LN* (CR), 12 September 1989, 10A. For Corn Island trafficking, see "Police Say Islanders Have a Ton of Cocaine," *TT* (CR), 19 December 2003, 8; "Decomisan cocaína," *LN* (CR), 12 March 1991, 10A; and "Militares centroamericanos involucrados en narcotráfico," *La Hora* (Guatemala), 24 October 1990, 13.

245. See "Cocaína acosa Puerto Limón," 1.

uninhabited northern Caribbean zone, the canal and related waterways were used in the 1980s by contra suppliers headed toward Barra del Colorado. This small coastal settlement, in turn, is connected to the Río San Juan, which runs from Lake Nicaragua to the Caribbean, winding past dense tropical forests through which numerous tributaries run. During much of the Nicaraguan civil war the contras controlled the river, which forms a sizable portion of the boundary. Afterward the San Juan continued to be used for arms smuggling from San Carlos, Nicaragua, to the Caribbean, with the weapons then moving on to Colombia.[246] Drug traffickers found that cocaine could pass down these inland waterways as well, moving in dugout canoes and other small vessels.[247]

The police presence in this far northern corner of Costa Rica has been erratic and sometimes virtually nonexistent. In 2007 the task of patrolling the 156 square miles of the Barra del Colorado National Wildlife Refuge fell to two park rangers.[248] And the long-running dispute over whether or not Costa Rican authorities had the right to send armed river patrols along the San Juan, which police sources have noted is one means for exporting drugs, decreased already paltry vigilance.[249] For these reasons only very occasionally have authorities scored counternarcotics successes, and these have more often been attributable to luck or trafficking mishaps than to planned interdiction strategies.

For instance, in 2005 a speedboat carrying Colombian cocaine developed engine problems and came ashore in Laguna de Samay, just south of the refuge. Police happened upon the abandoned boat within the lagoon and were tipped by locals to 2.5 tons of cocaine buried in boxes in the sand. Eventually, eight suspects were arrested, including an American, a Nicaraguan, two Costa Ricans, and four Colombians, each later convicted of trafficking.[250] (Here we see how globalized drug-trafficking networks have become, encompassing Colombians or Mexicans, associates from multiple Central American states, and occasionally Americans or Europeans.)[251] In late 2009, 197 kilos of cocaine were found floating in this same area, and shortly thereafter police discovered 21 kilos in the weeds of Samay after a passing patrol caught sight of footprints in the sand and followed them to a cache of drugs.[252]

By the twenty-first century, inhabitants of the upper Caribbean coast had found profits in the drug trade. In 2002 and 2003 investigative reporters discovered that fishermen in this area had taken subsidized gasoline from the Costa Rican Institute of Fisheries and Aquaculture and sold it to cocaine traffickers, a scam that was repeated in Limón in 2008 with representatives of the port authority and the independent fishermen's association allegedly involved. The scale of the fraud was remarkable: in 2008 Limón was responsible for a mere 3 percent of the twenty thousand tons of seafood caught annually in Costa Rica but was absorbing almost 6 percent of the subsidized gasoline meant to be directed to the fishing fleet. That same year, authorities discovered that in the Barra del Colorado vicinity, cocaine packages were being

246. See "San Juan River Used for Gun Running," *TT* (CR), 21 December 2001, 5; Cragin and Hoffman, *Arms Trafficking*, 23; and Honey, *Hostile Acts*, 206.

247. See DEA, *Resources, Costa Rica* (2003), 4.

248. See "Vast Caribbean Refuge at Risk," *TT* (CR), 23 November 2007, 1.

249. Because the Río San Juan is sovereign Nicaraguan territory, available for Costa Rican use by treaty, Nicaragua objected strenuously to armed Costa Rican patrols, a legal position the World Court upheld in 2009. Navigational and Related Rights (*Costa Rica v. Nicaragua*), 48 I.L.M. 1183. See also "Court Rules on River Rights," *TT* (CR), 17 July 2009, 1, and "San Juan River Dispute Leads to ICJ," *TT* (CR), 13 March 2009, 2. For drugs and the San Juan, see "Policía detiene a presunto contacto del cartel de Sinaloa," *LN* (CR), 15 January 2010, 16A.

250. "2.5 Tons of Cocaine," 4.

251. For another representative case of this phenomenon, with the arrest of Guatemalans, Costa Ricans, and the Mexican leader linked to at least 430 kilos of cocaine, see "Banda trasegaba cocaína en cargamentos de aguacates," *LN* (CR), 7 June 2008, 12A.

252. "Policía halla veintiún kilos de cocaína ocultos en Maleza," *LN* (CR), 24 December 2009, 17A.

transferred to speedboats en route to Guatemala and other points north. Moreover, drugs were washing up so frequently after traffickers botched water drops or jettisoned cargoes offshore when pursued by U.S. or Costa Rican authorities that fishermen in Barra and other villages could snare cocaine packets in gill nets and resell them.[253]

Even after Limón's role in the Caribbean drug trade had become well publicized, Costa Rica's Caribbean coast remained key to transshipment. When scrutiny of cargoes and port officials was high, drug networks opted for more creative methods and circuitous routes. When it was at a low ebb, more simple and direct approaches were utilized.[254] The frequent success of Limón drug transit is suggested by the fact that when leading Russian criminal organizations began to work with Colombian cartels to transship cocaine into Europe and also, occasionally, into the United States, they opted for this same route.[255] In 1993 a joint DEA-OIJ operation broke up a major smuggling ring, financed by Russian organized crime, that was exporting cocaine to Florida.[256] In this scheme the drugs arrived in Puerto Limón by speedboat from San Andrés, and rental cars brought the cocaine to San José to be flown to the United States. After seizing 91 kilos, OIJ director Rafael Ángel Guillén stated that this group had accounted for a significant slice of the Costa Rican cocaine trade at that time, and one of the Russians, Igor Abkumov, was found to possess a U.S. bank account containing $82 million. Another, Stefan Martirosian, eventually pled guilty, in a separate case brought by U.S. federal prosecutors, to charges of possessing cocaine with intent to distribute.

Russian participation demonstrates that by the early 1990s the Costa Rican cocaine trade had come to reflect the increasingly globalized nature of transnational crime. In the 1980s cocaine trafficking was transnational in that it involved criminal activities in South American supply countries, Central American bridge states, and North American markets. By the following decade the tentacles of organized crime reached not merely into western European consumer markets, but to Russia and prominent Russian criminal figures. The considerable advantages associated with moving drugs through Costa Rica, well known to Colombian cartels and of increasing interest to their Mexican counterparts, had come to attract criminal organizations headquartered far from the region. In fact, cocaine shipments utilizing Puerto Limón headed toward diverse parts of Europe. In early 1999 Swedish authorities discovered 243 kilos of cocaine, the country's largest seizure ever, in bananas shipped from Limón. In 2005 police found one Limón-based network to be hiding cocaine in boxes of pineapples and heart-of-palm tins and a different group to be burying cocaine in the soil of potted ornamental plants, all of these goods being shipped into Rotterdam.[257]

The magnitude of the Limón export trade limited customs inspections to a very small percentage of departing shipping containers. Occasional weighty seizures, although helping

253. "Banda aprovechó combustible subsidiado para traficar drogas," *LN* (CR), 27 August 2008, 4A; "Exoneración a pescadores cuesta ¢6.000 millones al año," *LN* (CR), 27 August 2008, 5A; and "Drugs Ousting Fishing in North Caribbean," *TT* (CR), 18 January 2002, 14.

254. For significant cocaine seizures in which the drugs entered Costa Rica from San Andrés, see "Descubierta empacadora," 10A; "Banda trasegó 550 kilos de cocaína," *LN* (CR), 19 July 1994, 10A; and "Decomisan 389 kilos de cocaína en bodega," *LN* (CR), 28 December 1996, 11A.

255. Cali traffickers established ties with Russian criminals as early as 1992, when authorities spotted a cartel member in Russia, and in 1993 a ton of Colombian cocaine was seized in St. Petersburg. Jordan, *Drug Politics*, 83–84. For more on Russian criminal activity in the region, see Bagley, "Globalisation," esp. 34–46, and Bagley, "Russian Mafia."

256. For more information, see "Desarticulada banda internacional," 12A, and *United States v. Martirosian*, 967 F.2d 1036. The term *Russian mafia* might mislead because "there is no capo di capi or ruling council, and often groups are independent organizations that may have as few as two members." Chepesiuk, *Hard Target*, 180.

257. "Tico Cargo Seized, Sweden's Biggest Coke Bust," *TT* (CR), 26 February 1999, 4; "Drugs Hidden in Exports to Europe," *TT* (CR), 30 June 2006, 1, 5.

the government appear to be vigilant to the public, have not sufficed to deter the multiple networks operating in this area, and considerable cocaine, undetected by authorities, has continued to transit this key maritime corridor. Moreover, in 2004 authorities discovered a Limón-headquartered smuggling ring that had been shipping heroin into New York, Florida, Ohio, Texas, and Delaware.[258] Clearly, for the better part of three decades, Puerto Limón has been one of the preeminent centers of drug trafficking not only in Costa Rica but in all of Central America.

The Pacific Coast

During the very years that Central America first witnessed extensive cocaine trafficking, Costa Rica completed a shift from an economy dominated by coffee and other traditional agricultural products to one marked by more specialized, diversified, and profitable undertakings in agriculture, service industries, and light manufacturing. While this development affected much of the country, the Valle Central, with its cities and fertile agricultural land, was the engine driving the changes. By contrast, many isolated pockets along Costa Rica's Pacific coast were largely left behind. Pollution, overfishing, and other problems caused the seafood industry to suffer downturns, and the banana production of prior decades tumbled. These traditional sources of income have been replaced, in part, by tourism associated with the beach communities. However, these developments have brought on economic dislocation, including unemployment and underemployment, in the midst of rapidly rising expectations.

These circumstances have affected the international drug trade in various ways. The boom in tourism has brought an increasing demand for drugs to sell to locals and visitors. And Costa Ricans along the Pacific coast have been recruited to assist in various transshipment operations and then compensated with drugs. Costa Ricans have helped traffickers to take over small landing strips on particular nights for refueling and other transshipment activities, and they have employed commercial fishing vessels and their crews to provide fuel for passing speedboats and other vessels.[259] Local associates have built hidden compartments and temporarily stored drugs awaiting export. They have assisted in transferring narcotics to shore after water drops or after off-loading from mother ships.

Foreign traffickers have often cropped up along the Pacific coast as well, overseeing ventures along particular routes, organizing, supervising, and paying off local conspirators, engaging in money-laundering activities, or hiding out from authorities.[260] For example, Colombian Silvio Montaño Vergara first entered Costa Rica in 2002, eventually presenting himself as the owner of a company manufacturing cell phones. While in his forties, he married an eighteen-year-old Costa Rican woman, thereby gaining citizenship, but he traveled constantly. Investigating authorities counted forty trips to Colombia, Panama, and Honduras and came to allege that he was, in fact, a key Costa Rican contact for Colombian and Mexican traffickers, overseeing cocaine transit by arranging associates, vehicles, and properties. Montaño reportedly worked in Limón for a period, coordinating drug shipments there, and then took over Pacific coast operations, supervising cocaine shipments from Colombia's

258. "Suspected Members of Heroin Ring Busted," *TT* (CR), 30 April 2004, 3.

259. For the arrest of the Costa Rican and Colombian crew of a fishing vessel carrying 2,313 kilos of cocaine, see *United States v. Moreno-Gomez*, 291 Fed. Appx. 938. Traffickers employed many small landing strips in Pacific beach communities, such as the town of Esterillos Este. See "Mysterious Flights Ignored," *TT* (CR), 7 May 1999, 4.

260. "Narcos pagan servicios con drogas en vez de dinero," *LN* (CR), 1 January 2009, 12A. Occasionally, Costa Rican authorities managed to arrest and extradite or expel foreign traffickers. See, for instance, "Gringo Cocaine Suspect Heading Back to U.S.," *TT* (CR), 2 May 2008, 5.

Chocó Department and Buenaventura port into Panama, Costa Rica, and Honduras. Just before Montaño's arrest in Cali in early 2010, investigations linked him to a late 2009 seizure of 2.6 tons of cocaine at the mouth of the Río Jesús María near Tiveves, just south of Puntarenas.[261]

The formidable difficulties of containing international drug trafficking along the Pacific coast are underscored by the fact that Costa Rica's offshore waters, including its exclusive economic zone, total 640,000 square kilometers, or more than ten times its land mass.[262] Although many of the country's most important seizures have occurred off its Pacific coast, authorities have concluded that far more drugs passed by undetected than have been interdicted.[263] Illustrative of this, in 2007, a year in which Costa Rica intercepted a record 27 tons of cocaine, Mexican authorities seized a single 22-ton shipment that had passed just north of Coco. The passage of drugs along the Pacific coast, however, was by no means confined to activities far offshore. Analysis of numerous trafficking schemes over three decades shows the diverse ways in which the Pacific coast was involved in the international cocaine trade.[264]

Nicoya Peninsula

The narrow, mountainous Nicoya Peninsula, forming much of Costa Rica's northern Pacific shore, has long attracted smugglers. The Santa Rosa National Park in the northern part of Nicoya lay on one popular overland smuggling route toward Nicaragua.[265] Numerous aerial cocaine loads have touched down on Nicoya airstrips, and rising numbers of maritime shipments have passed offshore, occasionally utilizing its beaches, bays, and harbors.[266]

While the runway at the Tamarindo beach community gained notoriety for its repeated use by different networks, drug rings have actually transshipped cocaine all along the peninsula, and arrests of American and Colombian traffickers have periodically occurred.[267] For example, in 1986 authorities seized 249 kilos of cocaine and two Colombian pilots who had flown a load from Cochabamba, Bolivia, into tiny Puerto Carrillo, near Sámara toward the southern end.[268] The following year an aircraft in distress, which eventually crashed near Playa Hermosa, abandoned as many as 500 kilos of cocaine into the sea.[269] In 1991 a Cali plane dropped 275 kilos into the waters of Gigante Bay. This time, undercover agents

261. "Cae in Colombia líder narco que obtuvo nacionalidad tica," *LN* (CR), 9 January 2010, 10A, and "Registro Civil pide anular cédula tica de líder narco," *LN* (CR), 12 January 2010, 17A.

262. "Country's Fisheries Dangle," 8.

263. By the twenty-first century the most widely accepted estimate was that Costa Rican authorities seized about 10 percent of the drugs passing through the country. See "Fear of More Drugs," 1. Naturally, the percentage seized was much higher in the airport confines than the vast Pacific reaches.

264. *INCSR* (2008), 162; "Barco Tico transportaba 4,5 toneladas de cocaína," *LN* (CR), 3 December 2007, 16A; "Fishing Boat Drug Bust Is the Year's Biggest," *TT* (CR), 7 December 2007, 6.

265. "Decomisan 101 kilos de cocaína," *LN* (CR), 22 September 1993, 10A.

266. See "C.R. Beaches Used by Foreign Drug Traffickers," *TT* (CR), 24 August 1990, 3.

267. Drug traffickers George Morales, Gerardo Durán Ayanegui, and José Ángel Guerra Laspuir were all linked to shipments through this airstrip. See Comisión Especial, *Segundo Informe*, 74–75. See also "Policía busca a piloto ligado con narcotráfico," *LN* (CR), 11 March 1987, 10A, and *La Prensa Libre* (Costa Rica), 11 March 1987, 8, quoted in "OIJ Reports Airports Used for Drug Trafficking," Foreign Broadcast Information Service (US), 24 March 1987, 2. Playa del Coco contained a rest house for the Carlton network's pilots and factored into the Dick Francis Jennings network. See "Traficantes compran protección," 10A, "Norteamericano preso almacenó cocaína aquí," *LN* (CR), 17 August 1990, 10A, and "C.R. Beaches Used," 3. For the arrest at Tamarindo of Stephen Lloyd Harman, a fugitive wanted in California on charges of trafficking 2.5 tons of marijuana, see "Capturan a estadounidense en playa de Tamarindo," *LN* (CR), 1 February 1996, 10A.

268. See "Policía tras nexos de los traficantes," *LN* (CR), 5 July 1986, 1, and "Policía conocía sobre aterrizajes en Nicoya," *LN* (CR), 7 July 1986, 1. The network had used this route on other occasions as well.

269. See "Presos admiten que llevaban cocaína," *LN* (CR), 20 November 1986, 1, and "Iniciada causa contra extranjeros por drogas," *LN* (CR), 27 November 1986, 10A.

had pierced the smuggling ring in a joint OIJ-DEA operation. Authorities confiscated the cocaine, and four Colombians were arrested and eventually convicted in Texas.[270] In the mid-1990s an investigation revealed that Playa del Coco, which had served in the 1980s as a base for an American trafficker, had joined the neighboring strip at Sardinal as a notable transshipment location.[271]

A number of these operations involved truly immense quantities of drugs. In 1990 a plane dropped a load of approximately 800 kilos of cocaine somewhere off Cabo Blanco at the southwest tip of Nicoya. Fishermen apparently scared off the contact and collected more than 100 kilos themselves.[272] The following year authorities broke up a Panamanian ring that had started to import enough cocaine through the Sámara and Puerto Carrillo airstrips to forward 300–400 kilos per week to Miami.[273] In 1992 traffickers botched a water drop, and 1.5 tons of cocaine vanished in the ocean near Playa Cuajiniquil.[274] As speedboat transport increased, additional substantial cocaine loads disappeared at sea. In June and July 2007 alone, two speedboat mishaps led to the loss of 3 tons of cocaine.[275] The sheer size of these shipments and the fact that so many of the most important losses occurred through the mistakes and accidents of traffickers, rather than the policies or vigilance of authorities, underscores the difficulties of countering the extensive cocaine trade along the northern Costa Rican coastline.

Puntarenas

Puntarenas, with nearby Puerto Caldera, has long served as Costa Rica's leading Pacific port and seafood center, with its fishing fleet bringing ashore 80 percent of the country's catch.[276] Puntarenas gained notoriety in the drug trade quite early. Frigoríficos de Puntarenas, a company purportedly in business to freeze and export seafood, actually served as a front for leading traffickers, with money launderer Ramón Milian Rodríguez using it to cleanse Medellín drug profits.[277] Carlos Soto and Ubaldo Fernández, both eventually convicted of trafficking, were the company's original owner-operators, along with Luis Rodríguez, who had once directed the largest marijuana-smuggling ring in Massachusetts history. Frigoríficos came to public prominence as a key cog in the southern front resupply effort, receiving $261,937 in humanitarian assistance from the U.S. State Department in 1986, funds later transferred to the contras. Authorities later learned that Frigoríficos was also exporting cocaine within seafood shipments, while Ocean Hunter, its sister shell company

270. See "Culpan en Texas a narcos detenidos por OIJ y DEA," *LN* (CR), 26 October 1992, 10A, and "Fuerte condena a red de narcotraficantes," *LN* (CR), 17 September 1994, 16A. The Costa Ricans received eleven to eighteen years in prison.

271. See "Embestida infernal," 4A.

272. See "130 kilos de coca pagados con $30 mil falsos," *LN* (CR), 22 November 1990, 10A; "Pescadores presos con cocaína,'" *LN* (CR), 23 November 1990, 10A; "Testigos respaldan a pescadores," *LN* (CR), 27 June 1991, 10A; and "Condenan a pescadores," *LN* (CR), 28 June 1991, 10A.

273. See "Investigan negocios de supuestos narcos," *LN* (CR), 29 June 1991, 10A, and "Más detenidos por red de presuntos narcos," *LN* (CR), 30 June 1991, 10A.

274. See "Cae pescador con catorce kilos de cocaína," *LN* (CR), 25 August 1992, 10A. For this and other water drops gone astray, see "Sospechan que avioneta lanzó cocaína en Quepos," *LN* (CR), 14 May 1993, 10A.

275. See "Narcos lanzaron desde lancha rápida cargamento de dos toneladas de cocaína," *LN* (CR), 27 August 2007, 14A; "Mar se deja más de una tonelada de cocaína," *LN* (CR), 28 August 2007, 18A; and "Drug Bust at Sea Washes Up Cocaine," *TT* (CR), 7 September 2007, 3.

276. "Country's Fisheries Dangle," 8.

277. Documents seized when federal agents arrested Milian showed he had transported $146 million from the United States to Panama between August 1982 and April 1983 alone. The U.S. Eleventh Circuit Court of Appeals noted that in "seeking to become a government informant, appellant proceeded to admit his deep involvement in an international narcotics and money laundering network, describing himself as the biggest money launderer in the country and characterizing his clientele as the 'who's who' of the South Florida drug underworld." *United States v. Milian-Rodriguez*, 828 F.2d at 680–81.

in Miami, was, according to the U.S. Senate, using "the intercompany transfers to launder drug money."[278]

From the mid-1990s into the new century, Puntarenas regained importance in the Costa Rican drug trade. As difficult, dangerous, and subject to ups and downs as a fishing career can be, it is not surprising that certain Costa Rican fishermen turned to moonlighting in the drug trade.[279] Some provided fuel and provisions to drug boats; others served as lookouts for authorities; still others actually carried drugs along the Central American coast.[280] In 2006 a high-ranking operative for the Fuerzas Armadas Revolucionarias de Colombia (FARC), Héctor Martínez Quinto, was arrested in Puntarenas and extradited to Colombia. During his time in Costa Rica, after arranging a marriage with a prostitute to gain Costa Rican resident status, he settled in the Puntarenas area, allegedly contracting with fishermen to transport drugs and trying to arrange for fishing vessels to be used in arms-for-drugs transfers.[281]

Puntarenas thus became involved in some substantial maritime drug-trafficking schemes, a number of which authorities uncovered. In 2003, in the largest seizure to date in the region, the DEA and Costa Rican Drug Control Police seized 3.5 tons of cocaine from a Costa Rican ship, the *Cocopepes VI*, in international waters off the Guatemalan coast.[282] In 2006 on four occasions Panama seized Costa Rican fishing vessels, all from Puntarenas, working in a chain of boats moving drugs north. In one of these cases the Panamanian Coast Guard, with assistance from the Colombian Navy, captured the Costa Rican vessel *Navegante I*, off Panama's Azuero Peninsula, carrying 621 kilos of cocaine and 34 kilos of heroin.[283] Even that confiscation was overshadowed by the seizure of the *Indio IV*, a Puntarenas fishing vessel captured off Playa Flamingo with 2 tons of cocaine.[284]

This type of maritime smuggling often brought Colombian and Mexican cartels together to undertake joint ventures capitalizing on the strengths of both. By the early twenty-first century, substantial cocaine shipments were regularly traveling north from Colombia toward Guatemala and Mexico, and Costa Rican fishing vessels and motorboats, usually hailing from Puntarenas, were involved. In 2007, for instance, the U.S. Coast Guard patrolling off the Guatemalan coast intercepted 800 kilos of cocaine on the *Veracruz II*, a fishing vessel with a crew of a Colombian and three Costa Ricans.[285] That same year, U.S. and Costa Rican coast guard officials seized a total of 4.5 tons of cocaine from the Costa Rican vessel *Yorleni II* and the Mexican boat *Judel IV*, 250 nautical miles off northern Guanacaste.[286] In a relay operation

278. For information on Frigoríficos, see U.S. Senate, *Law Enforcement: Report*, 45–46, 153, and Honey, *Hostile Acts*, 368. For allegations that Noriega helped establish Frigoríficos to market Cuban shrimp in the United States, see Koster and Sánchez, *In the Time*, 294. After interviewing Milian in prison, one journalist reported, "Drug money passed from other cartel companies was deposited into Frigoríficos accounts; then the so-called business transactions between it and Ocean Hunter were used to hide these profits. Eventually the funds moved to cartel companies on Caribbean island tax shelters. Some of this money was also passed to the contras as well as to Costa Rican politicians." Honey, *Hostile Acts*, 368.

279. See DEA, *Resources, Costa Rica* (2003), 4, and *INCSR* (2004), 8.

280. See, for instance, "Detienen a lancha con pinchingas de gasolina," *LN* (CR), 11 June 2008, 13A. For fifteen assaults on fishermen by Puntarenas criminals thought to be stealing gasoline and outboard motors with which to supply traffickers, see "Usan motores para abastecer a los narcos," *LN* (CR), 15 June 2008, 5A, and "Piratas del Pacífico aterrorizan a pescadores puntareneneses," *LN* (CR), 15 June 2008, 4A.

281. "Cae en Colombia líder narco," 10A. In 2008 Martínez was convicted in Colombia and sentenced to thirty-six and a half years for the 2002 Bojaya massacre in which FARC forces killed seventy-eight and wounded fifty-three.

282. "Autoridades confiscan cargamento de cocaína," *LP* (PA), 10 October 2006, 34A.

283. "Ticos se niegan a declarar," *LP* (PA), 8 October 2006, 5A.

284. "Amplían prisión por caso narco," *LN* (CR), 14 December 2007, 17A.

285. "EE.UU. entrega a pescadores detenidos con alijo de cocaína," *LN* (CR), 20 December 2007, 18A.

286. See "Barco Tico," 16A, and "Lancha Tica llevaba más de 1.6 toneladas de coca," *LN* (CR), 1 December 2007, 12A.

Colombian speedboats from Buenaventura had passed the drugs to the Puntarenas vessel and its crew of six Costa Ricans and a Nicaraguan, who, in turn, were to deliver the cocaine to the Mexicans off southern Nicaragua. In two 2008 incidents authorities seized 2,600 kilos of cocaine apiece from identical Colombian go-fasts operating sufficiently near Puntarenas to suggest a Costa Rican role in refueling.[287] Thus, Costa Rica was clearly playing a key logistical role in immense Pacific cocaine-trafficking endeavors.

Quepos

South of Puntarenas, a critically important aerial cocaine-smuggling route for a time ran through Quepos, a central Pacific Coast town originally built as a United Fruit banana port, but whose activities largely shifted to providing services for tourists visiting Manuel Antonio National Park.[288] In 1986 a DEA-OIJ operation intercepted 204 kilos of cocaine, wrapped in waterproof bags for delivery to Florida, that a small plane had deposited at La Managua airstrip in Quepos. The network, led by Cuban American Bienvenido Pita Gómez, planned to send 1,000 kilos to the United States and had arranged to transship the drugs through three Costa Rican runways.[289] The following year authorities surprised another cocaine plane at La Managua, seizing 500 kilos linked to Cali traffickers. Costa Rican ringleader Fernando Castro Zamora, a former Ministry of the Interior employee, had plotted an intercoastal scheme, planning to move the drugs across the country for export from Puerto Limón, hidden among perishable goods subject to expedited customs inspection. The OIJ reported that when the bust occurred, Castro Zamora's organization had already exported a ton through a Limón front company.[290]

Then in 1989 undercover DEA agents persuaded Juan Merino Noriega, a Medellín operative in San Francisco, that they could assist in transshipping large quantities of cocaine via Costa Rica's Pacific coast. The following year one of the agents, posing as a drug pilot, brought 450 kilos of cocaine from Peru into La Managua. In a controlled delivery the DEA and U.S. military planes then forwarded the load to Moffett Field Naval Air Station near San José, California, where a moving van carried the drugs to Merino Noriega's residence in San Francisco's Marina district. Rather than immediately seizing the cocaine, however, the agents persuaded the Colombian to request a second shipment, while the OIJ tapped the phones of suspected conspirators in Costa Rica. Thirteen days later, pilot Jannette Hernández Ávila flew another cocaine plane to La Managua, this one loaded with 550 kilos. Although Hernández expected to receive a $4 million payment from Colombian contact Farid Humberto Tawil Gómez, the OIJ already had him in custody. When the plane landed, waiting drug police arrested Hernández and her copilot and confiscated the plane and cocaine. After the DEA captured Merino Noriega and four close

287. "Police Seize 2,600 Kilos of Cocaine in Puntarenas," *TT* (CR), 5 December 2008, 4.

288. In 1987 witnesses reported suspicious planes dropping packages near Quepos beaches. "Alarma en Quepos por decomiso," *LN* (CR), 4 July 1987, 9A. In 1990 Costa Rican police reported that for some time traffickers had been using the La Managua strip. "Cae gran carga de coca," *LN* (CR), 17 March 1990, 8A. For continued trafficking and a sixty-nine-kilo cocaine seizure south of Quepos, see "Caen traficantes," *LN* (CR), 21 July 2000, 10A.

289. See "Decomisan cocaína por casi ¢3 mil millones," *LN* (CR), 14 May 1986, 1, and "Huge Cocaine Shipment," *TT* (CR), 16 May 1986, 21.

290. "Cocaína sería enviada en furgones a Miami," *LN* (CR), 4 July 1987, 1; "Detenido por cocaína fue inspector de autoridades," *LN* (CR), 9 July 1987, 10A; "Ex oficial tico era contacto de 'narcos,'" *LN* (CR), 7 December 1989, 10A; "Cocaína pertenece al cartel de Cali," *LN* (CR), 21 April 1990, 10A; "Capturado avión con cocaína en Quepos," *LN* (CR), 3 July 1987, 10A; and "Bust Yields Record Cocaine Haul," 4. Castro Zamora was eventually convicted and sentenced to thirteen years in prison. "Penas por noventa y un años a narcos," *LN* (CR), 14 December 1989, 10A.

associates in San Francisco and Fort Lauderdale, the special agent in charge characterized them as "significant players in the [Medellín] organization . . . looking to expand their market, . . . [into] the San Francisco Bay Area."[291]

While the use of the Quepos airstrip diminished as other trafficking methods came into vogue, by the early twenty-first century, Colombian networks had discovered the utility of the coast south of the city, largely marked by African palm oil plantations, and had started to send through some sizable cocaine shipments.[292] In 2007 authorities received information that cocaine trafficking had been occurring here for some weeks. After uncovering a site near Playa Matapalo used to supply speedboats carrying cocaine to Guatemala, police first engaged in a gunfight with traffickers wielding AK-47 weapons and then found forty-four containers of gasoline. A follow-up investigation soon led to the seizure of 1.5 tons of cocaine, which had been brought from Colombia by speedboats directed by global positioning systems to the tiny town of Ojochal. Three Colombians and three Costa Ricans were arrested.

Golfito and the Osa Peninsula

The features of Costa Rica's Pacific coast that have attracted substantial drug trafficking are especially pronounced in the country's far southern corner. Here, there are even more remote stretches, scattered settlements, and infrequent law-enforcement attention. Inland mountain ranges slope down to fertile lowlands, once largely dedicated to banana production, which themselves give way to a coastline where beaches are interspersed with mangrove swamps and small rivers running toward the Pacific. The coast supports such a wealth of birds and wildlife that the government has dedicated substantial tracts to national parks, with a negligible police presence. This far southern region has been well suited to water drops by passing aircraft and ideal for refueling speedboats. Smuggling organizations have focused especially on the old banana port of Golfito and the waters immediately bordering Panama.[293] Furthermore, the hilly and secluded Osa Peninsula has had little internal transport, relying largely on coastal trade, and law enforcement has been stretched thin.

Among those suspected of bringing the potential of far southern Costa Rica to the attention of leading traffickers was American fugitive financier Robert Vesco.[294] After fleeing the United States in 1972 to avoid a $243 million fraud lawsuit, Vesco allegedly bribed officials for protection in Costa Rica and the Bahamas,

291. "Cae gran carga de coca," *LN* (CR), 17 March 1990, 8A; "Biggest Ever Bay Area Cocaine Bust," *San Francisco Chronicle*, 17 March 1990, A6; "A $100 Million Cocaine Bust with Medellín Cartel Links," United Press International, 17 March 1990; "2,200 Pounds of Cocaine Seized," *CT* (US), 18 March 1990, 14C; "Cayó avión con coca . . . continuen operativo," *LN* (CR), 19 March 1990, 10A; "Five Hundred Kilos of Cocaine Nabbed," 30; "En Quepos cayó red de 'narcos,'" *LN* (CR), 29 March 1990, 10A; and "OIJ amplió informe sobre coca," *LN* (CR), 29 March 1990, 10A.

292. See "Lancha rápida y armas aparecen en Quepos," *LN* (CR), 23 June 2008, 15A; "Policía halla campamento narco en Playa Matapalo," *LN* (CR), 6 August 2007, 14A; "Narcos habitaron campamento en playa durante tres días," *LN* (CR), 7 August 2007, 16A; "Caen tres sujetos con dos toneladas de cocaína," *LN* (CR), 8 August 2007, 14A; and "Equipo satelital controlaba trasiego de droga por mar," *LN* (CR), 9 August 2007, 18A.

293. For the arrest and extradition of Alex Arosemena Saavedra, a fugitive and alleged cocaine trafficker in Playa Zancudo, just south of Golfito, see "Detenido 'narco' buscado por EE.UU.," *LN* (CR), 20 April 1991, 10A; "Hoy extraditarán a Alex Arosemena," *LN* (CR), 16 October 1992, 12A; and "Extraditó Arosemena," *LN* (CR), 17 October 1992, 10A. See also "Woman Rejoices; Husband to Return," *SLPD* (US), 2 April 1992, 3A; "Man in Costa Rican Prison May Be Extradited to U.S.," *SLPD* (US), 16 April 1992, 5A; and "Man Back from Costa Rican Jail, Charged Here," *SLPD* (US), 17 October 1992, 3A.

294. In one taped conversation President Richard Nixon told White House aide John Ehrlichman that Vesco had "bought" Costa Rican President José Figueres "lock, stock, and barrel," apparently by promising to make million-dollar investments. In 1974 Vesco moved into southern Costa Rica, living near Golfito until his presence became a presidential campaign issue in 1978, and he left for the Bahamas and, later, Nicaragua and Cuba. See Eddy, Sabogal, and Walden, *Cocaine Wars*, 137–38, and "Tape: Vesco 'Bought' Figueres," *TT* (CR), 5 March 1999, 1.

where he was later allegedly linked to traffickers in various countries.[295] In Costa Rica, Vesco sold certain Rancho del Mar real estate holdings in Pavón, Golfito, to American Daniel James Fowlie, who moved in along with his sons Danny and Gus.[296] Each of them would eventually be convicted of drug offenses in U.S. courts.[297] Authorities first suspected Fowlie of involvement in the drug trade through the Brotherhood of Eternal Love network, founded by Harvard University psychology instructor Timothy Leary and broken up with the arrest of forty-six individuals in 1972.[298]

In the late 1970s and early 1980s Fowlie purchased 3,700 acres, including fifteen miles of waterfront property, and set about building roads, piers, and bridges and initiating agricultural enterprises in items such as peanuts and cacao. In this way he became the largest landowner and employer in the Pavón area. His Costa Rican attorney Roberto Umaña later recalled, "Once I was with him when he flew his plane over the town and threw his money down on the people below. There's a myth about him now, that he'll return some day in a golden plane throwing money."[299] After what an FBI agent termed "a lengthy historical case showing a large conspiracy to import large amounts of marijuana and cocaine and distribute them," a U.S. Court of Appeals found that from 1981 to 1986, while Fowlie resided in Costa Rica, his organization had delivered at least thirty tons of marijuana, largely obtained from the Sonora cartel, to locations in the United States and Canada.[300] A jury found him guilty of fifteen drug-related offenses, and a U.S. federal court eventually sentenced him to thirty years in prison and a fine of $1 million.[301]

The growth of the drug trade in and around Golfito illustrates not only the important influence of expatriate foreign traffickers but the

295. A Florida grand jury indictment charged that Vesco helped Colombian traffickers to fly cocaine through Cuban air space. Vesco was also accused of having managed financial matters for various drug networks, underwritten cocaine purchases from the Suárez family in Bolivia and heroin from Southeast Asia's Golden Triangle, and set up a cocaine-refining laboratory in Nicaragua with a Sandinista official. Vesco lived on a Bahamas caye next to one owned by kingpin Carlos Lehder, with whom he was friendly. U.S. Customs investigated Vesco for helping the Sandinista regime to finance cocaine shipments to Belgium and the United States. See "U.S. Probes Vesco's Possible Drug Deal with Nicaraguans," *Wall Street Journal*, 15 October 1984, 1. For Vesco's U.S. legal problems, see U.S. Senate, *Law Enforcement: Report*, 15. In 1982 Vesco moved to Cuba, where in 1996 he swindled $974,000 from foreign business executives, and in 2008 he reportedly died. See "Las huellas de Vesco, Fowlie, y Caro," *LN* (CR), 26 July 1990, 8A; "Indictment Cites Vesco," *TT* (CR), 21 April 1989, 11; Eddy, Sabogal, and Walden, *Cocaine Wars*, 145, 149; "Finalizó juicio por estafa Robert Vesco," *LP* (PA), 5 August 1996, 4A; and "Shyster Robert Vesco Dies Ignominiously," *TT* (CR), 9 May 2008, 5.

296. The U.S. government seized Fowlie's 213-acre southern California ranch, valued at $6 million, and President George Bush dedicated it to counternarcotics training. See "Squatters Win Drug Suspect's Land," *TT* (CR), 15 December 1989, 13, and "Accused U.S. Drug Trafficker Reported Comfy," *TT* (CR), 4 May 1990, 32. Witnesses later claimed that, just before his arrest and extradition from Costa Rica, Sonora cartel kingpin Rafael Caro Quintero visited Fowlie's Rancho del Mar property, and a U.S. indictment explicitly linked the two men. See "U.S. Landowners Plead Guilty to Drug Charges," *TT* (CR), 8 September 1989, 14.

297. See "Vesco, Fowlie, y Caro," 8A, and "Una extensa tierra temida por muchos," *LN* (CR), 27 July 1990, 8A. In exchange for the government dropping twenty-four other drug-related counts, Fowlie's sons pled guilty to conspiring to distribute between 6.8 and 9 tons of marijuana. Because their father had taken the profits, his sons received relatively light prison terms of three and a half and two and a half years. "Sons of U.S. Landowner Sentenced on Drug Charges," *TT* (CR), 6 October 1989, 17.

298. See "Jury Convicts Fowlie," *LAT* (US), 20 April 1991, 1A.

299. "Ex-convict Returns to Claim Property," *TT* (CR), 10 June 2005, 1. Fowlie did, in fact, return, but authorities then barred him from further entry after he disputed who owned certain of his former properties, allegedly threatening Costa Ricans.

300. See "Jury Convicts Fowlie," 1A, and "Fugitive Financier Sold Land to Accused Drug Trafficker," *TT* (CR), 25 November 1988, 8. For FBI agent Bucky Cox's quote, see "Landowner's Son Faces Drug Charges in U.S.," *TT* (CR), 24 February 1989, 15. Although the case against Fowlie turned on marijuana-importing charges, Cox linked him to cocaine import and distribution as well.

301. Fowlie's conviction of running a continuing criminal enterprise was later upheld on appeal. *United States v. Fowlie*, 24 F.3d 1059, and *United States v. Fowlie*, 24 F.3d 1070.

way in which the drug trade has penetrated vulnerable communities with deteriorating economies. In the mid-1980s, shortly after United Fruit discontinued its area operations, leaving a depressed local economy attempting an awkward shift from banana to palm oil production, trafficking around Golfito accelerated. First, marijuana cultivation increased. Then, small planes began dropping cocaine in offshore waters. Traffickers would bring the drugs into Golfito and then continue up the Pacific coast to Quepos or Puntarenas by ground or sea. Although authorities rarely intercepted shipments, much less broke up networks, during the early 1990s all the earmarks of considerable transshipment could plainly be seen in Golfito.[302] Drug abuse rose sharply, numerous suspicious vessels entered the port, and suspect air traffic increased in the city's vicinity at odd hours, while shady foreigners bought nearby property.[303] The DEA eventually reported that cocaine smuggling into Golfito by fishing vessels commonly occurred from the mid-1990s to 2001.[304]

Occasional seizures and legal cases provide insight into what was actually occurring in the Golfito area. For instance, in 1990 undercover U.S. Customs agents in Tampa, Florida, engaged in a one-ton cocaine bust also participated in a sham real estate deal, in which a Costa Rican lawyer aimed to buy properties for Cali traffickers, including an island near Golfito with an airstrip.[305] The following year Costa Rican police noted that the drug trade had jumped in this region. With smuggling organizations enjoying largely free rein over 150 miles of nearby territorial waters, citizens were reporting the entry of vessels, planes, and helicopters, and reports of cocaine found floating off Golfito multiplied. At length, officials estimated that Colombian cartels were shipping up to 40 tons of cocaine annually through nearby routes.[306]

The Osa Peninsula lies directly across the Dulce Gulf from Golfito. Here, Corcovado National Park, the only virgin rain forest in Central America, has been associated with cocaine smuggling, as has Isla del Caño, a biological preserve just north of the peninsula. In 1990 authorities came upon five Colombians, two with international drug-trafficking records, supposedly fishing on the Río Sirena in Osa.[307] Despite suspicious circumstances, police failed to locate any drugs and deported the men after questioning. Shortly thereafter, however, 850 kilos of cocaine were found floating nearby. In 1994, after the DEA identified an operation shipping cocaine up the Pacific coast from Colombia to Guatemala, a joint Nicaraguan–Costa Rican operation captured several of those same deportees with 650 kilos of cocaine. Two years later, a shoot-out between cocaine traffickers and authorities near Osa's Punta Salsipuedes led to a 130-kilo seizure, and local inhabitants cited constant deliveries of drugs from Panama.[308]

302. "Alarma en el sur por narcotráfico," *LN* (CR), 29 September 1986, 1; "Guerra a la marihuana," *LN* (CR), 15 June 1991, 10A; and "Denuncian gran tráfico de cocaína en Golfito," *LN* (CR), 14 September 1986, 10A.

303. For a 1992 National Drug Assembly testimony of a local representative, see "Denuncian presencia de narcos en Golfito," *LN* (CR), 20 July 1992, 8A. See also "Narcos y ladrones," *LN* (CR), 8 November 1992, 10A.

304. DEA, *Resources, Costa Rica* (2003), 4.

305. For a proposed land purchase by Cali associates that was dropped after Tampa Bay arrests, see "Un caso no cerrado," *LN* (CR), 28 July 1990, 8A.

306. Albert Lorente, Costa Rican counternarcotics police director, noted "an amazing increase in trafficking and storage in this area." See "Hallan cocaína en el mar," *LN* (CR), 26 April 1991, 18A; "Cocaine Haul off Coast," *TT* (CR), 3 May 1991, 17; "Investigan base 'narco' en el Pacífico Sur," *LN* (CR), 2 June 1991, 10A; "Pacífico Sur a merced del narco," *LN* (CR), 9 June 1991, 5A; "Pescadores hallan dieciséis kilos de cocaína," *LN* (CR), 11 July 1991, 12A; and "C.R. Fishermen Find Cocaine at Sea," *TT* (CR), 12 July 1991, 4.

307. See "Dos narcos en lancha capturada," *LN* (CR), 1 December 1990, 10A. For a typical smaller smuggling case, see "Caen treinta kilos de cocaína," *LN* (CR), 31 January 1996, 10A.

308. "Capturan a panameño con lote de cocaína," *LP* (PA), 10 January 1996, 2A. Go-fasts occasionally delivered Colombian marijuana as well. See "Lancha desapareció de la playa," *LN* (CR), 6 June 2008, 16A, and "Aparece más marihuana," *LN* (CR), 7 June 2008, 14A

Although for many years the Costa Ricans behind drug smuggling on the far southern coast were unknown, or at least not publicly identified, in 1995 authorities succeeded in breaking up one important Golfito network, allegedly headed by six brothers in the Vargas Hidalgo family.[309] The case developed after a border police officer reported to San José antidrug officials that the Vargas family was not only deeply involved in the marijuana trade but also linked to cocaine traffickers. Furthermore, he alleged that the Vargas network had thoroughly corrupted local authorities. This homegrown Costa Rican organization, according to OIJ director Manuel Alvarado Blanco, had the capacity to distribute 200 kilos of cocaine per week within Costa Rica and had provided logistical support and protection for a Colombian organization transshipping large quantities of narcotics through Costa Rica and Guatemala and on to the United States.[310]

For all of the vulnerabilities exploited by traffickers moving drugs along Costa Rica's Pacific coast, the manner in which authorities pursued the Vargas network demonstrates the strengths of the Costa Rican criminal-justice system, with which drug rings also had to contend. Although the traffickers had bribed local police to ensure their cooperation, Costa Rica's elite antidrug officers were sufficiently clean and skillful that they could take confidential information, conduct further investigations, and eventually succeed in arresting, prosecuting, and imprisoning members of a prominent regional family. Such an outcome would have been highly improbable in much of the rest of Central America.

The chief problem in Costa Rica was not abysmal seizure totals, bumbling or corrupt police officers and judges, or a legal system wholly unable to prosecute and convict drug traffickers. Instead, the plethora of attractive smuggling opportunities enticed a great array of criminal syndicates that, together, overwhelmed the ability of the authorities to curb the drug trade. Domestic and foreign networks alike set up shop in Costa Rica, with traffickers convincing themselves that they could earn large sums, while using local knowledge and powerful international connections and while selectively deploying bribes, bullets, and intimidation to evade capture.

For law enforcement the volume of drugs passing along the Pacific coast has been sobering. Along with Golfito and the Osa peninsula, another notable landmark for drug networks active in the far southern waters of Costa Rica has been Punta Burica, located at the tip of the long, narrow peninsula that marks the country's southern border with Panama. In 1991 authorities discovered a downed helicopter, which had been carrying cocaine into Costa Rica, floating in Panamanian waters off the point. Then, as maritime Pacific transit climbed, transshipment of very large quantities of cocaine occurred. In 2000, ninety nautical miles from Punta Burica, authorities seized 513 kilos of cocaine off a vessel heading to Guatemala, the *Douglas I*, with Costa Rican officials eventually sending ten Colombian suspects to the United States for trial. This was followed by Costa Rica's largest seizure to date—fully 3.9 tons—taken off a vessel 150 miles southeast of Punta Burica, within Costa Rica's exclusive economic zone. The following year officials seized another 1,630 kilos of cocaine from two speedboats, with the arrest of ten, after a chase in Costa Rican territorial waters. In 2007 authorities recovered a speedboat with a ton of cocaine near Punta Burica.[311]

309. *INCSR* (1996), 126. See also "Policía incrimina a los hermanos Vargas," *LN* (CR), 15 March 1997, 10A, and "Implicados habrían ofrecido fuerte soborno," *LN* (CR), 18 May 1997, 10A.

310. See "OIJ golpea a importante organización de narcos," *LN* (CR), 3 November 1995, 10A, and "Presuntos narcos prófugos," *LN* (CR), 4 November 1995, 10A. This network aimed its activities at considerable domestic distribution as well as transshipment, attesting to the extent of national drug problems.

311. "Hallan helicóptero utilizado por narcotraficantes," *LP* (PA), 4 June 1991, 32A; "Drug Suspects Shipped to U.S. for Trial," *TT* (CR), 28 July 2000, 3; "Decomiso interesa a la DEA," *LN* (CR), 16 July 2000, 10A; "Huge Drug Bust Called Biggest Seizure Yet," *TT* (CR), 8 December 2000, 6; and "Caen diez por narcotráfico," *LN* (CR), 4 November 2001, 12A. "Hallan una lancha con una tonelada de cocaína," *LN* (CR), 22 December 2007, 14A.

To try to stem these activities, the Costa Rican government in 2001 chose to establish its new Coast Guard Academy in Golfito.[312] Yet neither the academy nor a coast guard station in Quepos have had nearly the resources to bottle up drug traffic along this sea corridor.[313] Instead, as in the case of Limón on the Caribbean, once a promising route has been established, traffickers have been loath to abandon it, although they have sometimes moved operations farther offshore. In 2002 U.S. radar located a thirty-six-foot speedboat heading up the Pacific coast 140 nautical miles from the coast. After interception and a seven-hour chase, the traffickers beached their boat, containing 1,200 kilos of cocaine, on the Osa Peninsula and attempted to escape into the Corcovado National Park.[314] Again, in 2004 a U.S. Coast Guard helicopter pursued a speedboat, this time for eleven hours, off Costa Rica's Pacific coast. It eventually dumped about a ton of cocaine into the ocean before entering Costa Rican territorial waters and eventually landing on Playa Malpaís, just north of Cabo Blanco at the tip of the Nicoya Peninsula.[315]

Despite the fact that joint U.S.-Costa Rican coast guard patrols have occurred since 1999, resulting in some very large seizures, well-entrenched smuggling groups have continued to send large quantities of drugs off these shores. While the fact that in 2004 authorities seized 4.7 tons of cocaine in Costa Rica's Pacific waters attests to an increased interdiction capability, it also underscores the important role that this route has continued to play in cocaine transit.[316] Sufficient shipments have eluded interception as to encourage continued trafficking. Indeed, telltale indicators of successful trafficking have abounded. For instance, in a nine-day span at the end of 2008, the Costa Rican Coast Guard came upon three abandoned boats, each with powerful engines and with registration numbers erased, one with Colombian food nearby, and another shot up in an unsuccessful bid to sink it and thus destroy evidence of drug transit.[317]

As was true throughout this bridge region, breaking up one domestic trafficking network had limited positive repercussions, as rivals usually stepped in or entrepreneurs sprung up to take advantage of new opportunities. Thus, despite the law-enforcement successes against the Fowlie and Vargas brother organizations, cartels clearly retained plenty of Costa Rican collaborators in this far southern corner. In this regard, while the stealing of cocaine in transit from traffickers or of seized cocaine from authorities has not occurred nearly as frequently in Costa Rica as in Panama and Guatemala, in 2009 five men in Golfito, armed with automatic weapons, stole from government agents 320 kilos of cocaine that had been confiscated four days earlier.[318] Such bold strikes attest to the power wielded by drug-trafficking organizations along the Costa Rican Pacific coast, while the prominent role of the Vargas family underscores how trafficking organizations in the bridge states, as in South American producer countries, valued the extra security that came from centering operations on a group related to one another.

Overland Entry and Exit

Although in Belize and Panama only a very modest percentage of imported narcotics arrived overland, the geography of the drug

312. *INCSR* (2002), 6.

313. For various recent cocaine-trafficking seizures in southern Costa Rica, see "Cayó más cocaína en la zona sur," *LN* (CR), 8 January 2004, 13A.

314. "Big Bust for Drug Patrol," *TT* (CR), 22 November 2002, 1A.

315. "Patrols Push Drugs into Deeper Water," *TT* (CR), 20 February 2004, 12. See also "Malpaís a Lawless, Copless Place," *TT* (CR), 4 April 2008, 1.

316. *INCSR* (2005), 10.

317. "Guardacostas decomisa tres lanchas narcos," *LN* (CR), 3 January 2009, 10A.

318. "Fear of More Drugs," 1. For the extradition request for a Panamanian arrested for killing seven and wounding three in an attempted cocaine robbery in the Ciudad Neily–Golfito area, see "Panamá prepara pedido de extradición por masacres," *LN* (CR), 8 June 2008, 14A.

trade was far more vexing in this respect for the Costa Rican government. Drugs could and did readily enter and leave the country across two long and porous borders, and they could be moved relatively quickly and securely along the country's fairly extensive road network. With the major cartels constantly probing for effective new routes and methods, with homegrown trafficking networks aspiring to greater profits and looking to capitalize on local knowledge and connections, and with freelancers aiming to join the trade, the potential for transporting drugs by land was bound to be thoroughly tested. In fact, particularly once peace came to Nicaragua and El Salvador, ground transit rapidly grew to become a third exceedingly important trafficking method in Costa Rica.[319]

While aerial smuggling has required pilots, aircraft, and arrangements for fuel and runways and while transport by shipping container has depended on well-developed networks to send off, transfer, and receive the drugs in ports in Colombia, Central America, and the United States, overland trafficking was especially well suited for lesser drug rings, as it has required fewer outlays and simpler measures within the bridge region. Successful ground transport has also put a premium on familiarity with highway checkpoints, secondary routes, border controls, and other relevant law-enforcement patterns and initiatives. For all these reasons, Central Americans tended to play very significant roles in overland trafficking.

When foreigners were involved in smuggling by land through Costa Rica, they were sometimes supervisors from the major Colombian and Mexican cartels, but they were also often associated with Panamanian, Salvadoran, or Guatemalan cartelitos. At times, they hailed from lesser Colombian organizations or drug rings in other Caribbean basin states, such as the Dominican Republic, that moved into Central America to take advantage of overland trafficking opportunities. One representative example occurred in 1997, when Costa Rican Drug Control Police broke up a cocaine network that for at least three years had used Costa Rican associates to assist in shipping overland loads of twenty to fifty kilos.[320] While the organization was allegedly led by Colombian Javier Darío Molina Cano, local individuals were in charge of transporting and warehousing the cocaine as well as distributing in Costa Rica those drugs not exported. Costa Rican police noted at the time that many similar drug organizations existed.

The leading overland route for narcotics passing into, across, or out of Costa Rica was along the Pan-American Highway. As an Allied country in World War II, Costa Rica had incurred considerable debt but had quickly built its two-hundred-mile portion of the Pan-American Highway, a project originally rationalized as providing a ground route to assist in defense of the Panama Canal.[321] Then, as Central American economies grew and became more interconnected, the highway gained importance for legitimate and illicit commerce alike. By the early 1980s it had come to serve as the principal overland artery to move drugs north. While originally much of the ground traffic was piecemeal work by lone mules or a driver and companion, carrying drugs on their persons or in their vehicles, over time drug rings began to transport much more considerable amounts by land much more regularly.[322] In particular, starting in the mid- to late 1980s, networks began to send cocaine shipments into Costa Rica in tractor trailers with the drugs hidden in secret compartments, buried deep inside

319. Aguilera Peralta, "Fighting the Dragon," 221.

320. "Caen con droga dos ticos y un colombiano," *LN* (CR), 8 January 1997, 10A. The five hundred thousand colones in small bills suggested significant domestic sales.

321. J. Bell, *Crisis in Costa Rica*, 72.

322. For the eight-year sentences plea bargained with four Costa Rican traffickers who had sent large quantities of cocaine overland from Panama, through San Isidro de El General and into the Valle Central, see "Cuatro aceptan cargo por narco," *LN* (CR), 11 August 1998, 10A.

loaded containers, or even stashed in the fuel tanks.[323]

In the 1990s the frequent success of overland trafficking schemes inspired cartelitos in Panama, Guatemala, El Salvador, and Nicaragua to invest heavily in trucking companies, which they dedicated to the ground transit of cocaine across Central America, often from Panama all the way to Guatemala.[324] By the middle of that decade authorities had exposed a new method—the transport of up to 300 kilos at a time in stolen cars. In 1997 José Luis Tobar Prieto, chief of the Salvadoran National Civil Police antinarcotics division, noted, "Some cars stolen in El Salvador and Guatemala are transported to Nicaragua and Costa Rica, where they are purchased with cocaine. Later, they steal other vehicles in these countries and transport drugs in them to Guatemala."[325] Thus, in the mid- to late 1990s and again by late 2003 overland cocaine shipments of 50–500 kilos were regularly passing through Costa Rica hidden in cars, pickups, and trucks.[326] In one of the chief seizures in 1999, authorities discovered 837 kilos of cocaine that had been trucked up the Pan-American Highway to Ciudad Neily.[327]

Bringing drugs by land from Panama was so readily accomplished that it grew to rival the aerial and maritime trafficking that had dominated the earlier years of the Costa Rican drug trade. Cocaine crossing the Panamanian border was then often shipped out of Limón or flown from San José. For a time, one popular route had Colombian cocaine shipped to Panama via the ports of Colón, Bocas del Toro, or other Caribbean entry points. Traffickers would hide the cocaine in produce or seal it in containers and truck the drugs into Costa Rica via Sixaola, with Guatemala as the eventual destination.[328] Much the same type of schemes were occurring on the Pacific side. In a notable 1996 case a joint DEA-OIJ undertaking intercepted one key overland cocaine shipment, capturing 645 kilos and bringing down an organization using an intercoastal overland route for more than a year. The network, led by Dominican traffickers, shipped Cali cartel cocaine up the Pacific coast of Panama, then trucked it to the border with Costa Rica, on up the Pan-American Highway to San José, then down to Limón for shipping to New York City inside boxes of yucca.[329]

Drug rings engaged in aerial trafficking from Costa Rica to the United States also sometimes imported cocaine by land. For instance, in 1989 a drug network, allegedly controlled by Sonio Nin of the Dominican Republic, arranged to have 137 kilos of cocaine trucked through Sixaola, then on to Limón. The traffickers' plan was to store the cocaine in the village of San Juan de Santa Bárbara de Heredia, just outside San José, then forward the drugs to Miami in suitcases loaded with 25 kilos apiece four times a week. Two members of the drug ring would fly to Florida to collect payment, and a third would

323. For an example of cocaine discovered at Paso Canoas in the fuel tanks of a truck bound for Guatemala, see "Incautan 120 kilos de cocaína en Costa Rica," *LP* (HO), 23 April 2001, 85A.

324. For representative cases from the summer of 2008, see "OIJ intercepta dos furgones con cocaína," *LN* (CR), 1 June 2008, 16A; "OIJ decomisa seis carros y 395 kilos de cocaína a narcos," *LN* (CR), 13 June 2008, 16A; "Trailero iba con 70 kilos de coca ocultos en carga de vidrio," *LN* (CR), 28 June 2008, 12A; and "Cae Trailero con 135 kilos de cocaína," *LN* (CR), 9 August 2008, 16A.

325. Various articles in Guatemala's *Siglo Veintiuno*, from January 17–18, 1997, quoted in "Vinculan al país con los robacarros," *LN* (CR), 19 January 1997, 10A.

326. *INCSR* (2007), 6; *INCSR* (2005), 12; and *INCSR* (2004), 8. For a typical case, in which authorities broke up "Los Sombrerones," a money-laundering, and arms- and drug-trafficking network linked to Colombian, Panamanian, and Mexican drug organizations, see "Banda despachaba cocaína a México," *LN* (CR), 4 August 2008, 18A.

327. DEA, *Resources, Costa Rica* (2000), 6.

328. For a representative case, see "110 kilos de cocaína hallados ocultos en maletas con frijoles," *LN* (CR), 2 August 2008, 12A.

329. See "Fuerte golpe a narcotráfico," *LN* (CR), 26 November 1996, 8A. See also "Procesados por tráfico de cocaína," *LN* (CR), 10 December 1996, 10A. In New York the container was consigned to a vegetable-importing company run by Dominican traffickers.

travel back to Panama to compensate the suppliers. Police using wiretaps cracked the ring, however, and airport customs discovered 50 kilos of cocaine in two suitcases belonging to Andres Cheves, an airport security officer. Curiously, Cheves had been ticketed to fly to Managua, but his luggage had been directed on to Miami. When police raided his house, they found another 87 kilos. Authorities arrested a Colombian, two additional Costa Rican associates, and two employees of LACSA, Costa Rica's national airline, who had allegedly changed the baggage tags on the suitcases to be directed to Miami. Rodolfo Jiménez, chief of Costa Rica's Public Security Ministry, reported that the traffickers had offered him a $1.1 million bribe to "look the other way" as the scheme was put into operation. Jiménez claimed to have played along with the traffickers; he then had the 137 kilos seized and nine suspects arrested.[330]

Because the characteristics of Costa Rica's far southern and northern zones differ, so do the challenges and opportunities for smugglers and law-enforcement agents. The central portion of the Costa Rican–Panamanian border runs through a remote mountainous region marked by few settlements or roads. Although neither country's authorities has exercised much control here, the lack of infrastructure has restricted the size of drug loads that can traverse the rugged terrain. Weighty shipments have instead tended to be trucked through the border stations at Sixaola near the Caribbean coast and at Paso Canoas along the Pan-American Highway. In circumstances analogous in certain respects to those found at the Santa Elena border crossing between northern Belize and Mexico, smaller vehicles could circumvent Paso Canoas and use any of the almost one hundred informal crossings.[331]

Because Panamanian businesses have long trucked many legitimate products to Costa Rica and points north, some drug rings, particularly smaller or entrepreneurial organizations, have relied on shipments slipping past otherwise occupied customs authorities at the primary border posts. For many years the sheer volume of cross-border traffic has overwhelmed customs officials at Sixaola, with streams of people and vehicles traversing the bridge in both directions and little control by authorities.[332] The border post at Paso Canoas has often been chaotic as well, contending with even greater numbers of trucks and other vehicles. More established and sophisticated criminal syndicates, trucking larger quantities of narcotics, have sometimes opted to corrupt border officials to ensure that loads pass through without confiscations.[333]

Highway checkpoints and police patrols have resulted in occasional busts within Costa Rica, particularly when police had advance information on a shipment. Generally, however, drug networks have found that cocaine shipments could traverse the entire country by road without much risk of interdiction.[334] This freedom has encouraged overland cocaine exports, although the northern border is not without challenges for drug smugglers plotting geotactics. Although the Nicaraguan border stretches for 186 miles, much of it is not conducive to ground transport since the countries are divided, for

330. "More Cocaine Seized; Probe Demanded," *TT* (CR), 17 November 1989, 4. One member of Costa Rica's Legislative Drug Commission questioned whether traffickers would have sent so much cocaine to someone like Jiménez if they had no prior relationship. See also "Intensifican pesquisas sobre presos por coca," *LN* (CR), 23 November 1989, 10A. For more on this case, see "Carga de cocaína entró por Sixaola," *LN* (CR), 14 November 1989, 12A; "Remiten a Alajuela causa por 137 kilos de coca," *LN* (CR), 22 November 1989, 10A; "Un preso más por tráfico de coca," *LN* (CR), 25 November 1989, 11A; and "La meta era cuatro cargamentos semanales," *LN* (CR), 26 November 1989, 10A.

331. See DEA, *Resources, Costa Rica* (2001), 5, and "Costa Rica: Paso vital del narcotráfico de Suramérica hacia Estados Unidos," *LP* (PA), 4 September 1991, 3A. For a representative instance, see "Incautados treinta y tres kilos de cocaína," *LN* (CR), 18 January 1990, 10A.

332. See "Frontera de Sixaola está abierta a ilegales y al narco," *LN* (CR), 1 June 2008, 4A.

333. For investigations concerning Sixaola and Paso Canoas corruption, see, for example, "Seguridad investiga a policías por narco," *LN* (CR), 14 January 1997, 10A.

334. For an example of the occasional bust of an overland shipment, see "Autoridades Ticas detienen a panameño," *LP* (PA), 3 June 2001, 5A.

many miles, by the Río San Juan and the swamps south of Lake Nicaragua. Moreover, no extensive Nicaraguan highway system reaches into its southeastern region. Although more than a dozen secondary border crossings exist from the eastern edge of Lake Nicaragua to the Pacific, none are suited for heavy vehicles, and most become largely impassable during the rainy season, when the official border crossing is often the only one that does not require four-wheel-drive vehicles.[335] Thus, the geography of the border has tended to funnel overland shipments toward the single official border crossing into Nicaragua at Peñas Blancas.[336]

Although this was always a "logical choke point for interdiction," Costa Rican authorities—resources stretched thin by the multitude of land, sea, and air routes—did not focus law-enforcement efforts on Peñas Blancas until the late 1990s. Installing density meters and other contraband detectors at the border stations then brought startling results, opening the eyes of authorities to just how much cocaine had been passing through. In a notable 1997 case border officials discovered 367 kilos of cocaine, and then another 200 kilos in storage, all brought into Costa Rica by speedboat to Limón and then hidden in small compartments in truck containers.[337] In another representative case of a Colombian ring shipping cocaine overland from Costa Rica into Nicaragua, a police wiretap brought about the seizures of 200 kilos, 130 kilos, and 25 kilos of cocaine.[338] Customs officials, who had started to inspect for cocaine traces even empty tractor trailers headed south, ultimately seized more than 7 tons in both 1997 and 1998.[339]

Capitalizing on these interdiction successes, the Drug Control Police established a new inspection post in 1999 and enhanced its sophistication five years later.[340] In one week in 2004 authorities at Peñas Blancas confiscated two shipments, totaling 550 kilos of cocaine, intercepted along the Panama-Guatemala truck route. Indeed, by August 2004 a ton of marijuana and more than a ton of cocaine seized by Costa Rican authorities that year had come as the drugs passed overland, with the cocaine shipments typically heading north from Panama. In 2007 authorities at Peñas Blancas seized 671 kilos from a truck headed north with a Guatemalan driver. That same year, overland heroin transport came to public attention, when considerable busts were made on the Nicaraguan and also the Panamanian border. In August authorities seized 10 kilos of heroin at Peñas Blancas, headed for the United States via Nicaragua, and then in December officials searching for a murder weapon in a bar along the Panamanian border happened upon 6 kilos.[341]

Costa Rica also created a Mobile Enforcement Team, drawing on customs and antinarcotics personnel, along with trained dogs and other specialized assistance. Unlike the prickly Belizean-Guatemalan relations, Costa Rica was a regional leader in cooperative antidrug initiatives. Thus, some further progress in stemming overland transit occurred with its neighbors at the bilateral level. In 2005 Costa Rica conducted eight cross-border joint operations with Nicaraguan and Panamanian counterparts, and six more in 2006.[342] The U.S. government is planning to finance construction of a state-of-the-art highway

335. See DEA, *Resources, Costa Rica* (2003), 9, and "Poverty in Border Areas," 6.

336. In 1994 Puntarenas authorities intercepted cocaine headed for Guatemala along this route. "Decomisan 107 kilos de cocaína," *LN* (CR), 17 May 1994, 16A.

337. See "Cuatro presos por decomiso de coca," *LN* (CR), 29 April 1997, 10A; "Policía hermética por decomiso de cocaína," *LN* (CR), 28 April 1997, 10A; "370 kilos de cocaína en Guanacaste," *LN* (CR), 27 April 1997, 10A; "Ocho detenidos con 200 kilos de cocaína," *LN* (CR), 27 April 1991, 10A; and "Capturan a narco guatemalteco," *El Diario* (Guatemala), 16 June 1997, 10.

338. See *United States v. Mejia*, 448 F.3d 436, and *United States v. Valencia-Rios*, 639 F. Supp. 2d 98.

339. *INCSR* (2002), 7, and DEA, *Resources, Costa Rica* (2000), 1.

340. "New Drug Control Checkpoint Opens," *TT* (CR), 23 April 2004, 3.

341. "Country Becomes Drug Destination," *TT* (CR), 2 April 2004, 1A; "Land-based Drug Seizures Increase," *TT* (CR), 20 August 2004, 1A; "Police Confiscate 949 Kilos of Cocaine in December," *NT* (CR), 4 January 2008, 2; "Amplían prisión por trasiego de heroína," *LN* (CR), 19 August 2007, 16A; "OIJ decomisa 6 kilos de heroína en un bar," *LN* (CR), 27 December 2007, 15A.

342. *INCSR* (2007), 5, and *INCSR* (2006), 7.

checkpoint in Golfito Province to stem overland trafficking from Panama.[343] With popular routes under enhanced scrutiny and vehicles of all varieties being much more thoroughly inspected, traffickers have had an incentive to find other routes or methods.

One result of these counternarcotics triumphs was that the export of drugs by courier rose markedly, though vehicles still retained a substantial share of the overland drug traffic.[344] As law-enforcement pressure at the official crossing increased, one group of Cali traffickers bought farm property on both sides of the border, near the towns of Puerto Soley, Guanacaste, and El Ostional, Nicaragua. After a dispute in 2000 concerning 74 kilos of missing cocaine led to a shooting, investigating authorities learned that the network was bringing the cocaine by car to Puerto Soley, taking it across the border on horseback, and then sending it on by vehicle to the United States. This form of smuggling has required ingenuity and patience, as smaller amounts were steadily accumulated. However, when confronted with a single choke point, trafficking organizations sometimes preferred to go to the trouble of circumventing it, rather than moving to a different smuggling method altogether.[345]

In 2008 authorities discovered that the Sinaloa cartel had arranged for cocaine to be imported via Paso Canoas, temporarily stored near the Panamanian border, and then carried in vehicles toward Los Chiles, near the Nicaraguan border. The drugs were sometimes transported across the border on foot or horseback, occasionally by boat up the San Juan and then out to an island in Lake Nicaragua. Authorities cracked the network with 56- and 74-kilo busts in Costa Rica, coupled with a much larger seizure by Nicaraguan officials of 1,400 kilos, headed from Lake Nicaragua toward Honduras. However, the route had clearly been used successfully for quite some time. And, as often occurred in the Central American drug trade, a dependable smuggling route attracted other traffickers, who put into effect variations of the earlier theme. In early 2010 Nicaraguan police seized 474 kilos of cocaine from a truck driven by a Costa Rican with convictions for drug trafficking and dealing. Investigations suggested that the network had been using twenty trucks and two boats to move cocaine both overland across the Costa Rican border and by sea into the small southern Nicaraguan port of San Juan del Sur.[346]

Conclusion

If ever there has been a Central American bridge state well positioned to implement a sustained antidrug strategy to curb transshipment, that country would seem to be Costa Rica. Here is a developed country with a strongly democratic political culture and a genuine concern with corruption, reflected in the convening of legislative commissions to investigate the drug trade. Here is a country whose governments almost uniformly have had excellent relations with producer states, with other bridge states, and with the United States and other market countries in North America and Europe. Here is a country with officials prepared to pay more than lip service to antidrug goals and to work earnestly to interdict drug shipments and investigate and break up foreign and domestic drug networks. Here is a country with a highly competent, elite

343. *INCSR* (2011), 204.

344. See "Narcos usan a vendedores ambulantes para trasiego," *LN* (CR), 3 August 2008, 16A, and "Narcos les pintan castillos," 21A.

345. "Indagan cartel de Cali aquí," *LN* (CR), 3 July 2000, 4A; "Cali Cartel Link Found," *TT* (CR), 14 July 2000, 3. The network allegedly included Colombian Gerardo Abrio Álvarez Rivero; former Nicaraguan police captain Esther Concepción Ruiz Téllez; her husband, Salvador Napoleón Silva Espinoza, a former Nicaraguan colonel; and former Honduran colonel Wilfredo Leva Cabrera.

346. "Cartel de Sinaloa abre nueva ruta para droga," *LN* (CR), 14 August 2008, 16A; "Expresidiario tico cae con droga en Nicaragua," *LN* (CR), 21 January 2010, 14A.

counternarcotics unit within the judicial police force. Yet for all the notable seizures and arrests, drug transit via Costa Rica has long thrived. Why exactly has that been the case?

In light of the demand for illegal drugs and the extraordinary profits to be made in supplying them, Costa Rican governments have been unable to accumulate sufficient deterrents to forestall smuggling through their country. Transnational criminal networks trafficking drugs—their numbers, abilities, and techniques—have overmatched even Costa Rica's institutions, procedures, and antidrug resources. Plainly, bribes, bullets, and intimidation have affected Costa Rica alongside the other Central American bridge states. In particular, the wealth of drug rings has distorted the workings of politics, the prisons, the Rural Guard, and the customs service. Furthermore, for all of its efforts Costa Rica has certainly failed to do all that might have been done to counter the drug trade: the laws targeting organized crime have long amounted to a particular vulnerability. Most important, however, stopping the flow of narcotics has been exceptionally challenging, given the multiplicity of available methods utilizing sea, air, or land routes.

Hall of Fame baseball player "Wee" Willie Keeler once described the essence of a batter's strategy as "Hit 'em where they ain't." The tactics of traffickers in the bridge states follow suit: move the drugs where the authorities are not expecting them. Traffickers have readily changed the way that drugs are hidden, and they have adeptly shifted from one to another route or method. Simply put, there have been too many networks, moving too many drugs, in too many locales for antidrug officials to curb drug transit very effectively.

Costa Rican authorities have become resigned to the fact that however many drugs have been seized, much more have probably been transiting undetected, whether by aerial, maritime, or overland means. At home, the domestic marijuana industry has been difficult to uproot. Countering it has diverted law-enforcement resources from efforts to stop cocaine transshipment, and it has provided a useful sideline for various domestic networks. With respect to international trafficking, even assuming that officials have been capturing the quite optimistic estimate of 10 percent, the ready supply and enormous profits in the remaining 90 percent has ensured that Costa Rica has remained a decidedly attractive bridge state. For all of Costa Rica's antidrug triumphs, and there have been many, traffickers have sent and continue to send substantial quantities of drugs through the country. Costa Rica thus underscores how limited are the possible accomplishments of an interdiction strategy in a prominent bridge state.

Costa Rica has enjoyed an admirable international reputation: a small, peaceful state of great natural beauty that abolished its military, long reveled in its elections, successfully promoted tourism, and joined the ranks of the developed world. Yet even this praiseworthy profile has attracted traffickers who have believed that air and sea shipments as well as passengers coming from Costa Rica would be viewed as less suspicious and, hence, less subject to official scrutiny than those from virtually any other Latin American state. In other respects, too, traffickers have seen opportunities to subvert institutions that are otherwise national strengths. Traffickers have succeeded in manipulating for their own purposes not only the country's intensely competitive elections but its criminal-justice system, scrupulously fair to defendants.

Given the importance of geotactics to the drug trade, Costa Rican geography has encouraged traffickers as well. This is not merely a country that happens to be located somewhere between South and North America. Rather, its geographic profile features sparsely populated hinterlands, border zones encompassing rugged territory, and Pacific and Caribbean coasts close to one another that offer opportunities for intercoastal smuggling. Costa Rica flanks Panama, that great southern engine of drug exports, and is situated a relatively short distance, by air or sea, from Colombia itself. Then, of extraordinary moment,

Isla de San Andrés lies close at hand, with longstanding connections to Costa Rica's principal Caribbean port of Limón. The country's position neighboring Nicaragua invites comment as well. At an early date drug-related activities connected to the Nicaraguan civil war brought trafficking networks into northern Costa Rica, with its multiple airstrips and limited law enforcement. Later, the ease of overland transport through Nicaragua and the poorly patrolled Río San Juan, running along much of the border, have attracted the attention of drug rings. And San José and the Valle Central have offered one of the most modern urban areas in Central America, including a busy international airport with extensive connections.

Thus, as early as the mid-1980s drug-trafficking organizations had initiated successful operations in Costa Rica. Over the years, many of the leading South American organizations have participated, often with resounding success. Starting with Medellín and Cali traffickers, Costa Rica attracted other Colombian organizations as well, including substantial rings from Bogotá and Pereira, as well as Colombian guerrilla and paramilitary forces.[347] Although by the mid- to late 1990s the initial primacy of Colombians in the national drug trade was waning in the northernmost Central American states of Belize and Guatemala, the Colombian presence in Costa Rica has proven to be more long-lived. Nevertheless, over time, the Mexican cartels have penetrated the country's drug trade, as have Panamanians, Guatemalans, and other Central Americans, Jamaicans, Dominicans, and even Russian criminals.[348] Although Costa Rica has posed singular sets of advantages and disadvantages for drug-smuggling networks, the country has become a transshipment center of great significance within the multipolar world of Central American drug trafficking, and it is very likely to remain so in the future.

347. Indeed, by 2008 of more than twelve thousands Colombians living in Costa Rica, between two hundred and three hundred had been imprisoned on drug charges, and an estimated 3 percent of Colombian visitors were thought to have links to the drug trade. "Crack is Country's Enemy No. 1," *TT* (CR), 15 February 2008, 6.

348. See, for instance, "Cartel de Sinaloa abre nueva ruta," 16A; "Police Take Bite Out of Mexico-Tied Drug Network," *TT* (CR), 22 August 2008, 4; and "Libertad condicional a mujer ligada a narcos," *LN* (CR), 24 August 2008, 15A.

4

Guatemala

Marked by deep and wrenching divisions from the Spanish conquest forward, Guatemala has differed strikingly from its Central American counterparts, postcolonial Belize and newly developed Costa Rica, with their relatively peaceful histories and solidly democratic regimes. The states of Central America have had certain distinctive economic emphases as well. Traditionally, the Honduran economy exported bananas, and the Belizean economy, mahogany and the logwood used to dye textiles. Panama long capitalized on its location as a commercial crossroads. As in Costa Rica, many Guatemalan elites, usually of European ancestry, made their fortunes in coffee. While abuses of agricultural workers occurred across the region, the labor drafts and indebted workers of the Guatemalan coffee-plantation system were particularly harsh.[1] Moreover, by the 1930s U.S. corporations engaged in the fruit trade, most notably the United Fruit Company, had bought large tracts, and poor conditions sometimes characterized their plantations as well. Thus, traditional exploitation of labor contributed to Guatemala's status as Central America's most fractured state.

Although the region's most populous country, with one of its largest economies, and fully twice the size of Costa Rica, Guatemala also became mired in the lengthiest civil war. In the 1980s Guatemala started to transition from a military regime to democracy. However, dire and longstanding social and economic difficulties have confounded civilian leaders, who have had to contend with vast disparities in wealth, alongside bitter ethnic and ideological cleavages and

1. See generally Paige, *Coffee and Power*. For the effects of the coffee-plantation labor system on one Guatemalan community, see Wilkinson, *Silence on the Mountain*.

GUATEMALA
MEXICO
Laguna del Tigre
La Honradez
MAYA BIOSPHERE RESERVE
Yaloch
Belmopan
Tenosique de Pino Suárez
El Naranjo
Sierra del Lacandón
R. Usumacinta
Melchor de Mencos
San Ignacio
Benque Viejo del Carmen
Lake Petén Itzá
Flores
San Francisco
BELIZE
R. Hondo
CHIAPAS
R. La Pasión
Sayaxché
Pípiles
Maya Mountains
Poptún
R. Salinas
PETÉN
Punta Gorda
Gulf of Honduras
Amatique Bay
Punta de Manabique
Ixcán
HUEHUETENANGO
Chisec
Lívingston
Puerto Barrios
Santo Tomás de Castilla
Santa Ana Huista
La Mesilla
ALTA VERAPAZ
El Golfete
R. Dulce
IZABAL
Lake Izabal
Cuilco
Huehuetenango
Cobán
R. Motagua
Izabal
Uspantán
Tacaná
QUICHÉ
Sierra de las Minas
Quiriguá
Los Amates
Sibinal
SAN MARCOS
BAJA VERAPAZ
ATLANTIC HWY
Sierra Madre
TOTONICAPÁN
El Carmen
Santa Cruz
ZACAPA
Zacapa
San Marcos
Quezaltenango
EL PROGRESO
HONDURAS
Ciudad Hidalgo
Santa Catarina Ixtahuacan
SOLOLÁ
CHIMALTENANGO
QUEZALTENANGO
GUATEMALA
Chimaltenango
JALAPA
CHIQUIMULA
Tecún Umán
Antigua
Guatemala City
Mazatenango
SACATEPÉQUEZ
Amatitlán
El Jocotillo
Puerto de Ocós
RETALHULEU
SUCHITEPÉQUEZ
PAN-AMERICAN HWY
Tiquisate
Pinula
Santa Lucía Cotzumalguapa
Escuintla
Jutiapa
Champerico
SANTA ROSA
JUTIAPA
San Cristóbal
La Gomera
PACIFIC COAST HWY
ESCUINTLA
Iztapa
Puerto San José
Puerto Quetzal
EL SALVADOR
Acajutla
PACIFIC OCEAN
N
0
50
100 mi

MAP 4.1

an extremely violent history. Widespread poverty, coupled with the entrenched privileges of elites, has made for a small tax base, and the armed forces have consumed substantial state resources. Operating on meager budgets, civilian government personnel have been plagued by inadequate training and compensation. Corruption has abounded, and most government institutions have operated for many years in dismal fashion.

While this profile of a deeply split and poorly functioning society caused many talented Guatemalans to emigrate and frightened away any number of potential foreign investors, it quickly attracted a multitude of drug organizations. By the early 1990s Guatemalan drug trafficking outpaced that of any other Central American state, with the possible exception of Panama. One local newspaper ruefully observed, "The records that Guatemala will never achieve in sports, they will obtain easily in this criminal activity."[2] In 2010 U.S. officials estimated that more than 60 percent of the cocaine passing through the Central American bridge states en route to the United States had transited Guatemala.[3]

Although Guatemala was clearly a bridge state ripe for transshipment ventures, surprisingly little has been written, to date, by scholars about the evolution and consequences of the drug trade. Which bridge-favoring factors encouraged drug organizations? When did marijuana, cocaine, and heroin trafficking take off, and how has each developed over time? Can their magnitude be estimated, and have the authorities had any success in thwarting their growth? What routes and methods have been utilized, and which syndicates have been most significant? How have the country's institutions responded, and how many drugs have been seized? Why has Guatemala outdistanced so many of the region's other bridge states in drug transshipment?

Bridge-Favoring Factors Relevant to Guatemala

Geography

As in the other Central American states, Guatemala's geographic features have helped to determine the magnitude of the drug trade. While its location in the northwestern corner of Central America, half the distance between Colombia and the United States, has fostered drug trafficking, Guatemala's position bordering Mexico has truly been of surpassing importance. The Mexican cartels have been able to move drugs so efficiently within their state and into the U.S. market that a country flanking Mexico has been exceedingly vulnerable to becoming entangled in transshipment schemes. Moreover, in recent years Mexican authorities have increased their vigilance against sea and air cocaine imports, and for traffickers this has increased the attraction of bringing cocaine supplies into Mexico by land.[4] Guatemala has border zones with Mexico, infrequently patrolled, that stretch for more than seven hundred miles. In this respect, it has been ideally situated to export drugs overland that could then be flown or driven across Mexico toward the U.S. border.

As in Panama and Costa Rica, Guatemalan authorities have had to deal with dual coasts, stretching thin their naval resources.[5] Furthermore, not only does the country have 350 miles of shoreline, but both the Pacific and the Caribbean coasts have certain advantageous features

2. "Guatemala: Decomisan cocaína por $3.826 millones," *La Prensa* (Honduras) (hereafter cited as *LP* [HO]), 31 December 1990, 13, quoting an editorial in Guatemala's *La Prensa Libre*, 29 December 1990.

3. U.S. Department of State, *International Narcotics Control Strategy Report* (hereafter cited as *INCSR*) (2011), 270.

4. *INCSR* (2011), 387–88.

5. For instance, the antidrug base opened in the Pacific port of Escuintla was charged with law enforcement along two hundred miles of coast as well as territorial waters. "Inauguran sede antidrogas en Escuintla," *Siglo Veintiuno* (Guatemala) (hereafter cited as *SV* [GU]), 22 January 2010, 6.

for trafficking. Amatique Bay forms the far southwestern corner of the Caribbean, with a long peninsula known as Punta de Manabique offering additional shelter from the open sea. Deep within the bay, Puerto Barrios, established by President Rufino Barrios in the late nineteenth century and further developed by United Fruit in the twentieth century, offers port facilities, as does neighboring Santo Tomás de Castilla. Various fishing communities and a pair of ports are strung along the country's Pacific coast, which also has many long and largely deserted stretches, including some quite close to the Mexican border.

Central Guatemala's rugged topography has influenced the drug trade as well. The so-called highlands—the central mountains, with their peaks, valleys, cliffs, and foothills—have often shielded low-flying planes from radar.[6] Guatemala is also the most volcanic state in Central America, with more than three dozen volcanoes, some quite active, and their rich dark soil has proven ideal for cultivating poppies, distinguishing Guatemala as the only Central American country in which opium has been grown.

Historically, imposing mountain ranges have divided Guatemalans, enhancing regional autonomy and weakening central authority. Not only do imposing mountains form much of the northwest boundary with Mexico, but the Sierra Madre volcanic chain also angles inland, rising above the piedmont coffee plantations, "with cliffs and ravines, volcanic debris, outcroppings and crevices, springs and waterfalls, thick forest and dense underbrush," running "like a corridor from the safety of the Mexican border into the heart of the country, right up to the outskirts of the capital."[7] During the civil war Guatemala's pronounced lack of integration provided opportunities for guerrilla forces that could elude the military in jungle-covered or steep, rugged, and forbidding terrain. These geographic factors both prolonged the internal fighting and encouraged the division of a half-dozen major domestic drug networks, divided from one another on regional lines, that stood ready to assist Colombian and Mexican organizations with transshipment.

Yet another bridge-favoring factor has been the many lightly populated expanses of the country in which drug trafficking could occur unobtrusively. While traffickers have utilized airstrips on ranches and farms and near small towns throughout Guatemala, the vast Petén region, by far the country's largest department, has proven to be an ideal target for drug planes. In 1990 Guatemala dedicated nearly 850,000 acres of northern Petén to an environmentally protected area called the Maya Biosphere Reserve. This tract, claimed to be the largest continuous tropical forest north of the Amazon, fronts the Mexican border. More than half of it has been designated a zone of strict protection, where settlements are barred. The lack of scrutiny by officials or a local population, however, has attracted illegal loggers, artifact looters, and drug traffickers.

While immigration has risen sharply across the Petén as a whole, the region remains quite sparsely populated for its size, with 390,000 inhabitants reported in the 2004 census. Although covering about a third of Guatemalan territory, the Petén has but three notable towns: Flores on Lake Petén Itzá, the gateway to the Tikal Mayan ruins; Poptún, on the principal road in eastern Petén and flanking the foothills of the Maya Mountains that stretch off into Belize; and Sayaxché, on the Río Pasión, the largest settlement in western Petén. At more than three hundred miles from Guatemala City,

6. See "Misteriosas naves sobrevuelan la Sierra de las Minas," *La Hora* (Guatemala) (hereafter cited as *LH* [GU]), 3 February 1989, 7, and "Drug Crackdown Forces Shipments into Guatemala," *Baltimore Sun*, 12 November 1989, 14A. Compared with the ease of employing radar in Florida with its flat topography and large expanses of surrounding water (Reuter, Crawford, and Cave, *Sealing the Borders*, 38), geographic difficulties greatly hamper its effective use in Guatemala.

7. Wilkinson, *Silence on the Mountain*, 233.

the Petén has long confounded central authorities intent on exercising control. Light planes might land on its hundreds of airstrips and dirt roads without much chance of interception. Once almost completely covered in jungle, the Petén has lost about half of its forest cover since the 1960s, as logging, cattle ranching, slash-and-burn farming, and oil extraction have increased. For instance, by 2005 about eight thousand illegal loggers were at work on the far western side of the Maya Biosphere in the Laguna del Tigre national park, about 40 percent of the 290,000 acres had been cleared for livestock grazing, and officials had located seven clandestine runways and thirteen abandoned jets.

Guatemala's inland waters have also factored into the geotactics of the drug trade. Traffickers have often formulated schemes to take advantage of rivers that run along international boundaries. Such waterways serve as easy points of entry into a neighboring country, enabling traffickers to evade official border posts. Boundary rivers also often stop pursuit by law enforcement. In Guatemala the Río Suchiate makes up much of the southwestern border with Mexico, as do the Río Salinas and Río Usumacinta farther to the north. Not only have these rivers formed convenient thoroughfares, but smugglers have crossed them to evade capture when authorities of one state or the other are near at hand.[8] Guatemala also contains Lake Izabal, the second largest in Central America. The Río Dulce actually connects Izabal with smaller Lake El Golfete and then with the Caribbean, and the lengthy river valley stretches inland from the coast, as does the Río Motagua valley just to the east. In this respect, geography has hampered tracking and intercepting drug flights because planes could fly in, low over the valleys, and then disappear onto runways on private land. Equally important, Guatemala's inland waters have been a magnet for water drops from passing planes and, in the Izabal region, for cocaine transit.

Civil War

For Guatemalans, bloodshed related to the country's civil war dominated much of the final half of the twentieth century. The land reform and other measures instituted by President Jacobo Arbenz Guzmán, starting in 1951, alienated many Guatemalan business and military elites and caused consternation among U.S. foreign policy makers, concerned at the potential encroachment of communism in Central America. After the 1954 coup assisted by the CIA, an authoritarian military regime dominated Guatemalan politics until the mid-1980s. In 1960 disillusioned junior officers formed one of the country's earliest revolutionary groups, operating mainly in the northern highlands, and two similar groups sprang up thereafter, though none had more than several hundred members. By 1966 Guatemalan military pressure had caused many left-wing guerrillas to move into urban areas, including Guatemala City, where some carried out assassinations and other terrorism. In the 1970s the fighting reverted to the highlands, and in 1982 the rebel groups coalesced to form the Guatemalan National Revolutionary Unity.

In the 1980s the military launched a series of brutal offensives in the highlands, seizing, torturing, and killing suspected leftists and sympathizers. At first specific individuals were targeted, but eventually the military attacked entire communities suspected of guerrilla support. A single counterinsurgency campaign in 1982 "killed an estimated 75,000, razed . . . 440 villages, and displaced over one million refugees."[9] During thirty-six years of fighting between 1960 and 1996, suspect citizens were

8. "U.S. investigators say smugglers move up and down the [Suchiate] river, using safe houses to lay low if they encounter border agents from either country." See, for instance, "Guatemala Is Key Drug Smugglers' Route," *The Reporter* (Belize) (hereafter cited as *TR* [BZ]), 13 November 2005, 30.

9. Schirmer, *Guatemalan Military Project*, 1.

denied the most basic human rights, and according to the Guatemalan Truth Commission, approximately two hundred thousand Guatemalans lost their lives.[10] Combatants did not confine the violence to themselves but instead assassinated or kidnapped, harassed or intimidated, thousands of civilians.[11] Although the army, civil-defense patrols, private death squads, and four revolutionary groups shared responsibility, soldiers, acting in their official positions or as vigilantes, amounted to the worst offenders.[12] Even when the pace of killing temporarily lulled, the collective memories of atrocities and the threat that political violence might soon be renewed hung over efforts to resolve hostilities.

This deep-rooted social conflict intersected with the drug trade in numerous ways. In the late 1970s and early 1980s government and military officials directed their attention chiefly to problems posed by the revolutionaries, rather than those related to organized crime. Furthermore, just as the Central American cocaine trade surged, relations between the United States and Guatemala were at a low ebb, the consequence of U.S. officials' cutting off military aid in 1978 on account of multiple grave human rights violations.[13] Consequently, early antidrug cooperation was sporadic, and at times grudging, curtailing the effectiveness of the DEA in Guatemala through much of the 1980s.

Guerrillas reportedly earned some income protecting Guatemalans cultivating opium and marijuana or transporting "opium gum on its way to Mexico for processing and marijuana to Mexico and Belize for onward shipment to the U.S. and other markets."[14] Even more important, the guerrilla fighting, particularly after the savage counterinsurgency campaign of 1982, was not so prevalent as to endanger transshipment flights or sea shipments. In contrast to the situation in El Salvador, Guatemala was large enough and the areas of combat sufficiently localized that traffickers could operate in numerous places without much risk of getting caught up in the fighting. And organizations that trafficked through Guatemala could find ways to capitalize on the country's turmoil. For instance, the counterinsurgency campaigns pacified much of the countryside, leaving military officers, themselves often corruptible, firmly controlling particular zones.

Moreover, during the civil war the Guatemalan Army became accustomed to acting with impunity in repressing its leftist opponents. Members of the armed forces were said to adhere to a code of silence with respect to transgressions, and the military habitually refrained from prosecuting its own for human rights abuses. If such a historically privileged position, "above the law" in most respects, could be transferred to drug trafficking, extraordinary sums might be earned. In fact, case files regarding drug allegations against military officers have been known to vanish, and few soldiers, including retired military, have been tried, much less punished, for trafficking offenses.[15] Naturally, the more that drug trafficking appeared to be risk-free, the more enticing involvement seemed.

10. Guatemalan Truth Commission, quoted in "U.S. Gives Military Aid After Twenty-Five-Year Ban," *Nica Times* (Costa Rica) (hereafter cited as *NT* [CR]), 30 June 2006, 3.

11. See Edwards and Butler, *Guatemala*, 1.

12. The Guatemalan Truth Commission attributed 96 percent of the human rights violations to the army and the rest to the guerrillas. "U.S. Gives Military Aid," 3. Juan José Rodil Peralta, congressional deputy and formerly minister of the interior and president of the Guatemalan College of Lawyers, estimated that government security forces were responsible for 80 percent of the political-violence killings before 1986, and insurgents for 20 percent. Rodil reported that police and military units would interrogate two hundred to three hundred people and then "shoot them in the street." Edwards and Butler, *Guatemala*, 12.

13. Castillo and Harmon, *Powderburns*, 105. This occurred as the administration of President Jimmy Carter incorporated human rights as a cornerstone of a new U.S. foreign policy.

14. *INCSR* (1989), 103.

15. See "Anunciada depuración," *SV* (GU), 27 March 2002, 4.One of the few drug prosecutions of an army officer involved Lieutenant Randolfo Adonirán Cordón Madrid, sentenced in 1998 by a Zacapa court for storing and trafficking cocaine. "Condenan a catorce años de prisión a ex oficial," *LP* (HO), 20 June 1998, 20A.

Democratization

In the 1980s Guatemala moved from its authoritarian military government to a democracy, with the first elected civilian government assuming office in 1985. However, even as the country has democratized, exceedingly serious problems have persisted. In 1990 conservative legislator Jorge Skinner Klee lamented, "In Guatemala, democracy is an alien plant which we are struggling to keep alive. People may have an intellectual commitment to it, but not an emotional or cultural one, so it is always in jeopardy."[16] As pressure groups vied with one another and with the vestiges of authoritarianism, public doubts concerning the future of elected government multiplied. Would power really be duly transferred after an election? Were the interests of labor, students, indigenous communities, the military, and agricultural and manufacturing elites really compatible? Could Guatemalans routinely engage in political compromise, even with those with whom they bitterly disagreed and had a long violent history?

In fact, although regular elections have been held, the deep democratization of a country like Costa Rica has remained conspicuously absent. Indeed, the give-and-take of a healthy democratic culture has not come naturally to Guatemala, and avoiding constant political gridlock has required more moderation and cooperation, dialogue and deal making, than has been readily forthcoming.[17] Unsurprisingly, wealthy, sophisticated, transnational drug organizations have managed to capitalize on the many travails of a newly democratic state.

The history of Guatemala's turbulent political system helps illuminate the opportunities available to drug traffickers. From its birth as a state Guatemala has often been characterized by an exceptionally violent political life. In 1839, just eighteen years after the country claimed independence from Spain, an English traveler wrote, "There is but one side to the politics in Guatemala. Both parties have a beautiful way of producing unanimity of opinion by driving out of the country all who do not agree with them."[18] A century and a half later, General Héctor Alejandro Gramajo Morales, a prominent minister of defense, bluntly declared to the U.S. Congress: "Political killing is a way of doing things in Guatemala[n] politics." Elsewhere, he summarized the military's thinking as follows: "Our strategic goal has been to reverse Clausewitz's philosophy of war to state that in Guatemala, politics must be the continuation of war."[19] Statistics detailing the assassinations of politicians and other public figures lend credence to Gramajo's observations.[20]

Nevertheless, as democratic movements and human rights campaigns gained regional and international attention in the late 1970s and early 1980s, military leaders changed their strategy. Seeming to tire of simultaneously

16. "Looking Ahead to the Past," *Boston Globe*, 8 October 1990, 2.

17. In a letter to the State Department explaining why Harvard University was terminating its improvement-of-justice program, Philip B. Heymann wrote, "Under current conditions there can be no democracy for the country—there can only be elections among a small privileged club. Without free speech and a right to organize for all non-violent sectors of the country, claims of democracy are a sham. Democracy cannot coexist with unpursued, unpunished terror." U.S. House, *Options*.

18. Goodwin, *Global Studies*, 37–38.

19. U.S. House, *Options*, 5–6, and Schirmer, *Guatemalan Military Project*, 1.

20. In three months in 1994 a UN mission to Guatemala "received reports of 22 political assassinations, 10 attempted assassinations and 68 death threats against priests, labor leaders, teachers, public prosecutors and human rights campaigners." "Secret Guatemalan Military Unit, Linked to CIA, Dies and Is Born Again," *New York Times* (United States) (hereafter cited as *NYT* [US]), 10 April 1995, 8A. In 2007, twenty-two years after Guatemala returned to a democratic regime, more than four dozen candidates and activists were killed during one round of national elections. "Guatemalan Businessman, Ex-general Head to Runoff," *Washington Post* (United States) (hereafter cited as *WP* [US]), 11 September 2007, A14. See also "High-Ranking Murders Stun Guatemala," *Tico Times* (Costa Rica) (hereafter cited as *TT* [CR]), 17 January 2003, 10..

trying to fight the civil war, fend off international critics, and attempt to cope, politically, with Guatemala's many domestic quandaries, the armed forces chose, instead, to appropriate "the imagery of the rule of law, of the mechanisms and procedures of electoral democracy."[21] The armed forces badly wanted an influx of U.S. aid. However, despite being deeply troubled by the situation in Nicaragua, U.S. officials remained hesitant to lavish assistance on a dictatorship extraordinarily abusive of basic rights. Regaining U.S. support was thus one factor influencing Guatemala's military leaders to choose to permit elections, perhaps with the expectation that a patina of civilian leadership could mask the actual control that the army might still exert.

After civilian Marco Vinicio Cerezo Arévalo gained the presidency for the Christian Democrats in 1985, Guatemalan citizens could claim to live in a democratic society, albeit one with a pervasive military influence. Cerezo's administration collaborated with the armed forces in important respects, and it avoided challenging various of their historical prerogatives.[22] Yet, even though the Council of Commanders has remained a potent power center, the most conservative elements of the armed forces have periodically pressed for a return to direct military rule.[23] On two occasions General Gramajo had to stifle coup plots. Furthermore, military officers and a powerful and extremely conservative land-owning class have long funded paramilitary death squads such as the Mano Blanco, or White Hand, linked to numerous terrorist activities and threats against politicians, government employees, military officers, and foreign diplomats.[24]

To a greater degree than in any other Central American state, Guatemala has either failed to assimilate or protect its indigenous population.[25] And, because many of the country's elites long exploited indigenous groups, including stripping them of ownership of the most agriculturally productive land, Guatemala's indigenous communities have tended to be fertile grounds for revolutionary movements. After generations of bloodshed, persecution, and discrimination, many indigenous Guatemalans, who have totaled over half the population, have become thoroughly alienated and isolated from the state.[26] They have also been divided from one another because few could clearly understand multiple indigenous dialects. In the more remote settlements, some have even been unfamiliar with the Spanish spoken by most officials.[27] Consequently, government institutions, especially the court system, have been extraordinarily inaccessible. In spite of democratization some of Guatemala's indigenous have been effectively disenfranchised by arcane and discriminatory voting regulations and informal practices, a state of affairs that is only now starting to change.[28]

Across Latin America, drug organizations have recruited the poverty-stricken and the deeply alienated, those who had little to lose,

21. Schirmer, *Guatemalan Military Project*, 2.

22. For instance, the army assigned a former military intelligence officer, Colonel Julio Enrique Caballeros Seigne, to serve as civilian police chief. When asked who would replace him, General Manuel Antonio Callejas y Callejas responded, "The army hasn't decided yet." Americas Watch, *Closing the Space*, 17.

23. See ibid., 204.

24. See "'Mano Blanca' revela amenazas en Guatemala," *La Nación* (Costa Rica) (hereafter cited as *LN* [CR]), 29 September 1989, 24A.

25. Wilson, "Guatemala," 506.

26. *INCSR* (1988), 125. The percentage of indigenous (who often call themselves *naturales* or *indígenas*, to avoid the stigma associated with *indio*) can only be approximated. For many years Guatemalans termed *ladinos* those who had left indigenous culture behind; some indígenas aspired to the upward social mobility associated with ladinos and chose to label themselves that way. See Wilkinson, *Silence on the Mountain*, 45–47.

27. In 1991 the National Statistics Institute of Guatemala reported that 32 percent of Guatemalans spoke an indigenous language: 29 percent spoke Quiché, 25 percent Kakchiquel, 14 percent Kekchí, and 8 percent Mam; the remaining 24 percent speak other languages such as Pocomchi, Pocoman, Tzutuhil, Chorti, Canjobal, Aguacteco, and Maya. "Estatísticas," *LH* (GU), 15 February 1991, 9.

28. Change came with the 2007 national elections, in which a million first-time voters registered. "For Guatemalan Villagers, Ability to Vote Is a Victory," *WP* (US), 10 September 2007, A11.

whether street children, gang members, or former criminals. Unsurprisingly, then, some Guatemalan indigenous groups became immersed in the drug trade, especially marijuana and opium production. One key military policy, although aimed at a different objective, ended up encouraging this development. As part of the 1982 counterinsurgency campaign General Efraín Ríos Montt organized and armed paramilitary forces called the Guatemalan Civilian Self-Defense Patrols. Hundreds of thousands joined, some of them under intense military pressure, including many indigenous groups, "very poor people who sided with the military for protection."[29] In the mountains of western Guatemala, rather than vigorously searching out guerrillas, these units sometimes opted to guard poppy fields, challenging not only those aiming to steal crops, but authorities sent to eradicate them.

To borrow the phrase used by one DEA agent in the country, key actors involved in the Guatemalan drug trade were "adept at exploiting chaos."[30] All of Guatemala's civilian administrations have confronted very serious domestic ills, led by what President Cerezo called "the scourge of poverty." By the twenty-first century the population approached fourteen million and was quite youthful: fully half under eighteen and almost a third, illiterate. Especially among the lower classes, legitimate prospects for economic advance were scarce. Thus, although from the early 1960s to the mid 1970s the Guatemalan economy expanded at a 5.7 percent annual average, the benefits seldom reached the masses. Instead, as also occurred in Panama, the gulf between rich and poor grew wider during military rule and immediately thereafter.[31] Guatemala consistently reported 60–80 percent of the population in poverty, with the United Nations reporting in 2008 that malnutrition afflicted almost half of Guatemalan children and nearly 70 percent of those from indigenous families.[32]

Although as Guatemala started to democratize it had a healthy intraregional export trade, the bankers, lawyers, factory owners, and other business elites were pocketing the vast bulk of the profits. Even as social expectations started to rise, the economy gradually slid into a marked downturn that alienated much of the middle class: merchants, shopkeepers, skilled laborers, and the like. Held back by a substantial foreign debt and with public attention focused on high rates of inflation and unemployment, democratic governments have often found austerity measures unpalatable.

President Cerezo tried to breezily dismiss three years of his administration, replete with strikes and lockouts, protests, demonstrations, and occasional riots as "the music of democracy," pointing out that a pluralistic democracy could not be built overnight.[33] However, to most Guatemalans, Cerezo's government appeared inept and beleaguered, unable to address effectively the country's deep-seated problems. While he managed to survive coup attempts, the president's popularity plummeted, and poor decisions irretrievably shattered his ability to bring progress to Guatemala. To make matters worse, in the late 1980s coffee prices bottomed out, while oil prices rose. The attention of leading U.S.

29. Castillo and Harmon, *Powderburns*, 116.

30. Ibid., 127. Celerino Castillo used the phrase "adept at exploiting chaos" with respect to alleged trafficker and G-2 operative Socrates Amaury Sofi Pérez.

31. Ebel, "Guatemala," 455, 470, and "Pit Stop on the Cocaine Highway," *WP* (US), 6 October 2004, A20.

32. "Report: Child Malnutrition Rampant in Guatemala," *NT* (CR), 11 April 2008, 6. In the mid-1980s the minister of the interior estimated that under military rule those living in poverty had risen from 66 to 80 percent of the population. A 1992 Guatemalan Planning Board study concluded that 75 percent were poverty-stricken, and 42 percent had no opportunity for education. By the twenty-first century the U.S. government estimated that 83 percent were impoverished, including 90 percent of the indigenous people. See Edwards and Butler, *Guatemala*, 18; "Crime Soars in Guatemala," *Miami Herald* (United States) (hereafter cited as *MH* [US]), 8 January 1992, 3A; Ebel, "Guatemala," 456, 470; and "A Country Turns Upside Down," *Economist*, 17 May 2003, 56.

33. "Guatemala President Stars in Political Drama," *NYT* (US), 24 June 1990, 14

policy makers was diverted away from Central America and toward the crumbling of the Soviet bloc. With the rejection of the Sandinistas in Nicaraguan elections, foreign assistance aimed at bolstering capitalist systems seemed less vital and began to wane. Mired in civil war well after peace had come to Nicaragua and El Salvador, Guatemala must have seemed to its increasingly cynical and alienated citizenry to be well-nigh ungovernable.

Although political violence had paused while the civilian government took power, within three years it had surged again.[34] When Jorge Serrano Elías, a conservative evangelical Christian, won the presidency in 1990, unemployment stood at 41 percent; inflation had increased fivefold in three years; the price of basic food items had risen 500 percent in four years; and the government, facing its highest deficit, had skipped short-term foreign debt payments. In 1991 Guatemala owed $787 million, yet could count only $2.6 million in the national treasury. The tax, customs, and criminal-justice systems were corrupted shambles; education, public health, and social security badly needed modernization. Law enforcement was wholly inadequate.[35]

A few bright spots stood out. Serrano initially succeeded in persuading the armed forces and the rebels to participate in genuine peace negotiations. The ongoing talks, coupled with a series of military victories over guerrilla forces, caused political killings to diminish noticeably for a period. Rigorous economic measures had brought about some encouraging national indicators. By the spring of 1993, however, the Serrano administration had become deeply unpopular. The president appeared unable to end the civil war, stem ongoing military human rights abuses, or even fashion the political compromises that might halt the constant strikes and protests.

As the government's grip slipped and rioting started in earnest, Serrano Elías attempted a "self-coup" that would have enabled him to rule by decree until a new legislative assembly could be elected. This not only further provoked his many opponents, but caused the United States to threaten trade sanctions if the democratic system were subverted. Eventually, the military negotiated a settlement that removed Serrano, who then avoided eleven pending criminal charges by accepting political asylum in Panama, and the Guatemalan Congress elected human rights activist Ramiro de Leon Carpio to serve out Serrano's term.[36] The country's third transitional president thereupon advanced new proposals that brought some progress in the peace talks. The next conservative president, Álvaro Arzú Irigoyen, dismissed eight of the country's sixteen generals and further shook up the lower officer corps.[37] After more protracted negotiations, the national government and the Guatemalan National Revolutionary Unity signed accords in 1996, ending thirty-five years of civil war.

And so, by the end of the century, a fragile peace prevailed in Guatemala. A Truth Commission was assembled to investigate civil war atrocities; however, assailants murdered one of its authors two days after its publication.[38] According to a United Nations verification team, four years after the peace settlement was signed, 119 provisions had yet to be

34. In 1990, although 550 investigations from 1989 remained unresolved, special prosecutor for human rights Ramiro de Leon Carpio opened 250 new murder investigations, noting, "In 1988, violence of all types began to escalate . . . threats and intimidation, disappearances, illegal detention and murders." "Guatemalan Violence on the Upswing," *Chicago Tribune*, 30 September 1990, 6C.

35. Ibid., and "Democracy in Guatemala," *Washington Times* (United States) (hereafter cited as *WT* [US]), 15 November 1990, G2.

36. "Guatemala reactivirá pedido de extradición de Jorge Serrano," *La Prensa* (Panama) (hereafter cited as *LP* [PA]), 12 April 1996, 4A.

37. "Guatemala's New President Shakes Up Army and Police," *NYT* (US), 7 February 1996, A11.

38. "Reaching the Untouchables: Guatemala and Organised Crime," *Economist*, 13 March 2010, 44.

implemented, and only 6 percent of Guatemalans polled felt the accords remained important.[39] During the peace process thousands of Guatemalan soldiers, paramilitaries, and guerrilla fighters had been demobilized, yet a huge number of weapons, perhaps as many as 1.5 million, were never recovered.[40] And peace, welcome as it was, delivered new problems, including rising drug use and rapidly climbing violent-crime rates. Also troubling was the fact that despite the disbanding of certain groups and disarming of others, many military and police authorities continued to act with impunity. The frequent political gridlock interfered with efforts to reform the administration of justice.

After its first peace-time elections in decades occurred in 1999, the country elected populist Alfonso Portillo to the presidency; he governed from 2000 to 2004. However, reflective of the deep splits in the population, voters chose former General Ríos Montt, a born-again Christian called "one of the last caudillos in Latin American politics," to lead the Congress.[41] Ríos Montt had taken the reins of the military in the early 1980s, a period marked by gruesome massacres during counterinsurgency. In his civilian political career, he had cultivated a no-nonsense popular image of refusing to yield to crime and corruption, and he used this reputation to revive his political fortunes.

This image gained the general political traction because, even by Central American standards, Portillo's administration had been spectacularly corrupt. When the president fled to Mexico in 2004, he faced charges of embezzling in excess of $15 million, and his vice president and nine other top officials were in jail charged with corruption.[42] Guatemala's most respected newspaper, *Siglo Veintiuno*, was alleging that military and civilian officials close to Portillo had secretly deposited millions from drug trafficking and embezzlement in a state bank prior to transferring the funds abroad. Portillo's name was eventually linked to $50 million in fourteen bank accounts, and in January 2010 Guatemalan authorities managed to arrest him on the point of land across from Puerto Barrios, as he prepared to flee by speedboat into Belize.[43]

Domestic problems during democratization have spilled over into international cooperation. Politicians have attempted to win votes and deflect attention from dire domestic problems by appeals to Guatemalan nationalism. Given their unsettled territorial claims, even civilian governments have thus typically had abysmal relations with neighboring Belize. Even more important, when interception rates flattened or outrageous narco-corruption surfaced, relations with the U.S. government turned frosty. For many years, because treaties signed at the turn of the nineteenth century governed extradition requests by the United States and other countries, relatively few criminal suspects were sent abroad to face justice.[44] Unlike many of its

39. See "Guatemalan Peace Promises Not Kept," *TT* (CR), 2 February 2001, 10.

40. Costa Rica's Arias Foundation for Peace and Human Progress suggested this figure; see "Region Takes Aim at Weapons Traffickers," *TT* (CR), 7 December 2001, 5.

41. "Country Turns Upside Down," 56.

42. The accusations in this "Panama Connection" case were aired not only in major foreign newspapers, such as the *Washington Post*, but also through investigative journalism jointly carried out by *Siglo Veintiuno* and Panama's *La Prensa*. See "Portillo en la mira de EE.UU.," *SV* (GU), 21 January 2004, 2; "Sacan dinero a Panamá," *SV* (GU), 5 March 2002, 2–3; "La conexión Panamá al desnudo," *SV* (GU), 10 March 2002, 7; "Conexión Panamá, un ejemplo de impunidad," *SV* (GU), 2 January 2003, 6; and "$50 millones vinculados a Portillo," *SV* (GU), 22 January 2004, 2–3. For his U.S. court case, see "Fiscalía de NY: Portillo robó y lavó 'decenas de millones,'" *SV* (GU), 26 January 2010, 2. See also "Endurance of Corruption Shakes Guatemala Anew," *WP* (US), 11 March 2006, A1.

43. "Portillo en la cárcel," *SV* (GU), 29 January 2010, 8.

44. Up to 2005 extraditions to Mexico proceeded under an 1895 treaty, thereby eliminating extraditions for such modern offenses as money laundering. See "Guatemala y México ratifican tratado de extradición," *SV* (GU), 31 March 2005, 6. Until a new extradition treaty was signed with the United States in 2008, a 1940 protocol to the U.S.-Guatemala extradition treaty of 1903 added narcotics crimes to the list of extraditable offenses. See *INCSR* (2006), 143, and *INCSR* (2009), 288. From 1903 to 1989 a mere sixteen Guatemalans were extradited to the United States. "Dieciséis guatemaltecos han sufrido ya la extradición a Estados Unidos," *LH* (GU), 11 February 1989, 4.

Central American neighbors, Guatemala failed to enhance cooperation with U.S. authorities through a bilateral mutual legal assistance treaty.[45] Even a maritime counterdrug agreement with the United States was not signed until 2003–4.[46] This, combined with few naval resources and erratic control of ports, helped make the country's waters an attractive target for traffickers.

Drug-smuggling organizations have readily exploited the vulnerabilities inherent in Guatemalan democratization. Overwhelmed governments, a fractured country, restive military officers, a violent society full of uncontrolled weapons: all of these were characteristics that those looking to establish promising Central American routes and then maximize the flow of drugs down them could capitalize on. The transnational drug organizations that found opportunities in postcolonial Belize and newly developed Costa Rica were highly unlikely to overlook the possibilities of slowly democratizing Guatemala.

Government Institutions

While across Central America key institutions have functioned in a manner that drug-trafficking networks could take advantage of, poor design, mismanagement, and corruption have been especially pronounced in Guatemala. Moreover, Guatemalan laws and procedures have often been crafted in a way that fostered high levels of drug trafficking. For example, traditionally, not only did the Guatemalan penal code not recognize the crime of conspiracy, but all prison sentences of five years or less were commutable, that is, could be cancelled or reduced by a per diem fine.[47]

As Guatemala democratized, even such fundamental institutions as the police, courts, and prisons lacked resources, transparency, and popular support. In 1991 Dr. Edmundo Vásquez Martínez, former president of the Supreme Court of Justice, argued that the administration of justice continued to resemble that of the colonial epoch, characterizing it as "bureaucratic, secretive, depersonalized, . . . slow, . . . overcrowded, lacking in the general confidence of the citizens, costly, divorced from social life, uncontrollable, [and] acting with impunity."[48] Prosecutors have been especially weak, the courts especially corruptible, and the tradition of elite impunity especially strong. These flaws plainly contributed to the grave difficulties Guatemala has experienced in stemming the drug trade. Although in minor cases of growing, dealing, or possessing drugs the penalties prescribed under Guatemalan law might be imposed, to try to convict local or foreign traffickers of any magnitude has often exceeded the capacity of the criminal-justice system, at least as long as authorities had failed to catch suspects with large quantities of drugs.[49]

Furthermore, military, political, and social elites have failed to promote, indeed have lacked much faith in, the ideal of a rule of law. Many have neither supported nor worked to develop a legal system with an independent and respected judiciary in which no individual is above the law, law enforcement is undertaken evenhandedly, individual rights are guaranteed, and the law protects individuals from the actions of others, including authorities.[50] Moreover, democratization has proceeded with little

45. Money-laundering legislation passed in 2001 contained limited conspiracy provisions, and in 2003 Guatemala signed a multilateral mutual legal assistance treaty under OAS auspices. *INCSR* (2004), 19.

46. In 2004 Guatemala signed the maritime agreement, in part to help get the country removed from the U.S. government blacklist for countries not cooperating against drug trafficking. "New deal with U.S. to combat drug trafficking," Intelligence Research (United Kingdom), 26 January 2004.

47. See Fowler and Bunck, "Legal Imperialism," 823. See also "Harris Verdict Expected Today in Guatemala," *TT* (CR), 30 January 2004, 12.

48. "Vásquez Martínez critica actual justicia penal," *LH* (GU), 23 November 1991, 7.

49. *INCSR* (1990), 178.

50. For more on the rule-of-law ideal, see Fowler, *With Justice For All?*, 7–8.

attention to improving institutional accountability. The government has not functioned such that supervisory entities have regularly and critically evaluated the way that assigned tasks were being implemented, nor have comprehensible critiques, meant to be absorbed and acted upon, been communicated to subordinates. In short, Guatemalan institutions have lacked accountability.[51] Thus, key ingredients, important for strengthened democratic governance, have been absent in Guatemala.

If malfunctioning institutions have formed one bridge-favoring factor, political instability has contributed to their problems. During its democratic transition Guatemala has experienced ongoing, extraordinary turnover in government personnel, even within the same administration. Between January 2000 and March 2003 the Guatemalan government had four ministers of government, seven directors of the National Civilian Police, and eleven directors of the key counternarcotics unit.[52] Such lack of continuity has badly hampered policy making and the investigation and prosecution of criminal organizations.

As regional drug-trafficking began to mount, Guatemalan law enforcement was shaky. Traditionally, the most publicly prominent of the several police forces was the Guardia de Hacienda, or Rural Guard, which by the mid-1980s totaled about eleven thousand officers. Not only have there been few police relative to a population of approximately nine million, but inadequate training and very low salaries have afflicted law enforcement and police morale. After years of negligent and brutal police work, the public has typically held officers in low esteem, with some scorning them as "subhuman."[53] Lack of faith in the criminal-justice system has been reflected in the frequency with which mobs have lynched criminal suspects, rather than subjecting them to the official administration of justice.[54]

Infrequent citizen cooperation has then contributed to faulty investigations in a mutually reinforcing negative spiral. In congressional testimony concerning a legal-assistance program in Guatemala that Harvard Law School had chosen to terminate, Philip Heymann, director of Harvard's Center for Criminal Justice, declared, "The most important failure is that citizens of Guatemala do not believe in their criminal justice system. They believe it is corrupt. They believe correctly that intimidation is everywhere. They believe that there are powerful people, including the security forces, who are immune to the criminal justice system. . . . As long as the citizens do not believe in the criminal justice system, even ordinary crime cannot be satisfactorily investigated. Citizen cooperation is simply the sine qua non for every country that I know of in investigating ordinary crime."[55]

Given deeply flawed work by the civilian police, the military long imposed much of the order that could be found. Within the country,

51. "For an entity to be seen as properly accountable, duties must be defined, a clear and effective hierarchy must be established in which one entity brings another to account, an adequate accounting to an appropriate body must occur, the results of the external evaluation must be communicated effectively to the entity being evaluated, and the assessment must then be absorbed and ideally acted upon in some productive manner." Fowler, "Different United Nations," 39.

52. See "EE.UU. asesora formación de la SAIA," *SV* (GU), 22 January 2003, 3, and *INCSR* (2002), 12.

53. By 1990 the salaries of ordinary police officers stood at several hundred dollars a month, and officers injured in the line of duty received only a third of their normal pay, not even as much as a sick worker on a coffee plantation would have received in the 1940s after President Juan José Arévalo's labor reforms. Wilkinson, *Silence on the Mountain*, 98; Fowler and Bunck, "Legal Imperialism," 823–24; "Crime Soars in Guatemala," *MH* (US), 8 January 1992, 3A.

54. U.S. House, *Options*, 5. In 2001 a Guatemalan Catholic Church human rights spokesperson noted, "Lynchings reflect the culture of violence that took root in Guatemala during the war." "Guatemalan Mobs Are the Law of the Land," *TT* (CR), 20 July 2001, 8. In 2005 the UN mission assessing compliance with the peace accords reported that mobs had lynched more than four hundred criminal suspects since 1996. "Suspected Gang Member Hacked to Death in Guatemala," *NT* (CR), 6 January 2006, N3. In 2009 mobs killed forty-nine criminal suspects. "Reaching the Untouchables," 44.

55. See generally "Secret Guatemalan Military Unit," 8A.

the most feared institution of the armed forces was the intelligence unit G-2, known to Guatemalans as La Dos (The Two) or El Archivo (The Archives).[56] For many years La Dos formed the institutional apex of Guatemala's military state. Relying on extensive wiretaps and numerous informants, the G-2 ran death squads and used its own agents to seize, interrogate, and often torture and murder suspected opponents of the regime, including criminals. The G-2's impact on the drug trade was mixed. While effective in tallying drug seizures and neutralizing particular traffickers and networks, military-intelligence officers could also be corrupted. Seized assets were not necessarily turned over to the state, and sometimes a portion of captured drugs was resold on the domestic market or planted on people that G-2 officers wished to arrest.[57]

The military, as a whole, while a strong and stable institution in certain respects, has also remained rigid and inflexible, insufficiently accountable, and prone to corruption as well as abusive behavior. During the civil war its dominant position with respect to matters of national security, broadly interpreted, led not only to tight control over particular zones of the country but to significant military influence in overseeing customs, ports, airstrips, and airports. Certain military officers were thus well positioned to assist, and profit from, the drug trade. As democratization occurred, as troop levels were drawn down, and as military officers looked about for new lucrative undertakings that might capitalize on their experience and connections, international drug trafficking proved to be an attractive option for some. Early in the twenty-first century a report from the Canadian Disarmament Information Service claimed that retired Guatemalan officers had converted their entire units into criminal enterprises: "These former soldiers possess intimate knowledge of the nation's facilities that in the past were used in covert operations, such as secluded landing strips, and safe houses for the monitoring of local populations. This knowledge, along with an easy access to weapons, has facilitated the expansion of the drug trade and incidents of political intimidation, making attempts to restrain drug trafficking more difficult."[58]

The signing of the peace accords in 1996 thus further highlighted institutional weaknesses welcomed by drug traffickers. Civilian police have usually been thoroughly overwhelmed by a quagmire of street crime, robberies, and murders. As the civil war receded, youth formed about four hundred street gangs—including branches of Mara Salvatrucha and Mara 18, active in Guatemala since at least 1990. Gang activities intersected with the drug trade and demonstrated how organized crime could confound authorities and threaten social order.[59] Smoking crack cocaine as well as selling it, some maras have gone to work for drug rings to gain the income needed to maintain their addiction.[60] Whether their target has been

56. For the G-2's handling of drug cases, see Castillo and Harmon, *Powderburns*, 122, 197–202.

57. For a summary of the Canadian Disarmament Information Service report, see "Outside View: Guatemala's Drug Woes," United Press International (United States) (hereafter cited as UPI [US]), 27 February 2003. U.S. counter-narcotics authorities likewise observed that demobilization "added to the nation's unemployment problems, and provided a large population vulnerable to international drug traffickers." DEA, *Resources, Guatemala* (2001), 3.

58. In the 1980s Salvadoran immigrants in Los Angeles created Mara Salvatrucha, also known as MS-13. "Salva" was short for El Salvador, and "trucha" is slang for "watch out." Branches of the gang soon sprung up in El Salvador, Guatemala, Honduras, and southern Mexico. See "Police Arrest Nine M.S. Gang Members in Miami," *NT* (CR), 21 January 2005, N-3. See also *Lopez-Soto v. Ashcroft*, 383 F.2d 230, and "Poor Neighbors Fall Prey to U.S. Gang Culture," *Guardian* (United Kingdom), 28 May 2003, 12.

59. According to leading drug prosecutor Fernando Mendizábal, some maras have worked for traffickers as assassins. See "Pit Stop," A20, and "ONU: Crece tráfico de drogas en maras," *SV* (GU), 2 March 2005, 16.

60. In 2000 U.S. government lamented the "mixture of corruptness and ineptness [that] has limited the effectiveness" of the special narcotics prosecutor's office, while citing an "intimidated and corrupt judiciary" as the reason the Guatemalan criminal-justice system had failed to prosecute and convict major traffickers." *INCSR* (2000), 165.

gang members, drug traffickers, or elites deeply involved in the drug trade, Guatemalan authorities have been unable to prosecute, convict, and imprison those engaged in organized crime at a rate that would deter others from joining.[61] In 2000 the Inter-American Development Bank listed Guatemala as one of the five most violent countries in the world.[62] By 2006 the country's murder rate had reached forty per one hundred thousand, four times the world's average, and it then ascended even more rapidly, reaching fifty-two per hundred thousand in 2006 and fifty-six per hundred thousand in 2008.[63]

In 1990 one participant in Guatemalan legal-reform efforts went so far as to state, "Worrying about defendants' rights is inappropriate in Guatemala since virtually no one gets convicted."[64] Indeed, horrendous conviction rates have reflected the system's many deep-rooted problems. In 1999 a U.S. government report noted that police officers had failed to execute arrest warrants "in an overwhelming percentage of cases." Among other problems, they could not pursue fugitives effectively, particularly in remote areas. In 2003 the national police released statistics stating that of 50,250 arrests, only 48 cases went to trial. In 2006 law professor Philip Alston, serving as the UN special investigator to Guatemala on extrajudicial, summary, or arbitrary executions, declared, "It's sad to say, Guatemala is a good place in which to commit a murder. Your chances of being committed and punished are staggeringly low." Indeed, when a serious conviction threatened, it was not unusual for suspects to deal with the problem by killing the prosecutor or judge.[65]

In fact, a key part of the problem with Guatemalan criminal justice is that the judiciary, a weak and harried institution, has often been intimidated and violently attacked, while repeatedly being denounced for its lack of autonomy, impartiality, and independence.[66] Pressure has often been exerted by criminals and officials alike; indeed, officials engaged in criminal behavior might have been the worst offenders.[67] In 2000, 76 judges reported threats, 1 was lynched, and 1 was attacked in a hail of seventeen bullets. Between 2001 and 2003 the Supreme Court reported that more than 130 judges had been threatened, and in 2003, after 27 judges had received death threats in a six-week period, Guatemala's human rights ombudsman, Sergio Morales, declared, "We are convinced of the existence of clandestine groups that operate without any type of control . . . formed by people in and out of government. . . . Their goal is impunity."[68]

Drug organizations, expert at wielding bribes, bullets, and intimidation, have repeatedly exploited Guatemala's weak judicial institution. In 2001 a judicial oversight body investigated one judge who in a six-month period had absolved numerous traffickers, including suspects

61. "The Most Violent Area in the Americas," *TT* (CR), 18 August 2000, 9.

62. See "Gang Riots in Guatemalan Prisons Claim Six Lives," *NT* (CR), 26 May 2006, 3; "Wave of Violence Grips Guatemala," *NT* (CR), 10 February 2006, 3; and "Istmo: País repunta en muertes violentas," *SV* (GU), 6 March 2009, 2.

63. Confidential interview, July 1990, Guatemala City, Guatemala.

64. *INCSR* (1999), 157; "Marero desnuda debilidad del sistema de justicia," *SV* (GU), 7 February 2005, 4; "U.N. Panel to Probe Guatemala Mob Crime," *TR* (BZ), 17 December 2006, insert 11; "Guatemalan Prosecutor Shot Dead," *TR* (BZ), 22 May 2005, 26; "Gunmen Kill Guatemalan Judge," *TR* (BZ), 1 May 2005, 27; "Se disparan ataques contra juristas," *SV* (GU), 10 August 2009, 2.

65. For criticism by the OAS Inter-American Commission on Human Rights, see Edwards and Butler, *Guatemala*, 2.

66. In 1991 Supreme Court president Vásquez Martínez publicly declared, "The authorities are the ones who threaten the judges and interfere with the administration of justice." "Vásquez Martínez: 'Las autoridades son las que amenazan a los jueces,'" *LH* (GU), 12 October 1991, 8.

67. See "Outside View," and "Armed Groups Threaten Guatemalan Judges," *TT* (CR), 21 February 2003, 10.

68. "Amplían protección a jueces," *SV* (GU), 16 March 2002, 8; "Leve sanción a magistrados," *SV* (GU), 9 March 2002, 7; "Suspenden libertad a jueza," *SV* (GU), 7 March 2002, 11; "CSJ suspende de nuevo a jueza," *SV* (GU), 30 July 2001, 10; "OJ sacude a cinco juzgadores," *SV* (GU), 4 July 2001, 2.

arrested with 380 and 937 kilos of cocaine, and found sixty-eight irregularities in drug cases. Later that same year, judges in Cobán released on bail four traffickers who had been caught transporting 170 kilos of cocaine. A Judicial Discipline Committee termed this a "grave" error, yet it imposed a three-month suspension, rather than firing the judges, concluding that they had acted ineptly and ignorantly, rather than in bad faith.[69]

As Guatemala has struggled with its democratic transition, pride, esprit de corps, and professionalism in government institutions have often been lacking. Guatemalan prisons have been a case in point. After 184 prisoners, including a number of drug traffickers, escaped the Guatemalan penal system in a seven-year period, a Commission on the Transformation of the Penitentiary System found that in 2000 prison guards were earning less than two hundred dollars a month and had been supplied with weapons in poor condition, little ammunition or communications equipment, not even any uniforms or boots to wear. Under such adverse conditions, despairing officials have sometimes given up. For instance, in 1996 prisoners were permitted to take over Pavón prison. While authorities controlled the perimeter, a committee of inmates took charge inside the complex. After a decade of this regime, prisoners had built shops, churches, and restaurants. However, one convicted murderer was reportedly earning $12,500 per month by renting inmates lots to build on. After complaints, three thousand Guatemalan security forces stormed the prison in 2006, and inmates resisted with guns, knives, and grenades. The authorities reportedly confiscated 150 guns and a cocaine facility, and a Colombian trafficker was killed in the shoot-out, emerging from his two-story house that featured high-speed internet and a widescreen television.[70]

In fact, Guatemalan prisons have been symptomatic of larger problems. With tax collection ineffective and evasion commonplace, in 2010 the central government budget amounted to just 13.7 percent of gross domestic product, the lowest rate in Latin America.[71] With revenues inadequate to enable the government to pay wages employees could live on, corruption has long infected virtually all government functions.[72] As it transitioned from authoritarianism, Guatemala has lacked transparent procedures, aggressive investigative journalists, and police and prosecutors prepared to uncover long-standing corrupt practices. So, when drug traffickers have reached police, judges, politicians, or prison officials with large sums in hand, they have found many officials eager to be bribed. In 1990, two-time chief of police and former G-2 director Julio Enrique Caballeros Seigne noted that drug-smuggling organizations have not needed a sophisticated intelligence system to determine which officials might be corruptible. "It's much easier than that," Caballeros maintained. "Just offer the money."[73]

Although on the whole Guatemala's institutions have functioned very poorly in contending with the drug trade, the record does seem to show this weak state retreating, persisting, and reasserting itself as it responded to transnational crime. Democratization did bring a number of notable institutional changes. Among the positive steps, in the mid-1990s a package of reforms to modernize the administration of justice included the creation of an office of special prosecutor for narcotics crimes. In 1997, of a total case load of more than 850, the drug prosecutors tried about three dozen cases of

69. "Guardia vinculada con fuga," *SV* (GU), 14 January 2000, 12; "Guatemalan Authorities Linked to Jailbreak," *TT* (CR), 13 July 2001, 11; "Guatemala Seizes Control of Jail," *TR* (BZ), 1 October 2006, 34; and "Pandilleros decapitan a subdirector de penal," *LP* (HO), 3 May 2008, 55.

70. "Reaching the Untouchables," 44.

71. *INCSR* (2009), 307. Not until 1995 did the government increase police compensation, including two levels of risk bonuses for antidrug work. *INCSR* (1996), 132.

72. Julio Enrique Caballeros Seigne, interview, 18 July 1990, Guatemala City, Guatemala.

73. *INCSR* (1998), 140; *INCSR* (1999), 155; *INCSR* (2000), 168; *INCSR* (2001), 5:20; and *INCSR* (2002), 5:22–23.

major narcotics trafficking, gaining thirty-two convictions and sentences ranging from twelve- to twenty-year prison terms. Similarly, a new Port Security Program (PSP) provided better interdiction capabilities against maritime drug trafficking, and international funding and cooperation helped to enhance the use of computers and intelligence sharing. In one eighteen-month period starting in 1998 PSP authorities seized a total of five hundred thousand dollars and fully 4.9 tons of cocaine. In 2001 a rapid response Antismuggling Unit had some success by randomly visiting sea and land border points and searching for drugs. Then in 2008, to transport antidrug personnel swiftly to remote transshipment locations, Guatemala created the Aerial Anti-drug and Terrorist Interventions Force, aimed at better projecting state power into the countryside.[74]

While beneficial, these initiatives have by no means reversed, or even halted, the trend toward ever more acute drug-trafficking problems. Chief among these has been endemic official corruption. Drug syndicates have readily penetrated the police, military, and judiciary; customs and immigration; and politicians. Unlike Costa Rica, with its legislative subcommittees leading assertive investigations, Guatemala has typically relied on the Ministry of Government to look into drug corruption.[75] But, the ministry, saddled with many other responsibilities, has evinced little interest in seriously investigating trafficking involving elites. Equally important, while the media's role in exposing corruption has been hailed in many countries, Guatemalan journalists have so regularly been threatened or killed that few have investigated and publicized narco-corruption.[76]

A thoroughly corrupt society exerts a magnetic pull on trafficking organizations, because corruption can neutralize legal reforms and law enforcement alike, while greatly diminishing interdiction risks. In Guatemala bribery by traffickers has been chronic, audacious, and seldom punished. Corrupted officials have sometimes so intervened in the drug trade as to metamorphose into traffickers themselves. Early in 2002 corrupt antidrug officers seized the tiny town of Chocón, north of Lake Izabal and less than ten miles from the southwestern corner of Belize. They tortured and killed two residents while attempting to steal two tons of cocaine stored there.[77] In another case, although Department of Antinarcotics Operations (DOAN) agents reported confiscating five hundred kilos of cocaine from a speedboat, in fact, investigations revealed that they had absconded with three-fourths of a two-thousand-kilo shipment.[78] Eventually, the U.S. government estimated that in 2002 DOAN employees had stolen twice the amount of cocaine they had reportedly seized.[79] That same year, both the United States and the European Union criticized the Guatemalan government's tolerance of the drug trade after fifteen tons of cocaine vanished from the police warehouse, and five hundred documents, including evidence of trafficking by civilian and military officials, disappeared from DOAN's antidrug information center.[80]

In 2003 assistant secretary of state Otto Reich reported to the U.S. Congress that in Guatemala drug traffickers had "very close ties

74. Interview with Roberto Adolfo Valle Valdizán (deputy, president of the Commission on Government, and former minister of government, 1988–89), July 1990, Guatemala City, Guatemala.

75. See the statements by OAS secretary-general César Gaviria and George Muñoz of the Overseas Private Investment Corporation. "Press Hailed as Graft Foe," *TT* (CR), 7 April 2000, 7.

76. See "Fiscal denuncia intimidación," *SV* (GU), 25 January 2003, 9.

77. *INCSR* (2002), 5:22–23.

78. *INCSR* (2003), 5:21.

79. See "Anunciada depuración," *SV* (GU), 27 March 2002, 4; "Auditan bodegas del DOAN," *SV* (GU), 28 March 2002, 5; "Guatemala admite roces con EE.UU.," *LN* (CR), 21 December 2002, 18; and "Estados Unidos y UE presignan a Guatemala," *SV* (GU), 21 January 2003, 4.

80. Agence France Presse, quoted in "Guatemalan President to Discuss Reich's 'Abusive Remarks' with U.S. President," *Financial Times* (United Kingdom) (hereafter

to the highest levels of government, and [they] exercise influence in decisions, especially those related to appointments in the Armed Forces and the Government Ministry."[81] Although President Portillo denounced Reich's "abusive remarks," shortly thereafter, Jorge Paredes, Guatemala's director of antidrug operations, declared of the Portillo years, "Guatemala was a paradise for . . . [drug smugglers]. There was total freedom, a green light for narcos for three full years. . . . The government of Guatemala lost its will to attack the problem."[82]

Eventually, top Guatemalan officials chose to disband the thoroughly discredited DOAN and replace it with the Anti-narcotics Analysis and Information Services (SAIA).[83] However, extensive efforts to remove suspect officers and to vet applicants through polygraph exams and other means could not forestall drug corruption for long. In 2005 corruption at the pinnacle of the SAIA surfaced when Adán Castillo Aguilar, director of the country's counternarcotics agency; his top deputy, Jorge Aguilar García; and Rubilio Orlando Palacios, the chief of police at the Santo Tomás de Castilla port, met with undercover DEA informants who allegedly extracted their promise to protect a cocaine shipment through Guatemala in exchange for a bribe of twenty-five thousand dollars. After a grand jury indictment had been procured, the DEA prevailed upon the three to attend a U.S. antidrug conference. Upon arrival, each was arrested on charges of planning to import cocaine, and after confronting the evidence, Castillo and Aguilar pled guilty.[84]

In 2008 Guatemalan legislators approved a United Nations–staffed International Commission Against Impunity in Guatemala (CICIG) to critique and assist in the administration of justice.[85] The 180 CICIG members were charged with strengthening the Guatemalan court system, while identifying and punishing criminal organizations at work within government institutions. Traditionally, the seriously understaffed office of public prosecutor had its role in the trial process interpreted quite narrowly, and prosecutors had rarely played a weighty part in most trial processes.[86] CICIG has helped to enhance the role of prosecutors, influencing the legislature to grant the ability to wiretap, plea-bargain, and use special courts.

Commission members have also investigated crime, including allegations of official corruption, in more competent, sophisticated, and even-handed ways. In 2009 Spanish jurist Carlos Castresana announced that CICIG had identified key clandestine groups active in Guatemala and would expose them and their leaders and bring them to justice.[87] The following year, however, Castresana resigned after Guatemalan officials disassembled the special team of CICIG prosecutors. Although CICIG did manage to take a leading role in certain important narco-corruption cases, whether its efforts will have a lasting impact

cited as *FT* [UK]). The United States was concerned about officials such as Francisco Ortega Menaldo, a close Portillo adviser, whose U.S. visa was revoked for suspected involvement in trafficking. "Nations' Efforts Against Drugs Slow," *WT* (US), 2 February 2003, A3.

81. "Sluggish Anti-drug Efforts to Help Guatemalan Smuggling Gang Flourish," Associated Press (United States) (hereafter cited as AP [US]), 2 September 2003.

82. See "EE.UU. asesora formación de la SAIA," *SV* (GU), 22 January 2003, 3.

83. *INCSR* (2006), 11, 143; *INCSR* (2009), 307; "Reaching the Untouchables," 44; "EU arresta al jefe antidrogas de Guatemala," *LP* (PA), 17 November 2005, 29A; "Endurance of Corruption," A1; "Guatemalan President Steps Up Fight Against Mexican Drug Cartels," BBC Monitoring Latin America, 15 October 2006.

84. See "UN Team to Investigate Organized Crime in Guatemala," *TT* (CR), 25 January 2008, 4.

85. Fowler and Bunck, "Legal Imperialism," 823. The mere forty-one prosecutors Guatemala employed in 1990 dropped the following year to twenty-four. See Heymann et al., *Criminal Justice Project*, 75, and "Procurador de la nación llegó a la policía," *LH* (GU), 28 February 1991, 8.

86. "CICIG ha identificado a grupos clandestinos," *SV* (GU), 7 November 2009, 3.

87. See "Reaching the Untouchables," 44. The Organized Crime Bill of 2007, as amended in 2009, approved the use of wire intercepts and enabled the state to reduce a sentence or choose not to prosecute should a suspect cooperate. *INCSR* (2009), 307.

remains to be seen. In fact, various suggestions for sweeping reforms met with foot-dragging, and the scope of the problems that must be addressed before Guatemala can effectively administer justice remains sobering.[88] Relations among the police, prosecutors, and judges have long been dismal, with each bitterly criticizing the other, and investigations have been particularly inept, with evidence frequently mishandled and arrest reports left incomplete.[89]

In 2009 U.S. counternarcotics authorities declared that weak Guatemalan law-enforcement agencies remained corrupted, intimidated, and underfunded, circumstances that cartels took advantage of to transfer more operations into the country. That August yet another scandal erupted after three police officers stopped a pickup on the Pan-American Highway and discovered three hundred thousand dollars in a secret compartment. National police chief Porfirio Pérez Paniagua, however, ordered the driver released, apparently because he was a personal friend. After receiving a tip about Pérez's actions, the Office of Professional Responsibility and then the CICIG investigated. Eventually, they alleged that Pérez had led a fifth column within the police, a criminal structure dedicated to stealing drugs and drug profits from traffickers.[90]

In 2010 evidence of narco-corruption in the top echelons of Guatemalan law enforcement surfaced once more. Five SAIA agents were ambushed and killed while apparently investigating a suspicious truck parked in an industrial complex on the outskirts of Amatitlán, a small city on a lake south of Guatemala City on the highway leading to the Pacific coast. Authorities who responded to the shooting found 353 kilos of cocaine and a huge arsenal that included eight land mines, eleven 30-caliber machine guns, and 584 hand grenades, as well as clothing, including bullet-proof vests, identical to that used by the national police.

Additional complexities soon surfaced. Curiously, the SAIA agents had not informed anyone that they were headed to the industrial park, nor were prosecutors immediately apprised of the incident. Eventually, investigators determined that the actual mission of the five dead agents had been to steal the drugs, that they had made off with 700 kilos and were killed as they returned for the remaining 350 kilos. Worse still, five officers from the antidrug division of the National Civilian Police were implicated in the murders. Further investigations suggested that the criminal structure within the force to which they belonged reached police chief Baltazar Gómez Barrios and the director of the Antinarcotics Analysis and Investigation Division, Nelly Judith Bonilla Estrada. They were both arrested, as was the director of the police's port authority in Izabal, Fernando Carrillo García.[91]

The Evolution of Drug Trafficking in Guatemala

The Guatemalan Marijuana Trade

Most Guatemalans living outside urban areas have belonged to poor subsistence farm families, and a number of these have long produced

88. For statements to this effect by a judge, the chief public defender, and the national police director, see "Persecución penal es inoperante," *SV* (GU), 8 February 2005, 6–7, and "Marero desnuda al sistema de justicia," *SV* (GU), 13 February 2005, 9.

89. "Juez envía a la cárcel a ex director de PNC," *SV* (GU), 29 August 2009, 2; "MP: Ex director de PNC lideraba grupo criminal," *SV* (GU), 13 November 2009, 2; "Capturan a director de la PNC y a jefe antidrogas," *SV* (GU), 3 March 2010, 4. Late in 2009 a judge found insufficient evidence of illicit association and drug trafficking and hence narrowed the case against Pérez to charges related to the money released. "Procesan a ex jefe de PNC por robo de droga," *SV* (GU), 27 November 2009, 6.

90. "Los Zetas acribillan a cinco agentes de la SAIA," *SV* (GU), 25 April 2009, 3; "Hallan 353 kilos de cocaína en Amatitlán," *SV* (GU), 26 April 2009, 3; "Caen 5 del DAÍA por el caso de Amatitlán," *SV* (GU), 22 January 2010, 3; "Fiscal implica a cinco policías muertos en 'tumbe' de droga," *SV* (GU), 23 January 2010, 7; "Capturan a director," 4.

91. For domestic marijuana consumption estimates, such as ten tons annually in the mid-1980s, see *INCSR* (1988), 126, and *INCSR* (1991), 148. For marijuana trafficking aimed at students, see "Policía intercepta marihuana que

marijuana, principally for domestic consumption.[92] Since growing marijuana has been one of their more potentially lucrative options, notable quantities have been produced all across the interior.[93] While substantial cannabis crops have emanated from the central Guatemalan department of Jalapa, just east of Guatemala City, the most significant marijuana for international trafficking has come from the northern reaches of the Petén, especially along the Belizean and Mexican borders.[94]

Drug organizations have often taken advantage of international boundaries by shifting operations from one country to another when pressured by law enforcement. In Guatemala this phenomenon has marked both transshipment and production, as events in its neighbors have deeply affected the Guatemalan marijuana and opium industries. During the 1980s, aggressive marijuana-eradication campaigns in Belize led to a flourishing cross-border trade in the Petén.[95] The lack of official vigilance combined with the northern Petén's climate and the growing deforestation of its lowland jungles have encouraged marijuana exports.[96] By the late 1980s Belizean drug organizations had started to provide seeds and weapons and to finance and oversee significant marijuana farming. They then imported the product, sometimes later transshipping it to the United States by plane or boat.[97]

By 1989 the DEA estimated that Guatemala was harvesting 600 tons of cannabis annually, and significant production continued in the 1990s and thereafter.[98] Despite the generally erratic performance of Guatemalan law enforcement across much of the country, authorities nonetheless succeeded in eradicating considerable marijuana fields. For instance, 200 hectares or more of cannabis were destroyed in 1993, 1995, and 1996, and 100 hectares or more in 1988, 1989, and 1994.[99] Officials have also periodically

iba supuestamente a la USAC [Universidad de San Carlos de Guatemala]," *LH* (GU), 13 April 1989, 7; *Guatemala v. de León Jimenez*, No. 692-D, 4th Penal Ct. of Sentencing; and "Procesos a traficantes," *LH* (GU), 17 September 1985, 1.

92. Traffickers have distributed cannabis seeds, and, upon harvest, wholesale prices have averaged $77 to $110 per kilo. See "Vasto operativo policiaco por plantación de mariguana," *LH* (GU), 5 December 1985, 4, and DEA, *Resources, Guatemala* (2001), 9. For representative articles concerning marijuana production in the Santa Rosa, Baja Verapaz, El Progreso, Huehuetenango, and San Marcos Departments, see "Un millón de quetzales en marihuana decomisan," *LH* (GU), 31 October 1990, 4; "Gigantesco plantío de marihuana," *El Gráfico* (Guatemala), 28 April 1990, 6; "Intensifican lucha al narcotráfico," *LH* (GU), 9 November 1990, 7; and "La DEA amenaza a Guatemala," *LH* (GU), 24 October 1989, 6.

93. Much of the Jalapa marijuana was grown around the city of Jutiapa. See, for instance, "Incineraron más de cinco millones de dólares en cocaína," *LH* (GU), 28 June 1989, 8; "SIPROCI [El Sistema de Protección Civil] busca armas y drogas en Jutiapa," *LH* (GU), 28 June1989, 6; "Decomisan gigantesca plantación de marihuana," *LH* (GU), 5 September 1990, 7; "Decomisan gran cantidad de mariguana," *LH* (GU), 12 September 1990, 32; and "Decomisan fuerte cantidad de mariguana," *LH* (GU), 22 July 1991, 7. See also "Guardia de Hacienda en abierta lucha contra el narcotráfico," *LH* (GU), 24 August 1991, 32, and "Decomisan gran cantidad de mariguana en Jalapa," *LH* (GU), 25 October 1991, 8.

94. *INCSR* (1989), 101. See, for instance, "En El Petén: Narcos utilizan selva virgen para sembrar mariguana," *LH* (GU), 9 October 1991, 8; "Decomisan valioso cargamento de droga," *LH* (GU), 30 September 1991, 8; "Millonaria plantación de marihuana," *LH* (GU), 20 September 1990, 32; "Incautan 12 millones de quetzales en marihuana," *LH* (GU), 20 June 1989, 7; and "Decomisan mariguana," *LH* (GU), 14 March 1986, 4.

95. Even well into the twenty-first century, U.S. antidrug officials lamented Guatemala's lack of control over northern airstrips. *INCSR* (2006), 8, and *INCSR* (2007), 11. For representative forays by Guatemalan authorities against marijuana production, see "Duro golpe al narcotráfico en Petén," *LH* (GU), 25 November 1988, 4. For the flight of Colombian traffickers from the Petén into Belize and southern Mexico, see "Sesenta narcotraficantes escapan del país," *LH* (GU), 30 November 1988, 7. For the destruction by the National Guard of 103,900 marijuana plants and 105 pounds of marijuana in seven plantations along the Belizean border, see "La Guardia de Hacienda incauta droga valorada en Q40 millones," *LH* (GU), 20 February 1995, 8.

96. For Belizean seizures of marijuana exported from Guatemala, see chapter 2 of this volume. See also *INCSR* (1988), 123, and "Ganga Growers Split," *TR* (BZ), 13 August 1989, 14.

97. "Cinco mil millones de dólares en cocaína originada aquí," *LH* (GU), 14 July 1989, 4.

98. See *INCSR* (1991), 150, and *INCSR* (2000), 170.

99. See *INCSR* (1991), 150, *INCSR* (2000), 170, and *INCSR* (2003), 5:27.

confiscated large quantities of processed marijuana: 1.3 tons in 1991, 1.76 in 1994, 2.1 in 1993, 6.8 in 1990, and fully 16.4 in 1996.[100]

When drug rings in Guatemala have transshipped marijuana toward the U.S. market, they have sometimes sent high-quality Colombian cannabis. Thus, in a major 1996 bust, Guatemalan authorities, acting on DEA information, assaulted and dismantled a Petén trafficking camp used for at least three years to transship marijuana and cocaine.[101] Just ten kilometers from the Mexican border and within the Maya Biosphere Reserve, the site at an abandoned petroleum concession on Laguna de Tigre proved to be virtually unapproachable by foot from Guatemala. Although this is an exceedingly remote corner of Guatemala, empty but for widely scattered indigenous settlements, across the border passable roads link more than half a dozen small Mexican communities with the Mexican city of Tenosique de Pino Suárez. Hence, traffickers in Guatemala could readily supply their camp from Mexico, yet could operate outside the jurisdiction of Mexican antidrug officials. The trafficking site featured a 2,500-meter-long runway, built in the midst of otherwise swampy terrain, with red flags and green chemical lamps to guide planes during nighttime deliveries. When the surprise assault occurred, traffickers attempted to defend their camp, opening fire on Guatemalan soldiers with AK-47 weapons. The military soon prevailed and found that tons of processed and packaged marijuana, including the noted Colombian Red Point variety, had been prepared for export.

By the late 1990s, however, aerial-spraying campaigns had taken a toll on domestic marijuana producers, and a 1997 U.S.-sponsored helicopter survey of known areas of cannabis cultivation revealed only twenty-one fields, amounting to 8.5 hectares. By 1999 U.S. officials were estimating that marijuana cultivation had stabilized at about 130 hectares. And, after substantial eradication efforts eliminated more than 280,000 cannabis plants in 2002 and more than 625,000 plants in 2003, the U.S. government concluded that all of Guatemala's marijuana crop was then being directed to the domestic market.[102]

The Guatemalan Heroin Trade

Far more disturbing to antidrug officials than Guatemalan marijuana trafficking has been the country's role in the heroin trade. Unique among the Central American states, Guatemalan farmers have capitalized on the country's climate, varied topography, and rich volcanic soil to grow opium poppies.[103] Unlike the situation in Afghanistan, Burma, Laos, and other primary producers, poppy growing has not been a traditional way of life in Guatemala, having first appeared in the early 1980s.[104] Enforcement efforts against poppy growers in Sinaloa and other high-production zones of Mexico had led heroin organizations to move operations south.[105] Although considerable market share eventually shifted to Colombia, some Mexican traffickers turned to Guatemala, providing seeds, financing, irrigation equipment, and an assured market.[106]

For Mexican drug syndicates, Guatemala has key advantages over other possible sites. The western mountains straddling the Mexican

100. See *INCSR* (1997), 132; "Golpe al narcotráfico en la frente de Guatemala," *SV* (GU), February 9, 1996, 4; and "Sembradío de marihuana estaba en terrenos concesionados a la BASIC," *SV* (GU), 10 February 1996, 4.

101. *INCSR* (1998), 138; *INCSR* (1999), 156; *INCSR* (2003), 14; *INCSR* (2004), 17.

102. *INCSR* (1990), 179.

103. "Drugs: The Trade Grows," Inter Press Service (United States) (hereafter cited as IPS [US]), 20 February 1991.See also *INCSR* (1993), 155.

104. For the seizure of 37,812 poppy seeds on the Guatemalan border, see *El Gráfico* (Mexico), quoted in "Poppy Plants Seized," Foreign Broadcast Information Service (US), 18 March 1987, 5.See also "Cinco mil millones," 4; "Narcos mexicanos financian cultivo de la amapola," *LP* (PA), 21 July 1991, 7A; and "Drug Crackdown," 14A.

105. *INCSR* (1990), 179.

106. See "Opium Production Rises in Guatemala Mountains," *WP* (US), 30 June 1989, A25. For opium growing in Huehuetenango, see "Un millón de quetzales," 4, and "Poppy

border are very difficult to patrol and quite suitable for poppy cultivation. The highlands not only contain many poverty-stricken farmers but feature indigenous communities that had become further alienated from the state when caught between military and guerrilla forces during the civil war. Thus, from the mid-1980s until intensive eradication campaigns decimated production a decade later, farmers in the highlands grew substantial quantities of Brown Star opium poppies. These were transported to Mexico for processing to heroin and export to market. In 2004 and 2005, as Mexican cultivation figures receded once more, Guatemalan production rose again. In this way Guatemala became an important secondary opium-cultivation zone.

Prime opium-growing territory lies in rugged, isolated terrain in Guatemala's mountainous far-western provinces of San Marcos and Huehuetenango, where fields can be most easily reached from Mexico.[107] In fact, the border has long stymied antidrug officials from both countries, who cannot themselves pursue counternarcotics activities in their neighbor without risking rows over sovereignty. The inaccessibility of the border region has posed particular problems for Guatemalan law enforcement, which is notably weak on the periphery. During the civil war guerrilla activity in this area increased the challenge to police, as did the many mines planted on the slopes of Tajumulco, Central America's highest volcano, and other areas of high-intensity conflict.[108]

During the lengthy growing season, farmers, ordinarily working small, remote plots, have been able to harvest as many as three separate crops, with an acre of opium poppies producing roughly four to six kilos of raw opium.[109] While an acre of tomatoes, the area's traditional export crop, might return $150, poppies might earn ten to fifteen times more. Thus, subsistence farmers have seen this as, potentially, an extraordinarily profitable undertaking. By the mid-1980s the DEA had embarked on regular aerial reconnaissance of Guatemalan poppy fields, and these were, at first, easy to locate.[110] A DEA agent active in Guatemala at the time later wrote, "The poppy fields glowed against the foliage, . . . [looking] beautiful from the air, red streaks against a green canvas." One partial aerial survey, carried out in November 1987, located 354 fields of opium poppies, amounting to about 740 acres, or approximately nine million plants.[111]

To thwart discovery and eradication, producers came to disperse their plots over wide areas. Some even draped plastic sheeting over the poppies when planes were near. More frequently, farmers tried to avoid detection by planting opium poppies in steep, narrow ravines at high elevations, even ten thousand feet or higher, or among legitimate crops such as corn, beans, squash, lettuce, and potatoes. Furthermore, while spraying could wipe out those poppy plantations the authorities had

Plantations," Foreign Broadcast Information Service (US), 13 May 1987, 6. For opium growing in San Marcos, see DEA, *Resources, Guatemala* (2001), 4, "Descubren gran plantación de amapola en Sacatepéquez," *LH* (GU), 8 October 1991, 7; "La Guardia de Hacienda decomisa millonario cargamento de amapola," *LH* (GU), 23 April 1991, 8; "Guardia de Hacienda localiza y destruye plantación de amapola," *LH* (GU), 22 June 1987, 3; and "Millonario decomiso," *LH* (GU), 9 June 1987, 1.

107. See Leffert, "Narcotráfico y el ejército," 1. DEA agent Castillo, who worked in Guatemala at that time, later observed, "The Guatemalan police generally left . . . [opium fields] alone. They didn't want to risk running into a guerrilla stronghold while trying to destroy a bunch of flowers." Castillo and Harmon, *Powderburns*, 115.

108. See DEA, *Resources, Guatemala* (2001), 9; *INCSR* (1995), 135; *INCSR* (1992), 154, 161; *INCSR* (1990), 180; and *INCSR* (1988), 127. For a major bust near Santa Catarina Ixtahuacan, close to the highest point on the Pan-American Highway, see "SIPROCI destruye gigantesco plantación de amapola en Sololá," *LH* (GU), 16 October 1990, 7.

109. *INCSR* (2005), 115, 188; DEA, *Resources, Guatemala* (2001), 4; *INCSR* (1995), 134; *INCSR* (1992), 154, 158; "Opium Production Rises," A25.

110. *INCSR* (1988), 124. The project was cut short before completion as the planes were needed elsewhere. Note that the U.S. BINM used the rough conversion measurement of thirty thousand opium plants per hectare. *INCSR* (2005), 17.

111. See "Drug Crackdown," 14A.

Fig. 4.1 Net production of opium in Guatemala, 1985–1995

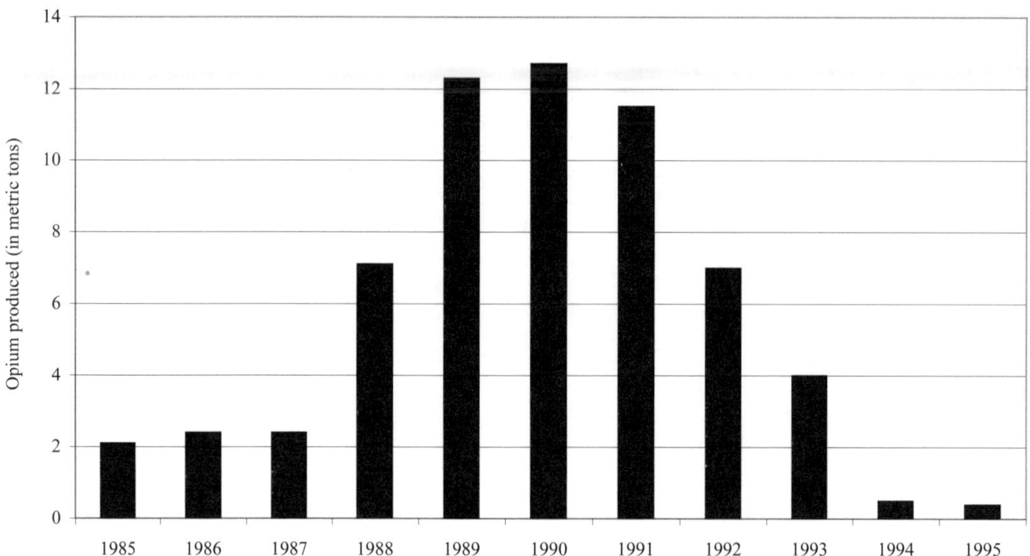

Sources: INCSR (1988), 127; *INCSR* (1990), 181; *INCSR* (1991), 21, 150; and *INCSR* (1992), 27–28, 161; *INCSR* (2000), 170; "Drug Trafficking and Poppy Growing Finding a Lush Home in Guatemala," *NYT* (US), 1 October 1989, 24; "US Targets Guatemalan Opium," *Christian Science Monitor*, 7 March 1990.

Note: Certain of the later reports corrected earlier estimates.

located, it could not stop farmers from immediately replacing the crop. Preventing replanting would require widespread arrest and imprisonment, not immediately forthcoming in Guatemala's antiopium campaign.

With wholesale prices of heroin reaching two hundred thousand dollars a kilo, by the late 1980s Guatemalan producers had made opium the country's third largest export, worth $100 million a year.[112] In the early years of the trade, however, heroin was not produced in Guatemala. Instead, Guatemalan farmers grew the poppies, occasionally doing initial processing, while Mexican organizations took charge of importing the crop, refining the morphine base into heroin, and eventually packaging and shipping it into the United States.[113] Not until 1989 did authorities following up on repeated rumors discover, between the towns of Tacaná and Sibinal in San Marcos Department, a laboratory for transforming raw opium into morphine base.[114] By the early 1990s antidrug officials acknowledged that traffickers were routinely exporting morphine base, rather than opium gum.[115] Income from

112. See *INCSR* (1988), 123, and *INCSR* (1992), 154. A DEA agent later wrote, "The Mexicans taught the locals how to score the hard pods with a blade, let the white sap ooze out, then scrape it off and knead it into a ball. The sap turned chocolate brown, and in short order [could be processed into] heroin." Castillo and Harmon, *Powderburns*, 115.For the seizure of Guatemalan opium in Mexico, see "Incautan fuerte cantidad de cocaína," *LH* (GU), 24 June 1989, 7.

113. *INCSR* (1990), 176.

114. For an account of Mexican police killing a Guatemalan trafficker in Chiapas with five kilos of opium paste, see "Narcotraficante Guatemalteco fue asesinado en México," *LH* (GU), 31 May 1988, 3.

115. See DEA, *Resources, Guatemala* (2001), 9, and *INCSR* (1992), 154. In 1987 some Mexican traffickers were paying Guatemalan opium farmers about $9,800 for each kilo of processed opium poppies. "Guardia de Hacienda," 3. See "US Targets Guatemalan Opium," *Christian Science Monitor* (US), 7 March 1990, 6, and "Drug Trafficking and Poppy Growing Finding a Lush Home in Guatemala," *NYT* (US), 1 October 1989, 24.

the trade increased substantially, as Mexican traffickers might pay $2,200 per kilo of opium gum, but $10,000 per kilo of processed poppies.[116] By 2005 seizures along the Mexican border indicated that Guatemalan laboratories had themselves turned opium into heroin.[117]

As fig. 4.1 illustrates, the 1985–95 period saw one crest in opium-poppy farming. Indeed, Guatemala temporarily moved into the top five opium-producing countries in the world.[118] In 1989, with poppy production nearly doubling in the country, the DEA estimated that Guatemalan farmers cultivated about 1,500 hectares of opium poppies—a quantity sufficient to produce as many as fifteen tons of opium.[119] By 1990 an estimated 1,930 hectares had been devoted to opium production, a figure that rose the following year to over 2,500 hectares.[120]

Although authorities attempted to increase manual-eradication efforts, they were for a time significantly outgunned. A 1988 incident in the mountains near Cuilco intimidated police when opium growers—or, according to one informant, the Civilian Self-Defense Patrol hired to guard poppy fields—killed six officers and their guide, punctuating their attack by thrusting a steel spike through the guide's head. Thereafter, the Rural Guard returned with 125 men, including DEA agent Celerino Castillo. A half-dozen armed members of the Self-Defense Patrol confronted the unit, demanding they leave the mountain. The police refused, spraying automatic-weapons fire at the feet of the indigenous group and continuing to the opium field, aiming to chop out the poppies with machetes.[121]

Castillo later wrote that hundreds of locals—"what looked like every villager on the mountain"—then massed on the slopes above the field, and snipers began to fire at the Rural Guard trying to eradicate the poppies. Castillo concluded, "A CIA helicopter found us, spotted the Indians, then lifted to a safe altitude and watched the villagers chase us all the way down the mountain. We reached Cuilco after eight hours, carrying soldiers with broken ankles and fractured legs. I passed out on a sidewalk, exhausted. The villagers made it very clear: Unless we marched into their plantations with an army, they were kings of this mountain." The U.S. government then grounded its spray planes stationed in Guatemala, because constant gunfire from opium growers had threatened the lives of U.S. pilots. Another sixteen-officer police detachment that entered the highlands to eradicate opium poppy turned back upon meeting sixty heavily armed growers; the police remained in their barracks thereafter.

With respect to the illicit global economy, state power has not so much steadily and generally eroded, as it has retreated, persisted, and reasserted itself in complex patterns.[122] The Guatemalan reaction to the opium trade is a case in point. Starting in 1990, larger and better-equipped units stepped up the government's effort against opium. DOAN officials sprayed herbicides from helicopters onto poppy plots. Spraying controversies ensued, as farmers and officials argued over whether the chemicals were adversely affecting honeybees and

116. For market shares, see the comparative statistics regarding Mexican and Guatemalan opium production in *INCSR* (2009), 34. For Guatemalan laboratories, see *INCSR* (2005), 180–81.

117. See DEA, *Resources, Guatemala* (2001), 4; "Drug Crackdown," 14A; and "Central America: A New Drug Focus," *NYT* (US), 16 December 1991, A10.

118. *INCSR* (1990), 176.

119. Castillo and Harmon, *Powderburns*, 4, 146; *INCSR* (1991), 21; "Guatemalan Army Called Best to Fight Drugs," *MH* (US), 26 April 1990, 3A; and "Cinco mil millones," 4.

120. Castillo and Harmon, *Powderburns*, 188–89; "Poppy Growing," 24; and "Opium Production Rises," A25.

121. Friman and Andreas, *Illicit Global Economy*, vii.

122. *INCSR* (1993), 154; "Opium Production Rises," A25; "US Targets Guatemalan Opium," 6; "Poppy Growing," 24; and "Graves peligros por la contaminación en Guatemala," *LH* (GU), 7 June 1989, 10. Note that in 1998 DOAN became one division of the National Civilian Police, formed as part of the peace accords.

legitimate crops. Aerial eradication did, however, succeed in reducing poppy production.[123]

In addition, for a period seven teams of more than a hundred men eliminated opium-poppy fields by hand three times a month. Although farmers at first simply planted more poppies to try to reduce losses, by 1994 spraying and manual eradication had dramatically reduced the crop. By the early 1990s Guatemalan authorities had also started to arrest more farmers for growing opium poppies, jailing forty-six in 1992 and more than sixty the following year. Frightened at the prospect not only of losing profits but of serving prison time, many farmers lost their enthusiasm for opium production.[124] By 1996 only isolated patches survived, and in 1999 a thorough U.S.-sponsored reconnaissance mission located a mere fifteen small poppy fields, thirteen of which were later sprayed and two manually eradicated.[125]

Nevertheless, once subsistence farmers had learned that they could earn much greater profits growing illicit crops, their tendency was to wait until law-enforcement attention dwindled and try again. Thus, in 2004, U.S. officials announced, "Cultivation of opium poppy is a problem that has returned to Guatemala." Indeed it had as, eventually, authorities eradicated over 5.4 million poppy plants. This amounted to 181 hectares, up from a single hectare the prior year. In 2005 and 2006, a time when Guatemalan officials identified Mexico's Sinaloa, Juárez, and Gulf cartels as recruiting indigenous farmers in San Marcos to grow poppies, they eradicated a combined total of 145 hectares. By later that year opium production so concerned officials that the Guatemalan government declared a state of emergency covering five western towns.[126] Cornelio Esteban Chilel, an alleged major producer, soon escaped, but the number of hectares dedicated to opium continued to rise. In 2007 U.S. authorities estimated that opium cultivation had rebounded to 600–800 hectares, of which 449 were eradicated. In 2008 authorities destroyed 536 hectares of opium poppies, and by 2009 fully 1,344 hectares were eradicated, a figure more than twice that of the largest eradication figure in the 1990s heyday of Guatemalan opium production.[127]

In the meantime, Guatemala had also become entangled in the transit of South American heroin. During the 1980s Guatemalans had occasionally been implicated in significant cases regarding the smuggling of Asian heroin. For example, in 1988 Australian authorities arrested former Guatemalan diplomat Jorge Mario Rueda, along with an Australian and three Hong Kong Chinese, in conjunction with a seizure of 31.6 kilos of 80 percent pure heroin.[128] By the 1990s, however, criminal syndicates had started to transship increasing quantities of Colombian heroin through the country, a trend eventually reflected in seizures.[129] In this regard, Guatemala was well positioned in

123. In 1992 the U.S. government reported that Guatemalan opium fields averaged 0.17 hectares, and in 1994 it suggested that most were in the 0.03 to 0.05 hectare range. *INCSR* (1993), 154. The government also noted that this represented "a significant portion of the land holdings of the average farmer in the area." *INCSR* (1994), 151.

124. See DEA, *Resources, Guatemala* (2001), 4, and *INCSR* (1999), 156. The U.S. government reported that from more than 2,500 hectares in 1991, Guatemalan opium production had steadily decreased to 12 hectares in 1996. *INCSR* (1997), 135.

125. "EE.UU. ve en Guatemala más cultivo de amapola," *SV* (GU), 1 March 2008, 3.

126. *INCSR* (2006), 12; *INCSR* (2007), 8; *INCSR* (2008), 169; *INCSR* (2009), 290; *INCSR* (2010), 308. Before the record eradication statistics of 2009, the largest number of hectares eradicated had been 576 in 1991. *INCSR* (2000), 170. For an interview with President Oscar Berger, see "A Merciless Fight," *Excelsior* (Mexico), 12 October 2006, quoted in "President Steps Up Fight."

127. "A luz detalles del caso de ex-diplomático traficante," *LH* (GU), 26 April 1988, 1.

128. In 1992 Treasury Police made their single largest confiscation to date, seizing nine hundred grams from a courier. *INCSR* (1993), 156.

129. "US Drug War Aims Its Sights at the Guatemala Connection," *Christian Science Monitor* (US), 17 April 1997, 8. See also "Detienen a mulas con heroína," *SV* (GU), 12 January 2000, 8. For a representative heroin-trafficking courier case, see "Aprehenden en aeropuerto a dos presuntos narcos," *SV* (GU), 12 March 1998, 55.

Central America, with a large international airport and a long history of couriers moving illegal narcotics.

According to officials in Guatemala City, Colombian trafficking organizations had trained mules to carry heroin (as well as cocaine) in their stomachs during flights into Guatemala. A Colombian doctor would administer a hunger-suppressing drug, and a Guatemalan doctor would eventually assist in removing the capsules. The organization would then pass the heroin along to another courier for the next leg, as one Guatemalan official put it, "like a relay race."[130] Thus, with time, U.S. officials reported numerous seizures of mules carrying heroin from Guatemala at airports and other U.S. entry points.[131] Indeed, as early as 1986 Carlos Humberto Orantes Arriaga, after his arrest, told U.S. authorities of a trafficking network regularly transporting heroin through Guatemala into the Pacific Northwest.[132] While Orantes was initially deported, he was rearrested in 1990 and convicted of conspiracy to possess heroin with intent to distribute, with a U.S. district court estimating that he had been selling 13 kilos of heroin a month in Texas between January and October 1990 and that his organization had supplied fully 267.9 kilos between 1985 and 1990.

As the magnitude of heroin trafficking via Guatemala came into focus, authorities devoted more resources to trying to curb it. By 1994 the DEA office in Guatemala had recruited confidential informants, who assisted in various arrests, including that of Colombian Diego Zapata, for smuggling heroin from Guatemala into New Orleans.[133] Other such heroin-trafficking rings were also active in Guatemala, and authorities seized 16 kilos or more in 1997, 2001, and 2002, and fully 52 kilos in 1999.[134] In 2000 authorities raided a Guatemala City facility dedicated to pressing heroin into pellets for couriers to carry into the United States.[135] Through the next decade Guatemalans continued to be arrested for involvement in Colombian heroin trafficking in Guatemala, elsewhere in Central America, and in the United States.[136]

The Guatemalan Cocaine Trade

While serious, Guatemala's heroin trade, even combined with the trafficking of marijuana and such other sidelines as the export of Ecstasy tablets, has paled in significance next to a truly extraordinary rise in cocaine trafficking.[137] As in other Central American countries, the drug's destination has typically been the United States, although to a significant though much lesser degree, various European markets have been targeted as well. Certainly, by the later 1980s cocaine transshipment via Guatemala was soaring. In 1987 U.S. government intelligence reported that traffickers had transshipped through Guatemala three extraordinarily large shipments that alone totaled about ten tons of cocaine.[138] By the end of the decade the $1.1 billion worth of estimated annual cocaine exports dwarfed all the country's other exports combined.[139]

130. See generally *INCSR* (2002), 13. For representative U.S. cases, see *United States v. Gomez-Galicia*, 2006 U.S. Dist. LEXIS 28412, and *Flores v. Texas*, 2004 Texas App. LEXIS 10565. In *United States v. Jurado-Lopez*, 338 F. Supp. 246, a Guatemalan gang was found to be coercing vulnerable women to serve as heroin couriers by compelling them to swallow pellets or forcing pellets into body cavities.

131. *United States v. Arias Villanueva*, 998 F.2d 1491.

132. *State v. Zapata*, 1991 U.S. App. LEXIS 4644.

133. *INCSR* (2000), 170; *INCSR* (2001), 5:23; *INCSR* (2002), 5:27; and *INCSR* (2003), 5:27.

134. DEA, *Resources, Guatemala* (2001), 8.

135. For an example of a courier arrested in Panama en route to Guatemala with briefcases of ornaments containing heroin, see "Detenido con cocaína agente de seguridad," *LP* (PA), 21 December 2006, 6A. Also see "Detienen a guatemalteco por narcotráfico," *LP* (PA), 11 September 2002, 11A.

136. See *United States v. Pofahl*, 990 F.2d 1456. Ecstasy is the popular name for 3,4-methylenedioxymetamphetamine (MDMA).

137. *INCSR* (1988), 123. The report noted, "A small quantity of cocaine HCL, probably about 600 kg annually, is manufactured in Guatemala from imported coca paste and exported primarily to the United States."

138. "Drug Crackdown," 14A.

139. "The New Frontier in the War on Drugs," *U.S. News & World Report* 109, 3 December 1990, 22. Other

In 1990 U.S. counternarcotics officials calculated that each year forty-eight tons of cocaine were transshipped through Guatemala, which, one declared, "has no interdiction capability."[140] In fact, authorities had seized just under a ton of cocaine in 1988, and in 1990 and 1991 they were to confiscate more than fifteen tons annually. The sharp rise in interdicted cocaine seems to have tracked a trend toward more transshipment. Indeed, the growth in the amount of cocaine passing through may have been even greater than the surge in seizures might suggest, since the percentage of drug loads that transited Guatemala without being interdicted was unknown. As cocaine trafficking via Guatemala took off, U.S. officials reported, "With hundreds of unmonitored airfields, an internal road network and river system leading to an uncontrolled border with Mexico, and with no air-search radar capability, Guatemala became the Colombian cartels' choice for cocaine transshipment in the early 1990s."[141]

A trend of this magnitude could not be kept secret, particularly in a country with advanced intelligence networks developed during the civil war. Through these means as well as information forwarded by the U.S. government, Guatemalan leaders were well aware that cocaine trafficking in their country was flourishing. In 1991 Guatemalan interior minister Ricardo Méndez Ruiz declared, "Drug trafficking has arrived in Guatemala. It's not casual and it's not sporadic. It's obvious that Guatemala is a major bridge now."[142] It had also become evident that Guatemalan authorities were intercepting only a small fraction of the drugs passing through and that narco-corruption was mushrooming into a sizable problem.[143]

A bridge state flanking Mexico and near the United States, with strictly limited law-enforcement capacity, secure places to hold drugs, and readily corrupted officials, was ideal for cocaine storage.[144] As early as 1989 antidrug authorities estimated that traffickers might have stockpiled as many as six tons of cocaine. To escape detection in market countries, traffickers hired chemists to blend cocaine into other products. After arrival at the destination, the chemical process would be reversed, with the cocaine restored to a pure state. The product used depended in large part on what would appear to be an appropriate export, unlikely to arouse suspicion. For instance, Medellín traffickers in Guatemala opted to mix cocaine with fruit pulp prior to smuggling.[145] Traffickers sometimes cut the cocaine prior to shipment to market, thereby increasing its quantity while reducing its purity. During storage drug networks have also sometimes divided a large shipment into smaller quantities for the final transit leg to increase the odds against the total load's being interdicted. Cocaine could also be warehoused awaiting an opportune moment to forward it, depending on the availability of purchasers, the current risk of

---

officials estimated that in this period five hundred kilos of cocaine transited Guatemala each week. "The President Vanishes," *Belize Times* (Belize) (hereafter cited as *BT* [BZ]), 30 July 1989, 14.

140. *INCSR* (1996), 131.

141. *INCSR* (1991), 146, and "Guatemala Is Latest Battlefield in War on Drugs," AP (US), 12 May 1991. See statements by interior minister Rodil Peralta in "Puente del narcotráfico," *LN* (CR), 8 January 1988, 18A, and Guatemalan OAS ambassador Eduardo Meyer in "Meyer: 'Centroamérica es puente del narcotráfico,'" *El Gráfico* (Guatemala), 14 March 1989, 11. For the DEA statement on the 1991 surge in Guatemalan trafficking, see "U.S. May Widen Anti-drug Drive in the Caribbean," *WP* (US), 1 June 1992, A4.

142. In 2002 U.S. State Department officials concluded, "Very large shipments of cocaine and heroin regularly pass through Guatemala without any law enforcement intervention." *INCSR* (2002), 5:21.

143. Confidential interview with a knowledgeable foreign law-enforcement official with regional responsibilities, 18 July 1990, Guatemala City, Guatemala, and from *INCSR* (2003), 14, and *INCSR* (2005), 17. For representative early busts of cocaine-storage houses in Guatemala, see "Cae cargamento de cocaína por 70 millones," *LH* (GU), 8 November 1990, 5, and "DOAN decomisa cargamento de cocaína valuado en Q60 millones," *SV* (GU), 14 July 1996, 1, 3.

144. Escobar, *Accountant's Story*, 61.

145. See Reuter, Crawford, and Cave, *Sealing the Borders*, 27.

interdiction, and the existing drug inventories in the market.[146] U.S. federal court cases eventually revealed that in repeated undercover operations in the early 1990s, DEA agents and informants had negotiated with cocaine-trafficking networks to purchase between 300 and 650 kilos of cocaine being held in Guatemala.[147]

The enormous flows of cocaine via Guatemala, as well as the storage of large quantities, came to involve an array of foreign and domestic drug rings. The U.S. method of breaking up such networks has involved arresting lower-level employees, gaining intelligence on operations, and slowly working up the chain toward the kingpins. Poor training, a dysfunctional court system, a history of endemic violence, and perhaps the need to protect domestic elites immersed in the trade has led Guatemalan authorities to a very different approach. On multiple occasions the G-2 and other authorities have simply summarily executed traffickers. DEA agent Celerino Castillo recounted that he would work undercover, arranging deals with cocaine suppliers and then tipping off the G-2 to upcoming meetings so they could make arrests. Instead, the G-2 would intercept the traffickers, torture and murder them, dump the corpses on city streets, and confiscate the cash and cocaine. Castillo wrote, "When I confronted the G-2 commanders, they brazenly admitted to the murders. They made no effort to lie or conceal their grisly work. They were the predators here. . . . When I insisted they stop ambushing my busts, they simply changed techniques. On the next bust, they staked out the meeting spot as planned, . . . wrestled the [traffickers] into the trunk of a car and screeched away. . . . They returned a short time later. The *traficantes*, they said coldly, had been eliminated."[148] Authorities who commit extrajudicial killings of this kind not only demonstrate their own profound contempt for the law and the criminal-justice system in which they operate but also put a premium on trafficking organizations systematically corrupting officials ahead of time to keep their people from being murdered. By 1990, with law enforcement contributing to rising drug-related violence, Guatemalan politician Edmond Mulet estimated that 20 percent of Guatemala's murders were somehow linked to the drug trade.

In the 1990s Guatemala's cocaine-trafficking problems worsened. As elsewhere in the region, foreign traffickers compensated local associates with cocaine, sometimes up to 10 percent of an entire shipment.[149] This stimulated the rise of local markets, especially in crack cocaine, and fostered drug abuse and higher crime levels, as addicts sought the money needed to buy drugs.[150] Furthermore, as aerial trafficking tapered off in Costa Rica, it thrived in Guatemala. More suspected cocaine flights arrived or refueled in the country, while some planes took advantage of the lax control of Guatemalan airspace to fly over the country en route to landing strips in Mexico. In the spring of 1991 U.S. military aircraft, outfitted with Airborne Warning and Control Systems, monitored flights toward the United States from South America. Their instruments counted hundreds of planes, including many suspected of carrying drugs, flying northward in the sixty-five-mile-wide corridor through the Caribbean basin toward Guatemala that standard U.S. radar did not then cover.[151]

146. See *United States v. Five Thousand Dollars ($5.000.00) in United States Currency*, 1996 U.S. Dist. LEXIS 12034; *United States v. Dominguez*, 992 F.2d 678; and *United States v. Vasquez*, 1992 U.S. App. LEXIS 26390.

147. Castillo and Harmon, *Powderburns*, 197. For one notable instance of authorities killing drug suspects, see "Guatemalan Police Chief Resigns in Wake of Killings," *NT* (CR), 5 October 2007, 4.

148. *INCSR* (2003), 5:23.

149. See *INCSR* (2005), 17–18. The first nationwide drug-consumption survey found that between 1998 and 2003 youth consumption of cocaine rose by 40 percent and marijuana by 50 percent.

150. *INCSR* (1991), 28; *INCSR* (1996), 132; "New Drug Focus," A10; and "U.S. Technology Gleans Data on Drug Corridor," *WP* (US), 26 June 1992, A25.

151. "Narcotráfico: 145 aviones aterrizan cada mes en Guatemala," *LP* (HO), 4 October 1991, 20; quote from "Central America: A New Drug Focus," A10.

Fig. 4.2 Cocaine seizures in Guatemala, 1987–2010

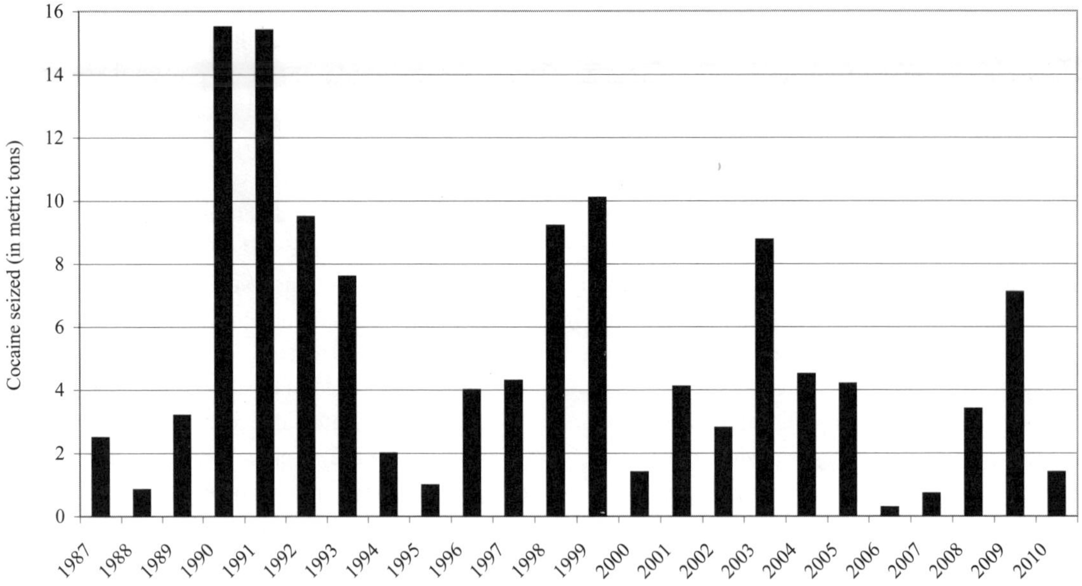

Sources: U.S. government statistics found in *INCSR* (1988), 127; *INCSR* (1991), 150; *INCSR* (2000), 170; *INCSR* (2001), 5:23; *INCSR* (2002), 5:27; *INCSR* (2003), 5:27; *INCSR* (2004), 155; *INCSR* (2006), 142; *INCSR* (2007), 160; *INCSR* (2008), 168; *INCSR* (2009), 289; *INCSR* (2010), 308; *INCSR* (2011), 272; DEA, *Resources, Guatemala* (2001), 2.

Eduardo Martí Guillo, Guatemala's vice minister of the interior, calculated that every month 145 planes loaded with cocaine arrived from Colombia, with another 160 flights leaving for Mexico and the United States. In light of estimates that one ton of cocaine was entering Guatemala each week, the DEA stationed there five permanent and six temporary agents. At the end of 1991 Torrey Shutes, DEA attaché at the U.S. Embassy, observed, "Three years ago, 100 kilos was considered a significant cocaine seizure in Guatemala. . . . Now, a seizure has to be at least 1,000 kilos—a metric ton—to be considered significant. That's getting to be a routine amount."[152] That more cocaine flights left than entered Guatemala likely indicated that cocaine was being stored and divided up for export and that it was also arriving by sea and overland prior to export by air.

Although Guatemalan authorities have freely conceded that only a small fraction of the cocaine passing through is being confiscated, fig. 4.2 shows that in some years significant amounts were being seized. As was true of counternarcotics work directed at the heroin trade, antidrug officials followed a distinctive pattern of at first falling back in the face of intensive cocaine trafficking but then reasserting themselves with rising annual cocaine seizures for a period, and then retreating once more as the bribes, bullets, and intimidation wielded by the traffickers temporarily gained the upper hand. Throughout these years, however, the U.S. DEA, customs, the coast guard, and other antidrug forces frequently traced seizures back to transshipment via Guatemala.

One might also note that drug-related arrests in Guatemala skyrocketed from 189 in

152. Cf. DEA, *Resources, Guatemala* (2001), 5, and "Subregion Grows as a Transit Route," *Latin America Weekly Report*, 22 August 1996.

1996 and 188 in 1997 to 5,917 in 2002 and 4,902 in 2003. In truth, however, the arrest and conviction of truly significant international traffickers occurred infrequently. The rise and fall of cocaine seizures seen in fig. 4.2 is most likely a result of more and less vigilant law enforcement, rather than dramatic peaks and valleys in the amounts of cocaine transiting Guatemala.[153] For example, after the 2005 arrests of top police officials during the U.S. DEA sting operation, cocaine seizures dropped from 4.2 tons to 281 kilos, suggesting that with police in disarray prior efforts to interdict cocaine had stalled.[154] And plunging interception rates could only encourage cartels to send yet more loads.

While Guatemalan cartelitos have answered to Colombian and Mexican cartels, their operations have not been confined to the national territory.[155] During the 1990s they extended their tentacles deep into regional smuggling operations, reaching even into Costa Rica and Panama. By 1999 Costa Rican antidrug official Rogelio Ramos observed of his country, "Of the last 30 drug enforcement operations, the kingpins in 17 of the cases were Guatemalan."[156] Lower-level employees of the minicartels fanned out across the bridge region as well. Between 2000 and 2005 Guatemalans were second only to Colombians in the number of drug couriers arrested in Costa Rica, and the same was true of Panama between 2004 and 2007.[157]

The trend toward the transshipment of ever more extraordinary quantities of cocaine continued into the new century. By 2000 U.S. State Department officials estimated that three hundred to four hundred tons of cocaine were passing through Guatemala annually. The next year the DEA declared, "Guatemala is the preferred Central American location for storage and consolidation of cocaine loads en route to the United States and Europe." In 2003, after identifying lackluster cooperation against drug trafficking, U.S. officials failed to certify Guatemala, although they ultimately granted a national-interest waiver rather than decertifying. Although reforms followed that brought about a dramatic increase in cocaine seizures, in 2005 the U.S. Embassy estimated that fully 75 percent of the cocaine entering the United States had transited Guatemala.[158]

Drug-Trafficking Organizations in Guatemala

Tracing the evolution of the Guatemalan marijuana, cocaine, and heroin trades suggests that the country separated itself from neighboring bridge states in how sharply cocaine transshipment climbed, as air and sea transit eclipsed movement by courier. We next explore the drug-trafficking networks and routes that lay behind this cardinal development.

153. At a 1998 Central American antidrug conference in San José, Costa Rica, Guatemalan officials stated that intercepting 2 percent of transshipped drugs would be satisfactory. "Heroin: A Growing Threat," *TT* (CR), 27 March 1998, 4. Note, however, that interdicting 280 kilos of perhaps 400 tons of cocaine passing through would amount to well under 1 percent.

154. *INCSR* (2003), 5:23.

155. "Drugs: Central American Region a Cocaine Warehouse," IPS (US), 21 April 1999.

156. See "Ambición destruyó la vida de 472 'burros' del narcotráfico," *LN* (CR), 15 January 2006, 20A, and "Uno de cada quince detenidos en Panamá es extranjero," *LP* (PA), 21 January 2008, 4A. Adding the totals of foreigners incarcerated in Panama in each year between 2004 and 2007, a period in which drug offenses were the most common crime for which foreigners were arrested, shows that 191 were Guatemalans, 172 Dominicans, 134 Mexicans, 131 Jamaicans, and 120 Costa Ricans. (Panamanian statisticians did not control for foreigners imprisoned for more than one year, who thus might be counted multiple times.)

157. *INCSR* (2000), 165; DEA, *Resources, Guatemala* (2001), 5–6; "The Untouchable Narco-State," *Texas Observer*, 18 November 2005, 6; "Once acciones contra el narco," *SV* (GU), 18 January 2003, 2; "Decomisos subieron 57.3% en un mes," *SV* (GU), 23 January 2003, 10; and "Guatemala: U.S. strikes Guatemala off drug blacklist," Intelligence Research (United Kingdom), 15 September 2003; *INCSR* (2004), 16; quote from *INCSR* (2001), http://www.state.gov/g/inl/rls/nrcrpt/2000/888pf.htm.

158. "Untouchable Narco-State," 7.

Involvement of Military Personnel

Active and retired military officers have held prominent positions in various Guatemalan cartelitos. One observer noted, "Guatemala is hardly the first military tainted by drugs; senior intelligence and law enforcement officers in many Latin American nations have been found colluding with organized crime. But what distinguishes Guatemala . . . is that some of its military suspects are accused not only of protecting large criminal syndicates but of being the ringleaders behind them."[159] Indeed, on the basis of drug-trafficking allegations, the U.S. government revoked the visas of two retired directors of G-2 military intelligence and one former air force general.[160] However, efforts to prosecute military officers, at home or abroad, have often been fraught with difficulties, as the following cases illustrate.

In December 1990 the Guatemalan military discharged air force captain Carlos ("Charlie") René Ochoa Ruiz after U.S. prosecutors had developed a drug-trafficking case allegedly implicating him. U.S. intelligence had suggested that Ochoa not only ran a stolen-car ring, bringing U.S. vehicles into Guatemala, but also was trafficking narcotics through his country, sometimes relying on his military documentation to bypass inspection checkpoints.[161] The DEA managed to penetrate a network that was transshipping Cali cartel cocaine via an airstrip on a farm in Escuintla Department. During the investigation a DEA agent reportedly watched Ochoa help load a small plane that flew to Tampa with five hundred kilos of cocaine on board, before anti-drug authorities seized it.

The U.S. government was unhappy that the Guatemalan government then simply discharged Ochoa. U.S. officials felt that simply firing a corrupt official amounted to a trifling sanction, given the extraordinarily lucrative criminal activities in which they were engaged. While this approach avoids personal, institutional, and national embarrassment, and circumvents the challenges of prosecuting and imprisoning elites, it is tantamount to winking at participation in the trade. Termination of employment has certainly not provided a sufficient disincentive to deter officials from participating in transshipment schemes or continuing to traffic drugs.

One dimension of a successful foreign policy is the ability to induce an otherwise reluctant foreign government to adopt a new course of action better aligned with one of the state's significant objectives.[162] Yet, although Guatemalan authorities did arrest Ochoa on international drug-trafficking charges in early 1991, the triumph for U.S. diplomacy was short-lived. U.S. authorities tied Ochoa to a significant cartelito linked to Cali traffickers and stated that federal prosecutors in Tampa had indicted him with respect to the transshipment via Guatemala of multiton quantities of cocaine. The U.S. Embassy thus requested Ochoa's extradition. However, despite the U.S. evidence and request, and the fact that Ochoa's name had been associated in Guatemala with a trafficking network known as the "narco-militaries," one Guatemalan court ordered him released, and two judges rejected the extradition bid.

Throughout Central America, even elites publicly accused of trafficking offenses have rarely withdrawn completely from the drug trade after earlier participation. Perhaps their connections in Colombia or Mexico have not permitted them to do so. Perhaps their feelings

159. The intelligence officers were reported to be Manuel Antonio Callejas y Callejas and Francisco Ortega Menaldo, and the air force officer was identified as Carlos Pozuelos Villavicencio. Ibid., 6–7, and Smythe, "Guatemala."

160. "Colonel Carlos Rene."

161. For information on the Ochoa Ruiz case, see *INCSR* (1998), 140; "Cae ex militar con cocaína," *SV* (GU), 21 March 1998, 51; "U.S. to Extradite Guatemalan Officer, Two Civilians," UPI (US), 24 December 1990; "Narcotics Trafficking and the Post-war Army," 8; "Untouchable Narco-State," 8; "A New Kingdom of Cocaine," *WP* (US), 26 December 1993, C4; Smythe, "My Enemy's Friends," 18; and "U.S. Drug Agency Tracks Guatemalan," *NYT* (US), 4 September 1995, 18.

162. Fowler, *Thinking About Human Rights*, 131.

of power and impunity within their countries and their contempt for laws and law enforcement have outweighed fear or caution. Perhaps their desire for future profits has proved too enticing to abandon trafficking altogether. In any event authorities have often had multiple opportunities to build cases against major figures. So it was with Carlos Ochoa Ruiz. In 1992 police discovered 2.8 tons of cocaine in a house owned by Ochoa near the old colonial city of Antigua.[163] At the time the retired officer was not actually occupying the premises, however, and Ochoa avoided arrest for the moment. Eventually, he appeared before a military tribunal, but this court dismissed the case forthwith for lack of evidence.

U.S. authorities continued to press Guatemala to deliver Ochoa to them for trial. And, eventually, the Ochoa Ruiz extradition case reached the Supreme Court. Epaminondas González Dubón, chief justice of the Constitutional Court, was one Guatemalan jurist who had clearly demonstrated his independence. He had previously ruled unconstitutional President Serrano's effort to mount his planned self-coup. The Constitutional Court reviewed Ochoa's case and, after a four-to-three verdict, Chief Justice González and the majority of the court ordered the alleged trafficker to be transferred to U.S. custody. But then nine days later, while driving near his home in Guatemala City accompanied by his wife and youngest son, the chief justice was assassinated. Eleven days later, the reconstituted court reversed the extradition decision. The intimidated judges simply inked out the verdict and date of the prior order in the court's register and rejected the extradition request without further comment. Although authorities at first tried to attribute González's killing to a carjacking by common criminals, this transparent effort to sweep the assassination aside was widely condemned. Eventually, one suspect in the killing was found dead, stuffed in a car trunk in Guatemala City, while two others were convicted and received twelve-year prison terms that, after a prosecutorial appeal, were increased to twenty-seven years apiece.[164]

In the meantime, Carlos Girón Méndez, Guatemalan police director, reported that Cali traffickers had infiltrated his force and ordered confiscated cocaine to be stolen, including evidence in the Ochoa Ruiz case. Ochoa then went free on a technicality, until a 1997 sting operation linked him to another thirty kilos of cocaine, and he was arrested again. A Guatemalan court eventually ordered that he serve fourteen years in prison, a sentence reaffirmed on appeal. Carlos Ochoa Ruiz thus stands as the most important trafficker a Guatemalan court has yet convicted. The killing of chief justice Epaminondas González Dubón, however, had a profoundly chilling effect: authorities thereafter failed to investigate, arrest, prosecute, and convict any major Guatemalan trafficker, including military officers involved in the drug trade, for more than a decade.[165] Nevertheless, that the state, at length, regrouped and reasserted itself is illustrated by the 2011 arrest of Juan Ortíz López, charged by U.S. attorney Robert O'Neill with trafficking tons of cocaine for more than ten years through Guatemala to Mexico and eventually the United States.[166]

Cartels, Cartelitos, and Other Drug Organizations in Guatemala

While the Medellín cartel was active in Guatemala in the 1980s, Cali traffickers were critically important to the surge in cocaine transition in the late 1980s and early 1990s. In the early 1990s a confidential informant, recruited by the U.S. government, provided information that led to a

163. DOS, *Country Reports*.

164. Smythe, "Guatemala," 1;

165. "Arrest of Guatemala's No. 1 Drug-Trafficking Suspect Shows Growing US Role in Region, "*Christian Science Monitor* (US), 31 March 2011, 1.

166. See *United States v. Orjuela* [*sic*], 809 F. Supp. 193.

1,500-kilo seizure of Cali cocaine in Guatemala, plus another 500 kilos that had already reached New York.[167] In 1993 U.S. diplomat Lee McClenny noted, "The vast majority of cocaine trafficking in Guatemala is Cali cartel-related."[168] In 1995 DEA sources publicly labeled Guatemala a prime "warehouse" for Cali traffickers, estimating that it had stored one-third of the cocaine then circulating in the United States.[169]

After his arrest, Cali kingpin Miguel Rodríguez Orejuela admitted to authorities that in 1987 he had bought an airline to send light planes carrying cocaine from Colombia to Guatemala.[170] There, a Panamanian export company transported the drugs to Miami, to be collected by Cali associates and distributed in various U.S. cities. Miguel Rodríguez further conceded that between 1987 and 1992, when two seizures occurred, he had collaborated with key associate Jorge ("El Pana") López and others in fifteen or sixteen cocaine shipments that had traveled by air from Colombia into clandestine runways in Guatemala and then on to Miami in refrigerated shipping containers of broccoli or melons. Then, between 1992 and 1994 he had supplied the cocaine for a venture in which a Cali exporter hid the drugs in coffee threshing machines sent from Barranquilla to Guatemala City, where the cocaine was extracted and forwarded overland to Houston. At a Colombian trial in 1996 Miguel Rodríguez further testified about thirty-two cocaine shipments via Guatemala and Honduras.[171] In 1997 Colombian authorities seized a seventeen-page document in a Bogotá prison holding Cali kingpins that identified Guatemala as their leading alternative to Mexico for transshipping and warehousing cocaine.[172]

As the new century approached, however, Mexican cartels were ascending rapidly in the international drug trade. Capitalizing on their weak southern neighbor, Mexican traffickers became ever more deeply involved in Guatemala, bringing cocaine trafficking to record heights and branching into new ventures, such as pseudoephedrine trafficking.[173] Guatemalan politicians, slow to reform extradition procedures and reluctant to sign bilateral antidrug accords, were so laggard in dealing with pseudoephedrine—waiting until 2009 to pass legislation requiring that its imports be justified—that Mexican drug rings had long since set up major transshipment operations. In 2009 Guatemalan authorities seized 11.8 tons of pseudoephedrine, while they confiscated another ton the following year, plus 1.5 million pseudoephedrine tablets.

Although multiple Mexican networks, including the Sinaloa, Tijuana, Juárez, and Gulf cartels, as well as La Familia, had important dealings in the country, by 2008 the Zetas were becoming dominant: sometimes partnering with Guatemalan networks, at other times seeking to replace them.[174] These particularly violent traffickers, with their roots in elite units of the Mexican Army, including some who had fought against the Zapatistas in Chiapas, have recruited former members of the *kaibiles*, Guatemala's ruthless

167. "New Kingdom of Cocaine," C4. See also Chepesiuk, *Drug Lords*, 104.

168. See "Has Guatemala Turned into the Warehouse?," 2, and "Guatemala es utilizada como bodega por narcotraficantes, afirma la DEA," *LP* (PA), 28 October 1991, 5A. For the statement of a U.S. Embassy official in Honduras, see "Costa Rica Linked with Money Laundering," 10A.

169. *Confesiones secretas*, 29, 33, 34.

170. "Desde Honduras envió cocaína, dice jefe de Cartel de Cali" *LP* (HO), 31 May 1996, 74A.

171. "Drug War Aims," 8.

172. See *INCSR* (2010), 308; "Decomisan A1.3 millones en pseudoefedrina," *SV* (GU), 28 October 2009, 7; "Capturan a cuatro hondureños con pseudoefedrina," *SV* (GU), 27 September 2009, 3; "Decomisan 1,500 cajas de pseudoefedrina," *SV* (GU), 7 September 2009, 2; "Sancionarán uso de pseudoefedrina," *SV* (GU), 14 April 2009, 8; and "MP vincula a mexicano con asesinato de abogado," *SV* (GU), 7 April 2009, 4.

173. For information on the Zetas in Guatemala, see generally "Zetas miran a Centroamérica," *LP* (PA), 1 December 2009, 2A; "Former Commandos Train Drug Traffickers," *TT* (CR), 4 November 2005, N-3; and Grayson, *Mexico*, esp. 184–88.

174. Garzón, *Mafia and Co.*, 95–96. Some Zetas previously worked for Mexico's Grupo Aeromóvil de Fuerzas Especiales (GAFE) and Grupo Anfibio de Fuerzas Especiales (GANFE). "De la 'A' a los Zetas," *LP* (PA), 1 December 2009, 2A.

counterinsurgency special forces.[175] Thus, former military personnel, shifting their allegiances from the state to transnational criminal enterprises, have again notably affected the drug trade. Their specialized training in weapons and tactics could be put to use by traffickers, as could their experience in intimidating and killing those within Guatemala who tried to resist them. Among the exploits attributed to Zetas in Guatemala were the robbing in 2007 of a maximum-security storehouse of military weapons and in 2009 of a national police outpost in Cobán, both to better arm their Guatemalan associates.[176]

Mexicans have long significantly influenced those parts of Guatemala that flank Mexico and are located far from Guatemalan central authorities. One such area—the swamps and tropical forests west of the Río Negro—has contained many undocumented Mexicans and immigrants as well as numerous settlements of Guatemalans repatriated from Mexico after the end of Guatemala's civil war. This was yet another set of circumstances that might attract drug traffickers. And, in 2009 the Zetas were found to have established a training camp at a farm right on the border with Mexico near the town of Ixcán, Quiché. Along with thirty-seven new recruits, authorities found five hundred fragmentation grenades and five AK-47s.[177] This training facility was symptomatic of a much larger problem. In 2010 the U.S. government concluded that drug organizations, most visibly the Zetas and the Sinaloa cartel, controlled entire regions of Guatemala.

To assist in operations, Guatemala's domestic trafficking networks, sometimes termed *cartelitos* and sometimes simply called *cartels*, have developed their own sets of Colombian and Mexican connections.[178] According to Guatemalan authorities, by the late 1990s five principal organizations had come to dominate the national cocaine trade, and at least two more had sprung up thereafter.[179] As in neighboring Belize, but more emphatically than has been the case with Costa Rican and Panamanian drug rings, Guatemalan cartelitos have been turf oriented, that is, they have attempted to stake out their primacy in particular zones. As the drug trade has evolved, some areas have been largely left to the devices of a particular organization, while others have been the subject of repeated violent challenges. This has depended, in large part, on how strategically important the area has become, an issue determined to a significant extent by the changing geotactics of the national drug trade.

In Guatemala City, the country's administrative heart and far and away its largest urban area, El Gallito cartel has often been behind major cocaine transshipment. Trafficking east of the city toward the Caribbean zone has often occurred through the Zacapa cartel, headquartered in Zacapa, capital of El Progreso Department in south-central Guatemala near the Honduran border. At the center of the country and surrounded by rich coffee plantations, the mountain town of Cobán is capital of Alta Verapaz Department and the birthplace of various noted Guatemalan traffickers. Here, the Cobán cartel has run many transshipment schemes, often working to link Colombian networks with counterparts in southern Mexico.[180] To the north the Sayaxché cartel has held sway in the Petén. Five powerful families have controlled much of the Petén trafficking: warehousing Colombian cocaine and financing plantations of marijuana and opium poppies in the department.[181]

175. See "Chocan Zetas con la policía," *SV* (GU), 7 March 2009, 3, and "Mexicano tendría rango de comandante," *SV* (GU), 12 March 2009, 6.

176. See "Hallan arsenal de Los Zetas," 28 March 2009, 3.

177. "El Salvador: PNC vincula a narcos con guatemaltecos," *SV* (GU), 9 January 2000, 6.

178. See "Cinco carteles de la droga hay en Guatemala," *LP* (HO), 29 June 1998, 100A, and "Guatemala Warns of 'Colombianization' of Country," *NT* (CR), 1 April 2005, N3.

179. "Ubican bodega del capo," *SV* (GU), 12 July 2001, 10.

180. "Drug War Aims," 8.

181. For the alleged trafficking of 450 kilos through Finca Samaria and of 220 kilos through Finca Amatilla,

Izabal Province, fronting the Gulf of Honduras, has housed the Gulf cartel, Guatemala's Gulf organization, whose traffickers have received Colombian cocaine and forwarded it to Mexico's Juárez and Sinaloa cartels. Gulf traffickers have had a presence on the Pacific side of the country as well, sometimes directing Colombian cocaine planes into places such as La Gomera in Escuintla Department. The city of Escuintla is strategically located at the junction of the Pacific Coast Highway and the highway that leads from Guatemala City to Puerto San José and Puerto Quetzal on the Pacific. Since Escuintla Department also forms the heart of an especially productive agricultural as well as industrial region, various drug rings have contested one another here, with a particular eye to the use of landing strips at nearby plantations.[182] Although unable to exert exclusive control, a notable organization the length of the Pacific coast has been the Luciano cartel, headquartered in Santa Lucía Cotzumalguapa, Escuintla.[183]

Violent Interactions Among Drug Networks

As this formidable array of domestic and foreign drug organizations rubbed up against one another in going about their business, violent incidents have multiplied. One notorious case in 2007 illustrates the links between Central American political elites, drug networks, and their police enforcers. Just off the highway from Guatemala City to El Salvador, three Salvadoran deputies to the Central American Parliament—including Eduardo José d'Aubuisson Munuguía, son of Salvadoran politician Roberto d'Aubuisson—and their driver were found murdered in the burned remains of a car.[184]

Authorities investigating the killings discovered that a traffic camera had caught the Salvadorans' vehicle being followed by a car containing four police officers and a driver. The officers were soon arrested.[185] Investigators further found that one suspect had called a Guatemalan legislator and other elites more than one hundred times the day the Salvadorans were killed. While the four were charged with the murders and placed in a maximum-security prison, three days later and hours before the U.S. FBI, which had been invited to assist, was to start its investigation, all of the suspects were murdered in their cells.[186] The official explanation was that imprisoned gang members had seized control of the prison to execute these police officers, afterward taking hostage five prison guards.[187]

However, an alternative version of what had happened soon emerged.[188] Witnesses claimed that two vehicles had driven to the prison entrance, which had been guarded by ten penal officials, while twenty-five military guards patrolled the perimeter. The men had entered the prison, controlled the inmates, and shot the jailed police, though cutting up the bodies so that it would look as though inmates, armed with crude weapons, had murdered them. They then left, having ensured that testimony of the imprisoned police would

---

both owned by Guatemalan bank Francisco Alvarado Macdonald, a close political associate of President Portillo, see "Narcotraficantes usaron finca de Alvarado Macdonald," *SV* (GU), 4 July 2001, 4. For a 728-kilo bust, perhaps of La Familia cocaine, being flown on a Colombian plane into nearby Pinula, Escuintla, see "Interceptan avioneta con 728 kilos de cocaína," *SV* (GU), 12 August 2009, 8.

182. For the arrest of Luciano kingpin Marcelo Magno Lemus Pérez, see Notimex, Mexico City, 19 June 1998, quoted in "Guatemala: 'Top Leader' of Luciano Drug Cartel Arrested," BBC Monitoring Latin America, 21 June 1998.

183. "Matan en el país a tres diputados al Parlacén," *SV* (GU), 20 February 2007, 2.

184. "Cops Nab Alleged Mastermind in Guatemalan Murders," *NT* (CR), 11 January 2008, 4.

185. "Policías anticrimen serían los asesinos," *SV* (GU), 23 February 2007, 2.

186. "Matan a los cuatro policías anticrimen," *SV* (GU), 26 February 2007, 4.

187. "Temen poder superior," *SV* (GU), 27 February 2007, 2.

188. See ibid.; "Capturan a 24 por asesinatos," *SV* (GU), 27 February 2007, 4; and "Escuadrones incluyen a evangélicos," *SV* (GU), 6 March 2007, 2.

not implicate the elites involved. According to this account, the prisoners took the hostages to try to avoid being blamed for the killings. In fact, laboratory analysis of the bullets that had killed the officers proved that they had come from a police gun.[189] In any event, the Salvadorans' murderers had been silenced. So, too, were three lawyers who had been consulting the police during the case; ultimately, hit men killed each of them.[190]

In late 2010 Guatemalan prosecutors, assisted by CICIG, convicted eight for the murders. Former Salvadoran legislator Roberto Silva Pereira, already imprisoned in the United States on drug charges, was accused of having contracted to have the Salvadoran legislators killed, as vengeance for d'Aubuisson's having supposedly turned him in to the DEA. The murders were then plotted out by former Guatemalan legislator Manuel de Jesús Castillo, the leader of a criminal organization involved in drug trafficking known as the Jalpatagua group. A Guatemalan court sentenced Castillo to 203 years in prison, with four gang members given between 17 and 208 years for their participation in the killings.[191]

The killing of the Salvadoran legislators was followed by a series of other high-profile drug-related murders. In 2008 a shoot-out between Zetas and Guatemalan traffickers who had laid a $1 million bet on a cockfight at a horse race in Santa Ana Huista, about ten miles from the border, left at least eighteen people dead, with bodies strewn across the road leading to Mexico.[192] The following month, a dozen assassins murdered Juan José León Ardón, a Mexican trafficker in charge of Guatemalan operations for Mexico's Gulf cartel, at a spa he frequented on the Atlantic Highway in Santa Cruz, Zacapa.[193] As they fled the scene in a stolen pickup, the hit men encountered a police patrol, and in the ensuing shoot-out ten more people were killed. Investigators believed that Mexican kingpin Joaquin Guzmán of the Sinaloa cartel had sent the gunmen to kill León Ardón to support the Zacapa cartelito, which had been pressured by Gulf traffickers.

With cocaine trafficking permeating the country, the crescendo of narco-violence led to a quick-trigger mentality. In another 2008 case drug traffickers came upon a bus, containing eleven Nicaraguans and a Dutch citizen, broken down along a major highway into Honduras. The traffickers, reportedly from the Taquero organization, a Guatemalan network that acted independently of the established cartelitos, deluded themselves into believing that these tourists were hiding drugs on the bus. After torturing them to reveal the location of the presumed drug shipment, the traffickers eventually killed all twelve.[194] While drug-related violence occurred across the country, the murder rates in places central to drug transit became staggeringly high. For instance, in 2009 the government reported that four different cities in the Petén led the country's homicide rates, each

189. "Con fusil de la PNC ultimaron a los diputados del PARLACEN," *SV* (GU), 15 March 2007, 8.

190. See "Acribillan a ex asesor policíaco," *SV* (GU), 27 October 2009, 6, and "Atentan contra asesores de PNC," *SV* (GU), 10 March 2007, 10.

191. "210 años de prisión a asesinos de diputados," *LP* (PA), 3 December 2010, 33A; "8 Sentenced in Guatemala for the Murders of Salvadoran Lawmakers," FoxNews.com, 2 December 2010, http://latino.foxnews.com/latino/news/2010/12/02/sentenced-guatemala-murders-salvadoran-lawmakers/. See also "CSJ remite extradición de Silva a Cancillería," *SV* (GU), 11 March 2009, 6.

192. See "Twenty-Six Massacred at Horse Race in Clash Between Guat and Mexican Drug Dealers," *Amandala* (Belize), 12 February 2008; "Fiscalía acusa a seis Zetas por narcoapuesta," *SV* (GU), 14 April 2009, 6; and "Quedan libres cuatro acusados por la narcoapuesta," *SV* (GU), 18 April 2009, 8.

193. See "Matanza deja nueve muertos," *SV* (GU), 26 March 2008, 8; "Narcomatanza involucró a tres cárteles," *SV* (GU), 27 March 2008, 2; and "Cae por proveer armas para la narcomatanza," *SV* (GU), 3 March 2009, 7.

194. See "Buscan a narcos en Zacapa," *SV* (GU), 23 November 2009, 6, and "Cateos están ligados a caso de nicaragüenses," *SV* (GU), 24 November 2009, 6.

registering more than two hundred violent deaths per one hundred thousand inhabitants.[195]

Networks Focused on Europe

While drug rings operating in Guatemala have directed as much as 90 percent of their transshipped cocaine to the U.S. market, they have supplied European distributors as well.[196] The Central American bridge states have had differing roles in cocaine trafficking into continental Europe, ranging from the negligible part played by Belize to much more robust participation by Costa Rica, Guatemala, and Panama. Among the significant variables have been the ease of air connections and the frequency of shipping. In the case of Guatemala, however, another key factor has been the presence of European expatriate communities. Groups of Guatemalans of European heritage date to the period when Guatemala was attempting to establish its coffee trade and officials were actively searching out and enticing skilled labor and capital and foreign investors to their country.[197] Many Germans and other central Europeans answered the call and settled in Guatemala, with quite a few rising to join the country's elites.

In 1997 the so-called German connection case came to public attention. After a tip to the DOAN antidrug hotline, Guatemalan officials discovered thirteen kilos of cocaine hidden in a shipping container headed to Germany, and investigations led to ten arrests in Guatemala, Costa Rica, and Germany. Turning the arrest of a prominent individual into a drug conviction has always been far from certain in Guatemala. In this case the Zacapa Court of Appeals chose to absolve the Swiss general manager of Nestlé in Guatemala, who had originally been sentenced to twelve years and an eighty-thousand-dollar fine for drug trafficking. Authorities went on to allege, however, that the figure actually behind many such European transshipment schemes was Hartmut Zersch, a long-time hotel proprietor in Antigua, who also owned a farm on the Costa Rican–Panamanian border. Investigators believed that Zersch had been deeply involved in transshipping Colombian cocaine via Central America to Germany, Switzerland, and Spain, under the cover of a legitimate enterprise exporting ornamental plants. Investigators alleged that this network had smuggled over $100 million in narcotics to Europe; in 1997 German authorities arrested Zersch on charges of trafficking cocaine between Guatemala and Europe.[198]

In fact, multiple drug organizations have moved cocaine from Guatemala into Europe, and the disruption of one sizable group simply opened possibilities for its rivals to gain market share. Hence, very substantial shipments have continued to flow toward different European destinations, such as one, intercepted by Italian police, in which 1.2 tons of cocaine had been secreted in a load of frozen fruit. Thus, having established itself as a prime transshipment center for cocaine headed to North America, Guatemala soon became embroiled in the effort by transnational drug syndicates to open and supply new markets in Europe.

Drug-Trafficking Methods and Routes in Guatemala

Whether narcotics have been transported to the United States or Europe, drug rings operating in Guatemala have not remain wedded to a single

195. "País duplica tasa de homicidios en AL," *SV* (GU), 11 August 2009, 3.

196. "Guatemala Warns," N3. In a notable 1998 bust a customs official at Santo Tomás de Castilla port decided to inspect an older vehicle scheduled to be shipped from Guatemala via Finland to Russia; thirty-seven kilos of cocaine were hidden in the fuel tank. *INCSR* (1999), 157.

197. See Wilkinson, *Silence on the Mountain*, 68–79.

198. For further information on this case, see *INCSR* (1998), 141; "Guatemalan Connection," Intelligence Research (United Kingdom), 23 September 1997, 3; "Narcotics Trafficking and the Post-war Army," 10; "Suiza pide juicio justo para sus ciudadanos," *SV* (GU), 1 February 1999, 2; and "Liberan a tres de la conexión alemana," *SV* (GU), 13 February 1999, 3. Prosecutors later claimed that pressure had been exerted on the Nestlé case judge, something that he denied. "Magistrado defiende fallo en conexión alemana," *SV* (GU), 17 February 1999, 4.

transshipment method. Although at any given time the trend might be toward one particular approach, even the same organization might employ air, sea, and land methods. To illustrate, in the late 1980s the DEA began to track the activities of Omar Pira-Palma, a young Guatemala City businessman, after a member of Pira-Palma's family had revealed to authorities his links to Cali traffickers. After being confronted with certain evidence against him, Pira-Palma offered to cooperate and relinquish a large quantity of cocaine. The Rural Guard then seized a ton of cocaine from inside a gasoline tanker truck parked in Antigua. DEA agent Celerino Castillo later wrote, "Pira-Palma agreed to cooperate, and sat down with me to explain how his system worked. It was ridiculously easy, he boasted. Sometimes, he used the cartels' planes to fly in the cocaine. He packed it in boats. He hired drivers to take [it] over the Texas border in loads of towels. He even stuffed it in boxes and shipped it by air freight."[199]

Much the same point could be made with respect to the more recent cocaine trafficking of Jorge Mario Paredes Córdova.[200] Paredes, a 330-pounder known as "El Gordo," led a substantial Central American network that for more than a decade brought many tons of cocaine into Guatemala by sea, air, and land routes. Paredes then either forwarded the drugs to the United States to be distributed through associates there or sold them in Guatemala to other drug rings. After the DEA offered $5 million for information leading to his arrest, Paredes fled to Honduras, where for a period he continued to run his organization while in hiding. However, U.S. antidrug officials dedicated significant law-enforcement resources against him, using fifty wiretaps and informants in ten states, and the DEA eventually located him in San Pedro Sula, Honduras. After being arrested and extradited to the United States in 2008, Paredes went to trial concerning a 265-kilo cocaine shipment into New York and was duly convicted.

In fact, as Guatemala's various bridge-favoring factors suggest, extraordinary opportunities have awaited traffickers looking to transship large cocaine loads. Moreover, as Mexican authorities have enhanced antidrug efforts, routes via Guatemala have become increasingly attractive. Transnational criminal organizations have proved able to adapt to their environment, and they have had the business acumen and essential resources needed to find and then seize promising opportunities, while avoiding places that have become relatively riskier. Not only have numerous drug enterprises accelerated their Guatemalan air and maritime transport, but they have implemented varied strategies to foil law enforcement. Sometimes they have eluded detection by changing transit methods, varying transshipment sites, or switching from air to sea to overland shipments. At other times, they have co-opted or systematically corrupted authorities who might otherwise have interfered with the flow of drugs.

To complete our portrait of the Guatemalan drug trade, we turn next to the routes that these and other trafficking networks employed. While the epicenter of early Guatemalan drug transshipment was Guatemala City and the international airport, starting in the late 1980s the transit of large narcotics loads spread across the country and along both coasts. As the drug trade evolved, Guatemala's multiplicity of entry and exit points overwhelmed counternarcotics efforts, and the country became not simply a revolving door in the drug trade, but one that could send off drugs, quite effectively, by air, sea, or land.

Air Routes

Courier Transport

During the 1980s networks frequently sent couriers through Guatemala City's La Aurora

199. Castillo and Harmon, *Powderburns*, 211.

200. See *United States v. Paredes-Cordova*, 2009 U.S. Dist. LEXIS 52415; "Un soplón hundió a Paredes y a otros narcos," *SV* (GU), 15 October 2009, 8; "Jorge Mario Paredes procesado en Nueva York," *SV* (GU), 26 October 2009, 2; and "Declaran culpable al Gordo," *SV* (GU), 7 November 2009, 4.

International Airport with a few kilos of drugs—usually cocaine but occasionally marijuana—on their persons or in their checked or carry-on luggage.[201] Although some of these mules were Guatemalan, they tended to be Colombian or Mexican citizens, and many were women.[202] Occasionally they were from such other South American states as Peru, Bolivia, or Venezuela.[203] One of the most popular routes brought cocaine into Guatemala on commercial flights from Colombia's Isla de San Andrés.[204] At times, Guatemala was simply a layover en route to the United States. At other times, couriers imported the narcotics and then turned the drugs over to Guatemalans to handle the next leg of the journey.[205]

In that initial decade of surging cocaine transshipment via Central America, the courier trade through Guatemala began to flourish, with mules who arrived on commercial flights, employing somewhat different methods to try to escape detection. To avoid customs officials turning up drugs in searches of luggage, couriers have transported cocaine capsules in their stomachs, although this could be deadly if the capsules leaked.[206] In Guatemala, as elsewhere in the region, mules with cocaine on their persons or in their bags have tried to merge into legitimate airport traffic and pass through customs without detection. Here, they have relied on devices such as double-walled suitcases and masking the scent of the drugs by enveloping them in other materials.[207] Larger quantities have been sent as cargo, with organizations hiding the drugs in secret compartments or relying on baggage handlers brought into their scheme. Associates at the destination airport have sometimes been alerted to marked bags or boxes, so they could

201. Traffickers occasionally attempted to export marijuana, despite its distinctive odor, right through the international airport. See, for instance, "Localizan mariguana en el aeropuerto," *LH* (GU), 22 July 1989, 7. For representative seizures, see "Gran cantidad de cocaína incautada," *LH* (GU), 28 May 1988, 3, and "Incautan cocaína y detienen a tripulación de carguero," *LH* (GU), 7 June 1991, 12. For fifty-seven kilos seized in a shipment of plywood doors on a commercial flight, see "Confiscan millonario cargamento de cocaína," *LH* (GU), 11 April 1990, 8. Mules caught in the United States often faced stiff sentences. See, for instance, *Uribe and Correa v. State of Texas*, Nos. A-14-83-100-CR, A-14-83-101-CR.

202. Mules are often poor, uneducated people out to make quick money. For the example of a Colombian street peddler entering a Houston airport from Guatemala and arrested with cocaine, see *United States v. Betancourt*, 592 F.2d 916. For representative cases of Colombian or Mexican couriers caught smuggling a kilo or two of cocaine in the mid- to late 1980s, see "Incautan cargamento de cocaína en aeropuerto," *LH* (GU), 21 March 1986, 1; "Más cocaína incautada," *LH* (GU), 12 July 1986, 1; "Mujer traficante de droga captura la policía en la terminal aérea," *LH* (GU), 5 September 1986, 4; "Narcotraficante mexicana detenida esta madrugada," *LH* (GU), 19 December 1988, 7; and "Cocaína por 290,000 dólares incautan anoche," *LH* (GU), 13 December 1988, 7.

203. For a representative case of courier cocaine smuggling from Peru, see *Guatemala v. Zorrilla Limo*, No. Z-127, 3rd Ct. of Ct. of App.s, and "Gran cantidad de cocaína incautan," *LH* (GU), 28 May 1988, 3. For a Bolivian woman attempting to smuggle two kilos of cocaine on a flight into Guatemala, see *Guatemala v. Montaño Ribera*, No. 1939-M, 1st Ct. of 1st Instance, and "Escándalo por adulteración de cocaína," *LH* (GU), 10 December 1986, 1.

204. For representative case reports of San Andrés smuggling, see *Guatemala v. González González*, No. 1843-L, Sup. Ct. of Jus.; *Guatemala v. Patiño Sánchez*, No. 1194, 10th Ct. of 1st Instance; and *Guatemala v. Prieto González*, Sup. Ct. of Jus. See also "Incautan cargamento de cocaína," *LH* (GU), 19 November 1985, 1; "Suspenden condena a traficante," *LH* (GU), 6 February 1986, 3; "Guatemalteco capturado con cocaína en el aeropuerto valorada en cuarto de millón de quetzales," *LH* (GU), 22 April 1986, 1; "Persiguen a traficantes," *LH* (GU), 16 July 1987, 1; "Incautan envió de cocaína," *LH* (GU), 16 February 1989, 7; and "Estudiante llevaba cocaína," *La Prensa Libre* (Guatemala) (hereafter cited as *LPL* [GU]), 17 February 1989, 19.

205. For instance, in 1989 authorities seized 11.5 kilos of cocaine from two couriers arriving on a flight from Colombia, who told the police their orders were to deliver the drugs to a contact at Guatemala City's Hotel España. "Capturan a colombianos con un cargamento de cocaína," *LH* (GU), 26 April 1989, 7.

206. For this cocaine-smuggling method, see *Dejesus v. Texas*, 960 S.W.2d 361; "Cuatro años de prisión para dos colombianos traficantes de cocaína," *LH* (GU), 7 April 1988, 3; and "Descubren tráfico de droga," *LH* (GU), 6 February 1986, 1. For an odd case of a courier both swallowing cocaine and packing it in luggage, see *Guatemala v. Godoy*, No. 1949-G, 10th Ct. of App.s, and "Castigan a colombiana," *LPL* (GU), 17 January 1989, 9.

207. See, for instance, "Capturan a 'correo' con cocaína," *LH* (GU), 19 February 1986, 1.

be separated from other luggage and smuggled to a prearranged drop point for retrieval.[208]

Apart from numerous flights of private planes, antidrug officials at La Aurora have had to contend with regular commercial flights entering Guatemala from other Central American and South American destinations, including Bogotá and San Andrés, and flights leaving to Houston, Washington, D.C., and other large cities, including some in Europe.[209] For drug organizations the continuous movement of small quantities of cocaine by courier has eliminated the risk of a single bust wiping out profits. Moreover, the mules have been viewed as expendable, indeed, as virtually interchangeable, so organizations have not felt obliged to bribe or intimidate authorities to try to free them after arrest. Although police and customs authorities were bound to seize some couriers, and judges to convict and imprison them, sometimes showing off their rigor with harsh sentences, such "successes" might deflect attention from far larger drug transactions.[210] Thus, the courier trade has been a low-risk effort to transport modest amounts of narcotics, slowly but continually, that could also keep authorities interdicting minor quantities and appearing to be diligent and effective, when in fact substantial shipments were passing through Guatemala undetected.

Despite persistent rumors that military officers and other influential citizens have been the contacts designing and assisting such trafficking schemes, Guatemalan authorities for the most part have been content to imprison couriers rather than to stage controlled deliveries or otherwise creatively investigate.[211] So long as couriers could be screened from knowledge of how the organization functioned or bribed or frightened into holding their tongues, such a transit strategy has ordinarily risked very little for drug-trafficking organizations. This method has worked particularly well in La Aurora Airport in Guatemala City, where an associate can stand in the balcony overlooking customs and immigration and determine whether an arriving passenger is having trouble with inspectors. If so, the associate could unobtrusively depart.

More extensive use of drug-sniffing dogs as well as the return of the airport to civilian control in 1998 brought about improved counternarcotics cooperation with the U.S. government.[212] However, while over the years numerous couriers have been arrested and prosecuted, their organizations have most often escaped unscathed. And, of course, many mules have passed in or out of Guatemala without detection. One notorious case at the end of the 1980s illustrates the manner in which cocaine has moved through the airport, the involvement of Guatemalan elites in the trade, and the dangers and difficulties inherent in prosecuting them successfully.

The Case of José Fernando Minera Navas

Long-standing rumors of official complicity in Guatemalan drug transshipment gained credence in 1989 as a middle-level official caught up in an airport-trafficking case publicly alleged that narco-corruption had reached the highest levels of Guatemalan society.[213] On August 1,

208. Castillo and Harmon, *Powderburns*, 124. This may have been the case with respect to a suitcase containing cocaine abandoned by a passenger arriving from Panama. See "Gran cantidad de cocaína incautan," *LH* (GU), 3 March 1989, 9.

209. For cocaine sent from Guatemala to Dulles Airport in a Maryland courier service mail pouch, see *United States v. Díaz-Calderón*, 2007 U.S. App. LEXIS 2240. For a case involving the Guatemalan courier service Air Express, see "Anulan sentencia por narcotráfico," *SV* (GU), 10 February 1999, 10. For drugs sent to Spain, see, for instance, "Arrestan narco con cocaína destinada a España," *LP* (PA), 25 February 1991, 5A. For three kilos of cocaine in luggage bound for Netherlands, see "Gran cantidad de cocaína incautada," *LH* (GU), 28 May 1988, 3.

210. In 1989 a court sentenced a courier to four years and a three-thousand-quetzal fine for possessing a mere ninety-five grams of cocaine. "Cuatro años de prisión por narcotráfico," *LH* (GU), 4 March 1989, 9.

211. For one exception, see the detention of Guatemalan politician Hugo César Padilla Gómez. "Más de Q.4 millones en cocaína incautados," *LH* (GU), 19 April 1990, 7.

212. *INCSR* (1999), 157.

213. For early media reports on the case, see "Traficantes de cocaína capturados en terminal aérea," *LH* (GU), 2 August 1989, 7; "Control Administrativo hará investigación

1989, José Fernando Minera Navas, employed, ironically, by the anticorruption police known as the Department of Administrative Control (DAC), made a special request to La Aurora employees of the state-owned airline, Aviateca. Minera Navas asked that a very heavy suitcase, being carried by DAC agent Rolando Moisés Fuentes de León, depart for Miami on a particular flight. The luggage tags showed the owners to be two American tourists. However, although they did hold Aviateca tickets, the tourists had already left for Miami on a different flight a half hour before Minera Navas made his request.

Suspicious of these circumstances, Aviateca employees called in narcotics agents, who opened the suitcase, discovered twenty-five kilos of cocaine, and immediately arrested Minera.[214] The immigration officer in charge then confided to the DEA that a leading military official, Lieutenant Colonel Hugo Francisco Morán Carranza, frequently arranged for bags to slip past customs to enable his associates to transport cocaine in commercial flights. Corroboration followed swiftly. During interrogation, rather than quietly accepting full responsibility, as underlings in drug-trafficking cases often did for fear or profit, Minera revealed Morán's involvement.

As another cover-up effort ensued, Minera Navas sent letters to Guatemalan newspapers from his jail cell. He alleged that high-level officials were protecting drug transshipment, and he claimed to be able to substantiate his charges. Minera declared that a key witness in his case, cargo loader René Estanislao López, had also seen "other unusual transactions at the airport involving public figures important in the political arena." However, before the police could interrogate him, the baggage handler was kidnapped, tortured, and killed. Juan Carlos Bernat, director of the prison where Minera was being held, thereupon prohibited the press from speaking with him. Various congressional deputies, along with Ramiro de León Carpio, then Guatemala's human rights ombudsman and special prosecutor, contended that this treatment violated the constitutional right to free speech. Thus, the Minera Navas affair metamorphosed into a cause célèbre among democratic reformers in Guatemala and a continuing embarrassment for the Cerezo government.[215]

The involvement of Lieutenant Colonel Morán Carranza lay at the root of the official consternation. Unlike the most conservative members of the Guatemalan military, who had scorned civilian rule and plotted coups, Morán had been one of the president's chief aides and closest confidants, considered, in the words of one diplomat, to be "Cerezo's eyes and ears." But Obdullor Chinchilla, an independent legislative deputy, publicly claimed that it was Morán who had stopped police from investigating Minera's charges. When confronted with this allegation, Morán tried to argue that the investigation had been suspended only because he had to attend a foreign conference.[216]

In fact, when Morán had attempted to procure a visa to enter the United States for military training at the Inter-American Defense College, embassy officials had turned him down, citing alleged drug offenses. Morán then reportedly threatened the DEA agent involved in cataloging the evidence for the U.S. ambassador. And three months later, Morán told a visitor to his office,

ante acusación a empleado por traficar de cocaína," *LH* (GU), 2 August 1989, 6; and "Cabecillas del narcotráfico detectados en aeropuerto," *LH* (GU), 10 August 1989, 8

214. For the interrogation and its aftermath, see Castillo and Harmon, *Powderburns*, 212–13.

215. "Guatemalan Officials Accused of Drug Trafficking Links," UPI (US), 15 March 1990; "Minera Navas intentará hablar hoy a la prensa," *LH* (GU), 4 April 1990, 6; "Si hubo violación a los derechos humanos en el caso Minerva," *LH* (GU), 9 April 1990, 7.

216. "Cocaine Makes New Roads," *St. Petersburg Times*, 11 May 1990, 1A; Castillo and Harmon, *Powderburns*, 185; and "Narcotráfico causa enfrentamiento verbal en Congreso," *LH* (GU), 31 October1989, 5. After his arrest Morán stated that Minera "is one of the most efficient employees of this office, and I give him total confidence." "Guatemala Seen Slipping into a Haven for Drugs," *Los Angeles Times*, 30 August 1989, 1.

who turned out to be a Guatemalan-American DEA informant wearing a recording device, that he would have the DEA agent ambushed and murdered on a visit to El Salvador, where the killing could be blamed on guerrillas. Thereafter, U.S. ambassador Thomas Stroock publicly stated of Morán, "We know, unfortunately, that he is involved in drugs." A diplomat from a western European country noted, "Our information is that there were a number of cocaine users very high in the government, and the Department of Administrative Control may have been used as a supplier."[217]

With controversy swirling around Morán, the Guatemalan Army then called him into active duty. Although this effectively immunized the colonel from civilian prosecution, it failed to quell the developing scandal. Another of Morán's subordinates was prosecuted but soon acquitted. The military then took up the case, first handing down a sixty-day suspension and then, after public outcry, discharging Morán. Although under Guatemalan law Morán's termination from the armed forces left a civilian prosecution possible, President Cerezo was in no position to confront the military. After announcing that the case was closed, Cerezo tried to dismiss the Minera Navas affair as nothing more than minor trafficking by a low-level government employee. Cerezo eventually appointed Morán to direct the port authority at Santo Tomás de Castilla, which has been not only Guatemala's busiest harbor but a notable location for maritime drug trafficking.[218]

In the meantime, in 1990, while in jail awaiting trial, Minera reported receiving death threats, as did his family.[219] Nevertheless, when the trial started, Minera again accused various members of Guatemala's political and military elites of complicity in the drug trade. Most sensationally, he claimed that President Cerezo's family, specifically his brother Milton, had engaged in drug trafficking. Minera further insisted that another prominent figure in political circles, Carlos Alfredo Cabrera, was deeply involved, as were certain military intelligence officers. He went on to allege that in his own case the police had failed to deliver to the court the total amount of cocaine that had been in the suitcase. All these charges added to the rampant public suspicion of the Cerezo regime and its ties to organized crime.

During the proceedings at Minera's trial, witnesses contradicted one another, and many details became clouded. Nevertheless, the essence of Minera's defense—that he was simply a pawn in a high-stakes game in which leading officials protected international cocaine traffickers and made fortunes with impunity—gained wide publicity.[220] Eventually, the Fifth Penal Court acquitted Minera. Although Guatemalan officials and others denied Minera's accusations and no case was ever developed against any member of the Cerezo or Cabrera families concerning the cocaine seizure at La Aurora, neither were Minera's charges convincingly swept aside as wholly unfounded.[221] However, with Minera adjudged not guilty of drug trafficking and set free, those behind the cocaine shipment seemed to have escaped punishment. Furthermore, the fact that the investigating judge, Víctor Hugo Pérez Aguilera, repeatedly received death threats

217. "Guatemala Seen Slipping," 1; Castillo and Harmon, *Powderburns*, 215; "Cocaine Makes New Roads," 1A; "Drug Crackdown," 14A.

218. "Drug Crackdown," 14A; "Cocaine Makes New Roads," 1A; "Derechos humanos y narcotráfico provocan enfrentamiento embajada EUA-Cerezo," *LH* (GU), 3 March 1990, 5. When U.S. officials informed Guatemalan counterparts of information linking Morán to trafficking, a minor diplomatic crisis ensued.

219. For Minera's statements, see "Involucran a parientes de Cerezo con el narcotráfico," *LP* (PA), 15 March 1990, 7A; "EUA no dará protección a Minera Navas y familia," *LH* (GU), 16 March 1990, 8; "Guatemalan Officials Accused," and "Esposa de Minera pide apoyo moral al pueblo," *LH* (GU), 17 March 1990, 7.

220. See "Ministerio Público inconforme con fallo," *LH* (GU), 10 April 1990, 32.

221. "Guatemala: Gobierno niega vinculación con narcotráfico," *LP* (PA), 16 March 1990, 3A.

regarding his further inquiries seemed to suggest that a well-connected drug ring wished to ensure that its activities remained hidden.[222]

In the meantime, however, other evidence indicated that one of those Minera had accused, Eric Alfredo Ralda Batres, was indeed implicated in cocaine trafficking. In June 1988, more than a year before Minera's arrest, antidrug agents working a controlled delivery at La Aurora had been watching to see who might collect two suitcases arriving on a flight from Panama that the agents had been informed contained more than sixty kilos of cocaine. When Ralda—variously identified as a farmer, a businessperson, and an intelligence officer—attempted to collect the luggage, he had been arrested and taken into custody. The case then took an interesting, though complicated, twist that touched a number of prominent political figures.[223]

In particular, in the summer of 1988 persistent rumors of complicity in the drug trade had been plaguing Alfonso Cabrera Hidalgo. Brother of Carlos Alfredo, that target of Minera's accusations, Cabrera was a lifelong friend and longtime political associate of Vinicio Cerezo and was then president of the Christian Democrat Party. In 1984 a U.S. federal court had convicted yet another member of the Cabrera family, Vinicio Cabrera, of narcotics trafficking after he was caught in Miami International Airport with ten kilos of cocaine.[224] Upon Vinicio's release from prison and return to Guatemala, Alfonso, then foreign minister, had appointed his brother to serve as cultural attaché in Guatemala's embassy in El Salvador. Alfonso Cabrera, who had become president of the National Assembly and secretary-general of the Christian Democrat Party, then decided to run for the Guatemalan presidency.[225] Viewed as Cerezo's handpicked successor, Cabrera soon proved to be a liability for the president and his administration. Both men came under intense criticism, with U.S. officials noting that Alfonso Cabrera was using a suspected trafficker's helicopter in his presidential campaign, and polls indicated his support had dropped to 6 percent.[226]

The controversy over the Cabrera family, its ties to the Cerezo regime, and its alleged links to cocaine trafficking continued to mount. While in custody Eric Alfredo Ralda Batres implicated Carlos Alfredo Cabrera in the sixty-one-kilo seizure at La Aurora. Ralda reportedly told investigators that this was the person who had given him the claim checks for the luggage, and witnesses confirmed that Carlos Cabrera had indeed been standing on the balcony above the baggage claim when Ralda had attempted to recover the suitcases.

The Ralda arrest, however, occurred just six weeks after an aborted coup attempt had underscored the instability of democracy in Guatemala. Despite suspicious circumstances and incriminating evidence, authorities failed to press drug-trafficking charges against Ralda and released him two days after his arrest. Officials familiar with the case pointed to the likelihood of a cover-up. Indeed, a diplomat who knew Cabrera declared, "It's not believable that he's just the piano player who didn't know what was happening upstairs."[227] Guatemalan investigators chose not to pursue the Cabrera's family possible drug connections. Not only had such elites traditionally enjoyed de facto immunity from criminal charges, but President Cerezo

222. Interview with Víctor Hugo Pérez Aguilera, Juez Sexto de Instrucción de Rama Penal, 6 July 1990, Guatemala City, Guatemala.

223. For more on the Ralda case, see "Drug Crackdown," 14A, and "Guatemala Seen Slipping," 1.

224. See "Cocaine Makes New Roads," 1A, and "Drug Crackdown," 14A.

225. See, for instance, "President Vanishes," 14. When asked if rumors about Cabrera trafficking drugs were false, a DEA spokesperson would state only, "We haven't cleared him," and a diplomat noted, "He hangs around with rotten apples." "Guatemala Seen Slipping," 1.

226. See "U.S. Pins Hopes on Guatemala Army," *NYT* (US), 5 July 1990, A6, and "Guatemala's Swashbuckling Evangelical Stages a Comeback," *U.S. News and World Report*, 1 October 1990, 49.

227. "Poppy Growing," 24.

may have felt that he could not afford to lose the Cabreras' political support and still retain office. Hence, Cerezo's aides began to deny that the incident had ever occurred.[228] Yet, by this juncture, trying to whitewash the incident caused a further drop in credibility.

Worse still, just over a year later, Ralda's name was again tied to drug incidents. In July 1989 Colombian pilot Rubencito Berveno crash-landed on Ralda's farm in a plane carrying a large cocaine load from Colombia to the United States. Before police arrived at the scene, five men, who had been seen hastily transferring the drugs into a black pickup, had vanished. Nevertheless, authorities who searched Ralda's farm found 54 kilos of cocaine paste, along with maps identifying transshipment airstrips. They also reportedly seized a quarter kilo of cocaine in Ralda's car. At length, antidrug officials located 365 kilos of cocaine on Guatemala's southern coast tied to this incident. Nonetheless, Guatemalan authorities opted not to pursue Ralda for international drug trafficking.[229]

The following October police arrested Ralda once more in another drug scandal related to the Cabrera family. This time police allegedly found the trafficker in possession of 273 grams of cocaine while he drove a car owned by Cabrera's wife. Although the Cabreras claimed that the car had been stolen, authorities declined to charge Ralda with larceny of an automobile, and by month's end a judge had thrown out the case for lack of evidence. Congressional deputy Edmond Mulet later observed, "The whole treatment of [Ralda Batres] . . . would indicate that this guy has some friends in very high places."[230]

Under Guatemala's prior military dictatorship an affair such as that involving Minera might very well have been quietly buried. With the country's new democratic opening, however, the military's grip on civil society had weakened somewhat. While the media did not vigorously investigate what had actually happened, Minera's charges were the subject of numerous press reports. Moreover, in conjunction with the Minera case, the U.S. government chose to publicize its suspicions about trafficking by Lieutenant Colonel Morán Carranza and other military officers. Hence, for many Guatemalans the Minera Navas affair came to symbolize how narco-corruption had penetrated the upper echelons of their society.

Transport by Small Plane

By the end of the 1980s light planes had eclipsed couriers as the drug-trafficking method of choice, and private aircraft have continued, ever since, to transship sizable cocaine loads via Guatemala. While courier trafficking has continued to occur, its characteristics have changed.[231] As drug networks opened European outlets, courier transit was the easiest way to begin to supply those markets.[232] The larger drug organizations, however, preferred to supply the United States through more lucrative approaches, leaving much courier transit to freelancers and smaller networks. Over time, transshipment by mules has thus involved a considerably smaller percentage of all the drugs transiting the country.

Since an antiquated radar system, with a cramped maximum range of several dozen miles, has long permitted flights to proceed

228. A Guatemalan congressman later stated, "For all intents and purposes, we pretend it didn't happen." "Guatemala Seen Slipping," 14A. For more on Cerezo's attitude toward the drug trade, see "Cerezo desmiente vinculos con el narcotráfico," *LH* (GU), 3 August 1989, 26, and "René de León: 'Cerezo no quiso combatir el narcotráfico,'" *LH* (GU), 28 September 1990, 32.

229. "Rastrean cuantioso cargamento de cocaína," *LH* (GU), 12 July 1989, 7; "Capturan a narcotraficante," *LH* (GU), 12 October 1989, 7; "Se intensifica búsqueda de narcotraficantes," *LH* (GU), 13 October 1989, 7.

230. "Rastrean cuantioso cargamento," 7; quote from "Drug Crackdown," 14A.

231. For representative later courier cases, see *United States v. Ramos*, 26 Fed. Appx. 80, and "Condenan a narcotraficante," *SV* (GU), 6 March 1999, 6.

232. For a representative case, see "Inglés capturado con Q800 mil de cocaína," *SV* (GU), 1 March 1998, 2, and "Sospechan que el presunto narcotraficante británico es un correo," *SV* (GU), 2 March 1998, 4.

undetected by domestic authorities, Guatemalan officials have not been able to follow all the flight paths through their airspace.[233] Then, even when authorities have managed to track a plane, the aircraft might fly over Guatemalan territory for only a short time.[234] Particularly before the 1992 introduction of U.S. Bell and then Black Hawk military helicopters, Guatemalan antidrug authorities often could not reach landing sites.[235] When officials have intercepted a drug plane, they have then often faced a firefight with well-equipped traffickers. In a representative 2001 case Guatemalan authorities engaged in a shoot-out with smugglers unloading a drug plane who had night-vision equipment and laser-guided weapons with which to defend themselves.[236]

While the presence of numerous uncontrolled airstrips has been a prime bridge-favoring factor throughout the region, Guatemala—with its many scattered ranches and small communities—has offered drug networks a plethora of aerial-trafficking targets. In one 1989 case involving the crash of a plane carrying 400 kilos of cocaine, police discovered maps identifying thirteen hidden airstrips the smugglers could choose among for refueling.[237] Even this, however, was a small fraction of all the country's clandestine runways. Some of these were newly created; others had been constructed long before. And officials disputed whether the total came to hundreds of airstrips or a thousand or more.[238]

During his period in Guatemala, DEA agent Celerino Castillo worked undercover, posing as a maintenance worker, and helped to refuel more than fifty small planes loaded with cocaine. All of these aircraft were associated with a single Guatemalan organization active in the mid-1980s. He later noted, "Most flights carried 300 to 500 kilos of cocaine, and . . . [were] charged $500 per kilo for delivery, plus expenses."[239] In 1989 another U.S. official declared of the many Guatemalan way stations in the cocaine trade, "Farm managers are routinely paid $50,000 to look the other way."[240] Two years later, another DEA agent stationed in Guatemala estimated that about ten airplanes carrying loads of cocaine were landing in the country each week.[241] A U.S. federal court case revealed further details concerning such transshipment operations, when a DEA confidential informant took possession of 770 kilos of cocaine at another Guatemalan airstrip.[242]

For aerial-trafficking schemes Guatemala has amounted to a very convenient midpoint from Colombia or Panama en route to northern Mexico and the United States. Trafficking networks

233. See DEA, *Resources, Guatemala* (2001), 3; "Poppy Growing," 24; and "US Targets Guatemalan Opium," 6. See also the comments of General Gramajo in "Guatemala: Falta de radar impide control de narcotráfico," *LH* (GU), 9 March 1990, 4A, and "Guatemalan Army Called Best," 3A.

234. For a similar observation about intercepting small planes smuggling drugs in the United States, see Reuter, Crawford, and Cave, *Sealing the Borders*, vii.

235. See "Anti-drug Drive," A4.

236. "Policía guatemalteca incauta cien kilos de cocaína," *LP* (HO), 10 April 2001, 41A.

237. "Rastrean cuantioso cargamento," 7.

238. In 2004 Guatemalan authorities calculated that their country contained 150 legitimate and 250 clandestine airstrips ("Guatemala Warns," N3, and "Logística inapropriada impide captura de narcos," *SV* [GU], 27 January 2004, 11), but these figures substantially underestimated the problem. In 1993 officials had counted 640 official runways and estimated 1,000, and possibly as many as 1,600, unsupervised strips. "Drugs: Guatemala Major Trans-shipment and Storage Site for Cocaine," IPS (US), 30 December 1993. Indeed, authorities from the Ministry of the Interior and Civil Aviation repeatedly figured the country had more than 1,000 clandestine runways, while a DEA attaché to Guatemala estimated the southern coast alone had more than 1,000. See "Narcotráfico: 145 aviones aterrizan," 20; "Denuncian que en Guatemala hay mil pistas clandestinas," *LP* (PA), 28 September 1991, 3A; "New Drug Focus," A10. In 1994 the DEA estimated that Guatemala contained a total of 1,200 clandestine airstrips. "Drug Flow Increasing," *TR* (BZ), 20 February 1994, 10. See also "DOAN: Cientos de pistas clandestinas facilitan el tránsito de la droga," *SV* (GU), 13 March 1996, 1, and "Policía busca pistas de aterrizaje usadas por narcos en Guatemala," *LP* (PA), 12 March 1991, 4A.

239. Castillo and Harmon, *Powderburns*, 123.

240. "Drug Crackdown," 14A.

241. "Guatemala Seizes Record Amount of Cocaine," UPI (US), 6 March 1991.

242. *United States v. Joelson*, 7 F.3d 174.

could arrange either to have a heavily loaded propeller plane refueled en route north or to have one plane fly a Colombia-Guatemala route, and another the next leg north. Alternatively, the drugs could be off-loaded in Guatemala and warehoused while awaiting future transport.[243] Over time, the quantities have increased, as have the sizes of the planes, with cocaine loads of 500–1,000 kilos becoming commonplace. Indeed, although traffickers have mostly employed small aircraft, occasionally larger planes have been used, substantially increasing the payload. In 1991 a C-46 cargo plane crashed, permitting officials to seize 2,500 kilos.[244]

Over time, the use of private planes to transship cocaine through Guatemala has ebbed and flowed somewhat. In 1993, for instance, U.S. government intelligence indicated that criminal enterprises were shifting cocaine trafficking away from aircraft and toward maritime and overland methods. By the mid-1990s some air traffic was bypassing Guatemala for locations in Mexico; however, planes continued to utilize landing strips in south-central and northern Guatemala, including Zacapa and the Petén. Then, in yet another indication of the quick adaptability of traffickers, in early 1997 the U.S. helicopters being used to transport antidrug units to transshipment sites were abruptly pulled from the country, and air traffic increased markedly once again. Soon, the DOAN was estimating that at least a planeload of cocaine was entering Guatemala each week. In 2001 Guatemalan attorney general Juan Luis Flores noted that drug syndicates were buying land along the country's borders and constructing additional airstrips there to transship cocaine.[245]

Many of the most notorious drug-trafficking airstrips have been located in the Petén, the Pacific lowlands, and the banana-growing region around Lake Izabal. While the central government often ignored Petén inhabitants, traffickers who owned large tracts there have curried favor by owning soccer teams, paying for electricity and health care, and sometimes allying with revolutionary groups.[246] In 2006 traffickers were found to have bought farms and created airstrips in the Sierra del Lacandón in the Maya Biosphere, south of Laguna del Tigre, near the Mexican border.[247] In some cases authorities have discovered traffickers to be using runways once utilized by oil companies.[248] However, drug-smuggling networks have taken advantage of runways across the country, with major air trafficking near communities in Quiché, San Marcos, Alta Verapaz, and Suchitepéquez.[249]

When concerns arose that authorities might interrupt a transshipment operation, an even more secure option was to drop narcotics to a ground crew, perhaps using a lake or waterway to avoid damaging the product. Thus, cocaine pilots have made water drops onto Lake Izabal

243. For a case involving this approach, see *United States v. Valencia-Quintana*, 136 Fed. Appx. 707. In 1991 undercover DEA agents contracted to export cocaine from Guatemala, using coordinates provided by Colombian trafficker to pick up 410 kilos of cocaine.

244. *INCSR* (1992), 154.

245. *INCSR* (1994), 149; *INCSR* (1996), 133; *INCSR* (1998), 137–38.

246. See "Endurance of Corruption," A1. For a seizure of five hundred kilos of cocaine, arms and ammunition, and subversive propaganda at a clandestine airstrip on Santa Amalia ranch near Laguna Colorado and the small settlement of San Francisco, about forty-five kilometers south of Flores, see "Guardia de Hacienda tras narcotraficantes," *LH* (GU), 2 July 1991, 8, and "Incautan quinientos kilos de cocaína en Guatemala," *LP* (HO), 3 July 1991, 18.

247. "President Steps Up Fight."

248. For 668 kilos of cocaine seized on the Chisec highway from traffickers using a clandestine strip at the Verapaces petroleum wells, see "Incautan cocaína con un valor de Q. 83.3 millones," *LH* (GU), 1 April 1991, 8. For an "inspection tour" carried out by traffickers in 1978 of potential airstrips that could handle a ten-ton DC-6, followed by the decision to use one, near Flores, constructed by oil companies, see *United States v. Elam*, 678 F.2d 1234.

249. For example, see "Decomisan 380 kilos de cocaína en pista clandestina," *LP* (HO), 28 April 2001, 44A; "Cuatro capturados con cocaína," *LPL* (GU), 22 January 1996, 8; "El DOAN y la DEA desentierran aeronave," *SV* (GU), 11 November 1996, 49; and "SIPROCI implementa nuevo sistema en lucha contra las drogas," *LH* (GU), 6 January 1989, 7.

as well as various smaller lakes and lagoons.[250] Cocaine has also occasionally been exported by river. In 2004 a Guatemalan aircraft followed a cocaine plane across the country. When the authorities had to stop to refuel, the traffickers landed near Pípiles, a town where the Ríos Pasión and Salinas merge to become the Usumacinta that then forms much of the Mexican border, to off-load a large cocaine shipment onto boats. When authorities finally arrived, a shoot-out ensued with the traffickers fleeing across the river into Mexico. Mexican and Guatemalan authorities eventually discovered 1.8 tons of cocaine, along with nearby wreckage of two other planes, burned by traffickers after earlier successful transshipment ventures.[251]

From the late 1990s on, as the Mexican Air Force began to chase suspected drug-smuggling planes more aggressively, Guatemala gained an increasing share of the aerial cocaine traffic heading north from South America. The country's law enforcement has lacked the planes and helicopters needed for extensive counterdrug operations, and in any event funds have been scarce for fuel and repairs. Consequently, authorities have interdicted only a small percentage of the cocaine passing through. For example, although in 1997 Guatemalan officials estimated that planes were delivering narcotics in Guatemala at least once a week, through the entire year they intercepted only three aircraft.[252] In 1999 the U.S. State Department figured that Guatemala was interdicting less than five percent of the drugs transshipped through the country.[253]

Nonetheless, given the sheer quantities of drugs in transit, drug organizations have slipped up on occasion, and other evidence of extensive aerial trafficking has surfaced. When planes have been loaded too heavily or have been caught flying in risky weather, pilots have often been forced to crash-land. These damaged aircraft have regularly been left behind, with the traffickers salvaging what they could of the cargo, and the authorities or local people taking the remainder. In 1998, for example, U.S. authorities tracked a twin-engine Cessna all the way from Colombia to Guatemala, where it crashed on a beach in the fog. By the time that antinarcotics officials reached the accident site, however, villagers had made off with an estimated ton of cocaine, and the two pilots had hitched rides to Guatemala City and disappeared.[254]

In March 2003 Guatemalan authorities forced a light plane carrying 1,095 kilos of cocaine to land near Lake Izabal. The next month they seized another 860 kilos from an airplane that had landed by accident on the southern side of that same lake.[255] In September of that year, the air force intercepted a Guatemala-registered DC-47 over Livingston, forced it to land in Izabal, and seized its cargo of 1,640 kilos of cocaine.[256] A few days later, police confiscated another 1.4 tons in the Petén. In 2009 Guatemalan authorities tried to seize a drug plane that had landed on a clandestine airstrip on a farm in the Río Dulce sector of Izabal. Although heavily armed traffickers, thought to be Zetas, fired on police and successfully escaped with the drug shipment, the plane was

250. See "Technology Gleans Data," A25. See also "Tres narcos mexicanos sentenciados en Cobán," *SV* (GU), 14 November 1996, 42. For a search of an alleged Cali associate thought to oversee the refueling of Petén drug planes, see "Fiscalía investiga nombres y direcciones encontrados al colombiano García Angulo," *SV* (GU), 22 August 1996, 3.

251. See "Decomisan novecientos kilos de cocaína," *SV* (GU), 26 January 2004, 8; "Logística inapropriada impide captura de narcos," *SV* (GU), 27 January 2004, 11; and "Drugs Seized in Guatemala," *TT* (CR), 30 January 2004, 12.

252. "Just What the Smuggler Ordered," *WP* (US), 2 August 1998, A1.

253. "Guatemala no tendrá financiamento adicional anti drogas," *SV* (GU), 1 March 1999, 6.

254. "What the Smuggler Ordered," A1.

255. ACANEFE, Panama City, quoted in "Guatemalan Police Seize 860 kg of Cocaine," Financial Times Information (United Kingdom), 9 April 2003.

256. See "Guatemalan authorities seize 1.64 tonnes of cocaine," Xinhua General News Service, 16 September 2003, and "Guatemala Triples Drug Busts in 2003," Financial Times Information (United Kingdom), 22 September 2003, noting also an earlier 920-kilo seizure.

seized, along with an arsenal of weapons that included eleven grenades and a MAG-30 submachine gun, a potent antiaircraft weapon.[257]

Trafficking organizations have sometimes employed the same drug planes repeatedly, as even those that authorities seized have then been available at government auctions at cut-rate prices.[258] However, the principal smuggling networks active in Guatemala have been so wealthy, and the loads of cocaine so valuable, that they have come to consider even their drug-carrying airplanes to be disposable. It has thus not been unusual for traffickers to land on remote airstrips, quickly unload the drugs, and then abandon or burn the aircraft.[259] The fire can eliminate potentially incriminating trace remnants of drugs and also the plane's identification numbers, making further investigation difficult or impossible. By 2004 so many derelict planes lay in the Petén's Laguna del Tigre that some termed it Guatemala's "airplane graveyard."[260] For at least two decades the Zacapa cartelito has been deeply involved in aerial cocaine trafficking through Guatemala, and its activities illustrate the magnitude of this trade and its connections within Guatemalan political and military circles.

The Zacapa Cartelito

In 1990 a group of campesinos living around nearby Los Amates, a city of seventy thousand, formally complained to local judicial authorities that the army was abetting the drug trade by building runways; moreover, those who learned of their activities were being intimidated, tortured, or even killed.[261] They specified that the ringleader was Zacapa's mayor—Arnoldo Vargas Estrada.[262]

A prominent rancher in southern Guatemala, Vargas had declared himself an evangelical Christian, a popular religious movement in the country, and had then entered politics. He was first elected in 1985, and then reelected in 1990, to serve as mayor of Zacapa. Vargas had longstanding ties with the local military, having collaborated with them from an early age and eventually being named a military commissioner, a designation used for paramilitary associates.[263] Vargas seemed to have considerable money of obscure origins, and in 1982 authorities under the Ríos Montt regime jailed him on illegal-enrichment charges. Nevertheless, when the general was deposed the following year, Vargas avoided serious penalty. When first elected mayor in 1985, he declared $1 million in assets and later claimed to contribute $350,000 to the community over his first term.[264]

In 1989, according to a U.S. federal court, traffickers from the organization of Colombian Luis Norberto Arboleda in Bogotá shifted from transporting cocaine in tractor trailers north from Panama to smuggling it by plane through south-central Guatemala.[265] Assisted by Colombians experienced in moving drugs through

257. "Incautan al narco arsenal y vehículos," *SV* (GU), 22 March 2009, 3.

258. See "Avioneta que vendió el OJ fue decomisada en otros países," *SV* (GU), 4 March 1998, 5, and "Investigan infiltración de los cárteles," *SV* (GU), 23 March 1998, 4.

259. See, for instance, "Decomisan 380 kilos," 44A.

260. "Pit Stop," A20. For more burned planes, see "Hallan dos narcoavionetas," *SV* (GU), 1 August 2009, 7; "Queman una narcoavioneta," *SV* (GU), 3 March 2009, 7; "Incendian avioneta en Mazatenango," *SV* (GU), 2 March 1999, 12; and "Localizan avioneta del narcotráfico," *SV* (GU), 5 February 1999, 4.

261. "New Kingdom of Cocaine," C4.

262. See "Guatemala Is Latest Battlefield." A member of the National Center Union Party, Vargas had been elected in 1986 and reelected in 1990. "Capturan alcalde vinculado al narcotráfico," *LP* (HO), 29 December 1990, 26. For useful accounts of the Vargas affair, see "Caso Vargas Estrada," *SV* (GU), 14 March 1996, 12, and "DEA: Duro golpe al 'Cartel de Zacapa,'" *LH* (GU), 7 March 1991, 7.

263. Guatemalan military commissioners are authorized to carry weapons and assist the armed forces with tasks including recruiting, guarding government installations, and reporting suspected criminal activity. *Hernandez-Recinos v. United States INS*, 1998 U.S. App. LEXIS 2967. One U.S. intelligence cable describes them as "the 'eyes and ears' of the military" at the grass-roots level. "Untouchable Narco-State," 18.

264. "Guatemala Keeps Watch on N.Y. Trial," UPI (US), 6 March 1996.

265. *United States v. Vargas*, 1998 U.S. App. LEXIS 25990.

the country, the organization approached Mayor Vargas, known as "Archie" to Colombian cocaine traffickers. They arranged with him to improve an airstrip and then to land planes on two of his farms, one near Los Amates and another near Zacapa.[266] In June 1990 this network shipped through 550 kilos of cocaine, with the mayor reportedly being provided fifty thousand dollars for providing the airstrip, ground assistance, and then protection and temporary storage for the cocaine, which was to be transported overland by tractor trailer through Mexico and into the United States.[267] Over the next three months, at least six more loads followed, with the cocaine winding up in Georgia, Texas, and New York.[268] These activities led to a 1990 New York federal grand jury indictment against Vargas.[269]

After a phone call was intercepted between Mayor Vargas and conspirator Ricardo Espinoza, DEA agents in the United States captured three Colombians, 700 kilos of cocaine, and $1.4 million.[270] To reduce his sentence and gain a spot in the Federal Witness Protection Program, Espinoza opted to collaborate with the government, and he identified to federal agents three clandestine runways and a narcotics warehouse nine miles from Guatemala City. In December 1990, after a U.S. extradition request, a hundred Guatemalan officers from the national police, treasury police, and military police arrested Vargas at his home, along with two close associates.[271] In a tunnel under one of the mayor's farms, authorities seized 287 kilos of cocaine; twenty-six firearms, including automatic weapons; and fragmentation grenades and other explosives.[272] About four months later, a second raid turned up much more cocaine: a total of 3,500 kilos.[273]

Despite the substantial evidence of warehousing narcotics, the effort to extradite Vargas soon stalled. His Zacapa organization allegedly provided such large bribes to those helping with his legal difficulties that U.S. ambassador Stroock characterized it as "spending money like a drunken sailor."[274] When bribery flagged in effectiveness, intimidation was employed. In early 1991 the Zacapa group claimed responsibility for a bombing campaign that it threatened to continue until Vargas was released.[275] Eventually, the extradition request came to court for decision. Judge Oscar López Lemus pointed to the technicality that the extradition request lacked the U.S. Embassy seal and ruled that incriminating tape recordings of the mayor's conversations were insufficient evidence.[276] In response, the Guatemalan government appealed the decision, while filing criminal charges against López, and the U.S. government stripped him of his entry visa. After a jailbreak in which investigators implicated Vargas's brother, congressman Elder Vargas, triggering his expulsion from the National Center Union Party, Guatemala finally extradited the former mayor to the United States in 1992.[277] A federal court then convicted Arnoldo Vargas Estrada of

266. An associate testified that trafficking planes had landed on Vargas's farms as early as July 1989. "Informan sobre pruebas contra Arnoldo Vargas," *LH* (GU), 13 February 1991, 5, and "Guatemala convertida en importante eslabón para el tráfico de cocaína," *LP* (HO), 17 June 1991, 26.

267. *United States v. Vargas*, 1998 U.S. App. LEXIS at 25992.

268. See "Drug Trade Routed Through Guatemala," *WP* (US), 25 May 1991, A27. Vargas was also allegedly supplying cocaine to Guatemalan drug markets. "Policía de Guatemala persigue narcos del Cartel de Medellín," *LP* (PA), 9 March 1991, 3A.

269. "U.S. Miffed at Guatemala in Drug Case," *Los Angeles Times* (United States) (hereafter cited as *LAT* [US]), 22 March 1992, 25.

270. See "En un mes decidirán sobre incidente de extradición," *LH* (GU), 13 July 1991, 4.

271. See December 1990 cable from U.S. Embassy to Washington officials. "Mayor of Zacapa Arrested."

272. See "Drug War Aims," 8; "Guatemala Seizes Record Amount"; "U.S. Wants to Extradite Mayor Accused of Drug Trafficking," UPI (US), 28 January 1991; "Guatemala: decomisan 3,500 kilos de cocaína en finca de alcalde," *LP* (HO), 7 March 1991, 20; and *INCSR* (1992), 148.

273. "Guatemala Is Latest Battlefield."

274. "Drug Trade Routed," A27.

275. "Challenge on Three Fronts for Serrano," *Latin America Weekly Report*, 31 January 1991, 10.

276. "U.S. Miffed at Guatemala," 25.

277. See "Guatemala: Weeding Out Corruption Looks Like an Endless Job," IPS (US), 3 September 1993; Juhn, "Central America," 395; "E.U. pide extradición de alcalde de Guatemala acusado de narco," *LP* (PA), 31 December 1990, 4A; and "En Guatemala, presunto jefe narco será extraditado a E.U.," *LP* (PA), 19 February 1992, 5A.

international cocaine trafficking, sentencing him to more than thirty years in prison.[278]

As elsewhere in Central America, however, even such a major counternarcotics triumph made no lasting dent in trafficking through the country. One DEA official wryly observed, "There are other people who jumped into their places very quickly."[279] The same group of campesinos that had earlier informed on Vargas wrote again to the DEA to report that the Zacapa network's smuggling operation, still linked to local military figures, had simply moved farther into the countryside. The attention of authorities attempting to determine who had taken over the Zacapa cartelito after Vargas's downfall eventually turned to his former close associate Byron Berganza Espina.[280]

Reportedly connected to the notorious Guatemalan death squad, the White Hand, Berganza had long administered Vargas's landholdings, which on occasion brought him into the public eye.[281] In 1991, for instance, a C-47 transport plane packed with 2.5 tons of cocaine crashed, killing six traffickers, on a landing strip on a Quiriguá farm, just a few kilometers from Los Amates. The farm had been owned by Vargas and was rented at the time to Berganza.[282] At this time, Berganza was also accused of aiding the Vargas operation by attempting to intimidate local citizens. For example, according to local farmer Celedonio Pérez, Berganza had ordered him kidnapped and tortured when Vargas came to believe that nearby residents had informed on drug shipments entering Zacapa.[283]

For quite some time Berganza seemed a most capable successor to Vargas. He was thought to have worked closely with the Colombians who had set up the Arboleda transshipment scheme, and later Berganza allegedly became a key Guatemalan connection for the Cali and Sinaloa cartels.[284] Over the next several years, the Zacapa organization grew in prominence, peaking in influence in the mid-1990s.[285] In 1996, however, on a farm owned by Berganza in Los Amates, authorities came upon a plane being refueled that contained 359 kilos of cocaine.[286] Authorities again opted not to arrest Berganza forthwith, and a Puerto Barrios judge eventually revoked an arrest warrant against him for drug trafficking and storage, a testament, perhaps, to the influence he wielded within the legal system.[287]

During the next two years, however, police confiscated approximately three tons from the Zacapa organization, sending Berganza into hiding and triggering internal battles for control of his enterprise.[288] After a lengthy investigation, the DEA learned that in September 2003 Berganza would be traveling from Guatemala to El Salvador. Tipped to his presence, Salvadoran antidrug officials arrested him, immediately expelling Berganza to the United States. Prosecutors charged that coconspirators, "acting under the direction of . . . Berganza . . . possessed approximately 1,020 kilos of cocaine, destined for the New York area."[289] In 2008 he was sentenced to nearly twenty-two years in prison for conspiring to import more than twenty tons of cocaine.[290]

278. See *United States v. Vargas*, 1998 U.S. App. LEXIS 25990.

279. "Drug Trade Routed," A27.

280. "Untouchable Narco-State," 19; "El poder tras el trono," *SV* (GU), 29 January 2004, 9. Certain antidrug sources claimed that Harold García, allegedly Cali's representative in Guatemala, also helped oversee Zacapa operations after Vargas's arrest.

281. "Poder tras el trono," 9. For Berganza and the White Hand, see "Antecedentes y relaciones," *SV* (GU), 28 January 2004, 3.

282. "Intensas investigaciones en caso de avión con cocaína," *LH* (GU), 12 October 1991, 7.

283. "Antecedentes y relaciones," 3.

284. See "Caso Vargas Estrada," 12.

285. "Poder tras el trono," 9.

286. See "Interceptan avioneta con cocaína valuada en más de Q50 millones," *SV* (GU), 28 July 1996, 47; "MP presenta acusación contra implicado en caso de narcotráfico," *SV* (GU), 14 November 1996, 5; and "GH [Guardia de Hacienda] duplica decomisos de cocaína en comparación con año anterior," *SV* (GU), 15 August 1996, 3.

287. "Antecedentes y relaciones," 3.

288. "Poder tras el trono," 9.

289. "Poder tras el trono," 3; quote from *United States v. Berganza*, 2005 U.S. Dist. LEXIS 2203, at 2221n4.

290. United States Attorney, Southern District of New York, "Guatemalan Cocaine Kingpin Sentenced to 262 Months in Prison," 11 April 2008, www.justice.gov/usao/nys/pressreleases/April08/berganzasentencingpr.pdf.

Although at times the leadership of Central American cartelitos might appear kaleidoscopic, continuing the drug trade hinged not on kingpin expertise so much as on routes and methods that succeeded far more than they failed. Hence, even with Vargas and Berganza imprisoned, major cocaine-trafficking operations still occurred in the same area between Lake Izabal and the Honduran border, still capitalizing on the encouragement and collaboration of powerful Colombian and Mexican organizations. And, while sea and land routes have gained popularity among trafficking organizations, the import of major quantities of cocaine by air has remained a key aspect of the Guatemalan transshipment business.

Sea Routes

At sea, to move cocaine via Guatemalan territorial waters, criminal syndicates have called on an array of vessels, from sailboats to coastal freighters to trawlers. Each vessel offers certain advantages. Authorities might be reluctant to tear apart an expensive yacht in search of a possible hidden compartment. Merchant ships sail regularly, full of legitimate products among which cocaine might be secreted. Commercial fishing vessels might unobtrusively relay drugs from mother ships stationed offshore. However, late in the 1990s and early in the new millennium, speedboat transport gained popularity as the fastest method to move a large load. Given Guatemala's lax law enforcement in its coastal and inland waters, maritime trafficking has proven to be sufficiently successful that traffickers have continued to use it regularly and have sometimes relied on it to transport shipments of increasing size.

Reflective of the country's geographic position and its considerable exports, especially agricultural commodities and light manufactured goods, Guatemala's ports on the Caribbean and Pacific coasts have handled considerable numbers of shipping containers. Concealing drugs in the containerized traffic had not yet become a particular problem in the 1980s, but by the following decade drug organizations were increasingly using legitimate shipping to camouflage their activities.[291] Thus, cocaine headed north from the island of San Andrés or Colombian mainland ports or such Central American trafficking centers as the Colón Free Zone in Panama has frequently been off-loaded in Guatemala.[292] Cocaine that has arrived in Guatemala by air, land, or sea has also been hidden in cargo directed to the United States and Europe. The vortex of Guatemala's maritime cocaine trade has long been the Caribbean coast, particularly Santo Tomás de Castilla and neighboring Puerto Barrios.[293] Occasionally, smugglers have also capitalized on Livingston, situated at the mouth of the Río Dulce connecting Lake Izabal with the Bay of Honduras. With a distinctly Caribbean flavor and a population that includes large numbers of Garífuna, Livingston is accessible only by boat and has ferry connections to Puerto Barrios and also to Punta Gorda, Belize, and, occasionally, to Omoa, Honduras, just southwest of Puerto Cortés.

As for Guatemala's Pacific coast, during the 1990s and especially in the new century, cocaine smuggling has increasingly occurred here with traffickers delivering loads of 500–1,000 kilos by sea and air.[294] Drug smuggling has been directed through Puerto Quetzal, in the

291. In the 1980s officials linked only a single large U.S. cocaine seizure to a shipping container originating in Guatemala. *INCSR* (1990), 176.

292. For one such scheme, see "Decomisan droga que venía para Guatemala," *SV* (GU), 5 March 1999, 2.

293. For a representative large seizure at Santo Tomás of a National Guard marijuana confiscation of five tons shipped into Guatemala from Colombia for transshipment to the United States, see "Marihuana en Guatemala," *LN* (CR), 25 July 1990, 20A. For one at Puerto Barrios, see "Incautan cocaína valuada en más de Q200 millones," *SV* (GU), 28 August 1996, 1–2. By 2009 in a typical month Guatemala might export through its ports more than 8 million tons and import 10–12 million tons. "Sube carga marítima hacia el extranjero," *SV* (GU), 24 September 2009, 12.

294. For example, on Guatemala's Pacific coast, an undercover DEA agent received 496 kilos of cocaine shipped from Colombia by Cali traffickers; see *United States v. Aguirre-Parra*, 763 F. Supp. 1220. See also

middle of the coast, and also such smaller communities as Champerico and Iztapa, as well as Puerto de Ocos near the Mexican border.[295] Southwestern Guatemala has confronted extensive drug trafficking as well, with large cocaine loads entering by sea or by combined sea-and-overland routes via El Salvador. Guatemalan ports on both coasts have also handled precursor chemicals, about half of them consumed by legitimate enterprises in Guatemala and the rest transshipped south for legal and illegal undertakings.[296]

While most of the narcotics shipped through Guatemala have escaped detection, occasionally traffickers have slipped up, providing glimpses of extensive maritime operations. For example, in 1992 the *Coloso I*, a Colombian vessel headed to Guatemala with 1.5 tons of cocaine, struck a reef off Costa Rica's Santa Elena Peninsula. Although the smugglers attempted to hide about 700 kilos on a nearby beach while they procured another vessel, authorities intercepted their communications, locating and detaining the group, while local fishermen stole much of the shipment.[297] In 1994 the DEA tipped Central American police forces to a Cali operation shipping cocaine from Buenaventura, Colombia, up the coast to Guatemala. After Costa Rican authorities chased one of the organization's vessels into Nicaraguan waters, authorities there confiscated 650 kilos.[298]

The cardinal point here is that traffickers opting for maritime geotactics could direct shipments through an extraordinary variety of targets along Guatemala's coasts. To choke off narcotics transshipment by sea was well beyond the capacity of counternarcotics authorities at work in the country. However, the incidents recounted earlier also underscore that traffickers moving cocaine by sea, although often successful, did have to reckon with the authorities. From very small numbers in the mid-1980s, the DEA presence in Guatemala grew rapidly to become the largest within Central America. Ties between the CIA and Guatemalan military intelligence have also sometimes benefited antidrug operations. From time to time confidential informants have provided leads on Guatemalan maritime trafficking. And yet these factors have often been counterbalanced by the narcocorruption of authorities—political, judicial, military, and law enforcement. The capture of the *Daring* illustrates a number of these points.[299]

The Case of the Daring

In 1987 counternarcotics officials were watching Guatemalan congressman Carlos Ramiro García de Paz, suspected of being an intermediary

"Decomisados 466 kilos de cocaína," *LP* (HO), 6 February 1992, 18; and "Incineran 400 millones de quetzales en cocaína," *LH* (GU), 7 August 1989, 5.

295. For a representative case of drug smuggling through Puerto Quetzal, see "Incautan supuesta droga," *SV* (GU), 18 April 2009, 8. For Champerico, see, for instance, "Cae avión que transportaba cocaína," *LH* (GU), 2 October 1991, 7, and "Tres Salvadoreños capturados por caso de cocaína incautada ayer," *LH* (GU), 3 October 1991, 8. For a large aerial shipment entering Guatemala into nearby Tiquisate, see "Guatemala: Incautan avioneta colombiana con 1,300 kilos de cocaína," *LP* (HO), 24 October 1991, 24. For Iztapa, where 893 kilos of cocaine shipped to Playa El Carrizo was discovered before a flight north, see "Descubrieron millonario contrabando de cocaína," *LPL* (GU), 16 November 1991, 6. See also "Millonario cargamento de cocaína decomisan," *LH* (GU), 18 November 1991, 8, and "Capturan a panameño y colombiano con cargamento de droga," *LP* (PA), 17 November 1991, 3A. For Puerto de Ocos, see "President Steps Up Fight."

296. *INCSR* (1990), 176, and *INCSR* (1991), 146.

297. Lacking tangible evidence, a Liberia court freed the Colombians. However, five Costa Rican fishermen who found and tried to sell the drugs were convicted and sentenced to eight to ten years. "Juzgarán por narco a pescadores Guanacastecos," *LN* (CR), 17 January 1994, 10A, and "Cuatro condenados por coca en Cuajiniquil," *LN* (CR), 18 September 1994, 10A.

298. See "Policía nicaragüense confisca cargamento de cocaína," *LP* (HO), 25 April 1994, 30A; "Gran operativo antidrogas," *LN* (CR), 23 April 1994, 10A; "Fishman pide devolver coca," *LN* (CR), 24 April 1994, 10A; "Nicaragua devolverá droga y narcos," *LN* (CR), 26 April 1994, 10A; "Narcos deportados por Nicaragua," *LN* (CR), 27 April 1994, 10A; and "Narcos con antecedentes," *LN* (CR), 30 April 1994, 10A.

299. Castillo and Harmon, *Powderburns*, 107–8; "Guatemala Seizes Record Amount"; "Secret Guatemalan Military Unit," 8A..

organizing ventures with Colombian traffickers.[300] Through wiretaps and informants, the DEA and G-2 learned of a large cocaine shipment to be sent by Medellín traffickers into Florida, by air and sea, via Puerto Barrios. In July the authorities permitted a small cocaine load they had detected to pass through, figuring that the cartel was testing the route, as Pablo Escobar often ordered. Then, in September García de Paz arrived in Puerto Barrios, and the G-2 blanketed his hotel and the port with nearly a hundred agents. Two Colombian traffickers who had been under surveillance in the town vanished, just as the *Daring*, a Panamanian-registered former Canadian Coast Guard cutter, entered the port. García de Paz then drove back to Guatemala City, and the Colombians reappeared with a Mexican trafficker, who had brought along his two daughters to appear to be a family vacationing.

Once the cocaine had been transferred, the G-2 moved in. They arrested the foreigners and also a Guatemalan Air Force reserve officer, who, under interrogation, admitted to having directed the Colombian traffickers to fly into an airstrip at a banana plantation behind Puerto Barrios. He reported that a small train had then transported three thousand kilos of cocaine to the port, and inflatable motorboats had ferried it at night to the *Daring*. The G-2, assisted by the DEA and a CIA agent expert in narcotics detection, boarded the boat, arresting the six Americans and one Canadian found there.

The *Daring* had been lavishly remodeled, and the G-2 went to work disassembling the wood paneling and stripping all other items of value. The cocaine, however, proved to be exceedingly difficult to find. At length, the Colombian and Mexican traffickers offered to reveal where the cocaine was hidden if the G-2 would sell it back to them for $5 million. G-2 officers pretended to agree to the terms. The traffickers then led the authorities to a hidden compartment bolted into the hold, and after calls to Colombia, the following day a Lear jet arrived from Medellín, carrying the cash.

The G-2 then double-crossed the traffickers. They seized the cocaine, officially reporting the total as 2,404 kilos, which amounted to the largest cocaine seizure in Central American history, to date, and the fifth largest that U.S. agents had ever participated in. Guatemalan authorities sent the North Americans to trial for drug trafficking, and the Sixth Court of Appeals in Zacapa convicted them, although imposing the exceptionally light penalty of six years in prison, but only eight months incommutable.[301] The arrested Latin Americans simply disappeared. However, a G-2 lieutenant later revealed their fate to the DEA agent involved. The daughters of the Mexican trafficker had been raped, and all the Mexicans and Colombians had been murdered. Guatemalan authorities had dismembered their bodies, sealed them in large, weighted drums, and disposed of them at sea. As for Representative García de Paz, Pablo Escobar, who had fronted the cocaine and money, reportedly summoned him to Costa Rica for an accounting. Thereafter, Escobar is thought to have sent hit men to Guatemala to murder all involved. The G-2, however, struck first, killing all the assassins but one, who was permitted to return to Colombia to report what had happened. García de Paz was not charged, although the White Hand death squad did publicly identify him as a drug trafficker and threaten his life.

300. For information on the *Daring*, see *Guatemala v. Chapelle et al.*, 6th Ct. of App.s; Castillo and Harmon, *Powderburns*, 159, 185–86, 190–95; "'Mano Blanca' revela amenazas," 24A; "Incautan cocaína por valor de 500 millones de dólares," *LH* (GU), 30 September 1987, 3; "Incautan cargamento de cocaína," *LH* (GU), 29 September 1987, 1; and *INCSR* (1988), 123.

301. Thus, sixty-four months of their terms could be cancelled by paying the court a modest sum to substitute for each day of prison time. See Fowler and Bunck, "Legal Imperialism," 823, and *United States v. Richardson*, 580 F.2d at 947n1.

The *Daring* incident illustrates a number of points about drug trafficking and the law in Guatemala. First, the G-2 was not bumbling, amateurish, or ridiculously ineffective. Rather, its agents, cooperating with U.S. counterparts, formed a reasonably competent and effective counternarcotics force by regional standards. Unlike bridge states completely dependent on DEA information, the G-2 could use its own assets and methods to gain some information on drug trafficking. G-2 members were also not intimidated, even by Escobar's organization, but instead repeatedly underscored the military's primacy within Guatemala. However, the G-2 was also savage and brutal. Taking orders from military commanders, it disregarded civilian laws and officials and carried out extrajudicial killings. While in the *Daring* case that modus operandi was aimed at stopping a trafficking venture, it could easily be put to the service of drug rings. The very effectiveness of the G-2 provided traffickers with the incentive to pay top dollar to corrupt it. As the quantities of cocaine transshipped via Central America soared in the 1990s and thereafter, an interdiction like that on the *Daring* seems not to have deterred cartels so much as spurred them toward more thoroughly and systematically corrupting Guatemalan authorities.

Other Trafficking at Sea

Another noteworthy aspect of maritime trafficking in Guatemala has been the periodic use of yachts to transport cocaine. For instance, in 1989 the Guatemalan Navy, off the country's Pacific coast, intercepted one sailboat, the *Lida*, transporting 788 kilos of cocaine from Guatemala to Los Angeles.[302] On the Caribbean side wealthy Guatemalans have established various marinas, and drug rings have used pleasure boats to carry cocaine across Lake Izabal and to traverse the Río Dulce. Thus, in 1991 a yacht called the *Ghost* sailed from Key Largo, Florida, cleared customs at Livingston, and then proceeded upriver to Lake Izabal. U.S. Customs agents had information that the crew was planning to traffic cocaine for the Colombians who had purchased the boat. They tipped Guatemalan military intelligence, which, in turn, alerted the navy. Its officials seized the *Ghost*, moored at the Hotel Tropical Izabal, discovering 343 kilos of cocaine in a secret compartment.[303]

Even much larger quantities of drugs have been exported on freighters that pass through Guatemalan ports, often headed north to Mexico or to U.S. ports in Florida or along the Gulf of Mexico.[304] In a key 1989 cocaine case U.S. Customs in Tampa confiscated 412 kilos from a refrigerator truck that had been driven onto a Honduran vessel, the *Carib Haven*, at Puerto Barrios.[305] Similarly, after an immense 1992 bust in Miami of 6.7 tons of cocaine, U.S. authorities traced the drugs, which had been hidden in frozen broccoli, to Guatemala, where the container had been loaded for shipment by sea.[306] That Miami seizure led to the arrests of top Cali operatives Francisco Guzmán and Harold Ackerman. A U.S. federal court convicted Ackerman—described by the DEA as "the Cali cartel's ambassador to Miami" and by U.S. Customs as Cali's "big player" in the city—of importing 22 tons of cocaine, sentencing him to six life terms.[307]

Significant busts of cocaine shipped via Guatemala have periodically occurred thereafter. In 1998 Guatemalan authorities discovered 2 tons

302. *INCSR* (1990), 177. See also "Narcotraficantes serán indagados," *LH* (GU), 29 July 1989, 7.

303. *United States v. Behety*, 32 F.3d 503, and *INCSR* (1992), 156.

304. DEA, *Resources, Guatemala* (2001), 4. For a DEA investigation of a Bogotá resident that revealed that large narcotics loads hidden among legitimate exports had been smuggled in the late 1980s via Guatemala, see *United States v. Pujana-Mena*, 949 F.2d 24.

305. See "En Tampa, Florida: Cocaína en camión enviado a Honduras," *LP* (HO), 4 September 1989, 64; "En portuaria podría haberse cargado cocaína incautada en EUA," *LP* (HO), 5 September 1989, 2; "No procedía de Honduras," *LP* (HO), 5 September 1989, 2; and "Tripulantes se declaran inocentes," *LP* (HO), 19 September 1989, 5.

306. *INCSR* (1993), 153. For information on this seizure, see "New Kingdom of Cocaine," C4.

307. Chepesiuk, *Drug Lords*, 157–59, 166. Chepesiuk pieced together Ackerman's career from court documents and interviews with him and the agents who pursued and debriefed him.

in a shipping container being prepared for export. That same year, they found 534 kilos in a container arriving at Santo Tomás de Castilla from Panama's Colón Free Zone. In 1999 authorities seized 1,225 kilos of stored cocaine that investigators believed the Zacapa cartelito had imported and transferred to Guatemala City. The following year DOAN officials confiscated 797 kilos in a container of transformers shipped into Santo Tomás de Castilla from Colombia. Authorities confiscated 3.2 tons from a Guatemalan-flagged vessel in 2004, and another 1,632 kilos off another Guatemalan ship in 2006. A 2006 U.S. federal court case involved the seizure by the U.S. Coast Guard in international waters of more than 2.5 tons from the Guatemalan-registered *El Almirante*.[308]

Negligible security ordinarily found at Guatemalan ports and Guatemala's erratic patrols of territorial waters invited extensive maritime drug trafficking. If information on an upcoming shipment could be screened from law enforcement, and if the U.S. Coast Guard could be evaded, the drugs would very likely transit unmolested. Not until 1995 did Santo Tomás and Puerto Barrios institute port-security measures of any note, and even these were soon criticized. In the late 1990s the Guatemalan government instituted a port-security program financed from a tax levied on shipping companies, and this came to cover Puerto Barrios, Santo Tomás, and Puerto Quetzal. Nevertheless, in 2000 U.S. officials reported that moving cocaine hidden in ship or truck containers remained "the best opportunity for smuggling drugs through Guatemala." Although the U.S. government provided training, technical assistance, and logistical support, State Department officials concluded in 2002 that the program had been "regularly stymied by port corruption." Nevertheless, it had led to a handful of major confiscations, including those at Santo Tomás of 979 and 997 kilos of cocaine in 2004 and 2005, or the total of 1,040 kilos seized in consecutive cases at Puerto Quetzal in 2009.[309]

To further complicate law-enforcement efforts, cocaine shipped out of Guatemala has often arrived in the country by indirect routes. The drugs might very well not have been imported into the same port from which they were exported; some have not even been brought into Guatemala by sea at all.[310] With respect to the twin Caribbean ports, cocaine has periodically arrived in Guatemala by air and has then been transported, sometimes via Lake Izabal and Río Dulce, to Santo Tomás or Puerto Barrios for export.[311] In 1999 Honduran authorities broke up a smuggling ring using helicopters to fly cocaine toward Puerto Barrios from La Mosquitia in northeastern Honduras.[312] Cocaine has also traveled from San Andrés to the Honduran northern coast, sometimes via Honduras's Islas de la Bahía, and then has proceeded overland to Guatemala's Caribbean ports.[313]

In light of the grave limitations to Guatemala's control of offshore waters, cigarette boats that

308. For the cases related in this paragraph, see *INCSR* (1999), 156; *INCSR* (2005), 179, 181; *INCSR* (2006), 144; *INCSR* (2007), 160–61; DEA, *Resources, Guatemala* (2001), 8; *United States v. Garcia*, 182 Fed. Appx. 873; "Fiscalía de drogas investiga a empresa de ZL," *LP* (PA), 4 December 1998, 5A; "Decomisan 1,225 kilos de cocaína," *SV* (GU), 17 February 1999, 2; and "Anuncian visita del director de la DEA," *SV* (GU), 18 February 1999, 8.

309. For information provided by the State Department, see *INCSR* (2000), 169; *INCSR* (2003), 14; and *INCSR* (2005), 17.

310. For thirty-two kilos carried from Costa Rica to Puerto Barrios by car, see "Libre supuesto contacto en Honduras de banda de narcos," *LP* (HO), 3 September 1990, 16.

311. For an example of the capture of a gun, speedboats, and a grenade launcher in an antidrug operation in Amatique Bay, Lake Izabal, see "Tres lanchas y AR-15 incautados a narcos," *SV* (GU), 2 July 1996, 39.

312. "Policía captura 'narco' prófugo y encuentra cincuenta kilos más de cocaína," *LP* (HO), 17 September 1999, 12A.

313. See the statement to this effect by Honduran legislator Carlos Sosa Coello, of the National Council Against Narcotics Trafficking. "A 1,800 kilos de cocaína valorada en $200 millones ascienden decomisos en el país," *LP* (HO), 22 June 1998, 11A.

could move shipments quickly and in a pinch outrun many pursuing vessels have clearly been an attractive option for traffickers. From the late 1990s on, go-fasts speeding along both Guatemalan coasts have contributed significantly to maritime cocaine transit.[314] Speedboats have proven to be far swifter than the small, slow, and antiquated vessels of the Guatemalan Navy and have usually been pursued, if at all, by the U.S. Coast Guard or Navy. For example, in 2002 a speedboat proceeded north to Guatemala from Buenaventura, Colombia, carrying more than 1,586 kilos of cocaine. A U.S. Navy helicopter sighted the go-fast, and the U.S. Coast Guard eventually seized it, also managing to recover the cocaine thrown into the sea during the chase.[315]

At times, speedboats have simply refueled in Guatemalan waters to continue on to Mexico or occasionally Belize. At other times, they have transferred cocaine to fishing vessels, better able to arrive in ports without raising suspicion, or they have dropped off the loads in remote locations on the Guatemalan coasts for warehousing before being moved north by vehicle, plane, or ship. In 1998 one counternarcotics patrol discovered an empty, beached go-fast, a nearby fishing vessel that had collected 140 kilos, and another 525 kilos hidden on the beach. In 2002, about two hundred miles south of Guatemala, a U.S. Navy frigate came upon a Guatemalan vessel, the *Martita Lau*, that was not fishing but was lying low in the water with large containers on deck. The vessel did not respond to being hailed, and navy personnel saw people scrambling to throw objects overboard. Eventually, 12.5 tons of cocaine were recovered. Four of the crew later testified that they had rendezvoused with a speedboat at sea to provide it with fuel but had ended up bringing the crew and cocaine on board, given the vessel's mechanical troubles.[316]

Speedboat traffic has often ranged far offshore, sometimes marking courses through Guatemala's exclusive economic zone or beyond. In early 2003 a joint Guatemalan-Mexican operation seized 242 kilos from two speedboats thirty-two miles from the Pacific coast, and one day later Mexican authorities seized another 1.5 tons from three speedboats in international waters off Puerto Madero, in far southern Mexico. In 2005 the U.S. Coast Guard, operating in the Pacific off Guatemala, intercepted four cocaine shipments amounting to 6 tons and arrested twenty-one individuals, most of them Colombian.[317]

Overland Routes

While Guatemala's rugged topography vastly complicated the development of infrastructure, authoritarian governments nonetheless pressed forward with road construction. Much later, large sums from the so-called peace dividend—that is, the millions of assistance dollars developed countries donated after the 1996 peace accords—were applied to road maintenance, improvement, and construction.[318] As trafficking organizations have become increasingly intent on getting drugs into and through Guatemala, its road network has thus offered considerable possibilities.

In particular, the two major highways that traverse Guatemala's southern departments have encouraged overland drug transport. The

314. In 1997 Guatemalan authorities interrupted one speedboat delivery of 1000 kilos of cocaine. *INCSR* (1998), 138. For a case of 1,513 kilos of cocaine seized by the U.S. Coast Guard in the Pacific off Colombia, headed to Guatemala, see *United States v. Perlaza*, 2006 U.S. App. LEXIS 31646. For another U.S. case involving a go-fast delivery of cocaine into Guatemala, see *United States v. Alegria*, 144 Fed. Appx. 801.

315. *United States v. Moreno*, 134 Fed. Appx. 339.

316. DEA, *Resources, Guatemala* (2001), 6; *INCSR* (1999), 157; *United States v. Revolorio-Ramo*, 468 F.3d 771.

317. "Incautan 242 kilos de coca," *SV* (GU), 2 January 2003, 5; "México confisca 1,500 kilos de cocaína," *SV* (GU), 3 January 2003, 9; "Caen 6,000 kilos de coca y veintiún narcos," *SV* (GU), 2 March 2005, 8.

318. Wilkinson, *Silence on the Mountain*, 215. Under President Jorge Ubico, who governed Guatemala from 1930 to 1944, the government compelled those unable to pay the "road tax" to provide a week's worth of free labor on a highway-construction crew (96).

Pan-American Highway and the Pacific Coast Highway run from the Salvadoran to the Mexican borders. The former, while winding for much of its length, takes drivers right through Guatemala City. The Pacific route is the country's fastest highway, enabling fairly rapid transit from El Salvador all the way to Mexico.[319] In addition, by early in the twenty-first century it had become possible to travel by highway into the Petén. One notable road ran from Cobán to Sayaxché, and in 2000 a new highway opened between Guatemala City and the Péten. This reduced driving time from eighteen hours to seven, providing an improved option for overland trafficking and bringing central Guatemala closer still to drug organizations in Chiapas, the Yucatán, and Mexico's Gulf coast.[320]

Although drugs have been smuggled in all varieties of vehicles, with time the larger organizations have come to favor tractor trailers. Relative to the other Central American states, Guatemala has had thriving export-import dealings, and with the advent of free trade, the truck traffic has increased further. Despite the occasional successes of roadblock interdictions, traffickers have found ground transit relatively easy and secure, and well-connected networks from Colombia, Mexico, and other Central American states have tried to take advantage of the ease of overland access to Guatemala.[321] For instance, in 2008 authorities in Costa Rica arrested Ricardo Alem, one of their most notorious traffickers and money launderers, alleging that his network had been trucking cocaine into Guatemala.[322]

Normally, drugs traveling overland have been imported into southern Guatemala through the customs post at San Cristóbal and the three other principal border crossings from El Salvador.[323] As Salvadoran violence tapered off in the early 1990s, this traffic surged.[324] Smugglers began to deliver sizable cocaine shipments into El Salvador either overland or by cargo ship, small plane, or commercial airliner.[325] These narcotics have then frequently crossed into Guatemala in trucks and other vehicles before being temporarily warehoused or continuing their passage north.[326] For example, in the early 1990s a Guatemalan cartelito headquartered in southern Santa Rosa Department was involved in a series of cocaine water drops off the Salvadoran coast; the cocaine was then delivered to Guatemala hidden in tractor-trailer cargoes.[327]

A stream of cocaine has flowed into Guatemala from Honduras as well. At times, trafficking organizations have shipped or flown cocaine

319. *INCSR* (2000), 167.

320. DEA, *Resources, Guatemala* (2001), 10.

321. In 1987 Guatemala initiated a roadblock-interdiction program that intercepted several large marijuana shipments and may have deterred overland drug transit for a period. *INCSR* (1988), 123. For an Atlantic Highway seizure of marijuana coming from the Caribbean, see "Incautados 190 kilos de marihuana," *LH* (GU), 30 March 1990, 8.

322. See "Alem detenido por decomiso de 170 kilos de cocaína," *LN* (CR), 10 August 2008, 12A.

323. See, for instance, "Mil kilos de cocaína decomisadas," *Al Día* (Guatemala), 15 May 1997, 8, and "DOAN decomisa cargamento de cocaína," *SV* (GU), 10 September 1996, 2. For early overland cocaine trafficking into Guatemala via El Salvador, see *United States v. Richardson*, 580 F.2d 946.

324. For Salvadoran-Guatemalan trafficking, see "El Salvador: PNC vincula a narcos," 6, and "Detienen a banda de narcotraficantes," *LH* (GU), 22 August 1991, 13.

325. For shipments smuggled overland, see, for instance, "Decomisan cocaína a guatemalteco," *LP* (HO), 9 September 1999, 28A. For a Costa Rican court upholding convictions of Guatemalan truck drivers who smuggled 100 and 110 kilos of cocaine and 13 kilos of heroin from Panama via Costa Rica toward Guatemala, see "Confirman condenas contra guatemaltecos 'narcos,'" *LP* (HO), 22 June 1998, 95A. For shipments traveling by cargo ship, small plane, or commercial airliner, see *INCSR* (1991), 28, 142. One popular route in the early 1990s involved flights into the mountainous northern region of El Salvador, especially Jinotega Department. See "Avioneta violó espacio aéreo de Nicaragua," *LP* (PA), 1 November 1991, 6A.

326. For 214 kilos of cocaine located in a house owned by Renato Moino Ruiz, alleged leader of the Cobán cartelito, see "Ubican bodega del capo," *SV* (GU), 12 July 2001, 10.

327. The case against Salvadoran trucking magnate José Irene Escobar Escobar is described in "Al descubierto la relación entre robafurgones y narcotraficantes," *SV* (GU), 9 May 1996, 2, and "López: Aquí funciona el narcocontrabando," *SV* (GU), 16 August 1991, 3. In 1991 authorities seized 2.9 tons of cocaine at the northern Salvadoran port of Acajutla. *INCSR* (1992), 151.

into Honduras, or into Guatemala's Caribbean ports, and had it trucked up the so-called Atlantic Highway into the central portion of the country. In a representative case in 2003, authorities seized 156 kilos of cocaine in a Honduran truck on the Atlantic Highway headed to Tecún Umán and thereafter located more than 800 kilos in a cistern just off the same highway.[328] Whether imported via El Salvador or Honduras, many of the largest cocaine loads have originated in Panama, traversing the length of Central America overland before entering Guatemala.[329] In a typical case in 1993 the DEA joined Guatemalan antidrug police to seize 137 kilos of cocaine transshipped in the tank of a fuel truck via Panama and El Salvador.[330]

Unlike the situation in neighboring Belize, the fairly extensive network of Guatemalan roads has provided trafficking organizations with multiple possible routes for transporting narcotics across the country. In one representative case Guatemalan authorities seized 450 kilos of cocaine headed to the United States and discovered a metal bunker under a mechanic's shop off the Pacific Coast Highway in Suchitepéquez Department, roughly forty miles from the Mexican border. As elsewhere in the region, over time, considerably larger loads have come to be confiscated. For instance, in 1997 counternarcotics officials seized a ton of cocaine hidden in a tractor trailer, and in 2002 they confiscated 838 kilos secreted in a tanker truck loaded with syrup.[331]

In contrast to the circumstances traffickers and law enforcement faced in Costa Rica, where the bottleneck at the northern border meant that narcotics entered the country somewhat more easily than they departed it, drugs in Guatemala have readily been exported to Mexico and on to the United States.[332] The country has numerous roads leading toward Mexico, with a handful of official border crossings and scores of unofficial ones, and considerable drug exports have left the country overland. Indeed, in Guatemala's largest cocaine bust to that date, in 1999 antinarcotics police seized 3.3 tons hidden in three tractor trailers heading for Mexico.[333] Smugglers have repeatedly employed such major border posts into Mexico as La Mesilla in Huehuetenango Department and El Carmen and Tecún Umán in neighboring San Marcos, rife with narco-corruption and intimidation. Tecún Umán, which lies just across from Mexico's Ciudad Hidalgo in Chiapas, has become so packed with bars, brothels, and illegal immigrants as to be nicknamed "Guatemala's Tijuana." In 1989 drug traffickers attacked the Tecún Umán police station with explosives in apparent retaliation for occasional seizures of cocaine and other narcotics.[334] Here, as one local judge noted, drug rings have come to control certain customs agents, and they transport their shipments through only when those agents are on duty. However, should these principal entry points not serve, traffickers have been able to take their pick from scores of others, since even

328. See "Incautan 156 kilos de coca," *SV* (GU), 24 January 2003, 5; "Inicia juicio," *SV* (GU), 10 January 2004, 6; and "Condenado a quince años de prisión," *SV* (GU), 21 January 2004, 10.

329. For representative cases in the 1990s, when this method grew especially popular, see "Decomisan 249 kilos de droga en Chiriquí," *LP* (PA), 11 November 1997, 2; "Narcos purgarán quince años de cárcel," *SV* (GU), 31 March 1998, 8; "Detienen a dos guatemaltecos con 276 kilos de cocaína," *SV* (GU), 3 March 1998, 9; and "Capturados dos panameños con 571 kilos cocaína," *LP* (PA), 12 April 1991, 1A.

330. See "Drugs: Guatemala Major Trans-shipment."

331. DEA, *Resources, Guatemala* (2001), 6, *INCSR* (2003), 17; "Caen cinco con 450 kilos de coca," *SV* (GU), 23 March 2005, 8; *INCSR* (1998), 140; and *INCSR* (2002), 14.For representative Pan-American Highway and Pacific Coast Highway busts, see "Narcos purgarán," 8, "Decomisan 200 kilos," *SV* (GU), 29 January 2004, 9.

332. See generally "Surge el Cartel de Santa Rosa," *Al Día* (Guatemala), 11 May 1997, 6. For representative cases involving the seizure of narcotics that had traveled north overland from Guatemala, see *United States v. Crooks*, 83 F.3d 103; *People v. Rivera*, 647 N.Y.S. 2d 943; *United States v. Ornelas-Rodriguez*, 12 F.3d 1339; and *United States v. Palomo*, 998 F.2d 253.

333. "Cocaine Bust Nets Tons in Guatemala," *Orlando Sentinel*, 18 March 1999.

334. See "Traficantes atacaron Tecún Umán," *LH* (GU), 11 February 1989, 7, and Leffert, "Narcotráfico y el ejército," 3.

the southern part of the Péten contains at least twenty unofficial vehicle crossings, plus at least a thousand footpaths.[335]

While the overland import of cocaine followed by its export to Europe occurred less frequently than to the United States, one such case surfaced in 2007 when Irma Ortiz, a trucking magnate in northern Panama, was arrested there for drug trafficking. Panama's lead drug prosecutor suspected the network of having operated for three years, trucking cocaine from Panama to Guatemala and then shipping it to Europe. Ortiz, who operated a fleet of 150 trucks and allegedly had fifty police on her payroll, owned multiple residences, a dozen farms, and an island. Authorities discovered at least $15 million in assets for which she could not account.[336] Her case shows how Central American trafficking networks were growing in size and in the scope of their transnational operations, while gathering significant wealth.

Although drugs traveling overland have normally been packed into merchandise or hidden in secret compartments or double walls deep inside tractor trailers, sometimes the methods have been more elaborate. In 1990 a drug-trafficking network that had been in business for nearly a decade was found to be accumulating cocaine loads of 300–500 kilos in Guatemala, then trucking the drugs north through Mexico and into Texas. The cocaine was first secreted in air-brake tanks of large trucks and then in metal containers inside the fuel tanks of large pickups. In the late 1990s Guatemalan authorities discovered two shipments of black cocaine hidden in the tires of eighteen-wheelers that had arrived from Panama. Traffickers intended to place the larger, 127-kilo load into double-walled shipping containers to be forwarded to the United States.

Then, in Operation Jump Start in 2005 authorities arrested one hundred, including a dozen in Guatemala, as they dismantled a Colombian ring that for three years had been transshipping cocaine and heroin through Guatemala and Mexico and into the southwestern United States. Police seized 61 kilos of heroin and 129 of cocaine that had been shipped from Colombia up the Pacific coast into Panama, and then overland to Guatemala, using compartments inside car batteries, some large enough to stash 5 kilos of drugs. The vehicles were then smuggled across Mexico and into the United States.[337]

Otto Roberto Herrera García

The most important Guatemalan kingpin deeply involved in the trucking of cocaine was alleged to be Otto Roberto Herrera García. With three brothers, Herrera ran four long-haul trucking companies, headquartered in Los Amates and operating throughout Central America. Herrera's trucks are thought to have started to smuggle arms and then moved into the even more lucrative cocaine trade. Eventually, "the Engineer," as Herrera became known, diversified his operation from overland transport to include air and maritime shipments. With time, he was reported to have become a key supplier for domestic traffickers from the Gulf and Sayaxché cartelitos and to be linked to Cali traffickers and the Sinaloa cartel.[338]

One key break for investigators came when a confidential informant closely familiar with

335. For a statement by President Oscar Berger, see "President Steps Up Fight."

336. See "Conectan droga con narco red," *LP* (PA), 27 January 2008, 1A, and "Los tentáculos de una narco red," *LP* (PA), 27 January 2008, 6A.

337. For the examples in this paragraph, see *United States v. Restrepo*, 994 F.2d 173, and "Arrestan a panameño en Guatemala," *LP* (PA), 13 May 1999, 5A. Occasionally, traffickers would attempt to hide cocaine, transforming it from white to black by mixing in a dark ingredient like charcoal dust. For information on this network, see "Narcos libres," *SV* (GU), 17 February 2005, 10; "Caen cincuenta y cinco narcotraficantes," *SV* (GU), 17 February 2005, 10; "Md. Men Named in Major Drug Case," *Baltimore Sun*, 16 February 2005, 1B; and "Guatemalan-Colombian Heroin and Cocaine Cartel Dismantled," DEA News Release, http://www.usdoj.gov/dea/pubs/pressrel/pr021505.html.

338. "DEA a la caza de peces gordos del narco," *SV* (GU), 29 January 2004, 8–9; "Guatemalan Drug Suspect Held in Mexico," *Guardian* (United Kingdom), 23 April

Herrera's organization provided the DEA with detailed information about ongoing cocaine trafficking from Colombia through Nicaragua, El Salvador, Guatemala, and Mexico and into the United States.[339] While the informant was soon murdered in Guatemala City, in 1999 Guatemalan authorities and DEA agents intercepted a shipment of 2,556 kilos of cocaine in the false floors of three shipping containers being trucked down the Pan-American Highway. The drugs had just crossed into Guatemala from El Salvador, headed ultimately to the United States. Law-enforcement officials suspected that, since the fall of 1998, Herrera's network had shipped cocaine in large vessels from Colombia to locations off the Salvadoran coast. Speedboats had then brought the drugs ashore, where the boats and their loads were towed behind pickup trucks to a temporary storage location on property rented by former Salvadoran official William Eliú Martínez. The cocaine would then be hidden in large trucks to cross into Guatemala.

Another step in building a case against Herrera came in 2000 when a drug plane was sighted over El Salvador. Although Salvadoran fighter jets could not force the pilot to land before the aircraft had left their airspace, the Guatemalan military succeeded in seizing it and the 1.1 tons of cocaine inside. An informant then reportedly linked the shipment to Herrera. Some time later, police raided the house of one of Herrera's reputed associates and found $14.4 million stuffed in file drawers. Herrera had been living, with his American wife, in an upscale section of Guatemala City, with his children enrolled in a top private school. But in the spring of 2003, as law-enforcement attention increased, he disappeared. With his reputed connections in Colombia, Panama, Mexico, and El Salvador, Herrera became, for a period, the most wanted Central American trafficker.[340]

At length, the DEA orchestrated Herrera's arrest, as he met a plane bringing his Mexican mistress to Mexico City from Guadalajara. At the time officials charged that Herrera's network had been transshipping cocaine by truck, plane, and speedboat through Panama and Guatemala into Mexico. U.S. attorney general John Ashcroft called Herrera, at the time of his arrest, one of the most significant drug traffickers and money launderers in the world. Although the United States promptly requested his extradition, after less than a month behind bars, Herrera escaped from a Mexico City prison in 2005. He seems to have made his way to Colombia, where he owned many properties, and investigators believed that he arranged to repatriate hundreds of millions in drug profits from his Colombian headquarters. Finally, working on a DEA tip, detectives from Colombia's Department of Administrative Security uncovered a deal, brokered by Herrera, in which a light plane was to fly $25 million in cash from Central America to Colombia. They managed to arrest the Guatemalan kingpin in a Bogotá parking lot, despite the trafficker's attempts to bribe arresting officers, earning about six thousand dollars a year, with first $2 million, then $5 million.[341]

In the meantime, authorities also succeeded in arresting Eliú Martínez, such a close associate of Herrera's that, some said, he had served as the Zacapa cartelito's chief of transportation. Sources within the Salvador's National Civil Police alleged that Eliú had been involved in at least thirty-six tons of cocaine exports to the United States. Many of the drugs had traveled by boat from Colombia to El Salvador, where they had been stored on farms and ranches Eliú

2004, 18; "Most Wanted Guatemalan Said to Have Connections in El Salvador," *Financial Times* (United Kingdom), 22 April 2003. Berganza had reportedly designated Herrera García to be his successor in leading the Zacapa organization. See "Poder tras el trono," 9.

339. *United States v. Martinez*, 476 F.3d 961.

340. "Guatemalan Drug Suspect"; "Sluggish Anti-drug Efforts." The United States offered a $2 million reward for his capture. "Pit Stop."

341. "Untouchable Narco-State," 19; "President Steps Up Fight"; "A $5-million Offer for Freedom Fell Flat," *LAT* (US), 27 June 2007, 3A; "Pedirán buscar aquí a cómplice de Herrera," *SV* (GU), 19 March 2008, 3.

controlled, before being trucked into Guatemala in double-walled containers. A U.S. federal court eventually convicted Eliú of drug trafficking, sentencing him to twenty-nine years in prison.[342]

Conclusion

As the drug trade climbed to new heights in Guatemala, it was sometimes said that the country had entered a process of "colombianization."[343] Plainly, Guatemala and Colombia experienced the common symptoms of growing narco-corruption and drug-related violence, and certain parallel factors help explain why the drug trade has flourished in both. Guatemalan and Colombian governments have both confronted long-standing regional divisions, and for long periods neither has been able to exercise extended control over great swathes of their countryside.[344] Traffickers have capitalized on lengthy internal conflicts, especially when the fighting has been largely confined to particular regions, since these clashes have diverted resources and attention and threatened state authority.[345] This was also true of the civil wars in both.

Government institutions in Guatemala and Colombia have also taken on, and then often fumbled, a large array of tasks. Thick webs of laws and regulations have been created, only to be disregarded in practice. Inefficient bureaucracies have been unaccountable and unresponsive to the public.[346] Extraordinarily rapid turnover in personnel has marked governance.[347] Such matters have weakened state authority, jeopardized political legitimacy, and widened opportunities for transnational criminals to operate successfully. More subtly, in describing modern Colombia, one scholar termed "the traditional use of violent means to accomplish personal and political ends" a national characteristic "embedded in . . . society and political culture," posing "some of the most difficult challenges to the country's democratic institutions."[348] Such a statement applies equally to Guatemala, where feuding in an effort to settle scores, inside and outside the drug trade, has become a bloody national pastime.[349]

As compared to the other Central American states, Guatemala has had to contend with a host of bridge-favoring factors—some familiar, others rather different than those found in its neighbors. As traffickers looked to open Central American routes, Guatemala was particularly vulnerable: a badly fractured society, suffering through the throes of civil war and, later, its aftermath. If the region's most peaceful and solidly democratic states have failed to curb drug transshipment, traffickers might be expected to take even greater advantage of its most deeply split country. In fact, Guatemala has been besieged by violence and grave social problems. Its government has been hampered by demoralized and underpaid bureaucracies, overseen by beleaguered and sometimes corrupt politicians, and the country has labored under an extraordinarily weak criminal-justice system with laws poorly tailored to combat organized crime. Not only has Guatemalan geography, particularly its position neighboring Mexico, been of

342. See "DEA a la caza," 8–9; *United States v. Martinez*, 476 F.3d at 963.

343. See, for instance, "Guatemala Warns," N3. At first glance, such a reference may seem odd because Colombia is one of Latin America's oldest democracies, while Guatemala has long struggled to attain a functioning democratic system.

344. See Strong, *Whitewash*, 9.

345. Gootenberg, "Talking Like a State,"109.

346. These statements echo points made by Colombian economist Francisco E. Thoumi, in his *Political Economy*, about his country: "A widening gap developed between the *de jure* and *de facto* socially acceptable behavior, and the underground economy greatly expanded" (172).

347. In the late 1980s, in the face of growing pressure from cartels, Colombia had eight ministers of justice in fourteen months. Duzán, *Death Beat*, 141.

348. Osterling, *Democracy in Colombia*, 261, cited in Crandall, *Driven by Drugs*, 47.

349. For an Izabalito attack by forty men armed with assault rifles and grenade launchers, as well as a Livingston mayor estimate that one drug-related murder per day was occurring, see "Sicarios atemorizan Izabal," *SV* (GU), 18 January 2003, 8.

paramount importance, but Guatemalan cartelitos have come to serve as crucial links between Colombian and Mexican drug enterprises.[350]

The country's most stable and well-endowed institution has been its armed forces, which have, in fact, offered notable assistance in certain antidrug efforts. Traffickers, however, have found the military's privileged position and extensive influence over Guatemalan society to be extremely useful. Particular officers have been corrupted to selectively enforce antidrug laws and skim money and drugs from law-enforcement operations. Some have gone to work for, or even led, prominent drug rings, with handsome compensation paid for their knowledge, expertise, and contacts. Thus, while civilian authorities have struggled to curtail the military, much less to dislodge or disband it, transnational criminal undertakings have readily subverted even Guatemala's most robust institution. If power is conceived in terms of an actor's ability to bring others to do as he or she wishes, traffickers have gained power over the military through bribery.

Guatemala has also been another Central American country deep in the midst of a difficult transition, a singular one in various respects, and the nature and challenges of the transitional era have often adversely affected counternarcotics work. During the transition to democracy and the subsequent move from civil war to peace, public and governmental attention has often been riveted on other domestic issues. Attempts to ameliorate such problems have then been vastly complicated by government institutions that have neither commanded nor deserved public faith. Indeed, the most fundamental pieces of the criminal-justice system have normally functioned poorly, if at all. This, too, has affected the drug trade, as investigation, prosecution, and conviction of traffickers has suffered, while those who tried to counter drug rings have too often been threatened or killed with impunity. Such circumstances have led many to look to enrich themselves from the drug trade, rather than resist it.

Abroad, Guatemala's enormous drug problems have reverberated through neighboring states. Guatemalan marijuana has entered western Belize, and both opium and marijuana have been exported to Mexico. Guatemalan cartelitos, well connected, with impressive warehousing and transportation abilities, have exerted a magnetic pull, drawing cocaine through Honduras and El Salvador. Indeed, by the mid-1990s Guatemala had become so saturated with cocaine that traffickers began to export surplus supplies south to El Salvador, sometimes in exchange for stolen cars.[351] Guatemala's central role in the drug trade, the reach of its networks, and the government's inability to counter the trade effectively have thus contributed to regional drug problems, raising tensions with all of its neighbors as well as with the United States.

At home, Guatemalans have found that drug smuggling has exacerbated many dire problems. Cocaine transit, in particular, has accelerated drug-abuse problems, while markedly increasing violence and corruption. Trafficking has greatly burdened penal, health, and criminal-justice systems. Drug enterprises have undermined often lackluster efforts to establish a rule of law, as elites have frequently participated in the trade, while avoiding penal consequences. Tightly knit networks of politicians, ranchers, and present and former military officials have been more intent on reaping profits from transshipment operations than ensuring that the political settlement serves as a springboard toward creating a new post–civil war society less rigid, violent, and authoritarian than Guatemala had traditionally been.[352] The drug trade

350. "El Salvador: PNC vincula a narcos con Guatemaltecos," *SV* (GU), 9 January 2000, 6, 13.

351. In 1997 José Luis Tobar Prieto, antinarcotics chief of Salvador's National Civil Police, estimated that as much as 80 percent of the narcotics consumed in his country came from Guatemala. "Tobar: Droga ingresando a Guatemala es transportada hacia El Salvador," *SV* (GU), 20 January 1997, 6.

352. This echoes an observation made by Michael Johnston of corruption in "elite cartel" societies. Johnston, *Syndromes of Corruption*, 89.

has thus contributed to a popular lack of faith in democracy.

In short, wealthy and powerful transnational criminal organizations have been able to exploit many characteristics of this deeply fractured state. Traffickers have found that police and the military could be bought, judges and the media could be bullied, politicians and government officials could be co-opted. Like bees to a hive, drug organizations have thus swarmed into the country.[353] Indeed, in this context it would have been astonishing had Colombian and Mexican traffickers failed to take advantage of the exceptional opportunities to transship drugs through this northernmost of the Central American states. As Guatemalan congressional deputy Edmond Mulet declared in 1989, "If I could pick an ideal country for the Colombian cartels, this would be it."[354] And so, wielding bribes, bullets, and intimidation, traffickers have turned Guatemala into one of the two most critically important bridge states in the region.

353. For the swarming metaphor, which we employ with respect to Guatemala and Panama, we are indebted to Watson, "Globalization of Finance," 35.

354. "Drug Crackdown," 14A.

5

Honduras

In certain respects Honduras has long typified Central America, with personalistic political leaders—some dictatorial politicians and some military strongmen—and an economy heavily dependent on bananas and other agricultural exports subject to the vicissitudes of international commodity markets. Yet in many other respects Honduras has developed quite a distinct profile. Traditionally, Honduran political elites were not as rapacious as were many of those in neighboring countries.[1] Furthermore, the Honduran population contains not only a highly influential Jewish minority, as Panama's does, but the largest percentage of inhabitants of Arab descent in all of Latin America. In 1843 Palestinians began to immigrate to Honduras, with particularly large influxes occurring during World War I and again in 1948, just after Israel gained sovereignty. As early as 1918 Arabs owned more than 40 percent of businesses in San Pedro Sula, the country's most vibrant commercial city, and to this day Arabs, many of them Christians, hold quite prominent business and government positions.[2]

In sociopolitical terms Honduras has neither suffered from sharp ethnic divisions to the extent Guatemala has, nor has it enjoyed the positive international reputation of Costa Rica. Although the country has experienced considerable labor turmoil, no significant revolutionary movement has coalesced to threaten the regime. Disappearances and human rights abuses have been quite serious, but they have not risen to the staggering levels of neighboring Guatemala

1. Ruhl, "Honduras," 519. In 1902 bananas accounted for 53 percent of Honduran exports, and in 1980 bananas and other fruit retained more than 30 percent of export income. Morris, "Honduras," 564.

2. "Palestinians Find Home in Honduras," *Tico Times* (Costa Rica) (hereafter cited as *TT* [CR]), 11 May 2001, 8. Hondurans of Middle Eastern heritage have developed the country's leading newspaper and risen to such positions as president of the Central Bank, minister of industry and commerce, vice president, and president (Carlos Flores Facussé).

MAP 5.1

and El Salvador.[3] Although the country's Caribbean coast and its Islas de la Bahía (Bay Islands) have shared characteristics with nearby Belize, Honduras has struggled to achieve its neighbor's democratic political culture.

In Honduras, as in various other Central American states, the end of the twentieth century and the beginning of the twenty-first marked a period of real transition. After about two decades of military rule, in the early 1980s Honduras moved decisively toward democracy with a constitution drafted in 1981, followed by a popular vote for president. While elections have been regularly held thereafter, the armed forces have maintained an important position in society.[4] Indeed, even under the 1981 Constitution, the leader of the armed forces, not the president, was to serve as commander in chief.[5]

Democratization has been stunted, in part, because political leaders and parties have made little progress in ameliorating the country's serious problems, and corruption has abounded. Hence, although their critics multiplied in the 1990s and civilian politicians succeeded in scaling back their political power, the Honduran armed forces have retained some notable popular support, especially when democratic administrations have floundered.[6] The 2009 political crisis was simply the most recent—as well as one of the more nationally popular—manifestations of military involvement in political affairs. Here, a coup halted President José Manuel ("Mel") Zelaya's attempt to convene a popular referendum to authorize a constituent assembly that he hoped would eliminate the constitutional limit of a single presidential four-year term. However, the military did promptly step aside, enabling the inauguration of President Porfirio Lobo Sosa in January 2010.

From the 1970s through the early 1980s Hondurans found themselves wedged in among the civil wars in Guatemala, Nicaragua, and El

3. Anderson, "Politics and Military," 426.

4. For steps toward the 1980s democratic transition, see ibid., esp. 425.

5. See Art. 277, *Constitución de la República de Honduras*.

6. See Ruhl, "Honduras," 520, 525.

Salvador. In terming Honduras "a crucible for Central American tensions," one observer noted that in the 1980s, it "hosted a volatile mixture of Nicaraguan contras, Salvadoran rebels, Sandinista spies, United States intelligence agents, mercenaries, and drug traffickers."[7] Although the country avoided the extent of revolutionary violence found just across its borders, from the 1960s through the 1980s military leaders repeatedly used the fear of encroaching communism to attempt to legitimize their own primacy and the repressive measures they imposed on society.[8] Most notoriously, death squads linked to the Honduran military eliminated particular left-wing sympathizers and activists who might have aimed to subvert the social and political order.[9]

For a country independent since 1821 yet plagued by scores of coups, deep-seated official corruption, and generations of personalistic rule by military dictators, developing a political culture conducive to democratic rule has been slow, erratic, and incomplete. Eliminating the military, as Costa Ricans did, has been impossible, and persuading it voluntarily to relinquish long-held duties has been a formidable task.[10] The weighty presence of the armed forces has strongly influenced, indeed sometimes cowed, politicians and has deeply affected the way that institutions function. Nevertheless, while accounting for the realities of power, the transition from military to civilian rule has very definitely moved forward. Over the past three decades politicians have progressed in making inroads on traditional military prerogatives, and some significant milestones have been reached. For instance, in 1993 an opposition candidate won the presidency. The Liberal Party then entered office, and the military refrained from direct interference, as it did when the Liberals again triumphed at the polls in 1997. In 1999 a constitutional reform subordinated the military to a civilian defense minister, while the prior position of chief of the armed forces was abolished and Liberal president Carlos Flores Facussé dismissed a number of high-ranking officers.[11]

Yet, unlike Belize, Costa Rica, and post-Noriega Panama, the Honduran armed forces, although diminished in power and numbers, have remained entrenched in national life. Not only has the military remained in charge of the intelligence agency, but officers have been central figures in the economy, with the armed forces controlling, and sometimes even operating, enterprises that have ranged over time from banks to hotels to export and telecommunications businesses.[12] The lack of a clear dividing line between military and civilian responsibilities is reflected in the fact that, traditionally, the police—known for many years as the Public Security Force—constituted a fourth branch of the military, along with the army, navy, and air force. The armed forces long pointed to communist threats to national security to justify their control over police work and such related matters as port and airport security. Even with the passing of the cold war, the armed forces have clung to various traditional powers. Not until 1998 did the Honduran Congress create

7. In noting that Honduran authorities feared "the 'contamination' from these foreign struggles," a diplomat stationed in Honduras declared, "There are an awful lot of out-of-work gunfighters here. . . . If you could wave a magic wand and send them all home, Honduras could go back to what it was. . . . But it will never go back." "Hondurans Shaken by Others' Wars," *Christian Science Monitor* (US), 16 February 1989, 4.

8. Human rights organization El Comité de Familiares de Detenidos Desaparecidos en Honduras (Committee of Relatives of the Disappeared in Honduras) has kept track of human rights violations. See "Persiste violación de derechos humanos," *La Nación* (Costa Rica) (hereafter cited as *LN* [CR]), 5 January 1997, 23A. The military intelligence unit Battalion 3-16 was particularly suspect. In 1998 U.S. Congress testimony, Leo Valladares Lanza, the national commissioner for human rights in Honduras, alluded to his office's 1993 report documenting 184 disappearances. U.S. House, *Government Information.*

9. See Americas Watch, *Human Rights in Honduras.*

10. See generally Solomon, *Política y militares*, and Rosenberg, "Honduras," 475–89.

11. Ruhl, "Honduras," 525–26.

12. Ibid., 528.

a civilian police force, called the Honduran National Police, and charge the civilian Ministry of Security with supervising law enforcement.[13]

With the rise of Central America in the international drug trade, transnational criminal groups have repeatedly exploited significant weaknesses within Honduran society. From a very early date drug rings have found transshipment operations through Honduras to operate so smoothly that knowledgeable observers have come to call the country a "trafficker's paradise."[14] The principal reasons, however, paralleled those that brought its neighbors to prominence in certain respects but differed in others. As in the other Central American countries, however, the manner in which the Honduran drug trade evolved has remained largely unexplored. When and how did extensive drug trafficking take hold in Honduras? Which traffickers and what organizations were active, and what routes and methods did they favor? Where and under what circumstances have significant seizures and arrests occurred? How did the distinguishing characteristics of Honduran society affect the development of the drug trade? How have traffickers and the law contended with one another? These are the questions to which the remainder of this chapter is devoted.

Bridge-Favoring Factors Relevant to Honduras

Geography

The first cardinal point with respect to Honduran geography and the international drug trade is that the country is right in the heart of Central America, very conveniently located between South and North America for the air, sea, and overland traffic in drugs.[15] Engaged in constant cat-and-mouse games with authorities, kingpins in the major organizations have figured that using a multiplicity of routes would result in the most drugs reaching market without interdiction. They have thus routinely spread their bets across the board. And, while Guatemala has been the primary entry point into Mexico, Honduras, like Belize, has stood as a next-best alternative.[16] This strategy underscores the great difficulties involved in curbing the drug trade through interdiction across an entire bridge region. With routes already blazed in numerous states, progress in one country has regularly resulted in increasing pressure on another.

Apart from its location within Central America, Honduras has other geographic assets relevant to drug transshipment. One of the largest and least densely populated of the Central American states, with one of the most mountainous terrains, the country has a long Caribbean coast, including various deep-water ports, long stretches of beach, and large tracts of uninhabited and virtually unpoliced jungle. The north coast is also marked by a series of prominent river valleys that angle inland from the Caribbean, providing excellent pathways into the interior for drug-plane pilots intent on entering the country unobtrusively. Honduras also features two major cities: the capital of Tegucigalpa, at more than 850,000, and San Pedro Sula, at 500,000. Each has factored into numerous drug-trafficking schemes.

The prohibitive cost of building and maintaining a speedy and extensive road network has brought many farms, ranches, and small communities to construct airstrips to accommodate light planes. Aerial trafficking has

13. DEA, *Resources, Honduras* (2000), 4.

14. "Honduras, paraíso de los narcos," *La Prensa* (Honduras) (hereafter cited as *LP* [HO]), 19 May 1996, 10A.

15. One diplomat stationed in the country explained, "Geographically, Honduras is a very tempting transshipment point. The drug lords know they will lose more if it goes straight from Colombia to the U.S." "U.S. to Open Outpost to Aid War on Drugs," *Chicago Tribune*, 27 November 1987, 36C.

16. U.S. Department of State, International Narcotics Control Strategy Report (hereafter cited as INCSR) (1994), 154.For a statement by former ambassador John Negroponte, see "EUA fortalecerá entes para luchar contra el narcotráfico," LP (HO), 6 June 2008, 2.

utilized roads as well as these runways and those on the country's Caribbean islands. In 1987 Honduran military authorities estimated that the northern portion of the country alone contained about 100 clandestine airstrips, some of them paved and lighted, and most well beyond official supervision or even radar coverage.[17] Shortly thereafter, Santiago Perdomo, the director-general of Aeronautics, noted that 215 airstrips had been counted, and acknowledged that authorities regularly watched only 3. In 2009, in his final public statement before being assassinated by hit men, Honduran counternarcotics director-general Julián Arístides González warned that drug traffickers were constructing additional runways on private farms across the country.[18]

Naturally, the most remote parts of Honduras have attracted considerable transshipment activity. Perhaps most important, Gracias a Dios Province on the northeastern Caribbean coast features lagoons and swampy coastal wetlands that have made it virtually inaccessible, except by boat or light plane. Though spanning almost a fifth of the country's land territory, this region, popularly known as La Mosquitia, has very few roads or settlements. These geographic conditions are matched by the neighboring Atlántico Norte Department of Nicaragua, creating a coastal swath of the two countries often called La Mosquitia.[19] Lightly populated and policed, this is home to the Miskitos, indigenous to this area, of whom about thirty thousand live in Honduras. In 2000 the DEA reported that Colombian traffickers were hiring Miskitos to move cocaine shipments along rivers and between Honduran islands in motorized dugout canoes. With negligible law enforcement to contend with, trafficking organizations have risked little in importing cocaine into this region, either by plane or speedboat. Indeed, in describing how authorities have been unable to police La Mosquitia, one foreign law-enforcement official stated ruefully, "There may be huge piles of cocaine on the beaches, for all that we know."[20]

For maritime traffickers Honduras has the most important archipelago off Central American shores—the Islas de la Bahía.[21] Lying about forty miles offshore, the chain includes more than five dozen small cayes and three major islands. The largest, Roatán, is flanked by Guanaja to the east and Utila to the west. Remote and poorly policed, the islands have provided a ready supply of the collaborators necessary to orchestrate water drops or to service vessels and planes.[22] Furthermore, by the late 1980s the Islas de la Bahía had become internationally popular locations for scuba diving and sport fishing. As elsewhere in the region, the tourist trade provided a convenient cover for those owning motorboats and light planes or found to be possessing

17. For the estimates on landing strips, see "Ejército detecta existencia de cien pistas de aterrizaje en Costa Norte," *LP* (HO), 4 December 1987, 83, and Centro, "Cronología," 10. Not all of these airstrips were connected to good roads, however, making them less useful as refueling spots during the rainy season. See *INCSR* (1995), 137, and "Ejército detecta existencia."

18. "Arístides había advertido que construían pistas en haciendas," *LP* (HO), 9 December 2009, 4.

19. La Mosquitia in Nicaragua contains 60 percent of that country's territory, but only 10 percent of its population. Basic infrastructure is in poor shape or completely absent, with fewer than three of ten houses having electricity. "Jail Conditions Scrutinized," *Nica Times* (Costa Rica) (hereafter cited as *NT* [CR]), 28 January 2005, 1.

20. Confidential interview, December 1991, Tegucigalpa, Honduras. Nine years later, the situation had not improved, with U.S. ambassador Frank Almaguer citing La Mosquitia and the Pan-American Highway as two key locations for drug trafficking. "Honduras hace esfuerzos para combatir el narcotráfico," *LP* (HO), 13 April 2000, 12A. For the facts in the rest of this paragraph, see "La Mosquitia: 'Puente' apetecido por narcotraficantes suramericanos," *LP* (HO), 4 May 1992, 3; "No es nuevo que narcotraficantes utilizan La Mosquitia como 'puente,'" *LP* (HO), 9 May 1992, 4; and DEA, *Resources, Honduras* (2000), 3. For representative trafficking here, see "Detectan misteriosa avioneta huyendo de pista clandestina," *LP* (HO), 30 May 1988, 18.

21. For trafficking on the Islas de la Bahía, specifically 297 kilograms of cocaine found in first three months of 1994, see "Caribe hondureño es puente para tráfico de cocaína sudamericana," *LP* (HO), 29 April 1994, 29A. See also "Aumenta el narcotráfico en los mares territoriales hondureños," *LP* (HO), 16 September 1992, 3, and "La Mosquitia," 3.

22. *INCSR* (1991), 151.

fuel, spare parts, and other supplies needed in the drug trade.

Poverty

Lacking mineral wealth, Honduras has lagged behind even its Central American neighbors since colonial times. More recently, the dismal state of the Honduran economy has amounted to another prime bridge-favoring factor. Lacking the vibrant national tourist trade of Costa Rica, the extensive banking and commerce of Panama, and the light manufacturing notable in Guatemala, Honduras has had to try to contend with serious problems. The Honduran economy has leaned heavily on largely extractive foreign investment in the textile and agricultural sectors. With unemployment and underemployment afflicting half the population by the twenty-first century, those with jobs were determined to retain them.[23] Unscrupulous employers could exploit employees, who had little effective legal recourse.

That annual imports have routinely exceeded exports has been a chronic drain on foreign-currency reserves. With few funds to address them, dire social problems have abounded, with illiteracy, malnutrition, and poor health care afflicting large sectors of the country's unusually youthful population.[24] Rural areas have lacked modern facilities and infrastructure; urban areas have had to contend with growing slums and extensive homelessness, including large numbers of street children.[25] Within this social context the foreign currency to be gained by participating in drug-transshipment activities has been especially attractive. And, over time, elites have become involved in money laundering, which, although not nearly at the level found elsewhere in Central America, has nonetheless started to grow to worrisome levels. To wit, in a single joint operation in 2010 with the DEA, the Honduran National Police seized $7,547,000 at the San Pedro Sula Airport.[26]

In fact, Honduras has stood out, even within Central America, as exceptionally poverty-stricken. Those joining drug rings have been extremely well compensated compared to what they could earn in legitimate employment, whether they have been low-level associates performing such tasks as off-loading cocaine, guarding storehouses, or transporting drugs through the country, or top judges or government or military officials corrupted to provide high-level assistance. In this regard the breadth and depth of Honduran poverty ought to be emphasized. Honduras has regularly ranked as the poorest state in the region on a per capita basis, with the Inter-American Development Bank calculating that eight out of ten Hondurans live in poverty.[27] In 2004 the United Nations Development Programme reported that more than two-thirds of Honduran children under the age of five were malnourished.[28]

Poverty has been compounded by a multiplying population. After registering the highest population growth in Latin America from 1950 to 1975, Honduras continued to grow rapidly: from 2.7 million citizens in 1974 to 5 million in 1992 to 7.8 million in 2010.[29] With few economic opportunities at home, much of the population has survived on remittances sent from relatives living abroad, which reached an estimated $800

23. Bureau for Latin American and Caribbean Affairs, *Gang Assessment*, 14.

24. In 2003, 49 percent of the Honduran population were under eighteen, and in 2006 41 percent were under fifteen. See ibid., and *INCSR* (2003), 146. The minister of health, Dr. Rubén Francisco García Martínez, later president of the San Pedro Sula Medical Association, noted that a dramatic drop in the infant mortality rate, from 130 per 1,000 to less than 80 per 1,000, had contributed to the increasingly youthful population. Interview, 16 December 1991, San Pedro Sula, Honduras.

25. For accounts of Honduran street children used for drug dealing in Vancouver, see "Niños hondureños llevados a Canadá se sienten en deuda con narcotraficantes," *LP* (HO), 22 July 1998, 4A, and "Smuggling of Honduran Kids Denounced," *TT* (CR), 16 April 1999, 9.

26. *INCSR* (2011), 293.

27. "The Most Violent Area in the Americas," *TT* (CR), 18 August 2000, 9.

28. PNUD, *Informe, Honduras*, 220, cited in Pine, *Working Hard, Drinking Hard*, 17.

29. See CIA, *World Factbook, 2010*.

million in 2003, then climbed to $1.1 billion, $1.5 billion, and eventually $2 billion in 2006.[30]

The massive destruction inflicted by Hurricane Mitch in 1998, which devastated urban and agricultural areas alike, exacerbated this already dire economic situation. Officials estimated that the hurricane affected about two-fifths of the country's population and caused $2 billion of damage.[31] This immense natural disaster seriously damaged the shrimp industry and virtually erased some coffee, banana, pineapple, and African-palm plantations. It destroyed hundreds of buildings and further debilitated the country's already inadequate infrastructure, wiping out roads and bridges. The repercussions of Mitch have not been easy to shake off, and the Honduran economy has continued to perform quite poorly through the first decade of the twenty-first century. In 2009 the United Nations estimated that three hundred thousand Hondurans lived in extreme poverty, that seventy thousand more had lost jobs that year, and another hundred thousand had dropped below the poverty line.[32]

The hurricane affected the drug trade as well. The ensuing economic convulsions caused soaring unemployment rates, expanding the pool of recruits for drug rings. Desperate for profitable economic activity, those in a position to assist traffickers have not been inclined to turn business away or to charge top dollar for their services. Furthermore, Hurricane Mitch caused law-enforcement resources to be directed toward the most immediate social needs of stopping looting and then providing vital assistance to grievously damaged communities.[33]

These socioeconomic characteristics have long contributed to growing drug consumption, which in turn has aided drug organizations, even those headquartered abroad, in various ways. It has formed a secondary market, especially for crack cocaine, creating Honduran associates eager to be compensated with drugs rather than cash. It has increased the numbers of those looking for money to support drug habits. And, by contributing to rising violent-crime levels, it has occupied law enforcement, diverting attention from other tasks, including interdiction. For these reasons traffickers have encouraged the use of drugs by Hondurans.[34] By 2000 foreign drug syndicates were routinely using cocaine to pay off those gang members who had helped them, and crack consumption was increasing in urban areas and along the north coast.[35]

Administration of Justice

With by far the fewest number of police officers per inhabitant of any Central American country, Honduras has been in no position to resist drug use, dealing, or trafficking very effectively through the regular operation of its criminal-justice system.[36] Rampant crime and uneven law enforcement led to a violent-death rate that, by 2000, had climbed to fifty homicides per one hundred thousand people.[37] By then, youth gangs—especially the contending Mara Salvatrucha

30. See *INCSR* (2003), Fin. Supp., 14; *INCSR* (2005), Fin. Supp., 12; *INCSR* (2006), Fin. Supp., 12; and *INCSR* (2007), Fin. Supp., 9.

31. "Huracán Mitch deja pérdidas multimillonarias," *LP* (PA), 6 November 1998, 2A.

32. "Honduras con 170 mil nuevos pobres en 2009," *LP* (HO), 27 May 2009, 15.

33. See *INCSR* (1999), 162, and DEA, *Resources, Honduras* (2000), 2.

34. In 1992 U.S. officials stated, "Reports indicate that traffickers are deliberately lowering the price of cocaine—as low as $1 per gram—to create a larger local market." *INCSR* (1992), 164.

35. *INCSR* (2002), 5:24; *INCSR* (2003), 5:29; and *INCSR* (2004), 157. U.S. officials reported, "Gang members are being utilized by organized crime rings to guard drug shipments in exchange for drugs and weapons." *INCSR* (2006), 14.

36. Honduras had 1 officer for every 791 inhabitants, as opposed to 1 for every 195 in Panama. PNUD, *Informe, Ámerica Central*, 232, quoted in "Centroamericanos, cada vez más desprotegidos," *LP* (PA), 26 December 2009, 6A.

37. See "Honduras: One of the Region's Most Violent Countries," *TT* (CR), 16 June 2000, 10, and "Police Purged Amid Soaring Crime," *TT* (CR), 22 September 2000, 6.

13 (MS-13) and Barrio 18 (B-18)—had proliferated to an estimated thirty-six thousand members, a figure that rose to fifty thousand by 2003. The Honduran legislature responded with draconian antigang legislation in 2003, further stiffened in 2005.[38] But by 2008 the murder rate had worsened, soaring to sixty-eight per one hundred thousand, the highest in the region.[39]

Reflective of Honduras's poverty, paltry tax revenues, and scarce public resources, the country's administration of justice has long been abysmal. Even in a region marked by rather lax standards, Honduran institutions, procedures, and officials have been exceptionally ill prepared to tackle organized crime.[40] The scandal-ridden police force has been characterized as "poorly trained, poorly motivated and under-equipped," and police have routinely engaged in extrajudicial killings during periodic "social cleansing" campaigns.[41] In a period of three and a half years in the late 1990s police were accused of participation or complicity in the killing of more than 820 street children and suspected gang members.[42] Then, in 2000 alone, rogue police officers resorted to perhaps as many as 1,000 extrajudicial killings of suspected gang members.[43]

The antiquated and horrendously overcrowded prisons have witnessed frequent violence, including extraordinarily bloody riots.[44] Corruption has been rampant, and in some cases institutionalized.[45] For example, the Central Penitentiary in Tegucigalpa has routinely rented rooms to solvent inmates, one among many irregular practices that have ranged from permitting prisoners to form for-profit businesses to providing prostitutes to inmates who could pay bribes to penal officials.[46] In 1988 José Victoriano Paz, deputy director of the San Pedro Sula penitentiary, accused director Juan Eduardo House Cuellar of selling privileges to inmates. Among other allegations, Paz claimed that House had allowed one trafficking suspect to leave the prison seventeen times in fifteen days for four-hour intervals. Paz also declared that House had been bribed to rent out the prison soccer field and had even accepted the gift of an AK-47 gun from an imprisoned cocaine trafficker.[47] While House denied many of the charges, he admitted taking the weapon, attempting to dismiss the incident as an "error of judgment."[48] In the mid-1990s Honduran authorities received complaints that one wealthy inmate not only owned a restaurant within the

38. "Honduras Stiffens Anti-gang Law," *NT* (CR), 28 January 2005, N3. The 2003 so-called *mano dura* law prescribed twelve-year prison terms for gang leaders and four-year terms for members; sentences increased to thirty and twenty years in 2005. Bail was also granted automatically to anyone who claimed self-defense or defense of family or property in killing a gang member.

39. "Istmo: País repunta en muertas violentas," *Siglo Veintiuno* (Guatemala) (hereafter cited as *SV* [GU]), 6 March 2009, 2.

40. As the U.S. government observed, "Honduran enforcement efforts are hindered by an underpaid and insufficiently trained police force, an inadequate judicial system, and widespread corruption." *INCSR* (1994), 154. In 1994 some police officers were being paid as little as sixty dollars per month (155).

41. On social cleansing, see Professor Jeff Stewart's testimony in *Castellano-Chacon v. Immigration and Naturalization Service*, 341 F.3d 533, and "Massacre Charged in Honduran Prison Riot," *TT* (CR), 11 April 2003, 8.

42. *INCSR* (1991), 153, and "Honduras Denies Death Squads," *TT* (CR), 10 August 2001, 9. The UN special rapporteur on extrajudicial killings and Casa Alianza, an award-winning nongovernmental organization aimed at safeguarding children's rights, investigated these murders.

43. See Bureau for Latin American and Caribbean Affairs, *Gang Assessment*, 14, and "Honduras Denies Death Squads," *TT* (CR), 10 August 2001, 9.

44. See, for instance, "Massacre Charged in Honduran Prison Riot," *TT* (CR), 11 April 2003, 8; "Reports: Police Killed Prisoners," *TT* (CR), 16 May 2003, 10; "103 Youths Die in Honduran Prison Blaze," *TT* (CR), 21 May 2004, 10; and "Honduran Prisons in Spotlight Again After Bloodbath," *NT* (CR), 13 January 2006, N3.

45. See "Reclusos tienen el control en el penal sampedrano," *LP* (HO), 3 May 2008, 55, and "Empirismo y corrupción han hecho colapsar el sistema penitenciario," *LP* (HO), 8 April 2003, 2. See also "Hacinamiento carcelario," *SV* (GU), 1 March 1998, 20.

46. "Corte de apelaciones dictó sobreseimiento," *LP* (HO), 2 April 1986, 2.

47. "Narcotraficantes planificaron asesinar dos jueces sampedranos," *LP* (HO), 18 November 1988, 19.

48. "'Mi error fue aceptar la AK-47,' dice House," *LP* (HO), 19 November 1988, 10.

San Pedro Sula prison but converted it into a nightclub each evening, "obliging" female prisoners into performing striptease dances.[49]

Unsurprisingly, inmates, especially drug traffickers, have frequently escaped from Honduran jails and prisons. In 1988 the Ministry of Government and Justice estimated that in recent years more than 1,500 inmates had paid their way out of the country's penitentiaries.[50] In the early 1990s Honduran authorities made curbing escapes a priority; yet by late 1991, 143 prisoners had fled that year. While amounting to a 2.7 percent annual escape rate, the director-general of Penal Establishments of Honduras noted that this represented a substantial improvement over past escape rates.[51] Imprisoned traffickers, who could draw on the bribery and intimidation wielded by their organizations, have proven to be the most difficult inmates to retain behind bars. In 1988 Deputy Director Paz stated that he had intercepted a letter, containing six hundred dollars in cash, sent from an escaped Guatemalan trafficker to the prison director.[52] The next year, sixteen inmates fled the Puerto Cortés prison, including nine Colombians who had been arrested on a ship with marijuana worth more than $10 million.[53] In 1996 Carlos Sosa Coello, director of the Honduran legislative commission investigating narco-corruption, estimated that 90 percent of escapees were traffickers.[54]

To counter these grave criminal-justice problems, the Honduran government, often with U.S. funding assistance, has created a host of antidrug programs, policies, and institutions: a chemical-control unit of customs in 1989; a ministerial-level National Drug Council the following year; a National Drug Task Force in 1991; a counternarcotics unit of the Public Ministry in 1996; a port security program in 2003; and a financial crimes task force and vetted police units in 2010.[55] Some of these, such as the showpiece canine drug-detection program and the small but remarkably effective Joint Information Coordination Center, have worked out quite well. More typically, though, the earlier reforms were chronically underfunded and, after an initial burst of activity, largely ineffective.[56] To their credit, Honduran officials have been willing to experiment with sweeping changes, as when the judicial system shifted from a purely inquisitorial toward a more accusatorial model in 2002. The hope was that the enhanced transparency of public exchanges in open court would reduce opportunities for criminals to subvert justice with behind-the-scenes bribery and intimidation. However, many of the long-standing problems hampering effective administration of justice have been intractable, rooted in such larger difficulties as continual budgetary shortfalls and the lack of education and technical resources.

49. "'Magnate' sigue siendo el rey en el penal sampedrano," *LP* (HO), 27 September 1996, 19A. The same prisoner was also allegedly involved in fatal shootings outside the prison while he was supposed to be incarcerated. "Libro de novedades del penal revela que 'El Magnate' salió de noche," *LP* (HO), 28 December 1995, 5A.

50. "Una 'Mafia' lo quiere echar del ministerio, denuncia Ortez," *LP* (HO), 29 September 1988, 5.

51. Interview with Carlos Quezada Aguilar (director-general of the Penal Establishments of Honduras), 12 December 1991, Tegucigalpa, Honduras. Of the 5,224 prisoners held during 1991, 143 inmates had escaped as of December 12. Statistics provided to authors by the Dirección General de Establecimientos Penales de Honduras under the Corte Suprema de Justicia.

52. "Narcotraficantes planificaron," 19.

53. "Frustran masiva fuga de reos," *LP* (HO), 23 September 1989, 9. Eventually, authorities recaptured all but four of the fugitives. "Recapturan diez prófugos de penal porteño," *LP* (HO), 25 September 1989, 9.

54. "Cárcel de seguridad para narcotraficantes centroamericanos construirán en La Paz," *LP* (HO), 29 March 1996, 21A.

55. See *INCSR* (1990), 182; *INCSR* (1998), 144; *INCSR* (1999), 162; and "Embajador Larry Palmer: 'Terminó' la piñata para narcos," *LP* (HO), 10 April 2003, 42.

56. For example, U.S. antidrug officials dismissed the efforts of the Directorate for the Fight Against Narcotrafficking, which had failed to establish working relationships with other Honduran law-enforcement agencies or U.S. counterparts, by declaring that it "suffers from weak leadership, inadequate funding, and unqualified personnel." *INCSR* (2004), 157.

Unlike states in which judges are senior, highly respected members of the bar, who customarily act within a judicial culture featuring personal integrity, principled contemplation of legal problems, and independence from political pressure, the Honduran judiciary has largely failed to develop such a culture. Judges have often lacked experience, and little public status has attached to their profession.[57] Bribes have often been offered in closed ex parte meetings between judges and defendants or their representatives. Indeed, when asked to comment on Honduran judicial corruption, one foreign official expert in antidrug matters declared, "I can't imagine it's any worse anywhere else in Central America. Here it's blatant bribery. Put the money on the table and *adios*. It extends all the way up through the judicial system and right up to the Supreme Court."[58] In 1998 the president of the Honduran Supreme Court, Oscar Armando Ávila, noted that all across the country, judges had been fined for negligently handling drug cases.[59] Attorney general Edmundo Orellano frankly attributed problems in administering justice to the cowardice, corruption, and ignorance of most Honduran judges.[60] In 2002 Vilma Morales, president of the Honduran Supreme Court, reported that in 2002 fully 1,823 complaints were lodged against judges for corrupt acts.[61]

Throughout the criminal-justice system the extent of Honduran corruption has been truly spectacular in its depth and extent, something noted by outside analysts as well as those within the system.[62] In 2000 the U.S. State Department—which over the years had funded and then assessed various programs for the improvement of justice—observed, "The judicial system is under severe strain due to corrupt, inefficient and overworked judges and lack of training and equipment."[63] That same year, Luis Morena, Latin American director of Transparency International, the nongovernmental corruption watchdog group, termed Honduran corruption "in a state of emergency."[64] His group ranked Honduras ninety-fourth of ninety-nine countries measured on its annual corruption index.[65] Almost a decade later, little had changed, with Transparency International once again designating Honduras one of the most corrupt countries in Latin America.[66]

Drug organizations have employed bribery, violence, and threats as levers to gain cooperation and defeat law enforcement. And those attempting to administer justice in Honduras have confronted real danger, particularly in narcotics cases. In 2007, for example, on the very day when the Honduran College of Lawyers was holding a vigil in front of the San Pedro Sula cathedral to protest the killing of fifteen lawyers that week, hit men ambushed and killed Judge Alba Leticia Bueso at an intersection elsewhere in the city, a murder linked to a drug case assigned to her.[67] The following year, prosecutors were receiving so many death

57. Dagoberto Mejía Pineda, director of the Public Defenders Service, noted that many Honduran law students have aspired to become judges after graduation to position themselves to become effective, experienced, and wealthy attorneys. Interview, 19 December 1991, Tegucigalpa, Honduras.

58. Confidential interview, December 1991, Tegucigalpa, Honduras. See also *INCSR* (2003), 5:28, and *INCSR* (2004), 156. The dramatic changes to the Criminal Procedure Code had the immediate effect of markedly increasing the number of trials, even during the transition period. *INCSR* (2003), 5:28.

59. "Por negligente separan al juez de Tocoa, Colón," *LP* (HO), 28 July 1998, 4A. In 2003 numerous judges were fired for being bribed by military officers and accused of crimes. "Cerca proceso penal por soborno de la justicia," *LP* (HO), 23 April 2003, 16.

60. "La mayoría de jueces no imparten justicia por corruptos, ignorantes, y cobardes," *LP* (HO), 29 July 1998, 4A.

61. "Denuncias por corrupción," *SV* (GU), 6 January 2003, 18.

62. *INCSR* (2005), 21.

63. *INCSR* (2000), 171. See also *INCSR* (1992), 158.

64. "Corrupción en Honduras está en estado de emergencia: Transparencia," *LP* (HO), 22 April 2000, 12A.

65. "Press Hailed as Graft Foe," *TT* (CR), 7 April 2000, 7.

66. "Es lamentable combate contra la corrupción," *LP* (HO), 10 December 2009, 18.

67. "Caso de narcotráfico provocó muerte a jueza," *LP* (HO), 20 May 2008, 20, and "Culpables asesinos de la jueza Alba Leticia Bueso," *LP* (HO), 10 September 2009, 8.

threats that the government resolved to rotate them more often, though transferring prosecutors from one jurisdiction to another proved to be of strictly limited value.[68] Then, in the most notorious drug-related killing of a leading government official in Honduran history, in 2009 motorcycle assassins on the streets of Tegucigalpa killed the Honduran antidrug director Julián Arístides González and then escaped.[69]

Trafficking organizations have manipulated promises of payments for cooperation and death threats for resistance, so they worked like two halves of a pair of scissors cutting through official antidrug procedures and institutions. Consequently, penal and judicial authorities have frequently assisted traffickers, and police have compromised DEA investigations.[70] U.S. counternarcotics officials declared, "Corruption is endemic in Honduras. Efforts to punish [it] . . . are ineffective, sporadic, and often inspired by personal considerations. Indeed, there is no national-level effort to prevent or punish corruption by public officials. Most Hondurans arrested on drug charges are released prematurely. Those convicted or awaiting trial frequently escape under suspicious circumstances."[71] The administration of justice in Honduras has thus proved to be a bridge-favoring factor of the first rank, encouraging traffickers to operate extensively in the country.

The Rule-of-Law Ideal

The virtual impunity with which military, political, and economic elites have long operated has undergirded these endemic criminal-justice problems. The absence of a rule-of-law ideal, much less any serious effort to adhere to such a principle in practice, has greatly encouraged elite participation in drug trafficking. Politicians as well as military officers have gained considerable wealth by becoming directly or indirectly involved in the trade. The routine trafficking of influence, common to Central American politics, has resulted in brisk sales of official credentials and diplomatic passports, and these have been employed in trafficking at airports and customs posts.

In these and other particulars, Honduran laws have been inadequate. Not only have they lacked breadth and precision in identifying corrupt acts, but they have failed to institute procedures to provide an effective structure and process for prosecuting and convicting the corrupt. Indeed, Honduran law traditionally shielded many officials from criminal complaints, including those involving the drug trade. In 2002 U.S. officials noted, "It is difficult to address corruption among public officials because all nationally elected officials enjoy legal immunity for all acts while in office. This creates a perverse incentive for people involved in illicit activity to run for office, and complicates enforcement efforts against suspected illegal narcotics activity."[72]

Officials have rarely been investigated, much less faced prison terms, for corrupt acts. On occasion, superiors have terminated the employment of a suspect individual. Other times, wrongdoers have been fined, publicly reprimanded, or transferred to another post. But almost never have they faced trial, conviction, and a severe penalty that might deter other officials contemplating corrupt behavior. Thus, in 2000 eight top law-enforcement officials were fired for suspected links to traffickers, including the minister of security, the deputy police commissioner, and the assistant director of police intelligence.[73] The following year the attorney general dismissed the counternarcotics

68. "Cambio en Fiscalía contra el crimen organizado," *LP* (HO), 3 June 2008, 51.

69. "Matan a jefe de lucha contra narcotráfico," *LP* (HO), 9 December 2009, 2.

70. *INCSR* (1994), 155. See also *INCSR* (1998), 144, and *INCSR* (2002), 145.

71. *INCSR* (1994), 155.

72. *INCSR* (2002), 5:25.

73. "Police Purged," 6.

director for suspected corruption, and the government opted to disband the entire Honduran Police Antinarcotics Force, terminating more than one hundred officers and shifting its duties to the Frontier Police.[74] However, neither thorough investigations of the suspected crimes nor prosecution and punishment of corrupt officials followed. Half measures have plainly failed to deter; instead, they have led rational actors to choose to reap the profits of assisting traffickers rather than resisting them. The challenges of revamping such a system—laws, institutions, procedures—so that corruption is better rooted out have been daunting, to say the least.

Frustrated at the incapacity of the Honduran system to deal effectively with drug trafficking as well as the inability of the U.S. government to change the situation, U.S. officials have resorted to such measures as canceling the U.S. visas of Hondurans suspected of drug-trade involvement. Thus, in 2001, after many years of the Honduran Congress's neglecting to pass money-laundering legislation, the U.S. Embassy stripped visas from various of those suspected of cleansing drug profits. (A new money-laundering bill became law the following year.) Again, in 2004 U.S. officials refused visas to about fifty Hondurans on suspicion of involvement in the drug trade.[75] Such a sanction, however, had modest utility. For some, being denied the ability to visit the United States simply amounted to an annoyance or embarrassment, and significant traffickers tended to avoid visiting the United States in any event for fear of arrest.

Early in the twenty-first century the Honduran legislature began to address some of the problems posed by impunity. In 2003 the Congress reformed laws that for forty-six years had shielded from criminal prosecution more than four thousand members of the armed forces and as many as twenty thousand public officials, including the president and other national politicians, the judiciary, mayors and municipal council representatives, and secretaries of state and their assistants.[76] Even then, however, the Honduran Congress did not immediately pass the implementing legislation needed to make the new regime effective.[77] Although such reforms made prosecution possible, the culture of the Honduran judicial system had to change before prosecution of official or elite wrongdoing became probable, much less automatic. Governments have often found, however, that cultures tend to be resilient, altered by government policy—if at all—quite slowly and through incentives that provide benefits to be gained from the revised way of thinking and behaving.[78]

To Hondurans, the costs inherent in challenging powerful interests were much more immediately obvious than just what might be gained by trying to expose corrupt or criminal conduct. The potential benefits, if they came to pass at all, would be long-term in nature. They would benefit individuals through their communities or society as a whole, and they would depend on like behavior by many others, which might not come to pass. In contrast, the potential risks involved in efforts to prosecute and convict elites or traffickers were quite immediate with the intimidation, injury, or death of individuals and close family members possibly at stake. The difficulties inherent in changing traditional culture and maintaining an effective rule-of-law ideal have clearly been enormous. The Honduran record plainly demonstrates that it has been easier to install a democratic voting process than to instill a culture with values conducive to a successful democratic regime.

74. *INCSR* (2002), 5:24.

75. "EE.UU. canceló visas a cincuenta hondureños corruptos en 2003," *SV* (GU), 9 January 2004, 20. See also "Corruptos no entrarón a EE.UU.," *SV* (GU), 13 January 2004, 15.

76. "Eliminan inmunidad en Honduras," *LP* (PA), 24 October 2003, 1A. "The decision was adopted for the good of the country," said the legislature's president, Porfirio Lobo Sosa. "Immunity was abused in the country and, for this, the hour had arrived to eliminate it."

77. *INCSR* (2005), 21.

78. See generally Bunck, *Fidel Castro*.

Military Influence

That the country's armed forces have held great sway over society has distinguished Honduras from certain other bridge states and allured traffickers. Absent accountability to civilians, the military has been left to regulate itself, a task it has undertaken erratically. Even officers have been found engaged in lucrative criminal activities, ranging from stealing cars to trafficking drugs; however, they have rarely been investigated, prosecuted, and punished.[79] Indeed, in 1996 the Honduran Supreme Court ruled that military personnel need not serve jail or prison time alongside common criminals but could instead be confined to barracks.[80] The impunity of a corrupted military could hardly help but attract the attention of traffickers weighing the advantages and disadvantages of transshipping through different bridge states.

As early as 1978, reports from numerous sources have accused military personnel of being vital cogs in major cocaine transit through the country, shielding traffickers from law enforcement, and providing muscle as rival drug networks clashed.[81] However, for a time, the importance of retaining Honduran military support in the Nicaraguan civil war seemed to curb the enthusiasm of U.S. officials for exerting pressure regarding officers involved in the drug trade.[82] In 1983 a DEA agent in Honduras investigated military trafficking and reported that, over fifteen months, officers had participated in smuggling more than fifty tons of cocaine. With the Honduran military helping the CIA to support the contras, the DEA, according to one insider, "promptly transferred that agent out of Honduras and closed the office."[83]

Thus, while bridge states sometimes find the counternarcotics policies of developed market countries to be contrary to certain of their other interests, the same phenomenon occurs in market countries. The objectives of a foreign policy may well be in tension with one another, and one may need to be sacrificed to another under a particular set of circumstances. This reality of international life frequently requires policy makers to prioritize and to resort to pragmatic behavior rather than principled or absolutist approaches.[84] With respect to efforts to curb the drug trade, however, this, too, injects stresses and strains into an interdiction strategy calling on multiple states to cooperate against transnational crime.

Not only has drug trafficking by Honduran military officers fostered corruption and obstructed the rule of law, but on one occasion it directly threatened the democratic regime. In 1984 the U.S. FBI thwarted a planned coup against President Roberto Suazo Córdova, arresting eight men in Florida and seizing three hundred kilos of Colombian cocaine flown into a remote south Florida airstrip. The cocaine would have financed the purchase of weapons, explosives, tanks, and planes for the Honduran ringleaders.[85] Honduran Gerard

79. See "Gozan de impunidad sin costo," *La Prensa* (Panama) (hereafter cited as *LP* [PA]), 23 January 1999, 6A, and "'Faceless' Judges Proposed," *TT* (CR), 3 July 1998, 8.

80. Bertha Oliva, president of the Honduras Committee of the Families of the Disappeared, declared, "This is a feather bed for all the genocidal criminals who violated laws in the last decade." "Accused Honduran Soldiers Avoid Jail," United Press International (United States) (hereafter cited as UPI [US]), 11 July 1996.

81. See, for instance, Morris, "Honduras," 569, and Scott and Marshall, *Cocaine Politics*, 10, 51–64. For activities of the "Gang of 13," Honduran military officers implicated in drug trafficking, robberies, and human rights abuses, see "'Faceless' Judges," 8.

82. Journalists and others have sometimes charged, though without documentation or other tangible substantiation, that drug transshipment was occurring on military bases. See, for instance, "Drugs, Torture, Extortion Mar El Aguacate Base," *TT* (CR), 17 September 1999, 9.

83. Levine, *Big White Lie*, 123.

84. Cf. Claude, "Principle and Pragmatism."

85. For information on this coup attempt, see *United States v. Perez*, 824 F.2d 1567. Cockburn and St. Clair, *Whiteout*, 293–94; "FBI Holds Eight in Plot on Honduras," *Washington Post* (United States) (hereafter cited as *WP* [US]), 2 November 1984, A1; "Army Ex-chief Sentenced in Coup Plot," Facts on File World News Digest, 5 September 1986; and "Narcotics: Terror's New Ally," *U.S. News and World Report*, 4 May 1987, 30.

Latchinian, an international arms dealer in Miami, conspired with Major General José Bueso Rosa, who had been demoted from armed forces chief of staff and ordered to serve as military attaché in Chile. Both were convicted and sentenced to lengthy prison terms for planning to assassinate Suazo and seize control of Honduras.

Despite the notoriety of this failed cocaine coup, a series of embarrassing incidents thereafter showed how entangled Honduran military officers and their family members continued to be in the international drug trade. In 1987 when police in Palmira, Colombia, detained Medellín kingpin Jorge Luis Ochoa for speeding and attempting to bribe the officers, he was driving a Cabriolet 911 Turbo Porsche sports car owned by Colonel William Said Speer, military attaché at the Honduran embassy in Bogotá.[86] The following year a U.S. State Department official told the *Los Angeles Times*: "We don't know the extent of the Honduran military's involvement in drugs. But our educated guess is that all of the senior officials have knowledge, many are involved . . . and they are all reaping the profits."[87] That same year, another U.S. official declared, "This is something that could get out of hand. We can't compete with the money the Colombian dealers are offering, and once the army is corrupted, we can't control it."[88]

Allegations were made, though never proven, concerning complicity in trafficking by General Humberto Regalado Hernández, chief of the armed forces.[89] However, the Honduran congressional commission charged in 1989 with investigating the national drug trade did implicate members of his family.[90] In 1988 U.S. Customs had arrested General Regalado's half brother, Colonel Rigoberto Regalado Lara, then serving as the Honduran ambassador to Panama, after he tried to enter Miami International Airport with slightly more than eleven kilos of cocaine in his luggage.[91] Investigations suggested that the cocaine had arrived in Honduras from Panama hidden in electrical appliances. Regalado Lara later told the Honduran drug commission that the general's daughter, Tania Regalado, had proposed the drug-smuggling plan. After a successful trial run, he allegedly obtained the cocaine from Tony Matteo, Tania's Cuban husband, who owned a seafood business in Trujillo, along the Honduran Caribbean coast, and then hid the drugs among coffee packages in his luggage.[92] However, an airport police dog smelled the cocaine, and because Regalado Lara was ambassador to Panama and not to the United States, he lacked diplomatic immunity in such circumstances. A customs search located the drugs, and Regalado Lara was

86. See "Narcotraficante Ochoa, arrestado en auto de diplomático hondureño," *LP* (HO), 25 November 1987, 14, and "Con auto de Said Speer se inició investigación de fraude millonario," *LP* (HO), 16 December 1987, 64. For Said Speer's defense and retirement, see "¡Miente Izaguirre, Said Speer es inocente!, aseguran FF.AA.," *LP* (HO), 7 June 1988, 4. Under Colombian law, foreign diplomats were permitted to import vehicles for free, though supposedly for personal use only. Between 1982 and 1987 Colombian car dealer Gabriel Taboada arranged to have forty-seven diplomats import luxury cars to sell to Medellín traffickers and others after a markup of twenty thousand to seventy thousand dollars, with kickbacks to the diplomats involved. "Diplomats Supplied Drug Lords' Cars," *WP* (US), 13 November 1991, A24.

87. "Honduras Drug Role Suspected," *Amandala* (Belize) (hereafter cited as *AM* [BZ]), 19 February 1988, 5.

88. Anderson, "Politics and Military," 427.

89. A U.S. State Department official alleged that Regalado Hernández "turned a blind eye to drug shipments," and continued, "We can only presume that he was paid a price for doing that. He wasn't doing it out of the goodness of his heart." "U.S. Aides Link Honduran Military Chief, Drug Trade," *Los Angeles Times* (United States) (hereafter cited as *LAT* [US]), 13 February 1988, 1, quoted in "Honduras Drug Role."

90. See "Narcotráfico en Honduras," *LN* (CR), 14 December 1989, 29A, and "Honduras Dismantles Narco Trafficking Bridge with S.A.," *The Reporter* (Belize) (hereafter cited as *TR* [BZ]), 28 January 1989, 6.

91. See "Embajador hondureño en Panamá capturado con cocaína en Miami," *La Hora* (Guatemala) (hereafter cited as *LH* [GU]), 17 May 1988, 12, and "En plástico y rodeada de café iba la 'coca,'" *LP* (HO), 17 May 1988, 3.

92. See "Hija del jefe de las FF.AA. entregó droga a Regalado Lara," *LP* (HO), 14 December 1989, 2. Regalado Lara initially declared that he had obtained the drugs from a "close friend" of the general's. "Denuncian a Regalado por corrupción," *LN* (CR), 16 October 1989, 26A.

convicted, sentenced to serve ten years, and dishonorably discharged from the military.[93]

The long-privileged position of the Honduran armed forces helps to account for the participation of officers in the drug trade. In 1995, for the first time, Honduran authorities successfully prosecuted a senior active-duty military officer and convicted him on drug charges. However, early the following year a Honduran judge slashed his sentence of twenty-one years in prison to five.[94] By the end of the century a mere five soldiers had been sentenced to prison terms on drug-trafficking charges. Some of these had been present when a drug seizure occurred, while others had been so deeply involved that their links could not be ignored. Beyond such blatant cases, military officers have usually continued to act with impunity.[95]

In one notorious 1998 case army officers were implicated in the murders of seven drug traffickers within seventy-two hours in and around the small city of Tocoa in Colón Department.[96] The prosecutor's theory was that members of a Honduran cartelito in Copán came to Colón to carry out a drug transaction with a north coast network headquartered in Tocoa, led by Honduran kingpin Juan Ramón Hernández Menjívar.[97] Although they were carrying a $240,000 payment, the Copán traffickers tried to double-cross their Colón counterparts by seizing the drugs but retaining the money. Hernández was thought to have responded by sending his alleged enforcer, Colonel Wilfredo Leva Cabrera, subcommander of La Ceiba military battalion, to recoup the drugs and money and kill the traffickers. Members of Leva's military unit then tracked down the Copán drug ring, torturing various people en route, including cutting off the testicles of one man.

Despite committing seven murders during this evening of settling scores, Leva and his subordinates were unable to find the money, which had been carefully hidden in the traffickers' vehicle. Police later combed over the car and located the cash, and after an investigation arrested Leva and five of his men. All five, however, escaped the National Penitentiary, and Leva himself obtained a false passport and the same day fled to Nicaragua through the border crossing at El Paraíso. While Leva was dishonorably discharged from the army in absentia, he then traveled quite freely through Central America, using an assumed name, despite an Interpol arrest warrant. In 1999 a group of former Honduran officials, including ex-president Carlos Roberto Reina, ran into Leva at the airport in El Salvador. They alerted the Honduran government, which asked Nicaragua to arrest Leva and return him to Honduras.[98]

A desperately poor country, with favorable geographic features, a malfunctioning criminal-justice system, and the long-standing impunity of elites, including influential military officers, amounted to a recipe for extensive drug trafficking. In fact, at a very early date large quantities of cocaine began to flow through Honduras, as this military-influenced transitional society proved to be one of the least capable states in the Caribbean region at resisting the drug trade. In 1988 one Honduran political leader commented, "This scale of drug trafficking

93. See "Coopera para hallar 'contactos,'" *LP* (HO), 18 May 1988, 3; "Baja deshonrosa para Regalado," *LP* (HO), 2 June 1988, 8; "Exembajador Regalado se declara culpable del tráfico de cocaína," *LP* (HO), 24 July 1988, 3; and "Diez años de cárcel para Regalado Lara," *LP* (HO), 2 September 1989, 2.

94. *INCSR* (1996), 137. For more on this case, see "Honduras Court Slashes Drug Sentence of Ex-security Chief," *Baltimore Sun*, 19 January 1996, 24A.

95. "Gozan de impunidad," 6A.

96. For information on this case, see "Teniente coronel Leva Cabrera sindicado en banda de 'narcos,'" *LP* (HO), 18 June 1998, 10A; "No se descarta que otros militares estén ligado al narcotráfico," *LP* (HO), 19 June 1998, 19A; and "Por detención ilegal y asesinato dictarán hoy auto de prisión a Leva," *LP* (HO), 11 February 1999, 27A.

97. "Teniente coronel Leva Cabrera," 10A.

98. "Prófugo Leva Cabrera se da el lujo de viajar por CA con funcionarios hondureños," *LP* (HO), 5 February 1999, 12A; "Leva Cabrera es capturado bajo el seudónimo José Jorge García," *LP* (HO), 6 February 1999, 6A; "Por detención ilegal y asesinato dictarán hoy auto de prisión a Leva," *LP* (HO), 11 February 1999, 27A; "'Faceless' Judges," 8; and *INCSR* (2000), 172.

can only be produced with the acquiescence or collaboration of high-level military and civilian officials. . . . This is more than a hypothesis. It is a fact."[99] A decade later, Honduran attorney general Edmundo Orellano declared, "The problem of narcotics trafficking is serious in Honduras, where the laws that exist are weak and are applied only to the mules, not to the big fish."[100]

The Evolution of Drug Trafficking in Honduras

The Honduran Marijuana Trade

Traditionally, Honduran farmers have grown low-potency marijuana in scattered locations virtually throughout the country and have harvested it twice a year. As elsewhere, cannabis plots have typically been hidden in rugged mountainous terrain or within legitimate agricultural crops in upland fields. Particularly notable production zones have included the following mountain ranges: Merendón flanking Guatemala; de la Flor in southern Yoro and northern Francisco Morazón Departments; and Nombre de Dios, inland from the Caribbean ports of La Ceiba and Puerto Cortés.[101] Almost invariably, the domestic crop has targeted Honduran consumers.[102] In the 1970s marijuana consumption rose steeply in Honduras, just as it did in Europe and North America. Significant markets developed in Tegucigalpa, San Pedro Sula, La Ceiba, and the Islas de la Bahía, and supply kept pace with demand. While dealers occasionally arranged for marijuana imports from Belize, many Belizeans had more lucrative outlets for their higher-quality cannabis, and Honduran growers produced most of the marijuana consumed at home.[103]

Although a rarely noted fact outside Honduran borders, cannabis production eventually grew quite sizable. Between 1986 and 2009 Honduran authorities confiscated more than a ton of processed marijuana in a dozen years, with seizures peaking at 4.65 tons in 1990 and more than 3 tons in 2008. Furthermore, despite the lack of thorough annual aerial surveys of possible planting zones, when so motivated, military and law-enforcement personnel have eradicated significant marijuana fields. For instance, in 1995 more than 2.6 million plants were eliminated, and in 2000 nearly 600,000 were destroyed.[104] However, the Honduran government frowned upon the aerial spraying of weed killer, and in certain years officials devoted little effort to locating and eliminating cannabis, such as 1993 and 1996, when a mere 4,203 and 2,309 plants were taken out. Hence, Honduran eradication has never reduced the marijuana crop to the maximum extent possible for any prolonged period.[105]

Also, unlike Belize or even Panama, Honduras never developed a marijuana-export trade of any significance. Although various long-standing marijuana-dealing organizations have existed,

99. "Honduran Drug Kingpin Poses Dilemma for US Pursuers," *Christian Science Monitor* (US), 7 March 1988, 9.

100. "El paraíso de los narcotraficantes," *SV* (GU), 23 March 1998, 23.

101. *INCSR* (1988), 130, and "Se han incautado en 1998 más de dos toneladas métricas de cocaína," *LP* (HO), 27 June 1998, 6A. In four major eradication campaigns in 1995 authorities seized over 3.1 tons of marijuana. *INCSR* (1996), 136–37.

102. We gained insights on domestic consumption during an interview with Dr. Dagoberto Espinoza Nourra (director of the Honduran Institute for the Prevention and Treatment of Alcoholism, Drug Abuse, and Drug Addiction), 12 December 1991, Tegucigalpa, Honduras. See also Centro, "Cronología," 2, 4, noting that by 1982 marijuana cigarettes, or *puritas*, were on sale for between $0.50 and $2.50, depending on supply.

103. For a 296-kilo shipment of Belizean marijuana seized at Puerto Cortés in 1984, see Centro, "Cronología," 4.

104. In a notable 1995 seizure DEA and Honduran officials broke up a Yoro marijuana operation, eradicating two hundred thousand mature plants and seizing more than nine hundred kilos of marijuana prepared for shipment. "A L. 40 millones llega valor de marihuana decomisada en Yoro," *LP* (HO), 5 March 1995, 3A, and "Decomisan seis vehículos, cincuenta armas de fuego, cuatro kilos de 'coca' y marihuana," *LP* (HO), 8 December 1995, 22A.

105. DEA, *Resources, Honduras* (2000), 1; DEA, *Resources, Honduras* (2001), 1; *INCSR* (2009), 305; *INCSR* (1996), 136–37; *INCSR* (1991), 154.

such as that allegedly directed by Wilfredo ("Choreta") Izaguirre Borjas, Hondurans have not produced high-quality marijuana.[106] Thus, although in Belize one's attention is focused on the manner in which the marijuana trade laid the foundation for cocaine transshipment, the interesting issue in Honduras is why the country never developed a marijuana-export industry. Not only were Honduran judicial and law-enforcement institutions weak and easily corrupted, but neither the soil nor the topography differ so markedly from those in Belize. One notable factor seems to be that the international marijuana-trafficking networks that helped Belizean growers to improve quality through better seeds failed to do so in Honduras. Perhaps Honduran growers lacked the connections or the initiative to follow the Belizean lead, or perhaps Mexicans and Americans with access to enhanced varieties had preexisting links to nearby Belize or otherwise preferred to assist Belizeans.[107] Perhaps traffickers saw the international marijuana market as already well supplied, with domestic production rising in the United States and Canada and with market shares already staked out in strains that marijuana consumers might recognize coming from Mexico, Jamaica, Colombia, Belize, and Panama. Perhaps a promising illicit business opportunity was simply overlooked. In any event, on account of its low THC content, no foreign demand has ever developed for Honduran marijuana. And only a small portion of the Honduran crop has been exported to its neighbors, much less to the United States.[108]

Honduras did, however, gain international prominence in the marijuana trade through transshipping the drug. Smugglers linked to Honduras long trafficked immense shipments of valuable Colombian cannabis to North America and even to Europe and Asia.[109] For many years politicians as well as military and government officials involved themselves in providing flags of convenience to vessels, including many at work in the maritime marijuana trade.[110] Table 5.1 lists some representative seizures of marijuana off Honduran vessels between 1980 and 1990, including enormous shipments of 45, 60, and 75 tons.[111] No doubt, many more vessels engaged in the trade escaped official detection.

106. See "Redada de narcotraficantes realizan en San Pedro Sula," *LP* (HO), 1 July 1987, 4, and "Un millón de marihuana 'de la fina' queman en la playa," *LP* (HO), 2 December 1987, 64. In 1991, after authorities charged Izaguirre Borjas with possessing 127 kilos of marijuana, the leading Honduran newspaper wryly observed that, despite a series of drug charges, Izaguirre "has always gained his freedom with the help of legal professionals and a bit of 'extra help' with which he has toasted the health of various judges, according to the police." "Hallan carro de narcotraficante 'Choreta' repleto de mariguana," *LP* (HO), 3 January 1992, 10.

107. For a thwarted 1986 effort by a prominent Belizean international marijuana trafficker to grow six acres of cannabis, presumably for export, in Honduras, see *INCSR* (1988), 128.

108. In 1985 the U.S. Coast Guard seized a ship, its five-man Honduran crew, and 9 tons of what the court identified as Honduran marijuana. *United States v. Euceda-Hernandez*, 768 F.2d 1307. For a representative case of domestic marijuana trafficking, see "Se incautan 210 libras de marihuana," *LP* (HO), 8 June 2008, 33.

109. As early as 1984 twenty-two Honduran sailors had been imprisoned, most in Britain and West Germany, on drug-smuggling charges, and in 1986 multiton shipments of marijuana had been seized off Honduran vessels in Italy (the *Fidelio*) and the Netherlands (the *Cornelia*). Centro, "Cronología," 4. For representative European seizures, see "Gran Bretaña: Arrestan carguero hondureño," *LP* (HO), 5 September 1988, 3, and "Hallan droga en barco hondureño," *LP* (HO), 7 September 1988, 4. In 1995 the crew members of a Honduran-registered vessel were involved in a marijuana-trafficking bust in Singapore. "Two Ship Engineers Caught with Cannabis Haul," *The Straits Times* (Singapore), 19 August 1995, 32.

110. In the late 1980s the Honduran government attempted to tighten "formerly lax registration and inspection procedures to reduce the use of a Honduran flag of convenience by smugglers." *INCSR* (1988), 129. See also "Investigan barco con bandera hondureña que llevaba cocaína," *LP* (HO), 23 April 2001, 26A.

111. Other relevant cases in which the weight of the marijuana seized was not immediately available include the 1980 seizure by the U.S. Coast Guard of the *Ocean Lady* ninety miles off Cuba, the 1983 seizure by Mexican authorities of the Honduran vessel *Escorpión* near the Yucatán, the 1983 seizure by New Orleans authorities of two drug-trafficking boats from Puerto Cortés, and the 1984 case of the Honduran ship *Rosangel*, seized by the U.S. Coast Guard with 114 bales of marijuana. See *United States v. Martinez*, 476 F.3d 961, and *United States v. Gonzalez*, 776 F.2d 931. Later that decade the U.S. Coast

Table 5.1 Major seizures of Honduran vessels carrying marijuana, 1980–1990

Date	Vessel name	Identifying information	Quantity seized (mt)
1980	*Jenny Conner* (or "*Four Roses*")	Headed to United States	25.9
1980	*Patricia*	Headed to United States (Maine)	18.7
1982	*Mary Anne*	Headed to United States (230 km from Puerto Rico)	15
1983	*Ocean Lady*	Headed to United States (seventy-five-foot shrimp boat from Tela)	11.8
1983	*Goloson*	Headed to United States	9.1
1984	*Lady Mac*	Seized off Mexico (Tampico)	25
1985	n/a	Headed to United States (Florida)	60
1985	*Sea Maid I*	Headed to United States (tugboat towing barge of marijuana off North Carolina)	75
1986	*Don Yevo*	Bahamas (seventy-foot Honduran vessel boarded by U.S. Coast Guard on high seas)	16
1986	*Fidelio*	Italy	10
1987	*Carmiel*	n/a	20
1987	*Kimberly*	n/a	15
1988	n/a	Vessel captured off Honduran coast in joint U.S.-Honduran exercise	15
1989	*Roatán*	Headed to United States via Dominican Republic	Precise amount not available
1989	n/a	Headed to Grand Cayman Island (vessel captured by Honduran Navy in transit from Cartagena with Red Point marijuana)	10
1990	*See Wonderer*	Headed to United States	45

Sources: *United States v. Hensel*, 699 F.2d 18; *United States v. Martinez*, 700 F.2d 1358; *United States v. Euceda-Hernandez*, 768 F.2d 1307; *United States v. Ospina*, 823 F.2d 429; *United States v. Mena*, 863 F.2d 1522; *Valencia v. United States*, 923 F.2d 917; *INCSR* (1988), 129; *INCSR* (1989), 183; Centro, "Cronología," 3–4, 6–7, 8–9, 12; Stephen Koff, "Twenty Thousand Pounds of Pot Seized," *St. Petersburg Times*, 23 May 1987, 1B, "Hunden barco que transportaban L. cuarenta y ocho millones en marihuana," *LP* (HO), 5 April 1989, 1, 5; "Decomisan veintidos mil libras de marihuana colombiano," *LP* (HO), 5 April 1989, 1, 5.

Occasional large seizures continued into the 1990s. For instance, in 1995 authorities took 2,534 kilos of marijuana off the Honduran-registered *Gato Negro*, just off Colombia's Guajira Peninsula.[112] By this point, however, the trafficking of Colombian marijuana by sea had established the Honduran merchant marine as an attractive option for cartels trafficking cocaine.

The Honduran Narcotics Trade

Where Honduras gained special notoriety in the drug trade was not in trafficking Colombian marijuana on its vessels, substantial as that was. Nor was it in money laundering, which, given the state of the Honduran economy, was long negligible, particularly in comparison with Panama. Instead, over the past four decades

Guard boarded the *Rose Marie 10*, with "Honduras" visible on the stern, in international waters off the Colombian coast and discovered marijuana. *United States v. Potes*, 880 F.2d 1475. See also *United States v. Pimenta-Redondo*, 874 F.2d 9.

112. *United States v. Amado Guerrero*, 114 F.3d 332.

Honduras has served as a vitally important cocaine-transshipment location, with very large quantities arriving and departing by air and sea.[113] The first salient point, in tracing the development of the Honduran drug trade, is that cocaine trafficking took hold at a very early date. In 1990 a special Honduran congressional commission assigned to investigate the drug trade concluded that South American suppliers had been using Honduras to send cocaine to North American consumers since the 1970s.[114] Honduras was also quite distinctive in that this early flourishing of trafficking may be attributed in part to the presence of the region's first true kingpin: Juan Ramón Matta Ballesteros.[115]

The Matta Ballesteros Era

It might be assumed that early Central American traffickers were usually subordinates, taking orders from and carrying out jobs for Colombian and Mexican cartels. In fact, Juan Ramón Matta Ballesteros was strikingly different. U.S. federal authorities came to characterize him as a "class I DEA violator," a designation also accorded Pablo Escobar, Jorge Luis Ochoa, and Carlos Lehder.[116] At his capture the DEA considered Matta to be among the world's ten most important traffickers. Despite his Honduran origins, the popular media referred to him as the "boss of bosses of Mexico's cocaine industry," and at its height his organization was thought to supply "perhaps one third of all the cocaine consumed in the United States."[117]

While the term *bridge state* is chiefly associated with the transit of illegal drugs, Central American traffickers also served to bridge the differences between South American organizations, especially in Colombia, and their North American counterparts, especially in Mexico. Indeed, Matta's career illustrates the key role played by those who could foster cooperative ventures among leading traffickers. His genius at facilitating narcotics deals also demonstrates how a Central American who had risen to the uppermost echelons of the drug trade could bring attention to the bridge-favoring factors associated with his country.

A boyhood pickpocket who grew up homeless on the streets of Tegucigalpa, Matta Ballesteros, as a young man, paired an incipient career as a narcotics chemist with one as a smuggler, transporting gems, gold, and jewels, and then drugs of different varieties.[118] In 1970 U.S. authorities arrested Matta at Dulles Airport outside of Washington, D.C., charging him with attempting to import 24.5 kilos of cocaine.[119] Although Matta prevailed on the drug charge at trial, federal prosecutors did convict him of illegal entry and the use of false documents. The following year Matta escaped from the minimum-security prison at Eglin Air Force Base in Florida.[120]

113. For the interception in 2004 of 2,640 kilos of cocaine off the Honduran-registered *Miss Lorraine*, located eighty nautical miles off Panama, see *United States v. De Jesus Matute-Santos*, 168 Fed. Appx. 343.

114. "Honduras Dismantles," 6. For an early case involving forty-two kilos of cocaine flown from Bolivia, see *United States v. Bollinger*, 769 F.2d 1394.

115. In Matta's heyday, before his controversial 1987 expulsion to the United States, the drug flow via Honduras increased dramatically. MacDonald, *Dancing on a Volcano*, 125. See also Centro, "Cronología," 9. The other possible contender for the first kingpin would be Alfonso Rivera, a prominent early South American cocaine trafficker who was born in Copán, Honduras, though his adult life was spent in Ecuador and Peru, and he actually became a Peruvian citizen. See Mills, *Underground Empire*, 862–64.

116. See "Matta desafía a tribunal en EUA," *LP* (HO), 6 May 1989, 2, and Scott and Marshall, *Cocaine Politics*, 10.

117. *Newsweek*, 13 May 1985, quoted in Scott and Marshall, *Cocaine Politics*, 42.

118. See "Pagó para hacer desaparecer fichas delictivas en la DNI [Departamento Nacional de Investigaciones]," *LP* (HO), 2 April 1986, 4; "Central American Drug Lord," UPI (US), 20 March 1988; and "Declaró Dimas Reyes: Por venganza Matta Ballesteros ordenó ultimar a los Ferraris," *LP* (HO), 2 April 1986, 4.

119. See the references to Matta in the 1983 U.S. Customs Service investigative report of Guy Owen. U.S. Senate, *Law Enforcement: Report*, 287. See also Government Sentencing Memorandum, 21 December 1989, in *United States v. Matta-Ballesteros*, 71 F.3d 754, and Scott and Marshall, *Cocaine Politics*, 208n25.

120. See *Matta-Ballesteros v. Henman*, 896 F.2d 255, and *United States v. Matta*, 937 F.2d at 569. See also "Presunto traficante hondureño Matta en cárcel de alta seguridad," *LH* (GU), 7 April 1988, 7; "Juez rechaza petición de Matta," *LP* (HO), 30 May 1988, 3; and "Matta, culpable de fugarse de la cárcel," *LP* (HO), 14 September 1988, 12.

Upon returning to Latin America, Matta Ballesteros continued to gain experience in different facets of the drug trade—transshipping cocaine, arranging joint ventures, even, reportedly, working as a hit man for Medellín traffickers and running a cocaine-refining laboratory. He again drew the attention of U.S. authorities, and in 1973 the DEA designed a sting operation to trap him. After that effort failed, Mexican authorities jailed Matta in 1974 on charges of selling 10 kilos of cocaine, and before his release a year later, Matta was suspected of killing two other prisoners.[121]

Matta's criminal background led him toward not only a thorough understanding of the different facets of the drug business but a wide circle of influential acquaintances deeply involved in it. In particular, Matta reportedly served as a key connection between an early Mexican cocaine kingpin, Cuban Alberto Sicilia Falcón, and coca suppliers in the Andes.[122] Matta also introduced Mexican traffickers to top Medellín boss José Gonzalo Rodríguez Gacha, thus helping to broker one of the initial arrangements by which Colombians paid Mexican smugglers to transport cocaine across the U.S. border.

By the mid-1970s Matta Ballesteros had risen to become an integral part of Mexico's chief cocaine- and marijuana-smuggling enterprise, the Guadalajara cartel. Most notably, Matta was tied to Miguel Ángel Félix Gallardo, who by this time had advanced from small-scale heroin trafficking in Culiacán to become a true cocaine kingpin. In 1975 Félix and Matta formed a partnership that made use of the Mexican's organization, growing rapidly in prominence at the time, and the Honduran's expertise and Colombian connections. In particular, Matta had access to enormous quantities of cocaine ready to ship to market. In 1977 Colombian authorities arrested him for possessing 1,173 kilos of cocaine and operating two cocaine-refining laboratories. The following year Colombian police discovered 800 kilos of cocaine on property Matta owned north of Bogotá. In 1979 a confidential source told U.S. agents that Matta was poised to deliver 125 kilos, and the next year officials in Bogotá arrested him while seizing 580 kilos of cocaine.[123]

Matta soon again demonstrated his abilities not only to avoid lengthy imprisonment but to work with different powerful networks of traffickers for his own profit, no easy feat in a drug underworld characterized by rumor, suspicion, and jealous rivalry and antagonism. Apart from his partnership with Félix Gallardo, Matta worked closely with his Guadalajara cartel colleague Ernesto Fonseca Carrillo and with the allied Sonora cartel, led by Rafael Caro Quintero.[124] In fact, in supervising the transit of many thousands of kilos of cocaine from Mexico into Arizona and southern California, Matta, drawing on his knack for devising smuggling schemes, was said to have thoroughly modernized the drug trade through Mexico.[125] As a native Honduran, Matta was credited with special expertise in trafficking through Central America, knowledge that proved of vital importance in the early 1980s, as Colombian kingpins came to favor pathways through Central America over their prior Caribbean routes.

Rather than taking citizenship in another country, Matta opted to keep his home base in Honduras. While from 1977 to 1986 Matta was often absent, he nonetheless intimidated

121. "Central American Drug Lord"; Scott and Marshall, *Cocaine Politics*, 55; U.S. Senate, *Law Enforcement: Report*, 287; Shannon, *Desperados*, 60–61; "Mexican Drug Traffickers Eclipse Colombian Cartels," *WP* (US), 30 March 1997, A1.

122. For a detailed portrait of Sicilia Falcón, see generally Mills, *Underground Empire*.

123. See the U.S. Customs Service investigative report reproduced in U.S. Senate, *Law Enforcement: Report*, 287; Centro, "Cronología," 5; and Shannon, *Desperados*, 61, 115–16. Matta later testified that in this period he visited Panama, attempting to resolve financial problems with a Panamanian bank and using Manuel Noriega's intervention to free from prison a trafficking associate. "Carlos Lehder recibe amenazas tras declarar contra Noriega," *LP* (PA), 7 March 1996, 1A. See also "Deniegan extradicción de Matta a Honduras y EU," *LP* (HO), 4 November 1985, 5.

124. *United States v. Matta-Ballesteros*, 71 F.3d at 760.

125. "Lo acusan de inundar el mercado con drogas por 70 millones de dólares," *LP* (HO), 28 July 1989, 76.

rivals and authorities while cultivating a network of Honduran associates, collaborators, and acquaintances in a position to assist him.[126] Some reports suggest that, after Matta's joint ownership of large real estate holdings with General Policarpio Paz García came to public attention in 1978, the Honduran kingpin financed the coup that brought Paz to power.[127] Thereafter, Matta is thought to have worked freely with Honduran military and political officials to ensure the smooth flow of substantial drug loads through the country. Then, from 1978 to 1981 Matta developed such a close relationship with the Honduran military chief of intelligence, Colonel Leonides Torres Arias, that CIA analysts reportedly believed the two were involved in joint Colombian drug deals.[128]

In hopes that Honduras, at least, would remain a reasonably safe law-enforcement refuge for him, Matta worked assiduously to minimize the evidence of his criminal undertakings there. In 1977, according to Lieutenant Juan Ángel Barahona, former Interpol director in Honduras, Matta paid five thousand dollars to officials at the Honduran National Department of Investigations (DNI) to "fix" his criminal records. Corrupt officials allegedly delivered to the kingpin all incriminating material about him in police archives, including tape recordings by witnesses.

For traffickers working in bridge states such knowledge can be a potent part of their power. Before potential informants and other witnesses step forward with information for police, they might take into account, and be dissuaded by, the key facts that a kingpin was apparently immune from conviction, was extremely dangerous and also extraordinarily well connected, and could readily find out who had said what about him. In fact, Matta's collaborators intimidated the few Hondurans who tried to publicize what Matta and his network were doing. After Lieutenant Barahona publicly stated that "the Chief of the Armed Forces has recordings and documents of officials who are linked to the drug trade and who have received money from the mafiosos," his superiors ordered him incarcerated in solitary confinement inside a military camp. When released, he chose not to speak further about these allegations.[129]

For a time larger foreign policy issues interfered with the DEA's investigation of Matta's Honduran connections. In 1981 DEA agent Tom Zepeda, then stationed in Honduras, filed a series of intelligence reports charging that senior Honduran Army and Navy officers, including Colonel Torres Arias, were protecting Matta and other traffickers. His superiors, however, chose not to pursue the matter. Critics alleged exposing the armed forces involvement might have undermined Honduran cooperation with the Nicaraguan contras, and in particular, the support offered by Honduran military bases. In fact, in various ways Matta's military connections helped to ensure his security.

126. For accusations by former Judge Izaguirre Fiallos that attorney general Rubén Darío Zepeda Gutiérrez and legislator Nicolas Cruz Torres had socialized with Matta at the beachfront hotel Villas Telamar in Tela, see "Juez Izaguirre: Políticos y magistrados 'mulas' del narcotráfico," *LP* (HO), 2 June 1988, 2. For angry denials by those accused, see "Es un canalla, acusa Zepeda," *LP* (HO), 2 June 1988, 5, and "Para Cruz Torres: 'Tiene una vil lengua,'" *LP* (HO), 2 June 1988, 5.

127. See Scott and Marshall, *Cocaine Politics*, 54. Paz García's predecessor, conservative general Juan Alberto Melgar Castro, ruled Honduras for three years but alienated other officers. Having a friendly general in power was in Matta's interests, as was operating in a weak democracy, and Paz spoke of returning Honduras to civilian control.

128. See "Prometan investigar narcotráfico en Honduras," *LN* (CR), 14 February 1988, 39A, and "Military Officers in Honduras Are Linked to the Drug Trade," *New York Times* (United States) (hereafter cited as *NYT* [US]), 12 February 1988, 1A. Torres Arias was also connected with Noriega, then Panama's chief of military intelligence, who is thought to have arranged trips to Cuba for him to meet Fidel Castro. In 1980 Noriega reportedly involved Torres in arms smuggling to leftist rebels in El Salvador, using airstrips in northern Honduras. In 1983 the military fired Torres after a trip to Cuba to confer with Fidel Castro, organized and inspired by Noriega, was publicized. Koster and Sánchez, *In the Time*, 284.

129. "Pagó para hacer desaparecer," 4; "Crimen de los esposos Ferrari deuda de Matta ante la justicia hondureña," *LP* (HO), 1 April 1986, 5.

Authorities granted the trafficker a permit to carry an automatic weapon. Matta also purchased a security company and hired retired military officers to serve as bodyguards.[130]

Matta Ballesteros and the Honduran armed forces shared interests in the Nicaraguan conflict, including profiting from assisting the contras. Werner Lotz, a Costa Rican pilot for Matta's partner Félix Gallardo, reported that his boss was a substantial contra supporter, having given Lotz $150,000 to forward to the contra cause. Furthermore, the U.S. Senate Committee on Foreign Relations later reported that Matta's air freight company, Servicios Ejecutivos Turistas Commander (SETCO), despite having already been implicated by the U.S. government in drug smuggling, was "the principal company used by the Contras in Honduras to transport supplies and personnel for the [Nicaraguan Democratic Front], carrying at least a million rounds of ammunition, food, uniforms, and other military supplies . . . from 1983 to 1985." In 1985 SETCO pilot Frank Versame Moss formed his own company, Hondu Carib, a subsidiary of Atlas Aviation, that was prepared to work alongside SETCO and step in if necessary. At the time ten law-enforcement bodies were investigating Moss for drug trafficking.[131]

This web of aerial import-export firms, with experienced pilots and multiple planes, all owned by or at the service of Matta Ballesteros, was ideally suited for his licit and illicit business dealings. The most lucrative, of course, was cocaine trafficking, and in this regard Matta enjoyed unparalleled connections in Colombia. By 1984 Colombian kingpins had sufficient faith in him to request the Honduran trafficker to negotiate an agreement with leading Mexican cartels to smuggle their cocaine into the United States for one thousand dollars per kilo.[132] That same year, Matta reportedly helped to orchestrate a meeting in Spain between Jorge Luis Ochoa and Gilberto Rodríguez Orejuela, who, though boyhood friends in Medellín, were leading the rival Colombian cartels.[133]

By their own accounts the Rodríguez Orejuela brothers had become closely familiar with Honduras, having already orchestrated drug-trafficking ventures through Tegucigalpa and San Pedro Sula.[134] Gilberto Rodríguez Orejuela later told prosecutors that in 1975, at the very beginning of his trafficking career, his first route involved flying cocaine shipments from Colombia into San Pedro Sula and that he had personally seen off shipments in Colombia and received them in Honduras. His brother Miguel reported that starting in 1982 he and Gilberto had been sending cocaine loads of fifty to one hundred kilos through the country. He also admitted that from 1984 to 1987 he had sent six shipments of one hundred to two hundred kilos of cocaine via Honduras into Miami.

While Matta had extensive ties with Cali traffickers, he associated with Medellín smugglers as well, having a hand in aerial-trafficking schemes that brought Colombian drugs through Honduras into the southeastern United States through Atlas Aviation and Hondu Carib.[135]

130. "The Traffic in Drugs," *NYT* (US), 10 April 1988, 1; Scott and Marshall, *Cocaine Politics*, 56, 63–64; Cockburn and St. Clair, *Whiteout*, 283. In claiming that there had been too little supporting evidence to pursue the charges, DEA director John Lawn later observed that Zepeda's allegations were similar to those that the DEA was receiving about many other militaries.

131. Quote from U.S. Senate, *Law Enforcement: Report*, 44; Scott and Marshall, *Cocaine Politics*, 41, 54–55; "What Will Congress Do About New CIA-Drug Revelations?," *San Francisco Chronicle*, 19 June 2000, A19. For all of the drug-trafficking investigations of Moss, he was never indicted.

132. Bonner, "New Cocaine Cowboys," 36.

133. See also "Los narcotraficantes Matta y Carlos Lehder estuvieron en España en 1984," *El País* (Spain), 5 May 1988, and "Matta y cartel de Medellín prepararon en España una base del narcotráfico," *LP* (HO), 20 May 1988, 14.Although Spanish police detained both Ochoa and Rodríguez, the former for illegally importing bulls and the latter for drug trafficking, both were eventually returned to Colombia and soon gained their freedom there.

134. *Confesiones secretas*, 23, 29, 40, 45.

135. For the material on Atlas Aviation, Honda Carib, and Guy Owen, see U.S. Senate, *Law Enforcement: Report*, 279–97.

Indeed, Matta's ability to cultivate connections and encourage cooperation, all while pocketing enormous profits, is illustrated by the activities of these air-transport enterprises.

In the spring of 1983 U.S. Customs agents joined with local police in Alabama, Georgia, and Mississippi to investigate Frank Moss and Guy Penilton Owen in relation to a series of flights from Honduras into their states. An airplane mechanic and pilot, Owen had risen to serve as part owner of Atlas Aviation and as president of Hondu Carib, which was supposedly importing shrimp and precious wood into the United States. In November 1981 Owen had arrived at New Orleans International Airport on a Beech aircraft from San Pedro Sula that a narcotics-detector dog indicated had recently carried drugs. Not only had Owen previously associated with various known or suspected traffickers, but he had been linked to aircraft that had apparently been altered for drug smuggling: stripped of seats, with enlarged cargo doors, expanded fuel capacity, and high-technology navigation equipment. However, a highly reliable source of the Intelligence Division of the Louisiana State Police tipped authorities that an Atlas DC-4 was to be used in a major marijuana- and cocaine-smuggling venture. The drugs were to be transshipped through La Ceiba, flown to the United States, and air-dropped at an isolated Louisiana farm owned by Adler Berriman ("Barry") Seal and his brother, alleged by the U.S. Customs Service at the time to be "major narcotics smugglers and distributors throughout the eastern and southern United States."[136]

In fact, Barry Seal was a leading pilot for the Medellín cartel, one who had graduated from flying 747 jets at age twenty-six for Trans World Airlines (TWA) to become one of the most skilled and trusted drug pilots. Known as "McKenzie" or "El Gordo" (The Fat Man), Seal earned up to half a million dollars per flight for smuggling tons of cocaine.[137] From a base at the Intermountain Regional Airport in Mena, Arkansas, he imported numerous drug shipments, regularly evading U.S. radar and dropping the loads to waiting ground crews in Texas, Arkansas, and Louisiana.[138] In 1983, however, the DEA arrested Seal for drug trafficking, and the following year he was convicted and sentenced to ten years. Shortly thereafter, the U.S. government accepted Seal's offer to become a DEA informant.

In June 1984, after the CIA outfitted a C-123 cargo plane with a remote-controlled camera inside the loading ramp, Seal took photographs showing Sandinista officials and Medellín traffickers transferring burlap bags of cocaine from a jeep into the plane, while it was parked on the military side of Managua Airport.[139] In late 1984, with Seal poised to testify against Jorge Luis Ochoa should he ever be brought to trial in the United States, top Medellín traffickers ordered his assassination.[140] In February 1986, after several failed attempts, Colombian hit men trapped Seal in the parking lot of a Baton Rouge Salvation Army halfway house and killed him with a machine gun.[141]

By the 1980s Matta had become extraordinarily wealthy. In 1982 DEA confidential sources reported that Matta had paid $50 million to

136. U.S. Senate, *Law Enforcement: Report*, 285.

137. See *Louisiana v. Velez*, 588 So.2d 116.

138. For CIA activities at this airstrip, see "Talk Lingers of CIA Link in Arkansas: Agency Says It Never Hired Drug Trafficker," *Dallas Morning News*, 10 November 1996, 1A.

139. U.S. House, *Nicaraguan Government*, 30. See also Gugliotta and Leen, *Kings of Cocaine*, 162, and Shannon, *Desperados*, 151.

140. Seal became a valuable U.S. witness in various cases, supplying information that helped prosecutors to indict Escobar and Ochoa and that led to the conviction of Medellín traffickers in Las Vegas. Seal was also instrumental in setting up the 1985 arrest on cocaine-smuggling charges of Norman Saunders, chief minister of the Turks and Caicos, British Caribbean islands south of the Bahamas. See *United States v. Herrera-Zuleta*, 1991 U.S. App. LEXIS 16090. For a firsthand account of Seal's assassination, see Mermelstein, *Man*, 195–204.

141. Prosecutors eventually convicted Colombians Miguel Vélez and Luis Carlos Quintero Cruz of first-degree murder, with Bernardo Antonio Vásquez adjudged guilty of second-degree murder. See *Louisiana v. Velez*, 588 So.2d 116. Two of the Colombian kingpins indicted for allegedly ordering the murder, Escobar and Rafael Cordona Salazar, were themselves shot and killed in Colombia without coming to trial on these murder charges.

Bolivian and other Latin American authorities for help in trafficking tons of cocaine.[142] A U.S. federal court of appeals later stated that Matta and Félix Gallardo were grossing more than $5 million a week.[143] In 1983 Colombian authorities again arrested Matta, seizing a ton of cocaine and $1 million worth of narcotics-tainted assets, though he soon managed to secure his release.[144] In 1982, in the course of confiscating $1.2 million in drug profits, U.S. authorities found that Matta had "provided 805 kilos of cocaine to the organization of Isaac Kattan Kassin based out of Los Angeles."[145] Born to a Jewish family in Syria but a Cali resident and naturalized Colombian citizen, Kattan was identified by federal prosecutors as being South America's leading drug financier.[146] U.S. Customs agents estimated that he "was handling . . . $100 million a year for a dozen large Latin organizations, among them the up-and-coming ring led by . . . Félix Gallardo and his partner, Juan Ramón Matta Ballesteros."[147]

A constant issue for true drug kingpins is how best to manage the enormous backflow of drug profits, and Matta spent considerable time and energy investing his illicit earnings. In addition to SETCO aviation, he accumulated coffee, tobacco, spice, and dairy- and beef-cattle holdings and founded construction and agro-industrial companies in Honduras.[148] He also tried to foster the popular image of a kindly and legitimate business executive, sympathetic to all raised in the poverty he had experienced, a man continually harassed by the U.S. government and others jealous of his success.

At its height Matta's business empire, including Matta Investments, employed as many as five thousand Hondurans, while enabling the laundering of drug money and gaining him respect, support, and acceptance in a cross-segment of Honduran society. In 1987 legislative deputy Dr. Félix Cerna Salgado admitted a close personal relationship with Matta, though denying that Matta had influenced him politically.[149] The prior year finance minister Reginald Panting had stated publicly that Honduras would gladly accept the millions in drug profits that Matta Ballesteros had supposedly reaped as the money "would be welcomed in our country because it would help us to improve our balance of payments." Panting proceeded to say, "If the gentleman wishes to set up gasoline stations here, I with pleasure will sell him mine."[150]

Because the Honduran economy could not easily accommodate all of Matta's resources, the kingpin also turned to foreign investment, first

142. Mermelstein, *Man*, 287–88.

143. *United States v. Matta-Ballesteros*, 71 F.3d at 760. After arresting Félix Gallardo in April 1989 and seizing $2.5 million in cash, Mexican authorities reported confiscating his assets, including 112 urban properties, 28 rural properties, fifty-six vehicles, and thirty bank accounts. "Confiscan bienes," *LN* (CR), 14 July 1989, 20A.

144. Centro, "Cronología," 3.

145. U.S. Customs Service investigative report reproduced in U.S. Senate, *Law Enforcement: Report*, 287.

146. DEA agents in Miami arrested Kattan, as he was participating in a modest cocaine deal that was under DEA surveillance, and U.S. prosecutors eventually convicted him of cocaine possession, with a federal court sentencing him to thirty years. See *United States v. Kattan*, 588 F. Supp. 127, and *United States v. Espinosa-Orlando*, 704 F.2d 507. For Kattan's money laundering at Miami banks, see *United States v. Kattan-Kassin*, 696 F.2d 893. See also "Regional News—Florida," UPI (US), March 19, 1981, and Shannon, *Desperados*, 79.

147. Shannon, *Desperados*, 79. A federal narcotics agent testified that an address book Kattan was carrying when arrested contained the names or phone numbers of at least eighty-eight convicted drug dealers, and his Miami financial offices were using five high-speed money-counting machines and a telex terminal for speculating in gold and foreign currencies.

148. "Cierran empresas de Matta," *LP* (HO), 10 June 1988, 3. See also "Major Drug Ring Leader Is Convicted," *LAT* (US), 7 September 1989, 1, and "Captured Honduran Wanted in U.S. Drug Agent's Murder," Associated Press (United States) (hereafter cited as AP [US]), 5 April 1988.

149. "Diputado nacionalista amigo íntimo de Matta," *LP* (HO), 29 August 1987, 5. Cerna Salgado, Olancho representative to the Honduran National Congress, submitted an affidavit at one of Matta's U.S. trials stating that the kingpin's apprehension "has been repudiated by the majority of the Honduran people and especially by public officers of the legislative, judiciary, and executive powers of the Republic." *Matta-Ballesteros ex rel. Stolar v. Henman*, 697 F. Supp. at 1043. He professed to know nothing of Matta's involvement with drugs. "Major Drug Ring Leader," 1.

150. "Ministro Panting quiere negocios con Ramón Matta," *LP* (HO), 3 April 1986, 4.

in Colombia, where authorities eventually found him to own properties valued at $10 million, then in Spain.[151] In 1979 Matta's wife bought a villa near Madrid, where her husband, using the alias Jairo Ríos Vallejo and the nickname "Don José," spent a considerable portion of the next six years.[152] Matta eventually took over businesses in Galicia in northwest Spain that imported luxury vehicles and Colombian tobacco.[153] He was also reported to have been associating with figures linked to Galician organized crime, including boss José Ramón Prado Bullago.[154] By 1985 Spanish police had Matta under surveillance and were forwarding U.S. authorities information.[155]

For all of Matta's ability to broker deals, solve problems, and win over rival traffickers, he dealt with perceived enemies ruthlessly. By 1986 Matta had been accused of thirteen killings in Colombia, two in the United States, and another pair in Honduras. However, given his ability to bribe and cow authorities, Matta had been brought to trial for murder on only a single occasion and then readily acquitted. This notable falling out occurred in 1977 with Mario Ferrari, a Honduran automobile dealer and alleged trafficker married to Mary González de Ferrari, niece of Mexico's former president, Lázaro Cárdenas del Río. Ferrari not only had co-owned a nightclub with Matta but had reportedly joined to smuggle weapons, emeralds, and drugs. Indeed, some credit Ferrari with helping to broker the deal in which Matta's police records had been destroyed. By the time Matta gained international prominence, Ferrari had become a prominent drug distributor in Honduras, purportedly with his own high-ranking army connections.[156]

The Matta-Ferrari clash reportedly had its origin in a drug deal in which Matta believed that Ferrari was trying to swindle a million lempiras from him. Ferrari was said then to have been involved in a sexual assault on Matta's wife. Matta soon divorced his spouse, and, some have claimed, met with associates in the G-2 military intelligence service to plan his vengeance against the Ferraris. According to hit man José Dimas Reyes Lazo, Matta hired him to kidnap the Honduran couple. On December 3, 1977, the Ferraris were seized in Honduras and taken to an airstrip near the Río Dulce, where a plane was waiting to fly them to Colombia to face Matta. After this "interview," Reyes Lazo claimed, the couple was flown back, because Matta wished them to die on Honduran soil. Six months later, after the wife of one of Matta's hired killers tipped police, searchers discovered the Ferraris' bodies in a well near Tegucigalpa. Although Matta was immediately suspected,

151. See "Ocupan diez propiedades de narcotraficante hondureño," *LP* (HO), 5 April 2000, 39A; "Gobierno colombiano expropia bienes de Juan Ramón Matta," *LP* (HO), 10 September 1999, 23A; and Centro, "Cronología," 5. Matta was later found to own seventeen Colombian farms.

152. "Matta organizó envíos de cocaína desde España," *LP* (HO), 5 December 1990, 46. See also *United States v. Matta*, 1995 U.S. App. LEXIS 36965.

153. *El País* (Spain), quoted in "Amplia red de empresas controla la familia de Matta en España," *LP* (HO), 1 December 1988, 8. In Spain, too, Matta carefully cultivated a positive image. For instance, surveillance photos caught him delivering Christmas presents to his Spanish employees. *United States v. Matta*, 1995 U.S. App. LEXIS 36965.

154. "Banco panameño vinculado con narcotráfico," *LH* (GU), 6 October 1990, 10. For Prado Bullago's arrests for drug trafficking, frequent presence in Panama, and list of his Central American holdings, see "Gobierno panameño oculta datos sobre capos gallegos de la droga," *LP* (PA), 19 August 1991, 1A; "Nexos con narco," *LN* (CR), 25 July 1992, 24A; and "Spanish Police Hold Drug Kingpin, Thirteen Accomplices, Two Boats in Major Operation," BBC Monitoring Europe, 16 August 2001.

155. At Matta's trial Spanish police officers testified about their wiretaps of his house and office. Forty-four conversations had been recorded, providing leads that assisted U.S. investigators. *United States v. Matta*, 1995 U.S. App. LEXIS 36965. See also "Matta organizó envios," 46. Although the legality of these recordings, made absent Spanish judicial authorization, did not affect his U.S. federal trials, that issue arose again when Spain attempted to seize Matta's holdings there. "Izaguirre: Grabaciones de pláticas de Matta, no lo afectan," *LP* (HO), 7 December 1990, 44.

156. "Según la propia versión de Matta Ballesteros: 'Milagrosa mano' abrió las siete rejas," *LP* (HO), 3 April 1986, 5; "En libertad hermanos Reyes, responsables de la muerte de los esposos Ferrari," *LP* (HO), 4 September 1996, 6A; "Pagó para hacer desaparecer," 4; "Declaró Dimas Reyes," 4. Ferrari's father later declared, "Certain men of high military rank were compromised with my son in the smuggling of cocaine." "Gozan de impunidad," 6A.

he then disappeared, and in the ensuing years officials could not or would not track him down for questioning.[157]

By the early 1980s, however, U.S. federal officials were developing a case against the Honduran kingpin that resulted in a 1984 drug indictment. In 1981 DEA agents raided a drug-distribution center in a Van Nuys, California, apartment, confiscating $1.9 million and more than 40 kilos of cocaine. Highly detailed, coded account ledgers showed that from January to September the organization had distributed 1,347 kilos of cocaine, grossing more than $73 million, of which Matta was thought to have received $22 million.[158] Authorities in Van Nuys arrested seven individuals; at trial, five pled guilty, and one was convicted. The accumulated evidence, including witness testimony, suggested that "El Negro," long one of Matta's aliases, had supplied the cocaine. An address book and papers found at the apartment contained phone numbers that corresponded to those assigned to a Cali business, whose owner was found to be Matta's new wife.[159] Although the raid disabled one part of Matta's organization, the scope of its operations may actually have increased thereafter. U.S. prosecutors later declared that between 1983 and 1985, "Matta was the leader and organizer of a cocaine ring that had smuggled massive quantities of cocaine from South America to Mexico, and from there into Arizona, Southern California, and New York."[160]

Ultimately, Matta's entanglements in the Mexican drug trade helped to bring about his downfall. Twice in October 1984 and then again in December of that year, leading members of the Guadalajara cartel, led by Ernesto Fonseca Carrillo, met to discuss seizing and interrogating DEA special agent Enrique Camarena, who had been investigating their operation and causing it devastating losses.[161] In particular, Camarena played an integral role in Operation Godfather, an investigation of Félix Gallardo and Caro Quintero that uncovered enormous irrigated marijuana farms in Chihuahua, which "had flourished with the connivance of federal authorities, local police, and the army."[162] U.S. federal prosecutors later claimed that Matta had been present at the traffickers' October meetings concerning Camarena.[163] Then, on February 7, 1985, off-duty police officers from the state of Jalisco, moonlighting for pay by Guadalajara traffickers, kidnapped Camarena as he left the U.S. Consulate.[164] Camarena's Mexican helicopter pilot, Alfredo ("Álvaro") Zavala Avelar, was also seized shortly thereafter.

Although DEA agents frantically investigated these disappearances, they were obstructed by corrupt Mexican officials and unable to locate the kidnappers.[165] A U.S. federal court declared, "Out-of-court statements, audiotapes and physical evidence, including hair, carpet fibers, sheet

157. "Esposos Ferrari," 5; "El caso Ferrari: Una historia de mafias, venganzas, terror, y romance," *LP* (HO), 1 April 1986, 2; "Gozan de impunidad," 6A; "Declaró Dimas Reyes," 4; "Solo tribunales nacionales pueden juzgar a Matta B.," *LP* (HO), 1 April 1986, 2. Although Honduran Interpol director Juan Ángel Barahona was accused of accepting a bribe to permit Matta's departure after the Ferraris' murders, an investigating committee of the Honduran armed forces could find no evidence to support this or allegations that the Honduran military assisted in Matta's departure. "Gozan de impunidad," 6A.

158. *United States v. Matta-Lopez*, 1995 U.S. App. LEXIS 38204. and "Matta Gets Life Term for Running Drug Syndicate," *LAT* (US), 17 January 1990, A3. See also "Hallan culpable a 'narco' hondureño," *LN* (CR), 7 September 1989, 25A, and "Matta enfrenta hoy otro juicio," *LP* (HO), 27 July 1989, 2. Assistant U.S. Attorney Manuel Medrano observed, "We've never seen such detailed, voluminous, sophisticated ledgers, in Spanish, in code." "Major Drug Ring Leader," 1.

159. *United States v. Matta*, 1995 U.S. App. LEXIS 36965.See also "Tribunal halla culpable a Ramón Matta de dirigir organización de 'narcos,'" *LP* (HO), 7 September 1989, 8, and "Hallan culpable," 25A.

160. *United States v. Matta*, 1995 U.S. App. LEXIS 36965.

161. For the Camarena killing, see Shannon, *Desperados*, esp. 204–13. See also "'Narcos' asesinaron a Camarena porque desbarataba el negocio," *Tiempo* (Honduras), 16 May 1990, 18, and "Las conexiones de Matta," *LP* (HO), 15 April 1988, 4.

162. Grayson, *Mexico's Struggle*, 27.

163. *United States v. Matta-Ballesteros*, 2000 U.S. App. LEXIS 4884.

164. Bonner, "New Cocaine Cowboys," 37.

165. In stating that a "large portion of the Jalisco state police force . . . was on the payroll of the Guadalajara cartel,"

fabric and rope strands, showed that Camarena had been taken to a house at 881 Lope del Vega in Guadalajara, where he was held, tortured, interrogated and finally killed."[166] While under police surveillance, Matta checked out of a Guadalajara hotel five days after the kidnapping. Shortly thereafter, U.S. agents used a telephone intercept to locate him in Mexico City, but the Mexican Federal Judicial Police failed to respond to the DEA tip in timely fashion, and Matta escaped.[167] When authorities finally located the house in which Camarena had been tortured, they found strands of hair, consistent with Matta's, in a bedroom and guest house.[168] One month later, Mexican peasants discovered the corpses of Camarena and Zavala in a shallow grave in a field seventy miles southeast of Guadalajara.

When a worldwide hunt ensued for the killers, Matta apparently fled to Spain with the likely assistance of corrupt Mexican police officers.[169] When the DEA closed in again, he moved to Colombia. In April 1985 authorities there located the kingpin in a Cartagena luxury apartment, arresting him on drug charges unrelated to Camarena's murder. When DEA agents questioned him, Matta denied responsibility for Camarena's murder. He did admit to some knowledge but refused to reveal particulars, claiming that he would be killed in retribution should he divulge anything more. While in La Picota Prison in Bogotá, Matta reportedly most feared U.S. extradition or being killed by U.S. agents. In fact, within weeks of his arrest U.S. officials did request extradition; however, Honduras also wanted him extradited for the Ferrari murders. In August 1985 the Colombian government opted to render Matta to Honduras, his country of origin, and the Supreme Court approved.[170]

Before delivery of the prisoner could occur, however, a motorcycle assassin killed the director of La Picota, Dr. Alcides Arizmendi. Some days before, Arizmendi had ordered a surprise inspection of Matta's cell, thereby frustrating an escape attempt. Authorities thus immediately suspected Matta of being implicated in the murder. In the meantime, U.S. diplomats in Honduras feared that Matta would intimidate and suborn the Honduran judicial system, perhaps ordering additional assassinations. Eventually, Honduras formally withdrew its extradition request. Yet in November 1985 the Colombian government denied the U.S. extradition request, opting instead to try Matta in Colombia for having operated a cocaine laboratory.[171]

For his part, Matta preferred to face murder allegations in Honduras than drug charges in the United States or even in Colombia.[172] According to Colonel Miguel Maza Márquez, director of Colombia's Department of

former DEA administrator Robert Bonner added, "The corruption extended beyond the state police and into the governor's office and even into the federal government, including the principal internal security agency, the Federal Directorate of Security." Ibid., 38.

166. *United States v. Matta-Ballesteros*, 71 F.3d at 761. Investigators later concluded that Camarena had been tortured for more than thirty hours to reveal information on DEA operations. Medical examination of the corpse revealed that Camarena's ribs had been broken, his skull fractured multiple times, and a hole driven into his head with a screwdriver.

167. Police director Manuel Ibarra stalled the proposed action, leading to speculation that he had been corrupted or feared an embarrassing shoot-out between the raiding party and police officers Matta had corrupted to provide him protection. See Shannon, *Desperados*, 214–15.

168. *United States v. Matta-Ballesteros*, 71 F.3d at 761, 766.

169. Caro Quintero so alleged during his interrogation after arrest. See "Huyó a España: Hondureño cómplice de Caro Quintero," *LP* (HO), 9 April 1985, 5.

170. *United States v. Matta-Ballesteros*, 71 F.3d at 761; "Narcotraficante Matta Ballesteros detenido en Colombia," *LP* (HO), 1 May 1985, 9; "Presunto traficante hondureño Matta," 7; "Matta Ballesteros reclama derecho de ser extraditado a Honduras," *LP* (HO), 9 October 1985, 10; "Colombia: Corte Suprema da visto bueno para extradición de Matta," *LP* (HO), 30 August 1985, 2; Centro, "Cronología," 5–6.

171. Gugliotta and Leen, *Kings of Cocaine*, 245; "Deniegan extradición de Matta a Honduras y E.U.," *LP* (HO), 4 November 1985, 9.

172. See "Matta Ballesteros reclama derecho," 10. Should Matta have been absolved in Colombia, he might then have been extradited to the United States.

Administrative Security, Matta's organization then bribed at least eighteen prison employees with about $2 million.[173] On March 18, 1986, Matta cut off his beard and escaped from the Bogotá prison, walking through seven security gates while disguised as a guard. Associates hustled the trafficker to a private airport at Guaymaral, northwest of Bogotá, and a private plane took him to Guatemala.

Just under two weeks later, after secretly crossing into Honduras, Matta Ballesteros, accompanied by his lawyer Carlos Díaz Lorenzana, turned himself in to Honduran authorities. He proclaimed his innocence of all charges, and preparations were made for trial. Although officials denied Matta bail, they periodically permitted him to return home at five hundred dollars per visit. Poor people then lined up in front of Matta's luxurious residence awaiting handouts, while behind the scenes Matta reportedly renewed ties to politicians and military leaders.[174]

In another example of the inability of the Honduran judicial system to convict the author of a crime rather than hired underlings, in August 1986 the judge and prosecutor agreed that, on account of insufficient evidence, the court should absolve Matta of the Ferrari murders and instead convict six others.[175] The kingpin then returned to private life. U.S. officials believed his net worth might exceed $2 billion, and one observed, "He now lives in a large house in Tegucigalpa where he gives parties and reportedly makes business deals."[176] After eighteen months passed, legislator Alfredo Landaverde declared that, given the total incapacity of Honduras to bring Matta to justice, the DEA should take him to the United States for trial.[177] However, since Honduran law did not permit the extradition of any citizen to another state for offenses committed abroad, Matta appeared to be secure in Tegucigalpa.[178] While the trafficker stated that he doubted that the United States would resort to kidnapping, he called on military associates to supply ten former members of the Israeli-trained Honduran Special Forces to act as his elite bodyguard team.[179]

Although the U.S. government had been providing substantial military assistance to Honduras for years, U.S. officials had been increasingly voicing their suspicions that military officers were deeply involved in the drug

173. For information on Matta's escape, see "Fuga de Matta, una vergüenza nacional," *LP* (HO), 2 April 1986, 3; "Dos millones de dolares empleó Ramón Matta," *LP* (HO), 29 April 1986, 5; "Un mexicano dirigió fuga de Ramón Matta," *LP* (HO), 30 April 1986, 2; "Presunto traficante hondureño Matta," 7; "He hecho algunos negocios que no son de drogas: Matta," *LP* (HO), 2 April 1986, 2; "Solo tribunales nacionales," 2; and "Sorpresa en Colombia," *LP* (HO), 2 April 1986, 3.

174. "Matta Ballesteros declara ante el juez," *LP* (HO), 1 April 1986, 3; "Aparece ridícula orden de Gobernación," *LP* (HO), 1 April 1986, 2; "Juzgado rechaza petición para liberar Ramón Matta," *LP* (HO), 28 May 1986, 2; "Una 'mafia' lo quiere echar del ministerio, denuncia Ortez," *LP* (HO), 29 September 1988, 5; "Lorenzana habría firmado su sentencia de muerte," *LP* (HO), 25 January 1989, 4; "Drug Deportation Sparks Anti-US Honduran Riots," Facts on File World News Digest, 8 April 1988, 231B1.

175. "Absuelto Ramón Matta," *LP* (HO), 23 August 1986, 4–5. The Ferrari hit men served approximately fifteen of their twenty- to twenty-four-year sentences and then were granted parole. See "En libertad hermanos Reyes," 6A; "Autorizan a Raúl Mata gestionar su libertad," *LP* (HO), 26 January 1992, 11; "Raúl Mata gestiona su libertad," *LP* (HO), 12 August 1994, 5A; "Raúl Mata anuncia su excarcelación," *LP* (HO), 16 August 1994, 13A; and "Policía acusa a Raúl Mata de dirigir banda robocarros desde el presidio," *LP* (HO), 18 August 1994, 34A.

176. "Military Officers in Honduras," 1A. Ironically, those deals included renting five of his Tegucigalpa houses to the unsuspecting U.S. Embassy. See "Central American Drug Lord," and "Kingpin Poses Dilemma."

177. "DEA debe llevarse a Ramón Matta," *LP* (HO), 1 March 1988, 4. Landaverde had his own score to settle with Matta, because he suspected that the kingpin had killed his brother—the regional president of the Committee for the Defense of Human Rights.

178. These would be Article 102 of the Constitución de la República de Honduras as well as the 1909 Honduras–United States extradition treaty, 37 Stat. 1616, 45 Stat. 2489, and the Inter-American Extradition Treaty of 1933, 49 Stat. 3111. See also "No puede ser extraditado," *LP* (HO), 1 April 1986, 4. For the statement of Honduran attorney general Rubén Darío Zepeda Gutiérrez, see "Extradicción de Matta violaría Constitución," *LP* (HO), 19 May 1986, 12.

179. See "Dope and Death Squads Rattle Honduras," AP (US), 27 February 1988, and *La Tribuna* (Honduras), 29 November 1986, cited in Centro, "Cronología," 8.

trade.[180] When General Regalado Hernández protested, U.S. diplomats are thought to have responded that deporting Matta would demonstrate that traffickers had not corrupted the entire military.[181] Apparently, after additional U.S. offers or pressure, Howard Safir, chief of operations for the U.S. Marshals Service and centrally involved since Matta had escaped from U.S. federal prison, persuaded the Honduran armed forces to expel the trafficker.[182] General Regalado ordered the army's Special Troops (or "Cobras") to capture and turn Matta over to the United States. The pinnacle of the Honduran high command seems to have to come to view Matta as threatening their military institution.[183] The magnitude of the kingpin's wealth, his unparalleled ability to corrupt officials, and the various killings he had been accused of may have come to be seen as endangering the regime, not simply embarrassing it.[184]

Very early on April 5, 1988, Matta left his Tegucigalpa residence to confer with his attorney. Although Matta's bodyguards then reported that his house was being watched, his lawyer told Matta that, according to his contacts, the authorities had been working on nothing more than a search warrant for weapons.[185] At about six in the morning Matta returned home, but as the trafficker emerged from the van, armed Cobras, accompanied by U.S. marshals, surrounded him, wrestling him to the ground when Matta resisted arrest and handcuffing him.[186] They then pushed Matta into a vehicle, putting a black hood over his head and perhaps using a stun gun on him, and two Honduran officers and two U.S. marshals drove the kingpin to the U.S.-run Soto Cano ("Palmerola") Air Force Base near Comayagua, forcing him to board a plane to the Dominican Republic.[187] By prior agreement with the U.S. marshals, Dominican officials termed the situation "irregular," because Matta lacked any passport, and promptly expelled him to the United States. Matta was arrested when the plane crossed into U.S. airspace, and within twenty-four hours of his abduction, he was imprisoned in the Marion,

180. Note that of the more than $1 billion in foreign assistance given to Honduras between 1980 and 1987, nearly 28 percent went to the military. "U.S. Clout on the Wane," *Christian Science Monitor* (US), 25 April 1988, 1.

181. "Drug Deportation Sparks."

182. The account of these negotiations that circulated in Honduras, although denied by the U.S. and Honduran governments, is that former U.S. ambassador to Honduras, John Negroponte, delivered the message to top military leaders that, unless Matta was delivered to U.S. officials, the U.S. government would publicize a list of Honduran military officials implicated in drug trafficking. See "Lorenzana habría firmado," 4; "No existe ninguna lista sobre narco-militares," *LP* (HO), 11 April 1988, 59; and *NYT* (US), 15 April 1988, cited in "No fui enviado a la Dominicana," *LP* (HO), 3 May 1988, 3. Another version is that the United States, in exchange for Matta, offered to forgive certain Agency for International Development loans and provide Honduras a list of military officers involved in trafficking. See "Estados Unidos comprometido a ocultar los narco-militares a cambio de Matta," *LH* (GU), 9 April 1988, 5.

183. "Clout on the Wane," 1.

184. Months before Matta's arrest, one U.S. official had stated, "We have warned that something must be done about Matta because, through the Colombian mafia, he has more money at his command to buy Honduran colonels and officials than the CIA and Pentagon." "Drugs and Money: The Honduras Connection," *U.S. News and World Report*, 11 January 1988, 31.

185. "Lorenzana habría firmado," 4.

186. For information on Matta's rendition, see *United States v. Matta-Ballesteros*, 71 F.3d at 761, 772–73, 775; *Matta-Ballesteros ex rel. Stolar v. Henman*, 697 F. Supp. at 1041; *Matta-Ballesteros v. Henman*, 896 F.2d at 256; "Matta enfrenta hoy," 2; and Shannon, *Desperados*, 451. When the plane crossed into U.S. air space, en route to New York, U.S. marshals then arrested Matta.

187. Matta later claimed that, while being transported to the air force base, his captors partially strangled him and repeatedly beat and shocked him with a stun gun all about his body, including his testicles; several of his former bodyguards offered eyewitness testimony supporting his claims. *United States v. Matta-Ballesteros*, 71 F.3d at 761, 764. U.S. officials responded that Honduras had arrested Matta and was responsible should any mistreatment have occurred, and various U.S. marshals filed affidavits denying Matta's claims that they had tortured him or seen him shocked. Nonetheless, upon Matta's arrival at the federal penitentiary, the attending physician noted abrasions on his "head, face, scalp, neck, arms, feet, and penis, as well as blistering on his back," injuries consistent with those that a stun gun might have caused. See *Matta-Ballesteros v. Henman*, 896 F.2d at 256, and *United States v. Matta-Ballesteros*, 71 F.3d at 764.

Illinois, maximum-security federal penitentiary. In the meantime, the Cobras entered the kingpin's house, appropriating three pistols, three shotguns, an AK-47, more than a kilo of cocaine, and a large ammunition cache.[188]

In Honduras Matta's irregular rendition was highly controversial.[189] About two thousand demonstrators, apparently fueled by money from Matta's network, surrounded the U.S. Embassy in Tegucigalpa, attacked two annex buildings, and set on fire and eventually pillaged one seven-story structure. After four hours of rioting, in which shop windows were smashed and cars overturned, Honduran authorities sent soldiers and tanks into the streets and then called a five-day state of emergency. This restored order, but not before five had been killed and at least ten injured. Many Hondurans resented that their politicians and military had bowed to yet another U.S. request.[190] Other Hondurans admired Matta's public-relations flair or his ability to rise from poverty to gain wealth and notoriety.[191] Still others saw the case as a major test of the rule of law in their new democracy and protested the cavalier manner in which their government had flouted constitutional guarantees.[192] In the National Assembly Matta's "public kidnapping" was denounced, with one legislator calling it "a negative and regrettable act against our country."[193] The very idea of extraditing drug traffickers turned highly unpopular.[194]

Early in 1989 Matta's chief defense lawyer, Carlos Díaz Lorenzana, was murdered. After parking on the street, the attorney had walked toward his house, and, witnesses reported, a hit man called out to him. When Lorenzana responded, the assassins fired multiple rounds from Uzi submachine guns. Although other plausible theories existed, many suspected that Matta had ordered the killing, suspicions heightened by the fact that the chief attorney for Matta's Mexican colleagues Felix Gallardo and Caro Quintero had also been murdered less than four months before. It was speculated that Matta had felt that his attorney had either double-crossed him or negligently failed to discover what was afoot. A Honduran police source observed, "A lawyer for the devil . . . should

188. "Enfrentará juicio," *LP* (HO), 6 April 1988, 2.

189. For information on the rioting, see "Amigos de Matta protestan," *LP* (HO), 7 April 1988, 5; "Azcona responsabiliza a narcotráfico de la violencia de anoche en Honduras," *LH* (GU), 8 April 1988, 1; "Gobierno de Honduras condena violentas protestas contra EUA," *LH* (GU), 8 April 1988, 12; "State Department Issues Travel Advisory for Honduras," AP (US), 8 April 1988; "Drug Deportation Sparks"; "Honduras molestó por actitud de EE.UU.," *LN* (CR), 29 April 1988, 32A; "Las conexiones de Matta," *LP* (HO), 15 April 1988, 4; and "Student Unrest in Honduras Follows Drug Baron's Expulsion," *TR* (BZ), 17 April 1988, 5.

190. Even right-wing politician Manuel Acosta Bonilla stated, "There has been complete submission to the U.S., and people are tired of it," while equating Honduras to "the circus dog that jumps through the hoops when its master tells it to." "Honduran Anger at U.S. Is Product of Washington Policy, Officials Say," *NYT* (US), 13 April 1988, A10. Another riot had occurred a few weeks earlier when 3,200 additional U.S. troops arrived. Quote from "Clout on the Wane," 1. One diplomat in Honduras stated of the Matta expulsion riots, "The reaction was surprising for Honduras. . . . But it's easy to understand for a country that's been kicked around for a long time."

191. Shortly after Matta's rendition, Honduran daily newspapers reprinted an upbeat letter from Matta to his wife with nationalistic and sentimental themes, instructing her to send flowers to all those maligning him. "Matta: 'Pongan flores a todos los que murieron a nombre mío,'" *LP* (HO), 18 April 1988, 72.

192. Cabinet minister Rodrigo Castillo had publicly stated, "The Constitution should be violated as many times as necessary for the good of the country." "Violent Honduran Anti-U.S. Protests the 'Culmination' of Resentments," *Latin America Regional Reports*, 5 May 1988, 1. But one student declared, "The Constitution is the most precious thing a country has." "Student Unrest in Honduras," 5. Following the incident, vice president Jaime Rosenthal resigned as an economic advisor to the president to protest Matta's expulsion. "Honduran Anti-US Protests."

193. "Comprometidos judicialmente quienes permitan extradición," *LP* (HO), 6 April 1988, 4. See also "FF.AA. negociaron salida de Matta el margen de la ley," *LP* (HO), 7 April 1988, 4, and "Diputados condenan acción contra Matta," *LP* (HO), 8 April 1988, 4.

194. A poll just before the operation showed nearly 80 percent of Hondurans favored the extradition of drug traffickers, but a CID-Gallup poll afterwards found nearly 70 percent approved the ban on extraditing Honduran citizens, with only 14 percent advocating that the law be changed. See "Correcto que se extradite a los narcotraficantes," *LP* (HO), 16 March 1988, 56, and "Cuestión de Matta no afectó relaciones hondureñas-EE.UU.," *LP* (HO), 10 September 1988, 2.

have spread a lot of money among judges, stenographers, and secretaries in the courts and even among the immediate neighbors so they maintain good information about every suspicious movement made against his client."[195]

At his U.S. federal trial Matta's defense counsel portrayed him as a legitimate and generous executive and cattle rancher, the largest employer in Honduras in 1988. However, the prosecution called as witnesses Héctor Barona Becerra, a Colombian who had managed pilots for Matta, and John Drummond, an American who had allegedly directed Matta's Arizona drug-distribution operation.[196] Barona testified that after two of his smuggling planes crashed, he was directed to travel to Cali to meet the kingpin. Barona's instructions took him to 5-55 Guadalupe Avenue, listed in the phone book as another business held in the name of Matta's wife. There, Barona interrupted a meeting of individuals he knew to be involved in trafficking, and he met their leader, Matta Ballesteros. On the basis of such evidence the jury found Matta guilty on all seven counts. In a presentencing memorandum U.S. prosecutors called Matta "perhaps the most significant narcotics trafficker in custody in the world," and the court ordered life imprisonment without parole and a fine of $225,000, a conviction and sentence later upheld on appeal.[197]

Prosecutors then held a second federal trial on charges that Matta had participated in the conspiracy to kidnap and kill Enrique Camarena.[198] Testifying for the prosecution was informant Héctor Cervantes Santos, who stated that Matta had been present as the murder was being planned.[199] Cervantes testified that when how best to handle Camarena was discussed, Matta simply stated, "Silence is golden." That reticence proved useful to his defense, and Matta was ultimately convicted only of racketeering. Nevertheless, a federal judge sentenced the Honduran trafficker to an additional three terms of life imprisonment, returning him to Marion Penitentiary. In 1990 the U.S. Supreme Court rejected Matta's final appeal.

Many applauded Matta's fate. Shortly before the trafficker's expulsion, a top U.S. official confided, "If two years from now [Matta] is

195. Quote from "Lorenzana habría firmado," 5; "De veinte balazos ultiman al abogado de Matta," *LP* (HO), 25 January 1989, 1; "Asesinan a abogado," *LN* (CR), 30 September 1989, 22A. Shortly before his death, Díaz had told a foreign journalist that he intended to testify before the Honduran Human Rights Commission to allege that the Honduran Army had killed Nicaraguan contra leader, Manuel Antonio Rugama Acevedo ("Comandante Aureliano"), a murder that occurred just ten days before his own. "Hondurans Shaken," 4. Thus, Díaz may have been murdered for reasons independent of Matta's extradition.

196. For information on Matta's trial, see *United States v. Matta-Ballesteros*, 71 F.3d at 761; *United States v. Matta*, 1995 U.S. App. LEXIS 36965; "Tribunal halla culpable," 8; and "Matta Gets Life Term," A3. Matta had already been found guilty of escaping a federal prison, for which he had been sentenced to three years imprisonment. *Matta-Ballesteros v. Henman*, 896 F.2d at 255. For more information on Drummond, see *United States v. Matta*, 1995 U.S. App. LEXIS 36965. Barona, although convicted of drug trafficking, served only seven months in prison and then entered the Federal Witness Protection Program in exchange for testifying against Matta. Nonetheless, the jury found his testimony credible. See "Major Drug Ring Leader," 1.

197. During the trial the U.S. government conceded to the court that the continuing-criminal-enterprise count should have sufficed to cover two conspiracy counts with which Matta had once been charged. Thus, the appellate court vacated the conspiracy convictions, while upholding the remaining convictions and sentences. *United States v. Matta*, 1995 U.S. App. LEXIS 36965. Quote from "Drug Kingpin Sentenced to Life in Prison Without Parole," AP (US), 17 January 1990. See also *United States v. Matta-Lopez*, 1995 U.S. App. LEXIS 38204; *United States v. Matta*, 937 F.2d at 567; and "Abducted Drug Trafficker's Conviction Upheld," *WP* (US), 3 December 1995, A28.

198. For information on the second trial, see "En caso Camarena: Matta declarado culpable," *LP* (HO), 27 July 1990, 4; "¡Cadena perpetua para Matta!," *LP* (HO), 17 January 1990, 3; "Condenan a tres perpetuas consecutivas a narcotraficante," *LH* (GU), 10 May 1991, 14; "Drug Kingpin Convicted in Camarena Kidnap, Acquitted of Murder," UPI (US), 26 July 1990; "Corte Suprema de EE.UU. rechaza apelación de Matta," *LP* (HO), 2 October 1990, 5; and "Drug Figure Loses Appeal Against U.S.," *NYT* (US), 3 December 1995, 43.

199. Cervantes Santos later tried to recant his testimony, something that the district court rejected as not credible, and Cervantes Santos himself eventually repudiated the recantation. *United States v. Matta-Ballesteros*, 2000 U.S. App. LEXIS 4884.

still there, Honduras will have a drug problem that it can't reverse." In the aftermath of Matta's convictions, Honduran President Rafael Callejas declared, "Matta has caused much damage to Honduras, to Honduran youth, and is a confessed assassin. [I am not going to] move one finger [to bring him back]." The following year one of the leading journalists in Honduras stated privately, "The expulsion of Matta was the best thing that happened to Honduras; otherwise, narco-corruption would have infected our politics as well."[200]

However, Central American trafficking has been such a firmly entrenched aspect of the international drug trade that the "decapitation" of a national kingpin often fails to eliminate his organization. In fact, even with Matta imprisoned in the United States, his network remained dangerous. During Matta's trial the U.S. Marshals Service received a tip that the trafficker's associates had concocted an elaborate escape plan. In exchange for a $5 million fee, three men on motorcycles, armed with automatic weapons, were to attack the van transporting Matta to the federal courthouse. The gunmen were to disable the van, blow off the side door, kill the deputy marshals, and free Matta Ballesteros. The effort was thwarted, however, when U.S. authorities learned of the scheme and changed plans, opting to transport Matta to the courthouse by helicopter.[201]

Although much less dramatic, the fate of the trafficker's property and possessions was also quite significant. Although Colombian, U.S., and Spanish prosecutors had moved expeditiously to confiscate the kingpin's assets held in their countries, Honduran authorities failed to seize anything that Matta owned in Honduras. Not until late 1989 did Honduran law specifically provide for drug-related assets to be confiscated, and not until 1994 was the law ever applied.[202] Indeed, since no Honduran court has ever issued a judgment against Matta Ballesteros, his wealth could sustain his organization.

In 1993 Colombian police arrested Jaime García García, Matta's brother-in-law, charging him with transshipping Colombian cocaine to the United States via Costa Rica. García was reported to have taken control of Matta's operation, and in congressional testimony DEA administrator Thomas Constantine alleged that García's network transported drugs for "a number of major Colombian traffickers." When a car bomb injured the son of retired General Regalado, Matta was suspected to have ordered the hit from his cell. Matta thereupon sent back to Honduras a recorded message saying that he knew Regalado was responsible for his kidnapping, but that he bore him no grudge and was in no position to plan such a "barbarity." However that may be, two years later a group calling itself the Revolutionary Patriotic Front stated that Americans living in Honduras would be killed if Matta were not released from prison.[203]

In 1997 Matta's efforts to avenge his U.S. rendition continued, as the attorney for Matta's family requested that kidnapping charges be filed against a number of former officials, including Regalado, police chief Julio Cesár Chávez, and President José Azcona del Hoyo, as well as two U.S. marshals. In their investigation Honduran prosecutors alleged that Captain

200. "Callejas no permitirá la repatriación de R. Matta," *LP* (PA), 23 June 1990, 5A; Kondracke, "Double Dealing," 17; confidential interview December 1991, San Pedro Sula, Honduras.

201. "En Honduras nadie ha denunciado que Matta esté lavando activos," *LP* (HO), 12 September 1999, 4A. For the recollection of U.S. marshal Samuel Cicchino, see "He's Fought in Wars, Against Drug Lords," *Columbus Dispatch*, 5 July 1998, 3E.

202. See *INCSR* (1989), 106; *INCSR* (1990), 182; and *INCSR* (1994), 137.

203. Quote from U.S. House, *Thomas Constantine*. See also Inravisión TV1, Bogotá, 5 September 1993, cited in "Drug Trafficker Arrested and Fourteen Aircraft 'Immobilized,'" BBC Summary of World Broadcasts, 7 September 1993; "Alleged Drug Kingpin Held in Colombia," *WP* (US), 4 September 1993, A10; "Ramón Matta dice que no guarda ningún veneor contra Regalado," *LP* (HO), 16 January 1993, 11; and "International News," AP (US), 1 October 1995.

Joselín Sierra Leva had planted the cocaine found at Matta's house during his arrest. Thereafter, the special prosecutor for human rights initiated court action against those involved in seizing Matta. In 1998 an unidentified assassin murdered the wife of Captain Sierra Leva. Although the police officer had likely made other enemies, he had come to public attention in the operation against Matta, and his return to the public spotlight had coincided with the allegations of evidence tampering in the Matta case.[204]

The career of Matta Ballesteros illustrates how important individual traffickers could be to the growth of bridge-state trafficking. The connections and experience that Mexican and Colombian cartels gained in Honduras during Matta's heyday has never been relinquished. Indeed, the Sinaloa cartel, with which Matta cooperated closely, continues to traffic large drug loads via Honduras twenty-five years after Matta's departure. However, the Honduran experience was singular in that no other Central American country produced a kingpin of international renown—a class I DEA violator—whose activities so greatly stimulated the growth of drug trafficking in Colombia and Mexico as well as Central America.[205] In addition, once a prominent Central American family has become immersed in the drug trade, relatives have often stepped in to keep their illegal undertaking active and profitable after a leading trafficker's arrest. In this regard one might note that in 2003 a drug plane landed on a highway in San Esteban, Olancho, directly in front of a farm owned by Matta's son, Ramón. Two years later, immigration director Ramón Romero was arrested for having allegedly permitted fourteen Colombians linked to Matta to enter Honduras without visas. It seemed that few wanted to challenge the organization formulated by Central America's leading kingpin, even many years after his expulsion.

Narcotics Trafficking Post–Matta Ballesteros

All who harbored hopes that the removal of Juan Ramón Matta Ballesteros would substantially curb Honduran drug trafficking were soon disappointed. In fact, as the cocaine trade took hold, Matta had often been traveling abroad. Many traffickers, foreign and domestic, had recognized the significant bridge-favoring factors associated with Honduran transshipment. Some, like the Rodríguez Orejuela brothers leading the Cali cartel, had already successfully transshipped large quantities of cocaine through the country and were poised to capitalize further. Thus, the cocaine flow continued apace after Matta's removal.

During the mid-1980s Honduran support for the Nicaraguan contras affected the drug trade by providing cover for traffickers like Matta and by strengthening the military's grip on society. The peace that came to Central America eased the Honduran transition to democracy; however, the aftershocks of the prior decades of fighting continued to influence society, including traffickers. In particular, immense numbers of weapons had been stored in Honduras during the neighboring civil wars. In 2000 authorities suggested that Hondurans

204. "Honduras to Indict Ex-president in Extradition Case," *LAT* (US), 12 February 1997, 8A; "Piden captura de nueve oficiales por entrega de Ramón Mata [*sic*]," *LP* (HO), 24 June 1998, 4A; "Ex jefes policiales declaran sobre captura de Ramón Mata Ballesteros," *LP* (HO), 23 July 1998, 13A; "Pistolero asesinan fríamente a la esposa del capitán Sierra Leva," *LP* (HO), 16 July 1998, 16A. For other cases Sierra Leva worked on that might have provided an alternative motive for his wife's murder, see "Policía presume que mafias mataron a la esposa del capitán Sierra Leva," *LP* (HO), 16 July 1998, 16A. See also "Honduran Legislator Detained on Drug-Traffic Charges," Agence France Presse, 7 July 2003; "Immigration Chief Arrested for Corruption," *TT* (CR), 6 May 2005, N3.

205. Panama and Noriega fall into a different category. As a senior U.S. antidrug agent expert in Colombian trafficking observed of the general on the eve of Noriega's trial: "At most this guy provided money laundering and other services to the cartel. Compared with other traffickers or even other corrupt officials in Mexico and Pakistan, Noriega was pretty ordinary—you're talking at most a couple tons of cocaine. Some guys move that every month." "Panama: Dirty Business as Usual," *WP* (US), 28 July 1991, 1A.

might own as many as one million high-powered arms, and despite an arms-control law aimed at registering guns, the government had no record of an estimated half million believed to be circulating.[206] The influx of arms contributed to rising violent-crime rates and also provided a cheap source of weapons for traffickers intent on protecting their operations and intimidating rivals and authorities.[207]

Equally important, the volume, quality, and availability of these arms came to the attention of Colombian guerrilla and paramilitary organizations that had access to large quantities of cocaine but needed a constant supply of weapons and ammunition. Thus, Hondurans became deeply involved in arms-for-drugs deals with Colombians. Occasionally, these transactions went sour, and details came to public light. For instance, in 2004 two assailants shot and killed Pedro García Montes, leader of a Honduran cartelito, in front of a Cartagena hotel shortly after his arrival from Medellín. Honduran police then searched García's Tegucigalpa residence and discovered a sizable weapons arsenal. Shortly thereafter, they arrested Colombian Ethalson Mejía Hoy, allegedly a key link between the Fuerzas Armadas Revolucionarias de Colombia (FARC) and García's drug network, although a judge promptly granted him bail, and he disappeared. The following year Honduran authorities broke up a network engaged in bartering weapons for drugs and managed to arrest the cell's alleged leaders, Colombians Diana Montoya and Gregorio Reyes.[208] Then, in 2008 Syrian international arms dealer Jamal Yousef became entangled in a DEA sting operation, agreeing to exchange automatic rifles, M-60 machine guns, antitank munitions, and grenades, including the rocket-propelled variety, for seven to eight tons of cocaine from the FARC, to which a confidential source working for the DEA purported to have access.[209]

Although such arms-for-drugs deals and the circulation of large numbers of weapons were one factor encouraging cocaine transit in the post-Matta era, so too did the track record of successful transshipment ventures. With organizations constantly changing routes and procedures to avoid detection, calculating with any precision the amounts of cocaine passing through Honduras has not been possible.[210] The Honduran attorney general's office suggested that at least four tons of cocaine was transshipped in 1990 and again in 1991, but these estimates seem quite low.[211] As fig. 5.1 illustrates, cocaine seizures have fluctuated dramatically; nevertheless, knowledgeable law-enforcement personnel, domestic and foreign, have agreed that authorities have interdicted only a very small percentage of the cocaine transiting the country. In fact, seizures at home and abroad, as well as evidence compiled in investigations and trials, demonstrate that Honduras has been a leading bridge state for decades.[212] During a trial in Colombia, Cali cartel leader Miguel Rodríguez Orejuela admitted to having directed thirty-two cocaine shipments through Honduras and

206. See "Cerca de quinientas mil armas circulan ilegalmente," *LP* (HO), 8 April 2003, 34, and "Police Purged," 6. In 1997 Honduran minister of defense Colonel José Luis Nuñez stated that between 1979 and 1990 the government of Nicaragua distributed 600,000 AK-47 rifles and recovered only 180,000. He estimated that 420,000 AK-47s were circulating in Central America. "Armas sin control en istmo," *LN* (CR), 1 February 1997, 17A.

207. See "Armas de la 'contra' avivan delincuencia y narcotráfico," *LP* (HO), 14 September 1990, 30.

208. "Honduras Arrests Two FARC Agents," *TT* (CR), 1 April 2005, N3.

209. *INCSR* (2004), 146; *INCSR* (2005), 186; "Hallan en Honduras arsenal de narco," *El Nuevo Diario* (Nicaragua), 22 August 2004, 1; "Two FARC Agents"; "García Montes se paseaba por CA," *El Heraldo* (Honduras), 20 July 2004, 1; "Las FARC tienen nuevo proveedor de armas," *El Heraldo* (Honduras), 19 April 2005, 1; *U.S. v. Yousef*, 2010 U.S. Dist. LEXIS 86281.

210. U.S. officials concluded, "There is no reliable estimate of the amount of cocaine being smuggled through Honduras." *INCSR* (1990), 182. See also *INCSR* (1991), 151, and *INCSR* (1992), 159, 162.

211. "Honduras: Cocaine Seizure Linked to Increased Drug Activity," Inter Press Service (United States) (hereafter cited as IPS [US]), 9 May 1992.

212. See *INCSR* (1990), 182, and *INCSR* (1993), 159.

Fig. 5.1 Cocaine seizures in Honduras, 1986–1995

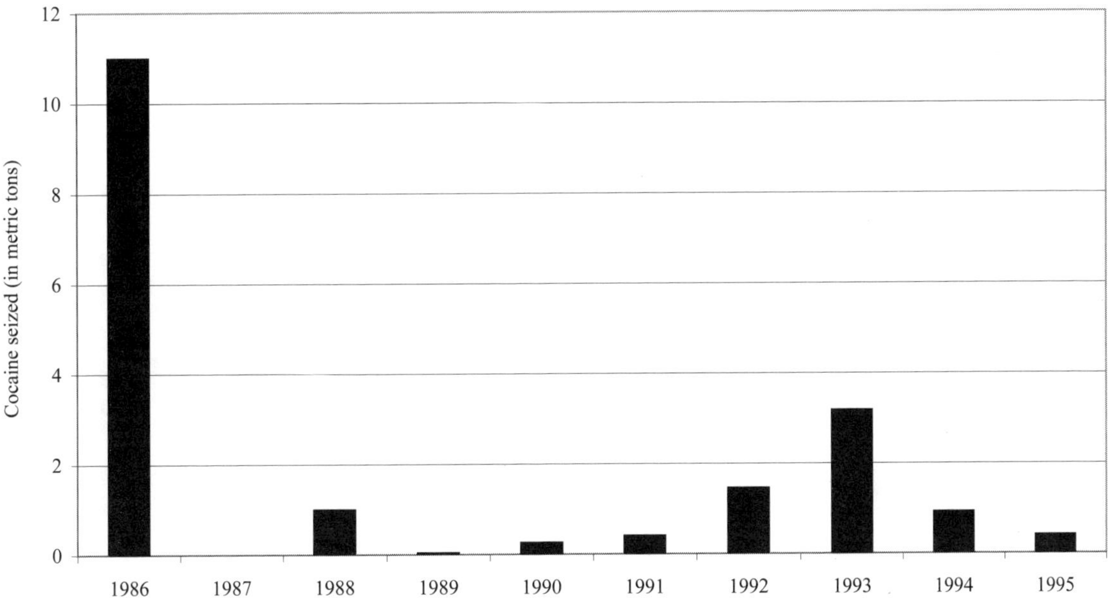

Sources: *INCSR* (1996), 139; *INCSR* (1990), 184; *INCSR* (1988), 184.

Note: The DEA updated certain of the statistics for the mid-1990s that the State Department had listed in its earlier reports. Note also the caution with which the U.S. government cited all these statistics: "Figures for arrests and seizures come from the Honduran Police Anti-Narcotics Unit. The statistics are neither comprehensive nor reliable." *INCSR* (1993), 161.

Guatemala.[213] By the early 1990s sufficient cocaine was on hand that traffickers could purchase substantial quantities from supplies secreted in the country.[214]

Figs. 5.1 and 5.2 reveal the same basic pattern of law-enforcement responses to cocaine trafficking observed in the other Central American bridge states—challenge, retreat, persistence, and then reassertion of state authority. Nevertheless, through the 1990s the cocaine traffic surged further, with Honduran authorities estimating in 1999 that an average of one hundred kilos a day might pass through the country or its territorial waters. That year a special committee of the National Congress flew over the Río Plátano in north-central Honduras, noting numerous clandestine runways. However, no follow-up actions were taken, something that national legislator Matías Fúnez Valladares attributed to fearful policy makers. In the meantime, cocaine seizures dropped markedly, to an embarrassing 182 kilos in 2001 and a microscopic 76 kilos in 2002.[215] Such nonfeasance simply encouraged drug networks to send more cocaine. In 2002 U.S. ambassador Larry Palmer declared, "The shipment of cocaine by air, sea, and land continues without any significant action by the government. . . . Seizures have dropped to their lowest level in three years, and they're the lowest in Central America. . . . Corruption continues to be a problem in the government, the police, the judiciary, and the armed forces, and that is the first impediment to any kind of cooperation."[216]

213. See "Desde Honduras envió cocaína, dice jefe de cartel de Cali," *LP* (HO), 31 May 1996, 74A.

214. See *United States v. Diaz*, 26 F.3d 1533.

215. *INCSR* (2003), 5:28.

216. "Politics-Honduras: U.S. Military Aid," IPS (US), 7 September 1999; "Con miedo difícilmente se podrá combatir

Fig. 5.2 Cocaine seizures in Honduras, 1996–2010

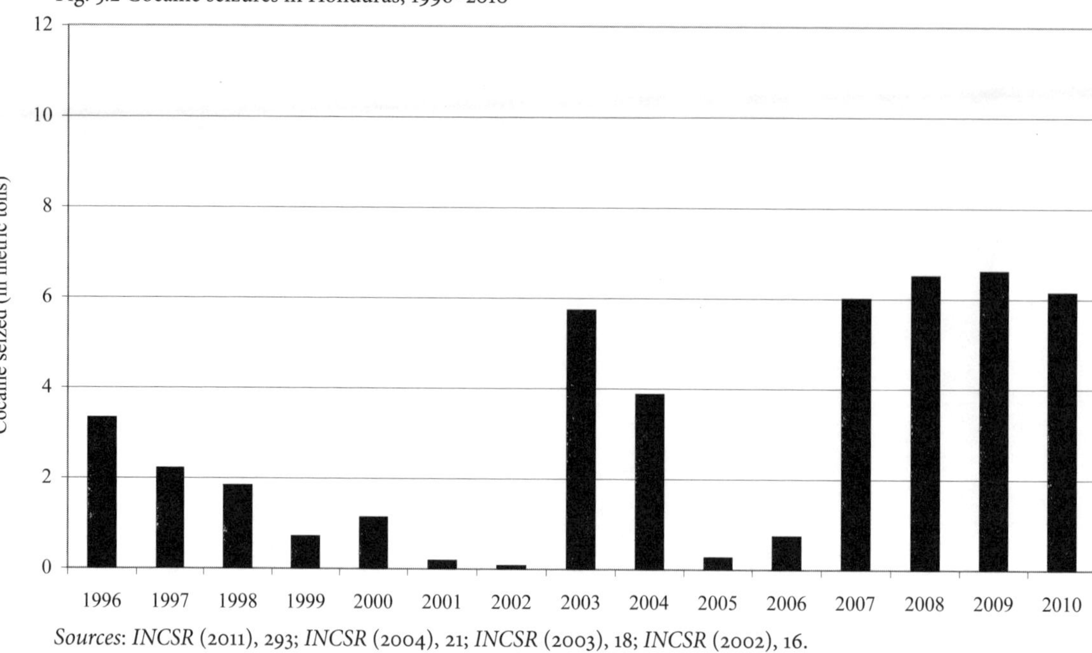

Sources: *INCSR* (2011), 293; *INCSR* (2004), 21; *INCSR* (2003), 18; *INCSR* (2002), 16.

Shortly thereafter, U.S. diplomats publicly declared that the country had failed to make sufficient efforts to combat cocaine trafficking, resulting in the passage of 80–100 tons per year, a staggering increase from the estimates a dozen years before.[217] Concerned that other vital foreign policy concerns, such as the future of the Central American free trade pact, might be at stake, Honduran authorities stepped up interdiction efforts. In 2003 and the first half of 2004 authorities seized nearly 10 tons of cocaine, a figure greater than the amount confiscated in the eight prior years combined.[218] While this underscored the lackluster prior efforts, all indications were that a high percentage of drugs transshipped via Honduras continued to escape interdiction. Although U.S. officials estimated that the total quantity of cocaine exported from South America decreased by at least 5 percent in 2007 and 2008, the percentage estimated to pass through Honduras climbed rapidly, from more than 180 tons in 2008 to more than 200 tons the following year.[219]

Alongside cocaine transit, though always in much smaller quantities, came Colombian heroin trafficking. While the typical case involved Honduran couriers or transit via Honduran airports, the country was occasionally involved in larger shipments.[220] For instance, in 2003 César Díaz, a Honduran legislator from 1997 to 2001, then serving as deputy to the Central American Parliament, approached the Costa Rican border crossing into Nicaragua at Peñas Blancas. When Costa Rican authorities tried to

el narcotráfico," *LP* (HO), 21 September 1999, 12A; "Two Convicted Drug Traffickers Flee After Armed Gang Stops Prison Van," AP (US), 31 May 2003; "U.S. Ambassador Slams Honduras' Anti-drug Efforts, Corruption," AP (US), 3 March 2003.

217. "Central America: Blacklisted Countries Make Big Drug Seizures," Intelligence Research (United Kingdom), 16 April 2003. Honduran antidrug official Ofelia Gutiérrez offered a somewhat lower estimate of sixty tons annually. "Se enreda lucha antidroga," *LP* (HO), 7 April 2003, 74.

218. "Honduras Proposes 'Faceless' Court System," *TT* (CR), 6 August 2004, 10.

219. *INCSR* (2010), 330.

220. For a representative case, see "Cargaba heroína en su estómago," *LP* (HO), 2 September 2009, 66.

search him, Díaz flashed his diplomatic passport and claimed immunity. As police called to get authorization from superiors for further action, Díaz reportedly fired a gun in the air and fled into Nicaragua. Alerted to these events, Nicaraguan officials found and detained him and soon discovered that he was carrying more than seven kilos of heroin. Díaz was eventually convicted of international drug trafficking and sentenced to ten years.

As in other Central American countries, by 2008 Honduran authorities were also confronting the new challenge of stopping pseudoephedrine passage. That year, officials at the Tegucigalpa airport seized one seventy-five-box shipment containing 1.2 million pills, thought to be headed from Chinese suppliers to Mexican traffickers. Shortly thereafter, police intercepted another load of a million pills being sent from Bolivia to a San Pedro Sula drugstore. In 2009 Guatemala prohibited pseudoephedrine imports, and later that year Guatemalan officials arrested four Hondurans in possession of two hundred boxes. This reflected a major new drug-trafficking trend, as in 2008 and 2009 authorities captured a total of nearly 5.3 million pseudoephedrine pills, and in 2010 they seized fully 29.7 million pills, plus another 12 kilos in bulk form.[221]

Shortly thereafter, national security adviser Alfredo Landaverde likened the drug trade in Honduras to an oil spill spreading in all directions and said that Honduran networks, working for Mexican and Colombian cartels, had infiltrated the prosecutors, the judiciary, and even private businesses.[222] Drug-trafficking organizations seem to have recognized that the distribution of bridge-favoring versus disfavoring factors had turned even more promising in Honduras than in various other Central American bridge states.

Drug-Trafficking Routes and Organizations in Honduras

As transshipment schemes along an array of Honduran routes continued to succeed, a host of drug organizations came to use them. Some of these were Honduran drug rings, either independent or quasi-independent operators or the more established cartelitos, offering assistance in transshipping drugs. Others were cells of foreign cartels, working on a particular venture or series of transactions. While some Honduran groups worked exclusively in the drug trade, others were transnational networks engaged in a range of criminal activity. For instance, in 2008 law enforcement received an anonymous tip that a Honduran vessel was sailing to Panama carrying money to be used to buy drugs. Officials then managed to intercept the *Capítan Ryan* off the Honduran coast and found $459,580 on board. Further investigations revealed that the network, allegedly led by Milton Merari Girón Zelaya, was suspected of having committed crimes in both Honduras and Panama: trafficking drugs and arms, counterfeiting and falsifying documents, and committing murder-for-hire, with twelve killings attributed to its members in the prior five years.[223]

For all of the attention devoted to trafficking by the Colombian and Mexican cartels, the study of Central American bridge-state trafficking spotlights how many other organizations were involved in the drug trade. These were lesser groups, encompassing fewer individuals, and moving smaller quantities per year. They tended to be less vertically integrated, in the sense that they lacked the detailed organizational hierarchy sometimes ascribed to cartels, and outsourced more tasks, rather than carrying them out "in-house." Yet these traffickers moved

221. "Incautan cargamento de seudoefedrina en Toncontín," *LP* (HO), 5 June 2008, 59; "Incautan otro lote de pseudoefedrina," *LP* (HO), 20 June 2008, 82; and "Capturan a cuatro hondureños con doscientos cajas de pseudoefedrina," *LP* (HO), 28 September 2009, 81; *INCSR* (2009), 305; *INCSR* (2010), 328; and *INCSR* (2011), 293. See also "Decomisan diez kilos de pastillas con pseudoefedrina," *LP* (HO), 7 June 2008, 63.

222. "Cae avión cargado con cocaína en Olancho," *LP* (HO), 21 October 2009, 68.

223. "Red de narcos ligada a desapariciones," *LP* (HO), 12 May 2008, 86.

significant amounts of cocaine. One such group, active in Honduras, was led by four individuals who had met in Cuban prisons: Roberto Ramírez, Jesús Ortiz, Alcides Cruz, and Manuel Ángel Tellechia. In the early 1980s Cruz and Tellechia belonged to a network that was shipping large marijuana loads into Florida through the Bahamas. When the DEA broke up the operation, with certain conspirators opting to become informants, Cruz and Tellechia opted to move into cocaine transshipment via Honduras.[224]

The pair first set up cover businesses engaged in exporting such items as plantains and then receiving such imports in Miami. By 1986 Cruz and Tellechia were flying Colombian cocaine into Honduras and then shipping it to the United States in containers. Although the Honduran military intercepted one cocaine load that year, the scheme worked on various other occasions. In 1987, for instance, a 1,148-kilo cocaine shipment reached the United States, to be distributed in Chicago and New York. One year later, the U.S. Customs Service stumbled upon 2,268 kilos, with a wholesale value of $61 million. In a controlled delivery counternarcotics agents followed the cocaine all the way to a fruit-and-vegetable dealership in Fulton Market, Chicago, where they made what was then the largest cocaine seizure in U.S. history.

As in the Matta Ballesteros case, Honduran authorities, with DEA assistance, eventually disrupted various key organizations by capturing or killing the local kingpin. For instance, Honduran authorities arrested Juan Ramón Hernández in 1997, and he was killed in 1999. Two years later, they captured Manuel de Jesús Rodríguez ("El Profe").[225] More recently, Fredy Donaldo Mármol Vallejo, the presumed leader of the so-called Northern cartel, operating along the Caribbean coast, had relocated to Guatemala to avoid Honduran authorities investigating activities, including a 2006 delivery on the beaches west of La Ceiba.[226] However, in 2009 the Cobras caught Mármol, along with his four heavily armed bodyguards, celebrating his son's birthday at a Puerto Cortés fast-food restaurant, and arrested him on drug charges. These successes, however, were tempered by the fact that replacement leaders or rings typically sprang right up. Furthermore, the debilitated Honduran penal system has enabled certain traffickers to continue to direct operations from within the country's penitentiaries.[227]

While authorities might be tipped to, or might stumble upon, particular shipments of drugs, curbing transshipment over any extended period has been exceptionally problematic. To avoid detection, many of the leading criminal syndicates have continually changed the locations in which they operate and occasionally altered their methods as well. When viewed over the perspective of nearly four decades of extensive drug trafficking, however, certain prominent features of Honduran drug transit stand out.

Sea Routes

A seafaring nation, Honduras has long had extensive fishing interests, a merchant marine moving cargo all about the Caribbean basin, and an export trade, especially in bananas and frozen seafood. This helped the country toward a much lengthier history of maritime drug trafficking than found in neighboring states. As early as 1933, the U.S. chargé d'affaires in Honduras sent a cable to the State Department warning that a prominent Honduran politician had

224. *United States v. Tellechia*, 1998 U.S. App. LEXIS 18786; *United States v. Izquierdo*, 1992 U.S. Dist. LEXIS 2797; *United States v. Gonzalez*, 933 F.2d 417. See also *INCSR* (1988), 128.

225. "Se enreda lucha," 74.

226. See "Cae presunto jefe narco y lavador de activos," *LP* (HO), 14 September 2009, 84; "Al centro penal manda juez a Fredy Mármol," *LP* (HO), 15 September 2009, 60; and "Fredy Mármol fue enviado a prisión," *LP* (HO), 22 September 2009, 63.

227. *INCSR* (2008), 174; *INCSR* (2009), 307; and *INCSR* (2010), 331.

imported two kilos of cocaine, two of heroin, and thirty-two of opium and that, in all likelihood, the drugs would be smuggled into the United States on United Fruit steamers. Two years later, four assassins killed Dr. Francisco Sánchez, dean of the University School of Medicine, director of the Government Hospital, and the Honduran official in charge of granting licenses to import narcotics. His murder was widely attributed to threats he had made to expose leading officials implicated in the drug trade.[228]

Decades later, in the early 1980s, as Colombian cartels grew disenchanted with Caribbean smuggling paths, routes via Honduras were enticing. Not only had Honduran vessels and crews been deeply involved in freight shipments around Central America and to the United States, but they had vast experience in trafficking Colombian marijuana. Honduras has direct maritime links with the United States and lies right along sea routes to Guatemala and Belize.[229] Cocaine has often been hidden within the legitimate cargo on board large container vessels. For traffickers, an ideal product has proven to be frozen seafood, which could not be thoroughly checked without risk of ruining it, something for which the Honduran government could ill afford to compensate.

Alternatively, traffickers have long concealed cocaine in hidden compartments on a ship or in its cargo. In 1991, for instance, Honduran authorities broke up a Panamanian cocaine-smuggling ring, which imported American vehicles to Panama, and after modifications, shipped them back to the United States, via Honduras, with cocaine hidden in some. In 2005 the U.S. Coast Guard intercepted the Honduran vessel *Babouth* off of Puerto Rico.[230] After a lengthy search, one of the crew members tipped authorities to a bolted manhole cover, hidden in the floor under more than six inches of sand, sawdust, and ammonia. Upon opening the hatch, the officials found more than nine hundred kilos of cocaine.[231]

Because Honduras has never produced significant quantities of drugs for foreign markets, its exports have not been subject to as rigorous scrutiny by customs as those from Colombia.[232] Much of coastal Honduras has always been sparsely populated, and the Honduran Navy has been small, inadequately trained, equipped with a handful of poorly maintained patrol boats, and often confined to port, lacking money for fuel and repairs.[233] Drugs could thus be easily smuggled into northern Honduras with only a slim chance of official detection. Even private sailboats could move offshore freely, taking advantage of following Caribbean trade winds from Cabo Gracias a Dios, at the Nicaraguan border, all the way to the Gulf of Honduras three hundred miles west.

In contrast to the geotactics of the drug trade employed in Belize, with its offshore reef and shallow waters, traffickers along the Honduran Caribbean coast have capitalized on its multiple deep-water ports. Depending on the size and draft of the vessel and the tactical issue of choosing remote or busy locations, traffickers might opt for Puerto Cortés, Puerto Lempira, or the city of La Ceiba. Alternatively, traffickers' purposes might be served by the small port of Tela, the quiet coastal town of Trujillo, or Puerto Castilla, tucked into the lee side of the peninsula that forms Trujillo Bay. Of

228. DOS, General Records of the Department of States, RG 59, 815.114, Narcotics/66, and RG 59, 815.114, Narcotics/304, cited in Walker, *Western Hemisphere*, 80–81, 85.

229. For a Panamanian ship caught in the high seas off Honduras carrying 2,442 kilos of cocaine in a ballast tank, see *United States v. Herrera Aguilar*, 2008 U.S. App. LEXIS 16318, and *United States v. Niebla Narvaez*, 285 Fed. Appx. 720.

230. See *United States v. Vilches-Navarrete*, 413 F. Supp. 60, and *United States v. Vilches-Navarrete*, 523 F.3d 1.

231. *INCSR* (1992), 164; "El tráfico de drogas se ha incrementado en Honduras," *LP* (HO), 23 April 1992, 37.

232. *INCSR* (1988), 128.

233. See *INCSR* (1995), 137, and *INCSR* (1996), 136. Extensive U.S. training of Honduran counternarcotics personnel began in 1999. See DEA, *Resources, Honduras* (2001), 6.

these, despite the nearby Honduran Navy facilities, Puerto Cortés has been the most popular for shipments headed directly to the United States or Europe.[234] The largest container port in this part of Central America, it encompasses Honduras's only duty-free zone, is located close to the Guatemalan border, and services San Pedro Sula, the country's most vibrant business center.

With so many options for imports and exports, the northern coast of Honduras has amounted to one of the most attractive drug-trafficking zones in all of Central America. As the DEA noted in 2000, this area "is very sparsely populated, has no roads in many areas, and is poorly policed." Whenever smugglers have feared official scrutiny in one port, they have been able to transfer operations quickly to another.[235] The scale of maritime cocaine-trafficking operations through Honduras, the involvement of leading foreign cartels, and the multiplicity of routes and smuggling methods involved are nicely illustrated by the following notable case.

Puertas de Castilla Network

Scarcely four months after the unprecedented Fulton Market bust of cocaine shipped via Honduras, the U.S. Customs Service, acting on a DEA tip, made yet another record-shattering seizure, confiscating two shipments that had arrived in Port Everglades, Florida, aboard the *Stena Mariner*, a Honduran vessel. Authorities confiscated more than 3.8 tons of cocaine, valued at $1.4 billion, hidden in containers of high-quality cedar for woodworking.[236] The shipment was traced to a business called Puertas de Castilla, operating out of the Puerto Cortés duty-free zone and run by Spaniard Luis Pérez Montevelve, Nicaraguan Alfredo López Rodríguez, and Peruvian pilot Carlos Florian.

As illustrated by the trafficking of Mike Tsalickis recounted in chapter 1, sending cocaine to market hidden in hollowed lumber was a specialty of the Cali cartel. At first, these shipments tended to depart from the Colombian Pacific port of Buenaventura, allegedly controlled by Cali associate Víctor Patiño Fómeque, and were then often transshipped via Panama or Mexico.[237] The Puertas de Castilla ring also operated under the ultimate direction of Cali overseers.

Further investigations revealed that the group had already sent at least two prior sizable cocaine loads, and Honduran judge Miguel Ángel Izaguirre Fiallos observed, "According to our information, the shipment was 8,000 kilos. . . . So more than half of it got through."[238] The nearly 9 tons of cocaine that the Puertas de Castilla conspirators shipped to the United States had arrived in Honduras by various routes. Some had been flown from Colombia into one of various landings strips; other loads had been shipped from Colombia in Honduran and Panamanian vessels. Smaller quantities had arrived via commercial airliner. Conspirators had packed about half of this cocaine into hollowed boards, specially manufactured in

234. The regular passage of modest shipments occurred alongside the occasional immense load. For the arrest of Hondurans trafficking twenty-eight kilos of cocaine from Cartagena through Puerto Cortés inside tar barrels, see "Siete detenidos en La Ceiba por tráfico de drogas," *LP* (HO), 4 March 1989, 5; "Declaran supuestos traficantes de cocaína," *LP* (HO), 8 March 1989, 11; and "Encuentran más drones de los usados para introducir cocaína a La Ceiba," *LP* (HO), 30 March 1989, 34. For the thirteen kilos of cocaine seized on the *Atlantic Trader* in Puerto Cortés in 2003, see "Honduran Authorities Arrest Eleven Aboard Boat Carrying Colombian Cocaine," AP (US), 11 October 2003.

235. Quote from DEA, *Resources, Honduras* (2000), 3; "75 kg of Cocaine Seized in Colón," BBC Monitoring Latin America, 3 February 2004.

236. See "Twenty Accused of Plan to Import Cocaine from South America," *NYT* (US), 20 November 1987, 22D; "Hallan cocaína en barco hondureño," *LP* (HO), 20 November 1987, 5; "U.S. to Open Outpost," 36C; "Mayor decomiso de cocaína en EE.UU.," *LN* (CR), 20 November 1987, 1; and "En zona libre no está maderera involucrada en carga de cocaína," *LP* (HO), 25 November 1987, 5.

237. *Confesiones secretas*, 202, 218.

238. See "Capturado principal cabecilla del narcotráfico en Honduras," *LP* (HO), 15 December 1987, 5. Quote from "Honduran Judge Says He Fights to Keep Drugs off U.S. Streets," AP (US), 15 March 1988.

the small town of El Corozal just east of La Ceiba, and trucked to Puerto Cortés to be loaded onto the *Stena Mariner*.[239]

Authorities identified the network's chief in Honduras as Rafael Arturo González, a naturalized Honduran of Cuban American descent.[240] González's partner was a Colombian professional singer, quite popular in Honduras and Colombia—Luis Carlos ("Lucho") Guerrero Franco. Although a trio of Bolivian pilots apparently stood on call in Honduras, waiting to help any of the traffickers who might suddenly have to flee, the Honduran police, assisted by the DEA, managed to arrest and interrogate both of the principals.[241] After a judge promptly freed González, police officers, exasperated by the workings of the court system, immediately rearrested the trafficker and expelled him to the United States.[242] This extrajudicial rendition of a Honduran citizen initiated the debate over whether the government should violate its own laws to bring to justice well-off criminals who seemed impervious to the country's judicial system, a controversy that would crescendo in the Matta case four months later.[243]

As for singer Lucho Guerrero, investigating authorities found sophisticated communications equipment and an array of weapons: five revolvers; three rifles with scopes, including one outfitted with a laser-aiming device; and even a crossbow and arrows.[244] A search of Guerrero's house turned up false identification that did not simply permit Lucho to pass freely through restricted areas of Honduran airports, but showed the singer to be chief of Internal Operations for the Honduran director-general of Civil Aviation. Police also uncovered a map highlighting six cocaine-entry points: Laguna de Brus on La Mosquitia, the San Pedro Sula and La Ceiba airports, the Armenta airstrip just outside San Pedro Sula, the Gulf of Fonseca, and a runway near Cholomo belonging to the company Centroamericana Agropecuria.[245] Investigators discovered that Guerrero had close ties to Medellín traffickers and had met with Manuel Noriega in Panama.[246] In 1987 he had been depositing $250,000 weekly in a San Pedro Sula bank.[247]

In 1988, just after a court in Tela had cited insufficient evidence and set Guerrero free, Honduran officials deported the singer to the United States, where he was prosecuted for importing large quantities of cocaine into Tennessee between 1984 and 1986.[248] At the trial Miami lawyer Eddy Cantera testified that

239. See "Encuentran más tablones para camuflar cocaína," *LP* (HO), 7 December 1987, 5; "Dictan prisión contra traficantes en Honduras," *LN* (CR), 4 December 1987, 52A; "Nos llamaban para 'dorar la píldora,' dicen agentes," *LP* (HO), 1 December 1987, 10; "DNI remite al juzgado auto de supuestos narcos," *LP* (HO), 21 July 1989, 63; and "El 'Cartel del Atlántico,'" *LP* (HO), 12 December 1988, 4.

240. Rafael González had left his Puerto Rico residence to become a naturalized Honduran citizen. See "Los cabecillas del narcotráfico financiaban guerrilla hondureña," *LP* (HO), 16 December 1987, 5, and "Desde trabajadores hasta empresarios desfilaron por el juzgado de Tela," *LP* (HO), 2 June 1988, 3. Notwithstanding the Matta case, the advantage to a drug trafficker of Honduran citizenship would be the constitutional ban on extradition of nationals.

241. "Comando de 'Cartel del Atlántico' declaró y fue remitido a prisión," *LP* (HO), 17 December 1987, 10. González, supported by an associate, claimed that authorities in Tegucigalpa tortured him, nearly paralyzing his hands. "Implicados en narcotráfico protestan auto de prisión," *LP* (HO), 23 December 1987, 4.

242. "'Rey de la coco' deportado a EE.UU.," *LP* (HO), 19 January 1988, 12.

243. Attorney general Zepeda Gutiérrez stated, "Although this man is pernicious for society, the process utilized, far from helping the cause of the improvement of justice in our country, left much to be desired." See Palacios Moya, *Reseña histórica*, 10.

244. See "Hasta armas al estilo de James Bond usaban supuestos 'narcos,'" *LP* (HO), 22 December 1987, 5, and "Cartel del Atlántico," 10.

245. "Mapa con puntos por donde entraba la droga tenía Lucho," *LP* (HO), 22 December 1987, 5.

246. See "Honduras deportó a cantante acusado de narcotràfico," *LP* (PA), 9 February 1988, 5A, and "Golpe en Honduras al 'Cartel de Medellín,'" *LN* (CR), 27 November 1987, 34A. See also "Desde el seis ordenaron la captura de 'Lucho,'" *LP* (HO), 16 December 1987, 5.

247. See Centro, "Cronología," 10; "Payique estuvó en reunión de 'narcos' junto con Noriega," *LP* (HO), 26 October 1988, 10; and "Declaran viciado juicio contra 'Lucho' Guerrero," *LP* (HO), 17 June 1988, 67.

248. For more on the Guerrero cases, see *Guerrero v. United States*, 383 F.3d 409; "Por 'llenar de cocaína' el Estado Tennessee entrega a 'Lucho' a la DEA," *LP* (HO), 8 February 1988, 5; and Palacios Moya, *Reseña histórica*, 11.

he had laundered more than $1 million for Guerrero, using a secret account in a German bank branch in Panama. The federal court convicted Guerrero and sentenced him to 175 years and a $2 million fine. In the meantime, Honduran police uncovered another 342 kilos of cocaine, hidden under the warehouse where the boards in the *Stena Mariner* case had been hollowed out. The army immediately sent the 105th Infantry Brigade to guard the site, and the following night the soldiers successfully repulsed an attempt by heavily armed traffickers to recover the drugs.[249]

With the Puertas de Castilla group behind bars, Judge Izaguirre concluded, "We believe we've cut the head off the main drug trafficking conspiracy in Honduras."[250] Although this may well have been the case, the disruption of any single drug ring has never had a lasting impact on the Central American cocaine trade. While popular attention is drawn to traffickers and their organizations, in reality, the balance of bridge-favoring and bridge-disfavoring factors is of paramount importance. So long as Honduras remains a very attractive transshipment venue, a slew of drug organizations will step in, seize market shares, and reap the profits of moving cocaine north, until they are disrupted with key arrests.

Other Caribbean-Coast Cocaine Trafficking

For much of the last three decades immense cocaine loads have been transshipped via the Honduran Caribbean coast. According to an FBI report, in the spring of 1984 a representative for the Honduran chief of police contacted expatriate Faiz Sikaffy, later implicated in the aborted cocaine coup against President Suazo, in Miami to determine how to sell more than a ton of cocaine in the United States. Then, in May Honduran authorities discovered 1,080 kilos and $560,000 in cash on the *Carib Freeze*, at anchor in Puerto Cortés, headed from Colombia to the United States. Among the crew members were five Hondurans and five Colombians, along with a Nicaraguan, a Guatemalan, and a Dominican. In February 1985 presiding judge Marcos Delgado had freed ten of the thirteen, and all the foreigners immediately left the country. The three remaining Hondurans were fined and sentenced to prison terms of twelve years and two months. The following August, however, Judge Ángel Guillermo Tróchez Medina freed each of them. When his actions were questioned, Judge Tróchez Medina later claimed that he was simply carrying out orders from the then president of the Supreme Court, Carlos Manuel Arita, who had told him to absolve the trio for "humanitarian reasons."[251]

But this was only the most notorious of numerous substantial maritime cocaine-trafficking cases. In 1984 U.S. authorities found 2 tons of cocaine hidden on a Honduran ship carrying bananas. In 1986 a Honduran vessel being pursued by authorities dumped more than 600 kilos of cocaine into the sea off Florida. In 1988 U.S. officials arrested a Honduran captain from the Islas de la Bahía in relation to a 250-kilo cocaine shipment discovered in Miami. In 1989 U.S. agents in Tampa located 412 kilos hidden in a truck shipped from Puerto Barrios, Guatemala, on board the Honduran vessel

Because nothing in the Honduran Constitution forbade the expulsion of an alien, the Guerrero case differed from those of Matta and González.

249. See "Encuentran millonario cargamento de cocaína en sótano de bodega abandonada," *LP* (HO), 10 August 1988, 4–5; "Encuentran 752 libras de cocaína," *LP* (HO), 10 August 1988, 1, 4; and "Narcos atacan soldados que custodian bodega," *LP* (HO), 11 August 1988, 1, 5. A trafficking network later offered one machine gun used in the attack to the San Pedro Sula prison director as a bribe. "Narcotraficantes planificaron," 19.

250. "Honduran Drug Arrests," *WP* (US), 16 December 1987, A47.

251. For information on this case, see "Arita Palomo me ordenó liberar supuestos narcos," *Tiempo* (Honduras), 15 December 1989, 10; "Hallan cocaína," 5; "El Cartel del Atlántico," *LP* (HO), 19 December 1988, 4; and Centro, "Cronología," 4.

Carib Haven. For the mid-1980s these were large shipments, their size attesting to the confidence traffickers already had in maritime smuggling through the country.[252]

Sea freight is inherently suspect, though port and customs authorities have been regularly overwhelmed by the sheer number of containers passing through their harbors. Fishing vessels have a somewhat different balance of advantages and disadvantages. Numerous commercial fishermen constantly come and go through the offshore waters of Central American bridge states, although any particular vessel would be easier to search for drugs than a freighter holding hundreds of containers. Drug organizations have thus recruited numerous Honduran fishermen to participate in the trafficking of tons of cocaine.

In 1989 undercover U.S. Customs agents penetrated an operation that shipped cocaine into Louisiana in shrimp boats that had been meeting a mother ship 150 miles off La Mosquitia. In 1993 authorities seized 2 tons of cocaine off the *Queen Anitra*, a Honduran fishing boat, intercepted 70 miles off Roatán by United States and Honduran authorities, and 2.25 tons of cocaine from yet another Honduran-flagged ship. In 2004 the U.S. Coast Guard intercepted a Honduran fishing vessel, the *Miss Lorraine*, about 80 miles off Panama and found 2.64 tons of cocaine in a hidden compartment inside a fuel tank.[253] Then, in 2008 Honduran authorities operating in international waters seized 900 kilos on *Miss Alyssa*, a fishing boat from La Ceiba. Several months later, a joint Honduran–U.S. Coast Guard operation seized 4.6 tons from the Honduran vessel *Eclipse*, located 160 miles north of Honduras and headed from Maracaibo, Venezuela, to the United States. Authorities also intercepted a Honduran fishing vessel that had removed a ton of cocaine from a speedboat and started to return to shore.[254]

For all of these eye-catching seizures, a regular traffic in more modest quantities of cocaine has also long been occurring, and the sum of these shipments has also been quite significant. For instance, in 1990 counternarcotics authorities discovered 38 kilos of cocaine flown from Colombia into Tegucigalpa, then brought overland to Puerto Cortés for export.[255] Two years later, another smuggling scheme reversed the port city's role, a move reflecting the manner in which drug rings have continually tried to cross up authorities by altering routes and methods so that drugs pass where authorities are not watching. In this case, however, U.S. officials discovered 62 kilos of cocaine, packed in grease, on an American Airlines flight from Honduras to Miami. Investigations revealed that 429 kilos had originally been shipped from San Andrés to Puerto Cortés, where the drugs had been divided into eight smaller shipments, two to be sent to the United States from Guatemala and six via Honduras.

Yet another case representative of the constant smuggling of small- to medium-size shipments along the Caribbean coast occurred in 1990. According to a suspect implicated in the case, Alejandro Francisco Aguilera Amaro, owner of El Bucanero restaurant in Trujillo, imported from San Andrés 21 kilos of cocaine on a vessel with a U.S. flag. Although the Honduran crew took a cut, most of the drugs traveled overland to San Pedro Sula, there to be seized by police.

252. *United States v. Garate-Vergara*, 942 F.2d 1543; *United States v. Castro*, 874 F.2d 230; "Capturan capitán de barco 'Coquero' detenido en Miami," *LP* (HO), 1 June 1988, 11; "En Tampa, Florida: Cocaína en camión enviado a Honduras," *LP* (HO), 4 September 1989, 64; "No procedía de Honduras," *LP* (HO), 5 September 1989, 2; "Honduras Coast Guard Seizes Coke Worth $80 Million," *TR* (BZ), 23 May 1993, 15; *INCSR* (2000), 172. In 1998 U.S. authorities also seized ninety-one kilos off another Honduran ship, the *Sea Viking*. "Agents Peel Cocaine Off Freighter at Port," *Fort Lauderdale Sun-Sentinel*, 23 May 1998, 3B.

253. *United States v. Matute-Santos*, 168 Fed. Appx. 343; *Matute-Santos United States v.* 2006 U.S. Dist. LEXIS 39220; and *Najara Haylock v. United States*, 2005 U.S. Dist. LEXIS 48437.

254. *United States v. Casildo-Suazo*, 332 Fed. Appx. 571.

255. "Según la policía: TAN SAHSA y Toncontín usados para el tráfico de cocaína," *LP* (HO), 23 January 1990, 48.

Apparently, the network had been operating for some time, with one member murdered, allegedly on Aguilera's orders, in a dispute over a different 6-kilo shipment. After six months in prison, Aguilera secured his freedom, only to be tied in 1993 to a 900-kilo cocaine shipment seized in Puerto Madero, just north of Belize.[256]

In fact, people all along the Honduran Caribbean coast were somehow involved in the drug trade, supplying fuel, performing mechanical services, helping to hide or store narcotics, and otherwise assisting with passing drug planes or vessels. Indeed, authorities in 2000 even found that a vessel owned by the nongovernmental organization Corazón a Corazón, supposedly bringing food, clothing, and other charitable donations into this area of Honduras, also had on board seventy-nine packages of cocaine.[257]

Speedboat Trafficking

By the late 1990s powerful motorboats, sometimes camouflaged with blue paint, traversed Honduran territorial and international waters carrying cocaine. Some Honduran go-fasts darted out to meet mother ships bringing cocaine up the Caribbean coast, then sped to shore.[258] Other speedboats traveled all the way from San Andrés or other Colombian ports, some carrying drugs north to Mexico, others using Honduran, Guatemalan, or Belizean ports for eventual shipment to North American or European markets.[259] Speedboats often landed in Gracias a Dios Department, depositing large cocaine loads that were then transported into La Ceiba and other Caribbean ports to be sent on either overland into Guatemala or in container ships bound for the United States.[260]

In early 2001 a bilateral maritime counternarcotics agreement finally came into force, enabling U.S. vessels to enter Honduran territorial seas in hot pursuit of suspected traffickers. The United States might exercise law-enforcement functions in Honduran waters so long as an accompanying Honduran law-enforcement official, a "ship rider," was on board.[261] While this amounted to a potent new counternarcotics tactic, drug organizations have countered by enhancing their intelligence networks along the Caribbean coast. Some have reportedly supplied coastal residents with communications radios and satellite telephones to inform on the movements of coast guard and navy vessels.[262]

While some local people have earned extra money by cooperating with traffickers, others have condemned what have sometimes been described as around-the-clock drug operations. Among the smaller communities that dot Honduras's Caribbean shores, the cocaine trade has most affected the Garífuna settlements. The Garífuna trace their heritage to slaves who were

256. For more on this incident, see "Decomisan veinte kilos de cocaína en operativo," *LP* (HO), 14 March 1990, 1–2; "Libre supuesto contacto en Honduras de banda de narcos," *LP* (HO), 3 September 1990, 16; "Danzan nombres de cocaineros en presentación de banda de narcos," *LP* (HO), 20 March 1990, 5; "De supuesto 'narco' resulta ser cadáver dejado frente a hospital," *LP* (HO), 24 October 1990, 10; "Habría muerto por seis kilos de 'coca,'" *LP* (HO), 25 October 1990, 44; and "'Narco' hondureño preso en Guatemala fue 'huésped' de presidio sampedrano," *LP* (HO), 18 February 1993, 8.

257. "U.S. Charity Staff Arrested on Drugs Charges," *TT* (CR), 22 September 2000, 6.

258. See, for instance, "Detienen embarcación por supuesta droga," *LP* (HO), 4 March 2008, 44.

259. See *INCSR* (2000), 171, and "Panamá y EUA revisan acuerdo marítimo de lucha antidroga," *LP* (HO), 18 April 2001, 60A. For the representative case of a Colombian go-fast, carrying 1,634 kilos of cocaine and heading to Belize and captured off Honduras, see *Angel v. United States*, 2007 U.S. Dist. LEXIS 9092. For the case of the U.S. Coast Guard capturing a Colombian go-fast heading north off the Honduran coast and carrying 1,954 kilos of cocaine, see *Antonio v. United States*. See also "One Dies, Three Arrested in Huge Honduran Seizure," AP (US), 29 July 2003.

260. *INCSR* (2003), 5:29.

261. *INCSR* (2002), 5:25.

262. See the statement to this effect by Nicaraguan authorities after their capture of a speedboat carrying a large cocaine load off the Corn Islands and the arrest of six armed Honduran traffickers and one Nicaraguan. "Caen seis hondureños con narcolancha," *LP* (HO), 19 May 2008, 90.

forcibly expelled or escaped from St. Vincent and other British Caribbean islands and sometimes intermarried with Caribs. Many fled or were deported to the Islas de la Bahía, and while some settled there, others made their way to the mainland, starting communities along the Honduran and Belizean coasts that featured distinctive language, customs, and culture.

For purposes of the drug trade, traffickers arranging maritime or aerial transshipment schemes have been attracted to these communities, often poor and seldom receiving much law-enforcement attention from central authorities. In 1998, while terming the Caribbean coast a "drug-trafficking corridor," one Honduran drug prosecutor noted that speedboats sometimes operate all night importing narcotics through these communities.[263] In one representative 2008 case, more than thirty people and two cars were reported to have waited near the Garífuna village of Punta de Piedra for a speedboat delivery of a ton of cocaine. By the time the police arrived, the boat had been emptied and the associates had vanished, although four kilos, thought to be payment for local assistance, were found buried on the beach.[264] The following year, Honduran officials located a drug plane, large enough to handle a ton of cocaine, on the coastal highway just outside the neighboring Garífuna town of Ciriboya. The very next week another pilot lost control of his Venezuelan plane and crashed near Ciriboya, with authorities finding thirty kilos of cocaine in the wreckage.[265]

The Islas de la Bahía

Excepting only the cities, towns, and villages of the north coast, the Islas de la Bahía archipelago has been the most significant focal point for Honduran maritime trafficking. For many generations, Islas de la Bahía inhabitants, as in so many other Caribbean locales, have been involved in contraband smuggling of some variety. Although marijuana trafficking took hold quite early, by the 1990s this had been far overshadowed by cocaine imported from Colombia, often via San Andrés. Although much of the trafficking, as well as the drug-financed foreign investment, has involved inhabitants on the largest island of Roatán, individuals in the smaller communities on Guanaja and Utila have played significant roles as well.[266]

The extensive poverty on the islands, the historical social acceptance of smuggling, and the early development of crack-cocaine markets encouraged growth of the drug trade. The economy of the Islas de la Bahía has also differed from that of mainland Honduras. Not only has a growing tourism trade, focused on offshore diving and fishing, promoted high prices, but apart from seafood and certain locally grown fruits and vegetables, most daily consumption items have had to be brought onto the islands. Unsurprisingly, drug rings have found a ready supply of collaborators to off-load cocaine shipments, transfer them from vessel to vessel, or fuel or provision drug boats.[267]

A sample of the most prominent cases helps to illustrate the magnitude and variety of trafficking

263. For information on the Garífuna of Honduras and their links to the drug trade, see Centro, "Cronología," 9, and "Comunidades Garífunas son corredores del narcotráfico," *LP* (HO), 7 July 1998, 10A. See also England, *Afro Central Americans*, 235–36.

264. "Hallan cuatro kilos de cocaína enterrada," *LP* (HO), 2 March 2008, 32.

265. "Cae una narcoavioneta con un mil kilos de cocaína," *LP* (HO), 7 October 2009, 66; "Caen otras dos narcoavionetas venezolanas en la zona norte," *LP* (HO), 19 October 2009, 90.

266. "Decomisos de cocaína y lucha del narcotráfico en posiciones desiguales," *LP* (HO), 1 April 1996, 16A; "'Narcos' and Politics: Honduras May Be Next in Line for a Major Scandal," *Latin American Weekly Report*, 21 March 1996, 121; and DEA, *Resources, Honduras* (2000), 3. For representative cases, see Centro, "Cronología," 2; "Utilizaba su restaurante para traficar con 'coca,'" *LP* (HO), 17 April 1989, 58; "Decomisan ocho kilos de cocaína," *LP* (HO), 5 February 1991, 19; "Denuncia Sosa Cuello: Juez de Guanaja fue presionado para deshacerse de caso de narcotráfico," *LP* (HO), 17 February 1994, 10A; and "En casos de isleños hallan armas y treinta y ocho kilos de cocaína," *LP* (HO), 19 February 1994, 6A.

267. DEA, *Resources, Honduras* (2000), 3.

occurring here. In 1992 authorities discovered 400 kilos of cocaine near Trujillo, and the local Honduran Navy commander suggested that another 800 kilos might still be present in that city of twenty-three thousand. Immediately thereafter, the navy apprehended a vessel in nearby waters carrying 463 kilos of cocaine and bound for Guanaja. Small cayes surrounding the Islas de la Bahía have been implicated as well. In 1996 a police helicopter spotted a buoy in the mangroves between two tiny islands off Roatán. An investigation uncovered 2,418 kilos of Colombian Red Point marijuana, then worth more than seven hundred dollars a kilo.[268]

Between the north coast of Honduras and Roatán lie the Cayos Cochinos, about a dozen small islands, in which speedboats have occasionally been found abandoned after cocaine runs.[269] In 1998 the U.S. Coast Guard seized 1.3 tons of cocaine near Cayo Gorda in Honduran territorial waters off the north coast. Considerably farther offshore, and hence much closer to San Andrés, lie two more Honduran possessions—tiny Islas del Cisne (Swan Islands) and the neighboring Islas Santanilla. These too have become transit points, with Islas del Cisne gaining such notoriety that the United States tried to assist Honduras by installing a mobile radar unit on the island in 1993.

The Islas de la Bahía have been ideally situated for aerial-smuggling schemes as well. In 2008 police investigating an abandoned drug plane on Utila interviewed frightened inhabitants who declared that constant drug flights were not diminishing in the slightest. All absolutely refused to identify the ringleaders on the island, although they conceded that everyone knew who they were. The following year island residents further reported that competing groups of traffickers had been using their runway and sometimes fighting with one another. That spring, one Venezuelan aircraft attempted to land, then circled the airstrip numerous times and crashed on its next attempt, killing the pilot and two Colombians on board. Police found 1,647 kilos of cocaine in the burned wreckage.[270]

Generally, police work on the Islas de la Bahía has left much to be desired. Local officers have not moved aggressively against entrenched trafficking groups, nor have potential witnesses and informants often emerged. A part of the problem is that Hispanic authorities from the mainland have not easily penetrated criminal networks composed of people of a markedly different culture. The culture and kinship ties of those on the Islas de la Bahía have long gravitated toward the Caribbean. Historically, the resentment of the ethnic minority has encouraged contraband smuggling, and breaking up entrenched drug organizations has been quite difficult. In 1992, citing the low salaries of local police in comparison to the high cost of living on Roatán, Guanaja, and Utila, Honduran general Luis Alonso Discua Elvir conceded that island traffickers can "break the arm of whatever authority [is sent to combat them]."[271]

In the mid-1990s antidrug law enforcement on the islands did improve with the creation of an Islas de la Bahía task force, funded by the United States, which resulted in certain substantial seizures and important arrests.[272] However, institutional deficiencies were but one part of the Islas de la Bahía drug-trafficking problem, and vigorous investigation of local

268. "Habría ochocientos kilos de coca circulando en Trujillo," *LP* (HO), 24 October 1992, 4; "Policía incauta cocaína valorada en 80 millones," *LP* (HO), 7 November 1992, 12; "Droga hallada en Roatán valdría L. 50 millones," *LP* (HO), 11 March 1993, 15; "U.S. Seizes Drug Runner in Honduran Waters," *Honduras This Week Online*, http://www.marrder.com/htw/mar98/national.htm; "Hay pista en isla de Barbareta que puede ser usada por 'narcos,'" *LP* (HO), 14 May 1992, 16; *INCSR* (1994), 156.

269. See, for instance, "Policía investiga supuesta narcolancha," *LP* (HO), 3 March 2008, 91.

270. "Dejan abandonada narcoavioneta en Utila," *LP* (HO), 10 September 2009, 70; "Incineran 1,647 kilos de cocaína de avioneta," *LP* (HO), 12 May 2009, 68.

271. "Isleños están en las 'garras' de la droga," *LP* (HO), 12 November 1993, 30A.

272. See *INCSR* (1999), 162. See also *INCSR* (1996), 138, and *INCSR* (1997), 139.

drug-trafficking and distribution networks has remained the exception, not the rule.

Air Routes

In 1939 U.S. diplomat Stuart Fuller wrote that the Honduran national airline TACA (Transportes Aereos Centro-Americanos) was "in the minds of police administrations throughout the world . . . identified with the smuggling of narcotic drugs."[273] By the 1980s the magnitude of the air traffic in drugs via Honduras or on Honduran airlines had increased immensely. Given air connections from Honduras south to Colombia and north to various U.S. cities, trafficking organizations used couriers to send cocaine through the international airports in the capitol of Tegucigalpa and the commercial center of San Pedro Sula.[274] By the early 1990s the courier traffic had come to target Europe, and it eventually included heroin passage.[275] Although occurring less frequently, larger cocaine loads have also been secreted within air-cargo shipments passing through Honduras.[276]

In the mid-1990s, as airport authorities began to rely on drug-sniffing dogs, the hope was that at least the courier traffic might diminish in importance.[277] In 1998, however, officials of the National Commission Against Drug Trafficking reported that drugs were again flowing freely through Toncontín Airport in Tegucigalpa. It seemed that airport security had not wanted to bother with the formalities and paperwork required by international conventions. Furthermore, private air companies have often transported civilian and military officials, and, traditionally, their flights have been neither registered nor inspected, as these passengers might perceive this as an affront.[278] Thus, a weak rule-of-law ideal combined with the traditional deference to elites accustomed to acting with impunity have adversely affected antidrug activity associated with courier trafficking.

Even more important to aerial drug smuggling has been the use of small planes or helicopters that have often arrived in Honduras either directly from San Andrés or other Colombian points of embarkation or with intermediate stops in the more southerly Central American bridge states. One often utilized flight route has been up the Caribbean and then bending around Cabo Gracias a Dios. Alternatively, planes have cut across sparsely populated northern Nicaragua before entering western Honduras. In either case the aircraft have usually angled to land somewhere on the Caribbean coast, often in the rough rectangle formed by the cities of Puerto Cortés and San Pedro Sula to the west and San Esteban and Trujillo to the east.[279]

273. See DOS, General Records of the Department of States, RG 59, 815.114, Narcotics/516, cited in Walker, *Western Hemisphere*, 87.

274. For a representative case, see *United States v. Moreno*, 185 F.3d 465.

275. For representative cases of Honduran couriers attempting to fly with drugs to Europe, see "Detenido en España matrimonio hondureño con 6.2 kilos de cocaína," *LP* (HO), 23 April 2001, 14A, and "Acusados de 'narcos' pagaron por libertad a magistrados sampedranos," *LP* (HO), 13 September 1999, 4A. In 1992 Carlos Leiva was arrested in the Houston Intercontinental Airport coming from Honduras with just over a kilo of heroin. "Heroin Busts at Airport Up for Holiday," *Houston Chronicle*, 31 December 1992, A23.

276. In 1996, for instance, police seized 167 kilos of cocaine in a Toncontín airport warehouse. See "Via Miami iban 167 kilos de 'coca' incautados en Toncontín," *LP* (HO), 13 March 1996, 18A, and DEA, *Resources, Honduras* (2001), 4.

277. *INCSR* (1998), 144. U.S. Customs recognized the Honduran canine program as the best in Central America. *INCSR* (1998), 144.

278. See "Toncontín un punto fácil para el narcotráfico," *LP* (HO), 31 July 1998, 14A, and "Aviones privados pueden ser registrados por agentes antinarcóticos: Carlos Sosa Coello," *LP* (HO), 4 July 1998, 11A.

279. See "La Mosquitia," 3. For an illuminating map of air routes, see DEA, *Resources, Honduras* (2001), 3. For a particularly notable drug-smuggling flight into San Esteban, Olancho, that eventually resulted in the prison murder of a former legislator involved in the shipment, see "Honduras Investigates Ex-congressman's Killing," *TT* (CR), 16 July 2004, 12. For seizures of four hundred to five hundred kilos from Colombian planes landing near Trujillo in 2003, see "Authorities in Northern Honduras Seize Cocaine, Arrest Six Aboard Small Plane," AP (US), 26 June 2003.

When one reviews more than three decades of aerial trafficking through Honduras, a number of points stand out. First, with the continued success of aerial schemes and the accumulation of experience, drug rings have moved toward more frequent use of larger planes with greater payloads. Thus, over the years typical air shipments of 200–300 kilos have given way to loads twice that size or more. In 2009 Honduran authorities came upon a Russian Antonov 14 cargo plane from Venezuela, which they believed had brought 3.7 tons of cocaine into the country.[280]

More broadly, even though cartels moved decisively toward maritime and overland transport in Honduras, as well as in other Central American bridge states, in the early to mid-1990s, aerial schemes had worked so well there that drug networks returned to this approach before long, with air trafficking rising to another crescendo through the first decade of the twenty-first century.[281] With such a small and immobile police force trying to cover such a large country, intercepting aircraft that can land at any time on numerous roads or airstrips is exceedingly challenging and, in fact, law-enforcement officials have usually arrived at the scene too late to do anything other than sift through the smoldering remains of an airplane that traffickers had crashed or purposefully set on fire.

In fact, drug planes have landed at places across a very wide swath of northern Honduras, making interdiction quite challenging. For instance, some have touched down in the Río Aguán valley, which angles inland from the Caribbean coast. In 2002 authorities arrested a Guatemalan and took almost 500 kilos from a Nicaraguan helicopter in this area, finding a burned Colombian drug plane nearby. The following year the pilots of another Colombian airplane apparently confused the small cities of Tocoa and Olanchito in this same large river valley. While Honduran associates armed with AK-47 weapons were waiting on a different road, burning tires to try to get the pilot's attention, the plane flew over the Standard Fruit property several times, searching for the proper landing area, and finally touched down on a road near Arenal, veering onto the shoulder when a vehicle unexpectedly appeared. When police arrived an hour and a half later, they found 397 kilos of cocaine in the plane, although the traffickers had fled to the small town of El Retiro and then disappeared. By 2003 authorities were reporting that hundreds of unidentified small planes were crossing Honduran airspace, perhaps carrying a total of as much as 100 tons of cocaine toward the United States.[282]

At the root of the problem of aerial-smuggling schemes via Honduras is the large number of uncontrolled landing spots, whether clandestine airstrips or isolated roads, that traffickers can choose among.[283] Although U.S. military planes operating from Soto Cano sometimes detect and monitor suspicious flights and in 1991 the United States helped Honduras install additional radar on a hilltop outside Trujillo to help track air traffic, law enforcement has remained unable to respond quickly enough to the remote locations where intelligence indicates the planes are landing.[284] Some cocaine planes simply refuel before flying on to Florida or to sites in Mexico en route to the United States. Other smuggling groups arrange for ground crews to off-load the cocaine to be trucked into Guatemala.[285] Some cocaine planes

280. "Cae avión cargado," 68.

281. Between 1993 and 1996 the U.S. State Department reported a lull in aerial cocaine trafficking through Honduras; however, by 2000 it stated that drug-smuggling rings were "frequently" employing Honduran airspace. Compare *INCSR* (1993), 158; *INCSR* (1994), 154; *INCSR* (1995), 137; and *INCSR* (1996), 136; with *INCSR* (2000), 171.

282. "Abandonan avioneta con 397 kilos de cocaína," *LP* (HO), 4 April 2003, 65.

283. See *INCSR* (2001), 146, and DEA, *Resources, Honduras* (2001), 4.

284. *INCSR* (1992), 163, and confidential interview with foreign law enforcement official closely familiar with Honduran antidrug operations, December 1991, Tegucigalpa, Honduras.

285. "FF AA pide ayuda contra narcotráfico," *LP* (HO), 31 May 2009, 47.

have simply crossed Honduran airspace en route to Guatemala or Mexico, and some traffickers have taken advantage of the lax coastal security to execute water drops in the country's Caribbean waters.[286] Information on incoming flights supplied by the U.S. government to Honduran officials have led to seizures, but not with the frequency needed to curb the aerial drug trade to any substantial extent.

Instead, transnational criminal organizations have often stayed a step ahead of authorities by using an array of aerial-trafficking schemes.[287] Although landing sites abound all along the Caribbean coast, from the Trujillo area through La Ceiba, Tela, and Puerto Cortés, the most risk-free zone for aerial drug traffickers has been farther east in La Mosquitia. In 1988 Judge Miguel Ángel Izaguirre Fiallos, for a period the most prominent Honduran investigating judge of drug matters, revealed a prominent aerial transshipment route from Tiburón Cove, Colombia, through Laguna de Brus in Gracias a Dios to Isla Mujeres, Mexico.[288] In 1996 Honduran authorities announced the seizure, with DEA assistance, of 2 tons in La Mosquitia. Nevertheless, the following February indigenous Hondurans complained that Colombian traffickers were buying up their ancestral lands to establish landing strips for cocaine planes.[289]

In one notable case in 1999 a helicopter registered to a Guatemalan business flew from Managua, Nicaragua, into La Mosquitia, touching down on a remote airstrip and collecting close to 500 kilos of cocaine, after local villagers, thought to be storing the drugs, took a cut.[290] While flying toward Puerto Barrios, the pilots had trouble with the helicopter, landed in central Honduras, and hid the drugs in a mill near a tiny village. Locals, however, thought the helicopter might be bringing supplies to help them recover from Hurricane Mitch. When they inquired and were turned away, suspicions were aroused and the police called in. Eventually, authorities arrested a Mexican and a Nicaraguan pilot, plus alleged Nicaraguan ringleader Juan Carlos Monterroso, while recovering 419 kilos.

In 2009 Honduran authorities made a startling discovery in La Mosquitia that illustrates the scope and ambition of transnational drug networks and underscores the importance of aerial trafficking on the Caribbean coast. After a number of suspect planes had been sighted flying in this northeastern corner of Honduras and the burned remnants of others had been located on the ground, authorities were alert to additional flights, particularly because two half-ton cocaine seizures had previously occurred in this area. When an airplane flew over the Miskito settlement of Warunta in Gracias a Dios, antidrug officials, supported by the Honduran Navy, responded. They found that the traffickers had already departed with the cocaine, and the plane had been set on fire. In searching the nearby jungle, however, the

286. As U.S. officials observed in 1992, "Honduras . . . has a long, virtually unguarded Caribbean coastline and poorly policed off-shore islands with a history of contraband smuggling. Also, there are vast open land areas. Transfers of illicit narcotics between small aircraft and boats can easily occur undetected. Loads can be consolidated for onward shipment overland, or by ship or plane." *INCSR* (1992), 162.

287. For a representative case, see *United States v. Bollinger*, 769 F.2d at 1394. For the account of one Honduran plane abandoned with 649 kilos of cocaine on board at Mexico's Puerto Vallarta Airport, see Centro, "Cronología," 12. See also the detailed statement by Carlos Sosa Coello of the National Council Against Narcotics Trafficking in "A 1,800 kilos de cocaína valorada en $200 millones ascienden decomisos en el país," *LP* (HO), 22 June 1998, 11A.

288. For a profile of Judge Izaguirre Fiallos, see "Honduran Judge Says."

289. "El Cartel del Atlántico: Siguen confesiones y más implicados," *LP* (HO), 17 December 1988, 4; "Decomisan 350 kilos de cocaína en Guasule," *LP* (HO), 18 April 1996, 4A; and "Drug Lords Buying Up Land: Indians," *TR* (BZ), 2 February 1997, 25. See also "Colombianos se apoderan de Sico y Paulaya," *LP* (HO), 2 March 1995, 4A; and "Valle Sico y Paulaya convertidas en depósitos y pista de 'coca,'" *LP* (HO), 24 January 1996, 11A.

290. See "Helicóptero encontrado en pista yoreña trajo alijo de 294 kilos de cocaína," *LP* (HO), 14 September 1999, 62A; "Faltan cinco fardos con cocaína por encontrar en montañas yoreñas," *LP* (HO), 16 September 1999, 20A; and "Policía captura 'narco' prófugo y encuentra 50 kilos más de cocaína," *LP* (HO), 17 September 1999, 12A.

authorities discovered an entire drug-transshipment camp, complete with a lighted runway, fifty-five barrels of aviation fuel, eight tents, a kitchen, and an electricity generator.[291]

Police came to believe that one of the Mexican cartels had joined with Guatemalan and Honduran associates to set up the camp to refuel the cocaine planes that had long utilized the various runways around the remote La Mosquitia indigenous communities of Samil and Warunta. Later that month, as the investigation continued, antidrug officials operating in this area discovered several "airplane cemeteries" in the jungle, the largest one less than seven miles south of Laguna de Brus. To conceal evidence, traffickers had paid local people, often compensating them with drugs, to dispose of dozens of planes. Some were helicopters; others were one- or two-propeller light planes; still others were cargo aircraft. Some were intact; others were damaged. Some of them had been burned, and others buried.[292]

Later in 2009 authorities found yet another base of operations for the Sinaloa cartel near the small town of Naco just outside San Pedro Sula. The Honduran legislator who had owned the farm had been murdered. He had left the property to his chauffeur, who, in turn, had sold it to the Mexicans, who had outfitted the property with a heliport and an excellent broad and lengthy runway.[293] Yet, although suspected cocaine flights continued to touch down across the country, La Mosquitia has remained the focal point. In 2008 U.S. military authorities tracked thirty-one suspicious flights into Honduras. That figure rose to fifty-four in 2009 and seventy-five in 2010, with U.S. officials noting their increasing concentration in La Mosquitia.[294]

After drugs have been flown into Honduras, traffickers have sometimes moved them overland, clear across Guatemala and into Mexico. At other times, cocaine that arrived by air has then been shipped or flown to the United States either from Honduras or Guatemala. Two shipments interdicted in 2000, of 283 and 630 kilos, illustrate this intermodal, or combined air/ground transportation, approach.[295] In the larger of these busts, Colombian guerrillas used three small planes and a helicopter to bring the cocaine from Colombia to a drop point near San Ignacio in Yoro Department. Cars and a small truck then transported the cocaine to a storage site, where it was eventually loaded into secret compartments inside tractor trailers. The plan was to truck the cocaine into Guatemala and then on to Mexico, where Tijuana traffickers would import the drugs into the United States. In this case, however, antidrug agents executed a controlled delivery, eventually stopping the trucks and seizing the drugs near La Flecha in Santa Barbara.

The problem of airborne trafficking grew to such dimensions that the Honduran Air Force, on several occasions, forced down or shot down suspected drug planes.[296] In 1986 Honduran fighter jets compelled a plane to land that was found to be carrying 900 kilos of cocaine. Within three months, however, the arrested Colombian pilots had been freed from jail and vanished. Frustrated with judicial corruption, the military began to shoot down suspected cocaine planes that failed to heed orders to land. In early 1987 a C-47 transport plane crossed the Nicaraguan border near El Paraíso on a flight path south of Tegucigalpa toward Guatemala.

291. "Ordenan la destrucción de dos pistas clandestinas," *LP* (HO), 1 October 2009, 62; "Desarticulan campamento de droga en La Mosquitia," *LP* (HO), 2 October 2009, 69; "Hallan cementerios de narcoavionetas," *LP* (HO), 26 October 2009, 90.

292. "Hallan cementerios de narcoavionetas" 90.

293. "Encuentran pista del cartel mexicano de Sinaloa en Naco," *LP* (HO), 14 December 2009, 114. Neighbors reported that Mexicans were arriving at the farm by car throughout the night.

294. *INCSR* (2011), 293.

295. See *INCSR* (2001), 146; "Incautan seiscientos kilos de cocaína escondidos en compartimientos falsos en dos cabezales," *LP* (HO), 12 April 2000, 59A; and "Avioneta de guerrilla colombiana transportó 'coca' a Honduras," *LP* (HO), 13 April 2000, 12A.

296. See "Derriban en alta mar una avioneta cargada con drogas," *LP* (HO), 8 May 1992, 3, and "U.S. to Open Outpost."

When Honduran Air Force jets intercepted the flight, the pilot ignored repeated orders to land and instead hurried toward the border. Eventually, the air force shot down the plane, killing three, including the American pilot.[297] Likewise, in 1992 Honduran fighter jets downed a twin-engine plane, loaded with over 500 kilos of cocaine, headed from La Guajira, Colombia, to Guatemala via Islas del Cisne, that had apparently intended to execute a water drop within Honduran territorial waters.[298]

While in effect, the shoot-down policy may have deterred some smuggling organizations.[299] However, the advantages of aerial ventures led numerous traffickers to assume the risk of interception. In 2001, near the Salvadoran border, the Honduran Air Force destroyed another plane, carrying a ton of cocaine, killing the Colombians on board.[300] That same year, however, Peruvian authorities shot down a small plane that turned out to be transporting American missionaries rather than cocaine, and the U.S. Congress voted to withhold data collected from satellites and radar installations from countries that fire upon unidentified aircraft suspected of drug running. Even so, in 2003 a Honduran fighter jet chased a Colombian plane crossing Honduran airspace and carrying extra fuel tanks and more than a ton of cocaine. After the pilot failed to respond to radio communications and made for the Salvadoran border, the plane either crashed or was shot down.[301] After the incident, President Ricardo Maduro announced that Honduras would no longer attack such aircraft, although he maintained that states had the right to do so and blamed the U.S. policy for increased aerial cocaine transit.

In 2005 the Venezuelan government stopped most cooperation with the DEA, increasing Venezuela's role as a transit state. Cocaine was then typically transshipped via Central American bridge states, and Honduras soon developed into a particular target. By 2009 such an enormous influx of Venezuelan drug planes had entered northern Honduras and the Islas de la Bahía that the Honduran government lodged an official protest with Venezuela.[302] In the first ten months of the year authorities received reports of more than thirty Venezuelan planes landing on roads or unsupervised runways, and by the end of that year police had found fifty abandoned drug planes, most hailing from Venezuela or Colombia.[303] In one representative case a plane carrying about a thousand kilos of cocaine and pursued by two helicopters crashed near the town of El Negrito in Yoro.[304] The pilot was killed and all but one hundred kilos of cocaine burned. Traffickers frequently returned to the same area on multiple occasions, indicative not only of their continued success but of the presence of networks of local associates. The following fall another Venezuelan plane landed

297. See "Drug-Smuggling Plane Downed, Honduras Says," *WP* (US), 11 March 1987, A14; "Colombia: Discovers Link to Plane Downed by Honduras," IPS (US), 11 March 1987; and "Derribado avión del narcotráfico," *LN* (CR), 11 March 1987, 1.

298. For an example where radar in Trujillo had located the plane, see "Derriban en alta mar," 3. See also "Capturan a tripulantes de aeronave derribada," *LP* (HO), 11 May 1992, 5, and "Honduras: Cocaine Seizure." The cocaine had been wrapped in beeswax to fool any drug-sniffing dogs encountered on the route further north. See also "Detectan otra avioneta en zona de reciente derribamiento," *LP* (HO), May 11, 1992, 3, and "'Somos inocentes,' dicen tripulantes de avioneta," *LP* (HO), 16 May 1992, 5.

299. *INCSR* (1992), 158–59, and *INCSR* (1995), 137.

300. "Honduras Wants U.S. Policy Change on Suspect Drug Planes," Agence France Presse, 21 August 2003.

301. See "Derriban avioneta con un mil kilos de cocaína," *LP* (HO), 15 April 2003, 12; "Incineran cocaína de avioneta derribada," *LP* (HO), 16 April 2003, 12; "Small Plane Carrying Cocaine Crashes, Killing Two, After Interception by Honduran Air Force," AP (US), 14 April 2003; and "Central America: Blacklisted Countries Make Big Drug Seizures," Intelligence Research (United Kingdom), 16 April 2003; and "U.S. Policy Change."

302. "Gobierno protesta por lluvia de narconaves [*sic*]," *LP* (HO), 22 October 2009, 67.

303. "Narcoavionetas podrían ser derribadas por FAH," *LP* (HO), 20 October 2009, 60.

304. "Cocaine-Carrying Plane Crashes in Honduras," *TR* (BZ), 15 March 2009, 31. Two months later, authorities found another Venezuelan drug plane in this area. "En Yoro cae narcoavioneta con bandera venezolana," *LP* (HO), 29 May 2009, 86, and "Es común que aterricen avionetas, dicen vecinos," *LP* (HO), 30 May 2009, 69.

at night on the main highway just outside the neighboring town of Morazán, although this time the cargo had been off-loaded before authorities arrived.[305]

The vast profits of the cocaine trade have thus been reflected in the attitude traffickers have come to take toward the airplanes used to transport drugs. In this regard, the larger the quantities of drugs sent to market, the more per kilo transportation costs are defrayed.[306] As shipments increased in scale from the 1990s on, the value of the plane relative to that of the cocaine load dropped dramatically. The intersection of criminal-justice concerns with the economics of the drug trade became evident in the numbers of abandoned aircraft found in Honduras and the other bridge states. With the only evidence left at the scene the burned remnants of the plane that had been used, arrests rarely occurred.[307] But the presence of all these planes plainly demonstrated that authorities had been unable to interdict more than a very small percentage of air-shipped cocaine.

Overland Routes

Throughout the bridge states the repeated success of particular routes and methods persuaded traffickers to send larger shipments in hopes of maximizing profits. In Honduras the control exercised by customs officials at the border posts into Nicaragua, El Salvador, and Guatemala has been strictly limited, whether on account of corruption or of heavy traffic and inadequate resources. Eventually, under the terms of regional free trade accords, trucks have frequently passed through Honduran border posts with sealed cargoes that have not been subject to routine inspection. Several attractive paths across the country have been utilized, as have multiple entry and exit points. Much ground transshipment in the 1980s involved loads of 100 kilos or less; indeed, shipments of 5, 10, or 20 kilos were commonplace.[308] By the following decade, however, traffickers were trucking through much larger loads, even of multiton dimensions, using more sophisticated methods of hiding the drugs in spare fuel tanks, double-walled shipping containers, and truck frames.[309]

Trafficking organizations did, of course, sometimes slip up, and significant cocaine seizures have periodically occurred. For instance, in 1992 authorities seized a total of nearly a ton of cocaine at Honduran border crossings. Occasional large busts led various networks to revert to splitting up loads in an effort to minimize risk. Early in the twenty-first century, the DEA reported, "Seizures in 2000 throughout Honduras and the rest of Central America indicated that drug traffickers using overland vehicles are moving cocaine in shipments that range between 100 kilograms and 200 kilograms."[310] Although such trends have been discernible, so many narcotics were successfully passing across Honduras overland that calculating the relative percentages of large, modest, and small shipments has been impossible.

At the borders the interception of a small fraction of the cocaine likely to be passing

305. "Caen otras dos narcoavionetas," 90.

306. "A pilot who demands 500,000 U.S. dollars for flying a plane with 250 kilograms is generating costs of only 2,000 dollars per kilogram, about 2 percent of the retail price. Even if the plane has to be abandoned after one flight, that adds only another 2,000 dollars to the kilogram price." Reuter, "Political Economy of Drug Smuggling," 132.

307. For representative Honduran instances of burned planes suspected of carrying drugs or drug money, see "Cae otra narcoavioneta en Cuero y Salado," *LP* (HO), 30 October 2009, 14, and "Otra narcoavioneta cae sobre La Masica," *LP* (HO), 26 September 2009, 66.

308. For representative cases, see "Decomisan setenta kilos de cocaína," *LP* (HO), 18 September 1991, 1, 46; "Incautan cincuenta y ocho kilos de cocaína escondidos en vehículos VW," *Tiempo* (Honduras), 18 May 1990, 2; and "Hay más implicados en narcotráfico," *LP* (HO), 23 May 1990, 1, 26.

309. *INCSR* (1996), 136; DEA, *Resources, Honduras* (2001), 4; *INCSR* (1995), 137; *INCSR* (1992), 159; "Drug Trafficking Growing in Honduras," UPI (US), 13 March 1996.

310. DEA, *Resources, Honduras* (2001), 4.

through is sometimes attributed to too much traffic, which overwhelms customs inspectors. At other times it is associated with too little traffic, which does not seem to warrant extensive border controls. Both explanations are valid along different parts of the boundary lines. With respect to the long Nicaraguan boundary, authorities have very few resources to devote to controlling the border crossings, many of them used quite infrequently. A large flow of marijuana and cocaine has thus traveled overland en route to El Salvador or Guatemala, and often in Guatemalan vehicles or with Guatemalan drivers.[311]

In 1990, for instance, authorities stopped two Guatemalans in Danlí as they drove through Honduras on one of the main highways from Nicaragua and arrested them for trafficking 272 kilos of cocaine, most of it found in a spare fuel tank in their truck. In 1996 authorities found 225 kilos of cocaine in a load of onions supposedly traveling from Panama to Mexico. The following month a Guatemalan at the same Guasule customs post was found to be carrying 350 kilos in a truck coming from Costa Rica. In 1999 Honduran authorities intercepted a drug caravan, arresting seventeen Mexicans in three vehicles and seizing 241 kilos of cocaine.[312]

Despite the plethora of problems at the border, authorities have occasionally uncovered the overland schemes of trafficking organizations, usually through confidential informants or vehicle inspections. In 2003, to curb the overland drug trade, the Honduran Frontier Police installed a Pan-American Highway checkpoint.[313] However, the extent to which this has deterred traffickers—as opposed to persuading them to divert loads to other routes or to corrupt officials systematically—remains unclear. Traffickers do not usually discard a long-successful approach without first trying to make adjustments to determine if it can still be made to work effectively. And for many years a steady stream of narcotics has passed through the inland cities of Choluteca and Comayagua and at the Guasule and La Fraternidad customs posts on the country's southern border, as well as at the notorious El Amatillo border crossing into El Salvador, which some have called "the most corrupt in all Central America."[314]

One of the indicators that much more cocaine is transiting overland than is being interdicted is that authorities in neighboring countries

311. See DEA, *Resources, Honduras* (2000), 2, and "Narcoactividad, corrupción, y tráfico de ilegales campean en El Amatillo," *LP* (HO), 18 July 1998, 7A. For the cases mentioned, see "Caen narcos guatemaltecos," *El Gráfico* (Guatemala), 28 April 1990, 7; "Incautan 600 libras de coca escondidas entre mercancias," *Tiempo* (Honduras), 26 April 1990, 10; "Decomisan otros 225 kilos de cocaína en Guasule," *LP* (HO), 13 March 1996, 18A; and "Decomisan 350 kilos," 4A.

312. *INCSR* (2000), 172.

313. *INCSR* (2004), 156, and *INCSR* (2005), 185.

314. For narcotics in Choluteca, see, for instance, "Honduras, paraíso," 10A, and "Incautan cargamento de coca," *LP* (HO), 31 July 1992, 8. For the increase in trafficking through Comayagua, see "Honduras seguirá siendo puente del narcotráfico, pero lo combatiremos," *LP* (HO), 18 October 1989, 52. For narcotics passing through the Guasule customs post, see "Honduran Police Confiscate $10 Million Worth of Cocaine," AP (US), 23 September 1991; "Decomisan setenta kilos de 'coca' en Guasule," *LP* (HO), 5 June 1992, 1; "Guasule: Decomisan setenta kilos de 'coca' a tres mexicanos," *LP* (HO), 8 June 1995, 1, 18A; "Otros treinta y un kilos de 'coca' caen en Guasule," *LP* (HO), 23 June 1995, 1, 19A; "Decomisan cincuenta kilos de 'coca' en Guasule," *LP* (HO), 9 May 1996, 16A; "Guasule: 'Coca' decomisada valorada en L. 150 millones," *LP* (HO), 3 August 1996, 1; and "Capturan a guatemaltecos con sesenta kilos de cocaína," *LP* (HO), 24 August 1996, 10A. For narcotics passing through La Fraternidad customs post, see "Falta de logística promueve tráfico de drogas en el país," *LP* (HO), 24 September 1999, 39A, noting that important posts, including La Fraternidad, at times all but abandoned the task of inspecting vehicles. For a flurry of activity at La Fraternidad in 1992, see "Otro cargamento de 'coca' incautado en La Fraternidad," *LP* (HO), 9 August 1992, 1; "Detienen camión con cien kilos de cocaína," *LP* (HO), 3 September 1992, 8; "Entre $4.4 y $6.4 millones valoran coca decomisada en La Fraternidad," *LP* (HO), 2 December 1992, 55; and "Otro millonario decomiso de cocaína en Choluteca," *LP* (HO), 8 December 1992, 3. For trafficking at El Amatillo border crossing, see "Aduana de El Amatillo es la más corrupta de Centroamérica," *LP* (HO), 24 July 1998, 6A.

have frequently intercepted large cocaine loads in trucks from Honduras, driven by Hondurans, or having just crossed Honduran territory. In 2008, 1.2 tons were confiscated from a Honduran truck passing through Nicaragua.[315] The following year, in the largest seizure of its kind in Guatemalan history, authorities followed a suspicious tractor trailer that had entered Guatemala from Honduras, escorted by a luxury car. A police inspection turned up a double-walled shipping container with 1,691 kilos of cocaine packed inside.[316]

Particularly with respect to immense loads traveling by truck, some important Central American trafficking networks have arranged the ground transport of cocaine via Honduras. While typically headquartered in El Salvador or Guatemala, these businesses have operated extensively in Honduras. For example, in 2009 authorities in Tegucigalpa arrested alleged Salvadoran kingpin Reynerio de Jesús Flores Lazo, owner of Transportes de Jesús and a suspected leading Central American contact of Mexico's Gulf cartel, expelling him to El Salvador to face criminal charges there.[317]

Although occasionally suspect vehicles have entered Honduras via sparsely populated northern Nicaragua into Gracias a Dios Province, traffickers have very much preferred two primary land routes. On the one hand, if the drugs have been headed to eastern or central Guatemala, including Guatemala City, drug rings have customarily sent the shipment across southern Honduras and through El Salvador. Here, the Pan-American Highway traverses the narrow southern neck of Honduras, which opens onto the Gulf of Fonseca, providing a means to transport a drug load from Nicaragua into El Salvador in several hours. On the other hand, if the drugs are to be exported by air from the Izabal region of Guatemala or by sea from a Caribbean port, perhaps Puerto Cortés or Puerto Barrios, traffickers have typically opted for more northerly ground passage. They could send a shipment into Honduras through the border crossings at El Paraíso or Danlí, then on toward San Pedro Sula along the highways leading through Tegucigalpa and Comayagua. From there, the drugs might head toward the Honduran coast or angle into Guatemala by any of various routes. Indeed, just as was true of entry through Nicaragua, so in exit via Guatemala trafficking organizations could take advantage of a border honeycombed with unsupervised entry points.[318]

Conclusion

Significant quantities of other drugs have been exported to market from the Central American republics, but cocaine transshipment has turned this area into the world's leading bridge region. In this regard Honduras ranks as the prototypical Central American bridge state. The country has never developed the export-quality marijuana of Belize and Panama. It has had none of the opium production of Guatemala, and Honduran heroin trafficking has paled next to that of Panama or even Costa Rica. Nevertheless, from a very early date Honduras witnessed truly extraordinary flows of cocaine. Substantial quantities transited from the late 1970s on, and as early as 1984 Honduran authorities had confiscated cocaine loads of 100, 500, and 1,000 kilos.[319]

Furthermore, while significant amounts of cocaine have arrived either by small planes or

315. "Detienen barco con 4.6 toneladas de cocaína," *LP* (HO), 29 June 2008, 36.

316. "Incautan 1,691 kilos de droga en Guatemala," *LP* (HO), 22 September 2009, 62.

317. "Capturan capo salvadoreño más buscado por Interpol," *LP* (HO), 7 May 2009, 94, and "Capo salvadoreño fue extraditado," *LP* (HO), 8 May 2009, 110.

318. Honduran campesinos living along the border have traditionally taken their produce—grains, beans, chiles, tomatoes, and the like—into Guatemala in search of higher prices. "Granos se van por puntos ciegos," *LP* (HO), 25 June 2008, 2.

319. See "Honduras Dismantles," 6, and Centro, "Cronología," 3.

by vehicles, including tractor trailers, Honduras, like Panama, has long featured maritime transport. Colombian cocaine has regularly been shipped via the "Honduran triangle"—marked by Trujillo to the east and Puerto Cortés to the west along the Caribbean coast and extending out to the Islas de la Bahía—one of the region's leading trafficking zones.[320] As maritime trafficking increased in importance as a percentage of the total drug trade, Honduras became further entrenched as a key Central American bridge state.

The early prominence of Honduras in cocaine transshipment may be attributed not merely to the presence of Juan Ramón Matta Ballesteros, significant as that chapter in the Central American drug trade was, but to a series of bridge-favoring factors that influenced transnational criminal organizations to do business in the country and that have remained significant over the years. First, Honduras has had the geographic prerequisites, in its case low population density, the Islas de la Bahía archipelago, a mountainous interior, various deep-water ports, and the safe haven of La Mosquitia.

Another central factor elevating Honduras in the regional drug trade has been its extensive poverty. The poorest country in Central America, Honduras has also had to try to overcome the highest population growth. Weak exports, high illiteracy rates, poor nutrition, homelessness, and substandard living conditions have plagued Honduras, creating widespread vulnerabilities. Its high unemployment, youthful population, and growing gangs have presented a ready workforce for traffickers. By the twenty-first century Honduras had become so violent that criminals stealing drugs occasionally victimized even trafficking organizations.[321]

Although the work of police forces and penal and judicial authorities have rarely stood out as the strength of Central American societies, the Honduran administration of justice has been nothing short of appalling. The scarcity of public resources, coupled with a lack of professionalism among many officials, especially within the country's judiciary, has created a system wholly unprepared to meet the challenges of transnational organized crime. Authorities have been linked to narco-corruption as well as to major human rights abuses, greatly reducing the incentives for citizens to assist in countering the drug trade. The government has infrequently prosecuted, and judges have rarely convicted and sentenced, traffickers of real magnitude, whether from foreign drug organizations or Honduran cartelitos. Horrendous prison conditions have led to routine escapes by prisoners, especially traffickers. Honduras has lagged in creating an effective legal regime to counter organized crime, including drug-related offenses, and in outlining an effective process for identifying and prosecuting corrupt acts. Because officials have rarely been convicted and punished, for many, the benefit of engaging in corruption continues to outweigh the potential costs, a systemic weakness that pulls foreign drug organizations into the country, while fostering homegrown talent.

Finally, the central role of the armed forces has distinguished Honduras from various other Central American bridge states. Continuing military influence has shaped Honduran society and influenced the role and nature of its drug trade. Military officers and their immediate and extended families have formed a powerful elite largely isolated from the rule of law. Accordingly, they have been in a unique position to work closely with traffickers, protecting shipments, carrying drugs in diplomatic pouches, and serving as vital cogs in transshipment

320. For the statement of Carlos Sosa Coello, see "La Ceiba, Trujillo, Islas de la Bahía es el 'triángulo' del narcotráfico," *LP* (HO), 3 April 1992, 4. For specific instances, see "Siete capturan en La Ceiba por tráfico de drogas," *LP* (HO), 4 March 1989, 5, and "Decomisan veinte kilos de cocaína en operativo," *LP* (HO), 14 March 1990, 1–2.

321. In one representative 2005 case a group of *delincuentes* intercepted a speedboat and robbed the traffickers of their cocaine before themselves being caught after a shoot-out with the Honduran Navy. "Roban droga a *narcos*," *SV* (GU), 7 February 2005, 36.

schemes. Although a few military officers have been convicted of drug crimes, in nearly every case they have served a significantly reduced sentence or avoided prison time altogether.

Set apart in many ways from Belize and Costa Rica, and distinct from Guatemala and Panama as well, Honduras presents us with yet another profile of a Central American bridge state. Yet exploring the evolution of drug trafficking within this military-influenced transitional society is especially important because Honduras typifies a variety of weak state that is quite vulnerable to the drug trade: a very poor country, with an entrenched military, caught in a political transition, with weak civilian authority and underfunded and inefficient government institutions.

As has been seen in Eastern Europe as well as in Latin America, transitional societies have been particularly vulnerable to organized crime. Those institutions that had previously maintained order have vanished or been transformed or scaled back, and yet new institutions, with revamped structures and procedures, have not yet developed to the point at which even basic functions can be performed effectively. In Honduras the military took steps to withdraw from various of its traditional tasks, including controlling all law-enforcement activities. But rather than being disbanded or dramatically downsized, the armed forces have continued their involvement in what are normally considered private-sector activities, while the civilian Ministry of Security has often appeared weak and ineffectual. A military elite—enjoying impunity, looking to make money, intimidating with weapons, maintaining long-standing international connections, and coming from a history of narco-corruption—is a recipe for drug-trafficking problems.

To reduce poverty, attract foreign investors, and become more commercially vibrant, Honduras's institutions, including those engaged in the administration of justice, will need to function more effectively. As the country plots a course aimed at establishing a more developed country, the government has been willing to implement sweeping changes, such as those in 2002 that aimed to transform a hidebound inquisitorial legal system into a more modern accusatorial one. However, although legislators could mandate changes in court procedures, it was also vitally important to change a legal culture that had traditionally featured slipshod investigations, passive prosecutors, weak and inexperienced judges, a protected military, and the extensive trafficking of influence within the court system. Promoting cultural change, though, even within its own ranks, is a tall order for any government, and it has thus far exceeded the capacity of Honduras in various respects.[322]

With respect to the ongoing transshipment of large loads of narcotics, the wealth of drug traffickers and their potent ability to influence officials have ensured that traditional problems have gone largely unresolved. In 1999 Alfredo Landaverde, representing the National Comission Against Drug Trafficking, declared, "But here nobody wants to do anything. The prosecutors say they can't move against the people linked to drug trafficking because there are no cases against them, but they could check in the United States and other countries that these are drug traffickers, and to build cases against them all you need to do is to ask for more details."[323] Transforming the Honduran legal culture to turn it from a bridge-favoring to a bridge-disfavoring factor presents an extraordinarily challenging task when traffickers intent on subverting the reforms have been able to respond with bribes, bullets, and intimidation.

322. See generally Bunck, *Fidel Castro.*

323. "Por miedo Fiscalía no captura a narcotraficantes," *LP* (HO), 20 July 1999, 6A.

6

Panama

For all of the trafficking elsewhere in Central America, Panamanians certainly might claim to live in the most important transshipment location for criminal groups moving drugs to North American and European markets. Yet, once again, the profile of Panamanian society differs in interesting respects from those of its neighbors. An economist would immediately note that Panama's annual growth rate has routinely led, and sometimes far outpaced, those of the other countries in the region.[1] A sociologist might add that with the exception of a handful of families at the pinnacle of society, social hierarchies have tended to be less rigid than those of its neighbors, and the middle class, larger. Panamanians have also tended to be better educated than the average Central American, a consequence of an emphasis on literacy, more public funds spent on schooling, a large university, and, normally, more freedom of expression.

Political scientists and historians might emphasize that, of our five case studies, Panama has also had the most complex and multilayered relationship with the United States, one with its own tensions and conflicts. In fact, the U.S. government has long riveted economic and geopolitical attention on Panama. It has not been the Panama Canal alone that has ensured that the country's strategic importance has dwarfed its negligible military power and small population of just over 3.1 million. Although for many decades U.S. soldiers were ostensibly present to defend the canal, in reality, the nine U.S. military bases were put to broader purposes. From 1963 to 1997 the Canal Zone was headquarters for the Southern Command, responsible for U.S. military affairs in Latin America and the

1. Within Latin America only Chile exceeded Panama's economic growth rate from 1990 to 2005. "Eaton: No revocamos visas caprichosamente," *La Prensa* (Panama) (hereafter cited as *LP* [PA]), 31 October 2006, 4A.

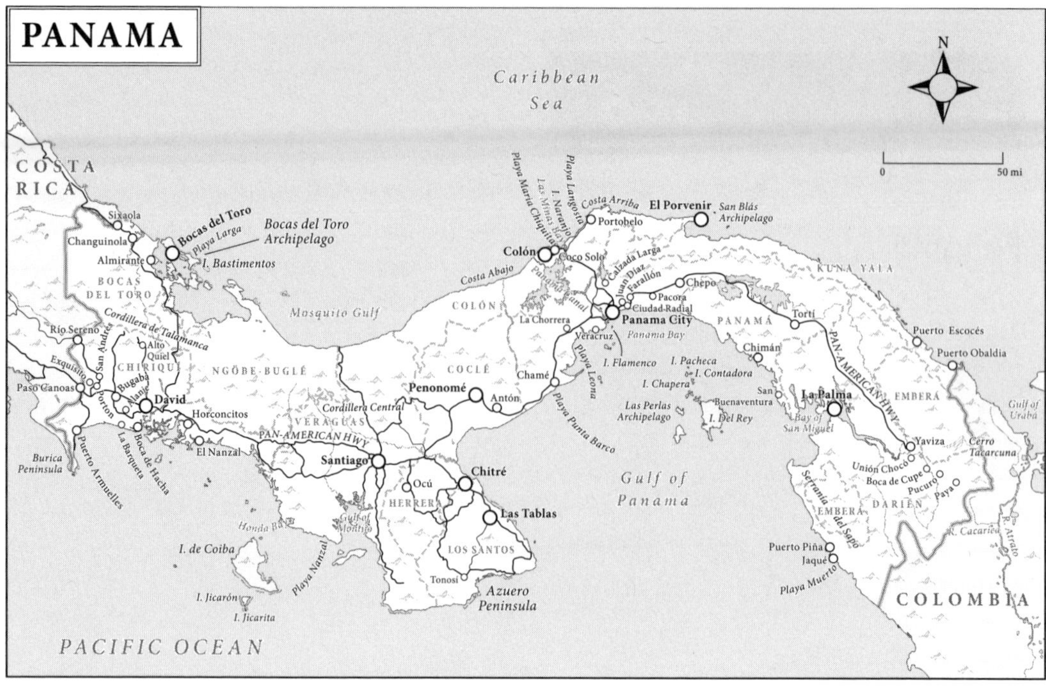

MAP 6.1

Caribbean. The U.S. National Security Agency (NSA) used high-technology equipment to overhear targeted conversations, with personnel on the bases analyzing as well as gathering intelligence.[2]

Unlike other Central American states, Panama suffered neither from a cold war civil war nor its aftermath. However, regional conflict in the 1980s did fan fears within the U.S. government that communism might spread through Central America and perhaps even threaten the canal. Thus, for a period U.S. foreign aid into Panama surged, increasing from $12 million in 1984 to $75 million the following year, and amounting to $150 million over the period from 1983 to 1987.[3] Nevertheless, in contrast to the largely subservient role of the Honduran armed forces, Panama's military regime took a more Machiavellian and independent-minded approach, regularly supplying weapons in Latin American wars and collecting payoffs for providing intelligence and other services.

Indeed, through much of the twentieth century, Panama stood as Latin America's unparalleled center of intrigue and espionage. Panamanian elites frequently assisted South Americans in *contrabandista* schemes involving the import of luxury items without payment of duties.[4] The U.S. antidrug office, established in 1972, was the first in Central America, predating even the existence of the DEA. For many years Palestinian, Colombian, and Salvadoran

2. See Hersh, "Panama Strongman Said to Trade in Drugs, Arms, and Illicit Money," *New York Times* (United States) (hereafter cited as *NYT* [US]), 2 June 1986, 1A; Kempe, *Divorcing the Dictator*, 301; Shannon, *Desperados*, 165; and Buckley, *Panama*, 19.

3. See Koster and Sánchez, *In the Time*, 204, and "U.S. Probes Panama Strongman on Drug Ties," *Washington Post* (United States) (hereafter cited as *WP* [US]), 11 November 1987, A1.

4. See Clark and Horrock, *Contrabandista*, 81. A Panamanian historian wrote, "Contrabanding and smuggling have in Panama such power we cannot consider it to be a marginal activity practiced by a small group of marginal persons in a clandestine way." Pérez, "Drugs," 150.

revolutionaries might be found in Panama, as might Cuban, U.S., Israeli, and Libyan intelligence agents.[5] During the cold war Panamanians regularly assisted Cubans not simply to circumvent the U.S. embargo but to transfer U.S. high-technology items to the Castro regime, some of which were then sold to the Soviet bloc for substantial profit.[6]

Former Panamanian vice president Ricardo Arias Calderón termed Panama a "transactional" society, and one academic has noted that Panamanian entrepreneurs have traditionally sought "quick short-term profits in businesses which require little initial capital or investment."[7] Even in the post–cold war era, plots, schemes, and rackets have abounded, many tied, directly or indirectly, to the drug trade. Certain bankers and lawyers have eagerly helped clients maneuver through the country's lax legal provisions and inadequate enforcement, avoiding foreign taxes, setting up shell corporations, creating doctored financial statements, and secreting the illegal earnings of kidnappers, drug traffickers, and white-collar criminals alike.[8] Although Panama has never been an industrial powerhouse, by the 1980s its busy import-export trade, coupled with the extensive underworld contacts of military and business elites, stimulated the passage of significant quantities of the precursor chemicals needed by South American cocaine producers.[9]

Some—referring to the highly profitable trade in dealing and transshipping weapons—have dubbed the country an "arms bazaar."[10] Panamanian flags of convenience have been extensively conferred to foreign vessels, bringing Panama considerable income and a merchant fleet of about eleven thousand, but also adding to the roll call of Panamanian ships found to be transporting drugs.[11] Moreover, Panamanian visas and passports have sometimes been sold to criminals, including the Italian mafia, as well as to émigrés from China, Taiwan, Cuba, and other countries.[12] In 1996 the director of immigration noted a brisk trade in forged passports, something of such benefit to drug organizations that a leading judicial official termed Panamanian citizenship "in the hands of narcotics traffickers."[13]

As one Panamanian academic observed, his has been a country of very lenient laws with an indulgent tolerance for the maladministration of public funds.[14] Typically, the government has welcomed exiled political and military leaders, various of whom had absconded with immense

5. For the Colombian M-19's extensive Panama connections, see Murillo, *Noriega Mess*, 376–82. For a meeting in Panama between members of the Chicago street gang, El Rukns, with Libyan officials to plan terrorism in the United States for pay, see *United States v. McAnderson*, 914 F.2d 934.

6. See the statement by U.S. assistant secretary of state Elliott Abrams, in U.S. House, *Situation in Panama*. See also Shannon, *Desperados*, 165; Koster and Sánchez, *In the Time*, 145; and "Strongman Said to Trade," 1A.

7. Arias Calderón, "Panama," 329; Pérez, "Drugs," 151.

8. For more on Panamanian shell companies, see *INCSR* (1998), 164; Dinges, *Our Man in Panama*, 361; Koster and Sánchez, *In the Time*, 284–85; and "Panama's Banks Remain a Conduit for Cocaine Traffickers' Billions," *WP* (US), 1 August 1996, A18 . By the mid-1990s in Russia the word "panamá" signified a corporation created for illegal purposes. "Panamá podría tener otro Noriega si no se limpia de 'narcodelitos,'" *LP* (PA), 8 April 1996, 1A.

9. See U.S. Department of State, *International Narcotics Control Strategy Report* (hereafter cited as *INCSR*) (1988), 146, and Strong, *Whitewash*, 122.

10. See "Panama Gains Reputation as Bazaar for Central American Weapons," Reuters, 19 April 2000, and Dinges, *Our Man in Panama*, 117–18. Reflective of this trade, Panamanian companies have been deeply involved in many arms ventures, including the U.S. government's efforts to ship weapons in the 1930s to Britain and in the 1980s to Iran. "Panama Still a Conduit for Cocaine Profits," *WP* (US), 20 September 1993, A1. As early as 1948, during the Colombian civil war, Panamanian arms traffickers were grossing sixty thousand dollars a month. Koster and Sánchez, *In the Time*, 54–55.

11. See Murillo, *Noriega Mess*, 666; "How the Cocaine Is Coming in This Time," *NYT* (US), 5 November 1989, 4; and *United States v. Pretelt*, 939 F.2d 233.

12. See Murillo, *Noriega Mess*, 673; "Nacionalidad panameña está en manos de narcos: Márquez," *LP* (PA), 6 September 1996, 2A; and "Narcos usan pasaportes panameños," *LP* (PA), 21 April 1996, 5A.

13. "Nacionalidad panameña," 2A.

14. Murillo, *Noriega Mess*, 83.

amounts. Reza Shah Pahlavi of Iran, Fulgencio Batista of Cuba, Juan Perón of Argentina, Abdalá Bucaram Ortíz of Ecuador, Haitian dictator Raoul Cédras, ex-chief of Haitian intelligence Philippe Biamby, intelligence director Vladimiro Montesinos of Peru, and former Guatemalan president Jorge Serrano Elías all moved to Panama.[15] Since the government has not been vigilant in excluding people on the run, fugitives have frequently hidden out in Panama, sometimes after payoffs to officials.[16]

Traditionally, an oligarchy, loosely known as Panama's "twenty families," thoroughly dominated Panamanian society—economically, socially, and politically. Many of the bankers, lawyers, developers, insurers, and others who have profited from Panama's various economic booms have been drawn from this social elite. Moreover, numerous wealthy or influential Panamanian citizens or residents have become enmeshed in incidents and allegations regarding the drug trade. Before becoming president, Guillermo Endara served as lawyer, director, and board secretary of Interbanco, a Panama City bank founded by a Colombian tied to members of the Cali and the Medellín cartels. Endara's law firm also created front companies allegedly used by Cuban American kingpins Augusto Guillermo Falcón and Salvador Maglutta to launder $2.4 billion.[17] Yet another prominent political figure, Rogelio Cruz Ríos, served as legal adviser and board secretary to First Interamericas Bank, a Panama City bank founded by Cali kingpin Gilberto Rodríguez Orejuela. Although Panamanian authorities closed First Interamericas in 1985, Cruz is said to have ensured the following year that $7 million in deposits were returned to Rodríguez. After accusations that Attorney General Cruz had freed a dozen drug suspects and perhaps as much as $62 million in funds frozen from companies or individuals that the DEA had identified as linked to the Cali cartel, he was forced to resign in 1992. Although he was eventually found guilty of abuse of authority and prohibited from holding public office, he became a leading criminal-defense lawyer.[18]

One particular problem has been the symbiotic relationship in which Panamanian elites have been eager to take "easy" money to serve as directors, treasurers, or attorneys for banks, corporations, or shell companies, while traffickers and launderers have been eager to recruit them to serve in those positions to help legitimize their financial dealings. When connections with the drug trade have surfaced, the elites have professed to have no knowledge and no responsibility for daily business dealings. One

15. See "Prófugos buscan refugio en Panamá," *LP* (PA), 22 July 2002, 21; "El paraíso fiscal panameño," *Siglo Veintiuno* (Guatemala) (hereafter cited as *SV* [GU]), 9 March 2002, 5; and "Sunny Playground of Deposed Dictators," *Guardian* (United Kingdom), 7 August 1996, 9.

16. For an article alleging that at least one hundred fugitives from Colombia, Costa Rica, Cuba, Ecuador, Guatemala, Haiti, Mexico, Nicaragua, Peru, and other countries were living in Panama, see "Panamá, refugio de los delincuentes," *LP* (PA), 22 July 2002, 1A. In 1984 Panama granted asylum to six Spanish separatists from Basque Homeland and Liberty (ETA), apparently a favor by Noriega to the Spanish and French governments. Murillo, *Noriega Mess*, 391–92.

17. See "Panama: Dirty Business as Usual," *WP* (US), 28 July 1991, C1, and "Endara pudo haber ayudado a narcos según revista de E.U.," *LP* (PA), 1 December 1991, 1A. Labeled a drug kingpin by prosecutors, Falcón was indicted for importing 75 tons of cocaine to the United States, and the government sought forfeiture of extensive Florida real estate and more than $2 billion in alleged drug profits. Although the Falcón-Magluta organization, which the government estimated controlled gross assets of $55 billion, hired hit men to eliminate various possible witnesses to cocaine trafficking, Magluta was eventually convicted of money laundering and obstruction of justice and sentenced to more than 150 years in prison. See *Ramirez v. United States*, 2009 U.S. Dist. LEXIS 117570; *Magluta v. United States Federal Bureau of Prisons*, 2009 U.S. Dist. LEXIS 49170; and *Falcon v. United States Bureau of Prisons*., 852 F. Supp. 1413.

18. See "Cruz critica a la Corte por no resolver denuncia," *LP* (PA), 30 January 2004, 3A; "Panama's Attorney General Faces Drug Charges," *WP* (US), 30 December 1992, A16; and "Acusan de nuevo por abusos al fiscal auxiliar Herrera," *LP* (PA), 20 November 1991, 28A. Cruz claimed that, while serving on Interamerica's board, he did not know that majority shareholder Gilberto Rodríguez Orejuela was a leading trafficker.

case in point occurred when Mayor Alfredo Alemán, presidential adviser and head of the central bank, was forced to resign for business dealings that intersected with those of traffickers.[19] Foreign minister Ricardo Arias Calderón had been president of a company that owned more than a fifth of the stock of the Banco Agro Industrial y Comercial de Panamá (Banaico), which accepted large deposits for various traffickers, including from the Cali cartel, and collapsed after $50 million disappeared from its accounts. A U.S. official later commented, "Banaico was a money-laundering operation masquerading as a bank. As long as millions of dollars flowing through maintained the capital flow, it looked all right. When the flow stopped, it collapsed."[20]

Another important dynamic in Panamanian society involved the military coup of 1968, which empowered officers from the lower classes. During the dictatorship, members of the armed forces had looked to join those capitalizing on the country's licit and illicit economic activity. For National Guard officers, this meant becoming involved in the fencing of stolen goods and the supply of luxury items from abroad, while evading the country's tariffs.[21] In a natural progression toward ever more lucrative criminal undertakings, assisting drug traffickers was a sideline that grew to overwhelm the other, earlier, criminal initiatives.

Whether through old or new elites, transnational criminal organizations have found Panamanian society to be readily penetrable, with bankers, executives, and officials offering inviting targets. As Rodrigo Arosemena, former director of Panama's Customs Service, observed in 1991, "The truth is there are a lot of people in the system protecting and actually helping narco-traffickers." Fifteen years later, little had changed, with U.S. officials commenting, "The use of bribery and coercion in the drug trade contribute [*sic*] to pervasive public corruption and undermine [*sic*] . . . [Panama's] criminal justice system." That providing assistance in the drug trade has long been a lucrative means to gain assets, climb the social scale, or enjoy luxuries was brought into sharp relief for Panamanians in late 2009 when Mexican authorities arrested four, including the cousin of President Ricardo Martinelli Berrocal, on charges of transporting profits for a Mexican cartel.[22]

In addition, in Panama, as elsewhere in Central America, vulnerable institutions and laws drafted without organized crime in mind have stood out as bridge-favoring factors, contributing significantly to the flourishing of transnational crime. During the military regime and thereafter, those engaged in shady undertakings took advantage of a weak judicial system in which the trafficking of influence and other forms of corruption had thrived and that generally levied only the most modest of penalties.[23] A constitutional privilege against nationals being extradited to any foreign country contributed to the view among elites that they were quite unlikely to be penalized severely for crimes, so long as they cultivated positive relations with influential military officers. With the administration of justice slow, overloaded, and prone to

19. A federal grand jury indicted Trans Latin Air, which Aléman partly owned, for assisting Colombian traffickers to purchase a plane.

20. Quote from "Panama's Banks Remain," A18; Pérez, "Drugs," 155; "Banaico: Un lavador de dinero con fachada de banco," *LP* (PA), 3 August 1996, 2A; "Scandal Sours U.S. Ties with Panama Adviser Accused of Drug Links," *Miami Herald* (United States) (hereafter cited as *MH* [US]), 10 June 1996, 1A.

21. Murillo, *Noriega Mess*, 250.

22. "Cocaine Is Again Surging Out of Panama," *NYT* (US), 13 August 1991, 1A; quote from *INCSR* (2006), 158. See also "Fiscal sigue caso de Ramón Martinelli," *LP* (PA), 3 December 2009, 6A; "Otro detenido en el caso de Ramón Martinelli," *LP* (PA), 6 December 2009, 5A.

23. By the twenty-first century, penalties for international narcotics trafficking stood at eight to ten years in prison, with money laundering five to twelve years. "Panameño encararía cadena perpetua," *LP* (PA), 30 January 2007, 6A. Inmates rarely served even half of lengthy sentences, something that occasioned public complaints. See "Hay que revisar la pena máxima en Panamá," *LP* (PA), 23 July 2002, 9A.

oversights, corruption, and manipulation, the drug trade was poised to soar, as cartels began to look into regional opportunities.

Over the last three decades of the twentieth century Panama thus became, in the words of the U.S. Department of State, "a crossroads for transnational crime, such as drug trafficking, money laundering, illicit arms sales, and alien smuggling."[24] This chapter explores Panama's role as one of the region's most pivotal bridge states. We address the following questions: What aspects of Panamanian society have made the country a vital point for drug transshipment? How has the Panamanian government confronted drug trafficking? To what extent did Manuel Noriega's career shape Panama's role in the drug trade? Which organizations have been most active in the country, and where, and what routes and methods have they employed?

Other Notable Bridge-Favoring Factors Relevant to Panama

Geography

Perhaps no country has been more closely tied to its geography than Panama, a territory that might never have attained sovereignty had it not occupied the narrow base of the Central American isthmus. With respect to the drug trade, the most outstanding feature of Panamanian geography has simply been its position flanking Colombia. As with Guatemala and Mexico, so Panama's proximity to Colombia has very much shaped its role in international drug trafficking. Criminal syndicates scheming to move drugs from Colombia to market have long been attracted to air, sea, and ground routes departing from Panama.

Nevertheless, the Colombian border is but one highly relevant aspect of Panama's geography. The country also has strikingly lengthy Caribbean and Pacific shores, totaling more than 1,700 miles of coastline, far more than any other Central American state. Moreover, bays and inlets, coves and beaches, and fully a dozen deep-water ports have provided traffickers with a plethora of opportunities to elude authorities and smuggle cargoes in and out of the country, as has the fact that as early as 1971 Panama had more than a hundred largely uncontrolled airstrips.[25] These bridge-favoring factors alone would have enticed traffickers, even had the country not been located next door to Colombia.

Panama's more than 1,500 islands are yet another geographic feature meriting special attention. Throughout Central America maritime traffickers have been drawn to archipelagos. Like the Belize cayes and the Honduran Islas de la Bahía, so Panama's island chains, lying off both coasts, have frequently factored into geotactics. On the Pacific side lie the Islas de las Perlas, within easy reach of Colombia and central Panama, including the canal and Panama City. On the Caribbean, the San Blás archipelago contains more than 350 islands close offshore. The administrative unit known as the Comarca de San Blás includes a narrow coastal strip extending from the Caribbean border between Panama and Colombia about 135 miles along the northern shore. The islands and accompanying territory form Kuna Yala, a semiautonomous region inhabited primarily by about thirty-five thousand largely poverty-stricken indigenous Kunas.[26]

Then, of course, there is that extraordinary constructed feature of the Panamanian landscape—the Panama Canal. Completed in 1903 under U.S. government supervision and financing, this fifty-mile waterway has been of transcendent importance to Panama, a unique national asset that has helped it to become

24. *INCSR* (2000), 188.

25. Dinges, *Our Man in Panama*, 336.

26. According to the Panamanian Ministry of Health, in 2002 more than 86 percent in Kuna Yala lived in extreme poverty and more than 95 percent in general poverty. "Pobreza y desnutrición en Kuna Yala," *LP* (PA), 28 July 2002, 7A.

Latin America's chief commercial crossroads. In 1977 the United States agreed by century's end to relinquish its historical supervision of the canal, along with the surrounding military bases. With the canal's reversion to Panama, the government gained soaring revenues, as well as an infrastructure bonanza in the heart of the country: roads, docks, airstrips, a railroad, power and water-treatment plants, and a wealth of other buildings, including schools and hospitals.[27] At the same time, however, drug shipments have passed through the canal in a range of vessels.[28]

Economy

Transnational criminals have been attracted to the most poverty-stricken states in Central America, such as Honduras, and the most well-off, such as Costa Rica. In fact, drug-transshipment schemes can readily take advantage of poor and wealthy bridge states alike. Panamanian economic vitality has attracted traffickers, just as it has foreign investors, who have flocked to the country for many years from Asia, Europe, and the Americas.[29] Panama's extensive commercial activity, particularly in Panama City and the Colón Free Zone, home to most of its many air- and sea-freight companies, has camouflaged cocaine transshipment to the United States and Europe, the transit of precursor chemicals, and the laundering of hundreds of millions in drug profits.[30]

The free trade zone, in particular, merits further comment. As the twentieth century progressed, Panama developed an enormous duty-free port at Colón, the country's second largest city. Situated at the canal's Caribbean mouth, this port has grown to become second in size only to Hong Kong. The more than three thousand businesses located within the Free Zone's walled enclave have come to employ fifteen thousand Panamanians, and by 2009 had reached $16 billion in trade, contributing to about 15 percent of the gross domestic product. The free trade zone has not only greatly stimulated the Panamanian economy but provided incomparable opportunities for traffickers. In addition to exporting Central and South American products, Free Zone businesses have funneled luxury and consumer goods into Latin American markets. Many hundreds of shipping containers a day have routinely entered or exited Free Zone premises, often completely overwhelming antidrug controls and thus providing an array of options for smugglers. Furthermore, because about a fifth of the transactions typically occur in cash,

27. Canal revenues are determined by transit tonnage. During the transition to Panamanian control the United States increased its annual annuity to Panama from $2.3 million to $10 million. By 2006, with the Panama Canal Management Authority (PCMA) in control, the average ship's toll had reached sixty-seven thousand dollars. From 1904 to 1999 Panama earned $1.5 billion from U.S. payments. From 2000 to 2009 the PCMA collected $10.8 billion, of which $3.27 billion went to government revenues. The 190 million tons of cargo and thirteen thousand ships traversing the canal annually in the 1990s had risen to about 300 million tons carried by fifteen thousand ships in 2007 and 2008. See "Voters in Panama Hold Key to Future of Canal's Locks," *WP* (US), 21 October 2006, A10; "U.S. Not Eager to Participate in Panama's Canal Party," *The Daily Yomiuri* (Japan), 22 November 1999, 14A; and "Panama Canal Forecasts Drop in Shipping Traffic," *Nica Times* (Costa Rica) (hereafter cited as *NT* [CR]), 30 January 2009, N6.

28. For instance, Bolivian cocaine traveled to Europe via Africa, Chile, and the Panama Canal. Strong, *Whitewash*, 125. In 2008 federal authorities in Brooklyn broke up a ring that had been hiding cocaine on ships traversing the canal en route from China to New York. "Frustran plan para introducir droga a EU," *LP* (PA), 11 January 2008, 5A.

29. By the mid-1980s direct U.S. investment, most prominently by the United Fruit Company, had reached higher per capita levels in Panama than in any other Latin American state. See Dinges, *Our Man in Panama*, 41 and 331; Murillo, *Noriega Mess*, 244; and Ropp, *Panamanian Politics*, 108–13. The $2.2 billion investment by American businesses equaled $1,325 per capita, or more than twenty-five times more U.S. investment per capita than in Mexico.

30. The U.S. government stated of the numerous deposits: "hundreds of millions of dollars of which are almost certainly narcotics related." "DEA se reúne con empresarios de Zona Libre," *LP* (PA), 13 January 1994, 3A. Quote from *INCSR* (1993), 176.

these businesses have provided extraordinary opportunities to launder drug profits.[31]

Even apart from Free Zone commerce, Panama has long been the most globalized and cosmopolitan state in Central America, with vibrant ethnic communities, steady immigration from people of different classes, and many more foreign contacts than found elsewhere in the region. By 1990 Panama City had grown into one of Central America's largest metropolitan areas, and Tocumen (formerly Torrijos) Airport, just outside the city limits, amounted to the busiest regional air hub.[32] Situated at the Pacific terminus of the canal, Panama's capital experienced a late twentieth-century construction boom unparalleled in the region, rapidly growing upward as well as outward. No other Central American capital had the skyline of Panama City or its roster of hotels and casinos. Indeed, by the turn of the millennium Panamanians could claim to have one of the most modern urban areas in the Caribbean basin.

Through all of this development, a large, vigorous, and never especially scrupulous banking establishment in Panama City has attended to the financial needs of Panamanians and foreigners alike. From 1971 on, Panama has welcomed foreign banks, and, alone in Latin America, it has gained global renown as a truly international center of finance, known for its use of the U.S. dollar as currency, its highly restrictive business-secrecy laws, and its laissez-faire regulatory environment.[33] As early as 1986 Panama City hosted fully 121 banks, employing nearly ten thousand people, with an annual payroll exceeding $200 million.[34] Total deposits reached $45 billion in 1987, dipped to $12 billion by the time the 1989 invasion capped two years of social instability and economic sanctions, but then two years later had climbed back to $16 billion.[35] Over the years certain Panamanian banks have, alongside many legitimate deposits, helped clients hide funds to evade tax or other authorities.[36] Such banking services have enticed criminal enterprises, including drug traffickers, to open numerous accounts.

However, while Panama's role in the drug trade has boosted the banking industry, contributed to an unparalleled construction boom, and injected hard currency into the economy, these developments have not brought wealth to the lowest classes. Drug rings recruiting locals to serve as mules, enforcers, off-loaders, and assassins have found recurring severe unemployment, as well as unequal income distribution markedly exacerbated by years of military rule, to be a boon.[37] In fact, right alongside significant

31. "Droga: Libre de impuesto," *LP* (PA), 12 October 2003, 6A; "Panama Still a Conduit," A1.

32. Early in the twenty-first century, annual air traffic via Panama exceeded 2 million passengers, and by 2005 2.7 million passengers, encompassing 58,216 planes, and 100,063 tons of air cargo. "Tráfico aéreo de pasajeros creció en 14%," *LP* (PA), 1 May 2006, 8A.

33. "Paraíso fiscal," 5. Torrijos overhauled Panama's banking laws to attract offshore cash by not requiring depositors to furnish names or addresses and by penalizing bank employees who violated depositors' secrecy with fines and prison terms. Even the Colombian black market then recognized the worth of Panamanian bank secrecy, valuing more highly checks drawn on Panamanian accounts. *United States v. Awan*, 988 F.2d at 1418. For the history of the U.S. dollar financial policy, dating to 1904, see Pérez, "Drugs," 155–56, and MacDonald, *Mountain High*, 100.

34. See "Senate Probe Says Panama Cleaning Up on Laundering," *Chicago Tribune* (United States) (hereafter cited as *CT* [US]), 15 June 1986, 14C, and Pérez, "Drugs," 156.

35. "Cocaine Is Again Surging," 1A.

36. Buckley, *Panama*, 260. See also "Paraíso fiscal," 5. Of 392 accounts investigated in 2004 for possible money laundering, officials reported that 40, containing approximately $10 million, were linked to ex-Nicaraguan president Arnoldo Alemán, and 14, containing $50 million, to ex-Guatemalan president Alfonso Portillo. "Investigan 392 cuentas por blanqueo de capitales," *LP* (PA), 21 January 2004, 1A. Panama's former president, Ernesto Pérez Balladares, was found to hold $12 million in 1 account and more than $20 million in total, all sums deposited during his presidency that he neglected to report on the assets list filed upon leaving office. "Pérez B. deberá explicar origen de más de 20 millones," *LP* (PA), 7 January 2004, 1A.

37. See the statement by drug prosecutor Patricio Candanedo, linking recruitment of mules to high unemployment. "Costas son vulnerables al narcotráfico, dicen autoridades," *LP* (PA), 27 July 2002, 4A. See also generally "Narcotraficantes eran protegidos por Noriega: Rodrigo Arosemena," *LP* (PA), 17 July 1990, 1A. Police in 1997

pockets of mounting wealth, Panama City has long been plagued by some of the most violent and lawless slums of any Central American metropolis. Drugs have circulated freely through poverty-stricken neighborhoods in its Curundú, Calidonia, and Chorillo sections, as well as in Santa Ana and San Miguelito.[38] The city has regularly been inundated by a veritable tide of narcotics, accompanied by a backflow of profits from local sales.

From time to time all of the Central American economies have stagnated under the burden of falling commodities prices, coupled with the high-interest payments due private and public lending institutions. Indeed, few states accumulated higher foreign debt payments per capita than did Panama under its military regime. Thus, Panama has not wholly avoided regional economic downturns, and traffickers have been quick to capitalize on this.[39] By the same token, the country's commercial strength has enabled it to emerge from regional slumps with less anguish than many of its neighbors have experienced. Yet in this regard Panama's economic development, especially its vibrant free trade zone and enterprising banking sector, have presented to drug rings a singular set of incentives that have very much encouraged them to include Panama in their trafficking schemes.

Types of Drugs Trafficked Through Panama

The Marijuana Trade in Panama

As early as the 1960s marijuana consumers had come to value Panama Red, a strain cultivated particularly in Las Perlas archipelago and especially in its large Isla del Rey.[40] But although some Panamanian marijuana has been exported, usually to the United States, cannabis plots scattered through the inland mountains have primarily targeted domestic consumption.[41] On occasion, the military regime suppressed marijuana production, sometimes to impress the public or U.S. officials and occasionally to provide cover for the lucrative joint ventures that military leaders had brokered with leading international traffickers.

Even more important, smugglers have frequently brought shipments of high-quality marijuana from La Guajira and other notable zones of Colombian production through Panamanian territorial waters or into Panama to be stored temporarily and then transported to market.[42] Certainly, Panamanian vessels have been deeply involved in marijuana trafficking. For example, in 1987 U.S. authorities intercepted the Panamanian tugboat *Coloso II*, which then tried to discard 5,818 kilos of marijuana into the Caribbean, and in a controlled delivery off Hawaii the next year they seized almost 16

identified two prominent Panama City youth gangs, Amor de Madre and Sangre Negra, as supplying killers-for-hire to trafficking organizations. "Dos nuevas bandas operan en la capital," *LP* (PA), 23 May 1997, 4A. By 2002 16 percent of all citizens of working age were unemployed, with unemployment in Colón Province at more than 20 percent and in Panamá Province at 16.4 percent. See "Violencia y desempleo en Panamá," *LP* (PA), 7 August 2002, 13A, and "Crece el disempleo," *LP* (PA), 16 July 2002, 1A. At the end of the dictatorship Panama trailed only El Salvador in the difference between the income distribution of the richest fifth and poorest fifth of society. See Murillo, *Noriega Mess*, 928.

38. See, for instance, "Decomisan 98 kilos de droga y caen nueve narcos," *LP* (PA), 28 April 2005, 6A, and "Detienen a cuatro adultos y dos menores que tenían una subametralladora Uzi," *LP* (PA), 18 December 1998, 4A. For a large Tocumen Airport seizure, see "Aduanas captura 198 kilos de cocaína que iban hacia Haití," *LP* (PA), 17 July 1990, 1A.

39. In addition, the economy faltered from the extensive sanctions imposed by the U.S. government on the Noriega regime between March 1988 and December 1989.

40. See "Incautan 385 kilos de cocaína," *La Prensa* (Honduras) (hereafter cited as *LP* [HO]), 24 September 1999, 75A.

41. For a period U.S. soldiers in the Canal Zone supplied marijuana to other military personnel stationed elsewhere. Murillo, *Noriega Mess*, 125. Indeed, by the early 1970s narcotics cases accounted for about a third of the Canal Zone prison population. Tully, *Secret War*, 134.

42. See "Incautan 150 libras de marihuana en Chiriquí," *LP* (PA), 25 June 2001, 8A.

Fig. 6.1 Marijuana seizures in Panama, 1982–1995

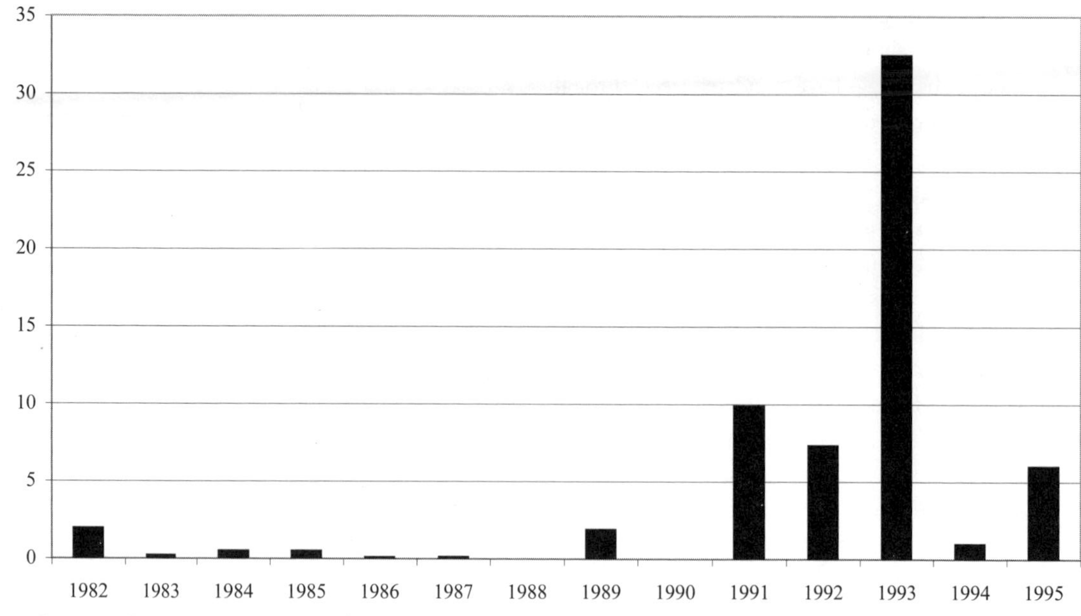

Sources: DEA, *Resources, Panama* (2000), 3; *INCSR* (1988), 149; *INCSR* (1990), 202; *INCSR* (1991), 187; *INCSR* (1994), 172; *INCSR* (1997), 160; *INCSR* (1999), 190; *INCSR* (2007), 19; *INCSR* (2008), 185; *INCSR* (2009), 467; *INCSR* (2010), 498.

tons of marijuana off the Panamanian coastal freighter *Christina M.*[43] The deposing of Manuel Noriega in 1989 by no means ended the maritime marijuana-transshipment trade: authorities soon captured more than 1.8 tons of marijuana off the tugboat *Concord*, arriving in Pascagoula, Mississippi, from Panama.[44]

In general, however, the post-Noriega governments have moved more consistently against the marijuana trade. Among the significant eradication efforts, authorities in 1993 eliminated more than sixty hectares of cannabis on the Colombian border. Indeed, periodically, officials have destroyed considerable quantities of marijuana from Las Perlas and elsewhere.[45] Furthermore, as figs. 6.1 and 6.2 illustrate, after Noriega's departure, exponentially more Colombian marijuana has been intercepted. In the last five years of the dictatorship, marijuana seizures totaled 0.67 tons, yet between 1991 and 1993 Panamanian authorities captured almost 50 tons, and they repeated the feat between 1996 and 1998.

Truly substantial seizures of Panamanian and Colombian marijuana continued in the new century, with 20.74 tons confiscated between 2004 and 2007, including some of the largest marijuana busts in the region.[46] For instance, in

43. See *United States v. Atkins*, 923 F.2d 650, and *United States v. Corpus*, 882 F.2d 546. For the substitution of marijuana in Panama for Colombian marijuana after Colombian authorities in 1986 seized a vessel due to deliver drugs to Louisiana, see *United States v. Valdez*, 861 F.2d at 430.

44. *United States v. Andrews*, 22 F.3d 1328.

45. See "Panamá y EU erradicaron cultivos de coca en Darién," *LP* (PA), 14 September 1996, 4A; "Panamá, puente para el narcotráfico," *LP* (PA), 24 October 2004, 6A; "Decomisan 240 kilos de marihuana," *LP* (PA), 28 December 1998, 8A; and "SAN [Servicio Aéreo Nacional] destituye veintisiete hectáreas de marihuana," *LP* (PA), 4 January 1999, 1A. In 1999 authorities eradicated 120,000 marijuana plants on Isla del Rey. "Incautan 385 kilos," 75A. Again, in 2004, 19,900 such plants were destroyed there. "Queman cultivos de marihuana," *LP* (PA), 1 October 2004, 2A.

46. For seizures from 2000 to 2004, see "Decomisan 900 kilos de marihuana," *LP* (PA), 3 October 2000, 2A; "Decomisan mil 734 kilos de marihuana en Bugaba," *LP* (PA), 16 March 2002, 8A; and "Decomisan 751 kilos de marihuana," *LP* (PA), 26 October 2004, 3A.

Fig. 6.2 Marijuana seizures in Panama, 1996–2009

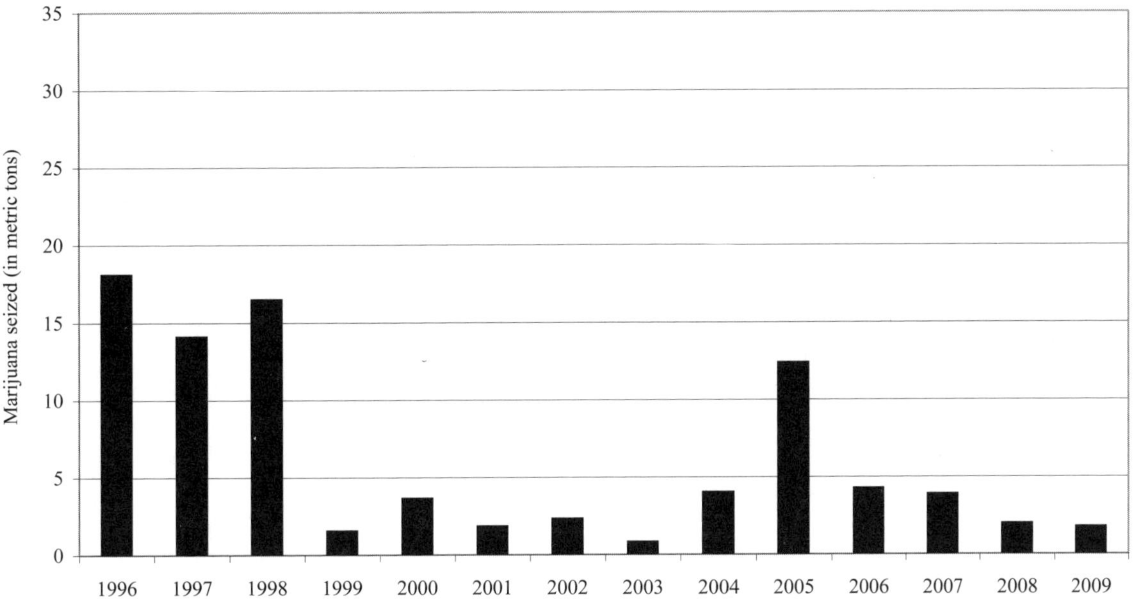

Sources: DEA, *Resources, Panama* (2000), 3; *INCSR* (1988), 149; *INCSR* (1990), 202; *INCSR* (1991), 187; *INCSR* (1994), 172; *INCSR* (1997), 160; *INCSR* (1999), 190; *INCSR* (2007), 19; *INCSR* (2008), 185; *INCSR* (2009), 467; *INCSR* (2010), 498.

2000 authorities found 900 kilograms of marijuana on a fishing boat off Isla Pacheca in Las Perlas. After a 1,734-kilo seizure in 2002, one official noted that Colombian guerrillas were supporting marijuana fields near the border, with the product exported via Panama. In 2004 antidrug personnel discovered 751 kilos near the border town of Río Sereno. The following year saw at least six marijuana busts of 300–500 kilos, a development that the Judicial Technical Police (PTJ) attributed to overproduction in Colombia and expanding international markets.[47] In fact, although earlier Colombian transshipment via Panama had been directed largely to North American and European markets, by the twenty-first century, Panama had become not only a market in its own right but a clearinghouse for overland deliveries north into Central America.[48]

Accounts of these 2005 and 2006 seizures suggest just how widespread Panamanian marijuana trafficking had become.[49] In one case the canal police seized more than 335 kilos near Veracruz, just southwest of Panama City. Shortly thereafter, Panamanian authorities captured 334 kilos from two Colombians and a Costa Rican, in Pacora on the Río Chico. Later that same month, transit police at Ocú on the Pan-American Highway stopped a truck carrying 462 kilos of marijuana, while national police in

47. "Aumentan decomisos de marihuana," *LP* (PA), 29 November 2005, 1A.

48. In 2005 the Paso Canoas border post intercepted sixty-two kilos of cocaine headed into Costa Rica, and fully four tons of marijuana. "La frontera tico-panameña continúa desatendida," *LP* (PA), 26 September 2005, 1A.

49. For 2005 and 2006 seizures, see "Policía se incauta marihuana," *LP* (PA), 2 November 2005, 5A; "Capturado un segundo cargamento de marihuana," *LP* (PA), 3 November 2005, 4A; "Policía decomisa marihuana," *LP* (PA), 8 November 2005, 10A; "Frustran entrada de drogas en Panamá," *LP* (PA), 6 January 2006, 6A; "Autoridades se incautan de treinta toneladas de droga," *LP* (PA), 6 December 2006, 4A; "Autoridades decomisan drogas y tortugas vivas," *LP* (PA), 28 January 2006, 5A; and "PTJ decomisa armas y drogas de la guerrilla colombiana," *LP* (PA), 4 April 2006, 8A.

Chiriquí intercepted a 397-kilo marijuana shipment heading to Paso Canoas for export to Costa Rica. Officials seized 485.2 kilos on a mangrove island off San Buenaventura, near Chimán, and then on New Year's Eve stopped a 367-kilo marijuana shipment that was to be divided between reexport and domestic consumption and that had arrived from Colombia into Playa Leona, twenty miles west of Panama City. Then, in 2006 in Puerto Obaldía on the Caribbean coast, Panamanian police seized almost 400 kilos and arrested five Colombians from an organization trafficking marijuana and endangered species. That same year 150 bales of marijuana that had been destined for reexport to Central America were seized in an arms-for-drugs deal with Colombians from the Fuerzas Armadas Revolucionarias de Colombia (FARC).

By the early twenty-first century additional new challenges had arisen, such as the smuggling of *pegón*—that potent mixture of marijuana, cocaine, and additives such as shoe glue. Cannabis for pegón would often arrive in Panama unprocessed, complete with branches, seeds, and resin, and would then be manufactured into squares for domestic sale and for export. In 2005 Panamanian prosecutor Patricio Candenado reported that authorities had intercepted five pegón shipments heading to Costa Rica and then on to Europe. In another two immense pegón seizures that year authorities confiscated two tons off a speedboat at Playa de Muerto, Jaqué, and a like amount heading to the United States.[50]

Perhaps because so much of Central American cannabis has been consumed at home, observers have often underestimated the magnitude and vitality of the regional marijuana trade and overlooked the considerable law-enforcement resources devoted to curbing it. Panama stands as a case in point. In six years between 1990 and 2008 Panamanian law enforcement actually seized more marijuana than cocaine, including in 1993, when authorities confiscated more than five times as much, and in 1996, when they took more than double.[51]

The Heroin Trade in Panama

While Guatemala has been the only Central American state to grow and export opium, Panama has been the country best situated to traffic Asian and South American heroin. Not only was the military regime tied to international heroin smugglers, but certain members of Panama City's sizable expatriate Chinese population have been linked to Asian traffickers. By the 1980s Chinese criminal organizations were found to be transporting heroin from Southeast Asia into the United States via Panama, a development that occasioned a 1987 Interpol warning.[52] Of crucial importance, Panama City has served as one of Latin America's principal international air hubs. The canal has regularly provided passage for ships from Asia, and vessels have often departed to Europe and North America from the Colón Free Zone. In the 1960s and 1970s one extremely important smuggling route for heroin traffickers crossed the Atlantic from France to the middle of South America—Argentina, Paraguay, or Uruguay—and then proceeded on to the United States, often via Panama.[53]

By the 1990s, however, the transshipment of Asian heroin had paled in importance compared

50. "Panamá, puente," 6A; "Confiscan otros cuatrocientos kilos de pegón," *LP* (PA), 1 March 2005, 5A; "Confiscan dos toneladas de drogas," *LP* (PA), 24 February 2005, 4A; "Decomisan 2.4 toneladas de drogas," *LP* (PA), 25 January 2005, 3A; "Decomisan 170 paquetes de pegón," *LP* (PA), 22 October 2004, 3A; "Decomisan cargamentos de cocaína y marihuana," *LP* (PA), 21 September 2002, 1A; "Policía decomisa marihuana," *LP* (PA), 18 July 2001, 2A.

51. At first, marijuana- and cocaine-smuggling networks active in Central America could be readily differentiated. During the 1990s, however, various syndicates began to traffic both drugs, and sometimes heroin as well. In 1999, for instance, authorities arrested an American, a Panamanian, and six Colombians and seized two speedboats, 10.5 kilos of heroin, and 385 kilos of cocaine. "Decomisan 385 kilos de cocaína," *LP* (HO), 18 September 1999, 24.

52. "Chinese Now Dominate New York Heroin Trade," *NYT* (US), 9 August 1987, 1.

53. Clark and Horrock, *Contrabandista*, 192–93.

Fig. 6.3 Heroin seizures in Panama, 1992–2009

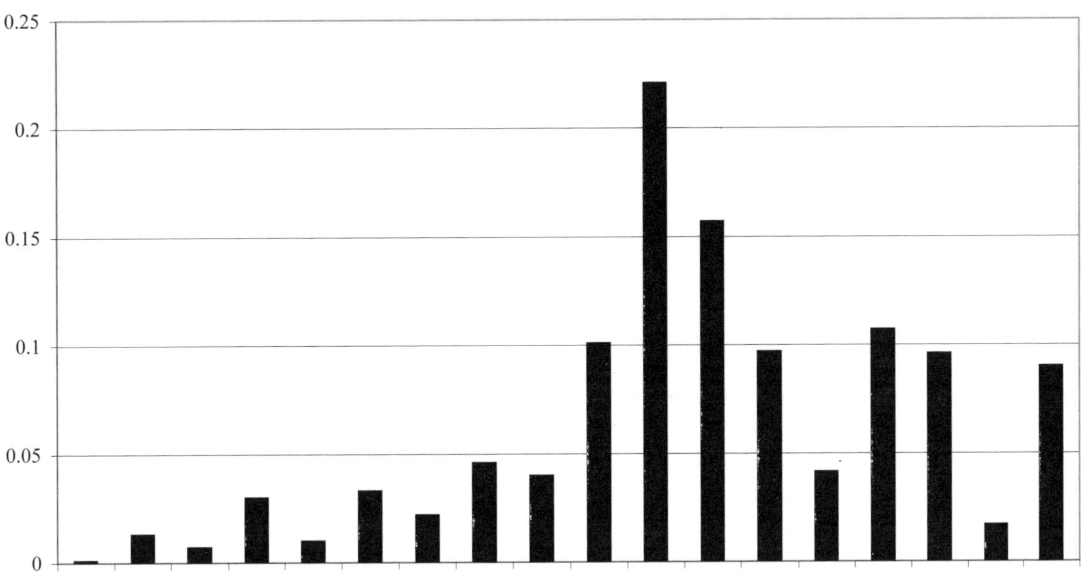

Sources: DEA, *Resources, Panama* (2000), 3; *INCSR* (2007), 19; *INCSR* (2008), 185; *INCSR* (2009), 467; *INCSR* (2010), 498; "Panamá, Puente para el narcotráfico," *LP* (PA), 24 October 2004, 6A; "Agentes antidrogas desmantelan banda que traficaba heroína," *LP* (PA), 4 January 1999, 4A.

to the trafficking of Colombian heroin. As Colombian cartels diversified, heroin transshipment surged throughout Central America, but in no other bridge state did it rise higher or more rapidly than in Panama. As early as 1992 Panamanian authorities seized eight kilos of Colombian heroin.[54] Although the greatest profits have been in exports, drug networks have developed a domestic market as well, useful because considerable quantities have been stored in Panama awaiting shipment to market. Thus, in 1999, after authorities had witnessed an alarming rise in local heroin dealing, Ronaldo Reyna, chief of the PTJ Narcotics, declared, "Heroin is a drug that is beginning to worry us."

Most heroin entering Panama, however, has been heading on toward the North American market. Panamanian trials of heroin smugglers en route to the United States have periodically occurred.[55] From the mid-1990s forward, U.S. prosecutors have brought to trial numerous couriers stopped at various U.S. airports attempting to import heroin via Panama.[56] Drug rings that have become leery of airport security have sometimes opted for overland transit north. For instance, in one week in 2005 Costa Rican police caught a Guatemalan who had just crossed the Panamanian border with 2.3 kilos of heroin in a suitcase, and Panamanian authorities arrested a Colombian trying to export through Paso Canoas two gallons of liquid heroin, hidden inside bottles of automobile oil.[57] As fig. 6.3 illustrates, heroin confiscations in Panama have ebbed and flowed, something

54. *INCSR* (1993), 175.

55. See "Agentes antidrogas desmantelan banda que traficaba heroína," *LP* (PA), 4 January 1999, 4A. For one interesting case, see "Cae con droga secretaria de magistrado," *LP* (PA), 17 May 2005, 1.

56. See, for instance, *United States v. Tenorio*, 69 F.3d 1103; *United States v. Jimenez-Rodriguez*, 1995 U.S. App. LEXIS 33668; *United States v. Torres*, 1996 U.S. App. LEXIS 32767; *United States v. Aguado*, 62 Fed. Appx. 39; *United States v. Rodriguez*, 342 F.3d 296; *United States v. Rodriguez*, 107 Fed. Appx. 295; and *United States v. Matthews*, 181 Fed. Appx. 171.

57. See "Detenido ciudadano guatemalteco," *LP* (PA), 29 May 2005, 3A, and "Un detenido con heroína liquida," *LP* (PA), 25 May 2005, 3A.

true of other Central American states as well. As fig. 1.3 in the introduction shows, however, on various occasions Panamanian seizures have amounted to more than half of the region's total confiscations.[58] By 1998, after a year in which heroin seizures by October had surpassed two and half times the total for 1996 and exceeded the 1995 total by 50 percent, the U.S. State Department was characterizing the country as a major transit and storage point for Colombian heroin-smuggling organizations.[59]

Depending on supply and demand, a kilo of heroin could be worth between eight thousand and twenty thousand dollars per kilo in Panama and one hundred thousand to three hundred thousand per kilo in the United States. With these tremendous smuggling incentives, enterprising heroin traffickers started to move much larger loads through Panama by plane and especially by sea, with shipments frequently emanating from the Colombian cities of Turbo, Pereira, and Medellín. In maritime transport heroin has often been transferred from larger to smaller vessels well out at sea, because smaller boats could more easily approach the coast without attracting attention. Panamanian heroin rings have constructed hidden cellars below beach houses and other residences for temporary storage. Then, the heroin has been packaged and supplied to couriers, who might swallow fifty to a hundred small capsules and fly to the United States on commercial aircraft.[60]

The dynamics of the developing heroin trade in Panama have emerged from a series of significant cases. In 2002 Panamanian authorities made their largest heroin bust to date, 14 kilos from a U.S. plane headed to Mexico, and capped the year with three 8- to 10-kilo heroin seizures, two by customs agents searching raincoats in Colón and overcoats at the Paso Canoas border crossing, and another off a small boat brought by Colombians into Coclé Province on the Pacific coast.[61] The Coclé case turned out to be an arms-for-drugs transaction, and investigators located an underground storage site containing eighty-seven AK-47 weapons and fifty Dranof rifles, as well as more than 700 kilos of heroin, cocaine, and marijuana. The following year Tocumen officials found 13 kilos of heroin hidden in furniture en route from Medellín to Miami.[62] Then, in one of the larger Central American heroin seizures of 2004, Costa Rican police at Paso Canoas stopped a truck headed from the Colón Free Zone to Honduras and discovered 1,039 packets of heroin hidden in the truck's batteries.[63] In 2004 authorities in Amador seized 15 kilos of heroin, ready to be swallowed by couriers, and the following year airport officials searched a group of four Dominicans, finding each to be transporting heroin.[64] That same year, in Operation Jump Start antinarcotics police in four countries arrested fifty-five people and broke up a network shipping heroin and cocaine from Colombia, up the Pacific coast to Panama, then on to the United States via Guatemala. Investigations suggested that the ring had sent a ton of cocaine as well as an average of 100 kilos of heroin annually. The prior year 120 kilos of heroin had been transshipped, hidden in car batteries. In early 2006 New York authorities,

58. See the table in "Tormenta de polvo blanco," *LP* (PA), 11 August 2002, 3A.

59. *INCSR* (1998), 165, 168.

60. Compare the figures in "Detienen a traficantes panameños," *LP* (PA), 28 January 2006, 3A, and "Decomisan heroína pura en Chiriquí," *LP* (PA), 31 October 2004, 9A. Also see drug prosecutor Patricio Candanedo's account in "Tormenta de polvo," 3A.

61. See "Juicio por tráfico de armas," *LP* (PA), 14 October 2005, 6A; "Piden condenar a presuntos narcos," *LP* (PA), 15 October, 2005, 8A; "Se incautan de ocho kilos de heroína en Chiriquí," *LP* (PA), 6 July 2002, 8A; "Los narcos amenazan a aduaneros," *LP* (PA), 2 July 2002, 1A; "Decomisan diez kilos de heroína en playa de Antón," *LP* (PA), 26 June 2002, 4A; and "Tormenta de polvo," 3A.

62. For 2003 heroin busts see, "Decomisan trece kilos de heroína en Tocumen," *LP* (PA), 27 May 2003, 2A, and "Capturan dominicana con heroína," *LP* (PA), 7 October 2003, 5A.

63. See "Decomisan mil treinta y nueve comprimidos de heroína," *LP* (PA), 18 January 2004, 9A.

64. See "Incautan quince kilos de heroína," *LP* (PA), 4 March 2004, 4A; "Dominicanos tratan de introducir droga," *LP* (PA), 10 April 2005, 7A; "Operación internacional desmantela a narcotraficantes," *LP* (PA), 17 February 2005, 6A; and "Narcos libres," *SV* (GU), 17 February 2005, 10.

Fig. 6.4 Cocaine seizures in Panama, 1982–1995

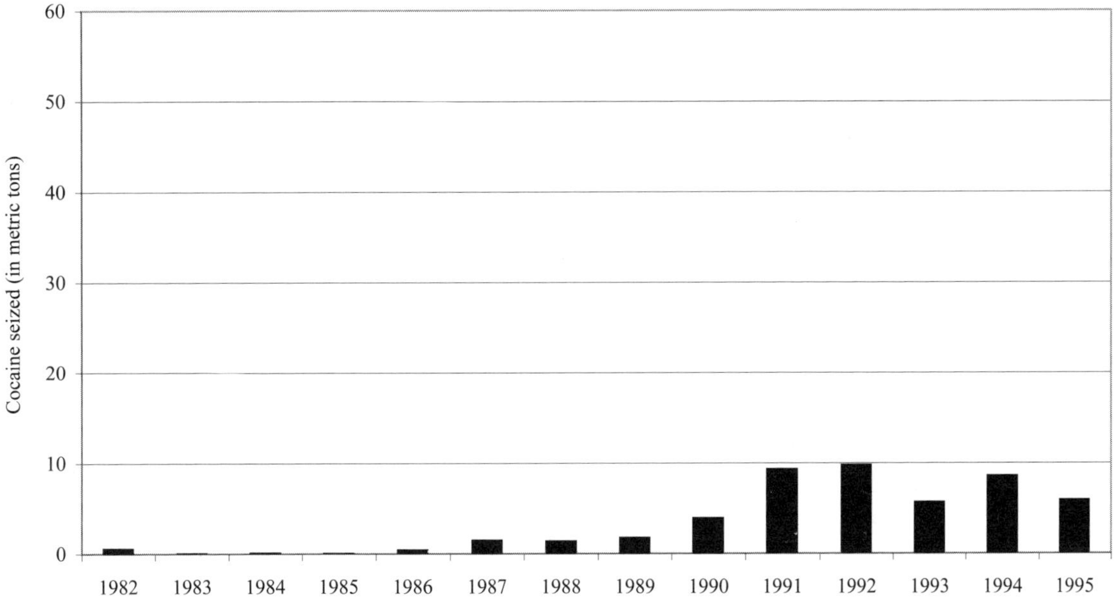

Sources: DEA, *Resources, Panama* (2000), 3; *INCSR* (1991), 187; *INCSR* (1994), 172; *INCSR* (1997), 160; *INCSR* (1999), 190; *INCSR* (2007), 19; *INCSR* (2008), 185; *INCSR* (2009), 467; *INCSR* (2010), 498.

supported by the DEA and PTJ, broke up another major heroin-trafficking ring, arresting twenty, most of them Panamanian or dual Panamanian-U.S. nationals.

The Cocaine Trade in Panama

The quantities of hard drugs interdicted in Panama have clearly attested to the country's status as an extraordinarily prominent bridge state. Alone in Central America, Panama has experienced both notable marijuana trafficking and considerable heroin transit. When authorities began to crack down on pseudoephedrine smuggling, Panama was one of the first states involved and immediately recorded extremely large seizures, including one of 10 tons in 2007.[65] All this reflects the country's myriad array of significant bridge-favoring factors. Nevertheless, as in all the other bridge states of the region, cocaine transit clearly is the most troublesome sector of the drug trade.

As figs. 6.4 and 6.5 illustrate, the quantities of cocaine interdicted under the military regime were much less than those interdicted under the later democratic governments. Over its last five years the Noriega regime seized, on average, about one ton of cocaine. Between 1990 and 1994 Panamanian authorities captured 32 tons of cocaine, heroin, crack, and hashish.[66] Then, from 1994 to 1999 officials destroyed just over 100 tons of drugs of all varieties.[67] The democratic governments seized an average of 7.47 tons of cocaine from 1990 to 1994, 6.14 from 1995 to 1999, and 6.34 from 2000 to 2004. Thereafter, seizures skied to an average of more than 54 tons from 2007 to 2009.

Furthermore, alone in Central America, Panama has witnessed repeated efforts to grow

65. "Hallan diez toneladas de sustancia base del éxtasis," *LP* (PA), 17 March 2007, 8A.

66. "El narcotráfico ha aumentado 'escandalosamente' en Panamá," *LP* (PA), 5 January 1997, 1A.

67. "'Mini carteles' colombianos operan desde Panamá," *LP* (PA), 10 January 2000, 5A.

Fig. 6.5 Cocaine seizures in Panama, 1996–2010

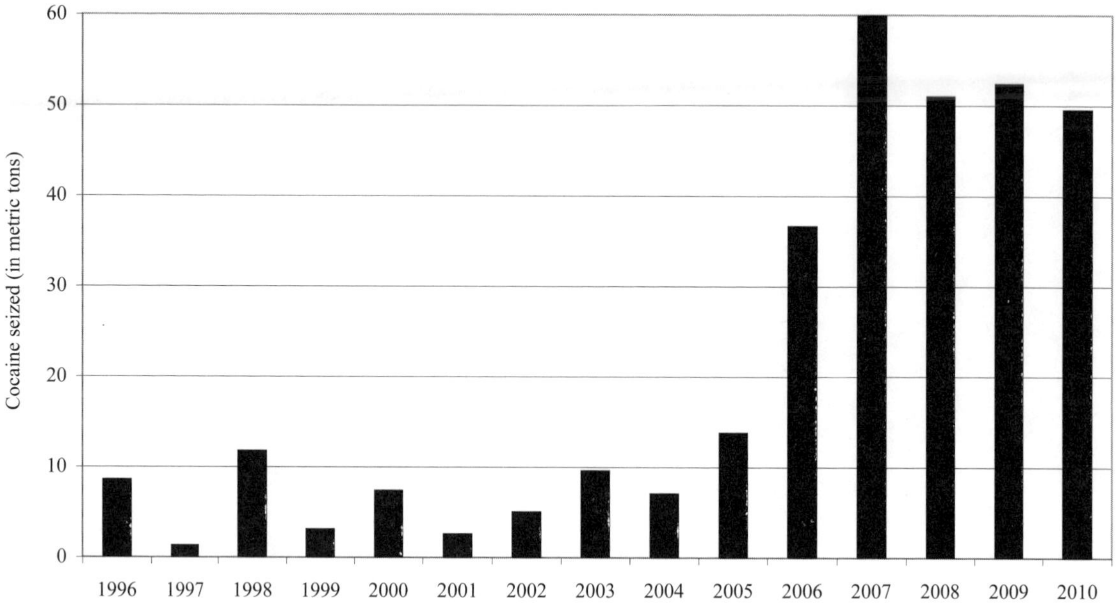

Sources: DEA, *Resources, Panama* (2000), 3; *INCSR* (1991), 187; *INCSR* (1994), 172; *INCSR* (1997), 160; *INCSR* (1999), 190; *INCSR* (2007), 19; *INCSR* (2008), 185; *INCSR* (2009), 467; *INCSR* (2010), 498; *INCSR* (2011), 439.

Note: Given Panamanian reporting timetables, the seizure figures obtained by the U.S. State Department for its March narcotics reports reflected seizures only through October of the prior year. The State Department reports in subsequent years sometimes give corrected seizure figures for the full-year periods. For Panama's own figures, including the 1999–2003 period, see "Panamá, Puente para el narcotráfico," *LP* (PA), 24 October 2004, 6A.

or to process cocaine. In 1984 the Noriega regime colluded with the Medellín cartel to establish a substantial laboratory in Darién, although the DEA and uninvolved Panamanian officials broke up that effort. Then, in 1993 counternarcotics forces burned seven cocaine-processing laboratories near the Colombian border, and law-enforcement agents, investigating a kidnapping by Colombian guerrillas on Cerro Tacarcuna in the far southern mountains of Darién, discovered the first coca grown in Central America.[68] During that and the following year, a joint Colombian-Panamanian-U.S. endeavor eradicated about 150 hectares of coca.[69] Helicoptering in units to burn coca fields and then extricating them before nightfall, to avoid likely counterattacks by heavily armed growers, have not been easy operations. Dense, triple-canopied jungle, limited Panamanian resources, and formidable Colombian insurgents have made coca cultivation difficult to wipe out entirely.[70] However, with the help of regular overflights and the use of U.S. intelligence, subsequent plantations have not amounted to a significant problem, and installing cocaine labs in Panama did not prove fruitful for Colombian traffickers.[71]

68. "SAN destituye," 1A.

69. See "SAN espera destruir más sembradíos de coca," *LP* (PA), 3 January 1994, 4A; "El Darién de las interrogantes," *LP* (PA), 9 April 1996, 6A; "Panamá lava miles de millones de dolares: Gelbard," *LP* (PA), 8 April 1996, 4A; and "Panamá y EU erradicaron cultivos de coca en Darién," *LP* (PA), 14 September 1996, 4A.

70. *INCSR* (2006), 23.

71. See "Darién de las interrogantes," 6A. See also *INCSR* (2006), 23; "Policía comprobará quema de plantaciones en Darién," *LP* (PA), 15 January 1995, 2A; and "Panamá y EU erradicaron," 4A.

Instead, the true challenge—one that has proven well beyond the capacity of Panamanian law enforcement to counter—has been the Colombian cocaine that has flooded the country. Rising seizures since the early 1990s suggest that the volume of cocaine passing through Panama may have been rapidly increasing. They also indicate that authorities in post-Noriega Panama have markedly enhanced their antidrug efforts. The level of cooperation between the United States and Panama has improved, law enforcement has become more effective, and officials have pursued interdiction more seriously and enthusiastically. Yet, plainly, Panama's counternarcotics successes have not deterred drug organizations from using the country as a key transshipment location. Drug shipments lost to authorities can be replaced more readily the closer the drugs are to South American producers. By the same token, the farther a drug shipment travels toward market, the more has been invested in its passage. Thus, the replacement costs for a seized load is higher. The economics of the drug trade therefore suggest that Panama, with its geographic position neighboring Colombia, has been particularly poorly situated to curb cocaine transshipment.

The Evolution of Drug Trafficking in Panama

Just before the Central American drug trade started to crescendo, a Panamanian military regime grasped political power and soon proved itself intent on accumulating wealth for its leaders and ensuring impunity for its crimes. In particular, certain National Guard officers had feared that the reelection of populist former president Arnulfo Arias Madrid would lead to their punishment for corruption or for torture, rape, murder, and other abuses perpetrated in efforts to suppress Arias's supporters. In 1968 two mid-level officers, Omar Efraín Torrijos Herrera and Boris Néstor Martínez Salazar, capitalized on the military discontent to mount a coup. Shortly thereafter, Torrijos seized power from Martínez. As Central American drug trafficking climbed, the influence of the military was second only to geography among Panama's bridge-favoring factors.

The Torrijos Military Regime

From the late 1960s until his death in a 1981 plane crash, Brigadier General Omar Torrijos Herrera led the armed forces, and he, rather than a civilian president, served as commander in chief. From 1968 to 1978 Torrijos enlarged the National Guard from 5,000 to 15,000 soldiers and from a $10 million budget to more than $100 million, while a bloated government bureaucracy beholden to the general tripled in size to about 150,000. Foreign lenders provided the regime with a total of about $6 billion, which financed popular public works projects from which the officer corps skimmed large sums. Since fortunes could still be made under military rule, the regime co-opted certain influential members of the business and banking elites. A thoroughly inadequate and corrupted judicial system was compelled to do the National Guard's bidding, while officers looked benevolently on illegitimate activities once they had received an ample cut of the expected profits. However, economic stagnation followed: wages fell, unemployment rose, inflation steadily climbed, the gap between rich and poor grew, and growth plummeted from 8 percent, when the military took over, to 0 percent by 1975.[72]

At about nine thousand soldiers the Panamanian National Guard was not sufficiently large or well equipped to affect international relations, but it came to repress dissent ever

72. Kempe, *Divorcing the Dictator*, 88; "Cocaine Is Again Surging," 1A; Koster and Sánchez, *In the Time*, 122, 186, 248–49; Murillo, *Noriega Mess*, 928–30.

more efficiently at home. According to the national Truth Commission, as the military consolidated its hold, more than one hundred opponents simply disappeared.[73] More common still were bullying and intimidation tactics designed to produce a cowed and compliant population. The regime employed thugs to threaten, harass, and beat those who might trouble its leaders, including journalists and civil society leaders. Although the dictatorship was largely unpopular, Torrijos did succeed in appealing to some Panamanians through populist slogans and rhetoric and government jobs, projects, and programs. He also crafted a reasonably positive international reputation by projecting the image of a nationalistic and at least nominally nonaligned leader, working to return the canal to Panama.

Through the Torrijos period the tentacles of military control entwined key aspects of society. Despite periodic elections and even opposition parties, politicians could not cross the military without repercussions, and the armed forces regularly manipulated voting results. Military officers involved themselves deeply in much of the daily government business that democracies traditionally keep in civilian hands. The Torrijos regime handpicked candidates for electoral offices, up to and including the presidency, while parties allied with the military dominated the legislature. The military supervised virtually all law enforcement, including the police, prisons, and customs and immigration, while issuing passports, administering Panama Canal matters, and regulating civilian aircraft.[74] The G-2 intelligence service conducted airport and other surveillance, and the military's National Department of Investigations carried out criminal investigations.[75] The military could arrest civilians without warrants and extract information "for motives of national defense and public security."[76]

With the armed forces astride Panamanian society, wealthy narcotics organizations targeted the military, and vice versa, and the roots of such dealings stretched far back into time. By the mid-twentieth century many military and political elites across Central America had engaged in occasional drug trafficking to earn money.[77] Indeed, the 1955 assassination of José Antonio Remón Cantera, a colonel in Panama's National Guard who had seized power in 1951 and had been elected to the presidency the following year, has been linked to his efforts to curb trafficking in the National Guard and perhaps in his own family as well.[78] However, the rise of the Torrijos regime corresponded with, and itself helped to stimulate, the extraordinary regional influx of drugs.

Trafficking organizations thoroughly penetrated Panama's officer corps and also the relatives and close associates of military elites.[79] During the Nixon administration U.S. antidrug authorities found that Panamanian officials—diplomats, politicians, and customs agents—were facilitating heroin transshipment. Various heroin couriers in the French Connection case had been outfitted with false Panamanian passports, and U.S. intelligence suggested that organizations might be transshipping through Panama as much as one-twelfth of the U.S. heroin supply.[80]

In December 1970 undercover U.S. agents, posing as Mafia members, approached Joaquín Him González, a Panamanian of Chinese descent,

73. "Sistema judicial es 'vergonzoso,'" *LP* (PA), 6 May 2003, 1A.

74. For a description of Law 20, placing ports, airports, customs, and immigration under military control, see Kempe, *Divorcing the Dictator*, 120.

75. See "Del Cid delata a Noriega," *LP* (PA), 20 September 1991, 1A; *United States v. Noriega*, No. 88-0079 OR-HOEVELER; and Dinges, *Our Man in Panama*, 119.

76. Koster and Sánchez, *In the Time*, 280.

77. For trafficking by elites in Mexico and Honduras in this time frame, see Walker, *Western Hemisphere*.

78. Murillo, *Noriega Mess*, 39.

79. For allegations of the arms and narcotics trafficking of Torrijos, including his ties to Cali traffickers, see Scott and Marshall, *Cocaine Politics*, 83, 88, 110; Dinges, *Our Man in Panama*, 114–15; and Murillo, *Noriega Mess*, 123–26, 233.

80. See Kempe, *Divorcing the Dictator*, 76; "Gobierno de Carter sospechaba vínculos entre narcotráfico y hermanos Torrijos," *LP* (PA), 8 July 2001, 1A; and the 1973 report of the Merchant Marine Committee, recounted in "Drug Trafficking in Panama."

who directed air traffic at the international airport and served as deputy director of Panama's Civil Aviation Authority.[81] An associate of Torrijos's older brother Moisés, Him González had reportedly long been engaged in the South American contraband trade. He then allegedly joined a trafficking network in which South American planes would be flown into the airport, often late at night, with drugs on board for special units to handle. When Him helped the agents set up a delivery of one hundred kilos of cocaine, a Texas grand jury indicted the Panamanian official, and in February 1971 U.S. agents orchestrated his arrest at a softball game in the Canal Zone. Him González was eventually convicted and sentenced to serve five years.

In an even larger case shortly thereafter, U.S. Customs agents arrested two Panamanians who had tried to pass through John F. Kennedy Airport carrying heroin. Nicolás Polanco was a former bodyguard for Moisés Torrijos who served at that time as a Panamanian ambassador to Argentina, and Rafael Richard González was the son of the Panamanian ambassador to Taiwan. Carrying a diplomatic passport signed by the foreign minister, González toted in his suitcases nearly seventy kilos of heroin supplied by Auguste Joseph Ricord, a French former Nazi collaborator turned South American heroin trafficker.[82] Upon arrest, González agreed to become a government informant and admitted to smuggling heroin into the United States on five prior flights. González's father, ambassador Guillermo Alfonso González López, who had once served as another bodyguard for Moisés Torrijos, then flew to New York, and while under surveillance, arranged to meet with Oscar San Martín, an Argentinian drug dealer in New York City. A controlled delivery of the heroin ensued, more arrests occurred, and a U.S. federal court indicted Moisés Torrijos. Eventually six persons were convicted and received prison terms, including twelve years for San Martín, seven years for González López, and fifteen years for New York intermediary Francisco Solimene, who was also found to have failed to report four hundred thousand dollars of income earned in 1971 from the heroin trade.[83]

These were only the most well publicized of a number of drug cases implicating Panamanian diplomats. In 1971 Danish authorities arrested Armando Moreno Guillén, Panamanian ambassador to Egypt and India, on charges of importing eighty-one kilos of hashish found in his suitcases. The following year U.S. Customs agents found cocaine and liquid hashish in the luggage of Manuel Rojas Sucre as he entered John F. Kennedy Airport under a diplomatic passport. Rojas was the son of Panama's consul general in Montreal and nephew of Panama's vice president, Arturo Sucre.[84]

Even more scandalously, Rafael González reportedly told U.S. authorities that Moisés Torrijos had been supplying heroin couriers with diplomatic passports so they could avoid customs searches.[85] A former U.S. official later declared that the incriminating evidence went well beyond providing passports, commenting, "We have one hell of a good case against Moises Torrijos." In March 1972, in reporting to

81. For information on different aspects of the Him González case, see Epstein, *Agency of Fear*, 97; Tully, *Secret War*, 33–34, 106; Clark and Horrock, *Contrabandista*, 114, 193–99; and Murillo, *Noriega Mess*, 125–27. See also "Drug Trafficking in Panama," and the statement of Leland L. Riggs Jr. in U.S. Senate, *Implementation*.

82. French-born former Nazi collaborator Auguste Ricord, implicated in the French Connection case, was deported to the United States in 1972, convicted of drug-smuggling charges, sentenced to twenty years, and eventually released in 1983.

83. *Solimne v. Commissioner of Internal Revenue*, 44 T.C.M. (CCH) 321. For information on the González case, see Tully, *Secret War*, 133–38; Murillo, *Noriega Mess*, 128–33; Koster and Sánchez, *In the Time*, 185; and Kempe, *Divorcing the Dictator*, 77–78. See also "Familia Torrijos tiene pruebas de la inocencia de 'Monche,'" *LP* (PA), 22 July 2001, 2A.

84. Murillo, *Noriega Mess*, 127, 133; Kempe, *Divorcing the Dictator*, 78.

85. Koster and Sánchez, *In the Time*, 185; Murillo, *Noriega Mess*, 132.

Congress the details of five heroin-smuggling cases via Panama, customs agents concluded that the González case "reached into the highest levels of Panamanian officialdom and included Moises Torrijos, the brother of General Omar Torrijos, and the Panamanian foreign minister, Juan Tack."[86] Shortly thereafter, all of the agents from the U.S. Bureau of Narcotics and Dangerous Drugs (BNDD), predecessor to the DEA, were expelled from Panama as personae non gratae. But in May 1972 a New York grand jury issued a sealed indictment charging Moisés Torrijos with involvement in heroin imports to the United States. The following month BNDD director John Ingersoll flew to Panama to lay out for General Torrijos the U.S. evidence that Moisés had been trafficking drugs since being appointed ambassador to Argentina in 1969.[87] Torrijos, however, was reported to have airily dismissed the charge, commenting to the U.S. ambassador that his brother had been trafficking a mere five kilos of heroin a week.[88]

Infuriated U.S. officials redoubled their pressure, and, at length, Torrijos agreed that U.S. antidrug agents could reenter his country; however, he named as liaison his key underling—Manuel Antonio Noriega Moreno.[89] This enabled Noriega to monitor U.S. intelligence reports on the Panamanian drug trade, particularly useful because allegations concerning the Torrijos regime continued to arise. A Senate Intelligence Committee report stated, "Over the years, several drug dealers have alleged that they were friends of Gen. Torrijos, that he was one of their customers, or that he protected them."[90]

Likewise, a secret DEA document, eventually declassified, that came to White House attention during the debate over the passage of the Panama Canal treaties, alleged that Omar Torrijos had been directly involved in drug trafficking. It implicated as well another brother, Hugo Torrijos, who owned a nightclub and directed Panama's casinos and lottery, all undertakings generating large amounts of cash. Furthermore, Cali trafficker Santiago Ocampo Zuluaga was thought to have given Omar Torrijos a racehorse and entered a joint venture with Hugo to operate an air-freight company, Aerolíneas Medellín, that could transport cocaine from Colombia to Panama.[91] In Washington, however, the Carter administration wished to avoid embarrassing inquiries into the Panamanian leader's drug connections when trying to negotiate the canal's future with him. In Panama few thought it wise to cooperate in investigations of the Torrijos family. Thus, the allegations were neither substantiated nor laid to rest.[92]

In 1988, however, DEA agent Tom Zepeda testified to Congress that a reliable informant had reported to him that General Torrijos had accompanied Manuel Noriega to Medellín on more than one occasion in the mid-1970s, presumably to meet with traffickers. Zepeda further declared that in 1977 he had watched a Panamanian government plane arrive in Medellín and had seen what he believed was a trafficker's vehicle pick up Torrijos and Noriega. Also in 1988 drug smuggler Michael Vogel told the U.S. Senate that in late 1979 he had met with Torrijos and Noriega in Panama to negotiate

86. Tully, *Secret War*, 139.

87. Classified report compiled by DEA investigator Michael DeFeo, cited in Kempe, *Divorcing the Dictator*, 79, 78, 430. See also Murillo, *Noriega Mess*, 156, and Shannon, *Desperados*, 164.

88. Murillo, *Noriega Mess*, 136, and Koster and Sánchez, *In the Time*, 140.

89. Kempe, *Divorcing the Dictator*, 80.

90. Murillo, *Noriega Mess*, 237. This Senate report referenced reliable intelligence indicating that Torrijos knew of drug trafficking by his brother and other Panamanian officials and failed to stop it, but it characterized the evidence linking Torrijos directly to trafficking as "largely secondhand and of varying reliability."

91. See Murillo, *Noriega Mess*, 233; MacDonald, *Mountain High*, and Scott and Marshall, *Cocaine Politics*, 82–83, 85–88.

92. See Murillo, *Noriega Mess*, 231–41. For summaries of the allegations and denials, see "Gobierno de Carter," *LP* (PA), 8 July 2001, 1A; "Pastor ignora si Omar tuvo nexos con narcos," *LP* (PA), 11 July 2001, 1A; and "Familia Torrijos tiene pruebas," 2A.

protection for transshipment. The potential deal fell through, however, when Torrijos and Noriega demanded one hundred thousand dollars per flight for their assistance.[93]

In 1981 a mysterious plane crash killed Torrijos. Shortly before the flight, the Panamanian leader had initiated an investigation into Noriega's support for traffickers César Rodríguez Contreras and Floyd Carlton Cáceres. Shortly after it, Noriega seized control of the military's inquiry into Torrijos's death.[94] However, no firm evidence has ever surfaced to substantiate allegations that Noriega was somehow involved in sabotaging the plane.[95] The De Havilland company that manufactured the aircraft sent independent investigators to Panama, who concluded that the crash was indeed accidental.[96] However that may be, for purposes of the evolving drug trade in Panama, the Torrijos years proved to be simply the prologue to a larger drama, as personalistic military rule was converted to a personalistic kleptocracy, headed by Panama's de facto military ruler—Manuel Noriega.

The Noriega Military Regime

Noriega's Rise to Power

In 1964, when the military had put Major Omar Torrijos in charge of intimidating Arnulfo Arias's supporters in Chiriquí Province, Manuel Noriega had become his most effective instrument of abuse and control. Thereafter, "my gangster," as Torrijos called him, tried to become distinguished from other rising officers by continuing to ingratiate himself to his boss.[97] During an aborted coup in 1969 Noriega strongly supported his patron, and by the following August, Torrijos had elevated him to G-2 chief.[98] This position was vitally important, because its holder could build a formidable power base while collecting embarrassing information on potential rivals.[99] As Demetrio Basilio Lakas later noted, "I was just the president. A puppet. . . . Torrijos used me to reach out to the Americans and the business community. . . . Noriega knew everything Lakas did, but Lakas knew nothing about Noriega's activities. After office hours, . . . the G-2 . . . ran the country."[100] In characterizing Noriega as the leading source of information on Latin America in the history of U.S. intelligence, retired U.S. Air Force colonel Matías Farías, formerly of the Southern Command, observed that Torrijos had increasingly become a figurehead, while Noriega actually governed Panama.[101]

In fact, U.S. officials recruited Noriega as an informant at the dawn of his career, while he was a military cadet studying in Peru in the 1950s and perhaps earlier still as a high school student able to infiltrate left-wing politics.[102] By 1967 Noriega had cultivated a significant

93. Dinges, *Our Man in Panama*, 352; Murillo, *Noriega Mess*, 233.

94. Scott and Marshall, *Cocaine Politics*, 110.

95. "Díaz Herrera reitera que Noriega está implicado en muerte de Omar Torrijos," *LP* (PA), 7 February 1988, 1A.

96. Dinges, *Our Man in Panama*, 122. Nicaraguan Eden Pastora believed Sandinista intelligence engineered the plane crash to kill him, because he had been scheduled to fly with Torrijos that day. Kempe, *Divorcing the Dictator*, 121.

97. Murillo, *Noriega Mess*, 41–42, 48, 65.

98. For the attempted coup and Noriega's role in thwarting it, see Dinges, *Our Man in Panama*, 44–48, and Koster and Sánchez, *In the Time*, 130–34. During the 1974 Panama Canal negotiations Noriega supported Torrijos's decision to send a message to the United States by initiating a relationship with Cuba and its intelligence service. Kempe, *Divorcing the Dictator*, 86–87.

99. Noriega subverted General Rubén Darío Paredes with information on his son Rubencito, who had been trafficking drugs with Noriega associate, César Rodríguez Contreras. In 1986 Medellín hit men killed Rodríguez and Rubencito Paredes, with General Paredes publicly accusing Noriega of having masterminded the killings. "Noriega Ordered Colombia Slaying," *NYT* (US), 5 February 1988, 1A. For Noriega's falling out with Rodríguez, see Koster and Sánchez, *In the Time*, 289–90.

100. Kempe, *Divorcing the Dictator*, 76.

101. "Noriega pide clemencia para poder regresar a Panamá," *LP* (PA), 9 December 1998, 1A.

102. The divergent accounts of just when U.S. military intelligence and the CIA recruited Noriega are thoroughly documented in Murillo, *Noriega Mess*, 63–64, 68–69 and esp. 947–48n13.

relationship with the CIA.[103] He eventually worked with other intelligence services as well, including some in Cuba, Israel, France, Taiwan, Nicaragua, and Great Britain.[104] During Noriega's thirteen years (1970–83) in charge of intelligence, he led the military's effort to capitalize on Panama's strategic assets and reorganize, modernize, and internationalize its espionage service. He also created G-2 divisions expert in civilian repression, electronic eavesdropping, and psychological warfare.

Noriega and Corruption

Most important for the drug trade, directing the G-2 placed Manuel Noriega at the center of the extensive web of military corruption, positioning him to collect bribes from smugglers in exchange for favors. As early as 1971 BNDD agents received a tip that a Miami charter service had rented a boat to traffickers smuggling marijuana out of Panama. When the suspects were taken into custody, they reported having bribed a Panamanian colonel with a pockmarked face, pointing to the name "Colonel Noriega" in their address book, which contained his direct phone numbers.[105] That same year General Torrijos's former chief of staff told the BNDD that Noriega had taken "overall operational control" of drug transshipment via Panama.[106] By 1972 the BNDD considered Noriega a significant obstacle to its counternarcotics efforts.[107]

In the early 1980s the U.S. National Security Council reviewed surveillance photographs of Panamanian soldiers loading narcotics and read transcripts of intercepted conversations between traffickers and officers.[108] Previously, the G-2 would routinely arrest drug vendors and then redistribute the captured narcotics to the armed force's own dealers, and as Noriega consolidated his power, such illicit activities escalated.[109] A 1983 U.S. Senate study concluded that the Panamanian military "provides warehousing for narcotics on their way north, assures the release, for bribes received, of drug traffickers arrested, guarantees the nonarrest of offenders wanted elsewhere who have paid a kind of local 'safe-conduct' fee, supervises the air transport of gold, arms, spies bound to and from North America, Cuba and Central America."[110] In August 1983 Noriega, now a general, took charge as commander in chief of the National Guard, which he renamed the Panama Defense Force (FDP).

For General Noriega the possibilities for corrupt activity must have appeared nearly limitless. As one U.S. source stated frankly, "The Panama Defense Force is the axle around which the wheel of corruption turns." By the mid-1980s DEA agents in Panama alleged that Noriega was raking in profits from prostitution, gambling, and other such businesses. In 1986 a U.S. official, referring to a classified Defense Intelligence Agency report, concluded, "Nothing moves in Panama without the instructions, order and consent of Noriega." Two years later, a U.S. military official in Panama testified, "Very little was going on of a commercial nature in Panama from which [Noriega] did not, in some sense, directly profit. [He] was certainly venal,

103. See testimony of Donald Harvey, former CIA station chief in Panama, on his weekly meetings with Noriega. *United States v. Noriega*, 40 F. Supp.2d at 1380. See also MacDonald, *Dancing on a Volcano*, 119, and Scott and Marshall, *Cocaine Politics*, 65–67. Some accounts claimed Noriega was paid two hundred thousand dollars. "Noriega estaba a sueldo de la CIA," *LP* (PA), 4 February 1988, 1A.

104. See Kempe, *Divorcing the Dictator*, 81, 119.

105. Ibid., 58. "In 1972, [BNDD] officials . . . considered Noriega a major hindrance to their efforts to shut down Panama as a staging area for shipments of heroin from Europe and cocaine from South America." Shannon, *Desperados*, 164.

106. Scott and Marshall, *Cocaine Politics*, 66. For BNDD's report that Noriega had freed a captured cocaine trafficker, see Dinges, *Our Man in Panama*, 60.

107. Shannon, *Desperados*, 164.

108. The information on the National Security Council's review is according to Norman A. Bailey, former chief economist for the Council, who saw the documents in question. "Fighting Narcotics," *NYT* (US), 10 April 1988, 1.

109. For testimony about these illicit activities at Noriega's trial, see "Blandón confirma cargos contra Noriega," *LP* (PA), 31 January 1988, 1A.

110. "The Underground Empire: Narco-dollars Upset Economy," *Toronto Star*, 20 July 1986, H5.

was involved in a lot of very, very shady kinds of undertakings."[111]

For a military leader intent on maximizing profits, facilitating the multimillion-dollar drug trade was simply a crowning variety of corruption. One observer perceptively noted, "Drugs didn't corrupt Noriega; rather, corruption led Noriega to the drug dealers."[112] As he gained power in Panama, Noriega, along with his close associates, met with the dominant Medellín traffickers. A U.S. federal appellate court later found that "from 1982 through 1985, with Noriega's assistance, the Medellín Cartel transported significant quantities of cocaine through Panama to the United States. It also utilized its relationship with Noriega to move ether for cocaine processing and substantial cash proceeds from drug sales from the United States to or through Panama."[113] Thereafter, Noriega provided sanctuary for Bolivian traffickers and, most notoriously, Medellín kingpins trying to evade law enforcement.[114] To deposit cash payoffs from drug organizations, he opened multiple bank accounts in his name and those of his family members.

Noriega and the Pacification of Panama

As with any authoritarian society, some potential threats to the military's power existed. A capable civilian government, particularly one relying on international lending agencies, might attempt to seize and privatize the various companies owned and operated by the armed forces, economic activity that ensured that the actual income of officers far exceeded their salaries.[115] Moreover, an independent democratic government, with its own wellsprings of popular support, might construct a criminal-justice system not so easily manipulated to conceal drug corruption and trafficking. Hence, although Noriega and other officers did periodically talk about turning over certain powers to civilians, they chose not to jeopardize their power by doing so.[116] Instead, the military regime aimed to ensure that civilian authorities, while useful figureheads for domestic and international observers, were, in reality, co-opted and intimidated.

In 1984 general elections occurred. While Arias, as opposition leader, emphasized the military's links to the drug trade, the regime tried to focus international attention on the seven presidential candidates and fourteen political parties represented.[117] However, with the military's handpicked candidate, Nicolás Ardito Barletta, running second, the FDP stopped counting votes, later simply announcing Barletta's victory.[118] Through such maneuvers, Noriega carefully avoided taking serious steps toward relinquishing political control. Indeed, Noriega and his associates persuaded various foreign traffickers to funnel money into Panamanian political campaigns, including Barletta's. Most notably, Jorge Luis Ochoa and Gustavo Gaviria Rivero of Medellín contributed two hundred thousand dollars to the presidential campaign of General Rubén Darío Paredes. However, when Noriega transferred the military's

111. "U.S. Probes Panama Strongman," A1; "Strongman Said to Trade," 1A; Shannon, *Desperados*, 165. See also "Central America: Noriega Is Under Suspicion—and Pressure," *WP* (US), 23 November 1987, 17, and Koster and Sánchez, *In the Time*, 123.

112. Kempe, *Divorcing the Dictator*, 188.

113. *United States v. Noriega*, 117 F.3d at 1210.

114. See Dinges, *Our Man in Panama*, 184; Shannon, *Desperados*, 360–65; and Murillo, *Noriega Mess*, 395–96.

115. See Dinges, *Our Man in Panama*, 116.

116. For the efforts in the final year and a half of the regime to coerce Noriega into stepping aside, see Kempe, *Divorcing the Dictator*, 315–31. See also "U.S. Deal with Noriega Crumbles," *CT* (US), 26 May 1988, 1C.

117. See letter to the editor by Ambassador Dominador Kaiser Bazan, "Attack on Panamanian Is Anonymous and Unproved," *NYT* (US), 15 July 1986, A28.

118. Barletta had previously served as one of Trujillo's cabinet ministers, yet had a clean, apolitical image. An internal U.S. Embassy study later concluded that the election had plainly been stolen from opposition candidate Arias. See Dinges, *Our Man in Panama*, 167–68, 194–95, 364–67.

support, one hundred thousand dollars was moved to Ardito's campaign, perhaps without the latter's knowledge.[119]

For the traffickers the contributions were investments in the Panamanian military regime. For the armed forces, not only did the money help ensure that the military's candidate would prevail, but Noriega could then wield dirty campaign-finance secrets to manipulate, control, and, if necessary, discredit politicians who began to act independently of his will. In addition, in the late 1970s and early 1980s Luis Carlos Noriega Hurtado, Manuel's older half brother, directed the country's electoral tribunal.[120] Under these circumstances elections were more than a sham: they served as an instrument of authoritarian rule, right alongside coercion, intimidation, and the political use of intelligence. Even puppet politicians, however, had to be kept firmly under the military's thumb and even disposed of regularly to prevent any of them from gaining an independent power base. Thus, between 1982 and 1988 the FDP installed, tired of, and then removed from office four presidents: Arístides Royo Sánchez, Ricardo de la Espriella, Nicolás Barletta, and Eric Arturo Delvalle.

Of these, the most important was Delvalle, scion of a wealthy and long-established Jewish sugar family, who as first vice president succeeded Barletta, who had resigned under FDP pressure in a wholly unsuccessful effort to deflect public attention from the military's brutal killing of Noriega opponent Dr. Hugo Spadafora, formerly a vice minister of health for Torrijos. Spadafora had been about to publicize evidence that the Noriega regime was involved in drug trafficking with contra supporters. However, his planned revelations were reportedly brought to Noriega's attention through officials the general had bought off in the Costa Rican security forces.[121] Soldiers were thus waiting for Spadafora when he reentered Panama in September 1985, seizing him from a bus near the Costa Rican border and eventually torturing and beheading him.[122] In the aftermath Delvalle could no longer coexist with Noriega. Police answerable to the general brutally broke up even peaceful antimilitary demonstrations and shut down inconvenient nongovernmental organizations, such as the transnational drug rehabilitation organization Parent's Resource Institute for Drug Prevention (PRIDE).[123] They ransacked and temporarily closed the country's leading opposition newspaper, *La Prensa*, harried editor Roberto Eisenmann into exile on two occasions, and even seized the television channel supportive of the president.[124]

119. See "Dinero de narcotráfico era para la campaña de Barletta: Purcell," *LP* (PA), 11 October 1991, 1A; "Barletta recibió dinero de narcos," *LP* (PA), 26 October 1991, 1A; and "Kalish compró protección oficial para actividades de narcotráfico," *LP* (PA), 6 November 1991, 1A. The other half of the money was used to reward FDP couriers who had brought the cash from Medellín and to assist other FDP-supported candidates. Barletta professed not to have known the source of these funds. See "Ex presidente Ardito Barletta refuta acusaciones de Ricardo Tribaldos," *LP* (PA), 28 October 1991, 1A, and "Tribaldos afirma que Ardito Barletta desconocía procedencia de fondos," *LP* (PA), 29 October 1991, 1A. But for Jaime Castillo's testimony that he had heard Colonel Julian Melo Borbua introduce Barletta to the two Medellín representatives who had transferred the money to him, see "Ardito Barletta y militares sabían que dinero era de narcotraficantes," *LP* (PA), 30 October 1991, 1A.

120. Murillo, *Noriega Mess*, 334, 347.

121. See the accounts of Noriega insiders José Blandón and Floyd Carlton. "Many Costa Rican Links to Noriega Charges," *Tico Times* (Costa Rica) (hereafter cited as *TT* [CR]), 12 January 1990, 13.

122. For Inter-American Commission on Human Rights proceedings, see *Spadafora Franco*, Case 9726, Inter-Am. C.H.R. 110, OEA/ser. 50/5/2.71 and OEA/ser 50/7, 74. For the criminal case in Panama, see "Corte confirma condena a asesinos de Spadafora," *LP* (PA), 16 January 1996, 2A. See also Koster and Sánchez, *In the Time*, esp. 26–27, and Murillo, *Noriega Mess*, 428–51. For secret U.S. National Security Agency intercepts allegedly linking Noriega to the killing, see "Strongman Said to Trade," 1A.

123. "Panama Welcomes Return of PRIDE Antidrug Group," *Belize Times* (Belize) (hereafter cited as *BT* [BZ]), 7 March 1991, 10. Noriega had claimed that PRIDE had become "too politicized."

124. *La Prensa* was closed from July 1987 to January 1988. See "Abre *La Prensa*," *LP* (PA), 20 January 1988, 1A, and "Dos presidentes y un amo," *Rumbo* (Costa Rica), 15 March 1988, 15. For many years Noriega had frequently clashed with *La Prensa*, and the dictatorship attempted to

Playing Both Sides of the Street

In the meantime, accounts of Noriega's abetting drug organizations multiplied. Luis Bernardo Londoño, an alleged Colombian trafficker who had been arrested in Panama in 1977, reported that he had bribed Noriega $140,000 to be released from jail.[125] After trafficking in two years about 150 tons of marijuana, American smuggler Stephen Michael Kalish came to Panama in 1983 to launder $10 million and to arrange to cleanse another $100 million in drug profits.[126] He later testified to Congress that in a personal meeting, Noriega had enthusiastically endorsed his plans and even provided three Panamanian passports, including diplomatic credentials, for $65,000. Kalish concluded, "It was obvious to me that there were no limits to what we could do in Panama."[127] Medellín leaders paid even more. Their cocaine typically entered Panama by air, with the traffickers utilizing small airstrips, like that at Calzada Larga; landing at Panama's domestic airport at Paitilla; or simply arriving at the international airport but then taxiing to the military base under Noriega's direct control. The aircraft would then be refueled or the drugs would be off-loaded to proceed to market by some other means.

Even while assisting traffickers, however, Noriega provided intelligence reports to the U.S. government on some significant drug activities. Not only could this also turn a profit, but it provided a ready excuse should U.S. officials question his meetings with suspect individuals.[128] The military regime also moved vigorously against those working independently of Noriega's network, whether small domestic groups, local marijuana producers, or international operators. Thus, the military regime always had antidrug successes ready to tout. For instance, when marijuana cultivation rose to 400–500 hectares in 1985, producing 190–290 tons of marijuana, Panamanian authorities claimed to reduce cultivation to about 250 hectares in 1986 and about 30 hectares thereafter.[129]

As rumors of the regime's involvement in the drug trade proliferated, Noriega selectively increased his cooperation with U.S. officials. U.S. narcotics-detector dogs began to be used in the airport, increasing courier arrests, and U.S. Coast Guard vessels were repeatedly permitted to board and seize Panamanian-flagged vessels suspected of drug trafficking. The government also cooperated in expelling to the United States various Colombians and others wanted on drug charges.[130] In the mid-1980s the DEA's Operation Pisces led to the seizure of tons of cocaine and almost $50 million in assets, along with the arrests of 115 traffickers and the indictments of Pablo Escobar and Fabio Ochoa. Panamanian counternarcotics agents supported the operation. Indeed, some were privy to such secret information as the identities of undercover DEA agents and yet neither leaked nor compromised it.[131]

But Noriega was engaged in a delicate and dangerous game. His "hidden transcript"—that is, his actual preferences and behavior—diverged sharply from his official stance or "public transcript."[132] With time, his effort to cultivate close working relations in Medellín

intimidate journalists who exposed official trafficking and corruption. MacDonald, *Dancing on a Volcano*, 115.

125. Dinges, *Our Man in Panama*, 352.

126. *United States v. Ellender*, 947 F.2d at 752.

127. Kalish anticipated shipping 180 tons of Colombian marijuana from Panama to New York City, where he had paid a bribe of eight hundred thousand dollars to a Teamsters intermediary allegedly representing a U.S. Customs official. When asked on cross-examination at Noriega's trial whether the general might have considered him simply a wealthy businessman, Kalish replied, "Mr. Noriega certainly knew it wasn't from bingo proceeds." "Marijuana Scheme Linked to Noriega," *NYT* (US), 10 November 1991, 29.

128. Kempe, *Divorcing the Dictator*, 189.

129. *INCSR* (1988), 148–49.

130. *INCSR* (1990), 200. As late as April 1989 Panamanian officials expelled to the United States fifteen individuals, most of them Colombians.

131. One assistant U.S. attorney noted, "The Panamanian officials we were dealing with were sincerely cooperative. They had information. They could have breached security, and they didn't." "Drug Cartel Leader Found Guilty of Laundering Money," *CT* (US), 2 April 1988, 1. See also Dinges, *Our Man in Panama*, 257.

132. For transcript concepts, see J. Scott, *Domination*, esp. xii, 2, 4–5, 14.

and Washington became widely known within both circles. Secretary of State George Shultz observed of the Panamanian leader, "You can't buy him; you can only rent him."[133] With Noriega's divided loyalties rankling his associates on contending sides of the drug war, he came to fear for his life. In April 1986 an intelligence report from the U.S. defense attaché in Panama stated, "Reportedly the General has been forced to move his headquarters to the small island of Naos [in] . . . a 'super' protected bunker with extremely limited access. Also each night around Noriega's residence at Altos de Golf . . . there are a half dozen radio patrol cars guarding all the side streets leading to his residence. Other police cars constantly patrol the surrounding areas."[134]

Opposition to Noriega Grows

In the latter half of the 1980s Manuel Noriega's problems multiplied. Whereas intelligence agents had long linked Noriega to drug dealings, exiled Panamanians, imprisoned traffickers, and disaffected former insiders now joined forces, publicly charging his regime with extensive complicity in the international drug trade. Before his 1986 murder, trafficking pilot Barry Seal declared that most of the Medellín cartel's cocaine transited Panama.[135] That same year, U.S. Customs helicopters intercepted a light plane, piloted by former PDF captain Antonio Aníbal Aizprua, on which a tracking transponder had been secretly attached. Aizprúa landed the plane, which was found to be carrying 408 kilos of cocaine, on a closed section of Interstate 75 in Florida. Although Aizprua, then working for the Carlton Cáceres smuggling network, escaped into nearby swamps and evaded capture for four months, he was eventually arrested at Miami International Airport. After opting to become a government witness, Aizprua reported that Noriega had ordered him to transport drugs when he was flying for the Panamanian Air Force.[136]

Insiders in the upper echelons of the Panamanian military also turned against the general. In May 1987 Noriega attempted to compel the resignation of long-time rival, left-leaning Colonel Roberto Díaz Herrera, a cousin of Omar Torrijos, who had served as chief of staff and also directed G-2 for a time. Díaz responded by frankly admitting his own corruption and then detailing to the media various charges against Noriega. For weeks opposition forces convened at his house, and anti-Noriega riots broke out in Panama City. In July the military stormed the residence, and Díaz was speedily convicted of crimes against state security and sentenced to five years. In fact, within a month he was exiled to Venezuela, where he publicly declared, "Noriega has got massive amounts of money from the drug business."[137]

As turmoil increased, the U.S. Senate demanded democratic reforms and the military to withdraw from Panamanian politics. Immediately thereafter, the U.S. Embassy came under attack, and human rights violations increased. But this caused the ranks of Noriega's U.S. supporters to dwindle further. Although the U.S. government had never recognized the general to be the de jure leader of Panama, officially considering his seizure of power illegal, through much of the 1980s influential figures, including CIA director William Casey and National Security Council

133. Shultz, *Turmoil and Triumph*, 1052. In 1988 the State Department noted, "The U.S. Customs Service believes that, despite the noted instances of Panamanian assistance, General Noriega and the PDF cooperate only when it is in their interest to do so." *INCSR* (1988), 246.

134. Dinges, *Our Man in Panama*, 383–84.

135. "Nuevas acusaciones vinculan a General Noriega con las drogas," *LH* (GU), 18 September 1987, 12. For information on Seal, see Scott and Marshall, *Cocaine Politics*, 98–102.

136. Murillo, *Noriega Mess*, 409, 592. The DEA debriefed Aizprua, receiving a detailed account of his trafficking. A year later, he testified before the grand jury investigating Noriega. *United States v. Morales*, 69 F.3d at 1428, 1430. See also "Nuevas acusaciones," 12; "Piloto panameño ligado a pandilla que operó aquí," *LN* (CR), 20 September 1987, 8A; and "Investigan a Noriega en los EE.UU.," *LN* (CR), 12 November 1987, 26A.

137. See "Central America: Noriega," 17; "U.S. Probes Panama Strongman," A1; and "Panama Frees Foe of Noriega," *CT* (US), 26 December 1987, 14C. Díaz's credibility suffered, however, because of his mystical beliefs. See Dinges, *Our Man in Panama*, 260–61.

aide Oliver North, had appreciated Noriega's assistance in intelligence and national-security tasks.[138] By the summer of 1987, however, Casey had died, and North had been dismissed in the wake of the Iran-contra scandal. Revelations concerning Noriega's assistance to left-wing fighters in Central America, both the Sandinistas and the leftist rebels in El Salvador, silenced former proponents, as did his ties to Libya.[139] In June 1987 Noriega refused to relinquish control of the armed forces to a successor, as previously promised, and the following month the Reagan administration suspended all economic assistance to Panama.[140]

The next fall the U.S. Senate heard testimony that Medellín kingpins had paid the general $1 million to protect cocaine trafficking.[141] Colombian money launderer Ramón Milian Rodríguez claimed that Medellín traffickers had paid $320 million to Noriega between 1979 and 1983.[142] In return, Milian asserted, Noriega had permitted the use of Panama's airports and banks and furnished the identities of DEA agents and schedules of U.S. Navy and Coast Guard ships operating in Panamanian waters.[143] In November 1987 General Paredes, retired but once in command of both Noriega and Díaz, called the allegations against Noriega "correct" and "legitimate," concluding, "He has acted to launder money, and plenty of it."[144]

As Noriega lost domestic and international support, increasingly vocal opposition coalesced. In early 1988 José Isabel Blandón Castillo, a former Torrijos advisor who had become Panama's consul general in New York and had served Noriega in tasks ranging from civilian intelligence to arms-sales negotiations, appeared before Congress and a Miami federal grand jury, testifying, "Noriega has turned Panama into a gigantic machine for all sorts of criminal activities and enterprises."[145] Blandón accused the general of helping top Medellín traffickers to evade the international manhunt after the 1984 assassination of Colombian attorney general Rodrigo Lara Bonilla, providing them sanctuary and even supplying bodyguards. He also revealed sensational details regarding the regime's release of nearly two dozen Medellín traffickers in 1984.[146] A key G-2 deputy, Colonel Julián Melo Borbua, had collected at least $4 million from the cartel for assistance in delivering materials and then building and protecting a cocaine-processing lab on the Río Quindío. But, on May 21, 1984, the Panamanian Air Force, accompanied by top DEA official James Bramble, took control of the site, hidden in the remote jungles of the Serranía del Sapo on the Pacific coast of Darién Province, about fifty miles from the Colombian border, seizing many millions of dollars' worth of equipment.[147] Noriega, out of

138. Although it formally considered Delvalle to be Panama's leader until August 31, 1989, the United States recognized no Panamanian government again until after the invasion. For legal repercussions of not recognizing Noriega, see the 1,211-kilo cocaine seizure in *United States v. Leuro-Rosas*, 952 F.2d 616.

139. Baker, *Politics of Diplomacy*, 184. Although relations ran hot and cold, Panama's military leaders from Torrijos's time forward had ties to the Sandinistas. See Murillo, *Noriega Mess*, 283.

140. Baker, *Politics of Diplomacy*, 179, and *INCSR* (1988), 147. Congress turned the Reagan policy into law later that year.

141. "Piloto vincula a Noriega con drogas," *LN* (CR), 18 September 1987, 23A.

142. Milian's testimony was not used in Noriega's indictments because the Florida U.S. attorney's office found him "wholly without credibility," and he failed a Kerry committee lie-detector test. See Dinges, *Our Man in Panama*, xi, and Scott and Marshall, *Cocaine Politics*, 194n24. We use his statements simply to illustrate the many voices raised against Noriega in the late 1980s.

143. "The International Cocaine Conspiracy," *WP* (US), 14–20 March 1988, 6. At Noriega's trial Carlos Lehder testified that the general had given Medellín leaders the names, addresses, and pictures of DEA agents in Panama. "Lehder: Cuba Cleared Drug Flights," *MH* (US), 22 November 1991, 1.

144. "Ex-general in Panama Backs Accusations Against Leader," *NYT* (US), 17 November 1987, 1A.

145. Shannon, *Desperados*, 168. For more on Blandón, see Murillo, *Noriega Mess*, 373, 375.

146. Blandón testified in February 1988 before the Senate. See "Blandón confirma cargos contra Noriega," *LP* (PA), 31 January 1988, 1A, and "Narcos le pagaron 1 millón mensual," *LP* (PA), 5 February 1988, 1A.

147. For a detailed account of the capture of the lab, see Kempe, *Divorcing the Dictator*, 185.

the country when the raid occurred, immediately feared assassination. He arranged, however, to scapegoat Colonel Melo and restore the traffickers' lost money; the military dismissed Melo, but he was quietly freed and never prosecuted, his earnings intact.[148]

In the meantime, prosecutors in Tampa, drawing on FBI and Customs Service investigations, assembled a federal criminal case against the general, while other prosecutors in Miami, drawing on DEA evidence, put together another. By February 1988 the Miami grand jury had indicted Noriega for permitting Colombian traffickers to use Panama to ship cocaine to the United States from 1981 to 1986 in return for bribes of at least $4.6 million. Simultaneously, the Tampa grand jury indicted Noriega for conspiring to import 1.4 million pounds of marijuana into the United States. Shortly thereafter, the U.S. government decertified Panama for failing to cooperate in antidrug efforts, and President Delvalle tried to discharge Noriega, but the general refused to cooperate. With the economy slumping further, in March 1988 Colonel Leonidas Macías, head of the FDP police, led a feeble coup attempt, quickly repressed by Noriega loyalists; the general then purged the officer corps by almost a quarter.[149]

Influential Panamanians continued the chorus of complaints against Noriega. In April 1988 archbishop José Sebastián Laboa, papal nuncio in Panama, characterized the regime as "rotten, but still hanging on the vine." He argued that so long as Noriega remained in Panama, curbing the drug trade would be impossible, because the traffickers had the state at their disposal. When Panamanian voters went to the polls the following month, blatant fraud, detailed by international election observers, muted another popular anti-Noriega message. To thwart the clear majority supporting corporate lawyer and former Arias aide Guillermo Endara Galimany, the FDP annulled the elections. The military regime also sent its Dignity Battalion thugs to brutalize opposition demonstrators and even a vice presidential candidate. The Noriega regime then installed as president the virtually unknown former comptroller Francisco Rodríguez, and the general's standing plummeted further.[150]

During the summer of 1988 the Reagan administration secretly offered a deal to Noriega: the indictments could be dropped in exchange for the general's exile from Panama, perhaps to Spain. After some vacillation, however, Noriega failed to agree. In early October a second and bloodier coup attempt occurred, led by a member of Noriega's security detail, Major Moisés Giroldi, who had helped to put down the Macías coup effort. The U.S. government provided a bit of the support that Giroldi had secretly requested, but it acted hesitantly, unsure of whether this was actually a Noriega plot to embarrass the incoming Southern Command leader, General Maxwell Thurman. While Giroldi and his forces briefly held Noriega and his Comandancia headquarters, they neither killed him nor delivered him to U.S. forces. During his brief captivity Noriega sensed the confusion and disorganization. He eventually taunted Giroldi, and after regaining control, Noriega immediately saw to his execution and those of ten other conspirators. He also ordered FDP intelligence to investigate, and it soon rooted out two other coup plots, torturing and imprisoning the participants.[151]

148. Murillo, *Noriega Mess*, 395. Melo was eventually arrested for involvement in an airport cocaine-trafficking scheme and was convicted and sentenced to four and a half years in prison. See "Melo Borbúa pide fianza de excarcelación para estar libre," *LP* (PA), 5 June 2001, 4A, and "Condenan a ex secretario de Noriega," *LP* (PA), 9 October 2003, 2A.

149. Sherman, "Inquiry Regarding," 393–428; "U.S. Probes Panama Strongman," A1; *United States v. Noriega*, 117 F.3d at 1209; "U.S. Decertifies Panama as an Ally in Drug-Fighting," *WP* (US), 2 March 1988, A17; Baker, *Politics of Diplomacy*, 179.

150. Quote from Shultz, *Turmoil and Triumph*, 1056; "Noriega entregó Panamá al narcotráfico, afirma Laboa," *LP* (PA), 8 January 1990, 1.

151. Baker, *Politics of Diplomacy*, 180, 187.

In December 1988, more than eight months before his term was to expire, President Delvalle, who had been in hiding in Panama, fled to the United States, declaring that under Noriega's tenure the Medellín cartel had "invaded" his country. The general responded that such charges were "imbecilic," evidence that his enemies were orchestrating a smear campaign and that the United States was manipulating drug allegations to retain control over the canal. Noriega also took the precaution of transferring about $20 million to European bank accounts. Through this period, while Panamanian drug-enforcement assistance continued, it did so selectively.[152]

The U.S. Invasion of Panama

Although the situation in Panama disturbed U.S. policy makers, the federal indictments seemed ineffectual. Within the Panamanian military most of those capable of subverting Manuel Noriega had been killed or imprisoned. Even if a civilian government were, miraculously, to effectuate his arrest, Panama could not lawfully render the general, because Article 24 of the Constitution and a 1904 U.S.-Panama treaty both prohibited extradition of citizens.[153] Thus, the U.S. government had aimed to increase the pressure on Noriega to step down. Various sanctions had been instituted. Exiled President Delvalle had agreed that the U.S. government should freeze Panamanian assets held in American banks. International lending institutions were pressured to register their displeasure with events in Panama.

As tensions climaxed in 1989, Noriega turned to anti-American rhetoric to try to retain some domestic support. Eventually, his handpicked legislature issued a declaration that a "state of war" existed with the United States. FDP soldiers also clashed with their U.S. counterparts from the Canal Zone, including an assault on the wife of one U.S. soldier and the shooting of another soldier who had panicked and attempted to drive through an FDP roadblock. The drug-trafficking indictments embarrassed various U.S. officials as well, who had long touted Noriega to be a loyal American ally. All this exacerbated criticism of the expensive but ineffective "war on drugs." Furthermore, a Panamanian was scheduled to take charge of the Canal Commission on January 1, 1990, and the military regime would doubtless appoint a Noriega supporter to that key post, portending future trouble.[154]

On December 20, 1989, the United States invaded Panama in what President George H. W. Bush termed "Operation Just Cause." Despite some resistance, U.S. forces rapidly took control. However, they were at first unable to locate Manuel Noriega. The general hoped Mexico, Spain, or Cuba would grant him asylum; however, U.S. soldiers were stationed around their embassies. Eventually, Noriega took sanctuary in the papal nunciature, inviolate under international laws of diplomatic privilege. With troops surrounding the compound, Laboa attempted to persuade Noriega that no country would take him.[155] In fact, Mexico did not respond to his asylum request, and Spain denied it outright, citing its extradition treaty with the United States. Furthermore, neither the United States nor the new Panamanian government would guarantee the general safe passage out of the country. Finally, in early January the general,

152. "Dos presidentes y un amo," 15; Dinges, *Our Man in Panama*, 252; "Drug Dealer Says He Gave Noriega 'Millions' in Bribes," *NYT* (US), 29 January 1988, 1A; *United States v. Noriega*, 117 F.3d at 1211. During 1989 U.S. counternarcotics authorities in Miami and New York confiscated at least 2 tons of cocaine transshipped via Panama; of these, 694 kilos were the result of information passed on by Panamanian authorities. *INCSR* (1990), 199.

153. For an analysis from Dr. Edgardo Molino Mola, University of Panama Dean of Law and Political Science, see "Noriega no sería extraditado, pero sí podría ser enjuiciado," *LP* (PA), 26 January 1988, 20A.

154. Baker, *Politics of Diplomacy*, 184.

155. U.S. troops played David Bowie and other loud rock music to make life inside less comfortable for the general. "A Cavalier View of Sovereignty," *Independent* (United Kingdom), 28 December 1989, 20.

in his military uniform, surrendered to U.S. authorities. He had convinced himself that asylum would not occur and that fighting U.S. drug charges would be preferable to trial and perhaps execution in Panama.[156] At Howard Air Force Base the DEA took charge of Noriega, who was arrested upon crossing into U.S. airspace and was soon imprisoned in Miami.

During the ensuing brief military occupation U.S. forces uncovered additional evidence of Noriega's links to drug trafficking, although much was inadmissible in court. Soldiers entered a house used by Noriega and reported finding 450 kilos of cocaine wrapped in banana leaves in a freezer. During a search of Panamanian military headquarters a letter apparently written by Noriega was recovered that laid out plans to develop a cocaine-refining lab that could produce 84 tons a year. Two months later, Colombian authorities arrested Medellín trafficker Jesús Humberto Vega Escobar, wanted in connection with the U.S. distribution of 6 tons of cocaine. Police found an organizational chart, showing Noriega's name in the midst of a complex transportation-and-distribution network. In this period the DEA also placed Noriega's half brother Eduardo under surveillance as he traveled through South America, and in September Peruvian police arrested him as he prepared to deliver cocaine to contacts of Medellín traffickers.[157]

Of more value in building legal cases against the general, prosecutors began to track down his assets. Although he had spent twenty-seven years working for the military for an official salary that peaked at $42,500 a year, Noriega had managed to accumulate hundreds of millions of dollars.[158] One banker eventually testified that Noriega had millions in accounts in the Bank of Credit and Commerce International (BCCI) alone.[159] After official requests France froze $44 million in Noriega's alleged assets, the Cayman Islands $35 million, the United States $20 million, and Switzerland, Luxembourg, and Austria a total of $14.4 million.[160] Among other holdings, Noriega was found to own three pleasure yachts; a $600,000 mansion in Panama City; a farm, an apartment, and a country estate in France; luxury apartments in the Dominican Republic; and several airplanes, including a Lear jet and a Boeing 727. Authorities searching one of Noriega's residences in rural Panama found hundreds of exotic animals and a cellar with 1,500 bottles of fine French champagne, 600 of which bore the general's name.[161] In 1996 a Panamanian court found Noriega guilty in absentia of illicit enrichment and corruption and ordered various assets seized, including bank accounts holding $15 million.[162] By 2001 Panamanian officials had identified another ten savings accounts, amounting to nearly $3 million, plus thirty-one farms, worth

156. See "Captura y juicio de Noriega son legales," *LP* (PA), 12 January 1990, 16.

157. "Confundieron cocaína con tamales," *LP* (PA), 24 January 1990, 16; "Manuel A. Noriega planeaba fabricar cocaína en Panamá," *LP* (PA), 13 December 1991, 1A; and "Noriega aparece en organigrama de narcotraficantes colombianos," *LN* (CR), 7 March 1990, 11. For Eduardo's arrest, see "Hermano de Noriega detenido por vinculación con Cartel de Medellín," *LP* (PA), 14 September 1990, 1A; "DEA pedirá al Perú extradición del hermano menor de Noriega," *LP* (PA), 15 September 1990, 1A; and Murillo, *Noriega Mess*, 821.

158. Noriega's salary totaled $648,583 over twenty-seven years. See "Noriega recibirá jubilación máxima," *LP* (PA), 11 October 1995, 1, and "Condenan a Manuel Noriega, a su esposa e hijas," *LP* (PA), 17 September 1996, 1A. Although estimates of his assets reached $480 million, various knowledgeable sources figured Noriega's wealth to certainly exceed $200 million. See "Fortuna de más de 480 millones tiene Noriega, revela a Procurador," *LP* (PA), 10 October 1990, 1A; "Contralor logra rescatar 1.2 millón de cuenta de Noriega," *LP* (PA), 12 June 2001, 1A; "Noriega millonario gracias a las drogas," *LN* (CR), 1 September 1989, 18A; and Dinges, *Our Man in Panama*, 388.

159. See also "El laberinto del dinero de Noriega," *LP* (PA), 17 December 1991, 2A. For the separate case including testimony regarding Noriega's BCCI accounts, see "Decenas de millones producto de drogas colocó Noriega en el BCCI," *LP* (PA), 29 September 1991, 32A.

160. "Contralor logra rescatar," 1A. Noriega also had significant assets frozen in Britain.

161. "Los lujos de Noriega," *LN* (CR), 18 March 1990, 27A. Located in Potrerillos de Chiriqui, the estate was called Finca La Escondida.

162. "Noriega acumula condenas por más de un siglo de carcel," *LP* (HO), 20 September 1996, 26A. Noriega's attorney was reported, in conferences with the U.S. federal judge, to have conceded that the general had put state funds to personal use. "Noriega usó dinero del Estado," *LP* (PA), 9 February 1992, 1A. See also "Noriega Lawyer Vows to Quit If Bank Letter Admitted," *MH* (US), 13 December 1991, 3A.

a total of more than $2 million, all owned by Noriega and his immediate family.[163]

The Trial of Manuel Noriega

At the general's U.S. federal trial much was learned of the functioning of the Noriega regime. Despite an array of useful witnesses, the government found convicting Noriega to be far from simple. The key prosecution challenge was the need to prove beyond a reasonable doubt that the general himself had known of, approved, and profited from the drug trade. However, as a career intelligence officer with extensive knowledge of organized crime, Noriega had painstakingly restricted information and frequently dealt with traffickers through intermediaries. Furthermore, the prosecution felt obliged to avoid certain potential witnesses who might speak of sensitive matters embarrassing to the U.S. military, law enforcement, or White House. Hence, to persuade a jury of Noriega's guilt, the prosecution had to assemble a jigsaw puzzle of largely indirect evidence.[164]

Max Mermelstein, the most important American in the Medellín cartel, stated that Jorge Ochoa and Pablo Escobar had confided to him that they had bought Panama's military institution and that he had personally seen Noriega's name in one of their account books.[165] He later related that a woman serving as Noriega's drug-enforcement director in Panama City had sold guns to Medellín traffickers, while serving as the chief contact for their cocaine planes transiting Panama.[166] Héctor López Valdez, a confidential employee for the Ochoas, testified that in 1986 he had bribed Pascual González, civil-aeronautics director, to guarantee security and to permit cocaine planes to be serviced and repaired at the international airport.[167] Anel Arcadio Pérez Castillero, lead air-traffic controller at Tocumen for a decade, testified that Colombian aircraft under Panamanian military protection regularly and flagrantly violated air-transit rules, including arriving without flight plans. Pérez also declared that on two occasions he had seen Noriega meet Ochoa on the tarmac and then fly away together in a military helicopter.[168] It developed at trial that the Noriega regime had offered Medellín traffickers unmarked planes to carry out operations at twenty-five thousand dollars per flight, and that G-2 agents had been poised to receive aircraft, sometimes with special tail markings, in particular prohibited-access areas, where distinctive green duffel bags of cocaine would be off-loaded.[169]

Convicted trafficker Floyd Carlton testified that the general had charged him one hundred thousand to two hundred thousand dollars per flight to protect four cocaine shipments, and former PDF deputy Luis Del Cid confirmed that he had delivered to Noriega two envelopes, apparently full of money, from Carlton.[170] Colombian car dealer Gabriel Taboada testified that at a face-to-face meeting with Medellín leaders in Colombia, Noriega had accepted half a million dollars from kingpin Gustavo Gaviria.[171] Pepe Cabrera alleged that he had seen Noriega welcoming top Medellín traffickers at the Contadora resort island in the Gulf of Panama.[172] Amjan Awan, director of the BCCI Panama branch

163. "Los bienes y las cuentas cauteladas de Noriega," *LP* (PA), 12 January 2001, 4A.

164. For further information, see "Lehder: Cartel Bribed Noriega," *MH* (US), 21 November, 1991, 10A, and Murillo, *Noriega Mess*, 831. Colonel Luis Del Cid observed that Noriega felt that the "right hand shouldn't know what the left hand was doing." "Las pruebas contra Manuel Noriega ¿son contundentes, or hay 'duda razonable'?," *LP* (PA), 22 December 1991, 2A.

165. "Noriega regresará a su país si es liberado: Frank Rubino," *LP* (PA), 9 March 1996, 1A.

166. Mermelstein, *Man*, 170.

167. "Pascual González protegía los vuelos con cocaína," *LP* (PA), 5 December 1991, 1A.

168. "Noriega recibió a Jorge Ochoa en el aeropuerto de Tocumen," *LP* (PA), 18 October 1991, 1A, and Murillo, *Noriega Mess*, 399.

169. "Pascual González protegía," 1A; "El G-2 se ocupaba de todo menos de la seguridad de los pasajeros," *LP* (PA), 23 October 1991, 2A.

170. "Del Cid delata," 1A.

171. "Los primeros testigos en el juicio a Noriega," *LP* (PA), 4 November 1991, 2A.

172. "Noriega regresará," 1A.

before being convicted of money laundering, reported that he had met Noriega each month to discuss his finances, including managing an account that reached $23 million.[173] Lehder testified that, prior to the Medellín cartel's understanding with Noriega, the Panamanian military had routinely detained and maltreated their people, then extorted money to free them.[174] After contemptuously dismissing the Panamanian leader as a "little policeman," Lehder further declared that Medellín traffickers had paid Noriega to secure Panama as a safe transit point, for which, he alleged, Noriega earned $1 million a month.[175]

Noriega's defense, however, exposed various weak points in the prosecution's case. Three of the general's assistants testified that they knew of no involvement by Noriega in drug trafficking, and numerous letters of commendation demonstrated that the Panamanian military leader had frequently cooperated in counternarcotics efforts.[176] Noriega had expelled various drug suspects to the United States and permitted undercover DEA operations to proceed. He had even seized shipments of precursor chemicals, even though possessing a product like ether did not violate Panamanian law. Retired admiral Daniel Murphy, former CIA deputy director, testified that Noriega had never refused a coast guard request to board a suspicious Panamanian vessel.[177] The general's subordinates had assisted in important money-laundering investigations, including in 1987 freezing accounts that belonged to Medellín traffickers, and from 1984 to 1988 Panamanian authorities had extradited seventy-five traffickers alleged to deal in multikilo amounts of cocaine.[178]

Prosecution witnesses not only occasionally contradicted themselves, but were in many instances confessed criminals themselves.[179] Noriega's defense team questioned the witnesses' credibility and highlighted plausible reasons for testimony against the general, including revenge, possible sentence reductions, or the prospect of a place in the Federal Witness Protection Program.[180] In that regard, Colombian Roberto Streidinger—once in the South Florida seafood business before becoming a pilot for Medellín traffickers—testified that, at Noriega's behest, he had transported French prostitutes to Colombia to consort with Pablo Escobar. He also confirmed Taboada's testimony regarding Noriega's meeting Escobar in Medellín.[181] However, prosecutors had helped to arrange for Streidinger to have

173. Awan testified at trial, but also appeared before the U.S. House Foreign Relations Committee where he used the figure $25 million. "25 millones, cuenta secreta de Noriega," *LP* (HO), 15 October 1988, 14. For more on Awan, see generally Mazur, *Infiltrator*.

174. See "Lehder confirma relación de Noriega con el Cartel," *LP* (PA), 20 November 1991, 1A, and "Lehder: Cartel Bribed," 10A. In 1990 Lehder declared in a television interview from his U.S. prison that Medellín had paid Noriega a salary for his services. "Noriega era un multi-espía y tenía sueldo de narcotraficantes," *Tiempo* (Honduras), 5 May 1990, 14.

175. "Carlos Lehder recibe amenazas tras declarar contra Noriega," *LP* (PA), 7 March 1996, 1A.

176. For example, in a May 1986 letter DEA administrator John Lawn praised Noriega's "vigorous policy" against drug trafficking, and a year later Lawn wrote the general, "DEA has long welcomed our close association and we stand ready to proceed jointly against international traffickers whenever the occasion arises." See "Panama Issues Report About Its Drug Battle," *NYT* (US), 10 August 1986, 12, and Koster and Sánchez, *In the Time*, 291.For the Noriega regime expelling a wanted trafficker to the United States, see *United States v. Zapata*, 1991 U.S. App. LEXIS 4644.

177. "Noriega Drug-Trafficking Case Chronology," UPI (US), 10 April 1992. For Murphy's 1987 trip to Panama to confer with Noriega, see Koster and Sánchez, *In the Time*, 294.

178. In the first half of 1986 Panama had deported thirty-six traffickers and thirteen fugitives. Murillo, *Noriega Mess*, 601. See also Shannon, *Desperados*, 165.

179. See "Contradicciones de testigos ayudan al acusado," *LP* (PA), 11 October 1991, 2A.

180. For sentence-reduction deals witnesses claimed the prosecution had offered, see "Lehder quizás atestigüe hoy en caso Noriega," *LP* (PA), 6 March 1996, 1A. The prosecution expended more than $1.5 million placing witnesses in the Federal Witness Protection Program. See "Noriega y 'la conexión sórdida,'" *LP* (PA), 27 September 1991, 2A.

181. See "Noriega regresará," 1A, and "Rubino intentará minar credibilidad del piloto colombiano R. Streidinger," *LP* (PA), 7 October 1991, 1A.

his sentence dramatically reduced in exchange for his testimony, a benefit that apparently backfired when he was murdered in Barranquilla in 1998.[182]

Among other problems for the prosecution, Héctor López Valdez could not demonstrate that the money used to bribe Pascual González had ever reached Noriega. Luis Del Cid admitted that he did not look inside the envelopes he had delivered from Floyd Carlton and instead had simply assumed they held money. Awan could not definitively link the money in Noriega's accounts to the drug trade, nor could the expert witnesses prove that Noriega's assets had not been not derived from another source, such as payments for intelligence work. Taboada's own former attorney, F. Lee Bailey, claimed that he thought his client had lied about Noriega meeting Medellín kingpins, though Taboada did later pass a lie detector test. Lehder's testimony was tainted by doubts as to the veracity of his statement that the U.S. government had permitted him to ship drugs so long as his island in the Bahamas was also used to supply the contras.

Such shortcomings troubled the jury, which deadlocked during deliberations. Only after Judge William Hoeveler instructed them to keep trying, did the jury, on April 9, 1992, convict Manuel Noriega on conspiracy, racketeering, and narcotics-trafficking charges.[183] After his sentence was reduced on two occasions, Noriega eventually served a twenty-year prison term in the United States.[184] Panamanian authorities also convicted him in absentia on various charges, and he was sentenced to a total of sixty years there, though a twenty-year term is the maximum that can be served under Panamanian law.[185]

The jury did not, however, convict Noriega of arms and cocaine trafficking relating to a Panamanian yacht called the *Krill*. When Colombian Customs officials captured the vessel at San Andrés, it was allegedly engaged in a barter of PDF weapons for 322 kilos of Medellín cocaine to be delivered to Florida.[186] Here, the deaths of key witnesses greatly complicated the prosecution's case. Because the onetime Noriega associates who had been involved—Cesár Rodríguez and Rubén (Rubencito) Darío Paredes Jr.—had already been murdered in Medellín, the key prosecution witness would have been Ramón Navarro, who had participated in buying the boat and the drugs. Navarro was prepared to testify that he had attended a meeting to discuss the *Krill* deal with Noriega, Brian Davidow, and William Saldarriaga, who from 1982 to 1984 had been married to Marta Ochoa, cousin of the Ochoa kingpins. The night before he was to be called to testify, however, Navarro was killed in an unusual one-car accident near the prison where Noriega was being held.[187]

182. When Streidinger disappeared on a visit to Colombia, three relatives had already been murdered, and when he was finally killed, his lawyer suspected a revenge motive. See "Desaparece importante testigo del juicio a Noriega," *LP* (PA), 11 January 1994, 1A; "Testigo contra Noriega denuncia al asesinato do dos familiares," *LP* (PA), 8 October 1991, 1A; and "Muerte de piloto pudo ser una verganza," *LP* (PA), 17 June 1998, 4A.

183. See "Noriega Guilty on Eight of Ten Counts," *WP* (US), 10 April 1992, A1, and "The Noriega Verdict," *WP* (US), 10 April 1992, A35. For an annotated list of the charges against Noriega and his codefendants, see "Pruebas contra Manuel Noriega," 2A.

184. Judge Hoeveler reduced the original sentence of forty years, to thirty and then twenty years, in part because of the disparity between the general's sentence and the reduced sentences served by so many prosecution witnesses and in part because Noriega was being held in modified solitary confinement. *United States v. Noriega*, 40 F. Supp.2d at 1380.

185. "Noriega iría directo a la prisión," *LP* (PA), 8 January 2007, 8A. Noriega's convictions and sentences in Panama included twenty years for killing Moisés Giroldi, fifteen years for ordering Hugo Spadafora's decapitation, and four years for participating in the "Albrook massacre," the killings after the October 1989 coup effort. "El General Noriega y sus lugartenientes," *LP* (PA), 26 January 2007, 6A.

186. For the facts in the *Krill* case, see *United States v. Saldarriaga*, 987 F.2d 1526. See also "Witness Says Noriega Approved Guns for Drugs, *MH* (US), 4 December 1991, 16A, and Murillo, *Noriega Mess*, 594–96.

187. Although a blood sample revealed no evidence of alcohol or drugs, Navarro was killed by a blow to the head, apparently caused by a falling light pole in a car accident. See "Muere Ramón Navarro, un testigo en el caso Noriega," *LP* (PA), 1 March 1991, 1A; "Defensa cuestiona credibilidad del testimonio de Amet Paredes," *LP* (PA), 8 March 1991, 1A; and "Witness Says Noriega," 16A.

Well after the trial, revelations concerning the testimony of lawyer and former Panamanian diplomat Ricardo Bilonick Paredes caused additional problems for the U.S. government. Identified by prosecutors as "the Medellín Cartel's representative in Panama," Bilonick by the early 1980s had become a leading money launderer, at first transporting suitcases laden with dollars from Miami to Panama on commercial airliners. Given the overwhelming volume of cash, however, Bilonick and his Colombian associates bought a freight airline to move cocaine north and payments south. Starting in late 1982, Inair smuggled at least 20 tons of cocaine into the United States, returning to Panama with drug money. In 1983 two Inair officials were indicted for conspiring to transport the profits of drug sales to Panama. Then, after U.S. Customs received a tip, a canine unit ferreted out 726 kilos of cocaine packed inside refrigerators being flown into Miami from Panama on an Inair flight. Panamanian officials arrested Bilonick, briefly placed him in a comfortable military cell, and then dismissed the case and released him.[188]

At Noriega's trial Bilonick testified that FDP intelligence officers would meet Inair planes upon arrival in Panama. He further reported that General Noriega had received five hundred thousand dollars for each of nineteen flights that delivered cocaine to Miami in appliances, as well as another half a million dollars for retrieving a drug shipment Panamanian Customs had seized. He also noted that Noriega had supplied Colombian traffickers with false Panamanian passports. It later came to light, however, that as Noriega's trial approached, Bilonick had been quite reluctant to testify and that prosecutors had conducted ten negotiating sessions with him in Panama before reaching an agreement.[189] Apart from offering spots in the Federal Witness Protection Program for Bilonick, his family, and maid, prosecutors agreed not to pursue Bilonick's remaining assets, despite their origins in drug transactions, and to reduce the maximum sentence he might face from sixty to ten years, while promising to recommend an even lower sentence. In fact, Bilonick eventually received a mere thirty months and was released after twenty-seven.

Additional controversy ensued from a 1996 federal court hearing that explored the possibility that the prosecution had secured Bilonick's testimony through a deal brokered during negotiations with Cali traffickers. The theory was that Cali figures, rivals to Noriega's Medellín connections, had paid Bilonick $1.25 million to testify against the general in exchange for the prosecution urging a reduced sentence in a case involving Cali kingpin José ("Chepe") Santacruz Landoño's half-brother Luis.[190] Informants, notably the Cali cartels' Chilean accountant Guillermo Pallomari, reportedly stated that Bilonick had indeed been paid such a sum, and a secret witness testified in federal court that "on behalf of the Cali Cartel, he had personally delivered $250,000 to Bilonick before Bilonick surrendered and later transferred $1,000,000 to Bilonick's wife after Bilonick testified against Noriega."[191] Although Bilonick denied having received Cali cartel monies,

188. Quote from "R. Bilonick se confesó culpable y declarará en juicio contra Noriega," *LP* (PA), 29 August 1991, 1A. For more on Bilonick's testimony, see also "Ricardo Bilonick se confiesa cómplice de Manuel A. Noriega," *LP* (PA), 15 November 1991, 1A; and "Declara Bilonick: Noriega recibía medio millón por cada cargamento de cocaína," *LP* (PA), 19 November 1991, 1A. See also Murillo, *Noriega Mess*, 402–4, and "Panama Envoy Tells of Noriega-Medellín Link," *Financial Times*, 20 November 1991, 8.

189. For additional details on the agreement, see "Noriega continuará en la cárcel," *LP* (PA), 7 April 1998, 1A; "Panama Envoy Tells," 8; "Ricardo Bilonick niega haber recibido dinero por testificar," *LP* (PA), 8 December 1996, 1A; and "Lehder quizás atestigüe," 5A.

190. "Ricardo Bilonick niega," 1A. For the response by prosecutor Michael Sullivan, see "Lehder quizás atestigüe," 1A. In 1996 authorities killed Santacruz Londoño after he escaped from Bogotá's La Picota Prison and then resisted rearrest in Medellín. "Muere el número tres del Cartel de Cali," *LP* (PA), 6 March 1996, 1A. See also Rempel, *At the Devil's Table*, pp. 67–70.

191. See "Ricardo Bilonick niega," 1A; quote from *United States v. Noriega*, 117 F.3d at 1220. The confidential witness testified that he had brought the million dollars in certificates of deposit to Bilonick's wife, who deposited

claiming simply that he had known Santacruz since 1981 and wanted to be of assistance, and although the prosecution denied that the two negotiations had been linked, the federal judges seemed to doubt that they were hearing the whole story.[192]

Ultimately, the Eleventh Circuit concluded that the U.S. government had indeed helped Santacruz Echeverri obtain a sentence reduction in exchange for the Cali trafficker's assistance in gaining Bilonick's cooperation in the Noriega prosecution. However, the defense introduced no evidence that Bilonick's testimony was false; indeed, even the witnesses who claimed that Bilonick had been paid stated that he had testified truthfully, and neither federal court found any reasonable probability that disclosing the arrangement would have brought about a different trial result.[193] In the final analysis, then, the Bilonick affair simply embarrassed the government and cast additional unwanted attention on the deals struck with witnesses in the Noriega case.

Noriega and Narco-Militarism

Once Manuel Noriega had served his prison sentence in the United States, the government extradited him to France in April 2010 to stand trial, but on money-laundering, not drug-trafficking, charges. After Noriega was sentenced to seven years in prison for laundering approximately $2.8 million through French banks, in July 2011 the French government signed an extradition order to return him to Panama.[194]

In retrospect, Noriega's trafficking activities may best be understood in the context of his background in intelligence and counterintelligence as well as his drive to gain wealth and power.[195] In the early 1980s Noriega had aimed to maximize his profits in weapon- and drug-smuggling ventures without jeopardizing his military position, possible given the extent of FDP corruption. With access to secret information and control of law enforcement, the G-2 leader was especially well positioned to profit from assisting leading traffickers. Only when rumors of Noriega's complicity in the drug trade threatened his efforts to consolidate or extend his power base did he pull back.

Noriega's political strategy was to use his money, military position, and international connections to woo, intimidate, or eliminate all potentially competing power centers until his influence was supreme within Panama. While Noriega had no scruples about dealing with traffickers, his relationship with U.S. government agencies, including DEA and CIA, contributed to his influence as well. The U.S. need for intelligence had initiated a lucrative symbiotic relationship, and yet the power of the U.S. government and its Canal Zone presence marked it as a potential threat as well. Noriega thus painstakingly compartmentalized information and minimized his direct contacts with traffickers, much preferring to use subordinates as intermediaries. For as long as possible, Noriega wished to extract as much money as he could from traffickers, but also to be, or sometimes

---

them in a Banco de Vizcaya security box requiring two keys, so neither Bilonick nor his wife could open the box without the other present. "Cartel compró testimonio de Bilonick contra Noriega," *LP* (PA), 5 March 1996, 1A.

192. During oral argument one judge stated, "The truth is that the Cali cartel helped to produce this witness. Isn't that the case?" and also "It is difficult for me to believe that the prosecution maintains that there was no relation between its negotiations with representatives of the Cali cartel and the fact that Bilonick appeared in Miami to testify." "Abogados insisten en que juicio a Noriega fue injusto," *LP* (PA), 5 December 1996, 1A.

193. "France Confirms It Will Extradite Panama's Noriega," Agence France Presse, 3 August 2011.

194. See "Noriega tuvo un juicio justo: Ex fiscales," *LP* (PA), 13 March 1996, 2A; *United States v. Noriega*, 117 F.3d at 1219; and "Niegan nuevo juicio a Noriega," *LP* (PA), 28 March 1996, 1A.

195. To the CIA and the National Security Council, Noriega portrayed himself as a bulwark against Central American communism, although he was simultaneously dealing arms to left-wing guerrillas in El Salvador and remaining on friendly terms with Fidel Castro and Colombian M-19 guerrillas. U.S. diplomat Frank McNeil once observed of Noriega: "He fed us every conversation with Fidel. And I'm sure he also fed Fidel every conversation with us." Dinges, *Our Man in Panama*, 341.

to feign being, a cooperative U.S. intelligence and law-enforcement asset. In this way he could protect himself against future difficulties whether in a court of law, in national-security decision making, or in public opinion at home and abroad. For a period Noriega earned millions from traffickers, continued to elicit support from the U.S. government, and even retained a place on the CIA payroll, all while consolidating his control over Panama. However, even so deft a juggler as Noriega could not keep such a difficult act going forever.

Noriega's legacy has sometimes been described as a new variety of political regime for Central America. In 1988 the exiled publisher of Panama's *La Prensa*, Roberto Eisenmann, then serving as a Nieman Fellow at Harvard University, described the Noriega regime in terms of "narco-militarism," that is, "a new phenomenon where drug lords take over the country's military apparatus . . . for the sole purpose of reaping profits from the enormously lucrative multinational narcotics business." Eisenmann pointed out, "Narco-militarism has an economy all its own, quite separate from the economy of the country. Panama could become a wasteland, but as long as the wasteland is owned by the Noriega gang, the gang's economy continues to flourish."[196] Certain singular aspects of military trafficking in Panama might be emphasized as well. The Noriega regime's narco-militarism amounted to a Panamanian manifestation of military involvement in the drug trade. Like different species of pine that have evolved differently in northern forests, coastal plains, and western mountains, military involvement in the drug trade assumed different forms in the varying circumstances found in different Central American countries. Although rank-and-file members of the Belize Defence Force have occasionally engaged in the transshipment of drugs, trafficking by higher-ranked officers seems not to have occurred, at least with any regularity. In the 1970s and 1980s leading officers in the Honduran armed forces were tainted by their association with Juan Ramón Matta Ballesteros and the cocaine trafficking that so rapidly enveloped their country. Eventually, midlevel military officers came to provide muscle and protection for local drug networks. And Guatemalan military elites capitalized on their extensive influence during and after the civil war to take leading roles in cartelitos. In Panama the personalistic role of Torrijos and then Noriega during the military dictatorship combined with a corrupted and avaricious officer corps and the country's extraordinary bridge-favoring factors to produce a narco-militarism that set Panama apart from the region's other bridge states. Thus, once again, the distinctive characteristics of our case studies are every bit as striking as their similarities.

The Panamanian Drug Trade Post-Noriega

Immediately after overthrowing Manuel Noriega, U.S. forces oversaw the inauguration of a new democratic regime under Guillermo Endara, on the reasoning that he had been elected president but never installed in office. Endara served his full term, surviving a coup attempt, a number of scandals, and growing popular discontent as democracy proved no panacea for Panama's problems.[197] After close but reasonably clean national elections in 1994, a peaceful transition occurred, with President Ernesto Pérez Balladares taking office. Thus did dictatorship formally give way to democracy.

In contrast to the situation in Guatemala and Honduras, the Panamanian transition from military to civilian rule was sweeping. Having so thoroughly alienated Panamanian society, the Panama Defense Force was completely disbanded. In the post-Noriega period the military was thus

196. "Panama and 'Narco-militarism,'" *Boston Globe*, 29 May 1988. For a similar view, see Koster and Sánchez, *In the Time*, 283.

197. See "Capturan narcotraficantes que desencadenaron aquí," *LP* (PA), 17 October 1991, 1A, and "G. Endara califica de 'injuria' vínculos con narcos cubanos," *LP* (PA), 18 October 1991, 1A.

in no position to seize power. It was not constantly interfering in politics, nor continuing to exert control over the police, courts, customs, and ports and airports. Unlike their counterparts in certain northern Central American bridge states, former PDF officers did not enjoy impunity, nor were they well situated to entangle themselves in business ventures, including major drug trafficking. Thus, the halting, incomplete, and potentially unstable transitions of Guatemala and Honduras were not replicated in Panama, which broke decisively away from military dictatorship.

As part of the effort to strengthen preexisting institutions and create new ones to enhance law and order, the democratic governments transformed Panama's antidrug apparatus. A civilian Public Force, composed of the national police, the National Air Service, and the National Maritime Service (SMN), replaced the disbanded Panama Defense Force. Then, within a month Endara had signed a comprehensive antidrug cooperation agreement with the United States. By the spring of 1990 the legislature had passed a law to control passage of precursor chemicals, while the executive branch provided records needed for foreign prosecutions of Cali and Medellín traffickers. The judicial branch established the PTJ to investigate crime. The new government recruited some fresh personnel, providing training and encouraging modernization.

In this environment police could interdict drug shipments and arrest traffickers, and they and the revamped prosecutor's office could build cases much more effectively than under the military regime. Not only did closer relations with U.S. officials help, but by 1993 the PTJ and Panamanian Customs were periodically capturing drugs independent of U.S. intelligence.[198] With time, signal counternarcotics triumphs followed these changes, temporarily enthusing authorities, including a twelve-ton cocaine bust in 1994 and two four-ton cocaine seizures in 1995.[199] It seemed that authorities were identifying routes and key networks and that drug syndicates no longer operated with impunity.

However, the initial applause regarding the progress of Panama's democratic transition overlooked stubborn flaws and weaknesses. With respect to drug trafficking, key bridge-favoring factors remained in place, and police, judicial, and political corruption continued to provide enticing opportunities for major trafficking organizations. Along with new dangers, traffickers saw possibilities for tremendous profit in the sweeping transformation of Panamanian society. As even more cocaine flowed through the country, Panama, post-Noriega, grew to become one of the region's two most important bridge states.

Obstacles During the Political Transition

Surprisingly, even as Panamanian institutions strengthened after Noriega's exit, drug trafficking soared, as the wealth, power, and influence of transnational criminals proved to be quite a match even for revamped law-enforcement agencies and redesigned laws, policies, and procedures. Drug organizations thus absolutely swarmed into post-Noriega Panama, stimulating the transit of even more narcotics than had been evident under the military regime. This development may be attributed to a number of factors.

One initial problem was that the U.S. military operations in the 1989 invasion, which killed a total of about three hundred Panamanian soldiers and civilians, also badly damaged certain sections of Panama City. Although some of this destruction occurred collateral to U.S. attacks, the Dignity Battalions caused extensive damage as well, spitefully setting fires in traditionally anti-Noriega neighborhoods such as El Chorillo. This, coupled with extensive looting and the presence of thousands of refugees,

198. *INCSR* (1994), 168. For a representative case reflecting these changes, see *United States v. Munoz-Solarte*, 1994 U.S. App. LEXIS 18128.

199. "Autoridades malogran," 20A. See also "En Darién ha disminuido tráfico de drogas e illegales," *LP* (PA), 13 October 1991, 40A.

helped to bring on further economic troubles. These problems lingered, though the U.S. government lifted its sanctions and freed frozen funds, and the U.S. military assisted in getting utilities functioning again. Although some sectors of the economy rebounded quickly, high unemployment, labor disturbances, and accumulated debts remained problematic.[200] The U.S. Congress also moved quite slowly in delivering on promises of financial assistance, delays caused by the demands of creditor banks, reports that money laundering was continuing apace, and frictions over the time the Panamanian government was taking to approve a Mutual Legal Assistance Treaty with the United States.

Another notable difficulty was that neither the personnel nor the budget could meet urgent social challenges. Authorities had to confront a wave of burglaries, robberies, and car thefts, primarily in Panama City, Colón, and environs. Rising crime rates reflected weaker law enforcement, mass prison escapes during the invasion, and unemployed and disaffected Norieguistas, many with military training and weapons.[201] The new Public Force, undertrained, poorly equipped, and stretched thin, trying to respect rights and adhere to new procedures, simply could not cope. Furthermore, the courts confronted enormous backlogs of cases, and prisons were filled far beyond capacity. In short, long neglected, mismanaged, or corrupted institutions—judicial, political, and penal—had to be retooled to avoid lapsing back into the Noriega regime's antidemocratic practices, and this could not happen with dispatch.

As for law enforcement, two years after Operation Just Cause, Panama's coast guard remained overwhelmed by the effort to control 1,800 miles of coastline. Apart from a handful of boats that patrolled the Panama City area, it consisted of one cutter, two rented shrimp trawlers, a yacht seized from traffickers, four patrol boats, and four small Boston whalers. The National Air Service found itself in similar straits, with three double-engine and four single-engine planes, three Bell helicopters, and a cargo plane. In 1997, after the government leased to developers the island on which the SMN had been headquartered, the coast guard lacked any permanent docking facilities on either coast.[202]

The enormity of the challenge for the immediate post-Noriega governments was soon starkly apparent. Bringing members of the dictatorship and their collaborators to account became bogged down. Reports were issued. Miscreants were fired. Occasional prosecutions occurred, and the media or government succeeded in shedding some light on past misdeeds. However, many people—not simply soldiers, officials, and other government workers, but bankers, politicians, and business executives—had cultivated ties with the military regime. As decisions were made as to who should be investigated and whose past misdeeds should be ignored, *amigoismo* and influence peddling ran rife. Many incriminating files were destroyed in a partially successful effort to cover up past corruption by some who anticipated future careers in law, politics, or government. Indeed, so many crimes were left unpunished and so many former officials remained influential that University of Panama law professor Miguel Antonio Bernal quipped, "The United States took out Ali Baba and left us the forty thieves."[203]

Then, hopes that Noriega's departure would break the grip of the drug trade were thoroughly dashed. As early as April 1991 a DEA official reported that trafficking and laundering in Panama had returned to the same levels as before the invasion.[204] Thereafter, the quantities

200. After comprehensively reviewing the issue of the number of deaths, Murillo concluded that 321 killed represented one of the more accurate counts. See his *Noriega Mess*, 824–26. For Dignity Battalion destruction, see page 793 and for delayed congressional support, see pages 855–57.

201. Ibid., 847–51.

202. *INCSR* (1998), 166.

203. Murillo, *Noriega Mess*, 834. For the burning of incriminating documents, see page 844, and for problems facing the new regime, see pages 850–52.

204. "EE.UU. revela auge de narco en Panamá," *LN* (CR), 19 April 1991, 18A.

of transshipped narcotics leapt upward. Even more drug shipments seized in other bridge states and in market countries had originated in Panama. The domestic price of cocaine fell, and local consumption grew.

The immediate post-Noriega years also proved to be an exceedingly difficult time for executive and legislative acts to be transformed into effective action to curb mounting drug transshipment. Laws on the books remained subject to infrequent and selective enforcement. Even when authorities did freeze assets, few proceedings resulted in forfeiture. Instead, defense attorneys frequently got assets returned to their owners.[205] Drug networks quickly grasped that large bribes no longer needed to be paid to operate successfully in Panama. Although interdiction risks grew for traffickers who no longer had Noriega's support, given law-enforcement weaknesses, those risks remained tolerable, while expenses plummeted.

Equally important, while Noriega's departure both contributed to and coincided with the decline of the Medellín cartel, this development was more than counterbalanced by the efficiency with which the Cali cartel began to move even larger cocaine loads. In particular, as Panama began its democratic transition, Cali and other traffickers shifted from relying primarily on aerial-trafficking schemes to maritime routes. Cocaine transit by sea had long been Cali's forte, and in the early 1990s Cali traffickers aggressively seized market share from Medellín. Given its proximity to Colombia, its extensive merchant marine and shipping facilities, and its canal and duty-free zone, Panama found itself at the heart of even more drug-smuggling ventures.

Then, as the fortunes of Cali traffickers ebbed in the later 1990s, other factors brought drug networks to become ever more deeply embedded in Panama. With the influence of the Colombian cartels dwindling, the drug industry there splintered, and the numbers of brokers linking farmers, chemists, smugglers, and distributors increased dramatically.[206] Panama was readily accessible and even familiar for many smaller drug rings that, at least initially, lacked the easy reach of their larger predecessors. Moreover, with the reversion of the canal to Panamanian control, the U.S. Southern Command left Panama, and so the drug center on Howard Air Base in the Canal Zone was shut down.[207] Negotiations to create a substitute institution died, and ultimately U.S. Air Force radar planes were stationed in El Salvador. Thus, although in 1996 Panama, alone among the Central American states, had installed radar covering 250 nautical miles, by 1999 U.S. military aircraft were no longer monitoring suspicious flights from Canal Zone bases, operations that had led to the interception of an average of fifty drug flights annually.[208]

The globalization of the cocaine trade spotlighted Panama as well. The country had long enjoyed extensive commercial links to Europe, including questionable European executives doing business in, networking in, and even residing in Panama. For instance, Spanish brothers Celso Luis and Manuel Celestino Fernández Espina owned the Celuisma hotel business, which included properties in Spain and Colombia as well as Panama City's Hotel Soloy. During the period that one of the brothers resided in Panama, Spanish police linked Celuisma accounts to the financial dealings of Honduran trafficker Matta Ballesteros. Indeed, the Fernández Espinas owned the house in Madrid where Spanish police arrested Medellín kingpin Jorge Luis Ochoa in 1986.[209] In 1989, just before Colombian police hunted down and killed

205. *INCSR* (1995), 152.

206. Decker and Chapman, *Drug Smugglers*, 39.

207. "E.U. cerrará centro antidrogas de Howard," *LP* (PA), 2 May 1999, 3A.

208. "Panamá tiene un nuevo radar," *LP* (PA), 9 August 1996, 2A. See also "EU mantiene centro antidrogas desde 1992," *LP* (PA), 26 September 1996, 2A; "Niveles del narcotráfico han aumentado, dice Ferro," *LP* (PA), 20 April 2000, 2A; and "Traffickers Set Up Shop in Panama," *Los Angeles Times*, 18 January 2000, 1A.

209. See "Panama: Dirty Business," C1, and "Matta Ballesteros residió hasta 1985 en Madrid," *El País* (Spain), 12 April 1990, 1.

Ochoa's colleague, Gonzalo Rodríguez Gacha, he had transferred $12 million to Interbanco in Panama, of which $7 million was reportedly loaned to the Fernández Espinas.

With connections of these sorts, as drug organizations opened cocaine markets on the continent, Panama was in a prime position to become deeply involved in European transshipment. Indeed, with time, certain Panamanians have come to lead drug networks involved in substantial European trafficking ventures. For instance, businessman Boris de Jesús Foguel Suengas organized the Camels to move drugs from Peru and other South American countries into Spain.[210] In 1999 workers at a frozen seafood business in Callao, Peru, found that 2.3 tons of cocaine had been hidden in a shipping container headed to Bilbao, Spain, each package marked with the picture of a camel. Peruvian intelligence and Panamanian authorities then joined to arrest Foguel, associate Pablo Mures Loaiza, and a Spanish couple who had served as the group's chief European contact. Eventually, all four were convicted, with Foguel receiving a sixteen-year sentence and his accomplices ten-year terms.

The ongoing civil war in Colombia also stimulated cocaine trafficking in Panama after Noriega's departure. Panama's prominent role as a weapons supplier eventually led to numerous arms-for-drugs deals, as paramilitaries and guerrillas traded cocaine for weapons.[211] Thus, in a single incident in 2002 authorities seized 139 guns, including AK-47 automatic weapons, as well as 279 kilos of cocaine and 239 of marijuana in the basement of a new beach house on the coast of Coclé.[212] In early 2003 the Colombian Navy seized a vessel linked to the FARC, heading to Panama with 158 kilos of cocaine, 280 kilos of marijuana, and a lesser quantity of heroin.[213] In the course of five operations later that year, Panamanian authorities arrested eleven—Colombians, Panamanians, and Mexicans—for participating in arms-for-drugs deals, while they seized nearly four hundred weapons and more than one million rounds of ammunition.[214] By 2007 Panamanian cocaine transshipment encompassed Colombian paramilitary forces, with 2,598 kilos seized over a three-day span, coming from the Autodefensas Unidas de Colombia (AUC) via Panama's Pacific coast.[215]

As this tremendous array of drug networks went to work, sometimes vying with one another, drug-related violence increased markedly.[216] From the late 1990s, some Panamanian criminal enterprises have dedicated themselves to stealing drugs in transit or storage and, occasionally, taking weapons or drug profits. Confident that the traffickers who have been robbed will not complain to authorities, these *tumbadores* sell the drugs to local dealers or to other international traffickers, or they forward them to foreign markets themselves. Not only have victimized drug networks responded violently to try to deter the practice, but drug robberies have increased police corruption, because the tumbadores need the intelligence on upcoming

210. For information on the Camels, see "Declaran legal detención de española," *LP* (PA), 6 April 2000, 3A; "Extraditarán a pareja de acusados españoles," *LP* (PA), 8 May 2000, 1A; "Enjuician a banda 'Los Camellos,'" *LP* (PA), 25 November 2003, 6A; and "Condenan a la banda de los Camellos," *LP* (PA), 26 August 2005, 6A.

211. See "La ruta panameña de las armas," *LP* (PA), 14 October 2000, 5A, which includes a list of Panamanian arms seizures from 1990 to 2000. Panamanian intelligence estimated that their authorities had intercepted only 10 percent of transshipped arms from 1980 to 2000. See, also, "Jefe de drogas en Darién en tráfico de armas," *LP* (PA), 17 May 2003, 1A, and "Policía Nacional decomisa armas y drogas en Tocumen," *LP* (PA), 31 January 2001, 4A.

212. See "Decomisan armas y droga en Coclé," *LP* (PA), 31 July 2002, 5A, and "Asestan duro golpe al crimen," *LP* (PA), 1 August 2002, 2A.

213. "Decomisan barco con cocaína," *LP* (PA), 28 January 2003, 4A.

214. "En el 2003 se decomisaron 393 fusiles," *LP* (PA), 3 January 2004, 3A.

215. See "El cargamento de los paramilitares," *LP* (PA), 12 August 2007, 9A.

216. In 2008 the minister of government and justice declared that 90 percent of Panama's violent crime was drug related. "Drogas están detrás de crímenes," *LP* (PA), 23 January 2008, 6A.

drug shipments to which police officers may have access.[217]

Isaac Jovannie Btesh Castillo, a Panamanian jeweler and former convicted drug trafficker, ran one prominent tumbadore network.[218] According to the DEA, Btesh partnered with Panamanian police officer Carlos Soto Vega, allegedly a double agent in the drug trade. Soto reportedly worked with Colombian traffickers, needing assistance in arranging the entry and exit of light planes; however, he also relayed information about their cocaine transshipment to Btesh, who organized robberies of the narcotics in transit. After concluding a forty-four-month sentence for cocaine trafficking in Louisiana in 2000, Btesh managed to accumulate at least $3.19 million in assets over the next six years, though authorities claimed he had no legitimate source of income to earn such sums, lacking even credit cards and bank accounts. Antidrug officials believed he was profiting from dispatching and receiving drug planes, while ensuring that some cocaine loads were stolen by tumbadores.

Thus, while the contours of the Panamanian drug trade shifted, the amount of drugs transiting the country soared, far exceeding what had traversed Panama in the Noriega years. In 1992 Leo González, chair of Panama's legislative narcotics commission, declared that money laundering and drug trafficking were reaching "horrifying dimensions." Five years later, Panamanian politician Francisco Sánchez Cárdenas referred to the "scandalous manner" in which drug trafficking and money laundering had climbed since the 1989 invasion. In 1998 retired U.S. colonel Matías Farías testified that triple the amount of drugs were passing through Panama than under Noriega's rule. Panama had become, in the words of U.S. representative Charles Rangel, "even more of a land of opportunity for drug traffickers."[219]

Center of Operations for Foreign Traffickers

For many years, to escape violence or law enforcement in their home countries, important traffickers not only held meetings and vacationed abroad but even temporarily transferred their locus of operations, including moving their families.[220] Far more of them chose Panama than any other bridge state. Scores of Colombian traffickers took residence there, as did Americans, Bolivians, Hondurans, Italians, Jamaicans, Mexicans, and others. We have noted that Medellín kingpins hid in Panama in 1984, under Noriega's protection, after the Lara Bonilla assassination. Pablo Escobar was said to have sent his son to be educated in Panama. In 1986 Bolivian traffickers, tipped to an upcoming antidrug offensive by the Bolivian Army with U.S. military support, hid out in Panama as well, and other Medellín traffickers also took advantage of the military regime's hospitality.[221]

Under the new democratic governments, Panama became a somewhat less reliable safe haven. Panamanian law enforcement officials, often aided by the DEA, have arrested numerous foreign traffickers stationed in Panama. In one

217. For information on the violence engendered by the tumbadores, see "El 'tumbo' y el crimen de la Calzada," *LP* (PA), 6 October 2006, 6A; "'Tumbadores' tratan de escapar del país por temor a represalias," *LP* (PA), 7 October 2006, 4A; "Los orígenes de los 'tumbes' se remontan a finales de los noventa," *LP* (PA), 6 October 2006, 6A; and "Intentaron 'tumbar' dinero a narcos," *LP* (PA), 3 October 2006, 8A.

218. For information on Btesh's ring, see "Corrup ción en la PN," *LP* (PA), 10 December 2006, 1A; "Comisionado Soto Vega era investigado desde 2005," *LP* (PA), 10 December 2006, 4A; "Soto Vega cobraba cifras de seis dígitos," *LP* (PA), 22 December 2006, 6A; and "DEA alertó sobre actos de comisionado de Policía," *LP* (PA), 5 August 2007, 8A.

219. "Panama: Corruption Returns," *MH* (US), 30 December 1992, 12A; "Narcotráfico ha aumentado," 1A; "Noriega pide clemencia," 1A; "Drug Traffic Rebounds: Two Years After the U.S. Invasion, Cocaine Trafficking Is as Bad as Ever," *Ottawa Citizen* 15 December 1991, A3.

220. See "Traffickers Set Up Shop," 1A.

221. See Dinges, *Our Man in Panama*, 184; Shannon, *Desperados*, 360–65, and Murillo, *Noriega Mess*, 233, 395–96. For one example of a Medellín trafficker under the top echelon hiding out in Panama, see *United States v. Reed*, 980 F.2d at 1573. See also "Prófugos buscan refugio," 2A.

representative case in 1999 the Panamanian Coast Guard stopped a go-fast and discovered numbers stored in the memories of cellular and satellite phones on board that helped investigators break up a network shipping one-ton cocaine loads from Cartagena through Haiti and the Dominican Republic into the United States. Culminating in 2004, Operation Bunker broke up another drug ring headquartered in Panama, with eight Colombians arrested and 1,639 kilos of cocaine confiscated. That same year, Panamanian police arrested Cristian Ortíz Guadamuz, allegedly a major Salvadoran trafficker connected to an operation that had sent at least six cocaine shipments overland through Central America and Mexico to the United States. Although Costa Rican and Guatemalan authorities seized three loads en route, the organization still had managed to transship a half ton of narcotics.[222]

In addition, starting in the late 1990s, at least seventeen traffickers quietly entered Panama to meet with DEA agents to negotiate their surrender to U.S. law enforcement.[223] All sought to become U.S. government informants to avoid violent competitors as well as antidrug authorities at home. They typically received a lower sentence, retained a portion of their assets, and gained a place in the Federal Witness Protection Program in return for information used to dismantle their former criminal enterprises.

One of the most important was Orlando Sánchez Cristancho. Cali kingpin Miguel Rodríguez Orejuela reportedly believed that Sánchez had ordered the shooting of his son, William Rodríguez Abadía, who for a period had ascended to the top echelon of Cali traffickers. In 1998 Sánchez entered and left Panama multiple times during extensive negotiations with U.S. authorities, before an agreement was struck for him to become a federal witness. Eight years later, Rodríguez Abadía himself entered Panama, arriving by speedboat from Colombia's Pacific coast. A fugitive since his father's arrest in 2002, wanted for drug trafficking and money laundering and a suspect in the murder of Guillermo Pallomari's wife, Rodríguez Abadía was very sick, suffering from kidney problems. In 2006, he, too, chose to deliver himself to the DEA and accept extradition to the U.S., where he became another important government witness.[224] Panama had thus become the favored site where deals might be brokered between Colombian traffickers and U.S. authorities.

Northern Valley Cartel Arrests

Among the most significant arrests of foreign traffickers in Panama who did not voluntarily surrender was that of Arcángel de Jesús Henao Montoya. A top leader of Colombia's Northern Valley organization, Henao Montoya had flown into Panama in 2003, supposedly as a tourist, under an assumed name. U.S. authorities wanted Henao for drug trafficking and money laundering, and Colombian prosecutors, for drug offenses and suspected links to a 1989 massacre of 130 campesinos in El Valle Department. With the Colombian drug trade fractured, Henao had also become a target for assassins in the increasingly bloody turf wars that Northern Valley traffickers were fighting. In 2004 U.S. intelligence tracked Henao Montoya to a nearly seven-hundred-acre country estate just off the Pan-American Highway in Tortí, near Darién, and twenty Panamanian Special Forces succeeded in capturing him as he breakfasted with an entourage of twenty-seven other Colombians. Four days later, Panama extradited Henao to the United States, where he was eventually

222. "Piloto de autos lideraba banda de narcos," *LP* (PA), 6 October 2004, 4A.

223. See "Sapos del Cartel," 4; "'Sapos' negociaron entrega a Estados Unidos en Panamá," *Panamá America*, 16 February 2009, 5; and "Paramilitares estarían en Panamá," *LP* (PA), 14 October 2006, 6A. See generally López, *Cartel de los sapos*.

224. For Sánchez and Rodríguez cases, see "Capo colombiano entró por mar a Panamá," *LP* (PA), 18 January 2006, 8A, and "Heredero del Cartel de Cali paseó antes de entregarse," *LP* (PA), 19 January 2006, 8A. See also Rempel, *At the Devil's Table*, pp. 317–18.

convicted of trafficking 136 tons of cocaine and sentenced to thirty years in prison.[225]

Then, in 2007 authorities in Panama City arrested Colombian José Nelson Urrego, allegedly the Northern Valley chief of communications. Wanted by the DEA since 1982 and accused of laundering $13 million between 2002 and 2006, utilizing Panamanian banks and shell companies, Nelson had spent $12 million to buy Chapera, a 270-acre island just south of Contadora in Las Perlas, where he planned to build a 320-room, five-star hotel. After his arrest, Nelson claimed that Panamanian politicians and businesspersons had recognized the development potential of Chapera and wanted to buy the island. When he refused to sell, Nelson claimed they had turned him in to authorities. A police investigation then produced photos of Nelson on the island, and confidential informants noted that drugs and weapons had been hidden there.[226]

Pablo Rayo Montaño

The extensive activities in Panama of another Colombian kingpin surfaced in Operation Twin Oceans, a three-year investigation by the DEA, Panamanian, Colombian, and Brazilian police, that resulted in more than one hundred arrests and the seizure of fifty-two tons of cocaine, more than 150 bank accounts, and assets reaching $70 million. The key target was Colombian trafficker Pablo Rayo Montaño, considered to be the successor to assassinated Cali kingpin Hélmer Herrera Buitrago.

Originally from a family of Colombian fishermen in Buenaventura, Rayo decided in 1999 to settle in Panama, where he had spent time since 1995. Colombian authorities were assembling a trafficking case against him. In addition, his brother William had returned to Colombia after serving a drug-trafficking sentence in Panama and had been immediately killed, a victim of the strife within the Colombian drug industry. Rayo thus assumed a false name, gained an investor visa, and assembled a battery of false credentials showing him to be Brazilian. Rayo posed as a legitimate businessman, investing in a popular Portobelo restaurant, Los Cañones, and a marina and sport-fishing business, NautiPesca. He bought a principal residence in Panama City, where his wife and daughter lived, and then he purchased at least thirty additional houses for his network, including nine from the government's Interoceanic Regional Authority.[227]

225. See "Detienen en Panamá a capo colombiano," *LP* (PA), 11 January 2004, 1A; "Capo ingresó como turista," *LP* (PA), 14 January 2004, 1A; "Un arresto en pleno desayuno," *LP* (PA), 14 January 2004, 2A; "Extraditan a EU a Henao Montoya," *LP* (PA), 15 January 2004, 1A; and "'Sapos del Cartel' dieron su último brinco en Panamá," *Panamá America*, 15 February 2009, 4. Meanwhile, the Panamanian Supreme Court freed Henao's sister, Lorena Henao Montoya, widow of the Northern Valley's original leader Iván Urdinola Grajales. The court claimed to lack sufficient evidence linking her to drug crimes, even money laundering, and ordered her deported to Colombia. Upon arrival, however, Colombian authorities immediately arrested her for bribery and money laundering, and she later confessed to having previously suborned Colombian judicial officers for protection. A luxury apartment in Paitilla, Panama City, contained boxes of incriminating evidence seized by the DEA and Panama police for use at trial. Her quick release in Panama thus became controversial. See "Los inútiles veintiocho tomos del caso Henao Montoya," *LP* (PA), 28 November 2005, 6A; "Las confesiones de la traficante que la Corte dejó en libertad," *LP* (PA), 6 March 2005, 2A; "Por qué Arjona objetó la liberación de Henao," *LP* (PA), 6 March 2005, 2A; "Arrestan a hermana de narco," *LP* (PA), 6 May 2004, 2A; and "Ilegal, detención de colombiana," *LP* (PA), 5 May 2004, 4A.

226. For the Nelson case, see "Capo tenía permiso para un 'resort,'" *LP* (PA), 17 September 2007, 5A; "Fiscalía indaga a capo colombiano," *LP* (PA), 18 September 2007, 8A; "Urrego, en el 'ranking' de los casos más sonados," *LP* (PA), 10 January 2008, 8A; "Empresarios de EU eran socios de José Urrego," *LP* (PA), 13 January 2008, 7A; "Urrego menciona a políticos," *LP* (PA), 23 January 2008, 6A; and "Interrogarán a agentes de la DIIP," *LP* (PA), 29 January 2008, 8A.

227. Capo colombiano compró islas panameñas," *LP* (PA), 18 May 2006, 8A; "Heredero de estirpe sangrienta," *LP* (PA), 25 May 2006, 6A; "Narcos compraron nueve casas a la ARI," *LP* (PA), 26 March 2004, 1A; "Formulan más cargos a Rayo Montaño," *LP* (PA), 7 December 2006, 5A; "Políticos y funcionarios vinculados a Rayo Montaño," *LP* (PA), 6 January 2007, 4A; "Narcos vivían como reyes," *LP* (PA), 19 May 2006, 6A; "Rayo Montaño y sus conexiones en Panamá," *LP* (PA), 21 May 2006, 8A; "Treinta casas de lujo tenía Rayo Montaño en Panamá," *LP* (PA), 23 May 2006, 6A; "Investigan a la pareja de Rayo Montaño," *LP* (PA), 24 May 2006, 6A.

Assisted by four key associates, Rayo Montaño then started to traffic drugs and arms and launder money from his new Panama headquarters. In importing cocaine via both coasts and exporting it to the United States, Rayo's organization relied on independent Panamanian networks as well as the Sinaloa cartel. While some aerial trafficking occurred, Rayo's real specialty was moving cocaine by sea. He thus bought three Caribbean islands, Las Tres Marías, situated just off the coast of Colón, which were used to hide and resupply his fleet of boats and to divide large cocaine shipments into smaller loads that could more easily be dispatched to the mainland. Rayo's organization operated extensively in the Pacific as well, bringing into Panama large quantities of cocaine, both by air and sea, from Buenaventura.[228]

While Rayo had generally adopted the low-profile, businesslike operations long associated with Cali traffickers, selective violence was used to protect his organization's interests. One informant accused Rayo of having ordered the murder of Franklin Brewster, chief of the PTJ Sensitive Unit, who was investigating a $2 million bank account and had already been responsible for the seizure of large cocaine loads, including one two-ton shipment. After detailing the links that Rayo's organization had in Panama's Public Ministry, Supreme Court, and National Assembly, this confidential witness reported that one of Rayo's Colombian associates had arrived in Panama with phosphorus and half a million dollars to finance Brewster's poisoning. PTJ officials Giovanni Véliz Ibarra and Keneth Brown were then allegedly hired to murder their boss.[229]

In late 2002 Panamanian authorities struck against Rayo's network. On the Río Chico near Chepo, just east of the Tocumen International Airport, officials seized 1,500 packets of heroin, 316 kilos of cocaine, and a weapons shipment destined for Colombian guerrillas. A week later $3 million was confiscated from one of Rayo's planes. Then, in the spring of 2003 officials arrested ten, and then another eighteen members of his organization, confiscating four boats, four businesses, and eleven residences, while seizing nearly $1.7 million. Rayo then fled to Brazil, where he was eventually arrested in São Paulo in 2006, with DEA administrator Karen Tandy declaring that his organization "had its own private rogue navy to run a drug business that was nearly as sophisticated as a small nation." In May 2009 Pablo Rayo Montaño was extradited to the United States to face extensive drug-trafficking and money-laundering charges.[230]

José Castrillón Henao

Although the final chapter of Rayo Montaño's criminal career occurred in Brazil, the most consequential arrest in Panama of a drug kingpin was that of Cali trafficker José Castrillón Henao. Early in 1992 in the Windward Passage of the Caribbean between Cuba and Haiti, a U.S. Coast Guard cutter, acting on a DEA tip, boarded a large Panamanian-registered freighter headed to Baltimore with a load of zinc. When the coast guard ship approached, the *Harbour*'s crew first set fire to the engine room, throwing flammable liquid into the main engines, and then tried to sink the ship by opening the sea valves. The coast guard, however, managed to douse the fire and eventually discovered the

228. "Panama Report Explains Drug Traffickers' Use of Runways, Airports," BBC Monitoring Latin America, 7 March 2008; "La historia del narcotraficante que construyó un imperio," *LP* (PA), 24 May 2006, 1A.

229. "Rayo Montaño mandó a asesinar a Brewster," *LP* (PA), 6 December 2006, 8A. The FBI brought into the Brewster case at the Panamanian government's request, was unable to identify the source of the phosphorus, because it is used in insecticides, weed killer, and more than 1,600 other products. "FBI no logra identificar el veneno en el caso Brewster," *LP* (PA), 12 December 2006, 8A.

230. "Narcos vivían," 6A; "Desmantelan célula de narcos colombianos," *LP* (PA), 8 November 2002, 8A; quote from "Drug-trafficking Suspect Released After Acquittal," *Washington Times*, 24 July 2008, A11. For more on his properties and connections in Panama, see "Pablo Rayo Montaño tenía propiedades en Coco del Mar," *LP* (PA), 22 May 2006, 8A; "La conexión de Rayo Montaño con el

Harbour to be carrying 5 tons of cocaine. After their arrest, the one Colombian on board and the ship's captain assisted the government to reduce their sentences. The trail led to a Chilean shipping company and an arm of the Cali cartel that had been sending cocaine to the United States and Europe for at least eight years. Investigators suspected the involvement of a Buenaventura businessman, José Castrillón Henao, who had first attracted attention by being linked to cocaine exports from Colombia in pleasure boats that arrived at different Panamanian ports.[231]

Then, in July 1995 in international waters near the Galápagos in the eastern Pacific, a U.S. Navy cruiser came upon the *Nataly I*, a 112-foot Panamanian-flagged long-lined vessel, a variety of boat that uses buoyed lines, sometimes fifty miles long, to catch large fish. Upon being intercepted, about 780 miles off of the coast of Peru, the captain acknowledged having left Panama six days earlier and consented to boarding by a U.S. Coast Guard team, which found a crew of ten Colombians, but no fish, insufficient ice and bait, and an industrial scale too small for large fish. A spray test performed on a forward hatch showed traces of cocaine. After Panamanian authorities approved a search of the ship, the coast guard drained an oil tank, finding two hidden compartments containing nearly 12 tons of cocaine, the largest seizure to date in U.S. history.[232] Further investigations revealed that in 1992 a Panamanian company, Pesqueros Aztecas, had bought a vessel called the *Malena* for one dollar from another Buenaventura drug trafficker, and the ship had been rechristened *Nataly I* and had joined Castrillón's fleet.[233]

In December 1995 authorities engineered a third major bust of Castrillón's operation, as the SMN intercepted a large catamaran, the *Michelangelo*, and seized 2.5 tons of Cali cartel cocaine. This vessel, with a crew of a Panamanian, a Colombian, and two experienced Austrian captains, who claimed to have been threatened by the drug traffickers, was en route from Colombia's Caribbean coast, through the Panama Canal. It was then to head north in the Pacific along Central America and Mexico. Investigators discovered that Castrillón Henao also owned the *Michelangelo*.[234]

Although sometimes referred to as "the Man of a Thousand Names," José Castrillón Henao was, in fact, a key Cali trafficker who had been in and out of Panama since 1983. By the mid-1990s, however, Castrillón had already earned millions and was eager to put the drug business behind him. After telling other Cali kingpins throughout 1994 that he wanted to quit and move to Panama, Castrillón finally got their approval and tried to retire in May 1995. By then, however, police and intelligence in the United States, Colombia, Costa Rica, Mexico, Ecuador, Honduras, and Panama had dossiers

'Divino Niño,'" *LP* (PA), 23 May 2006, 1A; "Las conexiones de políticos panameños con Rayo Montaño," *LP* (PA), 26 May 2006, 6A; and "Los 'fantasmas' espantan en Guanche," *LP* (PA), 27 May 2006, 7A.

231. *United States v. Huerta Rojas, et al.*, 801 F. Supp. 644; "Desarticulan red del cartel de Cali en Chile," *LP* (PA), 5 May 1998,1A; "Target: Cali Cartel," *Tampa Tribune* (United States) (hereafter cited as *TT* [US]), 17 June 2001, 1; "Millionaire Extradited for Drug Trial," *TT* (US), 20 March 2004, 1. For more information on the *Harbour*, see the affidavit of FBI special agent Roderick D. Huff, who helped to debrief Castrillón, in *United States v. Valencia-Trujillo*, No. 8:02-CR-329-T-17-EAJ (hereafter cited as "Huff affidavit"), 6–7. For the essence of that affidavit, see "The Confidential Witness," *TT* (US), 15 May 2005, 1.

232. See "Barco cargado de cocaína llevó a captura de Castrillón Henao," *LP* (PA), 26 April 1996, 1A; "Target: Cali Cartel," 1; and *United States v. Klimavicius-Viloria*, 144 F.3d 1249. The month before being seized, the *Nataly I* was housed at a secure closed deck on Panama's Caribbean coast, undergoing "repairs."

233. The vessel was owned by Kurt Alexander Abicht Aguilar, member of a network running drugs from Buenaventura into Panama until he decided to move into business on his own. Within the year hit men had killed Abicht, with police suspecting Buenaventura trafficker Víctor Patiño Fómeque. "La banda de los hijos de Rafaela," *El Tiempo* (Colombia), 25 June 1995, 1.

234. For information on the *Michelangelo*, see "Autoridades malogran," 20A; "Acusados de narcotráfico," *LP* (PA), 30 January 1998, 5A; "Hoy juzgan a diez socios de Castrillón," *LP* (PA), 30 January 1998, 5A; "Niegan nexos de Castrillón con diez sindicatos por narcotráfico," *LP* (PA), 13 January 1998, 5A; "Target: Cali Cartel," 1; and "Castrillón Henao dirigía vasta red de narcotraficantes," *LP* (HO), 25 April 1996, 48A.

on him, and U.S. officials were close on his trail. In fact, CIA agents had rented the apartment above Castrillón's, and after drilling a hole in the floor and inserting a tiny camera, had started to videotape his movements and contacts.[235]

Investigators believed that Castrillón had taken charge of at least thirty major cocaine shipments from Colombia to the United States and Europe. He had at least six million-dollar bank accounts and owned sixty-two properties in Colombia alone. Castrillón was also deeply engaged in Cali money laundering, using fishing, real-estate, and communications businesses—twenty-seven of them in Colombia, twenty in Panama, and four in Costa Rica—and moving at least $36 million through sixty-six bank accounts and 112 corporations.[236] In Panama, Banaico served as one of the principal banks for Cali traffickers.[237] Here, Divaldo Cano Saavedra, a well-connected Panamanian businessman, had vouched for Castrillón, who had opened seventeen accounts, totaling $2.6 million.[238]

In April 1996 Colombian National Police moved against Castrillón, searching his primary place of business in Buenaventura as well as various residences and offices. A subordinate promptly informed the kingpin, and the following day he fled his Panama City apartment, suitcase in hand. Police immediately moved in for the arrest, charging Castrillón with drug trafficking and money laundering. They discovered in his briefcase a financial statement listing numerous Panamanian assets, leading them into a labyrinth of financial dealings.[239] After a two-year investigation, authorities discovered that the kingpin had set up sixty-four shell companies in Panama, alongside a total of sixty in Colombia, the United States, Mexico, and Ecuador. His organization had held sixty-six accounts in thirteen Panamanian banks, alongside twenty-two accounts in eight other countries. While Panamanian authorities seized $8 million in assets, many more holdings had been hidden abroad.[240] A federal prosecutor in south Florida froze assets there worth $700,000, and authorities as far afield as Spain, France, and Germany discovered additional accounts held by Castrillón's organization. By 1998 cases against Castrillón or his subordinates were pending in Colombia,

235. Huff affidavit, 62, 85–86; "Castrillón, un atrapado en su propia red," *LP* (PA), 26 April 1998, 4A; "PTJ captura a miembros del cartel de Cali," *LP* (PA), 19 April 1996, 3A; "Target: Cali Cartel," 1; "Formulan cargos contra José Castrillón Henao," *LP* (PA), 25 April 1996, 1A;"De Veraguas a Quintana Roo," *LP* (PA), 17 January 1999, 6A; "Castrillón Henao dirigía," 48A; "PTJ captura," 3A; "Tampa-Run Probe Nets Alleged Cali King," *TT* (US), 1 February 2003, 1; "Colombia Cocaine Bust Nets Seven Arrests," *TT* (US), 13 December 2001, 1.

236. For the information on Castrillon's finances, see "'Patrimonio' de narco detenido asciende a millones de dólares," *LP* (PA), 20 April 1996, 1A; "Castrillón movió 36 millones," *LP* (PA), 12 May 2004, 3A; "Más de veinte empresas usó el cartel de Cali," *LP* (PA), 22 April 1996, 3A; and *LP* (PA), 28 September 2000, cited in "Castrillón-Henao Released in Exchange for Information," BBC Monitoring Latin America, 29 September 2000.

237. For Castrillon's banking, see Huff affidavit, 33–34; "Panama's Banks Remain," 18; and "Red de Castrillón tiene 36 millones en Banaico," *LP* (PA), 16 September 1996, 1A. But see "Expresidente de Banaico desmiente a *La Prensa*," *LP* (PA), 19 September 1996, 5A. For added security, eleven of Castrillón's accounts were numbered, with various held in false names or names of others, such as Castrillon's secretary, whose account totaled $1,736,000. See "Fiscal exige condena para Castrillón," *LP* (PA), 15 May 2004, 4A.

238. When Banaico collapsed in January 1996, after money launderers withdrew their holdings given ongoing investigations and U.S. indictments, Castrillón's accounts held $2.9 million. "U.S. Tolerant of Panamanian Leader's Links to Drug Trade," *WP* (US), 21 July 1996, A29.

239. For Castrillon's assets in Panama, see Huff affidavit, 88, 90; "Barco cargado," 1A; "Castrillón Henao dirigía," 48A; "Más de veinte empresas," 3A; "Castrillón Henao sufre segunda crisis de salud," *LP* (PA), 17 April 1998, 2A; and "Incautan 10 millones a organización de Castrillón," *LP* (PA), 15 February 1997, 1A. By 1999 Panamanian prosecutors had found nine luxury apartments valued at more than $2 million, four luxury automobiles worth $120,000, and seventeen boats. "Fiscalía de drogas administrará los bienes de Castrillón Henao," *LP* (PA), 23 January 1999, 2A.

240. For Castrillón's assets abroad, see "Desarticulan red criminal de Castrillón Henao," *LP* (PA), 28 May 1997, 3A; "Confirman nexos entre narco mexicano y Castrillón Henao," *LP* (PA), 19 September 1996, 1A; "Francia abre proceso penal a Castrillón Henao," *LP* (PA), 19 February 1997, 1A; and "Cómplice de Castrillón Henao fue asesinado," *LP* (PA), 18 April 1998, 2A.

Costa Rica, Canada, Ecuador, France, Germany, and Switzerland, as well as Panama and the United States, and an Italian court had already sentenced two collaborators to thirty years for drug trafficking.

Investigators also discovered that, to ensure smooth transactions in Panama, Castrillón had carefully cultivated business and political elites. In 1994 he donated $51,000 to Pérez Balladares's presidential campaign. According to his own later testimony, Castrillón frequented Le Trianon, a rooftop French restaurant at the Caesar Park hotel, mingling with the wealthy and influential and enjoying fine French cuisine and $175 bottles of champagne. Castrillón's attorney publicly stated that the trafficker's closest friends in Panama included former ambassador Félix Estripeaut and first vice president Felipe Virzi.[241] Another was businessman Enrique ("Kiki") Pretelt Araúz, a relative of President Pérez Balladares, who had been friendly with Noriega and had eventually pled guilty to drug trafficking and money laundering.

For the next two years, at a cost to Panama of $70,000 a month, Castrillón was imprisoned in Panama City.[242] Other than a brief hospital stay when a chronic back injury flared up, he had at first been guarded by sixty police in La Modelo Prison. However, after learning of escape plans, authorities moved the kingpin to a special maximum-security cell constructed right in national police headquarters, where he was put under guard twenty-four hours a day. In the meantime, Castrillón and his lead attorney, former attorney general Rogelio Cruz, tried to engineer his return to Colombia through the political system as well as the legal, pressuring Panamanian contacts to assist or face exposure of their past interactions. Reportedly, the Cali cartel tried to help out by bribing Panamanian officials on Castrillón's behalf. Various sources maintained that a Cali representative had arrived with a million dollars to be distributed once Castrillón was safely back in Colombia.[243]

In April 1998 the situation climaxed. Panamanian prosecutors, armed with eighty-five thousand pages of information drawn from authorities in seven countries, placed the kingpin on trial. Castrillón's immediate response was to file various medical complaints, perhaps in an effort to be moved to a hospital from which escape might be easier. However, doctors found him neurologically healthy, though he had fainted during a hunger strike. Then, in his opening statements at trial, Castrillón referred, generally, to his relations with the most important families in Panama. This seems to have been a threat that his past friends and acquaintances had better act quickly or Castrillón was prepared to reveal in court embarrassing details of their behavior, including perhaps criminal conduct.[244]

Almost immediately, plots were hatched to return Castrillón to Colombia. Certain legislators had inserted in a crime victims' bill an amendment that would have authorized Castrillón's

241. "U.S. Tolerant," A29; "La historia secreta del caso Castrillón Henao—primera entrega," *LP* (PA), 16 November 1998, 6A; "Noriega Codefendant Pleads Guilty in Tampa Case," *WP* (US), 9 June 1990, A11. Pretelt owned jewelry shops and duty-free stores in Panama; in 1990 he pled guilty to two drug-related counts in U.S. federal court. Castrillón, while in prison, sent a letter to Virzi, thanking him for offered assistance, that was reprinted in *La Prensa* on August 27, 1998. See also "La historia secreta del caso Castrillón Henao—segunda entrega," *LP* (PA), 17 November 1998, 8A.

242. For Castrillón's imprisonment, see Huff affidavit, 93; "Target: Cali Cartel," 1; "Castrillón fue sacado por Howard," *LP* (PA), 2 June 1998, 1A; "Castrillón debe ir al hospital, reitera jueza," *LP* (PA), 19 May 1998, 4A; "Asignan a sesenta policías para custodiar a Castrillón," *LP* (PA), 17 November 1996, 2A; and "Cruz denuncia complot contra José Castrillón Henao," *LP* (PA), 10 August 1996, 2A.

243. "Historia secreta—segunda entrega," 8A; "Target: Cali Cartel," 1; "Trasladarán a Castrillón a celda de máxima seguridad," *LP* (PA), 20 May 1997, 2A; "Policía niega traslado de Castrillón," *LP* (PA), 22 May 1997, 3A. When Castrillón was first denied medical assistance at La Modelo Prison, he was reported to have cried out, "Now I am the poor one, but when they needed my money, then I was not so poor." "Historia secreta—primera entrega," 6A.

244. "Cómplice de Castrillón Henao," 2A; "Castrillón Henao sufre," 2A; "José Castrillón Henao se desmaya," *LP* (PA), 16 April 1998, 2A; "Historia secreta—primera entrega," 6A.

expulsion from the country.[245] Documents were drawn up revoking his immigration status and ordering him deported forthwith. That plan was to be implemented on Holy Thursday, a date when the courts would be closed and no judge would be available to question or countermand the documents. However, a penal official refused to proceed without written orders from a superior. Nevertheless, because no U.S. extradition proceedings had been initiated, attorney Cruz remained confident that the trafficker would soon be expelled to Colombia. Indeed, a letter to Castrillón printed on official letterhead and apparently signed by Vice President Felipe Virzi declared that Virzi had been informed of Castrillón's interest in returning to Colombia and that new legal mechanisms made such a resolution possible.[246]

Others in the upper echelons of Panamanian politics, however, considered Castrillón to threaten national security as well as the government's reputation. Panamanian national security adviser Gabriel Castro reportedly flew to Washington, D.C., to urge haste in U.S. legal proceedings against the trafficker. In short order, a Tampa grand jury indicted the kingpin and fifteen associates on cocaine-trafficking and money-laundering charges. Ambassador William Hughes then sent a note to the Panamanian chancellery invoking the Mutual Legal Assistance Treaty and requesting that Panama transfer custody of Castrillón to the United States. Thus, on the evening of April 31, 1998, in a thirteen-minute operation under extraordinary security, the Colombian trafficker was moved—handcuffed, in a wheelchair, and under heavy guard—out of his prison cell. An ambulance conveyed him to a courtyard in the national police headquarters, where a Black Hawk helicopter awaited. Castrillón did not appear to be perturbed. He seemed to have believed that bribes, pressure, and threats had finally brought about his return to Colombia. In fact, however, the helicopter took him to Howard Air Force Base in the Canal Zone, and there FBI and DEA personnel accompanied Castrillón on a special jet to a Florida air base.[247]

The U.S. State Department trumpeted that José Castrillón Henao was the Cali Cartel's primary maritime smuggler, and antidrug officials went further, calling him the highest-ranking Colombian kingpin over which U.S. law enforcement had ever gained custody. When Castrillón first appeared in Tampa federal court, ten armed guards watched over the proceedings. For two months the kingpin refused to cooperate with U.S. officials, but in late 1999 he changed his mind, agreeing to provide information to the U.S. government on Cali drug traffickers and the Colombian and Panamanian officials involved with them. In exchange, he avoided a criminal trial, and the government offered to move him and three or four dozen family members into secret locations through the Federal Witness Protection Program.[248]

At that point Castrillón had strong incentives to provide full and truthful information to U.S. officials, because any deception might forfeit witness protection. He and various family members might then be deported to Colombia and face

245. The Law Concerning the Protection of Victims, Article 25, states that, to advance public order and social interest, the Executive Branch can extradite or otherwise deliver an alien despite ongoing penal process or a sentence not yet served.

246. "Trasladan a Castrillón Henao a EU," *LP* (PA), 1 June 1998, 1A; "Historia secreta—segunda entrega," 9A; "Target: Cali Cartel," 1.

247. "Trasladan a Castrillón," 1A; "Historia secreta—segunda entrega," 8A; "Castrillón fue sacado," 1A; "Historia secreta—primera entrega," 6A; "Castrillón fue expulsado de Panamá: William Hughes," *LP* (PA), 9 June 1998, 1A; "Tampa-Run Probe," 1; "Target: Cali Cartel," 1. For a description of the operation, see "Trece minutos duró traslado de Castrillón," *LP* (PA), 9 June 1998, 1A.

248. *INCSR* (1997), 155; "Target: Cali Cartel," 1; "Agentes armados custodian proceso a Castrillón en EU," *LP* (PA), 10 June 1998, 1A; Huff affidavit, 95; "Castrillón-Henao Released"; "Confidential Witness," 1. Doctors at the Springfield Medical Center for federal prisoners diagnosed Castrillón with a injury, noting also that he had previously been shot on either side of his groin. "Target: Cali Cartel," 1.

the wrath of traffickers there.[249] And so, Castrillón came to serve as the lead informant for Operation Panama Express, an immense law-enforcement venture aimed at dismantling the Cali cartel through collaboration between the DEA, FBI, and U.S. Customs Service and Coast Guard, as well as the police and intelligence services in numerous other countries.

During his debriefings, Castrillón related that from 1983 until 1986 he had worked distributing cocaine in Miami in partnership with Chilean Pedro Rafael Navarrete Venganzones. When seven associates were arrested in 1987, Navarrete had moved to Europe to launch drug-trafficking initiatives in Italy and Spain. Castrillón, however, had returned to Buenaventura, where his illicit earnings helped him to develop a Colombian seafood-exporting company, Inversiones Marítimas del Mar Pacífico, or Invermap. In early 1989 Cali and Northern Valley representatives called on Castrillón, asking to use his fishing vessels for smuggling cocaine from Colombia to Mexico. At Castrillón's suggestion Cali traffickers then bought a long-line fishing boat, the *Challenger II*, to move drugs.[250]

Dealings with the Cali cartel then multiplied. In December 1989 a hit man shot and almost killed Castrillón, and Cali associates sent bodyguards to the hospital to protect him. Less than a year later, Northern Valley traffickers kidnapped Castrillón from Invermap headquarters in the apparently mistaken belief that he had stolen a cocaine shipment from them. However, Cali kingpins intervened, through negotiations undertaken by a representative of Hélmer Herrera Buitrago. Eventually, Cali representatives offered five hundred thousand dollars to cover Northern Valley's costs, securing his freedom. Squarely in their debt, Castrillón was instructed to claim affiliation with Cali alone. He then began to assist the cartel more directly.

In particular, Cali traffickers had been flying cocaine profits from Miami to Panama City and on into Colombia; however, this route had become vulnerable. The cartel thought maritime operations might be preferable, and Castrillón agreed to carry money from Panama to Colombia on motorboats. Thus, on at least five occasions in 1990 and 1991 Castrillón claimed that he or his subordinates had traveled to Panama City and met with Divaldo Cano Saavedra to collect cardboard boxes full of currency sealed in plastic. These were placed on board Castrillón's boat at the Balboa Yacht Club, and the money, more than $15 million in total, then proceeded by sea to Invermap's headquarters in Buenaventura, to be collected by other Cali representatives.[251]

In the meantime, Castrillón had started to assist the cartel directly in cocaine smuggling. In 1991 he had agreed with Pedro Navarrete to partner once again, this time using Invermap, which continued to carry out some legitimate fishing for domestic and export markets but had come to serve primarily as a front business for cocaine trafficking. By November of that year, when the U.S. Coast Guard interrupted a one-ton shipment, Castrillón and Navarrete

249. Castrillón also faced a life sentence, to be reduced only for cooperation. Authorities repeatedly emphasized that any deception would nullify all the negotiated benefits, the contents of which were detailed in the Huff affidavit, 6–7. See also "Tampa-Run Probe," and "Colombia Cocaine Bust," 1.

250. Huff affidavit, 7–14, 22–23; "Confidential Witness," 1; "Castrillón, un atrapado," 2A. To shield Invermap and Castrillón, the *Challenger II* was sent to Panama, where it was owned by a shell corporation, supposedly run by two people. The first was Castrillón's maritime agent, Enrique Chang Ortiz, a Colón resident implicated in a 650-kilo cocaine seizure in Belgium in 1992. The second was Castrillón's mistress, Paola Tejada de Chong, who had once modeled cosmetics at a Panama City pharmacy but eventually served as director for nineteen companies, with a luxury Marbella Tower condominium and a Chase Manhattan bank account. Tejada was imprisoned until 2001, then placed under house arrest. "Liberan a 'compañera' de Castrillón H.," *LP* (PA), 9 July 2001, 5A.

251. Huff affidavit, 37, 39–41, and "Historia secreta—segunda entrega," 9A. In 1992 Panamanian authorities searched two shipping containers that had arrived from Miami at Las Minas Bay, just north of Colón, discovering a total of more than $7 million. Cano, after attempting to bribe customs officers, was arrested, and eventually imprisoned for two years. This interrupted Castrillón's money-moving operation.

had already successfully smuggled twice that quantity into San Diego, arranging for the cocaine to be transferred from Colombian vessels to sailboats for the final leg. Furthermore, the pair had helped Cali traffickers with three multiton cocaine loads that had been air-dropped to designated locations in the eastern Pacific, collected by fishing vessels, and transported into Mexico. Castrillón had especially strong connections there, including reportedly with Manuel Rodríguez López of the Tijuana cartel, who had assisted with investments in Mexico and also held accounts in Banaico and other Panamanian banks.[252] Castrillón's organization was also able to employ Mexican fishing boats to recover about five tons of cocaine that had been jettisoned by Colombian pilots intercepted by U.S. military aircraft. Then, in 1992 the partners turned to smuggling by freighter, using the *MV Harbour* for the five-ton load seized by the U.S. Coast Guard.

Thereafter, to minimize exposure to arrests and seizures by employing more secure shipping routes, Navarrete and Castrillón introduced the Pacific-pipeline scheme. Cocaine-carrying vessels would travel south from Colombia, then veer far out into the Pacific, before heading for Mexico. A smuggling boat would receive a cocaine load near Isla Gorgona, about 30 miles off Colombian shores. The shipment would then travel 400–600 miles out to sea, where Castrillón's fishing fleet, perhaps twenty vessels in total, would act as decoys, while watching for Colombian and U.S. patrol aircraft and ships. The cocaine load, ordinarily about 5 tons, would then be transferred to a long-line fishing vessel serving as a mother ship, which would travel to rendezvous points south of the Galápagos and transfer the drugs to Mexican fishing boats for the 1,200- to 1,500-mile run to Mexico. Castrillón informed U.S. authorities that this route had been used monthly between 1992 and May 1995 to export about a hundred tons of cocaine a year, or about a fifth of all the cocaine consumed in the U.S. annually. U.S. authorities had never intercepted these cocaine shipments, and Castrillón was paid expenses, plus a smuggling fee of $1–2 million, depending on the size of the load.[253]

Upon becoming a federal witness, Castrillón also persuaded various other cartel employees to cooperate with authorities, including his son-in-law, an accountant. Castrillón also reportedly persuaded a long-time employee to become an informant and provide tips on drug shipments leaving Buenaventura. Over the next two years U.S. authorities arrested more than a hundred sailors aboard fifteen vessels in the Pacific, loaded with more than a hundred tons of cocaine. In May 2005 authorities claimed that Operation Panama Express had led to 775 arrests and the seizure of four hundred tons of cocaine. Lead federal prosecutor Joseph Ruddy stated that no other informant had ever generated the results that Castrillón had.[254]

As the Cali cartel disintegrated, however, the key target for U.S. law enforcement was Joaquín Mario Valencia Trujillo. The husband of celebrity Luz Mery Tristan, a Colombian model and skating star, Valencia Trujillo by his midthirties ran a ranch breeding show horses, while he publicly served as a paper company's owner and operator. Behind the scenes, however, he

252. See "Red de Castrillón," 1A, and "Veraguas a Quintana Roo," 6A. Rodríguez and Castrillón had reportedly met at Cano's house. "Red de Castrillón," 1A. Although Cano denied that, he conceded that Castrillón had introduced him to Rodríguez, who became a "fishing buddy." "Gobierno sabía que Cano hacía los pasaportes," *LP* (PA), 20 September 1996, 1A. In 1996 Mexico's antidrug czar Francisco Javier Molina noted considerable evidence that Castrillón and Rodríguez had partnered in trafficking and laundering. See "Confirman nexos," 1A, and "Operaciones de narco son supermillonarias," *LP* (PA), 21 September 1996, 4A.

253. Huff affidavit, 43, 64; "Millionaire Extradited," 1; "Colombia Cocaine Bust"; "Confidential Witness," 1. For information from a former Invermap employee, knowledgeable of accounts, who became a confidential federal witness, see Huff affidavit, 55, 60, 64–68, 90–91. Compensation was provided either in assets such as fishing vessels—or, on one occasion, a tuna cannery in Ecuador—or, more commonly, in cash paid in Panama, Colombia, Mexico, or the United States.

254. "Colombia Cocaine Bust"; Huff affidavit, 6; "Tampa-Run Probe," 1; "Confidential Witness," 1.

was trafficking drugs. In late 1990 he approached José Castrillón Henao, scheming with him to air-drop cocaine into the Pacific for transport to Mexico in fishing vessels. The following year Valencia gained financing for a drug-smuggling operation via Chile by going to Banaico, where a bank manager ordered suitcases full of dollars to be presented to alleged Chilean trafficker Manuel Losada Martínez. After the downfall of the Rodríguez Orejuela brothers in 1995, Valencia rose rapidly in the Cali hierarchy, capitalizing in large part on Castrillón's efficient maritime shipping. Federal officials believe that he had used twenty-eight businesses as fronts for laundering proceeds from the drug trade, eventually accumulating $500 million in assets. On January 31, 2003, Colombian police arrested Valencia in Bogotá on drug-trafficking and money-laundering charges, as they did Pedro Navarrete, who had apparently taken over from Castrillón Henao the role of overseeing Cali's maritime transportation. On March 19, 2004, Joaquín Mario Valencia Trujillo was extradited to the United States, with DEA agent Dominic Albanese declaring, "I would say he's as big as Pablo Escobar, if not larger."[255]

Drug-Trafficking Routes Through Panama

As the transshipment of drugs began to take hold in Central America, large shipments of cocaine, marijuana, and heroin regularly entered Panama by sea or air, to be temporarily stored, sometimes repackaged or secreted, forwarded to the point of export, and finally sent along to market by plane, ship, or vehicle.[256] The bulk of the drugs have been directed toward the United States either directly or with intervening stops elsewhere in Central America or in Mexico. Another portion of the Panamanian trade has moved drugs to or via Caribbean islands, especially Jamaica, Haiti, and the Dominican Republic.[257] Then, some very large loads have headed to Europe.[258] Panama's bridge-favoring geographic factors are brought into sharp relief by examining the many routes that traffickers have employed.

In 2000 U.S. antidrug officials noted, "Panama's Canal, containerized seaports, the Pan-American Highway, an active international airport, and numerous uncontrolled airfields provide organized crime groups almost unlimited transportation options through the country."[259] In addition, while drug networks have frequently used Central American capital cities for transshipment, no other metropolis has approached the quantities of drugs sent through Panama City. Over time, virtually all parts of the city have been affected by the trade.[260] In 1996 officials reported that of the twenty-three total tons of illegal drugs seized, fully twenty tons had been discovered in or around the capital.[261] Thus, the constant economic activity of Panama City,

255. Huff affidavit, 1, 4, 48, 87–139; "Tampa-Run Probe," 1; "Confidential Witness," 1; quote from "Millionaire Extradited," 1. Even the arrest of Valencia did not plug the Pacific pipeline. In September 2005 the U.S. Coast Guard and Navy stopped two vessels off Ecuador, the *Lina Marie* and the *San José*, carrying fifteen and twelve tons of cocaine. Huff affidavit, 22, 33.

256. "Juzgarán a un oficial y a cuatro agentes de la Policía," *LP* (PA), 18 October 1995, 1A. See also *INCSR* (1995), 153. For a major marijuana shipment from Panama to the United States, see *United States v. Valdez*, 861 F.2d at 430.

257. See, for instance, "Decomisan droga," *LP* (PA), 20 May 1999, 4A; "Capturan a narcotraficante jamaicano en ZL," *LP* (PA), 19 April 1996, 4A; "Detienen a dos personas con 22 kilos de cocaína," *LP* (PA), 14 November 1996, 4A; and "Aduanas captura 198 kilos," 1A. Larger loads headed to Caribbean islands were then redirected to the United States. For an example of a Colombia-Panama-Haiti–United States route, see "Tres toneladas de drogas decomisa la policía," *LP* (PA), 24 November 1996, 4A.

258. In 1998, in Ireland's largest seizure, three hundred kilos of cocaine were captured on the fifty-foot catamaran *Gemeos*, headed to Liverpool in a transaction believed to be brokered by an English expatriate in Panama City to supply Liverpool and Manchester dealers. "Noriega Link to Pounds 100 m Drug Haul," *London Sunday Times*, 13 September 1998. For other major shipments to Europe, see "Policía decomiso alijo de cocaína y 'pegón,'" *LP* (PA), 22 April 2005, 6A, and "Fiscalías asestan golpe al narcotráfico," *LP* (PA), 22 February 2005, 1A.

259. *INCSR* (2000), 188.

260. In the small residential sector of Chanis alone authorities seized 320 and 748 kilos of cocaine in 1995, another 224 in 1996, and fully 1,800 in 1997. See "Decomisan 748 kilos de cocaína," *LP* (PA), 18 October 1995, 1A, and "Incautan 1,800 kilos de cocaína," *LP* (PA), 5 February 1997, 1A.

261. "Capturan este año veintitrés toneladas de drogas," *LP* (PA), 17 December 1996, 2A. That summer, after finding 333 kilos of cocaine in sacks of flour, police arrested twenty, seizing another 900 kilos. That fall, in two connected busts,

its international air and sea connections, its location on the Pan-American Highway, its wealthy banking and business sector, and also its slums have all encouraged drug trafficking.

Sea Routes

Given the canal, the numerous offshore islands, the lengthy coastlines, the position of neighboring Colombia, and the country's extensive shipping via deep-water ports, sea routes have always figured prominently in Panama's drug trade. Most drug imports have traveled from Colombia up the Pacific or Caribbean coasts in a range of vessels: container ships, freighters, trawlers, speedboats, yachts, skiffs, even motorized canoes.[262] In 1991 SMN commander José Rosas declared, "Lots of drugs are coming in. . . . The boats operate all day long, day and night."[263] When antidrug units have increased their scrutiny of vessels in one place, traffickers have rapidly switched areas of operation or tactics. For instance, they might start to divide loads into multiple shipments to be carried north in smaller boats. When authorities have noticed suspicious activity and approached to investigate, maritime smugglers have frequently jettisoned their cargoes. Hundreds of kilos of drugs in floating, often vacuum-sealed, packages have washed up on beaches on both coasts, even right along Avenida Balboa in downtown Panama City, and locals have sometimes collected large quantities, such as 1,227 kilos discovered in the Pacific fishing village of Playa Nanzal.[264]

Larger ships have carried the most significant cocaine exports. In 1989, shortly before the U.S. invasion, U.S. authorities seized 1,205 kilos of cocaine off the Panamanian vessel *Argovind*; 1,527 off the *Barlovento*; and 5,549 off the *Zedom Sea*.[265] Then, once Noriega had been deposed and Medellín traffickers were no longer operating under military protection, the Cali cartel soon came to dominate Panamanian transshipment, chiefly relying on bulk sea exports. Indeed, the Rodríguez Orejuela brothers later admitted to U.S. officials that in 1992 and 1993 they had exported large quantities of cocaine hidden in packaged coffee and shipped from Buenaventura to the United States, via the Colón Free Zone.[266]

Thus, in the post-Noriega period, Panamanian-registered ships have been found, even more regularly, to be transporting very large narcotics loads. For instance, in 1991 more than 5 tons of cocaine arrived off Long Island on the Panamanian-registered *Blue Crown*. In two 1999 cases the U.S. Coast Guard found 2 tons of Colombian cocaine headed to Canada on the Panamanian

---

authorities captured 500 kilos, and then interrupted Cali traffickers transferring 400 kilos outside a hotel. Later, officials seized 1,237 kilos being packed for export, another 950 in a refrigerator shipment, 800 mostly packed into truck batteries, and 136 in a pickup. See "Incautan 333 kilos de cocaína," *LP* (PA), 7 August 1996, 2A; "Policía captura 167 kilos de cocaína en Vía Argentina," *LP* (PA), 9 August 1996, 1A; "Detienen a policía, a estudiante, y pasantes por narcotráfico," *LP* (PA), 10 August 1996, 2A; "Capturan una tonelada de cocaína," *LP* (PA), 8 September 1996, 1A; "Confirman evasión de reo acusado de narcotráfico," *LP* (PA), 19 October 1996, 1A; "Capturan mil 237 kilos de cocaína en Tocumen," *LP* (PA), 20 November 1996, 1A; "Policía captura otros 950 kilos de cocaína," *LP* (PA), 22 November 1996, 1A; "Policía decomisa 169 kilos más de cocaína," *LP* (PA), 23 November 1996, 1A; and "Policía y PTJ decomisan 800 kilos de cocaína," *LP* (PA), 21 November 1996, 1A.

262. Interview with Judicial Technical Police narcotics detective, 27 February 1992, Panama City, Panama.

263. "Cocaine Is Again Surging," 1A.

264. See, for instance, "Policía encuentra droga en playa de Isla Coiba," *LP* (PA), 8 February 2005, 9A; "Decomisan cuatrocientos kilos de pegón en la Bahía," *LP* (PA), 16 October 2003, 2A; and "As F-16s Fly Out, Drugs Float In," *TT* (CR), 5 June 1998, 14.

265. See "How the Cocaine Is Coming in This Time," *NYT* (US), 5 November 1989, 4, and *United States v. Pretelt*, 939 F.2d at 233. The month before the U.S. invasion, federal authorities in New York seized 4,840 kilos of cocaine shipped from Panama to Philadelphia on *The New York Senator*, packed in 10-gallon drums of sodium hydroxide. See "Seizure of Cocaine Is Called Largest in New York City," 5 November 1989, 1; "Couple Sought in Record Drug Seizure in Queens," *NYT* (US), 6 November 1989, 1B; and "Drug Agency Faults Customs in Cocaine Case," *NYT* (US), 12 November 1989, 48.

266. *Confesiones secretas*, 28.

vessel *Adriatik*, and then 4 tons of cocaine on the Panamanian freighter *China Breeze*, heading to Portugal. In 2005 the U.S. Coast Guard stopped the *Lesvos*, a Panamanian fishing vessel, in international waters in the Pacific and found 4 tons of cocaine. A 2008 case involved the seizure of 2,442 kilos of cocaine on a Panamanian-flagged mother ship off Honduras, which had been outfitted with a directional finder antenna to locate nearby vessels and had rub marks on the hull consistent with smaller boats frequently loading and off-loading drugs.[267]

The most popular and long-standing method of exporting drugs by sea has been to hide them in large sea-freight containers. The sheer numbers passing through Panama's principal ports, combined with the lack of resources to police the traffic, have ensured a minimal risk of interdiction. Only when tipped off or confronting something clearly suspicious did officials search containers, most of which have been packed full of legitimate products.[268] Thus, while the DEA has supplied information on vessels in Panamanian waters to port authorities and law enforcement, and although Panamanian officials did intercept some immense shipments, these were random, occasional events.[269] No doubt, very large numbers of cocaine shipments passed through Panama without interdiction.

Around the Central American bridge states the destinations of maritime drug exports have been dictated in part by the extent to which globalization has affected that country. In contrast to Belize, where virtually all maritime drug exports have headed to the United States, Panama's position as Central America's most globalized state is reflected in the numerous drug loads proceeding toward other markets. Some have headed to Canada or Europe.[270] Others have been bound for Costa Rica and other Central American destinations. Although typically drugs have been hidden in shipping containers or in secret compartments on the ship, traffickers have occasionally launched more elaborate schemes. For instance, in 2007 the *Gatún Panamá*, a ship owned by Mexicans allegedly linked to the Sinaloa cartel, came through the Panama Canal, anchored off Panama's Pacific coast, and took on cocaine supplied by speedboats. When authorities eventually stopped and searched the vessel off Isla de Coiba, they found a prodigious shipment: fully 19.5 tons of cocaine.[271]

Panama has such extensive coastlines and so many islands, fishing villages, ports, and other coastal settlements that trafficking by sea has occurred constantly in many different locations. However, three particular sea routes merit special mention. Large quantities of narcotics have been transshipped via the Colón Free Zone, the San Blás archipelago, and along Panama's Pacific coast. While numerous seizures have occurred, the particular characteristics of each of these routes and the formidable quantities of narcotics being transferred have largely defeated the efforts by counternarcotics authorities in the

267. For the cases cited, see "New York: Incautan un barco panameño con cinco toneladas de cocaína," *LP* (PA), 26 July 1991, 24A; *United States v. Bustos-Useche*, 273 F.3d 622; *United States v. Perez-Oviedo*, 281 F.3d 400; *Kurdyukov v. United States Coast Guard*, 578 F. Supp. 114; *Granja-Portocarrero v. United States*, 2008 U.S. Dist. LEXIS 31788; and *United States v. Herrera Aguilar*, 2008 U.S. App. LEXIS 16318. In 1998 customs agents in Port Everglades, Florida, discovered 119 kilos of cocaine in a container on the Panamanian freighter *Arctic Sun*. "Port Everglades Bust Nets Millions in Cocaine," *Fort Lauderdale Sun-Sentinel*, 1 July 1998, 5B.

268. For example, in 2002, after officials at the Colón Container Terminal noticed a broken security seal on a forty-five-foot container headed to the United States, they found a black suitcase buried inside a sack of charcoal. It contained eighty-five capsules of heroin and twenty-five of cocaine. "Incautan a heroína y cocaína en Colón," *LP* (PA), 5 July 2002, 10A.

269. "Vigilan puertos para evitar narcotráfico," *LP* (PA), 7 October 1996, 5A.

270. See, for instance, "Acusan a marinos de trasegar cuatro toneladas de droga," *LP* (PA), 30 December 2009, 3A; "Hallan droga en barco panameño," *LP* (PA), 7 October 2006, 6A; "Decomisan droga en Manzanillo," *LP* (PA), 30 September 2005, 8A; *United States v. Perez-Oviedo*, 281 F.3d at 400, and *United States v. Bustos-Useche*, 273 F.3d at 622.

271. See "Droga no pasó por Canal," *LP* (PA), 23 March 2007, 8A, and "Extraditan a dos capos mexicanos," *LP* (PA), 12 May 2007, 3A.

post-Noriega period to choke off maritime drug shipments.

The Panama Canal and the Colón Free Zone
The Panama Canal, and especially the Colón Free Zone at its Caribbean terminus, has long played a vital role in drug trafficking. Even more important than narcotics passing through the canal, various drug organizations have set up, taken over, or infiltrated Free Zone businesses to store incoming cocaine from Colombia and then to hide the drugs in outgoing shipments.[272] In 1992 in the largest cocaine shipment seized to that date in the entire Caribbean basin, the Colombian office-supply company Celeste International was caught transshipping to Baltimore, via the Free Zone, containers of tiles within which authorities found 5,415 kilos of cocaine, wrapped in special paper to try to fool canine units.[273] After determining that the company's lawyer had been deeply involved, investigators eventually found that Celeste International had been money laundering as well, with Cali traffickers disguising incoming drug profits as payment for fictitious consumer goods. In 1996 one PTJ official observed, "In the world of the cartels . . . , it is known that one can transport illegal substances in the Free Zone of Colón quite easily."[274]

Under the dictatorship the National Guard took responsibility for Free Zone security. In practice, however, this encouraged collaboration with drug rings in laundering and trafficking. Eventually, the military regime incorporated its own Free Zone business, Transit, to benefit officers in various ways, including assisting in drug transshipment. Soldiers were frequently used to off-load cargoes from South American ships to Transit warehouses, where the drugs could then be extracted and stored awaiting export. In 1977 Leland Riggs Jr., U.S. Embassy customs attaché, testified to Congress about the Panamanian military's involvement in such activities. In particular, in the late 1960s U.S. Customs had learned that South American trafficker Yolanda Sarmiento, an associate of Auguste Ricord, had been sending 150- to 200-kilo shipments of heroin and cocaine to the United States, using a Panamanian airline crew.[275] She had laundered the drug profits through the Colón Free Zone, and by the early 1970s her network was flying narcotics into Tocumen, drugs which the National Guard would then truck to the Free Zone. U.S. authorities believed that Sarmiento was sending about 45 kilos of heroin to the United States monthly. Although after her U.S. arrest Sarmiento posted the bond of one hundred thousand dollars and fled to Argentina on a Panamanian aircraft, she was later extradited, tried, convicted, and imprisoned in New York.

As table 6.1 illustrates, throughout the post-Noriega period the Colón Free Zone has witnessed numerous cocaine seizures exceeding a ton.[276] Indeed, the PTJ reported that over a three-year period a single major network, reportedly directed by Colombian Alcides Masso, trafficked in excess of 20 tons of cocaine to the United States and Europe. In 1995 Masso allegedly offered fifty thousand dollars to two

272. For example, in 2000 major narcotics investigations targeted two Free Zone businesses, leading to a 663-kilo cocaine bust. "Droga: Libre," 6A.

273. See *INCSR* (1993), 173; *Confesiones secretas*, 30; "Droga: Libre," 6A; "Panama Still a Conduit," A1; and "Condenan a empresarios por introducir droga al país," *LP* (PA), 1 March 1996, 1A.

274. "Investigan carga de contenedor," *LP* (PA), 17 September 1996, 7A. See also the statement by the president of the Colón Free Zone User's Association in "Droga: Libre," 6A.

275. For the Sarmiento case, see Tully, *Secret War*, 99–103; "Drug Trafficking in Panama"; and the Riggs statement in U.S. Senate, *Implementation*. See also the related cases *United States v. Martinez-Carcano*, 557 F.2d 966, and *United States v. Torres*, 519 F.2d 723.

276. The table fails to include the many large seizures under the one-ton cutoff. For instance, in 1997 Colón authorities intercepted 754 kilos of cocaine being transported in a van, with a like quantity seized in Panamá Province the following day. "Capturan a cuatro panameños con 754 kilos de cocaína," *LP* (PA), 29 May 1997, 1A, and "Decomisan tonelada y media de cocaína," *LP* (PA), 30 May 1997, 2A.

Table 6.1 Cocaine seizures of more than one ton involving the Colón Free Zone

Date	Seizure location	Details	Quantity (kg)
1992	Colón	DEA-led operation brings about largest cocaine seizure to date	2,118
1992	Colón Free Zone	Largest cocaine seizure to date in Caribbean Basin	5,415
1992	Mexico	Cocaine shipment originating in Colón Free Zone	1,500
1993	United States Miami	Cocaine shipment originating in Colón Free Zone	5,200
1996	Cuba	Cocaine seizure off Panamanian ship flying Honduran flag	1,700
1996	Catavia, Colón Province	Two vehicles carrying cocaine try to flee from police; shoot-out and eleven arrested	1,056
1997	Colón Free Zone	Medellín trafficking operation brought in cocaine by sea with complicity of Colón Free Zone security guards	1,429
1997	Cativá, Colón	Cocaine seizure leading to eight-year and eight-month terms for three Panamanians and one Colombian, followed by controversial decision by Panamanian court to halve penalties on the grounds that international trafficking had not been proven	1,200
2003	Colón Free Zone	Cocaine find linked by investigators to Mexico's Sinaloa organization	2,487
2005	Porvenir, Colón	National Air Service and U.S. law enforcement interrupt transshipment operation	1,880

Sources: *INCSR* (1991), 172; "Condenan a empresarios por introducer droga al país," *LP* (PA), 1 March 1996, 1A; "Droga: Libre de impuesto," *LP* (PA), 12 October 2003, 6A; *INCSR* (1993), 173; "Panama Still a Conduit for Cocaine Profits," *WP* (US), 20 September 1993, A1; *INCSR* (1994), 167; "Cubanos descubren dos toneladas de 'coca' en embarcación Hondureña," *LP* (HO), 9 October 1996, 1; "Barco decomisado con cocaína en Cuba pertenece a compañía panameña," *LP* (HO), 10 October 1996, 55A; "Capturan una tonelada de cocaine," *LP* (PA), 8 September 1996, 1A; "Audiencia por narcotráfico," *LP* (PA), 24 September 2002, 4A; "Investigación interna en el Segundo Tribunal Superior," *LP* (PA), 29 May 1999, 5A; *INCSR* (2007), 22.

Colón Free Zone employees to assist in transshipping to Spain what turned out to be his organization's ultimate shipment.[277]

In fact, cocaine smugglers have frequently opted to penetrate Panama via locations near Colón: small islands, beaches and rivers, villages and towns, and harbors and bays.[278] In 1990, at a time when Panamanian police estimated that as much as 85 percent of the narcotics entering their country arrived via the Colón area, inhabitants of Portobelo, the next major town north of Colón, complained that Colombian boats were operating throughout the night, unloading drugs on their

277. "Droga: Libre," 6A.

278. Among the key locations, at different periods, were Coco Solo, Las Minas Bay, Playa Maria Chiquita, Playa Langosta, Puerto Piña, and Puerto Limón. See "Incautan veinte kilos de cocaína en Colón," *LP* (PA), 13 December 1998, 5A; "Incautan diez kilos de cocaína en Folk River," *LP* (PA), 14 April 1998, 8A; "Juzgarán a un oficial y a cuatro agentes de la policía," *LP* (PA), 18 October 1995, 1A; "Investigan caso de cocaína hallada en Bahía Las Minas," *LP* (PA), 2 September 1990, 15A; and "Denuncian acción de narcotraficantes en Playa Langosta," *LP* (PA), 15 July 1990, 11A.

beaches.[279] Drug organizations have varied target destinations for their imports to confuse law enforcement, and as time passed, they began to conduct their operations farther afield to the east and west of the city.[280] Furthermore, transshipment networks have frequently recruited Colón inhabitants to protect shipments and to construct, service, and repair boats. Some locals have even built piers in remote locations. In 1996 and 1997 antidrug officials destroyed four such piers along the Colón coastline, and the following year police discovered 350 kilos near the Río Guanche on the upper coast of Colón Province, with an additional 264 kilos intercepted early the following month.[281]

While some drugs have entered the duty-free zone by sea, traffickers have also imported narcotics to Panama by other routes, smuggled them into the zone, and then exported the drugs by sea. Within the Free Zone, goods to be exported are constantly being consigned to bonded warehouses. With narcotics hidden in containers, smuggling organizations then arrange for extraction at the cargo's destination.[282] While Free Zone trafficking operations have typically involved export by sea, occasionally drugs that entered the zone have been sent to market by other means. For instance, in 1996 Colón airport authorities seized 334 kilos of cocaine, hidden inside ceiling fans destined for Miami, and determined that the drugs had been imported via the Free Zone.[283]

To avoid patterns that might be easily detected, traffickers exporting from the Free Zone have also varied the maritime routes to market. Thus, while sometimes the cocaine has traveled directly to a U.S. or European port, at other times, it has been transshipped through a Caribbean island or another Central American site before heading to its final destination.[284] For example, in 2000 Salvadoran law enforcement seized a 360-kilo cocaine shipment that had been packed in Panama with the assistance of a corrupt Free Zone inspector. Indeed, some substantial cocaine shipments that were taking or had taken a Free Zone–Guatemala route have been intercepted.

By the twenty-first century, alongside the continuing trade in cocaine, traffickers had started to transport Colombian heroin into the

279. See "Uso y abuso de drogas se incrementó entre 60% y 70%, dice Famiglietti," *LP* (PA), 1 September 1990, 14A, and "Denuncian acción," 11A.

280. See "Investigan diversas playas utilizadas por el narcotráfico," *LP* (PA), 15 October 1995, 3, and "Autoridades malogran fin de año a narcotráfico internacional," *LP* (HO), 4 December 1995, 20A. Occasionally, authorities have intercepted these transactions, as in 1996 when two Colombians and 417 kilos of cocaine were found on the Colón coast. "Capturan una tonelada," 1A. See also "Investigan a colombianos y panameños por drogas," *LP* (PA), 23 February 2005, 3A, and "Capturan setenta y ocho kilos de cocaína en Colón," *LP* (PA), 13 April 1996, 2A.

281. See "Agentes antinarcóticos destruyen muelle clandestino en isla Naranjo," *LP* (PA), 13 April 1997, 4A; "Incautan 264 kilos de cocaína en Colón," *LP* (PA), 8 July 1998, 2A; and "Incautan 350 kilos de cocaína en la Costa Abajo de Colón," *LP* (PA), 25 June 1998, 4A.

282. Export loads have started at about 100 kilos, depending on the organization, destination, and smuggling method. See, for instance, the 1994 PTJ-DEA joint operation that uncovered 100 kilos of cocaine in shipping containers exported from the Free Zone. "Droga: Libre," 6A. In 1998 authorities found 500 kilos hidden in a refrigerated container of squash aboard the *Madison*, and in 2000 authorities found 376 kilos hidden in transformers headed to the United States. "Incautan 500 kilos de cocaína en Manzanillo," *LP* (PA), 6 January 1998, 1A.

283. See "Policía decomisa 334 kilos de cocaína en Colón," *LP* (PA), 14 August 1996, 1A, and "Arrestan a empresaria de ZL por narcotráfico," *LP* (PA), 16 August 1996, 4A.

284. "Droga: Libre," 6A. For example, in 1998 Tocumen customs inspectors found heroin and 113 kilos of Cali cocaine, apparently to be exported to Haiti from the Free Zone. "Decomisan 113 kilos de cocaína en Tocumen," *LP* (PA), 28 July 1998, 1A. In 1998 Free Zone officials found 294 kilos of cocaine in merchandise Guatemalans had prepared for export. Later that year, Guatemalan officials at the Santo Tomás de Castilla port searched incoming Free Zone shipping containers and discovered another 534 kilos. The following year a canine unit in Panama discovered 335 kilos of cocaine hidden in a Free Zone shipment of pants also scheduled to be reexported to Guatemala. Then, in 2005 Panamanian port authorities discovered an additional 770 kilos in a container directed to Guatemala. See "Incautan 289 [*sic*] kilos de cocaína en Zona Libra," *LP* (PA), 28 May 1998, 7A; "Fiscalía de drogas investiga a empresa de ZL," *LP* (PA), 4 December 1998, 5A; "Decomisan droga que venía para Guatemala," *SV* (GU), 5 March 1999, 2; and "Droga: Libre," 6A.

Colón area by boat, sometimes combining shipments of different varieties of drugs. In 2002 authorities discovered 24 kilos of heroin on a speedboat near Portobelo. Later that year, two stowaways in Balboa were found to have heroin taped to their bodies, while authorities seized 4 kilos from two Colombian "tourists" in Colón. The following year SMN agents spotted a boat acting suspiciously in the Samba Bonita port near Cativá, just north of Colón. On board were four Colombians carrying 28 kilos of cocaine and a waistcoat laden with heroin.[285]

The Colón Free Zone thus ranks as a great regional hub of drug activity with traffickers varying their modus operandi, when necessary, to keep ahead of authorities. Law enforcement has frequently intercepted amounts ranging from several dozen kilos to a hundred or more, headed to local dealers or to nearby warehouses.[286] The ready availability of cocaine in the Colón area has spawned a thriving local market that led the Cruz Blanca Panameña to report that the city had among the highest drug-consumption rates in all of Latin America.[287]

San Blás–Kuna Yala Trafficking

As for narcotics imports to Panama, the Comarca de San Blás lay on one leading maritime route. Drugs routinely passed from Colombia's Caribbean coast through the islands, many of them deserted, and also into small mainland ports, such as Puerto Obaldía. For historical reasons, antidrug efforts have been strictly circumscribed. After a 1920s uprising, Kuna Yala, inhabited primarily by indigenous Kunas, became a semiautonomous region. Relations with Panamanian central authorities have often been strained, and the Kuna have had long-standing ties to Colombia, exporting coconuts and importing merchandise. Law enforcement has traditionally been markedly underfunded, and many Kunas have failed to cooperate with Panamanian authorities, not recognizing even joint law enforcement to be legitimate. The key political body was the General Kuna Congress, and the Kunas have periodically underscored their separate governance by refusing entry to the Panamanian and U.S. coast guards. Moreover, local law enforcement has answered to the national director of Indigenous Police or to the traditional Kuna authorities known as *sailas*, and the latter have sometimes been implicated in the drug trade.[288]

A 1997 Panamanian government report concluded that many maritime drug imports were arriving in Panama via Kuna Yala, sometimes with local assistance.[289] While the Kunas' hollowed-out log canoes, known as *cayucos*, have sometimes been utilized, the typical vessel of choice has been a go-fast.[290] In one representative 1998 case a helicopter from a joint U.S.-Panamanian coast guard operation intercepted a speedboat off San Blás. The traffickers scuttled the boat, escaping in a second go-fast, although

285. "Decomisan heroína en Colón," *LP* (PA), 30 March 2002, 2A; "Detienen a polizones con droga en Balboa," *LP* (PA), 31 July 2002, 5A; "Decomisan cocaína en Colón," *LP* (PA), 5 May 2003, 9A.

286. For one such discovery at a routine traffic stop in Colón in 1996, see "Capturan 164 kilos de supuesta cocaína," *LP* (PA), 4 September 1996, 12A. For representative modest seizures, see "Policía captura 24 kilos de cocaína en Colón," *LP* (PA), 6 March 1996, 5A, and "Decomisan 38 kilos de droga en Colón," *LP* (PA), 13 July 2001, 7A.

287. "Colón: Violencia y silencio," *LP* (PA), 12 February 1996, 6A. Their poll showed 18 percent having used cocaine, 15 percent marijuana, and 3 percent bazuco.

288. For example, an unwritten rule developed that Kunas finding drugs could resell them so long as the sailas received a "tax" of two hundred to six hundred dollars. See "Narcotráfico amenaza a la comarca Kuna Yala," *LP* (PA), 3 October 2005, 1A, and "Las pacas que traen las olas del mar," *LP* (PA), 3 October 2005, 6A.

289. "El 80% de la droga se introduce por vía marítima entra por Kuna Yala," *LP* (PA), 20 January 1997, 4A. For one case of three Kunas arrested in the Azuero Peninsula with marijuana and cocaine, see "Capturan a tres narcos en las costas de Tonosí," *LP* (PA), 2 July 2002, 9A.

290. See "Investigan diversas playas," 3, and "Decomisan treinta y ocho kilos," 7A. In 1995 Pérez Balladares visited San Blás, noting the frequent drug runs by Colombian speedboats, as did U.S. Ambassador William Hughes the following year. "Narcotraficantes usan Darién y San Blás, declara Hughes," *LP* (PA), 10 April 1996, 1A.

divers eventually recovered nine hundred kilos from the wreck site.[291] Over the ensuing years, even though nearby coast guard stations multiplied, the drug trade has remained vibrant, with very large shipments passing through. In 2005 one joint operation among the United States, Panama, and Colombia resulted in two tons of cocaine being taken from a speedboat close to the border, and an even larger shipment was captured in a 2009 incident.[292]

The transit of cocaine, while providing employment to a few and increasing the circulation of hard currency, has also had deleterious effects on ethnic minorities across Central America, whether Mennonites, Garífuna, or Native Americans. In the Comarca de San Blás constant cocaine trafficking has vastly increased violence, crime, and drug abuse. As early as 1994, when almost two dozen Colombians were being investigated for trafficking on the islands, more than a quarter of all reported crimes were drug-related. By 2007 Kuna communities were requesting more antidrug support from the national government, including a permanent SMN presence off their coasts, and were discussing the possible creation of their own indigenous coast guard. Nevertheless, resources have been scarce, and public opinion, split. Some Kunas have profited from the drug trade. Many have continued to resent intervention by outside authorities. And few supported the idea that Panama would establish a naval base in Puerto Escocés, twenty-one miles from Colombia. Transnational criminals have been quite successful in penetrating the chinks in the armor of weak states. In San Blás the alienation, poverty, and lack of integration of the Kuna ethnic minority has hampered antidrug activities and eased drug imports.[293]

Pacific Coast Trafficking

Cocaine, marijuana, and pegón shipments have also traveled up Panama's Pacific coast, often having been exported from the major Colombian port of Buenaventura, located about 125 miles south of the border.[294] While a multitude of vessels have been involved, traffickers have often especially favored speedboats, which could quickly deliver drugs to beaches or ports, often operating late at night. Small freighters and other ships carrying cocaine have regularly employed the port of Chimán, about 125 miles north of the border, where smugglers could off-load the drugs onto Panamanian vessels engaged in the coastal trade.[295]

In so many parts of Central America it has seemed futile to lavish scarce resources on a task like trying to thwart drug transit through one particular border crossing, when traffickers could easily move their operations to any of a slew of neighboring entry points. Similarly, focusing counternarcotics attention on a port like Chimán has seemed of dubious merit because, in fact, the entire Gulf of Panama, including Las Perlas and Panama Bay, has formed an attractive target for maritime traffickers.[296] Considerable quantities of cocaine have been

291. "Recuperan del fondo del mar mil cien kilos de cocaína," *LP* (PA), 11 July 1998, 2A, and "Decomisan 472 kilos de cocaína colombianas," *LP* (PA), 17 July 1998, 1A. The amount recovered was eventually revised from 1100 to 900 kilos.

292. "Decomisan dos mil kilos de cocaína," *LP* (PA), 30 October 2005, 1A; "Se incautan más de dos toneladas de cocaína," *LP* (PA), 11 December 2009, 10A. For the new coast guard stations, see "Se multiplican las bases aeronavales," *LP* (PA), 2 December 2009, 6A.

293. "Piden crear policía comarcal," *LP* (PA), 24 January 2007, 8A; "Decomisan dos toneladas de cocaína," *LP* (PA), 19 January 2005, 1A; "Hay sectores Kunas que prefieren drogas en la Comarca: Giraud," *LP* (PA), 5 January 1997, 2A; "Reportan más de cien delitos por droga," *LP* (PA), 16 January 1995, 1A.

294. See "Incineran cuatro toneladas de drogas," *LP* (PA), 11 May 2000, 3A. For information on the multilateral Operation Buenaventura, see "Fiscal investiga a A. Portillo," *LP* (PA), 14 May 2003, 3A.

295. For a large Chimán seizure, see "Decomisan más de mil kilos de droga," *LP* (PA), 26 May 2004, 1A, and "Extensión de costas panameñas hace muy difícil su custodio," *LP* (PA), 16 December 1991, 44A.

296. See, for instance, "Decomisan 385 kilos," 24. For a 772-kilo pegón shipment that entered via Panama Bay and was being moved overland toward Honduras when intercepted, see "Decomisan tonelada y media de pegón," *LP* (PA), 2 August 2003, 2A.

shipped into or around Panama City, with the drugs sometimes off-loaded right beyond the city limits, either in communities such as Chepo or Veracruz, or in the mangrove swamps near Ciudad Radial.[297] The semiabandoned port of Juan Díaz, in a rough, violent area on the outskirts of Panama City, has amounted to another popular destination because it has lacked much police supervision, and even very many lights.[298]

Southwest of Panama City, some major transshipment operations have occurred in Coclé Province.[299] One involved the so-called Toral-Trujillo network, linked to Cali traffickers and allegedly led by Gilberto Toral Malek and Plinio Trujillo, fugitive nephew of former Dominican Republic dictator Rafael Leonidas Trujillo.[300] This organization transshipped cocaine through Panama into Costa Rica, before exporting it to the United States and Europe mixed in coffee shipments. Although the network at first opted for smaller loads, it suffered a bust of 2,086 kilos in 1994 in Coclé, followed by a related 2,733-kilo seizure in Bocas del Toro. In 1998 a Panamanian court convicted Trujillo and Toral in absentia, sentencing them to twenty-year terms.

For transshipment schemes in which drugs are bound for Central America by land or air, traffickers have aimed to import drug loads well to the north of Panama City, making onward transport more convenient. While some maritime transit of this type has occurred on the Caribbean side into Bocas del Toro, even more extensive drug trafficking has been directed into Panama's upper Pacific zone, including the coastline of Veraguas Province.[301] Unlike the remote jungle swamps and highlands that characterize much of Panama's borders, central Panama is more deforested and dotted with small villages. Nevertheless, for many years drug smugglers from at least ten networks have extensively targeted the Azuero Peninsula, which juts into the Gulf of Panama, sometimes buying up coastal properties and then bringing narcotics ashore by water drops or speedboats.[302]

Even farther into western Panamanian territorial waters, the immense, 110,000-acre Isla de Coiba, which through the end of the twentieth century housed a notorious penal colony, has been situated along one maritime drug-smuggling path, as have the islands of Jicarón and Jicarita, just to the south. Both water drops and transfers from mother ships to smaller vessels have frequently occurred in this vicinity.[303] In one representative case off Jicarita in 1998, Panamanian patrol

297. For a large bust in front of Panama City, see "Policía Nacional decomisa una tonelada de cocaína," *LP* (PA), 25 September 2007, 8A.

298. "Aumenta el tráfico de drogas en Juan Díaz," *LP* (PA), 25 August 1996, 13A.

299. See generally "Costas son vulnerables," 4A. For specific instances, see "Policía decomisa 315 kilos de cocaína," *LP* (PA), 16 March 2005, 5A; "Denuncian tráfico de drogas en Playa Punta Barco," *LP* (PA), 31 January 2003, 4A; and "Decomisan 232 kilos de cocaína en las costas de Farallón," *LP* (PA), 27 June 2001, 4A.

300. Rafael Trujillo's son, Rhademés, trafficked cocaine in Panama for the Cali cartel before his 1994 murder. Rempel, *At the Devil's Table*, 165–66. For accounts of the Toral-Trujillo network, see "Ministerio Público apeló la condena de narcotraficantes," *LP* (PA), 3 December 1998, 9A; "Amplían las sumarias en caso millonario de drogas en Coclé," *LP* (PA), 18 May 1997, 8A; "Acusado de narco se oculta en Costa Rica," *LN* (CR), 2 July 1994, 10A; "Cartel de Cali tenía una bodega en frontera sur," *LN* (CR), 1 July 1994, 10A.

301. For a representative case of transit into Bocas del Toro, see "Decomisan 399 kilos de cocaína," *LP* (PA), 7 April 2006, 8A. For cases in the upper Pacific zone, see, for instance, "Investigan casos de narcotráfico en Veraguas," *LP* (PA), 21 January 2000, 8A; "Aumentan casos relacionados con drogas en Veraguas," *LP* (PA), 3 January 2002, 10A; and "Policía encuentra droga," 9A.

302. Judicial statistics document how the trade soared: in 1994 prosecutors in Azuero tried twenty-nine narcotics cases, and by 2004—a year 777 kilos of cocaine and thousands of kilos of marijuana were seized—294 such cases jammed the courts' dockets. See "No hay recursos para combatir el narcotráfico en Azuero," *LP* (PA), 18 April 2000, 7A; "Investigan diversas playas," 3; "Detectan bandas que trafican drogas en la península de Azuero," *LP* (PA), 9 December 1996, 9A; "Buscan medidas para controlar tráfico de drogas en Azuero," *LP* (PA), 19 July 1991, 16A; "Costas sirven de corredor marino para narcotraficantes," *LP* (PA), 2 September 2002, 16A; "Panamá, puente," 6A; and "Aumentan delitos de drogas," *LP* (PA), 4 January 2005, 5A.

303. See, for instance, "Decomisan cocaína y detienen a tres personas," *LP* (PA), 7 October 2000, 9A; "Descubren cocaína en Coiba lanzada desde una avioneta," *LP* (PA), 11 June 1991, 18A, and "Policía encuentra droga," 9A.

boats, tipped to an incoming shipment, intercepted two Colombian vessels, seized 927 kilos of cocaine, and after a lengthy shoot-out, arrested seven Colombians and a Panamanian.[304]

Just north of Coiba and flanking Costa Rica's southern border, Chiriquí Province has also witnessed considerable maritime cocaine trafficking. While speedboat transfers and water drops have been most frequently employed, in 1995 authorities found shrimp trawlers bringing cocaine into Boca de Hacha. Then, in a notable 1998 case, police seized 300 kilos that had arrived via El Nanzal port in Horconcito, a month later discovering an additional 927 kilos in the same house. While the government has welcomed such counternarcotics triumphs, circumstances typical of all the Central American bridge states—overstretched authorities, an array of potential transshipment sites, and extensive local collaboration—have ensured that only a small fraction of the drugs passing through have been intercepted.[305]

Chiriquí's major port, Puerto Armuelles, with about twenty-two thousand residents, is located just south of the border, at the base of the Burica Peninsula.[306] In the early 1990s Colombian traffickers set up a base of operations there and soon had extensively corrupted local officials.[307] Later that decade, the faltering banana trade created grave economic troubles for the Puerto Armuelles area. By 2002 unemployment stood at 47 percent, and local drug dealing was commonplace, just as it was along the far southern Costa Rican Pacific coast.

Bridge-favoring factors can certainly stretch past national boundaries. Indeed, the cardinal point here is that traffickers can readily capitalize on a transborder factor such as a particularly depressed economic zone, hopscotching operations back and forth across the boundary, while adjoining authorities are likely to be less vigilant and less able to cooperate effectively in the face of dwindling local government resources.

Air Routes

The second most popular mode of importing drugs into Panama, and the favored approach for bringing in illicit profits, has been by air.[308] Smuggling, even by small planes, risks radar detection, which has been better in Panama than in much of Central America. Nevertheless, hundreds of kilos of cocaine can be moved from Colombia to Panama most quickly by air. Small, low-flying planes have thus continually touched down on the country's numerous airstrips to deposit loads. For instance, from the 1990s forward, landing strips in Bocas del Toro, conveniently flanking southern Costa Rica's Caribbean coast, have repeatedly been used for aerial cocaine transit.[309] The narcotics have then

304. "SMN decomisa 927 kilos de cocaína," *LP* (PA), 14 December 1998, 2A; "Incautan 927 kilos de cocaína pero se escapan cinco sospechosos," *LP* (PA), 14 December 1998, 7A. Another 927 kilos had been intercepted the prior year on Playa Nanzal from the same type of boat using the same engine, and that seizure was linked to cocaine busts of 1,227 and 300 kilos. "Hoy se inicia el juicio a siete colombianos narcotraficantes," *LP* (PA), 18 December 1998, 7A.

305. "Incautan 300 kilos de cocaína en Chiriquí," *LP* (PA), 27 April 1998, 2A; "Decomisan 927 kilos de cocaína a colombianos," *LP* (PA), 28 May 1998, 7A; "Investigan diversas playas," 3.

306. For information on drugs in the Burica Peninsula and Puerto Armuelles area, see "Punta Burica, un territorio que está a la deriva," *LP* (PA), 1 May 2006, 10A; "Puerto Armuelles, más que bananos," *LP* (PA), 26 August 2002, 8A; "Decomisan cocaína en una casa en Bugaba," *LP* (PA), 5 May 1997, 15A; "En Chiriquí: Denuncian nexos de Policía y PTJ con el narcotráfico," *LP* (PA), 4 June 1991, 32A; "Trasiego de drogas utiliza las costas de Veraguas y Chiriquí," *LP* (PA), 4 June 1991, 32A; and "Poca vigilancia policial en Chiriquí y Veraguas facilita tráfico de drogas," *LP* (PA), 17 June 1991, 28A.

307. Nonetheless, authorities later made occasional large busts, such as a four-hundred-kilo cocaine seizure in 1996.

308. See "Carteles colombianos utilizan a Panamá como puente para droga," *LP* (PA), 19 March 1991, 26A. For drug earnings sent to Panama City to be laundered, see "Investigan a sobrino de G. Ford por presunto trasiego de dólares," *LP* (PA), 16 September 1991, 1A. For a typical Colombia-Panama–United States aerial-transshipment scheme, see *United States v. Londono-Villa*, 930 F.2d 994.

309. See "Vuelos sospechosos siguen en Bocas," *LP* (PA), 30 January 1994, 2A. For representative cases involving Guabito and Changuinola, see "PTJ decomisa quince kilos de cocaína en la frontera," *LP* (PA), 4 December 2006,

normally been repacked, for instance, hidden in double-walled containers, before being exported north, often overland via Costa Rica.

The other common use of light aircraft has been in water drops coordinated with waiting speedboats, in which drugs have been brought ashore to a beach house or nearby farm for temporary storage, prior to export to market. In 1991 authorities broke up one sophisticated venture, finding 37 kilos of cocaine packed into three plastic tubes, emitting radio signals to guide associates, yet floating perpendicularly to avoid detection. While water drops protect pilots and planes, the risk of losing the drugs increases. The bales may break when they hit the water, particularly if incorrectly packaged or if the pilot flies too high.[310] One result is that, after botched water drops, narcotics floating at sea or washed up on beaches have frequently been collected, sometimes by authorities but often by fishermen or other residents who supply local drug markets. Thus, in late 1997 and early 1998 a total of 369 kilos of cocaine washed up in Bocas del Toro, all packaged to surface after a water drop. Early in 2003 the Panamanian Coast Guard discovered 30 kilos of cocaine floating off the Río San Roque near Colón, packed in the characteristic green insulating material. Shortly thereafter undercover officers came upon two liters of liquefied heroin floating near Isla Flamenco.[311]

In 2006 traffickers sent a series of cocaine flights out of Chiriquí Province. Since Colombian authorities had increased scrutiny of aerial-trafficking schemes, drug networks had started to ship cocaine into Panama by sea, prior to flying the drugs on to Mexico.[312] In April Panamanian Air Force personnel, tipped to the presence of a drug plane, helicoptered to a banana plantation near Puerto Armuelles and blocked the departure of a small Mexican aircraft. Crop dusters had once used the runway, but given low prices for bananas on the international market, thousands of acres of the surrounding plantation had been largely neglected. When the Cessna 206 tried to flee, the air force disabled the plane, also killing the pilot with machine-gun fire. Investigators determined that the plane had arrived from Mexico into the Chiriquí airport, been refueled and flown to the airstrip to collect cocaine trucked onto the plantation through an abandoned entrance. The Tijuana cartel had financed the operation, and the network of Costa Ricans, Panamanians, Colombians, and Mexicans had more than five years of experience. Traffickers have rarely been deterred by a single mishap, however, and later that year witnesses reported a light plane flying over La Barqueta in Chiriquí and then dropping packages on Playa Alanje, collected by men driving all-terrain four-wheelers.[313]

Apart from traffic through remote airstrips, Tocumen International Airport has served as yet another conduit for transshipped drugs, ever since Pan-American Airlines flights touched

8A, and "Policía captura a tres narcos en Bocas del Toro," *LP* (PA), 26 January 1994, 5A. For an Almirante 1997 case, see "Decomisan quinientos kilos de cocaína," *LP* (PA), 17 April 1997, 1A, and "Desmantelan banda de narcotraficantes," *LP* (PA), 18 April 1997, 2A.

310. Decker and Chapman, *Drug Smugglers*, 53.

311. *INCSR* (2000), 190; "Extensión de costas," 44A; "Panamá, puente," 6A; "Ruta de Centroamérica preferida para los carteles de la droga," *LH* (GU), 8 June 1991, 11; "Costas de San Lorenzo son usadas para traficar drogas," *LP* (PA), 23 November 1997, 14A; "Encuentran sesenta y nueve kilos de cocaína en Playa Larga, Bocas del Toro," *LP* (PA), 20 January 1998, 7A; "SMN decomisa treinta kilos de cocaína en Colón," *LP* (PA), 10 January 2003, 4A; "Policía decomisa heroína líquida," *LP* (PA), 31 January 2003, 4A.

312. "Narcotráfico en la frontera tico-panameña," *LP* (PA), 18 April 2006, 6A.

313. "SAN derriba avioneta con droga," *LP* (PA), 17 April 2006, 1A; "Moradores advierten sobre movimiento de traficantes," *LP* (PA), 17 April 2006, 8A; "La droga que cayó del cielo," *LP* (PA), 18 April 2006, 6A; "Detenidos niegan participación en tráfico," *LP* (PA), 21 April 2006, 8A; "Otro arresto por 'narcoavioneta,'" *LP* (PA), 26 April 2006, 6A; "La ruta de 'oro' hacia Estados Unidos," *LP* (PA), 30 April 2006, 8A; "Alcalde denuncia que narcos operan en Alanje," *LP* (PA), 2 August 2006, 7A.

down there from the 1950s on.[314] Traffickers have hidden considerable quantities of cocaine in private aircraft and also in the holds of cargo planes or commercial airliners landing here.[315] This became a prime transshipment method when the military regime controlled airport security. In that period such aerial-smuggling schemes were exposed, if at all, largely through the efforts of foreign law enforcement. Thus, in 1982 U.S. Customs agents in Louisiana searched a plane arriving from Tocumen and discovered 544 kilos of cocaine hidden in sacks of cattle feed. Despite repeated DEA warnings to military intelligence, presumed ringleader Jorge Baena Robinson, who operated an export-import firm at Tocumen, managed to escape to Venezuela.[316]

Until the Canal Zone bases reverted to Panamanian control, drug-trafficking scandals involving the U.S. military occasionally came to light as well. U.S. soldiers sometimes brought cocaine or marijuana onto military or commercial flights.[317] In a major 1989 case U.S. counternarcotics agents arrested twenty-six people, including two U.S. military personnel, for transporting 20–50 kilos of cocaine a month from Panama City into Washington, D.C., sometimes by military transport but mostly via commercial aircraft.

Although the transition to democratic rule failed to halt airport smuggling, hidden cocaine has been more regularly seized in cargo and from passengers at Tocumen. As a major regional air hub, with flights to Latin America, North America, and Europe, Tocumen has continued to be used for an array of smuggling ventures, with authorities reporting the discovery of sixty-five drug-trafficking cases in 1996 and the seizure of more than a ton of drugs throughout 1998.[318] In Operation Olé in 1996 an undercover agent infiltrated one Cali network that had been using an air-cargo business called SENTRACA to ship cocaine to the United States and Europe and found top customs, treasury, and PTJ officials on its payroll.[319] Indeed, as traffickers have opened European markets, passengers have frequently carried cocaine via Tocumen to

314. Gootenberg, *Andean Cocaine*, 273. In the late 1970s the military regime converted old Tocumen Airport into an air force base and cargo depot and built a new terminal. Although this was initially called Torrijos Airport, eventually Panamanians reverted to describing the entire airport complex as "Tocumen."

315. For one such case in which authorities seized one hundred kilos of cocaine at New York's Kennedy Airport in a plastic pipe-fittings shipment arriving from Panama City, see *Ramirez-Leon v. United States*, 1996 U.S. App. LEXIS 27138. For other representative air-transshipment cases, see "Aduanas decomisa B/1.1 millón en cocaína," *LP* (PA), 14 December 1990, 44A, and "Decomisan cuarenta y tres kilos de cocaína en aeropuerto," *LP* (PA), 24 May 1991, 32A.

316. *United States v. Morrison*, 946 F.2d 484; *Vines v. United States*, 28 F.3d 1123; and *United States v. South*, 28 F.3d 619. A DEA agent later recalled that in this case his organization had "asked for certain things to be done very quickly. They weren't done very quickly. . . . By the time the Panamanian forces got around to looking for this guy, . . . why, lo and behold, he had managed to escape to, they said, Caracas. . . . Nobody gets out of Panama that they don't want to get out, especially at Tocumen with all the controls they have there." Murillo, *Noriega Mess*, 398–99.

317. For instance, in 1992 a U.S. Navy enlisted man shipped ninety-five kilos of cocaine in television sets to Virginia via South Carolina. *United States v. Clark*, 911 F.2d 725. For other representative cases, see *United States v. Browne*, 891 F.2d 389; *United States v. Peart*, 888 F.2d 101; *United States v. Garcia*, 882 F.2d 699; *United States v. Mack*, 892 F.2d 134; *United States v. Smith*, 918 F.2d 1551; *United States v. McDowell*, 918 F.2d 1004; and *United States v. Pirre*, 927 F.2d 694. See also "Federal Agents Break Up Panamanian Cocaine Ring," United Press International (United States) (hereafter cited as UPI [US]), 16 May 1989; "Two Soldiers Face Charges in Duffel Bag Drug Operation," *Orlando Sentinel*, 8 March 1990, A3; and *United States v. Bethancourt*, 65 F.3d 1074.

318. See "En el aeropuerto de Tocumen: Detectan sesenta y cinco casos de tráfico de drogas," *LP* (PA), 29 December 1996, 5A, and "Panamá decomisa 28.3 toneladas de drogas," *LP* (PA), 31 December 1998, 4A. For a representative case, see "Más amenazas de muerte," *LP* (PA), 12 July 2002, 1A. Quantities discovered at Tocumen varied based on transshipment strategies and interdiction resources, human and technological. Thus, in 2003 a mere 3 percent of Panama's drug seizures occurred at Tocumen: 197 kilos of cocaine, 76 of heroin, and 8 of marijuana. "Bajo decomiso de droga en Tocumen," *LP* (PA), 5 January 2004, 2A.

319. See "Juzagarán a veinticinco personas acusadas de narcotráfico," *LP* (PA), 30 August 1996, 4A; "Juzgarán a veinticinco personas vinculadas a cartel de Cali," *LP* (PA), 19 September 1996, 3A; and "Abren causa criminal contra ex director de aduanas," *LP* (PA), 21 September 1996, 2A. In 1994 a group of Panamanians involved allegedly traveled to Colombia to meet Gilberto Rodríguez Orejuela.

Spain, Germany, the Netherlands, and the United Kingdom.[320] In a notable 1995 case, a Belgian citizen delivered a suitcase containing cocaine to undercover police agents. This led authorities to a far-flung network of Colombians, Panamanians, Spaniards, French, and Belgians that was coordinating courier deliveries of cocaine to numerous European destinations.[321]

The airport-trafficking schemes interrupted in the late 1990s illustrate the diversity of methods, networks, and destinations. In 1997 one ring regularly brought cocaine from Colombia into Tocumen, then shipped the drugs overland to Costa Rica via Chiriquí Province and the Paso Canoas border crossing. In the first half of 1998 Haitian authorities found cocaine on Panamanian airliners four times, including a 675-kilo load, the largest cocaine seizure off a Central American commercial aircraft. More typically, in two 1998 cases in Panama four individuals were arrested, convicted, and sentenced to eight-year terms for attempting to export just over 15 kilos of cocaine. One cache had been hidden in welding machines awaiting delivery to Spain and the other had been secreted in amplifiers to be flown to Honduras. The following year customs inspectors checked boxes of iced fish headed from Panama to Miami and found two to contain thirty packages of cocaine wrapped in rubber and adhesive tape.[322]

Aerial smuggling in Panama thus reflects in microcosm the evolution of the Panamanian drug trade. The delivery of narcotics by courier or in cargo dates well back into the twentieth century. The military regime abetted such trafficking, and the flow of drugs vastly increased. By the post-Noriega period the use of the busy international airport and the many unregulated airstrips and air-freight companies had become deeply entrenched and difficult to uproot. Indeed, in 2008 Mexican officials vowed to redouble efforts to inspect private planes arriving from Panama, because so many drugs were entering their country on Panamanian, as well as Colombian and Venezuelan, aircraft.[323]

Overland Routes

In comparison to maritime and aerial shipments, the overland import of narcotics into Panama ranked a distant third. Nevertheless, very large quantities of drugs have departed from the country, and traffickers have frequently used Panama's network of roads and highways, including the Transisthmian Highway from Panama City to Colón.

One particularly notable overland-export operation, broken up by authorities in late 2007 and early 2008 through judicially authorized wiretaps, involved a drug ring, allegedly led by Irma Ortiz, that brought large cocaine loads into Chiriquí by sea to be trucked north all the way to Quatzatenango, Guatemala, and then forwarded to Europe by sea.[324] According to Panama's chief drug prosecutor, the group had been sending narcotics along this route for three years. Panamanian officials arrested fifty associates, including ten national police officers, eleven PTJ officers, and two Mexicans, and in January 2008 alone they seized 1,327 kilos of

320. See *INCSR* (1998), 167, and *INCSR* (2006), 23. For cocaine smuggling from Panama to Miami and from Panama to Spain, see *United States v. Bristol*, 964 F.2d 1088, and *United States v. de Leon Davis*, 914 F.2d 340.

321. "Fiscalía indagará a César Guardia por narcotráfico," *LP* (PA), 6 December 1996, 1A. César Guardia was a Panamanian lawyer accused by Dobarro of obtaining couriers to carry the drugs to Europe. For Guardia's response, see "César Guardia niega nexos con banda de narcotraficante," *LP* (PA), 12 December 1996, 3A. For another representative case, see "Detenido en RFA un panameño por posesión de coca," *LP* (PA), 22 May 1991, 11A.

322. "Detienen a cinco mexicanos por introducir cocaína," *LP* (PA), 7 January 1997, 5A; "Decomisan cocaína en aerolinea panameña," *LP* (PA), 4 June 1998, 3A; "Anulan sentencia absolutoria y condenan a ocho años a narco," *LP* (PA), 10 July 1998, 2A; "Condenan a ocho años del cárcel a tres narcotraficantes," *LP* (PA), 16 June 1998, 4A; "Corte niega libertad a empresario sindicado por tráfico de drogas," *LP* (PA), 21 January 1999, 5A.

323. "Panamá apoyará lucha antidrogas de México," 17 January 2008, 4A.

324. See "Conectan droga con narco red," *LP* (PA), 27 January 2008, 1A, and "Los tentáculos de una narco red," *LP* (PA), 27 January 2008, 6A.

cocaine linked to this network. Upon being detained, the ringleaders could not account for as much as $20 million in seized assets, and Ortiz alone was found to have interests in illegal gambling and to own various residences, a dozen farms, an island, and 150 shipping containers, as well as a recently constructed and remodeled freight-truck depot.

Darién and the Colombian Border

Fronting the 140-mile-long Colombian border, the far southeastern province of Darién covers roughly a quarter of Panamanian territory. As of 2000 it contained a mere forty-one thousand inhabitants, many members of the Kuna, Embera, and Wounaan tribes. The border zone, often referred to as the Darién gap, is marked by extremely dense jungle, low mountains, and swampland. Some of the terrain is virtually impenetrable during the April-to-November rainy season. Because no major highways angle toward the border on either side, most narcotics entering Darién arrive by small plane to one of an estimated two hundred clandestine airstrips, or by speedboat, either to remote coves or beaches, to Puerto Obaldía on the Caribbean, or to Puerto Piña or Jaqué on the Pacific coast.[325]

The quantity of drugs crossing the boundary with Colombia overland rises during the dry season, when smugglers can travel by some combination of rivers and the rough trails linking indigenous villages. Thus, some narcotics have moved down Colombia's Río Cacarica by boat, then up and across the ridge dividing the countries by foot, and through the Chocó and Kuna settlements of Paya, Pucuro, Boca de Cupe, and Unión Chocó. From there, the drugs have usually been carried into the town of Yaviza in the center of the isthmus, thirty miles north of the Colombian border, which is the southern terminus of the Pan-American Highway.

During military rule, the drugs and contraband filtering through Darién stood as unwanted competition, a way to evade the bribes being collected at places such as Tocumen Airport and the Colón Free Zone. Hence, the armed forces cracked down on Darién trafficking: smugglers were beheaded, and corpses were left behind to deter others.[326] Although Panamanian officials claimed that immediately after the U.S. invasion the amounts of narcotics passing through Darién by land, sea, and air diminished even further, this did not last.[327] Through the 1990s and into the new century, as rival forces in the Colombian civil war vigorously contended for neighboring territory, what had once been a minor stream of narcotics entering Panama via Darién rose noticeably. In 1994 the Panamanian government established at Yaviza a 180-person border-patrol outpost, the Border Patrol Service, to curb trafficking and incursions by Colombians. However, the region is immense, the terrain difficult, and extensive smuggling of drugs, contraband, illegal aliens, and especially weapons has continued to occur, as Colombian fighters have vied with one another to control arms and drug flows along the border.[328]

325. Although Turbo, Colombia, on the Gulf of Urabá, is reasonably close to Panama, Puerto Obaldía is not connected with any sizable road network. Here, drugs are typically imported and exported by air or sea, as is true of trafficking via the Jaqué port on the Pacific. See "PTJ custodia las fronteras para evitar el narcotráfico," *LP* (PA), 11 December 1991, 2A. For trafficking in and around Jaqué, including Piña Bay, see "Desmantelan red de narcos en el Darién," *LP* (PA), 1 July 2002, 3A, and "Juzgado condena a cinco colombianos," *LP* (PA), 17 January 1998, 4A. See also "Narcotraficantes usan Darién y San Blás," 1A; "EU brindará entrenamiento antidrogas," *LP* (PA), 11 April 1996, 2A; "Jarvis confirma la existencia de pistas clandestinas," *LP* (PA), 13 April 1996, 4A; and "Hughes insiste en la existencia de pistas aéreas clandestinas," *LP* (PA), 16 April 1996, 2A. For multiple cases involving the speedboat *El Maicero*, see "Computadora ayuda a descubrir drogas en lancha," *LP* (PA), 10 October 1996, 3A.

326. Murillo, *Noriega Mess*, 445.

327. "En Darién ha disminuido," 40A.

328. For information on twenty-plus FARC incursions into Panama, see "Los ataques de las FARC," *LP* (PA), 5 January 2009, 4A. See also Cragin and Hoffman, *Arms Trafficking*, 34; "En Darién convergen fuerzas paramilitares y el narcotráfico," *LP* (PA), 6 December 1998, 1A; "Las fronteras inseguras," *LP* (PA), 27 January 1997, 6A; and "'Narcoguerrilla' mantiene 10 mil hombres armados," *LP* (PA), 27 October 1996, 4A.

While the drug loads transported down the network of trails and footpaths crossing the Darién gap have necessarily been modest in size, the risk of interception by law enforcement has been minimal as well, and the indigenous population has been paralyzed with fear, given drug violence.[329] Heavily armed men have often passed through carrying drugs, but there have been few authorities to report to, much less to offer protection should traffickers later return to exact vengeance. The other factor that has influenced the Darién drug trade has involved the establishment of cocaine laboratories in the border zone, controlled by irregular Colombian forces. In one notable 2007 case Colombian authorities reported seizing twenty to twenty-five tons of cocaine at a large laboratory near the Panamanian border.[330] With laboratories positioned nearby and with the FARC, in particular, markedly increasing its share of the Colombian cocaine industry, ground imports of cocaine have increased. However, Darién routes have proven to be sufficiently arduous and time consuming in comparison with the ease of sea and air transit that only a very modest percentage of all the narcotics entering Panama have arrived overland.

The Costa Rican–Panamanian Border

In contrast, considerable amounts of cocaine and occasionally notable quantities of marijuana have exited Panama via the exceedingly porous Costa Rican border.[331] Cocaine has traversed the major crossings at Sixaola on the Caribbean side and Paso Canoas on the Pacific, each marked by heavy traffic and lax controls. Additional loads have transited the many small central communities such as Río Sereno, Alto Quiel, Portón, San Andrés, and Exquisito.[332] Then, more than one hundred informal border crossings have had no customs and immigration controls whatsoever.[333] Not only has there typically been a negligible police presence, but some traffickers have created local intelligence networks to keep them informed of the occasional patrol schedules.[334]

Although cocaine has been exported overland by foot, horse, and vehicle, traffickers usually hid major loads in large trucks.[335] In 2001 Panamanian officials located 800 kilos of cocaine in the double walls of a tractor trailer

329. Estimates of the numbers of paths range from forty-seven officially identified by the Border Patrol Service to two hundred cited by others. See "Darién de las interrogantes," 6A, and Cragin and Hoffman, 35. For examples of drug violence, see "Darién de las interrogantes," 6A. For an alleged Colombian trafficker's kidnapping and killing, see "Secuestran a ciudadano colombiano en Darién," *LP* (PA), 18 January 1997, 1A, and "Encuentran cadáver de colombiano secuestrado," *LP* (PA), 31 January 1997, 4A.

330. "Decomisan el mayor cargamento de droga," *LP* (PA), 1 May 2007, 3A.

331. For an informative series on border problems, see "Una frontera sin control que vive al ritmo de la ilegalidad," *LP* (PA), 6 March 2005, 1A; "Drogas al norte; armas al sur," *LP* (PA), 8 March 2005, 6A; "Caballos usados como 'mulas,'" *LP* (PA), 9 March 2005, 6A; and "Irregularidades en la frontera," *LP* (PA), 11 March 2005, 6A.

332. See "Nuevo decomiso de drogas en la frontera con Costa Rica," *LP* (PA), 14 October 1990, 44A; "Guasule: 'Coca' decomisada valorada en L. 150 millones," *LP* (HO), 3 August 1996, 1. For representative border busts, see "Se incautan de 162 kilos de cocaína," *LP* (PA), 6 December 2006, 6A, and "Incautan 120 kilos de cocaína en frontera de Panamá con CR," *LP* (PA), 21 February 1996, 1A.

333. See, for instance, "Frontera Panamá–Costa Rica un paso sin restricción," *LP* (PA), 30 October 2000, 6A. The Paso Canoas border crossing, in particular, was extremely busy: here, more than eighty thousand people entered Panama annually. See "Estafan a turistas en Paso Canoas," *LP* (PA), 25 April 2005, 8A. A group of investigative reporters crossed the Panamanian border post into Costa Rica ten times without being stopped. "Drogas al norte," 6A.

334. See "Frontera tico-panameña continúa," 1A, and "Descubren 'venta' de información clasificada," *LP* (PA), 29 September 2007, 4A. In 2005 fourteen Panamanian officials had been assigned to attend to the seventeen thousand people crossing the border each month.

335. "Decomisan cuatro toneladas de cocaína en cuatro meses," *LP* (PA), 2 May 1998, 4A. For a representative sample of cases employing these different methods, see "Incautan ochocientos kilos de cocaína en Panamá," *LP* (HO), 21 April 2001, 46A; "Decomisan treinta y un kilos de droga y detienen a dos colombianos," *LP* (PA), 11 October 2000, 8A; "Acusado de narcotráfico se entrega a la policía," *LP* (PA), 15 May 1997, 15A; and *United States v. Cardenas*, 917 F.2d 683.

headed north, and the following year they found 256 kilos in the wheels of another truck proceeding toward Costa Rica.[336] Once peace came to Nicaragua and El Salvador, and as Central American governments loosened trade restrictions, drug rings bought up or infiltrated some trucking firms, and Guatemalan, Salvadoran, and Honduran drivers were periodically discovered to be exporting drugs within containers of merchandise or produce.[337] Given the total volume of traffic criss-crossing the border, however, much more cocaine has evaded detection. As one police source noted of drug seizures on this border, "When we trap a shipment, it is because we have a tip about it. We don't have the technical equipment or the personnel to do anything else. A truck full of bananas, we can't inspect banana by banana. The truck could have a double wall and nobody would know."[338]

The Central American drug trade has been sufficiently interconnected that developments in one country often grievously affect another. To stop the prodigious overland drug exports to Costa Rica, one Panamanian official declared, would require an officer every twenty meters.[339] The Panamanian and Costa Rican governments have lacked the resources needed to control a 225-mile border that weaves its way through jungle and mountains.[340] In the immediate post-Noriega years the Panamanian customs service had no vehicles whatsoever. Outside of the five official border posts, officers were simply occasionally patrolling on foot, while unpaid workers hoping one day to become customs inspectors had been put in charge of the customs stations near David.[341] Even decades later, resources have been scarce and corruption evident. Consequently, cocaine has streamed north in buses and passenger vehicles, with smaller quantities exiting via the foot traffic of undocumented individuals—street vendors, prostitutes, and others who have passed freely back and forth.[342]

Determining the magnitude of the flow has been especially difficult in light of all the cross-border drug loads, small, modest, and large in size. In 1994 Panamanian authorities estimated that as many as 1,500 kilos of cocaine flowed north into Costa Rica each month. That may have been an underestimate, however, as in a single case that year Coclé authorities seized more than 2 tons of Colombian cocaine that had arrived by sea on the Pacific coast and was being trucked north.[343] Indeed, for years and years police have stumbled onto significant shipments heading to the Costa Rican border, and many of the large truckloads of narcotics intercepted in the more northerly Central American states originated in Panama.[344] Although authorities seemed to be confiscating only a small percentage of the drugs crossing the border, given the quantities involved, even a fragmented and lackluster effort resulted in some notable seizures.[345] Plainly, drug rings have regularly used ground transport to move substantial cocaine loads into Costa Rica for export to market by land, air, or sea.[346]

336. "Camión llevaba 256 kilos de cocaína," *LP* (PA), 31 August 2002, 2A.

337. See, for instance, "Decomisan 103 kilos de cocaína," *LP* (PA), 9 June 2001, 5A; "Decomisan 100 kilos de cocaína en David," *LP* (PA), 10 July 1998, 8A; and "Decomisan 414 kilos de cocaína," *LP* (PA), 26 April 1998, 1A.

338. "Drogas al norte," 6A.

339. "Revelan que es imposible vigilar la frontera," *LP* (PA), 11 August 1996, 11A.

340. See "Disminuye incautación de drogas en Chiriquí," *LP* (PA), 12 January 1997, 7A, and "Una frontera ingobernable y silenciosa," *LP* (PA), 6 March 2005, 1A.

341. "Panama Drug Smugglers Prosper as Dictator's Exit Opens the Door," *NYT* (US), 21 August 1990, 1A.

342. "Carteles de la droga toman zona sur," *LN* (CR), 24 July 1994, 4A.

343. "Posponen audiencia de implicados en el tráfico de millonario de cocaína," *LP* (PA), 3 December 1996, 14A.

344. Ibid. See also "Crece narcotráfico por Paso Canoas," *LN* (CR), 11 November 1994, 10A. For a representative instance, see "Decomisan cocaína por L13 millones," *LP* (HO), 26 April 1990, 2.

345. In a typical 1997 case 1,339 kilos of Cali cocaine were discovered in La Chorrera, just west of Panama City. "Capturan a cinco personas con mil 300 kilos de cocaína," *LP* (PA), 24 March 1997, 4A.

346. See *INCSR* (1998), 167, and *INCSR* (1999), 187.

Conclusion

Although none of the Central American bridge states have been able to deter criminal syndicates from transshipping large quantities of drugs via their territory, skies, and waters, we have seen the drug trade evolving differently in each country. For its part, since the 1970s Panama has served as a critically important link between South American drug producers and North American and European consumers. Some of its bridge-favoring characteristics—pockets of rural and urban poverty, vulnerable judicial and penal systems, long-standing political corruption—parallel those that have enticed traffickers into the other bridge states. Yet the principal set of factors encouraging drug transshipment through the country has been quite distinct. Panama's geography has stood out, especially its location near Colombia, the presence of the canal, and its long coastlines and multiplicity of offshore islands. Furthermore, Panama's economic profile, especially Colón Free Zone commerce and Panama City banking, has attracted drug traffickers in singular fashion.

Panama has also been engaged in one of the most complex political transitions in the region. From its democratic past the country moved through the populist and personalistic rule of Omar Torrijos. Thereafter, the rise of Manuel Noriega from his prominent intelligence post in the Torrijos regime to become Panama's de facto ruler greatly exacerbated earlier trends. Not only did the military bully the population and dominate puppet civilian officials, but Noriega and close associates used their power primarily to enrich themselves. Noriega's tenure opened opportunities for wealthy criminal syndicates intent on securing assistance in moving drugs through the country, especially the then dominant Medellín traffickers. But, ironically, the same profit motive that brought enormous wealth to Noriega also curtailed the drug trade to some extent, because the military regime not only exercised authoritarian control but seized drugs and broke up organizations that had failed to pay off the military beforehand. Numerous lesser traffickers, as well as certain rivals to Noriega's partners, were arrested, and some were extradited.

The 1989 U.S. invasion that unseated Noriega brought on a difficult political transition, and, sensing instability and weakness, drug traffickers swarmed into a country replete with bridge-favoring characteristics but that now lacked authoritarian controls, as the new government struggled to reconstruct effective law-enforcement machinery.[347] Although drug transshipment in the post-Noriega period has not occurred with brazen involvement by the authorities, the destruction of the military regime actually spurred more cocaine transshipment, as the initial postinvasion governments could call upon only very meager resources to combat the drug trade.[348]

Hence, new opportunities arose for various foreign and domestic smuggling organizations. Once Noriega and his Medellín contacts moved out of the Colón Free Zone, Cali traffickers moved right in, taking advantage, even more thoroughly, of the extensive shipping into major North American and European markets. Furthermore, mixed signals emanated from the post-Noriega Panamanian governments as to how high a priority to place on antidrug policies. Although most officials wanted a sharp break from the Noriega years, and although the problems of drug abuse and drug-related violence were soon starkly evident, influential Panamanian citizens had reaped large, though often indirect, profits from the drug trade. Drug trafficking continued to encourage the banking industry

347. In 1991 Panama had 4,368 police, one officer for every 142.5 square kilometers, and police could call on a mere forty-three vehicles, thirty-three in poor repair. "Director de PTJ preocupado por la falta de recursos," *LP* (PA), 19 March 1991, 26A.

348. "Extensión de costas," 44A. In 1991 the DEA reported that trafficking and laundering in Panama had reached preinvasion levels. "EE.UU. revela auge de narco en Panamá, " *LN* (CR), 19 April 1991, 18A.

and construction boom in Panama City, and the repatriation of drug profits continued to contribute to the growth and vitality of the Free Zone. Hence, the extent to which antidrug rhetoric would be matched by the passage of laws and the implementation of policies has been an ongoing issue. Just as in Noriega's day, the official transcript has by no means necessarily coincided with the hidden transcript, and so, for instance, Panama's banks have continued to be a notable center for money laundering.[349]

Broader international developments, in the drug trade and beyond it, have also affected post-Noriega drug trafficking. The rise in intensity of FARC and AUC trafficking in Colombia and the increased interest in arms-for-drugs deals stimulated the drug trade, as no bridge state was more familiar or convenient than Panama for Colombian irregular fighters. Moreover, law-enforcement pressure in Colombia and the atomization of the Colombian drug industry brought leading traffickers to move to Panama, making it their sanctuary or even their new headquarters. Equally important, as Mexican cartels seized market share, they vigorously increased their presence in Panama, once so clearly the territory of Colombian traffickers. The country's prison population eventually reflected this trend, as did airport seizures of assets.[350] In the early twenty-first century, with the Colombian cocaine business in a state of turmoil, smuggling by Mexicans and by cartelitos from Guatemala and other Central American states further boosted drug transshipment.

In the final analysis, what stands out in Panama is the extent to which its geography, coupled with the vulnerabilities and incapacities of this transitional state, has ensured a central position in bridge-state trafficking. Although the country has consolidated its democratic and civilian regime and has repaired much of the damage inflicted by the dictatorship, it has proven incapable of significantly curbing the amounts of narcotics being sent across its territory, over its seas, and through its air space by the numerous transnational drug-smuggling rings attracted to the country by its many bridge-favoring factors. Indeed, exceedingly large quantities of cocaine have transited and continue to transit the country, while trafficking in heroin, pegón, and pseudoephedrine have come to pose new threats. Although progress has been made in laws, courts, and prisons, the new civilian governments have not been able to reverse rising crime rates or institute an effective criminal-justice system that can consistently counter powerful drug networks by moving effectively from investigation through arrest, prosecution, conviction, sentencing, and incarceration. Thus, in the post-Noriega era, although notable seizures have occurred, prominent figures have been arrested, and cooperation with the DEA and other foreign law-enforcement bodies have been undertaken more thoroughly than before, these efforts have not cancelled the array of bridge-favoring factors that have made transshipment via Panama so attractive and that have ensured that it has remained the primary Central American bridge state.

349. See *INCSR* (1991), 171. See also "Continua en Panamá lavado de dinero, según informe de E.U.," *LP* (PA), 13 March 1991, 1A, and "U.S.: Panama Still Money-Laundering Center," *MH* (US), 15 February 1992, 1A.

350. By 1997 Panama was incarcerating 346 Colombians, 271 for drug trafficking. By 2004, 552 Colombians were imprisoned, most for drug offenses. By 2007 the figure had diminished to 396, but as the number of jailed Colombians declined, Mexican prisoners increased from 27 in 2004 to 47 in 2007. The following year, in what a Panamanian prosecutor termed a "criminal migration," the number of imprisoned Mexicans jumped by 56 percent, while arrests of Colombians declined another 21 per cent. See "Morosidad judicial afecta a detenidos colombianos," *LP* (PA), 13 May 1997, 4A; "Repatriarán a veintisiete reos colombianos sentenciados," *LP* (PA), 7 May 2005, 5A; "Uno de cada quince detenidos en Panamá es extranjero," *LP* (PA), 21 January 2008, 4A; and "Aumenta la presencia de narcos mexicanos," *LP* (PA), 6 January 2009, 6A. In 2006, for the first time, Panamanian officials caught more Mexicans failing to declare large sums at customs than any other nationality. See "Arrestan a mexicano con $30 mil," *LP* (PA), 8 December 2006, 8A.

Conclusion

The time has come for a summing up. In exploring the trade in drugs in Belize, Costa Rica, Guatemala, Honduras, and Panama, the preceding chapters have aimed to answer the fundamental questions we initially posed concerning drug trafficking and the law in Central America. What conclusions might be drawn, then, from the record of the ways that drug organizations and law enforcement have contended with one another in these bridge states? Most basically, the Central American states have proven to be remarkably effective places in which to transship drugs from South American producers to North American and European consumers. Their attributes—geographic, economic, social, and political—have been quite well suited for drug transshipment, and they represent an array of prototypical bridge states.

As for law enforcement, confronted with the transit of millions of dollars' worth of illegal drugs, the Central American republics have not simply given up in despair. Instead, with some outside assistance, many marijuana, heroin, and cocaine shipments have been confiscated and numerous arrests have been made. Rather than a steady deterioration in state power, even the weakest of the Central American bridge states have "retreated, persisted, and reasserted [themselves] . . . in complex patterns."[1] While the history of Central American drug trafficking highlights the incapacities of states, one can also make out a dogged determination to counter this form of transnational organized crime, despite considerable costs. And, the complexities of these national patterns—that is, the particular years marked by low or high seizures and the length of the periods in between high and low marks—differ from country to country in relation to the shifting context of new trafficking challenges, revised policy-making priorities,

1. Friman and Andreas, *Illicit Global Economy*, vii.

different law-enforcement initiatives, and an array of regional and international pressures.

Nevertheless, although authorities have posed a very real threat to trafficking ventures and to particular drug organizations, the bridge states have failed to reduce markedly the overall amounts of drugs transiting the region. Law enforcement has become much more skilled at detecting smuggling by identifying patterns, drawing on past experience, and using more advanced technology, but the goal of significantly interrupting a sizable percentage of transshipment operations has become progressively more difficult as the decades have passed. And so, Central America witnessed larger drug flows at the end of the 1980s than at the beginning and still larger flows at the end of the 1990s—a trend that has continued into the twenty-first century.

While particular parts of Central America have been especially attractive transit zones—for instance, the Colón Free Zone in Panama, the San Andrés–Limón corridor in Costa Rica, La Mosquitia in Honduras, the Petén in Guatemala, and the cayes of Belize—drug smuggling has truly blanketed the region. Very few areas have been completely untouched by the trade. Trafficking has also evolved, with different varieties of drugs being transported by different methods and different routes in different periods. Although certain trends can be discerned across the region—the tapering off of the courier trafficking of cocaine, for instance, or the advent of speedboat transit—others have been quite country-specific. They have depended on the constellations of bridge-favoring and -disfavoring factors in one state or another at a given point in time. Thus, Panamanian drug traffickers may be far more involved in container shipments to Europe than Belizean counterparts. There might be relatively few aerial-trafficking schemes in Belize and Costa Rica at about the same time that Honduras and Guatemala confront a surge in them. The distinctive profiles of the bridge states help dictate national trends in drug trafficking.

As for the issue of which criminal organizations have been at work in the bridge states, the footprints of major Colombian and Mexican cartels have been most evident. Over varying time periods—some distinct, some overlapping—traffickers from Medellín, Cali, and the Northern Valley in Colombia have been quite active, as have their counterparts from the Sinaloa, Juárez, Gulf, and other major Mexican syndicates. However, this should not obscure the fact that scores of criminal groups have been trafficking cocaine, marijuana, and heroin in the region. Those foreign to the bridge states have been headquartered not only in Colombia and Mexico, but in an array of other countries: Russia, the United States, the Dominican Republic, and Jamaica, to list a few.

Still other vitally important drug organizations operating in Central America have been native to the bridge states. Some of these have been composed entirely of citizens of one state—a Belizean network refueling cocaine planes, for instance—while others have had members drawn from multiple bridge states, perhaps a group of Guatemalans, Hondurans, and Panamanians trucking cocaine the length of the isthmus. Some bridge-state drug rings have been cells of larger distant organizations, with foreign representatives present carrying out trafficking activities or at least supervising them. Others have been native cartelitos, offering transportation services within their home states to one or more foreign drug syndicates. Some prominent families in the region have been engaged in the trade in drugs for many years. Indeed, lesser organizations of many stripes have abounded—ad hoc and opportunistic networks, some of them entrepreneurial. A Central American trafficker might be associated with a trucking concern, a fishing fleet, a military unit, or an export-import business, among many other possibilities.

Naturally, broader trends in the illegal drug industry have been reflected in the characteristics of the organizations working in the Central American transportation phase of the business.

A transit operation today may have quite distinct characteristics from a 1980s predecessor. For instance, the shift in cocaine trafficking from somewhat more vertically integrated cartels to more numerous and autonomous networks that tend to interact horizontally, rather than control as many of the phases of the drug trade as possible, has had real repercussions for Central America. Because outsourcing transportation tasks to a cartelito is very much in sync with developments in the illicit global economy, Central American networks can expect to gain more business, not less, in the years ahead.

Relevant Characteristics of Bridge States

One important theme of our work has been to identify and analyze which characteristics of the Central American states have factored into the trade in drugs most centrally. Of course, initially at least, a Honduran cartelito, a Belizean street gang, or a Costa Rican crime family will normally look to take advantage of the opportunities to traffic drugs in their own country. But what of a major foreign drug syndicate, such as a Colombian or Mexican cartel, that has the expertise and wherewithal to opt for any of a number of routes through different bridge states? Other than stating that such traffickers like to spread their bets across the board, can we hypothesize as to what enters into their decisions to utilize this or that bridge state more or less frequently?

We would suggest that drug organizations have chosen to direct operations through one state or another based on an amalgam of variables, weighed somewhat differently by different traffickers. One has been whether a country has the geography, economy, or physical infrastructure appropriate for a particular drug-smuggling method that the drug ring views as promising at that point in time. Another has been personal risk, that is, the likelihood that foreign traffickers or local associates would be captured, arrested, prosecuted, imprisoned, or even killed in the course of a transshipment venture. While certain traffickers have thrived on danger and risk taking, and while drug rings have certainly tolerated the arrests or deaths of their operatives, personnel losses have the potential not only to weaken the organization but to bring unwanted attention to its leaders and its other operations. Hence, to maximize profits, drug syndicates have generally preferred routes that have promised less risk to their associates. Leading traffickers have been able to draw on the experiences of their own organization, and perhaps of others as well, to help estimate the risk associated with one route as compared with another.[2]

Drug organizations assessing which bridge states to utilize have had to consider costs as well. Certain outlays must be made to operate in a given country. The conspirators might need to rent an airstrip or a safe house, or pay local associates to conduct surveillance or receive a water drop. They might want to warehouse drugs temporarily. Traffickers might need to corrupt a judge or prison guard to free a member of their network or bribe police or military to gain advance warning of law-enforcement operations. The costs of these outlays vary over time and from one bridge state to another. For instance, while the Noriega regime offered Medellín traffickers secure transit via Panama, its services came at a considerable price, perhaps higher than transshipment costs via Honduras or Belize at that time.

Although the potential profits of a sizable shipment have far outstripped the costs of transporting the drugs, as in any business, minimizing the cost of getting the product to market has the effect of enhancing the ultimate return.[3] Estimates of the average costs incurred

2. Cf. Cave and Reuter, *Interdictor's Lot*, iii.

3. One might also point out that when authorities interdict a load of narcotics, the trafficking organization has to absorb not only the costs of procuring the drugs but all the transit costs tied up in the lost shipment, with no return whatsoever.

in smuggling drugs to market have ranged from a low of 15 percent to a high of 50 percent of the market price.[4] In fact, as Cali kingpin Miguel Rodríguez Orejuela told prosecutors after his arrest, the costs have varied year by year and from one bridge country to the next. By the mid-1990s the Cali cartel was figuring transportation costs at $6,000–$7,000 per kilo, with extra costs sometimes adding another $1,500 per kilo.[5] Clearly, the trafficking method selected has factored into costs, as have the number of tasks to be outsourced and the extent of the need to corrupt officials. In this regard, since considerable resources have had to be expended in changing routes and setting up new transshipment schemes, the use of reliable existing groups has been one approach aimed at minimizing transshipment costs. This, too, has benefited domestic networks within the Central American bridge states.

A singularly important variable in determining how many drugs to send through a given bridge state has been the risk to the drugs being transported as evidenced by the interception rate: that is, the percentage of drug shipments that authorities have interdicted and traffickers have lost.[6] When fewer drugs have been seized, organizations have been encouraged to send more to market along those paths. Interception rates have been a function of various changing factors, including the level of cooperation of bridge-state officials with the DEA; the degree to which a particular route has become congested with multiple trafficking ventures that might attract the attention of authorities; the motivation, efficiency, and honesty of antidrug personnel; and the type and amount of available law-enforcement resources.[7]

Interception rates have also varied among different trafficking groups, depending on how expert and creative they have been in devising and implementing transshipment strategies. Significant drug rings might opt for any of various methods or a mixture of them, and they might alter methods over time, all in an effort to minimize the chance of interdiction. Indeed, since trafficking involves continual efforts to stay ahead of authorities, organizations have sometimes estimated the likelihood of future interception, a calculation that might cause them to opt to vary transshipment patterns, even given tolerable past interception rates. They have thus opened new routes, changed the location of operations, and sometimes employed different bridge states to try to forestall seizure of large loads.

In sum, then, as traffickers from major organizations have considered the advantages and disadvantages of sending drugs through any particular state, the cost-benefit analysis has very much depended on the profiles of the bridge states under consideration. Among the key questions for traffickers have been the following: How appropriate is the fit between the trafficking plan and the characteristics of the bridge state through which it might be directed? Do geotactics suggest themselves that might make for successful drug transit? How risky to the individuals involved might the venture turn out to be, and how high are the estimated costs? Most important, what is the likely interception rate, and how might this compare to other potential routes? How traffickers have answered such questions has depended on such factors as the geographic attractiveness of the bridge state, its drug-related laws and policies, the competence of its authorities, the state of its economy, the nature and structure of its institutions, the potential for narco-corruption and its likely price, and the degree to which officials are cooperating with counterparts abroad, especially the United States and its large antidrug apparatus.

4. Thoumi, "Illegal Drug Industry," 119.

5. *Confesiones secretas*, 43.

6. Although our focus is on risk with respect to transshipment schemes in the Central American bridge states, we acknowledge that minimizing risk is an objective of customers and sellers in market countries at the distribution stage, and it factors into the street price of drugs in this and other ways as well. See Reuter, Crawford, and Cave, *Sealing the Borders*, 12–16.

7. Cave and Reuter, *Interdictor's Lot*, 5.

Drugs, Governments, and the Illicit Global Economy

What, then, might the record of bridge-state trafficking reveal about international relations, particularly about the efforts of governments to contend with the challenges posed by transnational drug organizations? Our study of the experiences of bridge countries has highlighted certain capabilities of organized crime and certain incapacities of Central American governments. What is immediately striking is how the abilities of drug-trafficking organizations are related not only to their wealth and weapons but to their agility and adaptability. Smuggling networks have learned from past experience, creating methods of moving drugs that have become more variegated and sophisticated over time.[8] Drug rings have often been able to shift operations from one place to another in a flexible, nimble manner that authorities have found difficult to counter effectively. In this game, one might say, the offense can capitalize on the element of surprise, while the defense cannot nearly cover the entire field. Equally important, drug-trafficking organizations have not been limited to carrying out transshipment ventures in any one particular type of country. Rather, they have been able to tailor their strategies to the specific possibilities that each bridge state has offered, while circumventing the potential problems it has posed. Traffickers have thus been able to choose from among many viable options regarding which routes to employ, which institutions to penetrate and exploit, and which officials to target for bribes, bullets, or intimidation.

As for the challenges faced by the bridge states, "the identification of drug trafficking as criminal activity seems to foster the simplistic notion that it can be curbed with sufficient law enforcement."[9] Although the numbers of antidrug units and personnel and the size of their budgets have certainly been relevant to the ways in which drugs and the law have contended with one another across Central America, bridge states have been buffeted by forces of supply and demand at work in the illicit global economy, as well as by the abilities of organized crime to flourish in the post–cold war world. The incapacities and deficiencies of these states have extended beyond inadequate police forces to encompass their erratic capacity to regulate their financial systems, their questionable record in creating real disincentives to narcocorruption, and their uneven abilities to prosecute, convict, and imprison wealthy and well-connected traffickers. The national security challenge has also been quite formidable. The zones through which drugs transit—land, sea, and air—have been immense and for various geographic reasons especially difficult to control.

Central American Responses to the Drug Trade

As for the issues of how the drug trade has been perceived within the bridge states and what government responses to it have been fashioned, certainly considerable time has been spent consulting and strategizing about how the Central American bridge states might best counter the drug trade. As the principal consumer state with the largest antidrug resources and programs, the United States has been deeply involved, and the governments of other market countries have occasionally participated as well. So, too, have international and regional organizations, such as the United Nations and the Organization of American States. Even nongovernmental organizations have taken part, especially those interested in health, crime, corruption, and other issues that have been related in one way or another to the drug trade.

Officials in each bridge state have been chiefly interested in the effects of the drug trade

8. See generally Kenney, *From Pablo to Osama.*

9. Center for Strategic and International Studies, *Transnational Drug Challenge*, 9.

on their own country. And, when assessed through a national lens, drug transshipment has actually delivered a number of benefits to bridge states. Drug organizations have paid top dollar to acquire goods and services. The trade has thus reduced poverty and unemployment to some degree, and it has brought influxes of hard currency into states contending with chronic balance-of-payments problems. The constant need of drug organizations to launder, repatriate, and invest immense drug profits has often advantaged particular sectors of a national economy. Extensive drug trafficking has had a multiplier effect within the economies of these transit countries, and this, in turn, has created certain supportive constituencies of elites, although these may often be invisible to the public eye.[10]

Yet cardinal disadvantages associated with trafficking in the bridge states have been very evident as well. Criminal organizations have exported to the bridge states increasing measures of the violence and intimidation first found in producer and consumer states. More widespread bribery has been employed, of both systematic and incremental varieties, and it may well have been targeted more effectively. As local markets have flourished, so too has violence related to drug dealing. Extensive narco-corruption has shaken faith in democratic governance. The patently inadequate health systems in most of these states have confronted the strain of enormous numbers of drug-abuse cases, including many related to particularly dangerous forms of consumption, such as the use of crack cocaine. Already inefficient criminal-justice systems have had to process numerous complex trafficking cases and dedicate scarce resources to prosecuting sophisticated transnational criminals. Overcrowded and atrociously underfunded prisons have had to make room for many drug offenders. They also have had to attempt to retain behind bars traffickers from dangerous criminal syndicates able to put extraordinary resources into orchestrating prison breaks or otherwise springing imprisoned associates.

When confronted with these problems, most officials in the Central American bridge states have been alarmed by trafficking in their countries and have searched for measures that might reduce it. Governments have thus negotiated scores of multilateral and bilateral treaties, and various forms of assistance have passed from the governments of market countries to those of the bridge states. A central goal has been to promote regional cooperation, to mount a campaign against drug trafficking that would bring together the region's republics to try to advance toward the common goal of curbing the drug trade across Central America. Toward this end, governments have hosted scores of conferences, to which numerous representatives have been sent, aimed largely at formulating agreements, some rhetorical, others aiming at the implementation of tangible, cooperative antidrug action.

Mounting any effective regional campaign faces the familiar generic difficulties of free-riders, differing priorities and strengths of feeling, and a tendency to adopt the least-common-denominator policies, that is, the approaches to which no one objects, rather than the most creative, innovative, or promising possible policy. Assembling an effective regional antidrug campaign in Central America has been more problematic still. Acute financial problems and long-standing nationalistic rivalries have contributed to the historical difficulties that these very different states have had in cooperating, bilaterally or multilaterally, on any of a range of matters. To ask them to overlook the potential for significant problems—including the very real possibility of corruption in a neighboring police force—and to cooperate extensively on highly sensitive issues regarding the trade in drugs, including the sharing of counternarcotics

10. This statement about the bridge states closely tracks the point made in Lee, "Colombia's Cocaine Syndicates," 14. See also Zabludoff, "Colombian Narcotics Organizations," 25

intelligence, is to expect quite a lot. Thus, while government representatives have succeeded in generating an impressive degree of rhetorical unanimity on antidrug issues, turning platitudes into effective regional practices and strategies has been far from automatic. Substituting cooperative antidrug rhetoric for real action has always been an option, although one that might not fool foreign officials for long.

Alongside regional initiatives have been national efforts to stem drug trafficking. These might be conceptualized as attempts to alter the advantages and disadvantages that criminal syndicates might perceive as they consider working within that state. National strategies to counter drug trafficking have aimed to influence drug rings to move the bulk of their transshipment ventures elsewhere. Bridge states have, to various degrees, passed new laws, reformed government institutions, and increased or differently distributed antidrug resources to discourage drug trafficking. They hope that better policing and improved criminal justice might persuade some major organizations to shift more of their operations to other states.

Although rarely discussed publicly, because it might be seen as undercutting or disrespecting international efforts, national antidrug-trafficking policies have a competitive aspect as well as a cooperative one. In a very real sense Central American governments aiming to curb the drug trade are vying with one another to discourage drug organizations from doing so much business within their borders. From time to time government policies do seem to have altered regional trafficking patterns. For instance, in 2000 U.S. counternarcotics authorities attributed a sharp decline in cocaine seizures in Costa Rica to successful interdiction in immediately preceding years that persuaded major trafficking organizations to direct a much higher percentage of shipments into Guatemala.[11] One can imagine the Costa Rican officials much more pleased with the result of that year's competition than their Guatemalan counterparts.

Conclusion

If national problems of drug trafficking are indeed like fingerprints, no two exactly alike, then national antidrug strategies ought to vary as well.[12] Officials should determine where their states are most vulnerable and adopt changes accordingly, including in how laws are written and how institutions function. They should then create approaches aimed at shoring up problematic areas, drawing not only on national resources but on foreign aid and assistance offered by foundations, other nongovernmental organizations, and regional and international organizations. Within Central America better progress might be made against the extensive trafficking now occurring if its governments ensured that the emphasis on fostering regional cooperation is coupled with a national focus on adopting those measures that may persuade drug organizations to send more of their product elsewhere.

For its part, as the largest market state, the United States is primarily interested in diminishing the flow of drugs throughout the region headed in its direction and is much less concerned with whether the narcotics crossed its borders after having passed through this bridge state or that one. The role of the United States might include not only providing assistance to help states fulfill their national strategic plans but also helping to disseminate information concerning the steps that the Central American governments are taking. Through its diplomats and its funding of grants and projects, the United States can help publicize which states are instituting what reforms to laws, policies,

11. See U.S. Department of State, *International Narcotics Control Strategy Report* (hereafter cited as *INCSR*) (2000), 44.

12. Calvani, foreword to *Island*, 1, cited in Maingot, "Decentralization Imperative," 147.

and institutions, with what results. Then, the United States might provide special assistance to the laggards in the race, helping them to strengthen areas in which they appear to be especially weak.

The most positive and hopeful aspect of the ways in which drug traffickers and the law have contended with one another in the bridge states is that the drug trade has stimulated reforms. The Central American republics have needed to institute changes in the administration of justice; in the functioning of the penal and customs institutions as well as of the police and judiciary; and in laws regarding money laundering, asset forfeiture, and official corruption—not simply to try to thwart drug traffickers but to continue their trajectories of development and modernization. It may be that future historians of Central America will view the passage to market of millions of dollars' worth of drugs as having forged new and improved, more efficient and more promising, paths to follow within these societies.

That said, it is important not to oversell the regional and national measures that have been taken or that might soon be taken, to imagine that there is a "solution" to the Central American drug trade that has eluded policy makers to date. Many of the bridge-favoring factors that we have analyzed appear to be well-nigh immoveable, certainly not conducive to change from a counternarcotics policy, no matter how enlightened. The cardinal fact remains that, although with outside assistance the Central American bridge states have been able to disrupt numerous drug transactions and arrest key members of particular drug-trafficking groups, their actions and resources have not nearly sufficed to reverse the flow of drugs through the region. These bridge states lack the capacities, their deficiencies are too many, and the scope of the problem is too vast for all the countries in the region simply to "push the traffickers out," as U.S. officials have sometimes urged.[13] There are simply too many criminal groups perceiving too many opportunities to make too much money to end the transit of drugs. That would require changes in demand in all of the market states, rather than enhanced interdiction policies or improved immobilization of drug organizations.

Foreign and domestic drug organizations have continuously tested each state, rooting out vulnerabilities and exploiting them, adapting to reforms and new tactics and strategies, and putting an array of transshipment schemes into operation. For the most part, they have also largely succeeded in evading authorities and moving enormous quantities of drugs from producers to consumers. Thus, for all of the seizures and arrests that have occurred, the overall picture of the drug trade in Central America underscores the pronounced incapacities of states in the post–cold war era. In the face of wealthy transnational criminal networks intent on maximizing profits by illicit means, these countries, thus far, have not been able to cope at all effectively with the deluge of drugs that have been crossing their borders, nor with the bribes, bullets, and intimidation wielded by the traffickers.

13. See, for instance, *INCSR* (2011), 439.

SELECTED BIBLIOGRAPHY

There follows a list of the books, journal articles, and documents from government and international organizations cited in the prior pages. The full citations for legal cases are listed in the Index of Cases. Treaties, interviews, wire-service reports, and articles from newspapers and news magazines are listed only in the chapter notes. Our work also draws on articles from the following Central American sources not listed in the bibliography: in Belize, *Amandala*, *Belize Times*, and the *Reporter*; in Costa Rica, *La Nación*, *Nica Times*, *La Prensa Libre*, *La República*, *Rumbo*, and *Tico Times*; in Guatemala, *Al Día*, *El Diario*, *El Gráfico*, *El Heraldo*, *La Hora*, *El Periódico*, *La Prensa Libre*, and *Siglo Veintiuno*; in Honduras, *El Heraldo*, *El Tiempo*, *Honduras This Week*, *La Prensa*, *Tegucigalpa This Week*, and *La Tribuna*; and in Panama, *Mediodía* and *La Prensa*.

Abrams, Elliott. "Drug Wars: The New Alliances Against Traffickers and Terrorists." Current Policy No. 792. Washington, D.C.: Bureau of Public Affairs, United States Department of State, 1986.

Aguilera Peralta, Gabriel. "Fighting the Dragon: The Anti-drug Strategy in Central America." In Griffith, *Political Economy of Drugs*, 218–29.

Allen, John L., and Elizabeth J. Leppman. *Student Atlas of World Politics*. 6th ed. New York: McGraw-Hill, 2004.

Americas Watch. *Closing the Space: Human Rights in Guatemala, May 1987–October 1988*. New York: Americas Watch, 1988.

———. *Human Rights in Honduras: Central America's "Sideshow."* New York: Americas Watch, 1987.

———. *Panama: Human Rights in Post-invasion Panama: Justice Delayed Is Justice Denied*. New York: Americas Watch, 1991.

Amnesty International. *1990 Amnesty International Report*. London: Amnesty International, 1990.

Anderson, Thomas P. "Politics and Military in Honduras." *Current History* 87 (December 1988): 425–31.

Andreas, Peter. *Border Games: Policing the U.S.-Mexico Divide*. Ithaca: Cornell University Press, 2000.

———. "Smuggling Wars: Law Enforcement and Law Evasion in a Changing World." *Transnational Organized Crime* 4 (Summer 1998): 75–90.

Andreas, Peter, and Ethan Nadelmann. *Policing the Globe: Criminalization and Crime Control in International Relations*. New York: Oxford University Press, 2006.

Arias Calderón, Ricardo. "Panama: Disaster or Democracy?" *Foreign Affairs* 66 (Winter 1987/88): 328–47.

Astorga, Luis. "Mexico: Drugs and Politics." In Vellinga, *Drug Industry*, 85–102.

Avirgnan, Tony, and Martha Honey, eds. *John Hull: El finquero de la CIA*. San José, Costa Rica: Varitec, 1989.

Bagley, Bruce M. "Colombia and the War on Drugs." *Foreign Affairs* 67 (Fall 1988): 70–92.

———. "Dateline Drug Wars: Colombia; The Wrong Strategy." *Foreign Policy* 77 (Winter 1989): 154–71.

———. "Globalisation and Latin American and Caribbean Organized Crime." *Global Crime* 6 (February 2004): 32–53.

———. "The Russian Mafia in Latin America and the Caribbean." In Vellinga, *Drug Industry*, 261–96.

———. "U.S. Foreign Policy and the War on Drugs: Analysis of a Policy Failure." *Journal of Inter-american Studies and World Affairs* 30 (Summer/Fall 1988): 189–213.

Bagley, Bruce M., and William Walker III. *Drug Trafficking in the Americas*. New Brunswick: Transaction, 1994.

Baker, James A., III. *The Politics of Diplomacy*. New York: Putnam's Sons, 1995.

Bartilow, Horace A., and Eom Kihong. "Busting Drugs While Paying with Crime: The Collateral Damage of U.S. Drug Enforcement in Foreign Countries." *Foreign Policy Analysis* 5 (2009): 93–116.

———. "Free Traders and Drug Smugglers: The Effects of Trade Openness on States' Ability to Combat Drug Trafficking." *Latin American Politics and Society* 51, no. 2 (2009): 117–45.

Belize Criminal Justice Act of 1994, no. 22. Belmopan, Belize: Government of Belize, 1994.

Bell, Griffin B. *Taking Care of the Law*. With Ronald J. Ostrow. New York: Morrow, 1982.

Bell, John Patrick. *Crisis in Costa Rica: The 1948 Revolution*. Austin: University of Texas Press, 1971.

Betts, Richard K. *Enemies of Intelligence: Knowledge and Power in American National Security*. New York: Columbia University Press, 2007.

Biesanz, Mavis Hiltanen, Richard Biesanz, and Karen Zubris Biesanz. *The Ticos: Culture and Social Change in Costa Rica*. Boulder: Lynne Rienner, 1998.

Bonner, Robert C. "The New Cocaine Cowboys: How to Defeat Mexico's Drug Cartels." *Foreign Affairs* 89 (July/August 2010): 35–47.

Bowden, Mark. *Killing Pablo*. New York: Atlantic Monthly Press, 2001.

Brana-Shute, Gary. "Narco-criminality in the Caribbean." In Griffith, *Political Economy of Drugs*, 97–112.

Buckley, Kevin. *Panama: The Whole Story*. New York: Putnam's Sons, 1990.

Bunck, Julie Marie. *Fidel Castro and the Quest for a Revolutionary Culture in Cuba*. University Park: Pennsylvania State University Press, 1994.

Bureau for Latin American and Caribbean Affairs. U.S. Agency for International Development. *Central America and Mexico Gang Assessment*. Washington, D.C.: U.S. Government Printing Office, 2006.

Calvani, Sandro. Foreword to *No One Is an Island*, edited by United Nations Drug Control Policy Office, 1–2. Bridgetown, Barbados: United Nations Drug Control Policy Office, 1997.

Castillo, Celerino, III, and Dave Harmon. *Powderburns: Cocaine, Contras, and the Drug War*. Buffalo: Sundial; Mosaic Press, 1994.

Castillo, Fabio. *Los jinetes de la cocaína*. Bogotá: Editorial Documentos Periodísticos, 1987.

Cave, Jonathan A. K., and Peter Reuter. *The Interdictor's Lot: A Dynamic Model of the Market for Drug Smuggling Services*. N-2632-USDP. Santa Monica: RAND, 1988.

Centeno, Miguel Angel, and Fernando López-Alves, eds. *The Other Mirror: Grand Theory Through the Lens of Latin America*. Princeton: Princeton University Press, 2001.

Center for Strategic and International Studies. *The Transnational Drug Challenge*. Washington, D.C.: Center for Strategic and International Studies, 1993.

Centro de Documentación de Honduras. "Cronología del narcotráfico en Honduras." *Boletín Informativo*, November 1991, 1–17.

———. "El narcotráfico en Honduras, 1982–1988." *Boletín Informativo*, August 1988, 1–16.

Chappell, James L. "The Colombian Heroin Threat: Demand and Supply." *Low Intensity Conflict and Law Enforcement* 5 (Winter 1996): 366.

Chepesiuk, Ron. *Drug Lords: The Rise and Fall of the Cali Cartel*. Preston, U.K.: Milo Books, 2005.

———. *Hard Target: The United States War Against International Drug Trafficking, 1982–1997*. Jefferson: McFarland, 1999.

Childress, Michael. *A System Description of the Heroin Trade*. Santa Monica: RAND, 1994.

———. *A System Description of the Marijuana Trade*. Santa Monica: RAND, 1994.

CIA (Central Intelligence Agency). Office of Inspector General. *Allegations of Connections Between CIA and the Contras in Cocaine Trafficking in the United States*. Document 96-0143-IG. Vol. 1, *The California Story*. Washington, D.C.: U.S. Government Printing Office, 1998.

———. *The World Factbook, 1991*. Minneapolis: Quanta Press, 1991.

CICAD (Comisión Interamericana para el Control del Abuso de Drogas). *Total de detenidos en Central América*. Washington, D.C.: Organization of American States, 1997.

Clark, Evert, and Nicholas Horrock. *Contrabandista!* New York: Praeger, 1973.

Claude, Inis L., Jr. *States and the Global System: Politics, Law, and Organization*. New York: St. Martin's Press, 1988.

———. *Swords into Plowshares: The Problems and Progress of International Organization*. 2nd ed. New York: Random House, 1961.

———. "The Tension Between Principle and Pragmatism in International Relations." *Review of International Studies* 19 (1993): 215–26.

Clawson, Patrick, and Rensselaer Lee III. *The Andean Cocaine Industry*. New York: St. Martin's Press, 1996.

Cockburn, Alexander, and Jeffrey St. Clair. *Whiteout: The CIA, Drugs, and the Press*. New York: Verso, 1998.

Cockburn, Leslie. *Out of Control: The Story of the Reagan Administration's Secret War in Nicaragua, the Illegal Arms Pipeline, and the Contra Drug Connection*. New York: Atlantic Monthly Press, 1987.

Código penal de Honduras. Tegucigalpa, Honduras: Lithopress Industrial, 1990.

Código penal de la República de Panamá. Panama City: Pérez y Pérez Gráficos, 2007.

Comisión Especial Nombrada para Investigar los Hechos Denunciados Sobre Narcotráfico. Legislativa Asamblea. Costa Rica. *Segundo Informe de la Comisión sobre el narcotráfico*. San José, Costa Rica: Editorial Universidad Estatal a Distancia, 1989.

Las confesiones secretas de Gilberto y Miguel Rodríguez Orejuela. 2nd ed. Bogotá: Quintero Editores, 2005.

Constitución de la República de Honduras. Decreto 131 del 11 de enero de 1982. Tegucigalpa, Honduras: Lithopress Industrial, 1991.

Cragin, Kim, and Bruce Hoffman. *Arms Trafficking and Colombia*. Santa Monica: RAND, 2003.

Crandall, Russell. *Driven by Drugs: U.S. Policy Toward Colombia*. 2nd ed. Boulder: Lynne Rienner, 2008.

DEA (Drug Enforcement Administration). Department of Justice. *DEA History Book, 1980–1985*. http://www.justice.gov/dea/pubs/history/1980-1985.html.

———. *DEA History Book, 1985–1990*. http://www.justice.gov/dea/pubs/history/1985-1990.html.

———. *DEA History Book, 1990–1995*. http://www.justice.gov/dea/pubs/history/1990-1995.html.

———. *DEA Resources for Law Enforcement Officers: Intelligence Reports; Belize*, March 2000, 2003; *Costa Rica*, April 2000, 2003; *Guatemala*, June 2001, 2003; *Honduras*, June 2000, 2001; *Panama*, April 2000, December 2001. Washington, D.C.: Intelligence Production Unit, Intelligence Division, DEA, 2000–2004.

———. "Evaluación de la amenaza del lavado del dinero." In *De Caro Quintero a Ricardo Alem*, by Carlos Roberto Loría Quirós, 236–41. San José, Costa Rica: Editorial Magenta, 2001.

———. *Illegal Drug Price and Purity Report*. August 31. Washington, D.C.: Intelligence Production Unit, Intelligence Division, DEA, 2003.

———. *Money Laundering in Costa Rica*. May. Washington, D.C.: Intelligence Production Unit, Intelligence Division, DEA, 2003.

———. Office of Intelligence. *Special Report: Black Tar Heroin in the United States*. March. Washington, D.C.: Intelligence Production Unit, Intelligence Division, DEA, 1986.

Decker, Scott H., and Margaret Townsend Chapman. *Drug Smugglers on Drug Smuggling*. Philadelphia: Temple University Press, 2008.

Democratic Monitoring Indicators Survey. *Latin American Public Opinion Project*. Vanderbilt University. Accessed July 11, 2011. http://www.lapopsurveys.org.

DHHS (Department of Health and Human Services). National Institute on Drug Abuse. *National Household Survey on Drug Abuse, 1979*. Computer file ICPSR06843-v3. 18 June 2008. Ann Arbor: Inter-university Consortium for Political and Social Research, 2008. doi:10.3886/ICPSR06843.

———. National Institute on Drug Abuse. *National Household Survey on Drug Abuse, 1985*. Computer file ICPSR06844-v2. 25 July 2008. Ann Arbor: Inter-university Consortium for Political and Social Research, 2008. doi:10.3886/ICPSR06844.

———. National Institute on Drug Abuse. *National Household Survey on Drug Abuse, 1990*. Computer file ICPSR09833-v4. 25 July 2008. Ann Arbor: Inter-university Consortium for Political and Social Research, 2008. doi:10.3886/ICPSR09833.

———. Office of Applied Statistics. Substance Abuse and Mental Health Services Administration Office. *National Household Survey on Drug Abuse, 1995*. Computer file ICPSR06950-v2. 23 October 2008. Ann Arbor: Inter-university Consortium for Political and Social Research, 2008. doi:10.3886/ICPSR06950.

———. Office of Applied Statistics. Substance Abuse and Mental Health Services Administration Office. *National Household Survey on Drug Abuse, 2000*. Computer file ICPSR03262-v4. 7 December 2006. Ann Arbor: Inter-university Consortium for Political and Social Research, 2007. doi:10.3886/ICPSR03262.

———. Office of Applied Statistics. Substance Abuse and Mental Health Services Administration Office. *National Household Survey on Drug Abuse, 2005*. Computer file ICPSR04596-v2.

12 August 2009. Ann Arbor: Inter-university Consortium for Political and Social Research, 2009. doi:10.3886/ICPSR04596.

Dinges, John. *Our Man in Panama: How General Noriega Used the United States—and Made Millions in Drugs and Arms*. New York: Random House, 1990.

Dirección Antinarcóticos. Policía Nacional de Colombia. *Amapola: Producción, procesamiento, y canales de distribución*. Presented at the International Technical Seminar on Illicit Poppy Cultivation in Latin America. Bogotá: Programa de las Naciones Unidas para el Desarrollo, 1993.

Dolan, Edward F. *International Drug Traffic*. New York: Watts, 1985.

Domínguez, Jorge I. "Smuggling." *Foreign Policy* 20 (Autumn 1975): 87–96, 161–64.

DOS (Department of State). Bureau of Democracy, Human Rights, and Labor. *2009 Human Rights Report: Costa Rica*. http://www.state.gov/g/drl/rls/hrrpt/2009/wha/136107.htm.

———. Bureau of International Narcotics Matters. *International Narcotics Control Strategy Report*. Washington, D.C.: U.S. Government Printing Office, 1985–2002.

———. Bureau of International Narcotics Matters and Law Enforcement Affairs. *International Narcotics Control Strategy Report*. Washington, D.C.: U.S. Government Printing Office, 2003–2010.

———. *Country Reports on Human Rights Practices*. February 23, 2001. http://www.state.gov/g/drl/rls/hrrpt/2000/wha/775.htm.

———. "Data on U.S. Maritime Drug Interdiction Agreements with Western Hemisphere Countries." Accessed December 2010. www.usdoj./gov/dea/pubs/intel/01019/usvi#usvi (site discontinued).

Duartes Delgado, Edwin, ed. *Jurisprudencia sobre narcotráfico*. San José, Costa Rica: Editec Editores, 1997.

Duartes Delgado, Edwin, Geraldo Campos Valverde, Johnny Rodríguez Vega, and Juan Carlos Arce Chavarría. *El tráfico de drogas en la jurisprudencia*. San José, Costa Rica: Editorial Investigaciones Jurídicas, 2002.

Duzán, María Jimena. *Death Beat: A Colombian Journalist's Life Inside the Cocaine Wars*. Translated and edited by Peter Eisner. New York: HarperCollins, 1994.

Ebel, Roland. "Guatemala: Politics in a Central American City-State." In *Latin American Politics and Development*, edited by Howard J. Wiarda and Harvey F. Kline, 453–74. 4th ed. Boulder: Westview Press, 1996.

Eddy, Paul, Hugo Sabogal, and Sara Walden. *The Cocaine Wars*. New York: Norton, 1988.

Edwards, George C., and William J. Butler. *Guatemala: A New Beginning*. New York: American Association for the International Commission of Jurists, 1987.

Ehrenfeld, Rachel. "Narcoterrorism and the Cuban Connection." *Strategic Review* 16 (Summer 1988): 55–63.

———. *Narcoterrorism: How Governments Around the World Used the Drug Trade to Finance and Further Terrorist Activities*. New York: Basic Books, 1992.

England, Sarah. *Afro Central Americans in New York City: Garifuna Tales of Transnational Movements in Racialized Space*. Gainesville: University Press of Florida, 2006.

Epstein, Edward J. *Agency of Fear: Opiates and Political Power in America*. Rev. ed. New York: Verso, 1990.

Escobar, Roberto. *The Accountant's Story: Inside the Violent World of the Medellín Cartel*. With David Fisher. New York: Grand Central, 2009.

Estievenart, Georges. "The European Community and the Global Drug Phenomenon: Current Situation and Outlook." In *Policies and Strategies to Combat Drugs in Europe*, edited by Georges Estievenart, 50–97. Norwell: Kluwer Academic, 1995.

———, ed. *Policies and Strategies to Combat Drugs in Europe*. Norwell: Kluwer Academic, 1995.

Everitt, John C. "The Growth and Development of Belize City." *Journal of Latin American Studies* 18 (May 1986): 75–111.

Farer, Tom, ed. *Transnational Crime in the Americas*. New York: Routledge, 1999.

Farrell, Graham. "The Global Rate of Interception of Illicit Opiates and Cocaine 1980–1994." *Transnational Organized Crime* 1 (Winter 1995): 134–49.

Federal Research Division. U.S. Library of Congress. *The Nexus Among Terrorists, Narcotics Traffickers, Weapons Proliferators, and Organized Crime Networks in Western Europe*. Washington, D.C.: Library of Congress, 2002.

Fowler, Michael Ross. "Bringing the Different United Nations to Account." In *Envisioning Reform: Enhancing UN Accountability in the Twenty-First Century*, edited by Sumihiro Kuyama and Michael Ross Fowler, 37–72. New York: United Nations University Press, 2009.

———. *Thinking About Human Rights: Contending Approaches to Human Rights in U.S. Foreign Policy*. Lanham: University Press of America, 1987.

———. *With Justice for All? The Nature of the American Legal System*. Upper Saddle River: Prentice Hall, 1998.

Fowler, Michael Ross, and Julie Marie Bunck. *Law, Power, and the Sovereign State: The Evolution and Application of the Concept of Sovereignty*. With a foreword by Inis L. Claude Jr. University Park: Pennsylvania State University Press, 1995.

———. "Legal Imperialism or Disinterested Assistance? American Legal Aid in the Caribbean Basin." *Albany Law Review* 55, no. 2 (1992): 815–47.

———. "Narcotics Trafficking, Central American Prisons, and the Law." *Suffolk Transnational Law Review* 25, no. 3 (2002): 433–90.

Friman, H. Richard. *Narcodiplomacy: Exporting the U.S. War on Drugs*. Ithaca: Cornell University Press, 1996.

Friman, H. Richard, and Peter Andreas, eds. *The Illicit Global Economy and State Power*. Lanham: Rowman and Littlefield, 1999.

Gamarra, Eduardo A. "Transnational Criminal Organizations in Bolivia." In Farer, *Transnational Crime*, 171–91.

Garzón, Juan Carlos. *Mafia and Co.: The Criminal Networks in Mexico, Brazil, and Colombia*. Translated by Kathy Ogle. Washington, D.C.: Woodrow Wilson International Center for Scholars, 2008.

Glassman, Paul. *Costa Rica*. Champlain: Passport Press, 1989.

Goodwin, Paul B., Jr. *Global Studies: Latin America*. 8th ed. Guilford: Dushkin; New York: McGraw-Hill, 1998.

Gootenberg, Paul. *Andean Cocaine: The Making of a Global Drug*. Chapel Hill: University of North Carolina Press, 2008.

———. "Talking Like a State: Drugs, Borders, and the Language of Control." In *Illicit Flows and Criminal Things: States, Borders, and the Other Side of Globalization*, edited by Willem van Schendel and Itty Abram, 101–27. Bloomington: Indiana University Press, 2005.

Grant, Cedric H. *The Making of Modern Belize: Politics, Society, and British Colonialism in Central America*. Cambridge: Cambridge University Press, 1976.

Grayson, George W. *La Familia Drug Cartel: Implications for U.S.-Mexican Security*. Carlisle, Pa.: U.S. Army War College, Strategic Studies Institute, 2010.

———. *Mexico: Narco-Violence and a Failed State?* New Brunswick: Transaction, 2010.

———. *Mexico's Struggle with Drugs and Thugs*. New York: Foreign Policy Association, 2009.

Griffin, Clifford E. "Democracy and Political Economy in the Caribbean." In Griffith, *Political Economy of Drugs*, 113–37.

Griffith, Ivelaw Lloyd. "Drugs and Political Economy in a Global Village." In Griffith, *Political Economy of Drugs*, 11–28.

———. *Drugs and Security in the Caribbean: Sovereignty Under Siege*. University Park: Pennsylvania State University Press, 1997.

———, ed. *The Political Economy of Drugs in the Caribbean*. New York: St. Martin's Press, 2000.

———. "The Political Economy of Drugs in the Caribbean: Problems Without Passports." In Vellinga, *Drug Industry*, 103–23.

Gross, K. Hawkeye. *Drug Smuggling: The Forbidden Book*. Boulder: Paladin Press, 1992.

"Guatemalan Army Lt. Colonel Carlos René (Ochoa) Ruiz." Files of the United States Government. MOR 1 DOCID 55819. National Security Archive.

Gugliotta, Guy, and Jeff Leen. *Kings of Cocaine*. New York: Simon and Schuster, 1989.

Gutiérrez Gutiérrez, Carlos José. *El funcionamiento del sistema jurídico*. San José, Costa Rica: Editorial Juricentro, 1979.

Hall, Kevin. "Drug-Busting X-ray Units Land at Port of Miami." *Journal of Commerce*, August 21, 1998, 1A.

Handelman, Stephen. *Comrade Criminal: Russia's New Mafiya*. New Haven: Yale University Press, 1995.

Henkel, Ray. "The Bolivian Cocaine Industry." *Drugs in Latin America* 37 (1986): 58.

Heymann, Philip B., Daniel McGillis, Carmen Ortiz, and Ana Maria Salazar. *Guatemala/Harvard Criminal Justice Project/Final Report*. Washington, D.C.: United States Agency for International Development, 1991.

Honey, Martha. *Hostile Acts: U.S. Policy in Costa Rica in the 1980s*. Gainesville: University Press of Florida, 1994.

Huxley, Aldous. *Beyond the Mexique Bay*. London: Chatto and Windus, 1950.

International Institute for Strategic Studies. *The Military Balance, 1985–1986*. London: Garden City Press, 1985.

———. *The Military Balance, 1989–1990*. London: Brassey's Defence, 1989.

———. *The Military Balance, 1994–1995*. London: Brassey's Defence, 1994.

———. *The Military Balance, 1999–2000*. Oxford: Oxford University Press, 1999.
———. *The Military Balance, 2004–2005*. Oxford: Oxford University Press, 2004.
———. *The Military Balance, 2009*. London: Routledge, 2009.
Johns, Christina Jacqueline. *Power, Ideology, and the War on Drugs: Nothing Succeeds Like Failure*. New York: Praeger, 1992.
Johns, Christina Jacqueline, and P. Johnson Ward. *State Crime, the Media, and the Invasion of Panama*. Westport: Praeger, 1994.
Johnston, Michael. *Syndromes of Corruption: Wealth, Power, and Democracy*. New York: Cambridge University Press, 2005.
Jones, Jill. *Hep Cats, Narcs, and Pipe Dreams: A History of America's Romance with Illegal Drugs*. New York: Scribner, 1996.
Jordan, David C. *Drug Politics: Dirty Money and Democracies*. Norman: University of Oklahoma Press, 1999.
Joyce, Elizabeth. "Transnational Criminal Enterprise: The European Perspective." In Farer, *Transnational Crime*, 99–115.
Juhn, Tricia. "Central America and Drug Trafficking." In *Drug Trafficking Research in the Americas: An Annotated Bibliography*, edited by Bruce M. Bagley, 385–405. Boulder: Lynne Rienner, 1997.
Kamstra, Jerry. *Weed: Adventures of a Dope Smuggler*. New York: Harper and Row, 1974.
Kempe, Frederick. *Divorcing the Dictator: America's Bungled Affairs with Noriega*. New York: Putnam's Sons, 1990.
Kenney, Michael. *From Pablo to Osama: Trafficking and Terrorist Networks, Government Bureaucracies, and Competitive Adaptation*. University Park: Pennsylvania State University Press, 2007.
Kirkpatrick, Sidney D. *Turning the Tide: One Man Against the Medellín Cartel*. With Peter Abrahams. New York: Dutton, 1991.
Knight, Alan. "The Modern Mexican State." In *The Other Mirror: Grand Theory Through the Lens of Latin America*, edited by Miguel Angel Centeno and Fernando López-Alves, 177–218. Princeton: Princeton University Press, 2001.
Kondracke, Morton. "Double Dealing: Drugs and Diplomacy." *The New Republic*, April 11, 1988, 17.
Koster, Richard M., and Guillermo Sánchez. *In the Time of the Tyrants*. New York: Norton, 1990.
Krasner, Stephen D. *Sovereignty: Organized Hypocrisy*. Princeton: Princeton University Press, 1999.
Krauthausen, Ciro, and Luis F. Sarmiento. *Cocaína y Co.: Un mercado ilegal por dentro*. Bogotá: Tercer Mundo Editores, 1991.
Law Concerning the Protection of Victims. Panama City: Pérez y Pérez Gráficos, 1998.
The Laws of Belize. Belmopan, Belize: Government of Belize, 1992.
Lawson, Chappell. *Losing the War on Drugs: The Political, Social, and Economic Impact of the Drug Trade in Latin America*. Princeton: Woodrow Wilson School of Public and International Affairs, Princeton University, 1988.
Layne, Mary, Scott Decker, Meg Townsend, and Caben Chester. "Measuring the Deterrent Effect of Enforcement Operations on Drug Smuggling, 1991–1999." *Trends in Organized Crime* 7 (Spring 2002): 66–87.
Lee, Rensselaer W., III. "Colombia's Cocaine Syndicates." *Crime, Law, and Social Change* 16, no. 1 (1991): 3–39.
———. "Perversely Harmful Effects of Counter-Narcotics Policy in the Andes." In Vellinga, *Drug Industry*, 187–210.
———. "Transnational Organized Crime: An Overview." In Farer, *Transnational Crime*, 1–38.
———. *The White Labyrinth*. New Brunswick: Transaction, 1989.
Leffert, Mike. "El narcotráfico y el ejército de posguerra." TNI Publications. Heinrich Böll Foundation. November 1997. http://www.tni.org/reports/drugs/folder4/guate.htm (site discontinued).
Levine, Michael. *The Big White Lie: The CIA and the Cocaine/Crack Epidemic*. With Laura Kavanau-Levine. New York: Thunder's Mouth Press, 1993.
———. *Deep Cover: The Inside Story of How DEA Infighting, Incompetence, and Subterfuge Lost Us the Biggest Battle of the Drug War*. New York: Delacorte, 1990.
Levitsky, Steven, and María Victoria Murillo, eds. *Argentine Democracy: The Politics of Institutional Weakness*. University Park: Pennsylvania State University Press, 2005.
Ley contra el lavado de dinero u otros activos y su reglamento. Guatelmala City: Librería Jurídica, 2005.
Ley contra la narcoactividad y sus reformas. Guatemala City: Librería Jurídica, 2007.
Ley sobre estupefacientes, sustancias psicotrópicas, drogas de uso no autorizado y actividades conexas. San José, Costa Rica: Editec Editores, 1991.

López López, Andrés. *El cartel de los sapos*. Bogotá: Editorial Planeta Colombiana, 2008.

Loría Quirós, Carlos Roberto. *De Caro Quintero a Ricardo Alem*. San José, Costa Rica: Editorial Magenta, 2001.

Lupsha, Peter A. "Drug Lords and Narco-Corruption: The Players Change but the Game Continues." In McCoy and Block, *War on Drugs*, 177–95.

MacCoun, Robert J., and Peter Reuter. *Drug War Heresies: Learning from Other Vices, Times, and Places*. New York: Cambridge University Press, 2001.

MacDonald, Scott B. *Dancing on a Volcano: The Latin American Drug Trade*. New York: Praeger, 1988.

———. *Mountain High, White Avalanche: Cocaine and Power in the Andean States and Panama*. New York: Praeger, 1989.

Maingot, Anthony P. "The Decentralization Imperative and Caribbean Criminal Enterprises." In Farer, *Transnational Crime*, 144–70.

Malamud-Goti, Jaime. "Reinforcing Poverty: The Bolivian War on Cocaine." In McCoy and Block, *War on Drugs*, 67–92.

Marshall, Jonathan. *Drug Wars: Corruption, Counterinsurgency, and Covert Operations in the Third World*. Forestville: Cohan and Cohen, 1991.

"Mayor of Zacapa Arrested for Drug Trafficking on U.S. Request for Arrest Pending Extradition." Files of the United States Department of State. 90 GUATEM 15523. National Security Archive.

Mazur, Robert. *The Infiltrator: My Secret Life Inside the Dirty Banks Behind Pablo Escobar's Medellín Cartel*. New York: Little, Brown, 2009.

McCoy, Alfred W., and Alan A. Block, eds. *War on Drugs: Studies in the Failure of U.S. Narcotics Policy*. Boulder: Westview Press, 1992.

Menzel, Sewall. *Cocaine Quagmire*. Lanham, Md.: University Press of America, 1997.

———. *Fire in the Andes*. Lanham, Md.: University Press of America, 1997.

Mermelstein, Max. *The Man Who Made It Snow: By the American Mastermind Inside the Colombian Cartel*. New York: Simon and Schuster, 1990.

"Mexico Arrests Alleged Cocaine Smuggling Kingpins as U.S. Unseals Indictment." *International Law Enforcement Reporter* 17, no. 8 (2001): 1.

Meyer, Kathryn. "Fast Crabs and Cigarette Boats: A Speculative Essay." In *Drug Control Policy: Essays in Historical and Comparative Perspective*, 64–88. University Park: Pennsylvania State University Press, 1992.

Meyer, Kathryn, and Terry Parssinen. *Webs of Smoke: Smugglers, Warlords, Spies, and the History of the International Drug Trade*. Lanham, Md.: Rowman and Littlefield, 1998.

Migdal, Joel S. *Strong Societies and Weak States: State-Society Relations and State Capabilities in the Third World*. Princeton: Princeton University Press, 1988.

Mills, James. *The Underground Empire: Where Crime and Governments Embrace*. Garden City: Doubleday, 1986.

Mollison, James. *The Memory of Pablo Escobar*. With Rainbow Nelson. London: Boot, 2007.

Morris, James A. "Honduras: Civil-Military Politics and Democracy." In *Latin American Politics and Development*, edited by Howard J. Wiarda and Harvey F. Kline, 562–80. 2nd ed. Boulder: Westview Press, 1985.

Muñoz-Guillén, Mercedes. "The Narcotizing of Costa Rican Politics." In *The Costa Rica Reader*, edited by Steven Palmer and Iván Molina, 342–43. Durham: Duke University Press, 2004.

Murillo, Luis E. *The Noriega Mess: The Drugs, the Canal, and Why America Invaded*. Berkeley: Video Books, 1995.

Nadelmann, Ethan. "The Case for Legalization." *Public Interest* 92 (Summer 1988): 3–31.

———. *Cops Across Borders: The Internationalization of Criminal Law Enforcement*. University Park: Pennsylvania State University Press, 1993.

———. "U.S. Drug Policy: A Bad Export." *Foreign Policy* 70 (Spring 1988): 83–108.

Natarajan, Mangai. "Understanding the Structure of a Drug Trafficking Organization: A Conversational Analysis." In *Illegal Drug Markets: From Research to Prevention Policy*, edited by Mangai Natarajan and Mike Hough, 273–98. Monsey: Criminal Justice Press, 2000.

Nicholl, Charles. *The Fruit Palace*. New York: St. Martin's Press, 1985.

Nordstrom, Carolyn. *Global Outlaws: Crime, Money, and Power in the Contemporary World*. Berkeley: University of California Press, 2007.

Odaffer, Douglas. "The Three Capitals of British Honduras." Master's thesis, San Francisco State University, 1970.

Office of National Drug Control Policy. *National Drug Control Strategy*. Washington, D.C.: U.S. Government Printing Office, 1999.

Osterling, Jorge P. *Democracy in Colombia: Clientelist Politics and Guerrilla Warfare*. Boulder: Lynne Rienner, 1989.

Paige, Jeffrey M. *Coffee and Power: Revolution and the Rise of Democracy in Central America*. Cambridge: Harvard University Press, 1997.

Palacios Moya, José Humberto. *Reseña histórica del narcotráfico en Honduras y su relación con el poder judicial*. Photocopy. Tegucigalpa: School of Law, National Autonomous University of Honduras, 1991.

Palmer, Steven, and Iván Molina. *The Costa Rica Reader: History, Culture, Politics*. Durham: Duke University Press, 2004.

Pérez, Orlando J. "Drugs and Post-intervention Political Economy in Haiti and Panama." In Griffith, *Political Economy of Drugs*, 138–61.

Perl, Raphael, ed. *Drugs and Foreign Policy: A Critical Review*. Boulder: Westview Press, 1994.

Philpott, Daniel. *Revolutions in Sovereignty: How Ideas Shaped Modern International Relations*. Princeton: Princeton University Press, 2001.

Pine, Adrienne. *Working Hard, Drinking Hard: On Violence and Survival in Honduras*. Berkeley: University of California Press, 2008.

PNUD (Programa de las Naciones Unidas para el Desarrollo). *Informe sobre desarrollo humano, Honduras 2006: Hacia la expansión de la ciudadanía*. Tegucigalpa: PNUD, 2006.

———. *Informe sobre desarrollo humano para América Central, 2009–2010*. Bogotá: PNUD, 2010.

Poppa, Terence E. *Drug Lord: The Life and Death of a Mexican Kingpin*. New York: Pharos Books, 1990.

Porter, Bruce. *Blow: How a Small-Town Boy Made $100 Million with the Medellín Cocaine Cartel and Lost It All*. New York: HarperCollins, 1993.

Reddy, Marlita, ed. *Statistical Abstract of the World*. New York: Gale Research, 1994.

Reuter, Peter. "The (Continued) Vitality of Mythical Numbers." *The Public Interest* 75 (1984): 135–47.

———. "The Political Economy of Drug Smuggling." In Vellinga, *Drug Industry*, 127–47.

Rempel, WIlliam C. *At the Devil's Table: The Untold Story of the Insider Who Brought Down the Cali Cartel*. New York: Random House, 2011.

Reuter, Peter, Gordon Crawford, and Jonathan Cave. *Sealing the Borders: The Effects of Increased Military Participation in Drug Interdiction*. Santa Monica: RAND, 1988.

Reuter, Peter, and John Haaga. *The Organization of High-Level Drug Markets: An Exploratory Study*. Santa Monica: RAND, 1989.

Reyes, Gerardo. *Nuestro hombre en la DEA: La historia de un fotógrafo que negoció la libertad de más de un centenar de narcos en Estados Unidos*. Bogotá: Editorial Planeta Colombiana, 2007.

Rice, Berkeley. *Trafficking: The Boom and Bust of the Air America Cocaine Ring*. New York: Scribner's Sons, 1989.

Rico, José Ma., Luis Salas, Enrique Gutiérrez, and Carlos Cruz. *La justicia penal en Costa Rica*. San José, Costa Rica: Editorial Universitaria Centroamericana, 1988.

Riley, Kevin Jack. *Snow Job? The War Against International Cocaine Trafficking*. New Brunswick: Transaction, 1996.

Robinson, Linda. "Central American and Drug Trafficking." In Bagley and Walker, *Drug Trafficking*, 445–54.

Robinson, Matthew B., and Renee G. Scherlen. *Lies, Damned Lies, and Drug War Statistics: A Critical Analysis of Claims Made by the Office of National Drug Control Policy*. Albany: State University of New York Press, 2007.

Ropp, Steve C. *Panamanian Politics: From Guarded Nation to National Guard*. Stanford: Praeger, 1982.

Rose-Ackerman, Susan. *Corruption and Government: Causes, Consequences, and Reform*. New York: Cambridge University Press, 1999.

Rosenberg, Mark B. "Honduras." In *Latin American Politics and Development*, edited by Howard J. Wiarda and Harvey F. Kline, 475–89. 4th ed. Boulder: Westview Press, 1996.

———. "Narcos and Politicos: The Politics of Drug Trafficking in Honduras." *Journal of Interamerican Studies and World Affairs* 30 (Summer/Autumn 1988): 143–65.

Rotella, Sebastian. *Twilight on the Line: Underworlds and Politics at the U.S.-Mexico Border*. New York: Norton, 1998.

Ruhl, J. Mark. "Honduras: Problems of Democratic Consolidation." In Wiarda and Kline, *Politics and Development*, 519–33.

Salas, Luis, and José Ma. Rico. *La justicia penal en Honduras*. San José, Costa Rica: Universidad Internacional de la Florida/Editorial Universitaria Centroamericana, 1989.

Salazar, Alonso J. *No nacimos pa' semilla: La cultura de las bandas juveniles de Medellín*. Bogotá: Centro de Investigación y Educación Popular, 1990.

Sarmiento, Luis Fernando, and Ciro Krauthausen. *Cocaína and Co.: Un mercado ilegal por dentro*. Bogotá: Tercer Mundo Editores, 1991.

Schirmer, Jennifer. *The Guatemalan Military Project: A Violence Called Democracy*.

Philadelphia: University of Pennsylvania Press, 1998.

Schreider, Helen, and Frank Schreider. *Exploring the Amazon*. Washington, D.C.: National Geographic Society, 1970.

Scott, James C. *Domination and the Arts of Resistance: Hidden Transcripts*. New Haven: Yale University Press, 1990.

Scott, Peter Dale. "Honduras, the Contra Support Networks, and Cocaine: How the U.S. Government Has Augmented America's Drug Crisis." In McCoy and Block, *War on Drugs*, 125–75.

Scott, Peter Dale, and Jonathan Marshall. *Cocaine Politics: Drugs, Armies, and the CIA in Central America*. Berkeley: University of California Press, 1991.

Scranton, Margaret E. *The Noriega Years: U.S.-Panamanian Relations, 1981–1990*. Boulder: Lynne Rienner, 1991.

Seligson, Mitchell. "Costa Rica." In Wiarda and Kline, *Politics and Development*, 450–63.

Shannon, Elaine. *Desperados*. New York: Viking, 1988.

Sherman, Mark Andrew. "An Inquiry Regarding the International and Domestic Legal Problems Presented in *United States v. Noriega*." *University of Miami Inter-American Law Review* 20 (1989): 393–428.

Shoman, Assad. *Party Politics in Belize*. Benque Viejo del Carmen, Belize: Cubola Productions, 1987.

———. *Thirteen Chapters of a History of Belize*. Belize City: Angelus Press, 1994.

Shultz, George P. *Turmoil and Triumph: My Years as Secretary of State*. New York: Scribner's Sons, 1993.

Skocpol, Theda. "Bringing the State Back In: Strategies of Analysis in Current Research." In *Bringing the State Back In*, edited by Peter B. Evans, Dietrich Rueschemeyer, and Theda Skocpol, 3–43. Cambridge: Cambridge University Press, 1985.

Slaughter, Anne-Marie. *A New World Order*. Princeton: Princeton University Press, 2004.

Smith, Peter H. "Semiorganized International Crime: Drug Trafficking in Mexico." In Farer, *Transnational Crime*, 193–216.

Smythe, Frank. "Guatemala, Home of Powerful Drug Runners." *Nieman Watchdog*. Nieman Foundation for Journalism at Harvard University. Last modified November 20, 2005. http://www.niemanwatchdog.org/index.cfm?fuseaction=Ask_this.view&askthisid=152.

———. "My Enemy's Friends." *The New Republic*, June 5, 1995, 18.

Solomon, Leticia. *Política y militares en Honduras*. Tegucigalpa: Centro de Documentación de Honduras, 1992.

Spector, Bertram I., ed. *Fighting Corruption in Developing Countries: Strategies and Analysis*. Bloomfield: Kumarian Press, 2005.

Stares, Paul. *Global Habit: The Drug Problem in a Borderless World*. Washington, D.C.: Brookings Institution Press, 1996.

Strange, Susan. *The Retreat of the State: The Diffusion of Power in the World Economy*. New York: Cambridge University Press, 1996.

Strong, Simon. *Whitewash: Pablo Escobar and the Cocaine Wars*. London: Macmillan, 1995.

Stutman, Robert, and Richard Esposito. *Dead on Delivery: Inside the Drug Wars, Straight from the Street*. New York: Warner Books, 1992.

Téllez, Édgar, and Jorge Lesmes. *Pacto en la sombra: Los tratos secretos de Estados Unidos en el narcotráfico*. Bogotá: Editorial Planeta Colombiana, 2006.

Thomas, Jon R. "International Campaign Against Drug Trafficking." *Department of State Bulletin* 85 (January 1985): 50–53.

Thomson, P. A. B. *Belize: A Concise History*. London: Macmillan Caribbean, 2005.

Thoumi, Francisco E. "Illegal Drugs in Colombia." In Vellinga, *Drug Industry*, 70–84.

———. "The Impact of the Illegal Drug Industry on Colombia." In Farer, *Transnational Crime*, 118–42.

———. *Political Economy and Illegal Drugs in Colombia*. Boulder: Lynne Rienner, 1995.

Todorovic, Alex. "Of Drugs and Thugs." *Mesoamérica* 9, no. 8 (1990): 1.

Toro, María Celia. *Mexico's "War" on Drugs: Causes and Consequences*. Boulder: Lynne Rienner, 1995.

Tully, Andrew. *The Secret War Against Dope*. New York: Coward, McCann, and Geoghegan, 1973.

United Nations Development Programme. *Democracy in Latin America: Toward a Citizens' Democracy*. New York: United Nations Development Programme, 2004.

United Nations Drug Control Policy Office. *No One Is an Island*. Bridgetown, Barbados: United Nations Drug Control Policy Office, 1997.

United Nations Office on Drugs and Crime. *World Drug Report 2007*. Vol. 2. Accessed July 11, 2011. http://www.unodc.org/pdf/WDR_2007/wdr2007_chap4_cocaine.pdf.

United States. Honduras–United States Extradition Treaty of 1909. January 15, 1909. *U.S. Statutes at Large* 37:1616.

———. Inter-American Extradition Treaty of 1933. December 26, 1933. *U.S. Statutes at Large* 49:3111.

———. Supplementary Extradition Convention between the United States of America and the Republic of Honduras. February 21, 1927. *U.S. Statutes at Large* 45:2489.

U.S. Department of Health and Human Services. National Institute on Drug Abuse. *National Household Survey on Drug Abuse, 1979*. Computer file. ICPSR06843-v3. June 18. Ann Arbor: Inter-university Consortium for Political and Social Research, 2008. doi:10.3886/ICPSR06843.

———. *National Household Survey on Drug Abuse, 1985*. Computer file. ICPSR06844-v2. July 25. Ann Arbor: Inter-university Consortium for Political and Social Research, 2008. doi:10.3886/ICPSR06844.

———. *National Household Survey on Drug Abuse, 1990*. Computer file. ICPSR09833-v4. July 25. Ann Arbor: Inter-university Consortium for Political and Social Research, 2008. doi:10.3886/ICPSR09833.

———. *National Household Survey on Drug Abuse, 1995*. Computer file. ICPSR06950-v2. October 23. Ann Arbor: Inter-university Consortium for Political and Social Research, 2008. doi:10.3886/ICPSR6950.

———. *National Household Survey on Drug Abuse, 2000*. Computer file. ICPSR03262-v4. December 7. Ann Arbor: Inter-university Consortium for Political and Social Research, 2008. doi:10.3886/ICPSR03262.

U.S. Department of Health and Human Services. Substance Abuse and Mental Health Services. Administration Office. *National Household Survey on Drug Abuse, 2005*. Computer file. ICPSR04596-v2. August 12. Ann Arbor: Inter-university Consortium for Political and Social Research, 2009. doi:10.3886/ICPSR04596.

———. *National Survey on Drug Use and Health, 2009*. Computer file. ICPSR29621-v1. November 16. Ann Arbor: Inter-university Consortium for Political and Social Research, 2010. doi:10.3886/ICPSR29621.

U.S. House. Committee on Foreign Affairs. *Nicaraguan Government Involvement in Narcotics Trafficking*. 99th Cong., 2d sess., 1990.

———. Committee on Foreign Affairs. *Options for United States Policy Toward Guatemala: Hearing Before the Subcommittee on Western Hemisphere Affairs of the House Committee on Foreign Affairs*. 101st Cong., 2d sess., 1990.

———. Committee on Foreign Affairs. *Situation in Panama*. 99th Cong., 2d sess., March 10 and April 21, 1986.

———. Committee on Foreign Affairs. *Testimony, June 22, 1994: Thomas Constantine, Administrator Drug Enforcement Agency*. Federal Document Clearinghouse Congressional Testimony. Washington, D.C.: FDCHE Media, 1994.

———. Committee on Government Reform and Oversight. *Access to Government Information and H.R. 2635: The "Human Rights Information Act." Congressional Record* 143. October 9, 1997, E1983–E1985.

———. Committee on the Judiciary. *Border Security and Deterring Illegal Entry into the United States*. 105th Cong., 1st sess., April 23, 1997.

———. Committee on the Judiciary. *Posse Comitatus Act: Hearing*. 97th Cong., 1st sess., 1981.

U.S. Senate. *Combating International Drug Cartels: Issues for U.S. Policy*. 100th Cong., 1st sess., 1987. Report prepared by Raphael F. Perl, Congressional Research Service, for a seminar held May 18, 1987, for the U.S. Senate Caucus on International Narcotics Control. Washington, D.C.: U.S. Government Printing Office, 1987.

———. "Drug Trafficking in Panama: An Appraisal of the Proposed Partner of the United States." *Implementation of the President's 1984 National Drug Control Strategy*. 101st Cong., 1st sess. *Congressional Record* 135 (October 5, 1989): S 12657–750.

———. Committee on Foreign Relations. *Corruption and Drugs*. Staff report, February 1996.

———. Committee on Foreign Relations. *The Drug Cartels*. 105th Cong., 1st sess., July 16, 1997.

———. Committee on Foreign Relations. *Drugs, Law Enforcement, and Foreign Policy: A Report*. 100th Cong., 2d sess., 1989.

———. Committee on Foreign Relations. *Drugs, Law Enforcement, and Foreign Policy: Hearings*. 100th Cong., 1st sess., 1987.

———. Committee on Governmental Affairs. Permanent Subcommittee on Investigations. *Structure of International Drug Trafficking Organizations*. 101st Cong., 1st sess., 1989.

———. Committee on Governmental Affairs. Subcommittee on Investigations. *Drugs and Money Laundering in Panama*. Washington, D.C.: U.S. Government Printing Office, 1989.

———. Committee on the Judiciary. *Narco-terrorism: International Drug Trafficking and Terrorism: A Dangerous Mix*. 108th Cong., 1st sess., 1989.

Vellinga, Menno, ed. *The Political Economy of the Drug Industry*. Gainesville: University Press of Florida, 2004.

———. "The Political Economy of the Drug Industry: Its Structure and Functioning." In Vellinga, *Drug Industry*, 3–22.

Waddell, David A. G. *British Honduras: A Historical and Contemporary Survey*. London: Oxford University Press, 1961.

Waldorf, Don, Craig Reinarman, and Sheigla Murphy. *Cocaine Changes: The Experience of Using and Quitting*. Philadelphia: Temple University Press, 1991.

Walker, William O., III. *Drugs in the Western Hemisphere*. Wilmington: Scholarly Resources, 1996.

———. "The Limits of Coercive Diplomacy: U.S. Drug Policy and Colombian State Stability, 1978–1997." In *The Illicit Global Economy and State Power*, edited by H. Richard Friman and Peter Andreas, 143–71. Lanham, Md.: Rowman and Littlefield, 1999.

Watson, Hilbourne A. "The Globalization of Finance: Role and Status of the Caribbean." In Griffith, *Political Economy of Drugs*, 29–57.

Webb, Gary. *Dark Alliance*. New York: Seven Stories Press, 1998.

Webster, Thomas C. *Honey Production Problems in Belize*. Photocopy. Belize Honey Producers Federation. March 15, 1988. National Library of Belize.

Weir, Carol. "Costa Rica and the Drug Trade." In Bagley and Walker, *Drug Trafficking*, 455–65.

Wiarda, Howard J., and Harvey F. Kline, eds. *Latin American Politics and Development*. 6th ed. Boulder: Westview Press.

Wilkinson, Daniel. *Silence on the Mountain: Stories of Terror, Betrayal, and Forgetting in Guatemala*. Durham: Duke University Press, 2004.

Williams, Phil. "The Nature of Drug-Trafficking Networks." *Current History* 97 (April 1998): 154–59.

———. "Transnational Criminal Networks." In *Networks and Netwars: The Future of Terror, Crime, and Militancy*, edited by John Arquilla and David Ronfeldt, 61–97. Santa Monica: RAND, 2001.

Wilson, Dwight. "Guatemala: A Second Decade of Spring?" In Wiarda and Kline, *Politics and Development*, 504–18.

Wilson, Suzanne, and Marta Zambrano. "Cocaine, Commodity Chains, and Drug Politics: A Transnational Approach." In *Commodity Chains and Global Capitalism*, edited by Gary Gereffi and Miguel Korzeniewicz, 297–315. Westport: Greenwood Press, 1994.

Wisotsky, Stephen. *Breaking the Impasse in the War on Drugs*. Westport: Greenwood Press, 1986.

Zabludoff, Sidney. "Colombian Narcotics Organizations as Business Enterprises." *Transnational Organized Crime* 3, no. 2 (1997): 20–49.

Zaitch, Damián. "Post-Fordist Cocaine: Labor and Business Relations Among Colombian Dealers." In Vellinga, *Drug Industry*, 148–74.

———. *Trafficking Cocaine: Colombian Drug Entrepreneurs in the Netherlands*. The Hague: Kluwer Law International, 2002.

INDEX OF CASES

INDEX OF NAMES

GENERAL INDEX

Page numbers in *italic* type designate figures, tables, and maps. See also the Index of Cases and Index of Names.